THE

Good
GARDENS
Guide 1990

―――――*Edited by*―――――
GRAHAM ROSE *and* PETER KING

BARRIE & JENKINS
LONDON

First published in Great Britain in 1990 by
Barrie & Jenkins Ltd
20 Vauxhall Bridge Road, London SW1V 2SA

British Library Cataloguing in Publication Data
Rose, Graham, 1928–
    The good gardens guide.
    1. Great Britain. Gardens — Visitors' guides
    I. Title   II. King, Peter, 1925–
    914.1′04858

    ISBN 0-7126-3506-8

Design by Clare Clements
Cartography: Malcolm Ward/Tek Art Ltd

Typeset by DP Photosetting, Aylesbury, Bucks
Printed and bound in England
by Mackays

Contents

Introduction 4

The Garden Scene 5

Top Grade Gardens 8

Using the Guide 9

THE GARDENS

Avon 13;   Bedfordshire 21;   Berkshire 23;   Buckinghamshire 31;
Cambridgeshire 41;   Cheshire 51;   Cornwall 61;   Cumbria 74;
Derbyshire 81;   Devon 88;   Dorset 103;   Durham 122;   Essex 126;
Gloucestershire 135;   Hampshire & Isle of Wight 148;
Hereford & Worcester 167;   Hertfordshire 178;   Humberside 185;
Kent 187;   Lancashire 203;   Leicestershire 208;   Lincolnshire 216;
London (Greater) 222;   Manchester (Greater) 251;   Merseyside 256;
Midlands (West) 260;   Norfolk 264;   Northamptonshire 277;
Northumberland 285;   Nottinghamshire 290;   Oxfordshire 297;
Shropshire 319;   Somerset 329;   Staffordshire 339;   Suffolk 344;
Surrey 353;   Sussex (East) 363;   Sussex (West) 372;   Tyne & Wear 388;
Warwickshire 391;   Wiltshire 403;   Yorkshire (North) 415;
Yorkshire (South & West) 424;   Ireland 432;   Scotland 448;   Wales 478

Acknowledgements 489

Your Comments 490

Report Forms 491

Introduction

There is nothing new about visiting gardens. Henry II and Rosamund did it, John Evelyn and his diary did it, even Dr Johnson and Mrs Thrale did it, so it is not surprising that millions today say 'Let's do it'. Nor is it surprising that, despite the vagaries of the British climate, this country should be one of the most popular amongst garden-lovers from other lands. Not only have some of the greatest designers in history worked here but the climate itself and the efforts of plant hunters have made this virtually a Botanical Garden of the World.

We decided to compile this guide because, both of us being by trade and by inclination avid garden visitors, we were constantly put off by the necessity of consulting several books at once in order to obtain the basic information needed to find the gardens of our choice. Why couldn't the facts be collected into one book? Small enough to keep in the car and with just enough information to whet our appetite, we thought it should also give some indication of the various features to be found so that choices could be made between the many wonderful offerings available to the public on a given day.

The result is a guide which we know is subjective. It is a compilation of the work of a large number of inspectors, each with different gardening interests, each with his or her favourites in the areas on which they have concentrated. This subjectivity we believe to be a benefit and we hope that our inspectors' enthusiasm will convey itself to the reader in a way which the modest descriptions written by the garden-owners themselves often fail to achieve.

Far more gardens are open to the public in the affluent south than elsewhere, and we have therefore tried to strike a balance by making a particular effort to find good gardens in other parts of the country. The same considerations apply to London and our other large cities where huge numbers of garden lovers live without gardens of their own. They find it hard to satisfy their craving for the luxury of being able to have a green thought in a green shade and our inspectors have therefore tried to help them by including parks and other public spaces which may well not be gardens in the strictest sense of the word. For this reason and others, comparison of standards between one county and another are bound to be uneven.

We have not, in general, included gardens which appeared to our inspectors to require substantial improvement, although sometimes their grading or comments indicate that a garden might have been given a higher rating if, for instance, its maintenance could be improved. Conversely the absence of a garden from our lists does not by any means indicate that it is not praiseworthy, as exclusion might have happened for all kinds of other reasons, our ignorance being the most probable.

We hope that future editions will be able to make up for any lapses noted by readers and we shall also aim to search diligently for newcomers.

Graham Rose and *Peter King*, London 1989

The Garden Scene

If you are reading this foreword you are probably both a keen gardener and an avid garden visitor. As such you are a tremendously important person because you are the raw material of a giant industry. Over six million of you visited gardens in 1988 and in the same year another twenty-eight million visited historic properties of one type or another in which the gardens are often the major attraction. Apart from the entrance charge (which averaged £1.50 per head) you spent money on meals and refreshments and a wide range of gifts in the shops which are often associated with such properties. In total it is estimated that you were responsible for a turnover well in excess of £100 million. So, apart from enabling many of the property owners to continue gardening on the grand scale or to keep their buildings in good repair, your expenditure had a salutary impact on many local economies. It provided work directly for gardeners, builders and guides. And very often the money you spent on the delicious sponge cake made by a good lady in the village permitted her to eke out a meagre pension and live a larger and more fruitful life. Indirectly, of course, the plants you buy as the result of admiring inspired planting in the gardens also brings valuable revenue to the horticultural community as a whole.

Gardens open under charitable trusts such as the National Gardens Scheme produce money for good causes – a total of £600,000 from NGS openings in 1988 which came from upwards of 300,000 visitors. The owners of these gardens have to be thanked for their public spirit which involves them in a great deal of preparatory work. A number of gardens open to the public are also registered as charitable trusts and this usually, but not always, means that all the income from admission charges goes to the running of the garden rather than some outside charity.

One of the major changes noted by our inspectors is that the majority of owners now maintain their property without help. The days when a grand park employed a hundred men or more are gone forever but so too is the availability of the odd job man who would cut the lawn, or weed the beds. Money for upkeep no longer goes to meet labour costs and is more likely to pay for electricity for power tools or bags of bark mulch to suppress the weeds. Despite this, most Britons do not seem to have dropped their standards and owners slave away at the labour-intensive chores to achieve that 'well-maintained' manicured look.

We may however have to change our ideas, not because of shortage of labour, but because we are becoming increasingly green. Organic gardening is not synonymous with tidy gardening. Diseases have to run their course; weeds are not verboten. The advent or re-invention of organic gardening will mean a change in the appearance of gardens which those whose passion is for order and spruceness may have to learn to accept.

Another hazard facing owners is that the British have become a nation of litter louts and they are not averse to practising their hobby in our parks and gardens. Black plastic bags do not do much for the charm of London squares.

Country gardens are not subject to abuse on quite the same scale but owners have to take the difficult decision whether to instal bins which are bound to detract from the scenery or to convey in some subtle way that the litter lout should wait until he reaches the tea room before disposing of his chocolate wrapper. Many of our inspectors sadly had to say that few public gardens still retain their 'former glory' because of the depredations of the litter lout, or worse still, the vandal, and the failure of councils to be able to spend adequate funds to overcome the problems.

These changes are paralleled, as we have noted, by a major growth in the scale of garden visiting - some individual sites alone attracting nearly half-a-million people in 1989. This explosion in interest causes us to pose the question - is your own interest in garden visiting adequately recognised and appreciated or are you sometimes greeted with a stiff tolerance?

The experience of the team of inspectors who helped to produce this guide was mixed. In the vast majority of cases they felt that owners seemed almost unduly grateful to visitors to their garden, permitting admission long after the advertised closing time, bending the rules to allow access to people who had travelled a long way on days when their garden was officially closed and always dealing patiently and thoroughly with questions.

There were other occasions when the anonymous inspectors felt that they were being greeted in a rather cavalier manner and that their presence in the garden was almost resented. This impression was particularly strong where the garden owners persisted in using their sports facilities during the hours when the garden was open to the public. A garrulous crowd of owners and their friends playing croquet can be an embarrassment to the garden visitors they are trying to ignore, and such owners really ought to be more considerate if they are charging for admission to their gardens.

Of course this criticism has to be made with some caution; if the admission charge is being handed straight on to a charity one could argue that the owners are, in these circumstances, entitled to act as they please towards the public. The visitors themselves would all agree that it is very pleasant to be permitted to sit drinking tea on the lawn of a grand house, surrounded by exquisite scenery, for a fraction of the price charged for any other form of Sunday afternoon entertainment, smug in the knowledge that a small contribution has been made to some charity or charities in the process.

Then again, the often seemingly bizarre opening times of some of the gardens (alternate Wednesdays from 2 to 5 except when there is racing at Ascot or Thursdays and Fridays only) was considered very irksome by some of our inspectors. Great gardens which are open for much of the summer season should, they felt, be open for at least some part of every weekend for the convenience of gardeners who find it difficult to make visits on weekdays. One owner, when criticised for opening for charity merely for one Sunday during the summer (his garden was otherwise open to the public every Thursday and Friday afternoon) became rather huffy and protested that 'We don't want crowds - just keen gardeners'. At first, our inspector felt this sounded somewhat hypocritical because clearly the grand garden was very costly to maintain and the visitors' entry fees must have helped towards paying for the squad of professional gardeners. What the owner appeared not to wish to admit was that when the family was in residence at the weekends it didn't want to share its home with strangers. While understandable, that is hardly a tenable position for an owner who at other times is appealing to the public for help and offering his accumulated garden experience in exchange for cash. So our plea, then, made in due recognition of the great generosity of spirit of almost all owners, is to the minority 'A little more openness please!'

It could be argued that the owners of great gardens have a clear choice. They can either be flexible and open them at times which are really convenient for the public or they can exclude the public altogether and enjoy their privacy which is a privilege to which they are entitled – but one for which they will have to pay in lost revenue.

On reflection, though, there is also the problem of what the National Trust calls 'over-visited properties'. Owners may well feel that their gardens suffer from too many visitors and indeed several actually requested to be excluded from our guide for this reason.

Asked to adopt a highly critical attitude, on the whole our inspectors reported that the major gardens which they visited were in a fine state with a great many of them looking particularly well after considerable refurbishment or restoration. The restored gardens at Belsay Hall in Northumberland and Ham House in Surrey were particularly praised. In general they felt that the substitution of mixed borders for purely herbaceous borders in order to reduce maintenance had done little to lessen the attraction of many gardens. They felt though that those gardens where extra dedication from the owners and their gardeners had allowed at least some area of traditional large-scale deep herbaceous beds to be maintained had an appeal and a quality unmatched elsewhere.

Almost without exception our inspectors praised the food offered at those properties which were open to the public regularly. It was the genuine 'homemade' quality of the refreshments which most impressed. As one inspector put it 'while the service was often slow and amateurish the food was nearly always worth waiting for'. The NGS gardens were particularly praised for the efforts made to offer teas, often on only one weekend afternoon in the summer.

If garden visiting is to continue to grow as an aspect of the British leisure scene and if it is also to be what the pundits call 'a growth market' for tourists, then the price to pay is eternal vigilance on the part of garden owners. Amateurism is all important in any activity on which our nation embarks, and gardening is no exception, but it must be mixed with a professional approach to what the garden visitor wants in terms of quality and value for money.

Top Grade Gardens

BERKSHIRE
Folly Farm

BUCKINGHAMSHIRE
Ascott
Cliveden
Stowe Landscape Garden
Waddesdon Manor

CAMBRIDGESHIRE
Anglesey Abbey
Peckover House
University Botanic Garden

CHESHIRE
Tatton Park

CORNWALL
Caerhays Castle Garden

CUMBRIA
Holker Hall
Levens Hall

DERBYSHIRE
Chatsworth

DEVON
Castle Drogo
Knightshayes
Marwood Hill

GLOUCESTERSHIRE
Hidcote Manor Garden
Kiftsgate Court
Westbury Court Garden
Westonbirt Arboretum

HAMPSHIRE
Exbury Gardens
The Hillier Garden and
    Arboretum
Mottisfont Abbey
Ventnor Botanic Garden

HERTFORDSHIRE
Hatfield House

KENT
Hever Castle
Sissinghurst Castle

LONDON (Greater)
Chiswick House
Ham House
Hampton Court
Royal Botanic Gardens
    (Kew)
St James's Park
Syon Park

MERSEYSIDE
Ness Gardens

NORTHAMPTONSHIRE
Castle Ashby Gardens

OXFORDSHIRE
23 Beech Croft Road
Blenheim Palace
Cornwell Manor
Oxford Botanic Garden
Rousham House

SHROPSHIRE
Hodnet Hall

SOMERSET
Forde Abbey
Hestercombe House
    Gardens
Montacute House

SUFFOLK
Helmingham Hall
Shrubland Hall
Somerleyton Hall

SURREY
Polesden Lacey
Royal Horticultural
    Society's Garden
The Savill Garden

SUSSEX (East)
Great Dixter
Sheffield Park

SUSSEX (West)
The High Beeches
Leonardslee Gardens
Nymans
Wakehurst Place Garden

WILTSHIRE
Iford Manor
Stourhead

YORKSHIRE (North)
Castle Howard
Studley Royal and
    Fountains Abbey

IRELAND
Anne's Grove
Birr Castle
The Burren
Castlewellan National
    Arboretum
Glenveagh Castle
Ilnacullin (Garinish
    Island)
Kilmacurragh
Mount Stewart House,
    Garden and Temple ...
National Botanic Gardens,
    Glasnevin
Rowallane

SCOTLAND
Brodick Castle
Castle Kennedy and
    Lochinch Gardens
Castle of Mey
Crathes Castle Garden
Drummond Castle
Edzell Castle
Inverewe Garden
Little Sparta
Logan Botanic Garden and
    Logan House
Mellerstain
Pitmedden Garden
Royal Botanic Garden
    (Edinburgh)
Younger Botanic Garden

WALES
Bodnant Garden
Powis Castle

Using the Guide

The *Guide* is arranged by counties. Within each county the gardens are listed alphabetically by the normal name of the garden/house.

The maps show numbers which refer to those given against each garden entry. For detailed information about how to reach gardens use the data given in the garden entry itself.

The information given is believed to be correct at the time of going to press but changes do occur – properties sold or ownership varied and routes improved by motorway extensions etc. There may also be closures of over-visited properties, or limitations imposed on opening times. Prices of entry may be varied without notice.

Gardens in Great Britain open by courtesy of the owners for the National Gardens Scheme [NGS], Scottish Gardens Scheme [SGS] and/or other charities are included where the gardens are of special interest even if, as on some occasions, they are open in this way on only one day in the year. However, many such gardens are also open at other specific times, such as for local charities or church restoration funds, and it is not generally possible to give dates for these locally-publicised openings. Readers should note that other nearby gardens, not listed in this guide for one reason or another, may well be open at similar times to those listed. Those so opened under the NGS scheme are usually marked by a distinctive yellow poster along nearby roads.

All the gardens listed have some special merits, but since it has not been possible to list every garden open to the public, exclusion does not imply that gardens unlisted have no merit. Readers are invited to advise the *Guide* of any gardens which in their opinion should be listed in future editions, and where possible arrangements will be made to review all suggestions.

It has not been possible for *Guide* inspectors to visit every garden which is open to the public at some time in the year, although the inspectors all have broad experience of garden visiting in their specific areas. In general, inspections have been made on an anonymous basis to ensure objectivity. Readers who would like to add information about gardens listed are warmly invited to write to the *Guide* with their comments, all of which will be acknowledged and may be used in future editions without attribution.

We have tried to make the *Guide* easy to use and the following notes will explain how we have organised all the detailed information offered about each garden.

Address This is the address given by the owner or some other reputable source.

Telephone Except where specifically requested to be excluded, telephone numbers to which enquiries may be directed are given for each property. To maintain the support and cooperation of private owners it is suggested that the telephone be used with discretion. Where visits are by appointment, the telephone can of course be used except where written application, particularly for parties, is specifically requested. Code numbers are given in brackets. For the Republic of Ireland when phoning from the United Kingdom dial 353

9

plus area code plus number (except Dublin numbers which are 0001 plus number). In all cases where visits by parties are proposed, owners should be advised in advance and arrangements preferably confirmed in writing.

Owners Names given are those available at the time of going to press. In the case of The National Trust, some properties may be the homes of tenants of the Trust. Some other gardens are owned or managed by other trusts.

Location This information has been supplied by inspectors and is aimed to be the best available to those travelling by car. The unreliability of train and bus services makes it unrewarding to include details, particularly as many garden visits are made on Sundays. However, many properties can be reached by public transport and National Trust guides and the Yellow Book [NGS] give details. Future editions of the *Guide* may include a special list of gardens easily reached by public transport if readers indicate that this would be helpful.

Maps Each county or country section begins with a map. The numbers on the maps correspond to the numbers to be found to the right of the name of each garden within each section. The maps show the proximity of one garden to another so that visits to several gardens can be planned for the same day. It is worthwhile referring to the maps of bordering counties to see if another garden visit can be included in your itinerary. The maps should be used in conjunction with a road atlas.

Access Times of access given are the best available at the moment of going to press, but some may have been changed subsequently. In the entries, the times given are inclusive – that is, an entry such as May-Sept means that the garden is open from 1st May to 30th Sept inclusive and 2 p.m. – 5 p.m. also means that entry will be effective during that period. Please note that many owners will open their gardens to visitors by appointment. They will often arrange to give a personally-conducted tour on these occasions. A few owners of gardens open under the NGS scheme have not been able to advise their opening times before the *Guide* went to press and in such cases the note N.A. (not available) indicates that so far as we know the garden will be open in 1990 but entry times must be checked.

Best season These are inspectors' suggestions though the garden concerned may well be highly attractive at other times and usually no garden will be open at a time when it does not merit a visit. The vagaries of climate prevent this information from being anything but a rough guide.

Entrance fees As far as is known, these are correct at time of going to press, but changes may be made without notice. Where there are variations, these will usually be upwards, but the amount of increase is small. Children are often charged at a lower rate, but are expected to be accompanied by an adult. Charges for parties are often at special rates. National Trust charges are explained in their literature with special concessions for members. Accompanied children are normally admitted by the Trust at half-price and this is why no specific charge for children is usually listed for Trust properties.

Charges in the Republic of Ireland are given in punts (IR£) IR£1 is approximately equal to 85p.

Parking No such entry means no close convenient parking.

Refreshments A guide only. Where Teas is marked, this normally implies that the owners have arranged to serve a simple tea on the property, or near at hand, at reasonable prices during opening hours. No such entry means that no specific refreshment arrangements are known to the inspector.

Toilet facilities Specific facilities are marked. Where there is no such entry there appear to be no specific toilets for visitors and enquiries will have to be directed to staff or owners.

Wheelchairs Inspectors have indicated where they believe a garden can be reasonably negotiated by someone in a wheelchair. No such entry means that the garden is probably unsuitable.

Dogs If dogs are allowed in a car park, or in the property on a lead, this is indicated. No such entry means dogs probably not allowed.

Plants for sale No such entry means plants not normally for sale.

Shop This entry refers to special shops on the premises, such as National Trust shops or shops selling souvenirs etc.

House open No such entry means that an adjoining house is not normally open to the visiting public. Where houses are open, there is often an extra charge, usually indicated here, but again subject to change without notice.

Grading This is the most subjective aspect of the *Guide* and one which may cause some disagreement on the part of owners as well as visitors. We stress that its purpose is to serve as an indication to visitors in order to give them some advance information about the status of the garden as viewed by our inspectors and editors. Readers will appreciate that direct comparisons cannot be made between a huge estate like Chatsworth with its staff of professional experts and a tiny plantsman's garden in a terraced house, tended with dedication by a single owner. This being said, both may be excellent of their kind and therefore be worthy of consideration for a visit, and considered by the *Guide* to be at the top of their class. Conversely a lesser grading does not imply any criticism of a garden but is an attempt to guide the potential reader as to its relative merits if a choice has to be made between several gardens. Broadly speaking the intention of the four grades is as follows:

Grade I Amongst the best gardens in the world in terms of design and content. Many are of historic importance, but some are of recent origin. Overseas visitors to Britain or Ireland are recommended to include them in their itinerary.

Grade II Gardens of high quality, though not perhaps as unique as Grade I, and worth travelling a considerable distance to visit. Sometimes the property as a whole, and the general ambience, make the visit particularly rewarding.

Grade III These are gardens which our inspectors suggest it would be worth driving fifty miles or more to visit. They may have some special feature of design or plant content while not being considered as justifying a higher grade overall.

Grade IV Gardens of considerable merit and well worth visiting when in the region.

Northern Ireland The National Gardens Scheme does not extend into Northern Ireland, but the local Garden Committee of the National Trust organizes the opening of small private gardens during weekends in spring, summer and early autumn. A leaflet is printed giving times and directions and this may be obtained from the National Trust, Rowallane House, Saintfield, County Down BT24 7LH. (Please enclose a stamped, self-addressed envelope). On all occasions there is a charge for admission (£1.00 or 25p for children). National Trust membership is not valid for these gardens, and dogs are strictly *not* allowed in any of the gardens). The Northern Ireland Tourist Board does not provide specific information about gardens in the province, but the Heritage Gardens Committee has issued a booklet describing some of the gardens and parks of outstanding historical importance (some of which are not open to the public). *Northern Gardens* published by Ulster Horticultural Heritage Society, Belfast is available for £1.50 (p&p included) by writing to Heritage Gardens Committee c/o Institute of Irish Studies, Queen's University, 8 Fitzwilliam Street, Belfast BT9 6AW.

Republic of Ireland There is no scheme operated in the Republic of Ireland similar to the National Gardens Scheme and Scottish Gardens Scheme in Britain or to the National Trust Scheme in Northern Ireland. The Irish Tourist Board does, however, issue annually a list of gardens open to the public; this may be obtained by writing to Mary Nash (Heritage), Bord Failte, Baggot Street Bridge, Dublin 2 (enclose a self-addressed envelope – and 40p (UK stamps) separately or 48p (Irish) stamps separately). This leaflet will give current admission times, entry fees, etc. for gardens in the Republic. Entry fees quoted in this guide for Ireland are the 1989 figures.

AVON

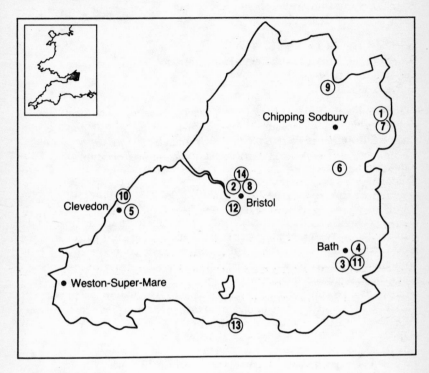

BADMINTON

Chipping Sodbury, Avon.
The Duke and Duchess of Beaufort

*5m E of Chipping Sodbury, B4040, M4 junction 18 ● Open 4th June, 2.00 –
6.00 p.m. (park only during Horse Trials) ● Entrance: £1.50, OAP £1.00,
children under 5 free ● Parking ● Teas ● Toilet facilities ● Suitable for
wheelchairs ● Grade II*

These two private gardens have been designed in the last four years to the
south and east sides of the house. Very cleverly planted, they manage to answer
both the grandeur and the muddle of the house. Two conservatories on the
east side of the house are exuberant with all the best conservatory plants –
large myrtle bushes in tubs and clambering cobea. On the south side a series
of enclosures or 'rooms' contain very successful mixed planting. Vistas
running down and across the garden lead the eye through to an urn or
doorway and glimpses of further excitement. Lilies burst out from the
alchemillas and annual mallows. A cool 'room' contains only blue and white
flowers. The furthest part is a heady mass of old-fashioned roses. Work is
starting on the walled garden, further from the house, with huge warm, brick

walls and a monumental gateway. In response to the massive scale of this garden a large allée of laburnum, wisteria and lilac has been erected. The development of this garden should be exciting.

BRISTOL BOTANIC GARDEN   2
Bracken Hill, North Road, Leigh Woods, Bristol, Avon.
Tel: (0272) 733682
University of Bristol

Cross the Suspension Bridge from Clifton, turn first right (North Road) and go 1¼m up on the left • Open Mon – Fri except Bank Holidays, 9.00 a.m. – 5.00 p.m. • Entrance: free • Parking • Partly suitable for wheelchairs • Become a Friend and get free plants. Otherwise plant sales are held twice a year • Grade III

The Botanic Garden moved to this site in 1959 and is very interesting for the keen plantsman. Collections of New Zealand cistus, sempervivums, campanulas. Everything is well labelled and agreeably set out. It aims to be educational, to represent most native trees and shrubs, and particularly the local flora peculiar to the Avon Gorge. Glasshouses contain ferns, orchids, bromeliads, epiphytic cacti, tender bulbs. The African stone plants are fascinating, small succulents resembling pebbles in shape and colour. There are also insectivorous plants and sensitive plants which move when touched. Altogether a fascinating place which needs a lot of support in these hard times – it costs only £10 to become a member of the Association of Friends.

CITY OF BATH BOTANICAL GARDENS   3
Royal Victoria Park, Bath, Avon.
City of Bath

Off Queen's Square • Open daily, dawn – dusk, Sun, from 10.00 a.m. • Best season: spring • Entrance: free • Parking • Toilet facilities • Suitable for wheelchairs • Dogs on lead • Grade III

Seven acres of fairly impressive botanical garden – but more a very extensive collection than a scientifically ordered exhibition. It is laid out as it might be in a private garden and not by families or places of origin as might be expected. There is a stream and pond and rockeries, herbaceous border and woodland garden. The magnolias are well worth a look, particularly as the pH is surprisingly high for them.

CLAVERTON MANOR   4
Claverton, Bath, Avon. Tel: (0225) 60503
The American Museum

3m E of Bath on A36, signposted American Museum • Open April – last Sunday in October, daily except Mon (but open Bank Holidays), 12 noon – 5.00

p.m. ● *Entrance: £1.00 (garden), £2.50 (house), OAP £2.00, children £1.50*
● *Parking* ● *Refreshments* ● *Toilet facilities* ● *Suitable for wheelchairs*
● *Herbs for sale* ● *Shop* ● *House museum open* ● **Grade III**

The house and garden are perched on the side of the Avon valley in a stunning
position. Parkland planted in the 1820s with cedars, beech and ilex slopes
steeply away from the house. A terrace runs along the south and east sides of
the house and small beds around the house harbour honeysuckles, clematis,
roses and other climbers which cover the ground floor walls. A handsome wall
abutting the south side backs a decent border 10 feet deep in which fastigiate
yews are planted at intervals, like buttresses up the walls. This feature appears
elsewhere. The 'Colonial Herb Garden' is easily missed as it is but a corner of
the terrace. Neatly done with box edges and clever pebble work on the patios
it is hardly exciting. The 'Mount Vernon' garden, named after George
Washington's garden, is rather lost to one side of the house. The planting is
interesting and supposed to be period with massed old-fashioned roses, very
good trained pear trees and box and beech hedges but it has the feel of a
reconstruction. The use of white palings at the boundary of the garden and
the summer house or 'school room' are features worth noting. There is also a
sort of grotto and an avenue of flowering cherry trees.

CLEVEDON COURT 5
Clevedon, Bristol, Avon. Tel: (0272) 872257
The National Trust

1½m E of Clevedon on B3130 ● *Open April – Sept, Wed, Thurs, Sun and
Bank Holiday Mon, 2.30 – 5.30 p.m. Last admission 5.00 p.m.* ● *Best season:
summer* ● *Entrance: £2.20* ● *Parking* ● *Unsuitable for coaches* ● *Tea and
biscuits at kitchen door 3.30 – 5.15 p.m.* ● *Toilet facilities* ● *Shop* ● *House
open* ● **Grade II**

Clevedon Court house is built upon a prehistoric foreshore which one can
easily imagine as the land in front stretches out flat for 10 miles towards the
Mendips and behind are towering ilex-clad cliffs. This highly dramatic and
commanding setting for a garden has been monstrously gashed by the M5
barely 200 yards from the house. Gertrude Jekyll recognised the quality of this
garden but despaired of the Victorian bedding to which it was subjected. Two
great terraces, of similar date and nature to those at Powis, rise monumentally
behind the house. These south-facing walls now harbour exotic and tender
plants – pomegranates, ceanothuses, arum lilies, *Magnolia grandiflora*,
myrtle, fuchsias and so forth. Originally they would have been used to grow
apricots and figs. Above the terraces the ilex woods rise magnificently several
hundred feet and are hot and dry with winding paths reminiscent of
Mediterranean woods. It is well worth looking carefully at the trees for almost
every one is a mature example of note. Weeping limes pour their fruity scent
onto the car park, an Indian bean tree flowers profusely. There is a mulberry
described as ancient in 1819. At the top of the terraces strawberry trees fruit

heavily and there are Judas trees. The charms of this garden are not necessarily immediately apparent but there is a lot here which has been created by the Elton family over 300 years.

DYRHAM PARK   6
Nr Chippenham, Avon.   Tel: (027582) 250
The National Trust

8m N of Bath, 12m E of Bristol on A46. Take M4 junction 18 in direction of Bath ● Park open all year, 12 noon – 5.30 p.m. or dusk, House and garden open 25th April – 4th Nov, daily except Thurs and Fri, 12 noon – 5.30 p.m. ● Best season: summer ● Entrance: £3.00, park only 60p ● Parking ● Refreshments in Orangery and picnics in park ● Toilet facilities ● Suitable for wheelchairs on ground floor of house and terrace only. Park suitable but many inclines ● Dogs in deer park on lead only ● House open ● Grade II

Only a tiny fragment of the London and Wise extensive 'Dutch' Garden shown in the view by Kip in 1712 survives. The terraces were all smoothed out in the early nineteenth century to form an 'English' landscape of now five mature Spanish chestnut, Lucombe oak, Red oak, Black walnut and ilex. Avenues of elms survived until the mid-1970s when they were wiped out by Dutch elm disease. They have since been replanted with limes. The cascade is still working and one can make out the form of the original garden and enjoy the terrace and the orangery which is almost certainly by Talman. It is the views towards Bristol and the elegance of the 'natural' landscape with the house tucked into the hillside that still make this an outstanding example of English landscape gardening. In all, 263 acres of ancient parkland.

ESSEX HOUSE   7
Badminton, Chipping Sodbury, Avon.   Tel: (045421) 288
Mr and Mrs James Lees-Milne

2m N of Acton Turville on B4040. M4 junction 18 ● Open by appointment only, May – July if seriously interested ● Toilet facilities ● Partly suitable for wheelchairs ● Grade II

Mrs Lees-Milne is to give up opening on the National Gardens Scheme which she has done for over 20 years but says that she really enjoys showing people who are seriously interested around the garden. Those that are will be impressed. Although not large and dominated by a mammoth cedar of Lebanon which casts a swathe of dry shade across the garden one could spend longer and learn more than in any number of more showy plots. It demonstrates what intelligence in dealing with site, sureness of hand in planting, lightness of touch in design can achieve. This garden is broken up by surprises but always maintains a consistency of thought behind it. Climbers, bulbs, alliums and annuals are woven throughout to reinforce the bones of the planting as the season progresses. The beds are full enough and the plants vigorous, everything is just in check but never too clipped or too manicured. This is a lesson to gardeners on how to achieve rampant growth and a sense of wealth (the back of the house is groaning with climbers like humulus) and yet fend off rank chaos. Clipped box and Lollipop euonymus maintain order, while a garden bench is lost in a cloud of mallow or honeysuckle. There are a lot of old-fashioned roses but their short-comings are disguised by accompanying floribundas such as 'Cardinal Hume' which soldier on until November. And all this in a spot discovered by the present owner only a dozen years ago which many would have declared impossible to garden without a full-time gardener.

GOLDNEY HALL   8
Lower Clifton Hill, Clifton, Bristol, Avon.   Tel: (0272) 303030
University of Bristol

In centre of Bristol at top of Constitution Hill, Clifton ● Provisional opening dates 7th and 13th May, 7th June. Grotto by special appointment for those with a serious interest ● Entrance: £1.50, OAP and children 50p ● Teas on NGS days ● Suitable for wheelchairs ● Grade III

Although not large or notably planted this is historically an important garden with much packed into it and a rare survival of a medium sized garden covering nine acres. The grotto is astonishingly elaborate, water really gushes through it and its walls are literally encrusted with shells and minerals. Its facade is a very striking example of early but sophisticated Gothic. The grotto is now justly famous but the entire garden (or what remains) is a thrilling discovery in the middle of this busy once bombed city. It is full of surprises not least of which is the small formal canal with orangery at its head. From the house one is lead through the shadows of an allée of Irish yews to the dank grotto entrance. Passing through the grotto and out by narrow labyrinthine passages, suddenly there is a terrace, a broad airy walk with magnificent views over the old dock. At the far end of this terrace is the Gothic gazebo and towering above the other end is the castellated water tower which holds the water for the grotto.

HILL HOUSE   9
Wickwar, Chipping Sodbury, Chippenham, Avon.
The Duchess of Westminster

4m N of Chipping Sodbury on B4060 ● Open for NGS. Date N.A. ● Best season: June ● Entrance: £1.00 ● Parking ● Suitable for wheelchairs ● Grade III

From the beginning of the drive when one notices the five weeping silver lime trees and the other newly-planted trees it is clear that this is the garden of someone who knows about plants. There is an astonishing array of rarely seen varieties of both shrubs and trees such as the Southern beech *Nothofagus antarctica*, and beneath these, floods of bulbs, and not just in spring. If you like variegation and golden foliage, there is much to inspire you. In the main garden to the west of the house, borders painted in careful choices of colour or foliage lap the lawn. The house itself is clad with the unusual climbing roses such as 'Mme Alfred Carrière', 'New Dawn' and 'Mermaid'. A remarkable collection of salix, including the creeping *S. repens* 'Argentea' cluster about a fountain. The second part of the garden, screened by a cedar and a row of thirteenth-century columns, has more recently created island beds and specimen trees dotted about. Despite the sheer quantity of good plants here, from massed hebes to golden dogwood, unusual buddleias and ceanothus, the choosing and planting is clearly informed and disciplined – nothing is leggy, invasive or wilful.

THE MANOR HOUSE 10
Walton-in-Gordano, Clevedon, Bristol, Avon.   Tel: (0272) 872067
Mr and Mrs S. Wills

2m NE of Clevedon on B3124. Entrance on N side of entry to village nearest Clevedon • *Open all year by appointment. Also 18th April – 28th June and 8th Aug – 13th Sept, Wed and Thurs, 10.00 a.m. – 4.00 p.m. and 6th, 7th, 27th, 28th May and 26th, 27th Aug, 2.00 – 6.00 p.m.* • *Entrance: 75p, children under 14 free* • *Parking. Coaches by appointment only* • *Suitable for wheelchairs* • *Plants for sale* • ***Grade III***

A most unusual plantsman's garden of about five acres which is basically only 15 years old although the owners have taken advantage of some plantings, mostly trees, which remain from the mid-eighteenth century onwards. The Wills have aimed mainly at an informal effect and they have planted ornamental trees, shrubs, herbaceous plants and bulbs to give colour and structure throughout the year. The colour in autumn is particularly remarkable. The new plantings to the south of the house, which include the White and Silver beds, retain something of the original layout but on the other side the owners have transformed the conventional sloping lawn and rose beds by a sensitive mixture of plants including many that are unusual. There is one formal area, called the Pool Garden, with rectangular pools and fountains,and, at one end, the raised Asian bank planted with pink, blue and white colours. The yew hedges round the area are still at an early stage. Overall the Wills have achieved a remarkably attractive garden, the very opposite of what is usually meant by the description 'plantsman'. Note too their emphasis on labour saving such as the gravel mulch in the White bed.

ORCHARD HOUSE 11
Claverton, Nr Bath, Avon.
Rear-Admiral and Mrs H. Tracy

3½m from Bath on A36, signposted to Claverton village, or follow signs to American Museum and proceed ½m down the hill • *Open every Wed in May,*

27th June, 4th July, 2.00 – 6.00 p.m. and by appointment for groups only but not for individual visitors ● Entrance: 80p, children 30p ● Plants for sale. Small wholesale nursery, retail on NGS days ● Grade III

On the edge of a pretty village and in the lea of an extended sixteenth-century Bath stone house this is an easy restful garden that slopes away in a series of lawns and effective rockeries. Begun as a retirement garden 40 years ago, the two and a half acres are planted with unusual plants and trees for a planned and stunning foliage effect. Vistas and a secret water garden offer surprises and the vegetable garden is a treat. The garden has views into the Avon valley and Rear-Admiral Tracy has added a viewing mound – a feature of walled medieval gardens. The glasshouses are full of alpines, new tufa gardens and are testimonials to Mrs Tracy's botanical expertise. The American Museum, Claverton House, is nearby – see entry.

THE RED LODGE 12
Park Road, Bristol, Avon. Tel: (0272) 223571
Bristol Corporation

Located in city centre ● Open July and Aug, Sat and Bank Holiday Mon, 10.30 a.m. – 1.00 p.m. and 2.00 – 4.00 p.m. ● Entrance 50p ● Parking in multi-storey next door ● Toilet facilities ● House open ● Grade IV

Good reconstruction of the seventeenth-century town garden of a merchant's house. Old varieties of fruit trees trained and espaliered. Trellis work recreated from seventeenth-century prints and similarly a knot garden.

SHERBOURNE GARDEN 13
Pear Tree House, Litton, Avon. Tel: (076121) 220
Mr and Mrs J. Southwell

15m S of Bristol, 7m N of Wells on B3114 beyond Litton and Ye Olde Kings Arms ● Open mid-June – mid-Sept, Sat – Mon, 2.00 – 6.00 p.m. ● Best season: June/July ● Entrance: £1.00, children 50p ● Parking in field ● Teas on Sat and Sun ● Suitable for wheelchairs ● Dogs on lead ● Gallery open with permanent exhibition of John Southwell watercolours ● Grade III

A rather surreal garden that displays a very personal choice of species trees, grasses and water garden features in a three and a half-acre site reclaimed from farmland. The owner gardeners are compulsive tree people who since 1963 have planted hundreds of species and exotic trees expanding the original cottage garden and pond into a mini-arboretum. Having purchased the original house because of the charm of the mature pear trees, the long narrow site now boasts a pinetum, a larch wood, nut hedges, splendid hip hedges and the latest manifestation, a prickly wood that offers 136 varieties of holly. (A list is provided for real holly lovers.) Most trees and plants are clearly labelled. This garden is an interesting example of how natural pasture land may be tamed and surface water channelled into ponds large enough to sustain fat carp. Worth a detour to read the signpost THE HOLLYWOOD – on Avon, and to see the evocative watercolours of winter painter, John Southwell, shown in a small gallery.

VINE HOUSE 14
Henbury, Bristol, Avon. Tel: (0272) 503573
Professor and Mrs T.F. Hewer

4m N of Bristol centre, in Henbury, next to Salutation pub • Open by appointment and 15th, 16th April, 27th, 28th May, 2.00 – 7.00 p.m. • Entrance: 60p, OAP and children 30p • Parking • Suitable for wheelchairs • Dogs on lead • Plants for sale • Grade III

Two acres of garden developed by the present owners since 1946 which although within the city has the good fortune to back on to the woodland of the large Blaise estate landscaped by Repton. This is a particularly interesting garden because its designers started by reducing it to 'brown earth' and planning the positioning of the planting by using sticks 'surmounted by caps of white paper as though they were trees and shrubs'. The result, surprisingly, is in 'large part a wild garden' although the specimen trees are labelled and one could call this an arboretum and botanical collection. There is a glade with bulbs, cyclamen and other small plants and a pond and water garden. Collection of herbaceous and hybrid tree peonies.

BEDFORDSHIRE

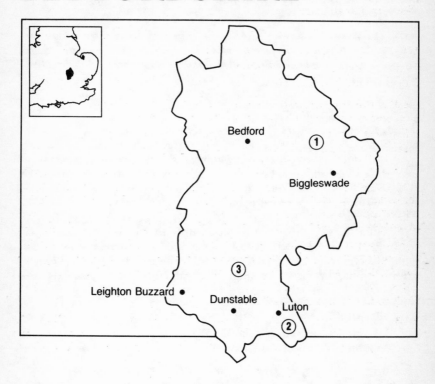

THE LODGE

Sandy, Bedfordshire. Tel: (0767) 80551
Royal Society for the Protection of Birds

1m E of A1 off B1042 Sandy – Potton road • Open daily, dawn to dusk • Best season: spring • Entrance: £1.50, OAP £1.00, children 50p • Parking • Toilet facilities • Suitable for wheelchairs • Shop • Grade IV

This is one of 60 reserves established by the RSPB throughout the country. The garden has many woodland walks and nature trails with extensive bird life and the rare Natterjack toad reintroduced and breeding happily. Nature trail and Nature Discovery Room. The Lodge was bought in 1934 by Sir Malcolm Stewart, who improved the garden and made a terraced fish pond on the south side. There is a Victorian terrace and fine trees in good lawns. Other features include a large weeping birch, Wellingtonias, azalea walks to a woodland heath, colchicums, acers, sweet chestnuts. A large begonia on the house. A huge wisteria, camellias and many big mature conifers. Two small walled gardens with *Garrya elliptica*, old wisterias and many *Clematis tangutica*. A very well planted vista of old cedar trees.

LUTON HOO 2
Luton, Bedfordshire. Tel: (0582) 30909
The Wernher family

2m SE of Luton, entrance W off A6129. Enter by Park Street gates ● *Open 16th April – 11th Oct, daily except Mon, 2.00 – 5.45 p.m. Last admission 5.00 p.m. Open Bank Holidays* ● *Best season: summer* ● *Entrance: £1.00, children 50p* ● *Parking* ● *Restaurant* ● *Toilet facilities* ● *Suitable for wheelchairs* ● *House open: £2.00, children £1.00* ● ***Grade II***

The house stands magnificently in a landscape by 'Capability' Brown with an abundance of large cedars, oaks, ashes and other mature trees. On the south side of the house is the formal garden with a large herbacous border, recently replanted, and two vast *Magnolia* x *soulangiana*. The lower terrace forms the rose garden in eight large beds edged with box and with a sheltering yew hedge. The walls of the terrace are covered in musk roses, *Garrya elliptica* and *Wisteria sinensis*. The rock garden, built early this century as a present for Lady Wernher from her husband, has small pools running through the centre with many water lilies. Some of the maples and dwarf conifers are the original planting, including *Juniperus horizontalis* and several different forms of *Acer palmatum*. There has been much new work with scree beds of *Iris reticulata*, sedum, lewisia, thymus etc. and peat walls with erica, abies, picea and pinus.

TODDINGTON MANOR 3
Toddington, Bedfordshire. Tel: (05255) 2576
Sir Neville and Lady Bowman-Shaw

1m NW of Toddington, 1m from M1 junction 12. First right in village, signed Milton Bryan ● *Open 24th June, 29th July, 12 noon – 6.00 p.m.* ● *Entrance: £1.50, children 50p* ● *Parking* ● *Teas on NGS day* ● *Suitable for wheelchairs* ● *Plants for sale* ● ***Grade III***

The Bowman-Shaws moved here in 1979 to find a wilderness, since reclaimed and planted with spring bulbs, flowering trees and other plants which lend colour on into the summer. They also inherited some wonderful old trees, especially beeches and Wellingtonias. They themselves made the pleached lime walk along a lovely old paved path, now bordered with pink and grey. A series of grey stone walled gardens are fully planted and mature with a good mixture of shrubs and plants, vines, viburnums, davidia, crinums, tree peonies, and *Hydrangea villosa*. In general planting has been of old favourites, but there are some rare and tender specimens in the greenhouse. Round the doorways between the gardens and in the borders, large daturas (both *sanguinea* and the semi-double 'Knightii') strike an unusual and interesting note. A herb garden, a nut walk and a wild garden are among newer projects. An island in a lake is planted with gunneras, amelanchier and hydrangeas.

BERKSHIRE

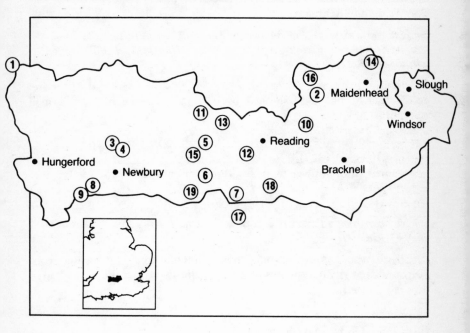

ASHDOWN HOUSE   1
Lambourn, Newbury, Berkshire. Tel: (0488) 72584
(some maps Oxfordshire)
The National Trust

*2½m S of Ashbury, 3½m N of Lambourn on W side of B4000   ● Open all year,
Sat – Thurs, dawn – dusk   ● Entrance: no charge for grounds   ● Parking 250
yards from house   ● Grounds suitable for wheelchairs   ● Dogs on lead   ● House
open April–Oct, Wed and Sat, 2.00 – 6.00 p.m. Closed Easter and Bank
Holiday Mon (charge for house entry)   ● Grade III*

The grounds of this seventeenth-century house are more a park than a garden.
A new box parterre behind the house was redesigned in 1960, based on a
simplified Victorian plan. Original west-facing lime avenue; other avenues
now being replanted with trees including oak and beech. Extensive woodland
walks, fine views. No flower or vegetable gardens.

BEAR ASH 2
Hare Hatch, Nr Reading, Berkshire.   Tel: (073522) 2639
Lord and Lady Remnant

2m E of Wargrave, ½m N of A4 at Hare Hatch ● Open 3rd June, 2.00 – 6.00 p.m. ● Entrance: 75p, children free ● Teas ● Toilet facilities ● Plants for sale ● Grade III

A delightful two-acre garden with a pleasant view over parkland. Silver and gold border. Shrubs, old-fashioned roses, swimming pool garden, and a small vineyard.

BUSSOCK WOOD 3
Snelsmore Common, Newbury, Berkshire.   Tel: (0635) 248203
Mr and Mrs W.A. Palmer

3m N of Newbury on B4494 ● Open 8th April, 2.00 – 6.00 p.m. ● Entrance: 50p, children 10p ● Parking ● Teas ● Toilet facilities ● Dogs ● Plants for sale ● Grade III

Wonderful views. A woodland garden with lily pond. Interesting trees. Surrounded by civilisation, it is hard to imagine that this was once a camp of the early Britons.

CHIEVELEY MANOR 4
Newbury, Berkshire.   Tel: (0635) 248208
Mr and Mrs C.J. Spence

½m from M4 in Chieveley village, Manor Lane by church ● Open 17th June, 2.00 – 6.00 p.m. ● Entrance: £1.00, children free ● Parking in field near house ● Teas ● Toilet facilities ● Suitable for wheelchairs ● Grade IV

Medium sized garden, including walled garden, swimming pool garden, herbaceous borders, shrubs and roses. Very well-maintained with new planting by present owners.

ENGLEFIELD HOUSE 5
Theale, Reading, Berkshire.   Tel: (0734) 302221
Mr and Mrs W.R. Benyon

Entrance is on A340, near Theale ● Open 10.00 a.m. – dusk, every Mon, and 22nd April, 20th May, 2.00 – 6.00 p.m. ● Entrance: £1.00, children free ● Teas in Long Gallery ● Toilet facilities ● Suitable for wheelchairs ● Plants for sale ● Grade II

A beautiful garden with a spectacular view. Deer park. Seven acres of woodland with interesting trees and shrubs. Stream and water garden. Terrace with borders, all excellently maintained.

FOLLY FARM 6
Sulhamstead, Nr Reading, Berkshire.

*7m SW of Reading. 2m W of junction 12 on M4. Take road marked
Sulhamstead at Jack's Booth 1m after Theale roundabout; entrance 1m on
right* ● *Open 22nd April, 28th May, 1st July, 2.00 – 6.00 p.m. Group
applications in writing* ● *Best season: spring/summer* ● *Entrance: £1.00,
children free. Parties at other times £2.00 per person.* ● *Parking* ● *Teas for
NGS* ● *Toilet facilities* ● *Partly suitable for wheelchairs* ● *Plants for sale on
open days* ● **Grade I**

A sublime example of the Lutyens and Jekyll partnership in its vintage years
before World War I. The intimate relationship of house and garden
personifies Lutyens' genius for design and craftmanship. A complex arrangement of spaces and courts is linked by herringbone patterned brick paths,
enhancing the vernacular origins of an attractive Edwardian country house.
The gardens retain much of their original character, although planting has
also been chosen to suit the taste of the present owners. The formal sunken
rose garden surrounded by a high yew hedge is particularly notable for its
masterful design on several levels. Other features include formal entrance
court, barn court, Dutch-inspired canal garden, flower parterre and tank
cloister. This is one of the country's most important twentieth-century
gardens.

FOUDRY HOUSE 7
Mortimer, Nr Reading, Berkshire.
Mr and Mrs J.G. Studholme

*6m SW of Reading, 4m from M4 junction 11 via Grazeley. At T-junction on
edge of village, from Grazeley, turn right. House 100 yards on right* ● *Open
6th May, 2.00 – 6.00 p.m.* ● *Entrance: 75p, children 10p* ● *Off-street parking
near church* ● *Teas* ● *Toilet facilities* ● *Suitable for wheelchairs* ● **Grade IV**

Attractive small collection of trees including acers, liquidambars, lirioden-
drons and eucalyptus, covering, in all, four acres.

FOXGROVE FARM 8
Enbourne, Newbury, Berkshire.   Tel: (0635) 40554
Miss Audrey Vockins

*Enbourne is 2½m SW of Newbury. From A343 turn right at The Gun Inn for
1½m* ● *Open by appointment Feb and March and 25th March, 14th April,
22nd May and one Sunday in mid-June, 2.00 – 6.00 p.m. Nursery open daily*
● *Entrance: 60p, children free* ● *Teas for NGS* ● *Suitable for wheelchairs*
● *Plants for sale* ● **Grade III**

This small garden adjoins a nursery run by the Vockins family. They specialize
in bulbs especially species snowdrops, also primroses, auriculas, alpines, and

small herbaceous plants. There is a delightful welcoming atmosphere and customers at the nursery are allowed to see the garden at times when it is not normally open to the public.

HAZLEBY HOUSE 9
North End, Newbury, Berkshire.   Tel: (0635) 253265
Mr and Mrs M.J. Lane Fox

6m SW of Newbury. From A343 Andover road outside Newbury take turning to Ball Hill and then road to Kintbury for ¼m ● Open 2nd July, 2.00 – 6.30 p.m. ● Entrance: £1.00, children 50p ● Parking ● Teas ● Toilet facilities ● Suitable for wheelchairs ● Plants for sale ● Grade III

A very attractive recently made garden with excellent plantings of shrubs and herbaceous perennials created by present owners. Each year there is another addition to excite the visitor.

HURST LODGE 10
Broad Common Road, Hurst, Berkshire.   Tel: (0734) 341088
Mr and Mrs A. Peck

On A321 Twyford – Wokingham road ● Open 13th May, 26th Aug, 2.00 – 5.30 p.m. ● Entrance: £1.00, children 10p ● Parking ● Teas ● Suitable for wheelchairs ● Dogs ● Plants for sale ● Grade IV

This old five-acre garden was developed by Lady Ingram who died in 1989. Her placing of trees and shrubs to give sensitive colour combinations makes for attractive views. The displays of flowers, bulbs, magnolias, hydrangeas, camellias and rhododendrons give a pleasing year-round effect. The most notable feature of the garden is the fine trees, a large cedar, old yews, copper beeches and scarlet oaks, a huge old oak and a Scots pine. Large kitchen garden. Lawns and a play area with several pieces of children's outdoor equipment make the garden inviting for young children, and overall there is an atmosphere conducive to a pleasant family day out.

LITTLE BOWDEN 11
Pangbourne, Berkshire.   Tel: (0734) 842210
Mr and Mrs M. Verey

1½m W of Pangbourne on the Pangbourne – Yattendon road ● Open by appointment and May Bank Holiday Sun and Sun nearest 9th July ● Best season: mid-May, late June/early July ● Entrance: £1.00 ● Parking: small groups in front of house. Open days parking in field ● Refreshments on open days ● Toilet facilities ● Suitable for wheelchairs ● Dogs on lead ● Grade III

Much of this three-acre semi-formal garden and three acres of woodland garden has been developed by the Vereys since 1949. But a glade with specimen trees and borders was developed by Percy Cane early this century. In May the canopy of the cherry wood is so thick with blossom, from far off it looks like snow; underfoot there is a carpet of bluebells with flowering shrubs, especially magnolias, azaleas, camellias. In July the herbaceous border along the whole length of the house is at its best, as are two other mixed borders of roses, shrubs and herbaceous plants; disaster struck the bed of *Cardiocrinum giganteum* last year, when the corms were accidentally deeply buried, but Mrs Verey hopes to rescue these over the next two or three years. In October the visitor should look out for the weeping lime. The terrace garden with original 1920s Italian olive jars and paved sunken garden with white flowers adjoins the house; also in the paved area is a pond with waterlilies, surrounded with plantings of roses and lilies. A silver plant border leads to a swimming pool area which is landscaped and sheltered by yew hedges and walls bearing roses, ceanothus and clematis.

THE OLD RECTORY 12
Burghfield, Reading, Berkshire.   Tel: (073529) 2206
Mr and Mrs R.R. Merton

5m SW of Reading. Turn S off A4 to Burghfield village and right after Hatch Gate Inn ● *Open last Wed in each month Feb – Oct, 11.00 a.m. – 4.00 p.m. and by appointment in writing* ● *Entrance: 50p, children 30p* ● *Parking* ● *Suitable for wheelchairs* ● *Plants for sale inc. unusual plants* ● *Grade II*

This garden has achieved wide renown and its maturity and the amazing generosity of plants skillfully planted are remarkable in a site started from scratch in 1950. Mrs Merton, described by herself as 'a green-fingered lunatic', has collected plants from all over the world notably some rare items from Japan and China. The terrace has a fine display most of the year, the herbaceous border and beds are impressive with collections of hellebores, pinks, violas, peonies, snowdrops, old roses and many others. In the spring there are drifts of daffodils and rather rare cowslips and so many other plants to see that it is well worth making a visit month by month if you live within reasonable range. There is something here for every type of gardener most of the year. The Mertons propagate everything so sales on open days are fascinating, and there is a 'mini-market' of stalls by other plantsmen.

OLD RECTORY COTTAGE 13
Tidmarsh, Pangbourne, Berkshire.   Tel: (0734) 843241
Mr and Mrs A.W.A. Baker

½m S of Pangbourne. Turn E down narrow lane ● *Open by appointment for garden societies only and on 15th April, 20th May, 24th June and 8th July, 2.00 – 6.00 p.m.* ● *Entrance: 75p, children free* ● *Parking* ● *Grade II*

Although this is not a large garden it is full of rare and exciting plants, many of them collected by the owner. It has a very dry area, with early spring bulbs, a wild garden round a small lake. Lilies, roses, unusual shrubs and climbers. It is worth visiting on each of the days it is open as there is always something new to stimulate the interest of a keen gardener.

ORCHARD COTTAGE 14
Sutton Road, Cookham, Berkshire. Tel: (06285) 21304
Mrs B.H. Samuel

In Cookham village, Sutton Road is the main road ● *Open by appointment and 5th, 21st Aug, 2.00 – 6.00 p.m.* ● *Entrance: 50p* ● *Parking in neighbouring roads* ● *Refreshments: tea and biscuits* ● *Toilet facilities* ● *Suitable for wheelchairs* ● *Plants for sale, especially herbs* ● **Grade III**

Mrs Samuel is replanting widely to widen interest and be more labour-saving. The roses, dahlias and 60 varieties of herbs for which the garden is famous remain, but there will be many new shrubs with a forest-bark ground cover for low maintenance. Peat block terraces filled with loose peat provide a home for gentians, lithospermums and camellias, to be accompanied by azaleas, rhododendrons for spring. Mrs Samuel's impatiens breeding has produced lovely double varieties, including a much- admired vermilion. A very unusual 'parrot' variety impatiens is in the collection; totally dissimilar to the more familiar blooms. The work involved in the fundamental restructuring seems daunting, but to Mrs Samuel, whose bungalow and garden were created from a derelict stable 25 years ago, it is 'all part of the fun of gardening'.

ST MARY'S FARM 15
Beenham, Nr Reading, Berkshire. Tel: (0734) 713705
Charles and Mary Keen

2m N of A4, halfway between Reading and Newbury ● *Open on written application only* ● *Entrance: 50p* ● *Parking* ● *Teas* ● *Plants for sale* ● **Grade II**

This eighteenth-century parsonage with fine trees and views has been given a wonderful uplift by the imaginative design and planting by the Keens. They have not been afraid of experimenting with bright colours, and the kitchen garden path flanked by apple trees holding hands, underplanted with scarlet poppies, is very striking if the garden happens to be open in poppy time. In any case, there is plenty to see and the herbaceous borders are particularly glorious.

SAVILL GARDEN
(see page 360)

SCOTLANDS   16
Cockpole Green, Berkshire.   Tel: (062882) 2648
Mr M. and the Hon. Mrs Payne

Halfway between Wargrave and Henley on A423. At top of hill take turning to
Cockpole Green ● *Open 28th, 29th April, 14th Oct, 2.00 – 6.00 p.m.*
● *Entrance: £1.00, children free* ● *Parking in meadow* ● *Teas* ● *Suitable for*
wheelchairs ● ***Grade III***

Well-planned and planted watergarden created by Mrs Payne from a mere
trickle. Astilbes, hostas, ferns, primulas, gunneras and many more moisture-
loving plants look very comfortable even after 1989's long dry summer. There
is hardly a space to be seen at the water's edge and in the surrounding shrub,
fuschia and ground cover borders even in October; a Humphrey Repton style
rustic summer house marks the merging of landscaped water garden with
natural woodland. Mown grass paths lead past the watergarden through the
woodland, around the pond and back up towards the house. On the other side
of the drive and nearest the house is the formal garden, terrace awash with
crevice plants, paved pool garden where a lead statue of a drummer boy holds
court among planted stone tubs, herbaceous borders and kitchen, herb and
flowers-for-cutting garden.

STRATFIELD SAYE HOUSE   17
Reading, Berkshire.   Tel: (0252) 882882
The Duke of Wellington

1m W of A33, halfway between Reading and Basingstoke. Turn off at
Wellington Arms Hotel ● *Open daily except Fri, May – last Sun in Sept, 11.30*
a.m. – 5.00 p.m. ● *Entrance: £3.00, children £1.50. Special rates for parties of*
20 or more ● *Parking* ● *Refreshments* ● *Toilet facilities* ● *Suitable for*
wheelchairs ● *Shop* ● *House open. Wellington Country Park, 3m from house*
caters for many tastes, and can be visited on continued entry ticket with house
and gardens ● ***Grade III***

You would expect to find Wellingtonias at the Duke's home and you will not
be disappointed. In this large area of parkland there are other fine trees
including a liquidambar reputed to be the largest in the country. As for the
gardens, these have been recently revived. The rose garden and the shrub
garden (once called the American garden) have been replanted. Perhaps the
most interesting area is the large walled garden, one half of which is laid to
grass and the other worked as a vegetable and fruit garden in the Victorian
manner. Down the centre runs a substantial herbaceous border. At one end is
a Camellia house, possibly built by Paxton whose boss, the Duke of
Devonshire, was a chum of the Iron Duke.

SWALLOWFIELD PARK 18
Reading, Berkshire.   Tel: (0734) 883815
Country Houses Association Ltd

5m S between Reading and Wokingham on A33 under M4; 2m then left to Swallowfield village. Entrance by the village hall ● Open May – Sept, Wed and Thurs, 2.00 – 5.00 p.m.   ● Entrance: £1.00, children 50p ● Limited parking in small courtyard in front of house ● Toilet facilities ● Suitable for wheelchairs ● Dogs on lead ● Grade III

The diarist John Evelyn called seventeenth-century Swallowfield 'a worthy house' and is said to have planted the row of yew trees (not the ancient yew hedge); Charles Dickens buried his dog, Bumble in the garden, and in the hot dry summer of 1989 BBC TV transformed the existing walled garden into a formal period garden of early nineteenth-century design. Despite the near drought conditions, new plantings have survived and are doing well. The gardens round the house, which is now divided into private apartments, are taken care of by the residents, and the main interest for visitors will undoubtedly be the 'new' walled garden.

WASING PLACE 19
Aldermaston, Reading, Berkshire.   Tel: (0734) 713398
Sir William and Lady Mount

3m S of A4 between Reading and Newbury. Turn off at Woolhampton ● Open 5th June, 1st July, 2.00 – 6.00 p.m.   ● Entrance: £1.00, children free ● Parking ● Teas ● Suitable for wheelchairs ● Plants for sale ● Grade II

This is a large garden on acid soil. Rhododendrons, azaleas and unusual trees and shrubs are at their best in spring. Magnificent cedars near the house. In summer the walled and kitchen garden, greenhouses and herbaceous borders all make this a beautiful place to visit.

BUCKINGHAMSHIRE

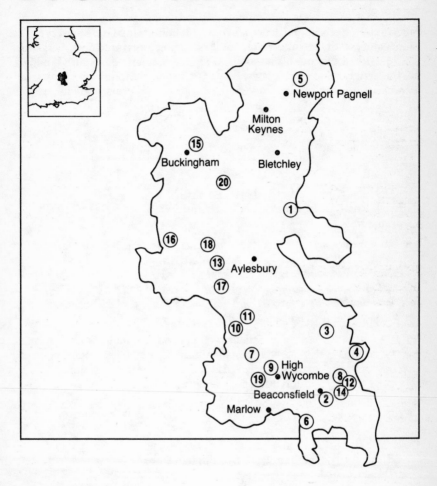

ASCOTT
Wing, Buckinghamshire. Tel: (0296) 688242
The National Trust

*½m E of Wing, 2m SW of Leighton Buzzard on S of A418 ● Open 4th, 11th
April and 23rd May – 29th Aug every Wed and last Sun in month and also
when house open. Also Bank Holiday Mon 27th Aug ● Best season: spring/
summer ● Entrance: £2.00, children £1.00 (grounds); £3.50, children £2.00
(house and garden) ● Parking 220 yards from house ● Toilet facilities
● Partly suitable for wheelchairs ● Dogs in car park only ● House and garden
open 14th April – 20th May and Sept; Tues – Sun, 2.00 – 6.00 p.m. Also Bank*

Holiday Mon 16th April and 7th May, 2.00 – 6.00 p.m. but closed Tues 17th April and 8th May ● **Grade I**

Thirty acres of Victorian gardening at its very best laid out with the aid of James Veitch and Sons of Chelsea. Formidable collection of mature trees of all shapes and colours set in rolling lawns. Fascinating topiary includes evergreen sundial with yew gnomon and inscription: 'Light and shade by turn but love always' in golden yew. Wide lawns slope away to magnificent views across the Vale of Aylesbury glimpsed between towering cedars. Formal gardens include the Madeira Walk with sheltered flower borders and the bedded-out Dutch garden. Two stately fountains were created by Story – one a large group in bronze, the other a slender composition in marble. Rock garden and fernery. Interesting all year, spring gardens feature massed carpets of bulbs.

BEKONSCOT MODEL VILLAGE 2
Warwick Road, Beaconsfield, Buckinghamshire. Tel: (0494) 672919
Church Army

From M40 take junction 2 for Old Beaconsfield. Signposted ● *Open March – Oct, daily, 10.00 a.m. – 5.00 p.m.* ● *Entrance: £1.60, OAP/student/ unemployed £1.00, children 80p. Parties of 13 or more £1.30 per person, children 65p* ● *Parking* ● *Refreshments: kiosk, hot and cold snacks, 11.00 a.m. – 4.30 p.m. most days. Picnic areas* ● *Toilet facilities* ● *Narrow wheelchairs available if required. Paths not very wide* ● *Souvenir shop* ● **Grade IV**

This one and a half-acre mini-village includes animals, buildings and people among imaginatively planted rockery landscapes. The oldest model village in the world and a masterpiece of landscape gardening in miniature. Of particular appeal to children and model railway enthusiasts. Narrow pathways may become congested in high season.

CAMPDEN COTTAGE 3
51 Clifton Road, Chesham Bois, Buckinghamshire.
Tel: (0494) 276818
Mr and Mrs P. Liechti

On A416 between Amersham and Chesham. Turn into Clifton Road by Catholic Church (opposite primary school). Close to traffic lights at a pedestrian crossing ● *Open by appointment for parties (but no coaches) and 25th March, 22nd April, 20th May, 10th June, 22nd July, 16th Sept, 2.00 – 6.00 p.m.* ● *Entrance: 80p, accompanied children free* ● *Parking in road, but on open days in school car park by arrangement* ● *Refreshments in Old Amersham* ● *Toilet facilities in Amersham on the Hill and Old Amersham* ● *Plants for sale* ● **Grade III**

Twenty one years ago the owner describes herself as 'never having given gardening a thought', and started to 'tidy' the neglected garden while builders took over the house. Straight lines have given way to a design adapted to take advantage of a magnificent weeping ash and the original network of stone paths has become a large York stone terrace surrounding the house. The owner's speciality is rare and unusual plants – when asked to point out those of interest in early September for a TV programme Mrs Liechti counted more than 400. She is also skilled in finding interesting associations of colour, shape and foliage.

CHENIES MANOR HOUSE   4
Chenies, Nr Amersham, Buckinghamshire.   Tel: (02404) 2888
Lt. Col. and Mrs MacLeod Matthews

Off A404 between Amersham and Rickmansworth. If approaching via M25, take junction 18 ● *Open April – Oct, Wed, Thurs and Bank Holidays in May and August, 2.00 – 5.00 p.m.* ● *Best season: summer* ● *Entrance: £1.00 (gardens only. House extra)* ● *Parking* ● *Teas* ● *Toilet facilities* ● *Suitable for wheelchairs* ● *Plants for sale* ● *Shop* ● *House open* ● ***Grade II***

The owners have created several extremely fine linked gardens in keeping with their fifteenth/sixteenth-century brick manor house. The gardens are highly decorative and maintained to the highest standards. Planted for a long season of colour and using many old-fashioned roses and cottage plants, there is always something to enjoy here. Formal topiary in the 'white' garden, collections of medicinal and poisonous plants in a 'physic' garden, an historic turf maze and a highly productive kitchen garden.

CHICHELEY HALL   5
Chicheley, Newport Pagnell, Buckinghamshire.   Tel: (023065) 252
Trustees of the Hon Nicholas Beatty and Mrs John Nutting

On A422 between Bedford and Newport Pagnell, 3m from M1 junction 14 ● *Open April, May, Aug and Sept, Sun and Bank Holiday Mon, 2.30 – 5.30 p.m.* ● *Entrance: £2.20, children £1.00. Parties special rates* ● *Parking* ● *Teas* ● *Toilet facilities* ● *Suitable for wheelchairs* ● *Shop* ● *House open* ● ***Grade III***

One of the best and least altered Georgian houses in the country is surrounded by an elegant park with fine avenues and views. Mature trees include oaks, cedars and limes. C-shaped canal lake attributed to London and Wise in 1709. Formal avenues (lime and laburnum) recently planted near the house.

CLIVEDEN   6
Taplow, Buckinghamshire.   Tel: (06286) 5069
The National Trust

2m N of Taplow on B476 ● *Open Mar – Dec, daily, 11.00 a.m. – 6.00 p.m. or sunset. Closed Jan – Feb* ● *Entrance: £2.50 (House £1.00 extra. Timed ticket)*

● *Parking* ● *Refreshments: light lunches, coffee, teas, in Orangery Restaurant*
● *Toilet facilities* ● *Partly suitable for wheelchairs* ● *Dogs in specified
woodlands only, not in gardens* ● *Shop* ● *House open April – Oct, Thurs and
Sun, 3.00 – 6.00 p.m. Last admission 5.30 p.m.* ● *Grade I*

A famous house built in 1666 by the Duke of Buckingham in the grand
manner overlooking the Thames which flows at the foot of a steep slope
below. The present house and terrace designed by Sir Charles Barry
incorporates a famous balustrade brought by the 1st Viscount Astor from the
Villa Borghese in Rome in the 1890s. The water garden, rose garden and
herbaceous borders are attractive in spring, summer and autumn respectively.
The formal gardens below the house and the Long Garden, fountains, temples
and statuary are pleasing throughout the year. Amongst famous designers
who have worked on the grounds are John Fleming (the parterre) Leoni (The
Octagon Temple) Bridgeman (walks and the amphitheatre) and Jellicoe (rose
garden). Part of the house is now a luxury hotel, and there is an Open Air
Theatre Festival in the summer.

GREAT BARFIELD 7
Bradenham, Buckinghamshire.   Tel: (024024) 3741
Mr Richard Nutt

*4m NW of High Wycombe. From A4010 at the Red Lion turn into village. At
bottom of village green turn right and walk down no through road* ● *Open
25th Feb, 7th May, 8th July, 2.00 – 6.00 p.m.* ● *Best season: spring and
summer* ● *Entrance: £1.00* ● *Parking next to village green* ● *Teas*
● *Suitable for wheelchairs* ● *Plants for sale* ● *Grade III*

This is a one and a half-acre plantsman's garden surrounding a modern house.
It is planted in contemporary style with wavy-edged borders, island beds and
immaculately kept lawns. Many climbing and shrub roses and herbaceous
plants. Borders planted for long season of interest.

HAREWOOD 8
Harewood Road, Chalfont St Giles, Buckinghamshire.
Tel: (02404) 3553
Mr and Mrs J. Heywood

*From A404 Amersham – Rickmansworth road, at miniroundabout in Little
Chalfont turn S down Cokes Lane. Harewood Road is 200 yards on left* ● *Open
by appointment and on 6th May, 17th June, 2.00 – 6.00 p.m.* ● *Best season:
spring to autumn* ● *Entrance: £1.00, children 25p* ● *Parking on street*
● *Teas* ● *Toilet facilities (W.C. for disabled ¼m away)* ● *Suitable for
wheelchairs once beyond gravel driveway* ● *Plants for sale* ● *Grade IV*

This one-acre garden has been developed over the last decade but specimen
trees planted a century ago and mature yew and box hedges give it a sense of
privacy and enclosure. Many unusual roses and clematis. Interesting hardy

plants have been chosen for foliage effect and climbers trained into neighbouring shrubs and trees. Other features include a pond garden. The condition throughout is very good all year round.

HUGHENDEN MANOR 9
High Wycombe, Buckinghamshire. Tel: (0494) 32580
The National Trust

1½m N of High Wycombe on A4128 ● Open March, Sat and Sun, 2.00 – 6.00 p.m., April – Oct, Wed – Sat, 2.00 – 6.00 p.m., Sun and Bank Holiday Mon, 12 noon – 6.00 p.m. Closed Good Friday. Last admission 5.30 p.m. ● Best season: spring – autumn ● Entrance: £2.50. Party rates on application ● Parking ● Toilet facilities inc. disabled ● Suitable for wheelchairs ● Dogs ● National Trust shop ● House open ● Grade II

High-Victorian garden created by Mrs Disraeli in 1860s and recently restored, dominated by a superb specimen cedar of Lebanon. Particularly pleasing is the human scale of house and gardens set in picturesque, unspoilt landscape. Woodland walks amongst ancient beeches and yews. Unusual chimaera shrub *Laburnocytisus adamii* produces yellow and mauve laburnum flowers and mauve sprays of *Cytisus purpureus* in late spring/early summer.

THE MANOR HOUSE 10
Bledlow, Buckinghamshire.
The Lord and Lady Carrington

½m from B4009 in middle of Bledlow village ● Open by written appointment, May – Sept, 2.00 – 4.30 p.m. and 15th April, 24th June, 2.00 – 6.00 p.m. ● Best season: spring – autumn ● Entrance: £1.00, children free. Lyde Garden open free every day ● Parking at farm next door ● Teas served on June open day ● Partly suitable for wheelchairs ● Grade II

With the help of landscape architect Robert Adams, Lord and Lady Carrington have created an elegant English garden of exceptionally high standard. Visit the highly productive and colourful walled vegetable garden, with York stone paths and central gazebo. Formal gardens are enclosed by tall yew and beech hedges. Mixed flower and shrub borders feature many roses and herbaceous plants around immaculately manicured lawns. The Lyde Garden (always open) is a wild area supporting a variety of species plants.

THE MANOR HOUSE 11
Princes Risborough, Buckinghamshire. Tel: (08444) 3168
The National Trust/Tenant Mr and Mrs R. Goode

From High Wycombe take A4010 to Princes Risborough. Turn left down High Street, left at the Market Square and then towards the church. The Manor is next to the church on right • By written appointment to the tenants, Wed, 2.30 – 4.30 p.m. (last admission 4.00 p.m.) and 13th May, 1st July, 2.00 – 6.00 p.m. • Best season: early summer • Entrance: 80p, children 20p • Public car park beside church • Teas for NGS on 1st July • Toilet facilities • Suitable for wheelchairs • Dogs by arrangement • House open by appointment on Wed, 2.00 – 4.00 p.m. • Grade III

Two acres of mature gardens surround this seventeenth-century manor house in the town centre restored by Lord Rothschild. The gardens are attractively laid out with mixed flower and shrub borders, box balls, orchard and wild area. Some mature trees. Recent planting includes new roses and herbaceous plants in pastel colours.

MILTON'S COTTAGE   12
Deanway, Chalfont St Giles, Buckinghamshire.   Tel: (02407) 2313
Milton Cottage Trust

½m W of A413, on B4442 to Beaconsfield • Open Mar – Oct, weekdays except Mon (but open Bank Holiday Mons), 10.00 a.m. – 1.00 p.m., 2.00 – 6.00 p.m., Sun, 2.00 – 6.00 p.m. • Best season: early summer • Entrance: £1.00, children under 15 40p, parties of 20 or more 80p per person • Suitable for wheelchairs • Shop • House open • Grade III

An historic cottage where Milton completed *Paradise Lost*, it houses many of Milton's artefacts. The half an acre of attractive gardens contain a large mulberry tree which was a cutting from Milton's famous tree at Christ's College, Cambridge. Planting is informal cottage style with rose arches, vines and tapestry hedges.

NETHER WINCHENDON HOUSE   13
Nether Winchendon, Nr Aylesbury, Buckinghamshire.
Tel: (0844) 290101
Mr and Mrs R. Spencer Bernard

5m SW of Aylesbury, 7m from Thame. Near the church in Nether Winchendon village • Open 15th April, 5th Aug, 2.30 – 6.00 p.m. and by written appointment for groups • Parking on street nearby • Suitable for wheelchairs • Grade III

Home of the Bernard family for centuries, the gardens surround a romantic brick and stone Tudor manor. Fine specimen trees include mature acers, catalpas, cedars, paulownias, liquidambars. Well-kept lawns, shrub and flower borders. Walled gardens include productive kitchen garden. Unusual avenue of dawn redwoods (not yet mature).

SPINDRIFT 14
Jordans Village, Nr Beaconsfield, Buckinghamshire.
Tel: (02407) 3172
Mr and Mrs E. Desmond

N of A40 in Jordans village, at far side of green turn right into cul de sac near school ● *Open for groups by appointment and 16th April, 4th June and 27th Aug, 1.00 - 6.00 p.m.* ● *Best season: summer* ● *Entrance: £1.00, children under 12, 25p* ● *Parking in school playground on open days* ● *Refreshments* ● *Toilet facilities* ● *Partly suitable for wheelchairs* ● *Dogs* ● **Grade III**

The house, built in 1933, was surrounded with trees and hedges and the present owners have extended the mature gardens on a sloping site with particularly interesting well-kept fruit and vegetable area. Productive vines under glass. Unusual trees and shrubs positioned throughout the garden. Collections of hostas and hardy geraniums.

STOWE LANDSCAPE GARDEN 15
Buckingham, Buckinghamshire.   Tel: (0280) 813650
The National Trust

½m from Buckingham on A422 ● *Open during school holidays, daily, 10.00 a.m. - 6.00 p.m. (last admission 5.00 p.m. or dusk if earlier) [1st - 10th Jan; 17th March - 17th April; 7th July - 4th Sept; 15th - 31st Dec; 1st - 8th Jan 1991.] During summer and autumn terms details on answering machine. Closed Good Friday and 25th, 26th Dec* ● *Entrance: £2.50* ● *Parking* ● *Refreshments during Easter and summer opening* ● *Toilet facilities in school* ● *Partly suitable for wheelchairs* ● *Dogs on lead* ● *House (Stowe School) may be open in holidays for extra £1.00* ● **Grade I**

The *Oxford Companion* says Stowe had an enormous influence on garden design especially after experiments there in 'natural' gardening in the 1730s. It continued to exhibit the changes of eighteenth-century taste and 'its final phase of idealized landscape still survives relatively intact'. It is a vast park with relatively few formal arrangements and the various changes made by the succession of distinguished designers who took a hand in it from the mid-seventeenth century are too numerous to be detailed. Viscount Cobham, Bridgeman, Vanburgh (who decorated the area with temples and other features) were followed by Kent who certainly designed buildings and probably the garden. 'Capability' Brown was head gardener from 1741 and his plantings were thinned out when he left 10 years later by the new owner Lord Temple. The latter also built a triumphal arch on the horizon, a focus for the main vista. Inevitably, as the work continued into the nineteenth century, the family money ran out, and the estate was sold to become a school in 1923. The governors, supported by money from the parents and ex-pupils, did well in their attempt to restore the 32 surviving buildings and the grounds so far as possible to their 1800 condition. The money that its successive owners have poured into Stowe justifies its reputation as a classic English garden. Now that the grounds are in the hands of the National Trust, which has launched an appeal for £1 million for Stowe, we may expect even greater things. If possible, the visitor should approach the gardens via the south portico of the school. The view then before him has been described as 'sudden and breathtaking' with, beyond the lawn, the Octagon Lake, the Lake Pavilions and Corinthian Arch. He may advance to walk in, and examine in detail, the Elysian fields. It is even possible to stay overnight in Stowe by renting the Gothic temple owned by a private group.

THE THATCHED COTTAGE 16
Duck Lane, Ludgershall, Buckinghamshire. Tel: (0844) 237415
Mr and Mrs D. Tolman

6m from Bicester, 13m from Aylesbury, 2m S of A41 ● Open 13th, 20th May, 17th, 24th June, 1st, 8th July, 26th Aug, 2.00 – 6.00 p.m. Parties by appointment on other days ● Best season: early summer ● Entrance: 75p, children free ● Parking on street ● Toilet facilities ● Dogs on lead ● Plants for sale at owners' nursery nearby ● Grade IV

Over the past decade the owners have restored the gardens surrounding their single-storey ancient thatched cottage. Their specialist nursery, located nearby, produces many interesting and rare herbaceous plants, some of which can be seen in the picturesque gardens round the cottage. Those interested in 'cottagey' plants will enjoy this garden.

TURN END 17
Townside, Haddenham, Buckinghamshire.
Tel: (0844) 291383/291817
Mr and Mrs P. Aldington

From A418 turn to Haddenham. From Thame Road turn at the Rising Sun into Townside. Turn End is 250 yards on left ● Open 8th April, 6th May, 1st July, 2.00 – 6.00 p.m. Also groups by appointment ● Best season: spring/early summer ● Entrance: £1.00, children 25p ● Parking on street ● Teas for NGS ● Toilet facilities ● House open once a year ● Grade II

Peter Aldington's RIBA award-winning development of three linked houses is surrounded by a series of garden rooms evolved over the last 25 years. A sequence of spaces, each of individual character, provides focal points at every turn. There is a fishpond courtyard, a shady court, a formal box court, an alpine garden, hot and dry raised beds and climbing roses. A wide range of plants is displayed to good effect against a framework of mature trees. This plantsman's garden is created within a one-acre town centre site.

WADDESDON MANOR 18
Waddesdon, Nr Aylesbury, Buckinghamshire.
Tel: (0296) 651211/651282
The National Trust

6m NW of Aylesbury on A41, 11m SE of Bicester. Entrance in Waddesdon village ● Open 4th April - 28th Oct. Grounds and aviary, Wed - Sat from 1.00 p.m. and from 11.30 a.m. on Sun. House times different. Good Friday and Bank Holiday Mon, 11.00 a.m. - 6.00 p.m. Note: closed completely on Wed following Bank Holiday ● Best season: spring - autumn ● Entrance: £1.50, children 5 - 17 75p, under 5 free (grounds and aviary) ● Parking ● Refreshments: light lunches and teas ● Toilet facilities inc. disabled ● Suitable for wheelchairs ● Dogs (but not allowed in aviary and children's play area) ● National Trust shop ● House open ● Grade I

Baron Ferdinand de Rothschild's remarkable chateau (built 1874-1889), which houses a formidable art collection, is set in an appropriately grand park with fountains, vistas, terraces and walks. The gardens contain an extensive collection of Italian, French and Dutch statuary. An ornate, semi-circular aviary of sixteenth-century French style, built 1889, provides a distinguished home to many exotic birds. The park today benefits from its 100-year old plantings of native yews, limes and hornbeams with a liberal sprinkling of exotic pines, cedars, Wellingtonias and cypresses.

WEST WYCOMBE PARK 19
West Wycombe, Buckinghamshire. Tel: (0494) 24411
The National Trust

At W end of West Wycombe, S of A40 Oxford road ● Open April - May, Sun and Wed, 2.00 - 6.00 p.m. June - Aug, Sun - Thurs, 2.00 - 6.00 p.m. Easter, May and Spring Bank Holiday Sun and Mon, 2.00 - 6.00 p.m. Last admission 5.15 p.m. Closed Good Friday ● Best season: spring - autumn ● Entrance: £2.00 (grounds), £3.50 (house and grounds) ● Parking ● Suitable for wheelchairs ● Dogs in car park only ● House open June - Aug, Sun - Thurs, 2.00 - 6.00 p.m. Last admission 5.15 p.m. ● Grade II

The park was largely created by the second Sir Francis Dashwood whose original designs, based on his experiences on the Grand Tour, were altered by Thomas Cook, a pupil of 'Capability' Brown, in 1779-80. Repton was called in by the next Dashwood but his plans never followed. The park survives as an important early example of the English Natural Landscape movement. Woodland and waterside walks lead to various classical temples. The music temple on an island in the lake is particularly fine. A small, pleasant park with views and vistas and a beautiful lake; this is not the place to visit if you seek flower gardens and rose beds.

WINSLOW HALL 20
Winslow, Buckinghamshire. Tel: (029671) 2323
Sir Edward and Lady Tomkins

10m N of Aylesbury, 6m S of Buckingham on A413 ● *Open by appointment for groups and 6th May, 2.00 - 6.00 p.m.* ● *Entrance: £1.50* ● *Parking* ● *Teas served in village* ● *Partly suitable for wheelchairs* ● *Grade III*

The original gardens were created around the house built in 1700 by Sir Christopher Wren, but the early work of London and Wise and others has disappeared. A sweep of lawn behind the house is bordered by shrubs and trees partly planted over the last 30 years by the owners, planting chiefly for foliage effect and autumn colour. Mixed shrub and flower borders and rose beds add summer interest.

THE GRADING SYSTEM

This is the most subjective aspect of the *Guide* and one which may cause some disagreement on the part of owners as well as visitors. We stress that its purpose is to serve as an indication to visitors in order to give them some advance information about the status of the garden as viewed by our inspectors and editors. Readers will appreciate that direct comparisons cannot be made between a huge estate like Chatsworth with its staff of professional experts and a tiny plantsman's garden in a terraced house, tended with dedication by a single owner. This being said, both may be excellent of their kind and therefore be worthy of consideration for a visit, and considered by the *Guide* to be at the top of their class. Conversely a lesser grading does not imply any criticism of a garden but is an attempt to guide the potential reader as to its relative merits if a choice has to be made between several gardens. Broadly speaking the intention of the four grades is as follows:

Grade I Amongst the best gardens in the world in terms of design and content. Many are of historic importance, but some are of recent origin. Overseas visitors to Britain or Ireland are recommended to include them in their itinerary.

Grade II Gardens of high quality, though not perhaps as unique as Grade I, and worth travelling a considerable distance to visit. Sometimes the property as a whole, and the general ambience, make the visit particularly rewarding.

Grade III These are gardens which our inspectors suggest it would be worth driving fifty miles or more to visit. They may have some special feature of design or plant content while not being considered as justifying a higher grade overall.

Grade IV Gardens of considerable merit and well worth visiting when in the region.

CAMBRIDGESHIRE

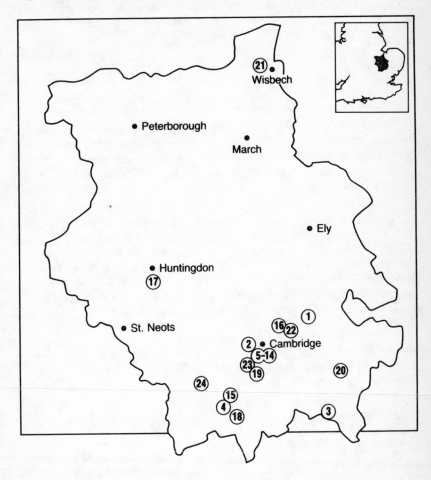

ANGLESEY ABBEY 1
Lode, Cambridgeshire.   Tel: (0223) 811200
The National Trust

In village of Lode, 6m NE of Cambridge, on B1102 ● Open 31st March – 15th July, Wed – Sun and Bank Holiday Mon, 12 noon – 5.30 p.m. Closed Good Friday. 16th July – 11th Sept, daily, 12 noon – 5.30 p.m. 12th Sept – 14th Oct, Wed – Sun, 12 noon - 5.30 p.m. ● Entrance: £1.50 (gardens only) ● Parking ● Refreshments: restaurant ● Toilet facilities ● Suitable for wheelchairs ● Plants for sale ● National Trust shop ● House open different times ● Grade I

The grounds cover 100 acres and were created in the last 50 years in the park of an abbey which was later converted to an Elizabethan manor. A very visual garden with magnificent vistas down avenues of mature trees and statuary and hedges enclosing small intimate gardens. 4500 hyacinths, spring bulbs and superb mature herbaceous borders. Silver pheasants.

THE BACKS   2
Cambridge.
University of Cambridge/Various owners

On W side of King's Parade. Either walk down Mill Lane or through King's College or approach by the W ring road. Or by punt down the Cam from the boathouse at Magdalene Bridge ● *Open all year* ● *Best season: spring* ● *Entrance: free* ● *Parking difficult* ● *Suitable for wheelchairs* ● *Dogs* ● *Grade II*

Although not a garden in the strict sense of the word, this open stretch was, like many garden/parks, the subject of 'Capability' Brown's interest in the late eighteenth century. In 1779 he prepared a plan to develop this splendid stretch of land which contains the River Cam and the 'backs' of the line of colleges to the east, but the individual colleges were reluctant to collaborate. Nonetheless the Backs today are one of the country's finest pieces of green space and the outcome is probably 'hardly less beautiful than even Brown could have made it' in the words of the *Oxford Companion*.

BARTLOW PARK   3
Nr Linton, Cambridgeshire.   Tel: (0223) 891609
Brigadier and Mrs Alan Breitmeyer

6m NE of Saffron Walden, 1½m SE of Linton, off A604 ● *Open 22nd April, 2.00 – 6.00 p.m.* ● *Entrance: £1.20, children 30p* ● *Parking* ● *Suitable for wheelchairs* ● *Grade II*

This garden was started 20 years ago by the Breitmeyers, helped by the renowned designer John Codrington, the former neglected garden being incorporated into the scheme. From the terraces there are splendid views of the park, through which run the headwaters of the River Granta. Other features include a formal rose garden, a tapestry beech and holly hedge, an old yew hedge and an avenue of sorbus, combined with many interesting trees and shrubs such as kolkwitzias, Judas and viburnums. There are good colour contrasts with *Acer platanoides, A.p.* 'Drummondii' and 'Goldsworth Purple', *Pyrus salicifolia, Robinia pseudoacacia* and many more. Good colour contrasts again in the border below the terrace, with piptanthus, *Cytisus battandieri, Clematis tangutica* and Michaelmas daisies for autumn interest.

BURY FARM   4
Meldreth, Nr Royston, Cambridgeshire.   Tel: (0763) 260475
Margaret Lynch

Just N of Royston on A10 to Cambridge, turn E signed to Meldreth. Opposite church • Open April – Aug, 1st Sun in the month and 17th June for Village event and by appointment • Best season: June/July • Entrance: £1.00, children 20p • Parking in back drive, or road • Toilet facilities • Suitable for wheelchairs • Plants for sale • Grade II

A plantsman's garden full of interesting and architectural plants – yuccas, acanthus, box, yew, euphorbias etc. A few ancient box trees remain from what was thought to be the parterre of the twelfth-century manor house. New yew avenue terminating in a box circle. Extensive shrub/herbaceous border in soft pinks and blues. Grey/white borders. Stone wall with appropriate planting. Good use of tender plants in garden and conservatory. Moat to be developed next. Collection of irises and campanulas. Monograph on campanulas just published by the owner.

CAMBRIDGE COLLEGE GARDENS
Most colleges are helpful about free access to their gardens although the more private ones, such as the Master's or Fellows', are rarely open. Specific viewing times are difficult to rely on because some colleges prefer not to have visitors in term time or on days when a function is taking place. The best course is to ask at the Porter's Lodge or to telephone ahead of visit. However, it is fair to say that some college gardens will always be open to the visitor, by arrangement with porters, even if others are closed on that particular day. There are also NGS openings at some colleges, when a charge is made, when Master's or Fellows' gardens may be open.
It has been said that the Cambridge college gardens are superior to those of Oxford because the former spend money on their upkeep while at the latter it is the upkeep of the Fellows that has the priority. Be that as it may, Cambridge also has the advantage of the Backs.

Parking is difficult • Refreshments in the town • All gardens suitable for wheelchairs • Access to college buildings, such as chapels, is often available by permission of porters and charges are now being made at some for this privilege. The college gardens have not been graded as they would probably be visited as part of a general visit to several colleges.

CHRIST'S COLLEGE   5
Tel: (0223) 334900

Open weekdays, 10.30 a.m. – 12.30 p.m., 2.00 – 4.00 p.m. Closed Bank Holidays and Easter week and May – mid-June.

An unusual garden originally formal but in 1825 relaid in Loudenesque style with large informal curved borders leading towards 'Milton's mulberry'. This was mounded up in 1856 to stop it leaning any more. Nearby is a cypress grown from seed from the cypress on Shelley's grave in Rome. Pool built in 1748 with summerhouse. Good clumps of hostas here. A clever canal in Charles Darwin's garden has false perspective to make it seem longer. In the roof garden on the new building plants grow well in one foot of loam, six inches of ash, nine inches of pea gravel. Good trees and lawns. Fellows' Garden never open.

CLARE COLLEGE FELLOWS' GARDEN 6
Tel: (0223) 333200

Open Mon – Fri, but closed Bank Holidays, 2.00 – 4.45 p.m. Open for NGS.

This two-acre garden was redesigned in 1946 by the then head gardener to give vistas and views. The north side has a long mixed herbaceous border edging the lawn. By the river are two spectacular red borders that are planted for autumn colour. A *Cercis siliquastrum* grows well here. Beyond the yew hedges is the sunken garden with a pond. Alpines are grown in the dry stone walling. There are blue/yellow borders and white borders, yew trees, a scented garden and a mass of things to see. Master's garden not open.

EMMANUEL COLLEGE GARDEN and
FELLOWS' GARDEN 7
Tel: (0223) 334200

Open daily during daylight hours except Fellows' Garden only open 14th July

Three large gardens with pools, a herb garden, herbaceous borders and fine trees including *Metasequoia glyptostroboides*. The Fellows' Garden has a great Oriental plane. Herb garden designed by John Codrington.

KING'S COLLEGE FELLOWS' GARDEN 8
Tel: (0223) 350411

Open daily until 6.00 p.m. Limited access mid-April – mid- June. Closed 8th, 9th Aug and 26th Dec – 3rd Jan.

One of the great architectural experiences which Britain has to offer, the garden is principally of lawns and magnificent old specimen trees. The Wellingtonias (*Sequoiadendron giganteum*) because of their huge size must have been planted here almost as soon as they were introduced into this country, thus dating them 1855-70. The *Koelreuteria paniculata* is also a venerable old tree which bears its golden flowers regularly – hence its popular name of Gold Rain tree. Spring bulbs. Splendid views of the Backs.

LECKHAMPTON (Corpus Christi) 9
37 Grange Road.   Tel: (0223) 335498

Open probably 6th May, 2.00 – 6.00 p.m.

COLLEGE GARDENS/CAMBRIDGESHIRE

Originally built as a private house in 1880 by F.W.H. Myers on land leased from the College, the garden layout was by William Robinson. The original garden covered seven acres but with the new buildings (1965) two further acres were added. The principal features of the Robinson design have been kept. There are lime and chestnut avenues and some fine trees including *Prunus* x *hillieri*, with bulbs, cowslips, oxlips and other spring flowers. A rose garden has been developed on an old tennis court site.

MAGDALENE COLLEGE GARDEN and FELLOWS' GARDEN 10

Open daily, 1.00 – 6.30 p.m., May and June, 1.00 – 5.00 p.m.

Some good hanging baskets and standard fuchsias in this tiny college of immaculate lawns. Odd to see ornamental cabbages here but Magdalene men have always had individual tastes.

PEMBROKE COLLEGE 11
Tel: (0223) 338100

Courtyard gardens with clever use of plants. Evergreen border. Good trees including the unusual golden elm. Dry walls around sunken garden planted with sages, grey plants and ivies. Wall planting excellent using unusual shrubs such as clipped euonymus and pomegranates. Purple-leaved pittosporum planted with the pink variety. Large catalpa with bunches of beans. Fellows' Garden never open, they say.

PETERHOUSE COLLEGE 12
Tel: (0223) 338200

Not a large garden, but varied. Apple avenue. Interesting hedge of escallonia and hebe. Some good trees and shrubs with contrasting foliage. Indigofera, parrotia, acers etc. A fairly new herb garden with pineapple sage, among many others, and a tree echium flowering but the laurel hedge is too big and coarse for a small area. Octagonal court cleverly planted. The hot side has tender plants, purple-leaved tradescantia and grey-leaved artemisias, cordylines, lanatas. The cooler side, hostas. A dramatic planting of orange-berried pyracantha with blue morning glory scrambling through it. The Fellows' Garden can be opened by arrangement.

ST JOHN'S COLLEGE 13
Tel: (0223) 338600

Open daily until 5.30 p.m. but although college closed to visitors May and June, entry from Backs possible.

45

This is a huge park-like garden, with eight acres of grass to be mown. Good mature trees – mulberries, chestnuts etc. Hundreds of bulbs flower in spring – more are planted each year – so a spring visit is worthwhile. The Fellows' Garden, never open to the public, has its original bowling green of 1630 now used as a croquet lawn. The wilderness was introduced by 'Capability' Brown and is massed with martagon lilies and other wild flowers. A rose garden – clematis and roses spilling over old walls. The Scholars' Garden designed in 1953 'by a lady' has a most unusual rose 'Brown Velvet'. Immaculately-kept lawns as in all Cambridge gardens.

TRINITY COLLEGE 14
Tel: (0223) 338400

A garden of 45 acres immaculately maintained by a staff of 10 gardeners. Although not officially open, dedicated visitors may see it by courtesy of the head gardener. Curved paths around shrubs and trees. Octagonal paved area planted with golden shrubs. Newly-planted bog area. Huge conical clipped yews. Fine avenues of planes, chestnuts and limes underplanted with cyclamen. The Master's garden has good herbaceous borders and a magnificent 60 ft beech hedge. Large mulberry.

CROSSING HOUSE GARDEN 15
Meldreth Road, Shepreth, Cambridgeshire. Tel: (0763) 61071
Mr and Mrs Douglas Fuller

8m SW of Cambridge, ½m W of A10 ● Open every day ● Entrance by collecting box ● Some parking ● Suitable for wheelchairs ● Grade II

This is a tiny garden, started by the present owners 30 years ago. No matter what time of the year you visit it there is always something fascinating growing. In all there are 5,000 species to see. It is also an eye-opener as to what can be achieved in such a small space – from the use of diminutive box edges, to the yew arches that are beginning to grow, to the three tiny greenhouses packed with unusual plants.

HARDWICK HOUSE 16
Fen Ditton, Nr Cambridge, Cambridgeshire. Tel: (0225) 2246
Mr L. and M.J. Drake

3½m NE of Cambridge. From A45 Newmarket Road turn N by the borough cemetery ● Open by appointment and 17th June, 2.00 - 6.00 p.m. ● Best season: spring/summer ● Entrance: £1.00, children 50p ● Parking in road ● Teas in Cambridge ● Toilet facilities ● Suitable for wheelchairs ● Plants for sale ● Grade II

This medium-sized garden can be visited at any time but particularly in the spring when the bulbs and the cherry blossom are out. Here is the National collection of aquilegias – over 80 different varieties – so they are worth a visit in themselves. There are hedges everywhere to protect the garden from the searing winds – hedges of beech, quickthorn and hornbeam. A pleached lime avenue is just beginning to take off, after 10 years. There is an attractive silver birch avenue too. Roses climb into trees. Old-fashioned plants, herbs and shrubs grow into the enclosures.

ISLAND HALL   17
Godmanchester, Nr Huntingdon, Cambridgeshire.
Tel: (0480) 459676/411675
Mr C. and the Hon. Mrs Vane Percy

On the main street in the centre of Godmanchester ● *Open May – Sept for parties by appointment and others Suns only and 10th June and 9th Sept, 2.30 – 5.30 p.m.* ● *Entrance: £2.00, children £1.00. No children under 13 in house* ● *Parking in municipal car park* ● *Teas* ● *Toilet facilities* ● *House open* ● *Grade IV*

In a tranquil riverside setting with its own island, the garden has been reclaimed from neglect and from the Nissen huts put there when the house was requisitioned in World War II. The terrace has been removed and replaced at a lower level with gravel – to the benefit of the house. Formal shaped borders planted with different box are either side of the gravel terrace. Gaps have been left in the gravel for fastigiate yew. New shrubberies have been planted with a walk through to white and blue borders – urns, hedges and vistas are there. The island is being cleared and wild flowers encouraged. An exact replica of the original Chinese bridge over the millstream has just been finished.

MELBOURN LODGE   18
Melbourn, Cambridgeshire.   **Tel: (0763) 260680**
Mr J. Keatley

3m N of Royston, 8m S of Cambridge. Off A10 in the middle of the village ● *Open 17th June, 2.00 – 6.00 p.m.* ● *Entrance: £1.00* ● *Parking difficult (not in main road)* ● *Suitable for wheelchairs* ● *Grade III*

A garden created by Mr Keatley who has built all the 'bones' himself: large and small walls, steps, paths etc. There are plans to put in York stone paths and pave a courtyard, as well as to find a suitable terracotta bird-bath to complement a terracotta sundial. The soil is dreadful – very thin over chalk – but the beautiful *Cornus controversa* 'Variegata' planted in 1970 seems to love it. Some new planting is being considered. The existing planting is mainly for leaf shape and interest rather than colour. Interesting statues.

NORTH END HOUSE 19
Grantchester, Nr Cambridge, Cambridgeshire. Tel: (0223) 840231
Sir Martin and Lady Nourse

*2m SW of Cambridge. Approaching on the A10 from S, turn left at
Trumpington (junction 11 on M11). If approaching from N on M11, take
junction 12 ● Open 24th June, 2.00 – 6.00 p.m. ● Entrance: not known
● Parking ● Teas ● Suitable for wheelchairs ● Grade II*

A good example of how to make a fairly small garden look interesting all the
year round. The bones of this newly laid-out garden are excellent with
beautifully maintained hedges, a small terrace imaginatively planted, a
rockery, pergola and herbaceous borders and a thickly planted shrubbery
totally concealing a tennis court. The swimming pool and conservatory are in
immaculate condition. A mirror carefully placed in an archway adds to the
illusion of space.

PADLOCK CROFT 20
West Wratting, Cambridgeshire. Tel: (0223) 290383
Mr and Mrs P.E. Lewis

*On the outskirts of the village by West Wratting Park ● Open March – Oct,
daily except Wed and Sun, 10.00 a.m. – 6.00 p.m. Wed and in winter by
appointment ● Best season: May – July ● Entrance: 60p, children 30p for
NGS. Free at other times ● Limited parking ● Teas for NGS ● Toilet
facilities ● Suitable for wheelchairs ● Plants for sale ● Grade II*

A two- to three-acre garden created during the last 50 years which holds over
280 varieties of campanula for the National collection along with a large
variety of alpines and other perennial plants. Many different environments
have been created for growing plants from all over the world including very
rare plants such as the St Helena ebony that was once thought to be extinct.
There is an experimental fruit cage with Chinese raised beds.

PECKOVER HOUSE 21
North Brink, Wisbech, Cambridgeshire. Tel: (0945) 583463
The National Trust

*In centre of Wisbech on N bank of the River Nene ● Open 31st March – Oct,
Sat, Sun, Bank Holiday and every Mon – Wed (garden only), 2.00 – 5.30 p.m.
Closed Good Friday ● Entrance: £1.50 ● Teas ● House open (principal rooms
only) ● Grade I*

For a hundred years or so this Victorian garden has been 'the product of
prudent tidiness, a period piece'. Given in 1943 to the National Trust by
Alexandrina Peckover, it had been in the same family since the second half of
the eighteenth century. A town house, with two and a quarter acres of garden,
it contains some very interesting trees. A maidenhair tree, one of the largest in

England, was planted a century ago by the donor's Peckover grandfather. Hardy palms withstand the English winter, and in the Orange House is an orange tree bearing fruit which was bought at the Hagbeach Hall sale and is at least 200 years old. In the conservatory are billbergias, daturas and monsteras. Another small house contains tender ferns. Trees and plants are rather in the Victorian taste, such as fern-leaved beech, Wellingtonias and Lawson cypresses, yuccas and spotted-leaved aucubas. The garden is divided by walls; imaginative planting of bulbs, climbers and herbaceous plants make for continuous interest throughout the year. An elegant summer-house is joined to the conservatory by matching borders edged with pinks.

THE RECTORY 22
Fen Ditton, Nr Cambridge, Cambridgeshire. Tel: (02205) 3257
The Revd. and Mrs L. Marsh

Off A45 Cambridge – Newmarket road. Turn N by cemetery into Ditton Lane
● *Open 17th June, and 1 day in July, 2.00 – 6.00 p.m.* ● *Best season: spring*
● *Entrance: £1.00 (fee of £1.00 for July opening covers combined admission to Hardwick House and Old Stables in the same village)* ● *Parking* ● *Teas*
● *Toilet facilities* ● *Suitable for wheelchairs* ● *Plants for sale when available*
● *Grade III*

The garden of this late seventeenth-century house is now reduced to one acre and is in the process of being restored. Some 35 varieties of old-fashioned roses and species roses have been planted with herbaceous plants to extend the flowering season. There are many rare plants including *Arisaema candidissimum*. Also good mature trees. Many fruit trees have been planted, mulberry, walnut and peach among others. Vegetables are grown organically and in sufficient amounts to provide vegetables for the whole year. Masses of bulbs in the spring.

UNIVERSITY BOTANIC GARDEN 23
Cambridge. Tel: (0223) 336265
University of Cambridge

In S Cambridge, on E side of A10 (Trumpington Road). There is also an entrance from Hills Road on the E ● *Open all year, weekdays, 8.00 a.m. – 6.00 p.m. in summer (closes 4.00 p.m. in winter), May – Sept, Sun, 2.30 – 6.00 p.m. for ticket holders only* ● *Entrance: free* ● *Parking in road* ● *Refreshments*
● *Toilet facilities* ● *Suitable for wheelchairs* ● *Grade I*

This garden covers a huge area (40 acres) and is so diverse that a brief description will not do it justice. It admirably fulfils its three purposes – research, education and amenity. A visit at any time is worthwhile – even in winter when the stem garden, especially on a sunny day, is dramatic. The various cornus with red, black, green and yellow-ochre stems contrast with *Rubus thibetanus*, while the pale pink trunk of the birch *Betula albo-sinensis* var.

septentrionalis is stunning. There is a splendid collection of native trees as well as exotic ones, including *Asimina triloba* and a good specimen of *Tetracentron sinense*. Among the collections is a fine one of salix and poplars. *Populus nigra* is now rare in England. A central area is reserved for research. There are also rockeries (both sandstone and limestone), a collection of tulip species, a scented garden, a fine range of glasshouses (hot and cool), a library and a herbarium of cultivated plants. Every specimen is clearly labelled. In 1990 a new Gilmour building will be partly completed, named after a director who greatly expanded the garden in the 1950s and 60s.

WIMPOLE HALL   24
Arrington, Royston, Cambridgeshire. Tel: (0223) 207257
The National Trust

7m SW of Cambridge signposted off A603 at New Wimpole ● Open 31st March – 4th Nov, daily except Mon and Fri, but open Bank Holiday Mon, 10.30 a.m. – 5.00 p.m. Closed Good Friday. Pre-booked guided tours 10.30 a.m., 11.45 a.m., 1.45 p.m., 3.00 p.m. with head gardener Michael Waites ● Best season: spring ● Entrance: £3.80 (Hall and garden) ● Parking ● Refreshments: teas and lunches ● Toilet facilities ● Suitable for wheelchairs ● Minimal number of plants for sale ● National Trust shop ● House open 25th March – Oct, daily except Mon and Fri ● Grade II

The gardens of this mid-seventeenth-century house followed almost every fashion in landscaping from 1690 to 1810. Today it is much changed due to Dutch elm disease. However, parterres, simplified by the National Trust, have been recently reinstated to the north of the house. Extensive and beautifully kept lawns but little else for the discerning plantsman. The surrounding landscape is of great historic and aesthetic interest and includes a two and a quarter-mile avenue, originally planted in elm in 1792, recently replanted with limes by the National Trust. Today, the Hall is used as a farm centre with a children's corner and agricultural museum. Also adventure playground and film loft.

CHESHIRE

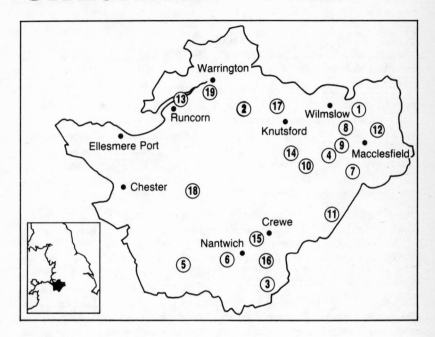

ADLINGTON HALL 1
Macclesfield, Cheshire. Tel: (0625) 829206
Mr C.F. Legh

5m N of Macclesfield off the A523. Signposted in the village of Adlington
● *Open Good Friday – Sept, Sun and Bank Holidays, 2.00 – 5.30 p.m., also Aug, Wed, Sat, Sun and Bank Holidays, 2.00 – 5.30 p.m.* ● *Best season: May/ early June* ● *Entrance: £2.00, children 95p, parties of 25 or more £1.50 per person* ● *Parking* ● *Refreshments in tea rooms* ● *Toilet facilities* ● *Partly suitable for wheelchairs* ● *Dogs on lead* ● *Shop* ● *House open* ● ***Grade III***

To the front of the house (fifteenth- and sixteenth-century with Georgian additions) a gravel drive encircles an oval of lawn with a sundial at its centre. Beyond there is more grass, then through a pair of iron gates is a short avenue of limes dating from 1688. After these a path leads eastwards to the Shell House, a small brick building dating from 1794, in which shells were stuck around its walls in the mid-nineteenth century. To the west is a wood through which there are walks open to the visitor. The walk along the small river bank is particularly pleasant. In the centre, close to a bridge is the Temple of Diana. East from the house across a cobbled area is a formal pool. A large statue of Neptune lies at the back with water pouring into the pool from a pitcher that he leans on. There are also bright beds of annuals and a small herb garden in this area. Not much interest, then, for the plantsperson but an attractive woodland park, mostly landscaped in the eighteenth century.

ARLEY HALL AND GARDENS 2
Arley, Nr Northwich, Cheshire. Tel: (056585) 353
The Hon M.L.W. Flower

5m W of Knutsford, 7m SE of Warrington on A50. Follow signs. Also signed from M6 junctions 19/20 and M56 junctions 9/10 ● *Open April – May, Sept – Oct, Tues – Sun and Bank Holidays, 2.00 – 6.00 p.m., June – Aug, Tues – Sun and Bank Holidays, 12 noon – 6.00 p.m.* ● *Entrance: £1.40, children under 17, 80p (grounds), £2.30, children under 17, £1.25 (Hall and grounds)* ● *Parking* ● *Teas. More elaborate meals by arrangement* ● *Toilet facilities* ● *Suitable for wheelchairs* ● *Dogs on lead* ● *Plants for sale* ● *Shop* ● *House open as gardens except June – Aug. Hall closed to 2.00 p.m.* ● ***Grade II***

The garden at Arley Hall contains what is believed to be the oldest, and is certainly one of the finest, herbaceous borders in England. One of the few remaining landed estates in Cheshire, this is the ancestral house of the Warburtons who built their first house there in the fifteenth century, though the present Arley Hall dates only from 1840. The gardens cover 12 acres and were awarded the Christie's and Historic Houses Association Garden of the Year Award. Bounded by old brick walls and yew hedges, there is a special predilection for the tonsured, as evidenced in the splendid avenue of pleached limes which form the approach to the house and the somewhat bizarre Ilex avenue which consists of 14 ilex trees clipped to the shape of giant cylinders. The walled garden, once a kitchen garden, now contains a variety of cordoned fruit trees, shrubs and herbaceous plants. There is also a collection of hybrid and species shrub roses, a rock garden planted with azaleas and rhododendrons, and a contemporary addition of a woodland garden which illustrates a continuous commitment to a family tradition.

BRIDGEMERE GARDEN WORLD 3
Bridgemere, Nr Nantwich, Cheshire. Tel: (09365) 239/381/382
Mr J. Ravenscroft

3m S of Woore on A51 between Nantwich and Stone ● *Open summer weekdays, 9.00 a.m. – dusk or at latest 8.30 p.m., Sun, 10.00 a.m. – dusk, winter weekdays, 9.00 a.m. – 5.00 p.m., Sun, 10.00 a.m. – 5.00 p.m. Closed Christmas Day and Boxing Day* ● *Entrance: 50p for display gardens (Garden Kingdom)* ● *Parking* ● *Refreshments: coffee shop* ● *Toilet facilities, inc. disabled* ● *Suitable for wheelchairs* ● *Plants for sale* ● *Shop* ● ***Grade III***

Begun in 1961 with one field of roses, this garden centre now claims to be Europe's largest. There are large areas with all types of plants for sale, garden ornaments, conservatories and greenhouses. Although some of these areas are attractively laid out, the main area of interest as a garden to view is the Garden

Kingdom. This has been made mainly to show what the plants offered for sale will come to look like, and most plants are labelled. There is a rose garden, including modern and old-fashioned shrub roses, rhododendron garden, winter garden, large herbaceous border, white garden, rock and water garden, cottage garden and a vegetable and fruit garden demonstrating some unusual ways of growing your own food. Most of these areas are, as is to be expected, very well kept.

CAPESTHORNE HALL AND GARDENS   4
Macclesfield, Cheshire. Tel: (0625) 861221/861439
Sir Walter and Lady Bromley-Davenport

7m S of Wilmslow, 1m from Monks Heath on A34 • *Open April, Sun, May and Sept, Sat - Sun, June - Aug, Tues - Thurs, Sat - Sun, 12 noon - 6 p.m.* • *Entrance: £1.20, children 5 - 16, 50p (Hall extra)* • *Parking* • *Refreshments: lunch, afternoon teas, supper by arrangement* • *Toilet facilities* • *Suitable for wheelchairs* • *Dogs in park only* • *Shop* • *House open as gardens but 2.00 - 5.00 p.m. only* • *Grade II*

Capesthorne is one of East Cheshire's fine historic parks showing the English style of eighteenth- and nineteenth-century landscape design with belts of trees enclosing a broad sweep of park and with the house as the focal element. The gardens are best enjoyed by following the suggested woodland walks, because the outstanding features are the range of mature trees, and the views and plant-life associated with the series of man-made lakes. There is much, too, to interest those with a taste for the history of gardens – for example the site of a conservatory built by Sir Joseph Paxton. There is a pair of outstanding rococo Milanese gates, and more conventionally a formal lakeside garden planned in the 1960s by garden designer Vernon Russell-Smith.

CHOLMONDELEY CASTLE GARDENS   5
Cholmondeley Castle, Malpas, Cheshire. Tel: (082922) 383/203
The Marquess of Cholmondeley

On A49 between Tarporley and Whitchurch • *Open Easter - 24th Sept, Sun and Bank Holidays, 12 noon - 5.30 p.m.* • *Entrance: £1.50, OAP £1.00, children 50p* • *Parking* • *Refreshments* • *Toilet facilities* • *Plants for sale* • *Shop* • *Grade III*

In spite of the ancient family name (pronounced Chumley), the Castle and more particularly the gardens are of relatively recent development, and understandably therefore they lack the maturity of other Cheshire parklands. As a site, though, it is magnificent, with the castle straddling a hill-top and a view across parkland to a distant mere, and the classic cricket square in between. Much has been done by the present owners to develop the gardens which consisted in the 1960s of but a few (but splendid) cedars and oaks and the creation of the Temple Gardens in particular – bordered walkways around a water garden – is most satisfying with its rock garden with a fine view of the lake that leads into a stream garden planted with moisture-lovers. The grass round the tea room is filled with wild orchids and backing away from this is a good planting of rhododendrons. The rose garden contains an interesting mixture of old and new.

DORFOLD HALL 6
Nantwich, Cheshire. Tel: (0270) 625245
Mr R. Roundell

1m W of Nantwich, S of A534 ● Open April – Oct, Tues and Bank Holiday Mons, 2.00 – 5.00 p.m. ● Best season: spring ● Entrance: £2.00 ● Parking ● Toilet facilities ● Partly suitable for wheelchairs ● House open ● Grade III

Dorfold Hall, impressive from the front, is approached through an avenue of limes with open parkland to each side and a large pool just to the west. The approach to the house is thought to have been laid out by William Nesfield who was chosen to design various parts of Kew. To the rear or south of the house is a large lawn at the east side of which is a statue of Shakespeare standing between two modern shrub borders. To the south is a low wall with a narrow border planted with shrub roses, beyond this is another large lawn from where there are views across a ha-ha to the flat countryside in the south. A broad grass walk leads eastwards to a dell. Here rhododendrons and other acid- loving shrubs have been planted amongst mature trees around a small stream, an area developed by the present owner. To the west is another grassed area with specimen trees; two fine gates lead to a disused walled garden.

GAWSWORTH HALL 7
Macclesfield, Cheshire. Tel: (0260) 223456
Mr and Mrs T. Richards

3m S of Macclesfield off A536. Signposted ● Open 7th April - 7th Oct, 2.00 – 5.30 p.m. ● Best season: midsummer ● Entrance: £2.50, children £1.25 (house and garden) ● Parking ● Refreshments: tearooms at pavilion in car park ● Toilet facilities ● Suitable for wheelchairs ● Small shop ● House open ● Grade III

Gawsworth Hall is approached by a drive leading between two lakes which arrives at the north end of the hall where there is a large yew tree and lawns sloping down to one of the lakes. A formal garden on the west side of the house has beds of modern roses edged by bright annuals and many stone ornaments including a sundial and circular pool with a fountain. Stone steps lead to a sunken lawn area with borders of shrubs and perennials. To the south is another lawned garden surrounded by a high yew hedge and herbaceous borders. A grassed area containing mature trees lies to the west of these formal areas, from where there is a view of the medieval tilting ground. Small conservatory with classical statues.

HARE HILL GARDENS 8
Hare Hill, Over Alderley, Nr Macclesfield, Cheshire.
Tel: (0625) 828981
The National Trust

N of B5087 between Alderley Edge and Prestbury at Greyhound Road • Open April - 28th Oct, Wed, Thurs, Sat, Sun and Bank Holiday Mon, 10.00 a.m. - 5.30 p.m. Special opening for azaleas 21st May - 8th June, daily, 10.00 a.m. - 5.30 p.m. Nov - Mar 1991, Sat and Sun, 10.00 a.m. - 5.30 p.m. • Best season: spring/early June • Entrance: £1.00 • Parking • Toilet facilities • Partly suitable for wheelchairs • Grade III

This garden consists of two distinct areas, a walled garden, once used for growing vegetables, and surrounding it a large woodland garden. The walled garden is rather sparsely planted. Climbing plants around the walls include vines, roses, ceanothus and wisteria, and in the centre are a few small rosebeds. A seat set into the north wall is surrounded by a white trellis pergola and nearby are two wire statues. The woodland garden is perhaps of greater interest. It contains over 50 varieties of holly, many fine rhododendrons and magnolias and there are spring flowering bulbs and some climbing roses growing high into their host trees. In the centre is a small pond spanned by two rustic wooden bridges.

HENBURY HALL 9
Nr Macclesfield, Cheshire.
Mr S.Z. de Ferranti

Turn S from the A537 by the Blacksmiths Arms. The entrance is 200 yards down the lane • Open for NGS, dates N.A. • Parking in field • Teas • Toilet facilities • Partly suitable for wheelchairs • Grade III

Henbury Hall was built in 1986 based on Palladio's Villa Rotunda and its light creamy stone goes well in its parkland setting. To the north of the hall the land slopes down to a lake. The area around is well-landscaped and planted with many mature trees and rhododendrons. There is a fountain in the centre of the lake and small ornamental bridges at each end. The land to the north rises again, and beyond more banks of trees and shrubs there is a walled kitchen garden. Close by is a unique design of tennis court and a large modern conservatory housing a swimming pool, a fernery and a grotto. At the other side of the kitchen garden is a cottage recently renovated in the gothic style. Altogether it is well worth waiting for Henbury Hall even though it has only one open day.

JODRELL BANK TREE PARK   10
Jodrell Bank Science Centre and Tree Park, Macclesfield, Cheshire.
Tel: (0477) 71339
Manchester University

On the A535 between Holmes Chapel and Chelford, 5m from M6 junction 18.
Signposted ● *Open Sat before Easter – Oct, daily, 10.30 a.m. – 5.30 p.m.*
Winter weekends and Christmas holidays open 12 noon – 5.00 p.m. ● *Entrance:*
£2.75, OAP £1.50, children £1.50 inc. science centre and planetarium
● *Parking* ● *Refreshments: self-service cafeteria* ● *Toilet facilities* ● *Partly*
suitable for wheelchairs ● *Shop* ● *Grade III*

The garden was begun in 1972 largely at the instigation of Professor Sir
Bernard Lovell and with financial support from the Granada Foundation. It is
set in a flat landscape with all views to the south dominated by the massive
radio telescope. Large collections of trees, heathers and old-fashioned roses
are its main attractions. There are broad grass walkways and many small
natural ponds in this 40-acre garden. The National collections of malus and
sorbus are here, together with the Heather Society Calluna collection. A visit
to Jodrell Bank represents good value when all its attractions are considered
and is a good day out for a family.

LITTLE MORETON HALL   11
Congleton, Cheshire. Tel: (0260) 272018
The National Trust

4m SW of Congleton on the E side of the A34 between Congleton and Newcastle-
under-Lyme ● *Open 2nd March – 8th April, Sat and Sun, 1.30 – 5.30 p.m.,*
14th April – Sept, daily except Tues, 1.30 – 5.30 p.m. Bank Holiday Mons,
11.30 a.m. – 5.30 p.m. Oct, Sat and Sun, 1.30 – 5.30 p.m. Last admission 5.00
p.m. ● *Entrance: £2.00 (£2.50 at weekends and Bank Holidays)* ● *Parking*
● *Refreshments: drinks and light meals* ● *Toilet facilities* ● *Suitable for*
wheelchairs ● *Dogs in car park and areas outside moat only* ● *Shop* ● *Herbs*
usually for sale ● *Grade II*

Little Moreton Hall is one of the best-known timber-framed buildings in the
country and its gardens too are very pleasant in their own quiet way. They
cover about an acre and are set within a moat. There is a cobbled courtyard in
the centre of the hall and to the west a large lawn with fruit trees and an old
grassed mound. To the north of the hall is a yew tunnel and the best feature of
all, a knot garden, laid out under the guidance of Graham Stuart Thomas
following a seventeenth-century model. It is a simple design of gravel and lawn
separated by a low box hedge. There are herbaceous borders around the hall
and a gravel walk that follows the inside perimeter of the moat. The garden is
largely the creation of the Trust and is a fitting complement to the house.

MELLORS GARDEN 12
Hough Hole House, Sugar Lane, Rainow, Nr Macclesfield, Cheshire.
Tel: (0625) 72286
Mr and Mrs G. Humphreys

Ten minutes from the centre of Macclesfield. Take the A5002 to Whaley Bridge. In the village of Rainow turn off to the north, opposite the church into Round Meadow Lane. Then turn at the first left into Sugar Lane and follow this down to the garden ● *Open Spring and Aug Bank Holiday Sun and Mon, 2.00 – 5.00 p.m. or by appointment for parties of more than 10* ● *Entrance: £1.00, children free* ● *Parking* ● *Refreshments* ● *Toilet facilities* ● *Partly suitable for wheelchairs* ● *Dogs on lead* ● ***Grade III***

Where can you pass through the valley of the shadow of death, climb Jacob's ladder, see the mouth of hell and visit the Celestial City all within 10 minutes of Macclesfield? Here in the second half of the nineteenth century, James Mellor, much influenced by Swedenborg, designed this allegorical garden which attempts to recreate the journey of Christian in Bunyan's *Pilgrim's Progress*. Most areas are grassed with stone paths running throughout. There are many small stone houses and other ornaments to represent features of the journey. At one end a large pond is overlooked by a small octagonal summerhouse. The garden stands in a small valley in a rugged but attractive part of the Peak District. Be sure to be shown round by the owner or buy one of the excellent guide books in order to get the best from this small garden.

NORTON PRIORY MUSEUM AND GARDENS 13
Warrington Road, Runcorn, Cheshire.   Tel: (09285) 69895
Warrington and Runcorn Development Corporation

From M6 at junction 11 turn for Warrington and follow Norton Priory signs. From all other directions follow Runcorn then Norton Priory signs ● *Open March and Oct, weekdays, 12 noon – 5.00 p.m., Sat, Sun and Bank Holidays, 12 noon – 6.00 p.m., April – Sept, daily, 12 noon – 4.00 p.m. Walled garden closed Nov – Feb* ● *Entrance: £1.20, OAP and children 60p. Walled garden 50p, OAP and children 25p* ● *Parking* ● *Refreshments: teas and snacks in Museum* ● *Toilet facilities, inc. disabled* ● *Suitable for wheelchairs* ● *Dogs permitted but not in walled garden* ● *Shop* ● *Museum open* ● ***Grade III***

Norton Priory was built as an Augustan foundation in the twelfth century and transformed into a Tudor then Georgian mansion before being abandoned in 1921. The 16 acres of gardens contain the ruins of the Priory, and also an authentic eighteenth-century walled garden. Originally designed by Sir Richard Brooke in 1757 it eventually fell into disrepair, but since 1980 the owners have restored it to reflect both the Georgian and modern designs and tastes. Its range of specialities include a culinary herb and medicinal herb garden, plants for household uses, a fruit arch and cordon fruit, a new orchard, and a number of herbaceous borders. And for a few pence more the visitor can make use of an impeccable croquet lawn!

PEOVER HALL 14
Peover Hall, Over Peover, Nr Knutsford. Tel: (056581) 2404/2611
Mr R. Brooks

3m S of Knutsford on A50 ● *Open May to Sept, Mon, 2.30 - 4.30 p.m., Thurs, 2.30 - 5.00 p.m.* ● *Entrance: £1.00 (hall, stables and garden £2.00)* ● *Teas on Mons* ● *Toilet facilities* ● *Partly suitable for wheelchairs (many grass paths)* ● *Dogs in park only* ● *Plants for sale on special occasions* ● *House open, Mon, 2.30 - 5.00 p.m.* ● *Grade III*

Peover Hall and its gardens are surrounded by a large expanse of flat parkland laid out in the early eighteenth century, but the gardens are mainly Edwardian. On the northern side of the hall is a forecourt, from where a broad grass walk leads through an avenue of pleached limes to a summerhouse. This overlooks a small circular lawn and both are enclosed by a high yew hedge. On the west side of the gardens is a wooded area containing many rhododendrons and a grassed dell that is particularly attractive. Clustered around the south and west of the hall are several small formal gardens, separated by brick walls and yew hedges. Some contain yew topiary. There is a rose garden, a herb garden, a white garden and a pink garden. The lily pool garden has a summerhouse with a tiled roof supported by Doric columns. A church stands in the centre of the gardens and there are fine Georgian stables.

QUEEN'S PARK, CREWE 15
Victoria Avenue, Wisterton Road, Crewe, Cheshire.
Tel: (0270) 583191 ext 486
Crewe and Nantwich Borough Council

2m W of Crewe town centre, S of the A532 ● *Open all year, 8.00 a.m. - sunset* ● *Entrance: free* ● *Parking off Queen's Park Drive* ● *Refreshments: cafeteria in park* ● *Toilet facilities* ● *Partly suitable for wheelchairs* ● *Dogs on lead* ● *Grade II*

Queen's Park is a very well landscaped Victorian park created in 1887-8 by the London & North Western Railway as a gift to the people of Crewe (BR are not so generous nowadays, and some might draw a contrast with their proposed despoilation of that Garden of England, Kent.) It is oval in shape and covers 48 acres, with large grassed areas and a wide variety of mature trees. From an ornate entrance with two 'gothic' lodges and a clock tower, a drive leads through an avenue of birches to the centre of the park. Here a modern café with a terrace looks down upon the large boating lake that is surrounded by banks of trees and shrubs. From the west of the park a stream runs through a lightly wooded valley to join the lake. A path linking the entrance to this valley passes some raised beds of heathers and goes through a tunnel of laburnum. It merits a high grade for the quality of landscaping, the trees and the Victorian buildings, but in essence it is a large municipal park where a fight against vandalism and litter is fought hard.

STAPELEY WATER GARDENS   16
92 London Road, Stapeley, Cheshire.   Tel: (0270) 623868
Mr R.G.A. Davies

*1m SE of Nantwich on A51 ● Open all year, daily except 25th Dec, Easter –
Sept, weekdays, 9.00 a.m. – 6.00 p.m., Sat, Sun and Bank Holidays, 10.00 a.m.
– 7.00 p.m., winter, weekdays, 9.00 a.m. – 5.00 p.m., Sat, Sun, 10.00 a.m. –
5.00 p.m. ● Entrance: fee for Palm Oasis only ● Parking ● Refreshments:
restaurant and café ● Toilet facilities ● Suitable for wheelchairs and some
wheelchairs available ● Grade IV*

This is an extremely large garden centre that has within it a few areas that are
attractive gardens in their own right. At the back of the centre are many pools
containing a good variety of aquatic plants and the land around is landscaped
with lawns and shrub borders. Another area has several small demonstration
gardens. Across the car park is the Palms Oasis, for which there is a charge to
enter. This huge greenhouse has none of the architectural merit of a Victorian
Palm House, but the main hall is quite impressive. It has a long rectangular
pool stocked with Koi and is flanked by high palm trees; on the right is a
rockery with streams and pools, on the left a tropical house with a giant
Amazonian water lily.

TATTON PARK   17
Knutsford, Cheshire.   Tel: (0565) 54822
The National Trust

*Signposted from Knutsford and from A556 ● Park open all year except 25th
Dec, April – 19th May, pedestrians, 9.00 a.m. – 7.00 p.m., others, 10.30 a.m. –
6.00 p.m. (Sun and Bank Holidays 10.00 a.m. – 6.00 p.m.) 20th May – 2nd
Sept, pedestrians, 9.00 a.m. – 8.00 p.m., others, 10.30 a.m. – 7.00 p.m. (Sun
and Bank Holiday Mon 10.00 a.m. – 7.00 p.m.) Garden, April and 3rd Sept –
Oct, 11.30 a.m. – 5.00 p.m. (Sun and Bank Holiday Mon 10.30 a.m. – 5.30
p.m.) 1st May – 2nd Sept, 11.00 a.m. – 5.30 p.m. (Sun and Bank Holiday Mon
10.30 a.m. – 6.00 p.m.) ● Entrance: £1.00, OAP 80p, children 50p
● Parking £1.20 per car ● Refreshments: hot and cold lunches and snacks
● Toilet facilities ● Partly suitable for wheelchairs ● Dogs on lead ● Plants for
sale ● Shop ● House open except Mons, April – June and 3rd Sept – 1st Oct,
1.00 – 4.00 p.m. (Sun and Bank Holiday Monday, 1.00 – 5.00 p.m.). Note that
special charges apply to events held here ● Grade I*

Described as Cheshire's 'showpiece', this contains over 2000 acres of deer
park, an eighteenth-century mansion, a fifteenth-century Hall, a home farm
and a mere on which sailing and swimming are allowed. It is also the venue for
many cultural events including the June Cheshire Show. The parkland,
landscaped by Humphrey Repton in the late eighteenth century, contains a
number of nature walks which in themselves justify a visit to the park. The
gardens, which are adjacent to the Georgian mansion, also comprise a number
of well-gravelled walkways which link a series of specialist features, such as

Paxton's Italian Terrace Garden and a Japanese garden with a Shinto temple (laid out in 1910 and probably among the best of its kind). There are also a number of restoration projects – the revival of the gardenesque design originally planned by the architect Wyatt in 1814, an arboretum and kitchen garden – all of which prompt a return visit. Tatton Park is financed, maintained and administered by Cheshire County Council.

TIRLEY GARTH 18
Utkinton, Nr Tarporley, Cheshire.   Tel: (08293) 2301
Tirley Garth Trust

3m N of Tarporley, just N of village of Utkinton on the road to Kelsall.
Signposted ● Open 19th, 20th, 27th, 28th May, 2.00 - 6.00 p.m. ● Entrance:
£1.00, children 50p ● Parking ● Teas ● Toilet facilities ● Partly suitable for
wheelchairs and a wheelchair provided ● Dogs on lead ● Grade II

Tirley Garth is a magnificent Edwardian house with gardens that complement it perfectly. They are still in much the same layout as originally designed by the architect T.H. Mawson and some of the stonework in the paths, ornaments and buildings is particularly notable. There is a circular courtyard at the western entrance and a small sunken garden to one side which leads to the large terrace on the south front which has lawns and rose beds. To the east is a lawned terrace with a view across the large semi-circular rose garden that spreads below it. Good views of the surrounding countryside.

WALTON HALL GARDENS 19
Walton Lea Road, off Chester Road, Walton, Warrington, Cheshire.
Tel: (0925) 601617
Warrington Borough Council

2m SW of Warrington on S side of A56 in the village of Walton ● Open daily,
8.00 a.m. - dusk ● Best season: spring and autumn ● Entrance: free
● Parking. A charge is made at weekends and Bank Holidays from Easter –
Sept ● Refreshments ● Partly suitable for wheelchairs ● Play equipment for
disabled children ● Toilet facilities ● Dogs on lead ● Shop ● House open
● Grade III

Walton Hall, the former home of the Greenhall family, is a dark brick house with a distinctive clock tower. In front is a large lawn and to one side a modern pool and rockery, with a variety of shrubs, alpines and aquatic plants. Behind the Hall is a series of formal gardens separated by yew hedges and planted with bright annuals. Further south is a lawned area with herbaceous borders, with a path leading under some large beech trees to a rose garden. This has beds of modern roses set in an area of grass enclosed by a high conifer hedge. A walk back around the west side of the garden passes through an attractive area of shrubs and trees amongst which are many acers. Banks of mature woodland and large parkland surround the garden.

CORNWALL

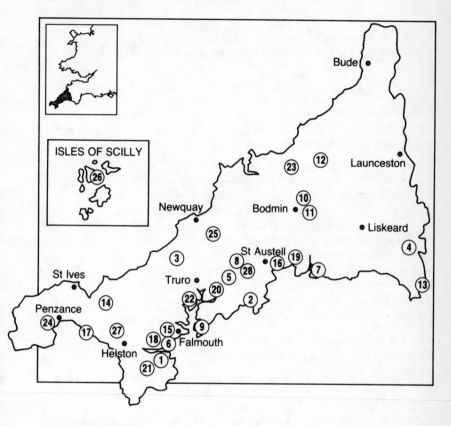

ISLES OF SCILLY

BOSAHAN

1

Manaccan, Helston, Cornwall. Tel: (0326) 23330
Captain and Mrs H.R. Graham Vivian

*10m SE of Helston, 1m NE of Manaccan village • Open 29th April, 2.30 –
5.00 p.m. Parties by arrangement • Best season: spring • Entrance: £1.00,
children 50p • Parking in field if dry • Teas • Partly suitable for
wheelchairs • Dogs on lead • Plants for sale • Grade II*

This valley garden of five acres started 100 years ago leads down to the
Helford river and will give pleasure to the keen plantsperson as it has both
mature and newer planted trees and shrubs, including some New Zealand
varieties. In spring colour is provided by masses of camellias, rhododendrons,
azaleas and magnolias along with bog plants in the water garden. There are
formal beds with herbaceous plants at the top of the garden and one walks
down through the valley to find the more mature specimens including

61

pittosporums and dicksonias. There is some additional colour from ornamental pheasants. Fine views from the top of the valley.

CAERHAYS CASTLE GARDEN   2
Caerhays, Gorran, St Austell, Cornwall.   Tel: (0872) 501310
Mr F.J. Williams

10m S of St Austell. On the coast by Porthluney Cove between Dodman Point and Nare Head ● *Open 15th, 23rd April, 13th May, 2.00 – 5.00 p.m.*
● *Entrance: £1.00, children under 14 free* ● *Parking at beach car park*
● *Refreshments at Beach Café* ● *Toilet facilities* ● *Suitable for wheelchairs*
● *Dogs on lead* ● *Plants for sale* ● **Grade I**

An internationally noted garden with unrivalled collections of magnolias and shrubs raised from seed and material brought back by such plant hunters as George Forrest and E.H. Wilson, who were assisted financially in their expeditions by the Williams. The woodland stretches down to the sea and there are many rare specimens to be seen including tree ferns, acers, oaks, azaleas and nothofagus. J.C. Williams originally specialized in the cultivation and hybridizing of daffodils, but turned his sheltered clearings over to a refuge for the nineteenth-century influx of new plants, and many in British gardens today originated at Caerhays. A plantsman's paradise.

CHYVERTON   3
Zelah, Truro, Cornwall.   Tel: (0872) 54324
Mr and Mrs N. Holman

1m W of Zelah on A30. Turn off N at Marazonvose, the entrance is ½m on right ● *Open by appointment only March – June* ● *Entrance: £2.50. For parties £2.00 per person. Visitors personally conducted around by owners* ● *Parking* ● *Dogs on lead* ● *Plants occasionally for sale* ● **Grade III**

The outstanding feature of this garden originally landscaped in the eighteenth century is its collection of magnolias, including some bearing the name of the property and also the owner's father 'Treve Holman'. Superb trees of copper beech, cedars of Lebanon, eucryphia, and a collection of nothofagus make a beautiful backcloth to a vast collection of camellias and rhododendrons. The garden is planted to give vistas and is always being further developed. A collection of acers is being planted and there are good colour combinations with azaleas and photinias. There is an unusual hedge of *Myrtus luma* and by the stream are vast gunneras and lysichitums. Trees and shrubs have room to develop freely here but it is hard to realise that this beautiful and vast garden is maintained solely by the owners.

COTEHELE 4
St Dominick, Nr Saltash, Cornwall.   Tel: (0579) 50434
The National Trust

1m W of Calstock, 8m SW of Tavistock, 4m from Gunnislake. Turn at St Anne's Chapel ● Open Good Friday and April – Oct, daily, 11.00 a.m. – 6.00 p.m. (5.00 p.m. in Oct) ● Best season: May/June ● Entrance: £2.00 (garden and mill) ● Parking ● Refreshments ● Toilet facilities ● Partly suitable for wheelchairs ● Plants for sale ● Shop ● House open except Fri ● Grade II

This ten-acre garden with terraces falling to a sheltered valley has developed gradually from Victorian times. It should give pleasure to most visitors with its combination of formal courtyards, fine terraces, walled garden, pools, herbaceous borders and valley garden. The grey granite walls of the house are a background to many climbers and from the rose terrace one walks down to the pool and dovecote. In the valley are giant conifers, hydrangeas, palms, acers and betula. There is a small acer plantation and yew hedges along with herbaceous borders.

COUNTY DEMONSTRATION GARDEN 5
Probus, Nr Truro, Cornwall.   Tel: (0872) 74282
Cornwall County Council Education Committee

Just E of Probus village on A390 ● Open May – Sept, daily, 10.00 a.m. – 5.00 p.m., Oct and April, Mon – Fri, 10.00 a.m. – 4.30 p.m. ● Best season: summer ● Entrance: £1.00, children free ● Parking ● Refreshments: drinks and biscuits ● Toilet facilities ● Suitable for wheelchairs ● Grade III

This seven and a half-acre demonstration garden was started from a field in the early 1970s to serve as an advisory and education centre. A unique and fascinating display garden covering methods of growing vegetables, pruning fruit, treating lawns, weed control, compost making, design of small gardens, layouts for many aspects and situations. Fencing and walls, artificial and natural windbreaks, heath and heather planting, hanging baskets, gardening for the disabled, tree planting and staking, cloches, mulches, shrubs for shade and pruning of shrubs, herbs, rock and scree garden – in fact all aspects of gardening including various plant collections and patio and container gardening. A place to visit to get ideas and advice on problems.

GLENDURGAN GARDEN 6
Helford River, Mawnan Smith, Nr Falmouth, Cornwall.
Tel: (0208) 74281
The National Trust

4m SW of Falmouth, ½m SW of Mawnan Smith on the road to Helford Passage ● Open March – Oct, Mon, Wed, Fri (except Good Friday), 10.30 a.m. – 5.30 p.m. ● Best season: spring – Sept ● Entrance: £1.50 ● Parking ● Toilet facilities ● Grade III

This 40-acre valley garden was originally planted by Alfred Fox in the 1820s with the village of Durgan at its foot alongside the Helford river. The wooded valley contains many specimen trees including *Dicksonia antarctica*, drimys, embothrium, eucryphia, conifers and a *Davidia involucrata*. In spring there is colour from primroses, bluebells, Lenten lilies and small daffodils while in late summer there are masses of hydrangeas. An unusual feature is the laurel maze. Vast camellias and magnolias provide early colour in the garden.

HEADLAND 7
3 Battery Lane, Polruan-by-Fowey, Cornwall.
Tel: (072687) 243
Mr and Mrs J. Hill

From the bottom of Fore Street in Polruan go along West Street and turn left up Battery Lane. Headland is almost at the end of the lane • *Open June – Sept, Thurs, 2.00 – 8.00 p.m.* • *Best season: June/July* • *Entrance: £1.00, children 50p* • *Grade III*

This cliff garden 100 feet above sea level, created from an old quarry on the headland, has been developed by the present owners since 1974. It is a great credit to the owners for the excellent range of plants they grow with sea on three sides of the garden where plants must withstand spray and gales. It is designed with narrow paths and archways leading round corners to discover secret areas with Australian and New Zealand plants – acacias, grevilleas and cordylines; sub-tropical succulents – agaves, echeverias, crassulas and lampranthus. There is 'Wattle Alley' with various eucalyptus and wattles. In crevices one sees sempervivum, sedum and erigeron. Monterey pines, tamarisk, Torquay pines, yuccas, fatsia and olearia all thrive and there are good plant combinations. It is surprising to find vegetables and fruit trees and bushes thriving on such a windswept slope. With the vast range of plants and clever design it is hard to believe the garden is only one and a quarter acres.

THE HOLLIES 8
Grampound, Truro, Cornwall.   Tel: (0726) 882474
Mrs N.B. and Mr J.R. Croggon

6m from St Austell on A390 Truro road in the village of Grampound • *Open 1st April, 20th May, 17th June, 15th July, 2.00 – 5.30 p.m.* • *Best season: spring* • *Entrance: £1.00, children free* • *Parking in side lanes – Creed Lane, Bosillian Lane, Pepo Lane* • *Teas* • *Toilet facilities* • *Suitable for wheelchairs* • *Plants for sale* • *Grade IV*

This garden has a charming 'cottage' garden effect created by the unusual design. There are island beds containing a wide range of trees and shrubs with underplanting of bulbs to provide interest and beauty throughout the year, although spring is the peak time. There are many rare plants, including alpines, to be enjoyed here.

LAMORRAN HOUSE 9
Upper Castle Road, St Mawes, Cornwall.   Tel: (0326) 270801
Mr and Mrs R. Dudley-Cooke

At garage above village of St Mawes turn right – signposted at Castle. In about ½m Lamorran is on left of road set behind a line of pine trees ● *Open 31st March, 28th April, 26th May, 30th June, 10.00 a.m. – 5.00 p.m.* ● *Best season: May – July* ● *Entrance: £1.50, children 75p* ● *Parking for cars in road. Coaches by prior appointment* ● *Toilet facilities* ● *Partly suitable for wheelchairs* ● *Plants for sale* ● ***Grade III***

This three-acre garden developed since 1980 contains a large and excellent collection of sub-tropical and warm temperate species which one would not expect to find on a hillside adjacent to the sea. There are 500 azaleas, many different palms and eucalyptus, yuccas, 250 rhododendrons, a wide range of conifers, a range of Australian and New Zealand plants and a fernery. There are little gardens and round every corner more unusual plants. A Japanese garden and water feature. The plantsman will enjoy this and so will other visitors as the owner has incorporated good design features and interesting colour and foliage combinations.

LANCARFFE 10
Nr Bodmin, Cornwall.   Tel: (0208) 72756
Mr and Mrs R. Gilbert

2m NE of Bodmin. Turn W off A30 signed Helland, then left hairpin towards Bodmin. After 200 yards, turn right signposted Norton and Holland, then bear left. Adjacent to Racecourse Farm ● *Open 29th April, 1.30 – 5.00 p.m.* ● *Best season: May/June* ● *Entrance: £1.00* ● *Parking. No coaches* ● *Refreshments* ● *Toilet facilities* ● *Dogs on lead* ● ***Grade III***

Walking through this four and a half-acre garden one can enjoy its wide range of plants from *Davidia involucrata* (pocket-handkerchief tree) to beds of roses. Some beautiful trees form a backcloth to a fine collection of azaleas, camellias and rhododendrons. There is a delightful walled water garden with shrubs and climbers on the walls. Hydrangeas, eucryphias, acers, *Desfontainea spinosa*, *Campsis radicans*, paulownias, various cornus and embothriums are some of the specimens to be enjoyed. A magnificent splash of colour in summer is provided by a long border of dahlias. The owners are continuing to develop this very pleasant garden.

LANHYDROCK 11
Bodmin, Cornwall.   Tel: (0208) 73320
The National Trust

2½m SE of Bodmin off A38, or off B3268 ● *Open April – Oct, daily, 11.00 a.m. – 6.00 p.m. (Oct 5.00 p.m.), Nov – March, daylight hours only* ● *Best*

*season: spring • Entrance: £2.00 (garden and grounds) • Parking inc.
disabled adjacent to garden • Refreshments • Toilet facilities inc. disabled
• Partly suitable for wheelchairs • Dogs on lead in park • Plants for sale
• Shop • House open (closed Mon except Bank Holiday Mon and closed Nov –
March) Extra charge • Grade II*

This superb 30-acre garden started about 1860 contains gardens within a
garden and has some exceptional trees and shrubs both in the park, woodland
and the more formal areas. The collection of trees started before 1634. Banks
of colour are provided by magnolias, camellias and rhododendrons, and this
is followed by roses which are in beds in the lawn adjacent to the house
interspersed with cone-shaped Irish yews. In the terraces beds of annuals are
edged with box. A circular yew hedge surrounds the herbaceous borders
which contain a wide range of choice plants and provide summer colour. The
woodland has walks amongst rare trees and hydrangeas and other flowering
shrubs. There is a stream with bog plants.

LOWER HAMATETHY 12
St Breward, Bodmin, Cornwall. Tel: (0208) 850218
Mrs M.A. Hall

*Take the St Tudy – St Breward road via Gam Bridge. Turn left ½m beyond
bridge • Open by appointment and 22nd April, 27th May, 10th June, 1st,
22nd July, 2.00 – 6.00 p.m. • Best season: spring/summer • Entrance: £1.00,
children free • Limited parking • Teas • Toilet facilities • Partly suitable
for wheelchairs • Plants for sale • Grade IV*

This garden lies in a narrow tree-sheltered valley and has a stream running
through it, which gives a feeling of peace. The bog garden contains primulas,
iris and astilbe. Terraces are planted with shrubs. There is a large rock garden
and in a shaded area are polygonums, hostas and gunneras, and ground cover
plants everywhere. Heathers, eucryphias, embothrium, acers and fuchsias,
rhododendrons and hydrangeas are among the range of plants to be seen and
climbers grow through the trees and up the house. Although not a weed-free
garden it has a sense of charm.

MOUNT EDGCUMBE COUNTRY PARK 13
Cremyll, Cornwall. Tel: (0752) 822236
Plymouth City Council and Cornwall County Council

*2m SE of Torpoint at end of B3247, or by passenger ferry from Plymouth
• Open, daily, 8.00 a.m. – dusk. Earl's Garden and House Easter – Oct, daily
except Mon and Tues, 1.00 – 5.30 p.m. Also Bank Holiday Monday
• Entrance: free. Earl's Garden and House £2.00, children £1.00 • Parking.
Coaches by appointment • Refreshments: lunches, teas and light refreshments
April – Oct in Orangery (0752) 822586. Picnics • Toilet facilities • Suitable
for wheelchairs • Dogs on lead • Shop • House open • Grade III*

The country park stretches four miles westward along the coast, a kind of landscaped peninsular, within which is a jewel of a garden all, except for nine acres around the house, open to the public. It is remarkable that this rare example of an early eighteenth century landscaped garden has survived intact since the house was gutted by fire in an air raid in 1941 and rebuilt in 1964 and purchased from the 7th Earl by local councils in 1971. Most of the work was done by the Edgcumbe family (established here in 1547) without the help of fashionable gardeners, although highly praised by Repton, who in 1803 designed parterre French and Italian character gardens which survive. Now it is being restored with new plantings to represent the family's connections with America and New Zealand. The Edwardian Earl's Garden is also being restored. There is a fine terrace walk with views of the sea, a ruin overlooking Drake's Island and a deer park. The National collection of the International Camellia Society is located here.

PENPOL HOUSE   14
Penpol Avenue, Hayle, Cornwall.   Tel: (0736) 753146
Major and Mrs T.F. Ellis

4m SE of St Ives. Turn left at White Hart, Penpol Road, then 2nd left into Penpol Avenue • *Open by appointment in June and July and on 1st July, 2.00 - 6.00 p.m.* • *Best season: May - July* • *Entrance: £1.00, children 50p* • *Parking in adjacent field* • *Teas* • *Suitable for wheelchairs* • *Plants for sale* • **Grade III**

This three-acre garden developed over the years by the owners has many different small gardens and interesting design features. There is a grey garden, cottage garden, an old walled garden with fruit, vegetables and a pool, a rose garden and herbaceous borders with collections of iris, delphiniums, shrubs and perennials. The old greenhouses contain a vine and some tender plants including plumbago, hoya and hibiscus. The average gardener should find plenty of ideas here.

PENWARNE   15
Mawnan Smith, Nr Falmouth, Cornwall.
Tel: (0326) 250585/250325
Mr and Mrs H. Beister

3¼m SW of Falmouth and 1½m N of Mawnan Smith off the Falmouth to Mawnan Smith road • *Open 29th April, 6th May, 2.00 - 5.00 p.m.* • *Best season: spring* • *Entrance: £1.00, children 50p* • *Parking. Coaches by prior arrangement* • *Toilet facilities* • *Partly suitable for wheelchairs* • *Dogs on lead* • **Grade IV**

There are many large trees including *Cryptomeria japonica*, beeches and oaks which form a backcloth to this woodland garden. The old walled garden has roses, clematis and lilies and there are banks of azaleas, rhododendrons and magnolias, together with shrubs from New Zealand. The pool with ornamental ducks and the stream running through the garden provide areas for primulas and tree ferns. There are fruit trees and bushes along with bamboos.

PINE LODGE 16
Cuddra, St Austell, Cornwall. Tel: (0726) 73500
Mr and Mrs R. Clemo

Just E of St Austell off A390 between Holmbush and Tregrehan • Open 29th April, 2.00 - 5.00 p.m., 13th, 20th May, 15th July, 1.00 - 5.00 p.m. or parties by arrangement • Best season: May - July • Entrance: £1.50 • Parking • Toilet facilities • Suitable for wheelchairs • Plants for sale • Grade III

This three-acre garden, started nearly 40 years ago but extended during the past 10 years, contains a wide range of plants and should be of interest to the keen gardener because there are good design features and original colour combinations. Plants labelled. Besides the usual rhododendrons and camellias so familiar in Cornish gardens there are herbaceous borders with rare and tender plants, a range of conifers, heathers, a pergola with clematis and hedera, and other climbers. Fish ponds, a bog garden and vegetable garden are other features to enjoy.

ST MICHAEL'S MOUNT 17
Marazion, Nr Penzance, Cornwall. Tel: (0736) 710507
The National Trust

½m from the shore at Marazion, ½m S of A394. Access by ferry or across causeway • Open April - Oct, Mon - Fri, 10.30 a.m. - 5.45 p.m. Last admission 4.45 p.m. Nov - March guided tours only. Special charity days most weekends during the season • Best season: spring/early summer • Entrance: £2.60 • Parking in Marazion • Refreshments: restaurant • Toilet facilities • Plants for sale • Shop • Castle and Abbey open but only to guided tours Nov - March when ferry may be difficult • Grade III

A unique and extraordinary 20-acre maritime garden which has been created in terraces just above the sea at the foot of a 300 ft perpendicular cliff. Here, in spite of apparent total exposure to gales and salt spray, sub-tropical species abound. A remarkable example of micro-climate effect is in itself a fascinating study for the keen gardener. Planting has been done amongst granite boulders, some weighing hundreds of tons. There are yuccas, geraniums, euryops, hebes, phormium and in spring sheets of wild narcissus. Kniphofia grow wild in the bracken and provide great splashes of colour.

TREBAH   18
Mawnan Smith, Nr Falmouth, Cornwall.   Tel: (0326) 250448
Major and Mrs J.A. Hibbert

4m SW of Falmouth, 1m SW of Mawnan Smith and 500 yards W of
Glendurgan Garden ● *Open end March – 3rd Sept, daily, 11.00 a.m. – 5.00*
p.m. ● *Best season: spring* ● *Entrance: £1.50, children 50p* ● *Parking*
● *Teas* ● *Toilet facilities* ● *Partly suitable for wheelchairs* ● *Dogs on lead*
● *Plants for sale* ● *Grade III*

A 25-acre ravine garden started by Charles Fox in the 1840s which contains
many beautiful and mature trees and shrubs that provide carpets of colour.
The deep ravine leading down to the River Helford is full of eucalyptus,
thujas, *Podocarpus totara*, tree ferns and trachycarpus. There are many tender
Australian and Asiatic plants as well as very large rhododendrons, many being
hybridized here. Azaleas, camellias and magnolias. The newish water garden
has some waterfalls and there is a range of bog plants. Fine views from the
terrace.

TREGREHAN   19
Par, Nr St Austell, Cornwall.   Tel: (072681) 2438
The Carlyon Estate

On A390 Lostwithiel to St Austell road. The entrance is opposite the Britannia
Inn. ● *Open 8th April, 6th May, 11.00 a.m. – 5.00 p.m.* ● *Best season:*
spring ● *Entrance: £1.50. Parties by arrangement* ● *Parking* ● *Toilet*
facilities ● *Suitable for wheelchairs* ● *Plants for sale* ● *Grade III*

The 20-acre garden was started by the family nearly 300 years ago and contains
many large and interesting trees and rhododendrons in addition to the large
collection of camellias raised by the late owner. There are woodland walks
carpeted with bluebells in spring and a walled garden. Other plants include
clivias and nerines, but the camellias, rare trees and vast rhododendrons are of
particular interest to the keen plantsperson.

TREHANE   20
Nr Probus, Cornwall.   Tel: (087252) 270
Mr D. Trehane and Mr and Mrs S. Trehane

Turn N off A39 between the Wheel Inn and Tresillian Bridge. Signposted
● *Open by appointment and 25th March, 15th, 29th April, 20th May, 3rd June,*
1st, 15th July, 19th Aug, 2.00 – 5.00 p.m. ● *Best season: spring/summer*
● *Entrance: £1.00, children 50p* ● *Parking in field* ● *Teas* ● *Toilet facilities*
● *Suitable for wheelchairs* ● *Dogs on lead* ● *Plants for sale* ● *Grade III*

This is a plantsman's garden containing a wonderful variety and many good
collections – geraniums, hemerocallis, romneyas and trilliums. There are
lovely camellias, many actually raised here. Interesting climbers cover the old

walls and in spring the woodland area is carpeted with bluebells, claytonias and campions. A very old *Pieris japonica* and davidia and vast rhododendrons, azaleas and magnolias provide a background to a large collection of herbaceous plants. This garden will also be enjoyed by the general visitor as it has a great sense of peace and half of its 10 acres is woodland.

TRELEAN 21
St Martin-in-Meneage, Nr Helston, Cornwall.   Tel: (032623) 255
Squadron Leader and Mrs G.T. Witherwick

7m SE of Helston on B3293. After 4m turn left for Mawgan • Open by appointment and 27th May, 12 noon – 6.00 p.m., 28th Oct, 12 noon – 5.00 p.m. Plantsman's walks on 27th April, 13th May, 30th June at 2.30 p.m. • Best season: spring/autumn • Entrance: £1.00, children 20p • Parking in lane • Teas • Toilet facilities • Dogs on lead • Plants for sale • Grade III

This 20-acre garden is for the keen plantsman as it contains a superb collection of beautiful and rare trees and shrubs including 14 different nothofagus, 50 different acers, various eucalyptus, cistus, enkianthus, olearias and robinias. As one winds down the steep paths one is surrounded on either side by ilex, hazels, Scots pine and many varieties of rhododendrons and 70 different conifers. As a complete contrast there are bananas and peaches in the conservatory. The owner, who started this garden from an area of woodland and bracken in 1980, is certainly creating a paradise for the botanist.

TRELISSICK 22
Feock, Nr Truro, Cornwall.   Tel: (0872) 862090
The National Trust

4m S of Truro on B3289 above King Harry Ferry • Open March – Oct, Mon – Sat, 11.00 a.m. – 6.00 p.m., Sun, 1.00 – 6.00 p.m., (Mar and Oct 5.00 p.m.) • Best season: April/May • Entrance: £2.20 • Parking • Refreshments • Toilet facilities • Partly suitable for wheelchairs • Plants for sale • Art and Craft Gallery in grounds open • Grade II

This 25-acre garden with woodland was originally planted with exotic things and became known as the fruit garden of Cornwall. Now it contains a wide variety of interest with its collection of hydrangeas, a dell, aromatic, fern and fig gardens along with some very large trees including *Quercus ilex, Fagus sylvatica* and a beautiful Japanese cedar *Cryptomeria japonica* in a lawn backed by herbaceous borders containing a range of perennials. Near the entrance is a lovely border of heliotrope – a tradition of Trelissick. The dell has tree ferns, hostas and hellebores and there are many beautiful shrubs. Woodland walk open Nov – March.

TREMEER 23
St Tudy, Nr Bodmin, Cornwall. Tel: (0208) 850313
The Haslam-Hopwood family

NW of St Tudy between A39 and B3266. Take Wadebridge road from the centre of St Tudy • Open April – Sept, daily, 2.00 – 6.00 p.m. • Best season: April – June • Entrance: 60p, children 30p • Parking in garden. Coaches at village hall by arrangement • Toilet facilities • Dogs on lead • Grade III

By Cornish standards this seven-acre garden is exposed and cold and has a high rainfall, but manages to produce vivid colour and pervading scent. A large bank of heathers is backed by dwarf rhododendrons and camellias. The terrace beneath the house looks out to a backcloth of fine mature trees. After crossing the lawn one walks through beautiful shrubs – rhododendrons, azaleas, camellias – and at the bottom of the garden is a pool with ducks. Primulas, hostas and other water plants. Herbaceous borders provide summer colour and the walls have good climbers and perennials beneath. The driveway to the house is lined by flowering cherries.

TRENGWAINTON GARDEN 24
Nr Penzance, Cornwall. Tel: (0736) 63021
The National Trust

2m NW of Penzance on B3312, or ½m off A3071 • Open March – Oct, Wed – Sat and Bank Holiday Mon and Good Friday, 11.00 a.m. – 6.00 p.m. (March and Oct, 5.00 p.m.) • Best season: spring • Entrance: £1.60 • Parking • Teas sometimes at Trengwainton Farm • Toilet facilities • Suitable for wheelchairs • Dogs on lead • Grade II

Trengwainton means 'House of the Spring' and was acquired by the Bolitho family in 1867. It will appeal to both the plantsperson and the ordinary gardener because it contains a magnificent collection of magnolias, rhododendrons and camellias and a series of walled gardens with many tender and exotic shrubs and plants that would not survive in less mild areas of England. The stream garden alongside the drive backed by a beech wood provides masses of colour from candelabra primulas, lilies, lysichitum and other bog plants. Many of the rhododendrons were raised from seed collected by Kingdon-Ward's expedition to NE Assam and the Mishmi Hills of Burma. New Zealand tree ferns, pittosporums from China, Japanese maples, embothriums, olearia, acacia, eucryphia, and Chatham Island forget-me-not are just a few of the beautiful plants to be seen during the spring and summer.

TRERICE 25
Nr Newquay, Cornwall. Tel: (0637) 875404
The National Trust

3m SE of Newquay via A392 and A3058. Turn right at Kestle Mill • Open April – Oct, daily, 11.00 a.m. – 6.00 p.m. (Oct, 5.00 p.m.) Last admission

½ *hour before closing* ● *Best season: summer* ● *Entrance: £2.80* ● *Parking*
● *Refreshments* ● *Toilet facilities* ● *Partly suitable for wheelchairs* ● *Plants*
for sale ● *Shop* ● *House open* ● **Grade III**

A small garden by Cornish standards developed around an Elizabethan manor
house where one can enjoy many unusual and lovely rare plants. It has been
planted with shrubs, climbers and perennials to provide very good foliage and
colour combinations. In the front walled courtyard are herbaceous borders.
An Elizabethan knot garden is currently being developed. The back court has
a range of cottage garden plants – fuchsia, lonicera, roses and climbers on the
house. An orchard has been planted with apples, pears, quince, plums in the
quincunx pattern used in the seventeenth century, and there are figs elsewhere
in the garden. The design features of the garden are of particular interest.

TRESCO ABBEY 26
Tresco, Isles of Scilly. Tel: (0720) 22849 (Head Gardener)
Mr D. Smith

On the Island of Tresco. Reached by commercial helicopter from Penzance or boat
from the Island of St Mary's ● *Open daily, 10.00 a.m. – 4.00 p.m.*
● *Entrance: £2.50, children free* ● *Refreshments* ● *Toilet facilities* ● *Suitable*
for wheelchairs (available at garden gate) ● *Dogs on lead* ● *Plants for sale*
● *Shop* ● **Grade II**

One of the most spectacular of all Britain's 'sub-tropical' gardens on an island
which lies in the warming Gulf Stream. Protected from the Atlantic gales by
the great hedges of *Cupressus macrocarpa*, the garden is arranged on several
terraces mounting a hillside which are linked by flights of steps. They serve as
a home for myriad exotic plants like proteus from South Africa, the tender
geranium *G. maderense* from Madeira and trees and shrubs from the North
Island of New Zealand which could not thrive out-of-doors in many places on
the British mainland.

TREVARNO 27
Helston, Cornwall. Tel: (0326) 572022
Mr and Mrs P. Bickford-Smith

3m N of Helston on B3303 and E of Crowntown ● *Open 29th April, 13th*
May, 1.30 – 5.00 p.m. Parties by arrangement ● *Best season: spring*
● *Entrance: £1.00, children 50p* ● *Parking. Coaches by arrangement*
● *Refreshments* ● *Toilet facilities* ● *Plants for sale* ● **Grade III**

This fine woodland garden of 15 acres includes a large ornamental lake at the
foot of the garden and alongside is the bog garden. It contains a vast range of
rare trees and shrubs along with a collection of oaks, species rhododendrons
and *Acer palmatum* 'Dissectum Nigrum'. There is a collection of ilex, a shady
garden and a grotto, and a collection of geraniums. Beside the waterfall are
primulas, rheums, astilbes and aruncus. A plantsman's garden.

TREWITHEN   28
Grampound Road, Nr Truro, Cornwall.
Tel: (0726) 882418/882585/ 882764
Mr and Mrs A.M.J. Galsworthy

On A390 between Truro and St Austell, adjacent to the County Demonstration Garden ● *Open March – Sept, Mon – Sat, 10.00 a.m. – 4.30 p.m.*
● *Entrance: £1.20* ● *Parking* ● *Toilet facilities* ● *Suitable for wheelchairs*
● *Dogs on lead* ● *Plants for sale* ● *House open April – July, Mon, Tues, 2.00 – 4.30 p.m.* ● *Grade II*

This is an internationally famous garden, known for its great collection of magnolias, rhododendrons and camellias along with many other beautiful and rare trees and shrubs. It is fitting that its founder George Johnstone named a camellia after his daughter 'Elizabeth Johnstone', and there are rhododendrons 'Alison Johnstone' after his wife, 'Trewithen Orange' and 'Jack Skelton' after his head gardener. The lawn in front of the house is edged with banks of a wide range of shrubs including viburnums, azaleas, potentillas, euonymus, berberis. There is a sunken garden with tree ferns, azaleas and acers. There are many nothofagus, embothriums, pieris, enkianthus, eucryphias, griselinias. The walled garden has a pool and some choice climbers including *Clianthus puniceus*, and *Mutisia decurrens*, and there is a pergola with wisteria. Newly planted beds of young trees of sorbus and birch, mahonia, cornus, phygelius and roses and island beds with heathers and dwarf conifers. The beech trees that provide shelter for the garden are magnificent. A half hour video describes the creation of the garden over the years.

TELEPHONE NUMBERS
Except where specifically requested to be excluded, telephone numbers to which enquiries may be directed are given for each property. To maintain the support and cooperation of private owners it is suggested that the telephone be used with discretion. Where visits are by appointment, the telephone can of course be used except where written application, particularly for parties, is specifically requested. Code numbers are given in brackets. For the Republic of Ireland when phoning from the United Kingdom dial 353 plus area code plus number (except Dublin numbers which are 0001 plus number). In all cases where visits by parties are proposed, owners should be advised in advance and arrangements preferably confirmed in writing.

London Telephone Codes: From May 1990 all London telephone numbers with the prefix 01 will be changed. The new prefix will be either 071 or 081. Details of these new numbers are available from British Telecom. During the changeover period in 1990 all London telephone numbers dialled with their 01 prefix will be redirected.

CUMBRIA

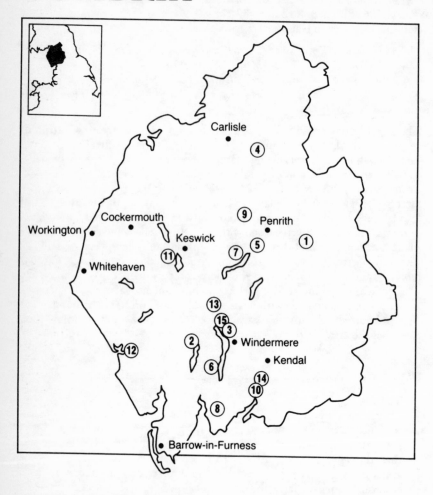

ACORN BANK GARDEN
1

Temple Sowerby, Penrith, Cumbria. Tel: (07683) 61893
The National Trust

6m E of Penrith off A66 N of Temple Sowerby ● Open April – 4th Nov, daily,
10.00 a.m. – 6.00 p.m. Last admission 5.30 p.m. ● Best season: spring and
early summer ● Entrance: £1.00 ● Parking ● Picnic area only ● Toilet
facilities inc. disabled ● Mostly suitable for wheelchairs ● Guide dogs only in
*gardens, on lead in picnic area ● Plants for sale ● Shop ● **Grade III***

The 'acorn bank' is the ancient oakwood sloping down to the Crowdundle
Beck behind the house. In spring it is a mass of daffodils and narcissi in many

varieties planted profusely in the 1930s (e.g. some 60,000 Lenten lilies). The walled gardens are then also a mass of blossom from the old varieties of apple, medlar, pear and quince in the sheltered orchards, with their carpet of wild tulips, anemones and narcissi. The orchard's trees include apple varieties which blossom late and are therefore suitable for cooler northern areas. Along the three sheltering walls are carefully modulated herbaceous and shrub borders, with good clematis and climbers. A bed of species roses (*Rugosa* and others) flanks the steps to a picturesque sunken garden (a pond and alpine terraces). Through a gateway lies a splendid herb garden – a well tended collection of some 250 medicinal and culinary herbs, all comprehensively labelled and documented.

BRANTWOOD 2
Coniston, Cumbria. Tel: (05394) 41396
Brantwood Trust

E side of Coniston Water off B5285, signposted ● *Open mid-March - mid-Nov, daily, 11.00 a.m. - 5.30 p.m., winter, Wed - Sun, 11.00 a.m. - 4.00 p.m.* ● *Best season: spring, autumn* ● *Entrance: 50p, children 25p* ● *Parking* ● *Tea room and restaurant* ● *Toilet facilities inc. disabled* ● *Dogs* ● *Plants for sale planned* ● *Shop* ● *House open, £2.00, children £1.00, family £5.25 (2 plus 5 maximum)* ● ***Grade III***

This is a superb site with wonderful views, atmosphere and potential. The rocky hillside behind the house is threaded with a wandering network of paths created by Ruskin (who lived here 1872 - 1900) to delight the eye and please the mind. Rhododendrons and azaleas flourish in the acid soil to make a lovely woodland garden. Now in the capable hands of Sally Beamish, it is being restored to its former glory after long neglect and enhanced by imaginative planting. The water features will also be revived. Given time and hard work it should become a classic.

BROCKHOLE 3
Lake District National Park Centre, Windermere, Cumbria.
Tel: (09662) 6601
Lake District Special Planning Board

1½m N of Windermere on A591 ● *Open Easter - early Nov, daily from 10.00 a.m.* ● *Best season: spring, early summer, autumn* ● *Entrance: £1.70, children 80p, family £4.00 (2 plus 3 maximum), groups £1.00 per person, children 50p* ● *Parking* ● *Refreshments* ● *Toilet facilities inc. disabled* ● *Partly suitable for wheelchairs* ● *Dogs* ● *Shop* ● ***Grade III***

A garden blessed with the Lakeland combination of western aspect and water to the hills beyond, in this case notably the Langdale Pikes. To frame this view Mawson worked closely (*c.*1900) with his architect colleague, Gibson. The ornamental terraces drop through rose beds and shrubbery to a wild flower meadow flanked by mature woodland. The original kitchen garden is being restored and other exciting developments being pursued by Sue Tasker include a herb garden and a cascade. Further specialities are the rock plants and half-hardy Chilean shrubs, and the constantly changing colour from spring rhododendrons and azaleas through to the late Chilean hollies.

CORBY CASTLE   4
Great Corby, Cumbria. Tel: (0228) 80246
Mr and Mrs John Howard

6m E of Carlisle, turn off A69 at Warwick Bridge to Great Corby village
● Open April – Oct, daily, 1.00 – 5.00 p.m. ● Best season: spring, early
summer ● Entrance: 40p (honesty box) ● Parking ● Dogs on lead
● Grade IV

Created by Thomas Howard in the early eighteenth century the grounds run along the River Eden for about one mile, with fine trees and architectural features. The cascade was restored in 1957 and takes the water from the park down a series of steps to the river.

DALEMAIN   5
Dalemain Estate, Dacre, Penrith, Cumbria. Tel: (08356) 450
Mrs Sylvia McCosh

On A592 2m N of Pooley Bridge on Penrith road ● Open Easter – early Oct,
daily, Sun – Fri, 11.15 a.m. – 5.00 p.m. ● Best season: early summer
● Entrance: Garden only £1.50, children free ● Parking ● Refreshments:
restaurant and tea room ● Toilet facilities ● Suitable for wheelchairs ● Plants
for sale ● Shop ● House open: combined ticket £2.50, children £1.50, family
£6.00 (2 plus own children) ● Grade II

Dalemain has evolved in the most natural way from a twelfth-century pele tower with its kitchen garden and herbs. The Tudor-walled knot garden is there, as is the Stuart terrace (1680s) and the Georgian orchard wall (1740s) where apple trees like 'Nonsuch' and 'Keswick Codling', planted in 1728, still bear fruit. The gardens have been finely re-established by Mrs McCosh with shrubs, species roses and other rarities, together with herbaceous replanting along the terraces and around the orchard. There is a wild garden on the lower ground featuring the Himalayan blue poppy in early summer and a walk past the Tudor gazebo into woods overlooking the Dacre Beck.

GRAYTHWAITE HALL   6
Ulverston, Hawkshead, Cumbria. Tel: (05395) 31248
Esthwaite Estate Company

4m up W side of Windermere from Newby Bridge, A590 ● Open April – June,
daily, 10.00 a.m. – 6.00 p.m. ● Best season: spring ● Entrance: £1.00,

children free ● *Parking. Coaches by appointment* ● *Toilet facilities* ● *Suitable for wheelchairs* ● *Dogs on lead* ● **Grade II**

Essentially a spring garden landscaped by the late Victorian Thomas Mawson in partnership with Dan Gibson in a beautiful parkland and woodland setting. Azaleas and rhododendrons lead to late cultivars of spring-flowering shrubs. Formal terraced rose garden. The finely wrought sundials and gate by Gibson, the Dutch garden and the stream and pond all add charm to this serene garden.

HOLEHIRD 7
Lakeland Horticultural Society, Troutbeck, Windermere, Cumbria.
Tel: (076883) 742 for information
Lakeland Horticultural Society Trust

2m N of Windermere on A592 Troutbeck road ● *Open all year, daily. April – Oct, 11.00 a.m. – 5.00 p.m.* ● *Entrance: free* ● *Parking* ● *Toilet facilities* ● *Partly suitable for wheelchairs* ● *Dogs on lead* ● *Annual plant sale 1st Sat in May* ● *Shop* ● **Grade II**

This is a garden run by members of a Society dedicated to promoting 'knowledge on the cultivation of plants, shrubs and trees especially those suited to Lakeland conditions'. It lies on a splendid site with a natural water course and rock banks looking over Windermere to Scafell Pike. The Society has part of the former orchard, the rock garden and now the walled kitchen garden. Much earlier planting has been preserved, including survivors from plant-hunting expeditions to China and many fine specimen trees (e.g. 66ft blue gum and 60ft handkerchief tree). Highlights are the summer-autumn heathers, winter-flowering shrubs, alpines and a large astilbe collection. The walled garden now has herbaceous specimens, herbs and climbers.

HOLKER HALL 8
Cark-in-Cartmel, Grange-over-Sands, Cumbria.
Tel: (05395) 58328
Mr and Mrs Hugh Cavendish

4½m W of Grange-over-Sands on B5278 between Haverthwaite (A590) and Grange-over-Sands ● *Open Easter Sun – Oct, Sun – Fri, 10.30 a.m. – 4.30 p.m.* ● *Best season: spring, summer* ● *Entrance: £1.95, children £1.00, group rates* ● *Parking* ● *Refreshments: cafeteria lunches, snacks and teas* ● *Toilet facilities inc. disabled* ● *Mostly suitable for wheelchairs* ● *Dogs* ● *Plants for sale* ● *Shop* ● *House open. Combined ticket £2.95, children £1.50, group rates (to change in 1990)* ● **Grade I**

Set in acres of parkland, the woodland walks and formal gardens have been constantly developed by the family ever since Lord George Cavendish established his 'contrived natural landscape' some 200 years ago. The woods now contain many rare and beautiful specimens, all tagged and chronicled in the excellent guide to the walks. Other features are the recent cascade, evocative of the Villa d'Este, and a beautifully contrived transformation of the croquet lawn into summer gardens. This combination of formal beds and inventive planting (e.g. spire lilies rising out of massed rue) make a wonderful Italianate-cum-English garden that typifies the spirit of Holker. There is also Mawson's rose garden, now being sensitively renewed (his pergola and balustrade still survive). The early blaze of rare rhododendrons and azaleas, carpets of spring bulbs and the colour and scent of summer and autumn displays provide year-round interest and pleasure.

HUTTON-IN-THE-FOREST 9
Skelton, Penrith, Cumbria. Tel: (08534) 449
Lord and Lady Inglewood

3m from M6 junction 41, along B5305 to Wigton ● *Open daily, 11.00 a.m. – 5.00 p.m. Closed 25th Dec* ● *Best season: summer* ● *Entrance: £1.00, children free* ● *Parking* ● *Teas* ● *Toilet facilities* ● *Suitable for wheelchairs up to house* ● *Dogs on lead* ● *Plants for sale occasionally* ● *Shop* ● *House open: June – 1st Oct, Thurs, Fri and Sun, 1.00 – 4.00 p.m. inc. Bank Holidays, £2.00, children free* ● ***Grade II***

This garden was inspired by William Gilpin, eighteenth-century pioneer of the picturesque, who was brought up in the Border Country. It has great visual appeal, with a magnificent view from the Victorian topiary terraces. There are good herbs and fruit trees in the walled garden. Some of the mature woodland trees were imported from the Indies by Henry Fletcher, an ancestor of the owners, in the early eighteenth century. Recent planting includes rhododendrons and other spring displays in the woodland low garden and there is an extensive park with forest walks, with conducted tours by arrangement. Other features include a seventeenth-century dovecote and pools.

LEVENS HALL 10
Levens Hall, Kendal, Cumbria. Tel: (05395) 60321
Mr C.H. Bagot

5m S of Kendal on A6 (M6 junction 36) ● *Open Easter Sun – Sept, Sun – Thurs, 11.00 a.m. – 5.00 p.m.* ● *Best season: summer* ● *Entrance: £1.60, children 80p, groups of 20 or more and others £1.40 per person* ● *Parking* ● *Teas* ● *Toilet facilities inc. disabled* ● *Suitable for wheelchairs* ● *Plants for sale* ● *Shop* ● *House open. Combined ticket £2.90, children and students £1.45, groups of 20 or more and others £2.40 per person* ● ***Grade I***

James II's gardener, Guillaume Beaumont, designed this famous topiary garden in 1692. It is one of very few to retain its original trees and design. The impeccably clipped yews and box hedges are set off by colourful spring and summer bedding and borders. Massive walls of beech hedge open to vistas over parkland. One avenue leads to the earliest designed ha-ha. There is a picturesque herb garden behind the house, and the kitchen gardens are being restored to their recently discovered seventeenth-century plan. The record of only 10 gardeners in 300 years, and the affectionate care by the Bagot family, account for the rare harmony of this exceptional garden.

LINGHOLM GARDENS 11
Lingholm, Keswick, Cumbria. Tel: (07687) 72003
The Viscount Rochdale

W side of Derwentwater, 1½m from Keswick off A66 ● *Open April – Oct, daily, 10.00 a.m. – 5.00 p.m.* ● *Best season: spring to autumn* ● *Entrance: £1.50, accompanied children free* ● *Parking* ● *Teas* ● *Toilet facilities* ● *Suitable for wheelchairs* ● *Dogs on lead* ● *Plants for sale* ● *Grade III*

A most pleasing lakeland garden with view south to Borrowdale. Colour from early spring with bulbs and long-lasting display of azaleas and rhododendrons (note *Rhododendron auriculatum* and *Rhododendron* 'Shilsonii') right through to August. Much other blossom and a particularly good mix of trees (e.g. silver firs, cedars and maples) keep up the interest throughout the season. Beatrix Potter stayed and wrote 'Squirrel Nutkin' here.

MUNCASTER CASTLE 12
Ravenglass, Cumbria. Tel: (06577) 614/203
Mr and Mrs Gordon-Duff-Pennington

15m S of Whitehaven on A595 ● *Open April – Sept, daily, 12 noon - 5.00 p.m.* ● *Best season: May and June* ● *Entrance: £1.50, children £1.00* ● *Parking* ● *Teas* ● *Toilet facilities* ● *Suitable for wheelchairs* ● *Dogs on lead* ● *Garden centre plants for sale* ● *Shop* ● *House open: Tues – Sun, 1.30 - 4.30 p.m. Combined ticket £3.00, children £1.50* ● *Grade II*

The splendid backdrop of Scafell and the hills, the acid soil and the Gulf Stream warmth provide ideal conditions. One of the finest collections of species rhododendron in Europe has been built up, many from plant-hunting expeditions to Nepal in the 1920s (Kingdon-Ward, Ludlow and Sheriff). There are excellent azaleas, camellias, magnolias, hydrangeas and maples, plus many unusual trees (e.g. *Nothofagus* species). The garden is at its best in May and June but intensive new planting is ensuring constant pleasure for visitors in all seasons. Tony Warburton of TV fame also runs an Owl Centre here – a national centre for breeding and conservation of endangered owls, including many worldwide species.

RYDAL MOUNT 13
Ambleside, Cumbria. Tel: (05394) 33002
Mrs Henderson

1m N of Ambleside on A591 ● *Open Mar – Oct, daily, 9.30 a.m. – 5.00 p.m., Nov – Feb, Wed and Mon, 10.00 a.m. – 4.00 p.m.* ● *Best season: spring*

● *Entrance: £1.80, children 80p, groups £1.50 per person* ● *Parking* ● *Toilet facilities* ● *Dogs on lead* ● *Shop* ● *House open* ● **Grade III**

The carefully maintained grounds of Wordsworth's house still follow the lines of his own plan and it is easy to imagine the poet wandering along the upper terrace walk (Isabella's) and down through winding, shaded paths to the lawns, or across a terrace to the ancient mound with its distant glimpse of Windermere. Apart from its poetic association the garden is also a visual delight with good herbaceous borders, shrubs and unusual trees (e.g. the fern-leaved beech). An addition to the spring display is the bank of dancing daffodils in nearby Dora's field. A word of praise for some good labelling.

SIZERGH CASTLE 14
Kendal, Cumbria. Tel: (05395) 60070
The National Trust

1m S of Kendal on A591 (M6 junction 36) ● *Open April – Oct, Sun, Mon, Wed, Thurs, 12.30 – 5.30 p.m. Last admission 5.00 p.m. Closed Good Friday* ● *Best season: spring to autumn* ● *Entrance: £1.25 (garden only). Parties of 15 or more reduced rate by arrangement* ● *Parking* ● *Teas: 1.30 – 5.00 p.m.* ● *Toilet facilities* ● *Partly suitable for wheelchairs* ● *Shop* ● *House open same days, 1.30 – 5.30 p.m.* ● **Grade II**

An exceptionally varied garden with colour from early spring daffodils to summer borders and climbers culminating in glorious autumn tints (the vine-clad tower all fiery red is a memorable spectacle). Other features encountered along shady paths are the Hayes' rock garden (Japanese maples, dwarf conifers, primulas, gentians, etc.) the long wall (*Clematis flammula, Hydrangea petiolaris*, brooms and much else) and the rose garden (specimen roses and clematis). The water and rose gardens seemed to have suffered from the long dry summer of '89, but will no doubt revive.

STAGSHAW 15
Ambleside, Cumbria. Tel: (05394) 32109
The National Trust

½m S of Ambleside on A591 ● *Open April – June, daily, 10.00 a.m. – 6.30 p.m. July – Oct, by appointment (please send SAE)* ● *Best season: spring, early summer* ● *Entrance: 70p* ● *Limited parking* ● **Grade III**

Created by C.H.D. Acland, this is a carefully blended area of azaleas and rhododendrons among camellias, magnolias and other fine shrubs on a west-facing hillside of oaks looking over the head of Lake Windermere. Rather difficult of access but worth the effort.

DERBYSHIRE

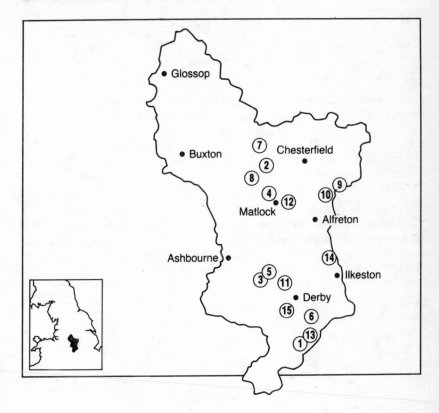

CALKE ABBEY

1

Ticknall, Derbyshire. Tel: (0332) 863822
The National Trust

9m S of Derby, off A514 at Ticknall • *Open April – Oct, Sat – Wed, 11.00*
a.m. – 5.30 p.m. Last admission 5.00 p.m. Also Bank Holiday Mon but closed
Good Friday • *Entrance: £3.50, children £1.70 (house and gardens)*
• *Parking* • *Refreshments: restaurant* • *Toilet facilities* • *Partly suitable for*
wheelchairs • *National Trust shop* • *House open* • ***Grade III***

Previously owned by an eccentric family and recently taken on by the Trust,
Calke House and park overshadow the gardens at present. These latter have a
long history and with a sympathetic approach could be another Trust jewel.
There are frames, pits, an orangery and grotto, and an auricula stand all
waiting to be restored. Only two gardeners are on the staff at present but the
work done in recent years is magnificent. The flower garden is delightful with
a pattern of beds and basket-weave ironwork round a little fountain pond. The

Trust hopes to restore the gardens to their former glory given enough funds, and for locals it will be worth making periodic visits to see its resurrection to eighteenth- and nineteenth-century glories.

CHATSWORTH   2
Bakewell, Derbyshire. Tel: (024688) 2204
The Duke and Duchess of Devonshire

4m E of Bakewell, 10m W of Chesterfield on B6012, off A619 and A6 ● Open Easter – Oct, daily, 11.30 a.m. – 5.00 p.m. ● Entrance: £2.00, OAP £1.00, children £1.00 (garden only) ● Parking: cars £1.00, coaches free ● Refreshments: salad and hot meals in the Stable Café, snacks near Orangery shop ● Toilet facilities ● Suitable for wheelchairs ● Dogs on lead ● Plants for sale ● Shop ● House open, Easter – Oct, £3.75, OAP £3.00, children £1.90 (house and gardens) ● Grade I

The 100 acres of garden at Chatsworth have developed over 300 years and many areas still reflect the garden fashions of each century. The seventeenth-century gardens of London and Wise remain only as the cascade and canal pond to the south. During the eighteenth century 'Capability' Brown destroyed much of the formal gardens to create a landscaped woodland park. Notable is the vista created by Brown from the Salisbury Lawn to the horizon, which remains unchanged as does the lawn itself since no liming or fertilizer has been used, allowing many varieties of wild flowers, grasses, mosses and sedges to thrive. The orange borders and blue and white borders are twentieth-century additions as is the terrace, display greenhouse, rose garden and old conservatory garden which has lupin, dahlia and Michaelmas daisy beds. The Duke and Duchess continue to work on the garden improving the arboretum and pinetum by removing the suffocating rhododendrons, laurels and sycamores and planting many new trees – labelling of these different trees is excellent. The serpentine hedge of beech was planted in 1953 and the double rows of pleached red-twigged limes were planted in 1952, both now rewarding features. Paxton's work still gives pleasure: there is the large rockery, some rare conifers, the magnificent 276 ft water jet from the Emperor fountain. Alas, the Great Conservatory was a casualty of the 1914-18 war and three and a half foot stone walls in the old conservatory garden are all that remain to give an idea of its size. There are plans to make a kitchen garden in a hitherto private area. A useful booklet 'The Garden at Chatsworth' can be bought in the shop before entering the garden.

DAM FARM HOUSE   3
Yeldersley Lane, Brailsford, Derbyshire. Tel: (0335) 60291
Mrs S.D. Player

5m SE of Ashbourne on A52. Opposite the Ednaston village turn, the gate is 500 yards on right ● Open by appointment and on 29th April, 20th May, 24th June, 22nd July, 2.00 – 5.00 p.m. ● Entrance: £1.00, children 25p ● Parking

in field next to garden ● *Teas* ● *Partly suitable for wheelchairs*
● *Plants for sale* ● **Grade IV**

The scree garden has a large number of choice alpines. Climbers are used abundantly for clothing walls, trees, pergolas – even spilling down over high retaining walls and all achieved in 10 years. Collection of old roses. Plenty of informative labelling.

DARLEY HOUSE   4
Darley Dale, Matlock, Derbyshire. Tel: (0629) 733341
Mr and Mrs G.H. Briscoe

2m N of Matlock on A6 to Bakewell, on right just past a garage ● *Open 30th March – Oct by appointment* ● *Best season: spring/ summer* ● *Entrance: 50p, children 20p. Special arrangements for private parties* ● *Limited parking beside entrance* ● *Refreshments: tea and biscuits* ● *Partly suitable for wheelchairs* ● *Plants for sale* ● **Grade II**

This serene garden was originally set out by Paxton in 1845. Plantsman's gardens can be bogged down by the sheer number of different plants but here, although there is a wealth of beautiful and unusual plants, all harmonise. There are a number of mature tender shrubs and plants which surprisingly survive the Derbyshire weather – thoughtful planting obviously paying dividends. Extensive seed list.

EDNASTON MANOR GARDENS AND NURSERIES   5
Nr Brailsford, Derbyshire. Tel: (0335) 60325
Ednaston Manor Gardens and Nurseries

Entrance on A52 between Ashbourne and Brailsford ● *Open Easter Sun – Sept, daily except Sat, 2.00 – 5.30 p.m.* ● *Best season: spring/summer* ● *Entrance: free* ● *Parking* ● *Teas on Suns* ● *Toilet facilities* ● *Suitable for wheelchairs* ● *Plants for sale* ● **Grade III**

The house was built by Lutyens during World War I, but the gardens were redeveloped in the 1950s. Acres of mature trees, flowering shrubs, rhododendrons and azaleas. Terraces and neat herbaceous borders complement the beautiful house. Erratic labelling (apparently the labels 'walk') – a pity not to know what species that peculiar conifer belongs to.

ELVASTON CASTLE COUNTRY PARK   6
Elvaston, Derby, Derbyshire. Tel: (0332) 571342
Derbyshire County Council

6m SE of Derby on B5010 between Borrowash A6005 and Thurlston A6. Signposted from A6 and A52 ● *Open all year, daily, 9.00 a.m. – dusk*

● *Entrance: free* ● *Parking* ● *Refreshments: Parlour tearoom, Easter – Oct*
● *Toilet facilities* ● *Suitable for wheelchairs* ● *Dogs on lead in Old English Garden* ● *Shop* ● **Grade II**

A fine garden to visit at any time of the year. Within the 200 acres there is a large variety of mature trees with many recent trees planted from donations as a memorial to a loved one – an excellent idea. A tree trail is planned. The Italian garden with its clipped yews has limited appeal visually. The original walled kitchen garden is now the Old English Garden containing herbaceous borders, rose garden and herb garden. The history of the garden is diplayed in the Information Centre; of particular interest is that in 1851 there were 90 gardening staff. William Barron, the professional gardener who developed the garden at that time, was an expert on transplanting mature trees – the cedars here were moved by the Barron method – Kew has a 'Barron transplanter'. He had erected 11 miles of yew hedge by 1850 and in 1880, when he had left his employment here, he caused a controversy by transplanting a 1000-year-old yew tree in Buckland churchyard to save the church.

FIR CROFT   7
Froggatt Road, Calver, Derbyshire.
Dr and Mrs S.B. Furness

4m N of Bakewell. Between the filling station and the junction of B6001 and B6054 ● *Open March – Dec, Sat, Mon, all day, Sun 1.00 – 6.00 p.m. and for NGS* ● *Best season: spring/early summer* ● *Entrance: by collection box for NGS and Rare Breeds Survival Trust* ● *Limited parking* ● *Partly suitable for wheelchairs* ● *Plants for sale at adjacent nursery* ● **Grade IV**

The owner is a botanist and botanical photographer who has put his expertise into an extensive alpine garden – a 'must' to visit if interested in alpine and scree gardens, particularly as the garden was started from scratch in 1985.

HADDON HALL   8
Bakewell, Derbyshire.   Tel: (062981) 2855
The Duke of Rutland

2m SE of Bakewell, 6½m N of Matlock on A6 ● *Open Easter – Sept, daily except Mon in April – June, and except Sun and Mon in July and Aug, but open Bank Holiday Sun and Mon, 11.00 a.m. - 6.00 p.m.* ● *Entrance: £2.60, OAP £2.00, children £1.50* ● *Parking: cars 30p, coaches free* ● *Refreshments: lunches and teas in Stables tearoom* ● *Toilet facilities* ● *House open*
● **Grade III**

The castle and gardens of seventeenth-century origin – reconstructed this century – stand on a limestone bluff. The gardens are mainly on the south side and are laid out in a series of stone-walled terraces with the River Wye at their feet. The thick stone walls of the castle and terrace walls face south and west and look well as a background for the extensive collection of climbing and rambling roses. The plants, shrubs and roses all have legible labels. The upper terrace with balustraded parapet and fine stairway is particularly memorable.

HARDWICK HALL   9
Doe Lea, Chesterfield, Derbyshire.   Tel: (0246) 850430
The National Trust

6½m NW of Mansfield, 9½m SE of Chesterfield. Approach from M1 junction 29 then A617 ● Open April – Oct, daily, 12 noon – 5.30 p.m. Car park gate closed 6.30 p.m. Country park open, daily, dawn – dusk ● Best season: summer ● Entrance: £1.50, children 70p (house and garden £4.00, children £2.00) No reduction for parties ● Parking. Gates close at 6.30 p.m. ● Refreshments in Great Kitchen of Hall on days Hall is open 12 noon – 5.00 p.m. ● Toilet facilities ● Suitable for wheelchairs ● Dogs in park only on lead ● National Trust shop ● House open April – 16th Sept on Wed, Thurs, Sat, Sun and Bank Holiday Mon, 1.00 – 5.30 p.m. ● Grade II

This famous Elizabethan mansion house was built for Bess of Hardwick by Robert Smythson in the late sixteenth century. Mature yew hedges and brick walls provide necessary shelter to an otherwise exposed hilltop site. The borders of the Great Court have spring-flowering shrubs to give colour for a longer period than herbaceous plants can provide. Some herbaceous borders have strong, hot colours as an overall grouping, others have soft hues. In order to rest the soil to rid it of a build-up of pests and diseases the borders were replanted in October 1989. The herb garden is outstanding in variety of plants and display. There is some 300 acres of country park.

THE HERB GARDEN   10
Hall View Cottage, Hardstoft, Pilsley, Nr Bakewell, Derbyshire.
Tel: (0246) 854268
Mrs Raynor

3m SE of Chesterfield. Turn off A619 and follow B6012 ● Open April to Oct, daily except Thurs, 10.00 a.m. – 6.00 p.m. ● Best season: summer ● Entrance: free ● Limited parking ● Plants for sale ● Shop ● Grade IV

A rich herb garden in a rural setting in the process of being greatly enlarged to include a parterre.

KEDLESTON HALL   11
Kedleston, Derbyshire.   Tel: (0332) 842191
The National Trust

4½m NW of Derby on the Derby-Hulland road between A6 and A52. Well signposted ● Open April – Oct, Sat – Wed, inc. Bank Holidays, 11.00 a.m. – 6.00 p.m. Closed Good Friday. Nov – 23rd Dec, Sat and Sun only, 12 noon –

4.00 p.m. Park only April – Oct, daily, 11.00 a.m. – 6.00 p.m. (vehicle entry charge £1.00) • *Best season: summer/autumn* • *Entrance: £3.50. Coach parties must pre-book by writing to the Administrator* • *Parking* • *Refreshments: tearoom, 12 noon – 5.00 p.m.* • *Toilet facilities* • *Not suitable for wheelchairs unless by prior written arrangement* • *National Trust shop* • *House open, 11.00 a.m. – 5.30 p.m., contains Curzon's Indian Museum* • *Grade II*

The ancient home of the Curzon family, their most famous member being George Nathaniel, one time Viceroy of India. The extensive gardens do not compete with this classical Robert Adam palace, but are of mature parkland where the eye is always drawn to the house. The rhododendrons when in flower are worth visiting in their own right, otherwise visit the gardens as a pleasurable way not only to view Adam's magnificent south front but his octagonal-domed summerhouse, his orangery, a Venetian-windowed water-side house, the bridge across the lake, the aviary – now a loggia – and the main gateway. The formal gardens have a heart-shaped sunken rose garden and beds by Lutyens (1925). The Hackforth Fountain is another attraction.

LEA GARDENS 12
Lea, Nr Matlock, Derbyshire.
Mr and Mrs Tye

5m SE of Matlock E off A6 • *Open 20th March – July, daily, 10.00 a.m. – 7.00 p.m.* • *Entrance: season ticket £1.50, children 50p* • *Parking. Coaches by appointment* • *Refreshments: light lunches, teas* • *Suitable for wheelchairs* • *Plants for sale* • *Grade III*

A collection of rhododendrons, azaleas, alpines and conifers are brought together here in a beautiful woodland setting.

MELBOURNE HALL 13
Melbourne, Derbyshire. Tel: (0332) 862502
Lord Ralph Kerr

8m S of Derby on A514, in village of Melbourne • *Open April – Sept, Wed, Sat, Sun and Bank Holiday Mon, 2.00 – 6.00 p.m.* • *Best season: spring/summer* • *Entrance: £1.00* • *Limited parking* • *Refreshments: hot and cold meals in tea room* • *Toilet facilities* • *Suitable for wheelchairs* • *Shop* • *House open, Aug, most days, 2.00 – 5.00 p.m., £1.50, children 75p, family ticket reductions* • *Grade II*

There has been very little alteration to Sir Thomas Coke's formal garden so this is a visual record of a complete late seventeenth- century/early eighteenth-century garden in the style of Le Nôtre laid out by London and Wise. It is in immaculate condition with avenues culminating in exquisite statuary and fountains including the lead urn The Four Seasons by van Nost whose other lead statuary stands in niches of yew. A series of terraces run down to a lake, the Great Basin. A grotto has an inscription thought to be that of Byron's troublesome mistress Caroline Lamb. Unique in English gardens is the Birdcage iron arbour of 1706 which can be seen from the house along a long walk hedged with yews. It is well worth buying the booklet 'Melbourne Hall Gardens' at the entrance, giving the history and a suggested guided tour.

210 NOTTINGHAM ROAD   14
Woodlinkin, Langley Mill, Derbyshire.   Tel: (0773) 714903
Mr and Mrs R. Brown

12m NW of Nottingham on A610 near Codnor. It is the first house past a garage on the left ● Open by appointment and 24th June, 2.00 – 5.00 p.m.
● Best season: late spring/early summer ● Entrance: 50p, children free
● Limited parking ● Suitable for wheelchairs ● Dogs on lead ● Grade IV

A plantsman's garden of half an acre with an emphasis on shrub roses – the garden is packed with many good examples. There are also some rarer shrubs and trees. Geraniums, hellebores, symphytums and similar plants provide all-year interest in the herbaceous section. The brick base of a disused greenhouse is used for a display of alpines.

57 PORTLAND CLOSE   15
Mickleover, Derbyshire.   Tel: (0332) 515450
Mr and Mrs A.L. Ritchie

3m W of Derby turn right off A516 into Cavendish Way then 2nd left into Portland Close ● Open by appointment only and 29th April, 2.00 – 5.00 p.m.
● Best season: spring/summer ● Entrance: 50p, children free ● Limited parking ● Plants for sale ● Grade IV

A small plantsman's garden with something unusual planted in almost every inch of it. The knowledgeable owner propagates most of the huge variety of hostas, primulas, auriculas, violas and cyclamen, with many of the plants for sale. Alpines, sink gardens.

DEVON

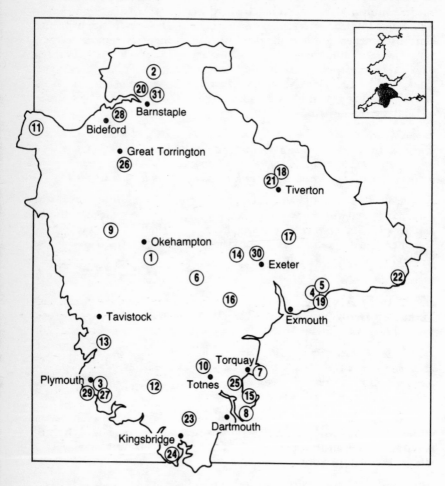

Map labels: Barnstaple, Bideford, Great Torrington, Tiverton, Okehampton, Exeter, Tavistock, Exmouth, Torquay, Totnes, Plymouth, Kingsbridge, Dartmouth

ANDREW'S CORNER
Belstone, Nr Okehampton, Devon. Tel: (0837) 840332
H.J. and Mr and Mrs R.J. Hill

1

3m E of Okehampton, signed to Belstone • *Open by appointment and 15th April, 6th, 27th, 28th May, 3rd, 24th June, 22nd July, 2.30 - 6.00 p.m.* • *Entrance: 50p, children 25p* • *Parking* • *Teas on open days* • *Suitable for wheelchairs* • *Plants for sale* • **Grade III**

Nine hundred feet above sea level, on north Dartmoor, facing to the Taw valley and across to the high moor. In its two thirds of an acre (amazing that it is not larger) grows a wide variety of plants of all sorts not normally seen at such an altitude. The sense of space is achieved by the division of the garden into different levels by rhododendrons and trees, each area being a small region with its own micro-climate, and all with glimpses through to other areas and to the wide landscape. There are herbaceous plants, many roses and lilies, conifers and heathers in island beds; in spring flowering bulbs and meconopsis; in autumn colour from maples and gentians. There are dry stone walls (a speciality of the area) a paved area and a pond with water plants and among the stone and paving are lewisias and other alpines. The owner does not like the description 'plantsman'; he says it is a hobby he loves – it is certainly an inspiration.

ARLINGTON COURT 2
Arlington, Nr Barnstaple, Devon. Tel: (027182) 296
The National Trust

6m N of Barnstaple on A39, turn E ● *Open April – Sept, daily except Sat but open Sat of Bank Holiday weekends, 11.00 a.m. – 6.00 p.m. Oct, 11.00 a.m. – 5.00 p.m. Last admission ½ hour before closing. Park open all year, daily during daylight hours* ● *Entrance: £1.80 (garden only)* ● *Parking 300 yards away* ● *Refreshments for parties by arrangement* ● *Toilet facilities in house* ● *Shop* ● *House open. £2.90. Less for parties by appointment* ● ***Grade III***

The Georgian house is set in a magnificent park where Shetland ponies and Jacob sheep graze. There are a number of woodland walks with many remains of the old stone-built water courses or leats that were used to irrigate the park in times of drought two centuries ago. The planned 'wilderness' was a popular eighteenth-century feature, a semi-wild area between the garden and the parkland. The woodland is managed to protect wildlife including red deer. The lake is approached by an avenue of monkey puzzle (araucaria) trees.

41 BEAUMONT ROAD 3
St Judes, Plymouth, Devon. Tel: (0752) 668640
Mr and Mrs A.J. Parsons

½m from Plymouth city centre, 100 yards from Beaumont Park. Take Ebrington Street exit from Charles Cross roundabout in city centre ● *Open 10th June, 2.00 – 6.00 p.m.* ● *Entrance: 50p* ● *Parking in nearby street* ● *Teas* ● ***Grade III***

A prize-winning garden in a north-facing, narrow Victorian backyard, 60 feet long. Plants intensively grown in pots and containers include clematis, ceanothus, parthenocissus. Variagated ivies grow out of tubs over arches; there is a rockery and even a pool and waterfall. Pieris, viburnums, camellias, many clematis, and scented plants such as philadelphus, *Viburnum farreri* and Regal lilies, make this matchbox garden an inspiration for small town garden owners. Mr and Mrs Parsons aptly quote Horace: 'This was one of my prayers: for a parcel of land, not so very large'.

BICTON COLLEGE OF AGRICULTURE 4
East Budleigh, Devon. Tel: (0395) 68353

By Sidmouth Lodge, halfway between Budleigh Salterton and Newton Poppleford on A376 • *Open all year excluding public holidays, Wed, 2.00 – 5.00 p.m., Fri, 2.00 – 4.30 p.m. and 28th April, 10.00 a.m. – 5.00 p.m., 2nd, 16th, 30th May, 13th, 27th June, 11th July, 12th, 26th Sept, 10th, 24th Oct, 2.00 – 5.00 p.m.* • *Entrance: free, on special open days £1.00, children free* • *Parking in visitor and student car park, through gate into arboretum* • *Toilet facilities* • *Suitable for wheelchairs* • *Plants for sale sometimes* • *Grade IV*

Linked to the Georgian house, the gardens are reached by a monkey puzzle (araucaria) avenue, and extend to the old walled garden and glasshouses via the arboretum which is half a mile long and planted with trees and shrubs including camellias, magnolias and flowering cherries. As this is the centre of the Horticultural department there is an enormous variety of plants in beds and borders, laid out for both teaching and visual effect. In Bicton Park nearby are more gardens and one of the finest glasshouses in Europe.

BICTON PARK 5
Bicton, Devon. Tel: (03954) 2789
Clinton Devon Estates

3½m N of Budleigh Salterton off A376. Entrance near St Mary's Church • *Open 28th March – Oct, 10.00 a.m. – 6.00 p.m.* • *Entrance: £3.25, OAP £2.75, children 3 – 14 £2.00. Special rates for parties of 20 or more* • *Parking* • *Refreshments: café for light lunches and teas late May – Sept* • *Toilet facilities* • *Suitable for wheelchairs* • *Dogs on lead* • *Shop* • *Museum open, extra charge* • *Grade II*

There is much to see here in the 50 acres – don't be put off by the 'fun and family entertainment'. The formal and informal gardens date from 1734 and the Italian garden is attributed to Le Nôtre; there is an Oriental garden with a 150 year old mulberry, azaleas, camellias, flowering cherries and a peony border (bush and tree); an American Garden established in the 1830s with a snowdrop tree (*Halesia carolina*), calico bushes and a handkerchief tree (*Davidia involucrata*); a Hermitage Garden with lake and water garden and a pinetum with some rare conifers including a Mexican juniper, yuccas, Korean thuya and Tasmanian cedar. The pinetum was established in 1838 and extended in 1910 to take the collection of the famous botanist and explorer 'Chinese' Wilson. Perhaps Bicton's greatest glory is the Palm House built between 1815 and 1820, one of the oldest in the country and recently refurbished; in it, Kentia palms up to 20 feet, tree ferns and bromeliads and outside an Assam tea plant. There are also geranium and fuchsia houses and a tropical and a temperate house for bananas, coffee trees and bougainvilleas. Bicton College of Agriculture is also open (see above).

CASTLE DROGO   6
Drewsteignton, Devon. Tel: (06473) 3306
The National Trust

4m S of A30 or 4m N of Moretonhamstead on A382, turn E to Drewsteignton ● *Open April – Sept, daily, 11.00 a.m. – 6.00 p.m. Oct, 11.00 a.m. – 5.00 p.m. Last admission ½ hour before closing* ● *Entrance: £1.50 (garden and grounds only). Reduced rates for parties by appointment* ● *Parking. Coaches by appointment only* ● *Refreshments: coffee and light lunches (licensed) and teas, 11.00 a.m. – 5.30 p.m.* ● *Toilet facilities inc. disabled* ● *Suitable for wheelchairs. Special parking and access by arrangement at shop. Scented plants for visually handicapped* ● *Shop sells brochure* ● *House open at extra charge. Croquet can be played with hired equipment* ● ***Grade I***

The last castle to be built in England (begun 1910) was designed by Sir Edwin Lutyens, with the great Gertrude Jekyll much involved with the garden design and planting. Apart from the evergreen oaks above the magnificent views over the Teign Gorge, and a valley planted with rhododendrons, magnolias, camellias, cherries and maples, there is a series of formal terraces and borders with walls of granite and sharp-edged yew hedges. One terrace has rose beds, with white flowers and arbours of yew and *Parrotia persica* 'the iron tree'. In the main formal gardens, with galleries round a sunken centre, paths are serpentine (an Indian touch typical of Lutyens who built New Delhi in the 1920s when he was supervising here), and herbaceous borders are full of old varieties of lupins, lychnis, campanula, hollyhocks and red hot pokers. Under the granite walls are perennials like euphorbias, hellebores, alchemilla and veronica, with spring bulbs. Steps lead to a second terrace with yuccas and wisterias and herb borders; more steps to shrub borders of lilacs, azaleas, magnolias and lilies, and finally a splendid circular lawn surrounded by a tall yew hedge at the top, a huge green circle and a perfect stage set for croquet.

CASTLE TOR   7
Wellswood, Torquay, Devon. Tel: (0803) 214858
Mr L. Stocks

In Torquay. From Higher Lincombe Road, turn E into Oxlea Road. Entrance is 200 yards on right with eagle-topped pillars ● *Open by appointment* ● *Entrance: 50p, children 25p* ● *Parking* ● *Plants for sale* ● ***Grade III***

Half a century ago the then owner of Castle Tor approached Sir Edwin Lutyens and asked him to design a smaller version of Castle Drogo; being too busy Sir Edwin nominated a pupil of his, Frederick Harrild, and the result is this fascinating architectural garden with magnificent views over Lyme Bay and Tor Bay. Gertrude Jekyll's ideas about garden colour – no violent juxtapositions or circular beds full of salvias – were incorporated, and the whole is framed in terraces of Somerset limestone (a pleasant change from granite) and cubic green walls of yew hedges; there is topiary in both green and golden (Irish) yew. There are architectural type follies like a pillared orangery with a domed roof and a tower with portcullis and gatehouse; best of all a long ornamental water course or small canal. Over the years the owner has collected suitable statuary and bright annual flowers are seen as bright accents in urns and tubs against the stone background.

COLETON FISHACRE GARDEN 8
Coleton, Kingswear, Dartmouth, Devon. Tel: (080425) 466
The National Trust

2m from Kingswear, take Lower Ferry Road and turn off at toll house ● *Open April - Oct, Wed - Fri, Sun, 11.00 a.m. - 6.00 p.m.* ● *Entrance: £1.80. Reduced rates for parties* ● *Parking* ● *Very limited for wheelchairs* ● *Grade II*

Oswald Milne who was a pupil of Edwin Lutyens designed the house and the architectural features of this garden for Sir Rupert and Lady D'Oyly Carte; the house was completed and the garden begun in 1926. Exceptionally mild and sheltered, it is in a Devon combe, sloping steeply to the cliff tops and the sea, and sheltered by belts of Monterey pine and holm oaks planted in 1925. There are many streams making a humid atmosphere for the moisture-loving plants like the magnificent bamboos (inch thick canes) and mimosas, and many other sub-tropical plants, rarely growing outside in this country. There is a collection of unusual trees like dawn redwood and swamp cypress and Chilean myrtle, and dominating all a tall tulip tree the same age as the house. Formal walls and terraces make a framework round the house for many sun-loving tender plants; there are various water features, notably stone-edged channels and a circular pool in the lawn in the herbaceous-bordered walled garden.

CROSSPARK 9
Northlew, Nr Okehampton, Devon. Tel: (040922) 518
Mrs G. West

8m NW of Okehampton. From Okehampton take A30 to Launceston for 1m, turn right onto B3218, then 2nd right to Northlew, then follow Highampton road for 1m ● *Open end March - Sept, Fri - Sun and Bank Holiday Mons, 2.00 - 6.00 p.m.* ● *Entrance: 50p* ● *Parking* ● *Toilet facilities* ● *Only a small area suitable for wheelchairs* ● *Plants for sale* ● *Grade III*

This plantswoman's garden, created from a field by the owner, would provide interest for a visit at most times of the year. A heather bed and pleasant separate colour beds and also an attractive white garden. The pool and waterfall are surrounded by a range of bog plants and there is a good selection of climbers on the house. Also dwarf conifers and a rockery.

DARTINGTON HALL 10
Dartington, Nr Totnes, Devon. Tel: (0803) 862271
Dartington Hall Trust

*2m NW of Totnes, E of A384 • Open daily, dawn – dusk • Entrance: free
• Parking. Coaches by appointment (0803) 863614 • Refreshments by
appointment • Toilet facilities • Dogs • Shop • Nature trail • Grade II*

The gardens were begun by Dorothy and Leonard Elmhirst in 1925 when the
Hall was derelict and the estate and parkland overgrown. Several garden
designers have been advisers – Beatrix Farrand designed the courtyard and
cobbled drive round the central lawn and opened up the woodland walkways.
There are three woodland walks using bay, yew, and hollies as a background
for a collection of camellias, magnolias and rhododendrons. Landscape
designer Percy Cane made the glade and the azalea dell. The overall design is
strongly architectural with sunken lawns and terraces and formal clipped yews
contrasting with the mature woodland. Fine sculpture by Henry Moore and
others attests to Dartington's artistic predilections.

DOCTON MILL 11
Spekes Valley, Nr Hartland, Devon. Tel: (02374) 369
Mr and Mrs N.S. Pugh

*Off A39 from Hartland village to Stoke, turn left and follow signs towards
Elmscott to Lymebridge in Spekes valley • Open April – Sept, daily except Fri
and Sat, 10.00 a.m. – 5.00 p.m. • Entrance: £1.00 (£1.50 in July and Aug),
children free • Parking • Plants for sale • Grade II*

Mr and Mrs Pugh took over this then derelict water mill 9 years ago and
embarked upon a large scale clearance of the waterways; there are ponds, leats,
footbridges over the river and many smaller streams as it is only 1500 yards
from Speke's Mill Mouth coastal waterfall and the beach. A boggy area was
drained to make a stream and a bog garden with ligularias and primulas and
ferns; the whole purpose has been to make everything as natural as possible,
integrating the garden into the wild with indigenous plants such as brooms,
cytisus and many grasses. Near the house the garden abounds in roses, mostly
old shrub roses, there is a hedge of 'Felicia' and 'Pax' hybrid musk roses and
a climbing 'Felicia' – a rarity. Roses are underplanted with many varieties of
perennial geraniums, another favourite plant, and these are also used on the
rockery which is wet clay and north facing so not suitable for alpines, together
with hebes and small conifers.

FARDEL MANOR 12
Ivybridge, Devon. Tel: (0752) 892353
Dr A.G. Stevens

*1¼m NW of Ivybridge, 2m SE of Cornwood, 200 yards off railway bridge
• Open 31st Aug, 11.00 a.m. – 4.30 p.m. and for specialist groups by*

appointment ● *Entrance: 75p, children 30p* ● *Parking* ● *Teas* ● *Plants for sale* ● **Grade III**

A five-acre garden, half of it recently planted, with secluded areas or 'rooms', including a herb garden, a formal fountain garden, herbaceous borders and shrubberies surrounding the fourteenth-century manor house. Climbing roses cover the south wall, joined by Canary creeper in late summer; there is an orangery with Black Hamburgh grapes and *Citrus mitis*, vegetable and fruit gardens and an orchard, a bog area with parsley, thistles, day lilies and wild iris and the giant *Gunnera manicata*. A stream leads to a lake surrounded with iris and primulas – a perfect habitat for waterfowl of all kinds. The cultivation is totally organic.

THE GARDEN HOUSE   13
Buckland Monachorum, Yelverton, Devon.   Tel: (0822) 854769
The Fortescue Garden Trust

10m N of Plymouth, W of Yelverton off A386 ● *Open April – Sept, daily, 12 noon – 5.00 p.m.* ● *Entrance: £1.50, children 50p* ● *Parking* ● *Partly suitable for wheelchairs* ● *Plants for sale* ● **Grade II**

An eight-acre garden created after 1945 by Lionel Fortescue, a great plant collector and perfectionist, the charming two-acre walled garden was originally part of a mediaeval monastery. It contains a good collection of herbaceous plants giving the appearance of a cottage garden. Hedges planted for shelter on different levels surprise one as new areas come into view. There are some lovely old trees and some unusual specimens, mainly shrubs, herbaceous and alpines. An alpine house is of special interest. Courses in gardening are held at specified times.

THE GLEBE HOUSE   14
Whitestone, Nr Exeter, Devon.   Tel: (039281) 200
Mr and Mrs S.J. West

4m W of Exeter, in village adjoining the church ● *Open 15th, 16th, 22nd, 29th April, 6th, 7th, 27th, 28th May, 3rd, 10th, 17th, 24th June, 1st, 8th July, 2.00 – 5.00 p.m.* ● *Parking but narrow lanes unsuitable for coaches* ● **Grade III**

A two-acre garden round a former rectory, fifteenth-century with a Georgian facade, and a listed fourteenth-century tithe barn, with splendid views to the south over the estuary of the Exe, and towards Dartmoor. On the lower level are lawns, trees and a heather garden; above, divided by coniferous hedges and windbreaks are walks among clematis, vitis and a collection of shrub roses – old-fashioned, species and modern hybrid. The middle level of the garden, with the house and tithe barn, features many varieties of climbing roses, clematis, jasmine and honeysuckle. The most impressive and memorable plant is an enormously vigorous *Rosa filipes* 'Kiftsgate' which is trained along the tithe barn, and which, in 1989 extended over 120 feet. Flooding the courtyard with scent when in flower in early July this must be one of the largest climbing roses in the South West.

GREENWAY HOUSE 15
Nr Greenway Ferry, Churston Ferrers, Devon.   Tel: (0803) 842003
Mr and Mrs A.A. Hicks

4m W of Brixham. From B3203 Paignton – Brixham road, take road to Galmpton, then towards Greenway ● Open 26th April, 3rd May, 2.00 – 6.00 p.m. ● Entrance: £1.00, children 50p ● Parking ● Teas ● Suitable for wheelchairs ● Plants for sale in nursery open Tues – Sat and by appointment ● Grade III

Another large (30-acre) and ancient Devon garden on a steep slope, on the bank of the tree-lined Dart river which has woodland walks. There are a large number of indigenous trees over 150 years old and a giant tulip tree. In the walled garden are many camellias, 30 varieties of early magnolias, ceanothus, wisterias and abutilons, and a cork oak. The banks of primroses and bluebells make it magical in spring. On the Georgian facade are *Magnolia grandiflora*, *Akebia quinata* and *Mutisia oligodon*; in the natural glades are foxgloves, white iris, herb Robert, pennywort, ivy and hart's tongue and male ferns.

HIGHER KNOWLE 16
Lustleigh, Devon.   Tel: (0392) 851222
Mr and Mrs D.R.A. Quicke

8m NW of Newton Abbot, 3m NW of Bovey Tracey on A382 towards Moretonhamstead. In 2½m, turn left at Kelly Cross for Lustleigh; after ¼m straight on at Brookfield for Manaton; after ½m steep drive on left ● Open 15th, 16th, 22nd, 29th April, 6th, 7th, 13th, 20th, 27th, 28th May, 2.00 – 6.00 p.m. ● Entrance: £1.00, children 50p ● Teas in village ● Grade IV

A woodland garden only 30 years old situated on a steep hillside with Dartmoor views. The old beech wood is carpeted with bluebells in spring, and magnolias and rhododendrons, ornamental cherries and heather banks; there is also a tall *Embothrium coccineum* flowering in early summer. A beech hedge encloses a lawn, with the main display of deciduous and evergreen azaleas. Giant Dartmoor granite boulders add much natural sculpture to the woodland walks.

KILLERTON 17
Broadclyst, Nr Exeter, Devon.   Tel: (0392) 881345
The National Trust

7m NE of Exeter, on W side of B3181 ● Park and garden open all year during daylight hours ● Entrance: £1.80 (park and garden). Winter rate £1.00

● *Parking* ● *Refreshments* ● *Toilet facilities* ● *Partly suitable for wheelchairs
but motorised buggy with driver available for higher levels* ● *Shop* ● *House and
costume museum open April – Oct, daily except Tues, 11.00 a.m. – 6.00 p.m.
(Oct 11.00 a.m. – 5.00 p.m.) Last admission ½ hour before closing. House
£3.40* ● ***Grade II***

This large garden was made on a hill with woods extending in all to 4000
acres, first by John Veitch in the 1770s and then by the famous Victorian
William Robinson. The actual garden area of 15 acres will provide interest and
pleasure to all, but to the tree and shrub enthusiast it is a haven of delight.
Beside the avenues of beeches there are Wellingtonias and Lawson cypresses
which provide colour and form and many fine broad-leaved trees including
oaks and maples as well as the usual conifers. Terraced beds provide summer
colour and there are dwarf shrubs and herbaceous specimens to follow the fine
display of rhododendrons. A garden to give pleasure at most times of the year.
There is a bear house.

KNIGHTSHAYES 18
Bolham, Tiverton, Devon. Tel: (0884) 254665
The National Trust

2m N of Tiverton, turn right off A396 at Bolham ● *Open April – Oct, daily,
11.00 a.m. – 6.00 p.m. (5.00 p.m. in Oct)* ● *Entrance: £1.80 (garden and
grounds only)* ● *Parking inc. disabled* ● *Refreshments: restaurant for coffee,
lunches and teas. Licensed* ● *Toilet facilities* ● *Suitable for wheelchairs* ● *Dogs
on lead in park only* ● *Plants for sale* ● *Shop* ● *House open, daily except Fri
but open Good Friday, at additional cost* ● ***Grade I***

This 40-acre garden should give pleasure to everyone with its extensive
parkland and large range of trees including Douglas firs, willows, cedar of
Lebanon, and nothofagus. The formal Victorian gardens were completely
transformed by the former owners, Sir John and Lady Heathcote Amory, and
continued by the Trust. An unusual piece of topiary – the Fox Hunt – leads one
on to masses of camellias, azaleas, magnolias, acers and rhododendrons. A
formal paved garden contains silver, lilac and pink plants and there is a circular
pool surrounded by a yew hedge. The borders have many tender and rare
specimens and in the peat-block beds are cyclamen, hellebores and primulas.
Something of interest at all seasons.

LEE FORD 19
Budleigh Salterton, Devon. Tel: (03954) 5894
Mr and Mrs L. Lindsay-Fynn

3½m from Exmouth ● *Open by prior appointment for parties only and 27th
May, 1.30 – 5.30 p.m.* ● *Entrance: £1.00, OAP 80p, children 50p. Parties of
20 or more 80p per person* ● *Parking* ● *Teas on open days, 3.00 – 5.30 p.m.*
● *Suitable for wheelchairs* ● *Plants for sale* ● ***Grade III***

Inspired by the Savill Gardens at Windsor, the present owner's father developed this wild woodland garden in the 1950s and 60s and it is one of the longest established open-to-the-public gardens in Devon, best seen perhaps in early summer when the magnolias are in flower. The mown glades are surrounded with masses of species and ponticum rhododendrons, and there is a large collection of camellias, many from the Channel Islands, including white camellias which are often in flower on Christmas Day. There is also a treat of an old-fashioned walled vegetable garden with an Adam pavilion.

MARWOOD HILL   20
Marwood, Nr Barnstaple, Devon.   Tel: (0271) 42528
Dr J.A. Smart

4m NW of Barnstaple. Turn off B3230 to Marwood ● Open daily except Christmas Day, dawn – dusk ● Best season: April – Aug ● Entrance: £1.00, children 10p ● Parking in roadway ● Teas on Sun and Bank Holidays or for parties by prior arrangement ● Partly suitable for wheelchairs ● Dogs on lead ● Plants for sale ● Grade I

With the wonderful collection of plants this 20-acre garden is of special interest to the connoisseur but could not fail to give pleasure to any visitor. Over 3000 different varieties of plants covering collections of willows, ferns, magnolias, embothriums, rhododendrons and hebes, and fine collection of camellias in a glasshouse. Tender plants from Tasmania, Australia and New Zealand are in another greenhouse and the walled gardens are clothed with a beautiful range of clematis and other climbers. A rock garden has been created from an old quarry and contains many alpines, and round the pools are primulas and bog plants.

MIDDLE HILL   21
Washfield, Nr Tiverton, Devon.   Tel: (03985) 380
Mr and Mrs E. Boundy

4½m NW of Tiverton, via B3221. Through the village of Washfield and the garden is 1½m on left ● Open end April – early Aug, Sun and by arrangement ● Best season: May ● Parking ● Partly suitable for wheelchairs ● Plants for sale ● Grade IV

This small garden has been created over 20 odd years to include some specialist plants. There are raised beds, a rockery, island beds growing gentians, ferns, hostas, clematis, crocosmias, penstemons, pittosporums and, being so exposed, shelter has been provided. Interesting colour and foliage combinations offer some good tips.

THE MOORINGS   22
Rocombe, Uplyme, Nr Lyme Regis, Devon.   Tel: (02974) 3295
Mr and Mrs A. Marriage

2m NW of Lyme Regis. Take A3070 out of Lyme Regis, turn right 150 yards beyond Black Dog pub, over cross roads, fork right into Springhead Road. Top gate to garden is 500 yards on right ● *Open by appointment and 15th, 16th April, 6th, 7th, 27th, 28th May, 4th Nov, 11.00 a.m. – 5.00 p.m.* ● *Entrance: 50p, children free* ● *Parking* ● ***Grade III***

Especially rewarding to visit in spring and autumn, this garden has been made by Mr Marriage since 1965 out of three fields on a sheltered, steep, west-facing slope. Impressively, most of the newly-planted arboretum trees have been grown from seed; there is a collection of eucalyptus, many unusual pines including umbrella and maritime pines (grown from seed gathered in the south of France) and nothofagus, including *N. obliqua* and *N. procrea*, and the woodland is underplanted with snowdrops. *Hibiscus* 'Pana Mutabilis' was first grown here; there are camellias and a 30 foot high magnolia, and a buddleia flowering rose-red in spring. A great point of interest is the collection of over 50 different species of fern, all grown from spores.

THE OLD RECTORY   23
Woodleigh, Nr Loddiswell, Devon.   Tel: (0548) 550387
Mr and Mrs H.E. Morton

3½m N of Kingsbridge, E off Kingsbridge – Wrangaton road at Rake Cross (1m S of Loddiswell), 1½m to Woodleigh itself ● *Open by appointment only* ● *Entrance: 50p, children 10p* ● *Parking* ● *Suitable for wheelchairs* ● ***Grade III***

A three-acre woodland garden, and walled garden, rescued from neglect 27 years ago. In the woodland are several individual glades of mature trees, underplanted with magnolias, azaleas, camellias and rhododendrons. There is great attention to form in the planting; evergreens and shrubs are planted for scent and winter effect, and the wild garden is most colourful in spring with crocus and daffodils, while the walled garden is designed with summer in mind. The garden is a haven for wildlife, and chemicals have never been used.

OVERBECKS MUSEUM AND GARDEN   24
Sharpitor, Salcombe, Devon.   Tel: (054884) 2893
The National Trust

1½m S of Salcombe, SW to South Sands ● *Open daily 10.00 a.m. – 8.00 p.m. or sunset if earlier* ● *Best season: spring – early summer* ● *Entrance: £1.80 (garden only)* ● *Parking. Coaches by appointment* ● *Picnic area* ● *Toilet facilities* ● *Dogs on lead* ● *Shop* ● *Museum open, April – Oct, 11.00 a.m. – 5.00 p.m. Extra charge* ● ***Grade II***

Palms stand among the bluebells in this exotic garden high above the Salcombe estuary, giving a strongly Mediterranean atmosphere. The mild, maritime climate enables it to be filled with exotics such as myrtles, daturas, agaves and an example of the large camphor tree, *Cinnamomum camphora*, a great rarity. The Himalayan *Magnolia campbellii* is nearly 90 years old and 40 feet high and wide and a sight to see in March. The steep terraces were built in 1901 and lead down through fuchsia trees, fruiting banana palms and myrtle trees to a wonderful *Cornus kousa*. In formal beds near the house is the Chatham Island forget-me-not – *Myosotidium hortensia* (hydrangea-like) with flowers as clear as blue china, phormiums, and tender roses among the rocks.

PAIGNTON ZOO AND BOTANICAL GARDEN 25
Totnes Road, Paignton, Devon. Tel: (0803) 557479

● *Open daily except 25th Dec, 10.00 a.m. – sunset* ● *Parking* ● *Refreshments: restaurants* ● *Toilet facilities* ● *Suitable for wheelchairs* ● *Shop* ● *Grade II*

Those not keen on zoos may be won over by Paignton; it is in the forefront of animal and plant conservation and one of the zoos worldwide involved in the breeding of endangered species. As well as the very healthy and happy animals there are the plants. Paignton (over 100 acres in size) was the first zoo in the country to combine animals and a Botanic Garden, laid out 60 years ago and added to over the years. Choice of plants has been dictated by their harmlessness to teeth and beaks and their ability to provide shade, perches and swinging and basking places; there are geographical collections of plants in the paddocks, and plants also make the fences safer. Hardy Chinese plants surround the baboon rocks. Paignton has the National Collection of sorbaria and buddleia. There are two large plant houses, one sub-tropical with tender plants and trees and magical birds flying, and a tropical house with a jungle pool and areas of tropical plants (indoor plants par excellence) and small areas of different plant families – orchids, African violets and lilies; everything is extensively and informatively labelled – both flora and fauna.

ROSEMOOR GARDEN 26
Great Torrington, Devon. Tel: (0805) 24067
The Royal Horticultural Society

1m SE of Great Torrington on B3220 ● *Open all year* ● *Best season: late May/ early June* ● *Entrance: £1.50, children 50p* ● *Parking* ● *Refreshments on Sun, Wed and Bank Holidays and for pre-booked parties* ● *Toilet facilities* ● *Suitable for wheelchairs* ● *Plants for sale in nursery* ● *Grade II*

This eight-acre garden was started by Lady Anne Palmer forty years ago with the help of the distinguished designer John Codrington. It contains over 3500 different plants. Masses of rhododendrons provide colour in the spring, followed by species and old-fashioned roses. There is an excellent collection of birches and sorbus and over 100 different ilex. Walking around the garden one is surprised by beds containing New Zealand plants, alstroemerias from Brazil and many other unusual plants. There is a silver and golden area, conifer beds, island beds with beautiful shrubs and perennials together with scree and raised beds with alpines.

SALTRAM HOUSE 27
Plympton, Plymouth, Devon. Tel: (0752) 336546
The National Trust

3m E of Plymouth. On A379 turn N to Billacombe. After 1m turn left to Saltram ● *Open daily except Fri and Sat, but open Sat of Bank Holiday weekends, 11.00 a.m. – 6.00 p.m. (Oct 11.00 a.m. - 5.00 p.m.) Last admission ½ hour before closing* ● *Best season: April – June* ● *Entrance: £1.20 garden only. Reduced rates for parties by appointment* ● *Parking* ● *Refreshments April – Oct* ● *Toilet facilities* ● *Suitable for wheelchairs* ● *Dogs* ● *Shop April – Oct* ● *House open April – Oct, extra charge* ● ***Grade II***

The original garden dates from 1770, slightly altered in the last century; there are three eighteenth-century buildings – a castle or belvedere, an orangery (due to the mild climate the orange and lemon trees are moved outside in the summer) and a classical garden house named Fanny's Bower after Fanny Burney who came here in 1789 in the entourage of George III. There is a long lime avenue underplanted with narcissi in spring, *Cyclamen linearifolium* in autumn and a central glade with specimen trees like the stone pine and Himalayan spruce. There is a beech grove, a Melancholy Walk, and walks with magnolias, camellias, rhododendrons and Japanese maples which, with other trees, make for dramatic autumn colour.

TAPELEY PARK 28
Instow, Devon. Tel: (0271) 860528
Mr H.T.C. Christie

2m N of Bideford S off A39 Barnstaple – Bideford road ● *Open Easter to Oct, daily except Sat, 10.00 a.m. – 6.00 p.m.* ● *Entrance: by collecting box* ● *Parking* ● *Teas in Queen Anne dairy. Picnic places* ● *Toilet facilities* ● *Suitable for wheelchairs* ● *Dogs* ● *Plants for sale* ● *House open. Tours for parties of 20 or more* ● ***Grade II***

The house is basically William and Mary, set on a splendid site above the River Torridge and Bideford, with much to see and a family with a fascinating history – the Christies of Glynbourne. There are three formal terraces, an Italian garden with ornamental water, yew hedges, an ilex tunnel, a shell house, ice house, and a variety of roses, fuchsias. lavender, dahlias as well as more exotic plants like *Abelia floribunda*, sophora and feijoa from Brazil. On the south of the house are yuccas, *Magnolia grandiflora*, agapanthus and mimosas; on the east, wisteria and *Drimys winteri*, a rare honeysuckle. A woodland walk is lined with camellias, hydrangeas and rhododendrons with primroses and primulas in spring under the giant beeches and oaks; this leads to a water-lily-covered pond in late summer, in the background tall firs and *Thuja plicata*. Walled kitchen garden.

TUDOR GARDEN   29
New Street, The Barbican, Plymouth, Devon.
Plymouth Corporation

In the centre of the old town ● *Open daily* ● *Parking difficult* ● *Dogs*
● *Grade III*

An integral part of an area of Plymouth that is being refurbished, this is an interesting reconstruction of the type of Tudor garden that would have existed behind the house in this ancient street. As far as possible only plants which grew in Elizabethan England have been established. Elsewhere in Plymouth the Corporation commemorates great Victorian seaside gardening with colourful carpet bedding by traditional methods.

UNIVERSITY OF EXETER   30
Northcote House, The Queen's Drive, Exeter, Devon.
Tel: (0392) 77911
University of Exeter

On N outskirts of Exeter on A396, turn E on to B3183 ● *Open daily* ● *Best season: April – June* ● *Entrance: free. Coaches by appointment only*
● *Parking* ● *Dogs on lead* ● *Shop open weekdays sells guide book* ● *Grade II*

There is much to see on a one mile tour of these extensive gardens based on those made in the 1860s by an East India Merchant millionaire who inherited a fortune blockade-running in the Napoleonic wars. The landscaping and tree planting was carried out by Veitch whose plant collectors went all over the world (among them E.H. 'Chinese' Wilson) and at that time many of the trees were unique in Europe. There is a series of lakes with wildfowl, dogwoods, birches, hazel and alder, callistemon shrubs (bottle brush) wingnut trees (*Pterocarya stenoptera*) from China in 1860 and a maidenhair tree (ginkgo) sacred in Buddhist China. Rockeries have collections of alpines; there is a banana tree (*Musa basjoo*), a large *Gunnera chilensis* and palm trees introduced by Robert Fortune in 1849. Formal gardens and bedding plants lead to a sunken, scented garden. Exeter will house the National collection of Azara, evergreens from Chile, with scented yellow flowers. There are, of course, rhododendrons, magnolias, camellias in a woodland walk; roses, eucalyptus and *Opuntia humifusa*, the prickly pear cactus flowering in summer.

WOODSIDE 31
Higher Raleigh Road, Barnstaple, Devon.   Tel: (0271) 43095
Mr and Mrs M. Feesey

Off A39 Barnstaple to Lynton road, turn right 300 yards above fire station
● *Open 13th May, 24th June, 22nd July, 2.00 – 5.30 p.m.*   ● *Best season:*
spring/summer ● *Entrance: 60p, children 20p* ● *Limited parking in road*
outside ● ***Grade III***

A sloping two-acre garden in a suburban area with an unusual collection of
plants including ornamental grasses, bamboos and sedges. Many parts of the
garden are shaded but rare dwarf shrubs, trees and conifers survive. There are
raised beds and troughs with alpines and peat-loving specimens. A collection
of New Zealand plants along with peat-loving shrubs make this a garden with
a difference.

TELEPHONE NUMBERS
Except where specifically requested to be excluded, telephone numbers
to which enquiries may be directed are given for each property. To
maintain the support and cooperation of private owners it is suggested
that the telephone be used with discretion. Where visits are by
appointment, the telephone can of course be used except where written
application, particularly for parties, is specifically requested. Code
numbers are given in brackets. For the Republic of Ireland when
phoning from the United Kingdom dial 353 plus area code plus
number (except Dublin numbers which are 0001 plus number). In all
cases where visits by parties are proposed, owners should be advised in
advance and arrangements preferably confirmed in writing.
   London Telephone Codes: From May 1990 all London telephone
numbers with the prefix 01 will be changed. The new prefix will be
either 071 or 081. Details of these new numbers are available from
British Telecom. During the changeover period in 1990 all London
telephone numbers dialled with their 01 prefix will be redirected.

DORSET

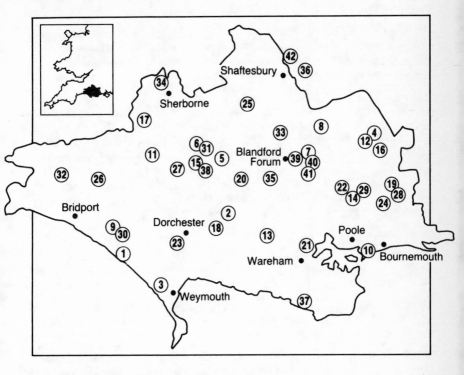

ABBOTSBURY GARDENS

1

Abbotsbury, Dorset. Tel: (0305) 871387
Holland House Estates

9m NW of Weymouth, 9m SW of Dorchester off B3157 ● Open mid-March –
mid-Oct, daily, 10.00 a.m. – 6.00 p.m. ● Entrance: £1.90, OAP £1.40,
children 50p ● Parking ● Refreshments ● Toilet facilities ● Partly suitable
*for wheelchairs ● Dogs on lead ● Plants for sale ● Shop ● **Grade II***

Proximity to the sea helps to provide the 'micro-climate' which makes
Abbotsbury so special. Within its 20 acres there is much of great interest to the
plantsperson in the many rare species on display, while amateur gardeners can
get pleasure from the banks of colour and the shaded walks – particularly in
the spring, but also at other seasons. People travel a long way to visit these
gardens – often called 'sub-tropical', but probably technically better described
as 'wet Mediterranean'. They are right to do so, although the initial
impression given by the cramped reception arrangements and sales area does
no justice to the quality of what lies beyond. There are big plans for an
extensive face-lift (Winter 1989/90), so hopefully the excellent quality of the
plants on offer will in future be more easily recognised.

ATHELHAMPTON 2
Puddletown, Dorchester, Dorset. Tel: (0305) 848363
Lady Cooke

On A35 1m E of Puddletown, near Dorchester ● Open Easter – mid-Oct, Wed, Thurs, Sun and Bank Holidays (Aug, Mon and Tues), 2.00 – 6.00 p.m. ● Best season: May/June ● Entrance: £1.25, children free (£2.50 house and gardens) ● Parking ● Refreshments ● Toilet facilities ● Partly suitable for wheelchairs ● Shop ● House open ● Grade II

Athelhampton garden was rescued and re-designed by Alfred La Fontaine in 1891, a process continued by subsequent owners, latterly the late Robert Cooke. Courts and walls follow the original plan with beautiful stonework in walls and arches. Apart from some of the most impressive topiary in England there are pools, fountains, a rectangular canal with water lilies and a pleached lime walk. It is not a great flower garden but rambling roses, clematis and jasmine (in their seasons) make it memorable. With one and a half gardeners instead of the original 12 you can't have everything!

BENNETT'S WATER GARDEN CENTRE 3
Putton Lane, Chickerell, Weymouth, Dorset. Tel: (0305) 785151
Mr John Bennett

1m W of Weymouth off B3157 ● Open April – Sept, except Sun and Mon ● Entrance: 80p, children 40p ● Parking ● Toilet facilities ● Partly suitable for wheelchairs ● Plants for sale ● Grade IV

First impressions are disappointing as the entrance and visible buildings are unattractive. A small shop sells fountains, fish etc and there is a restricted area displaying a good range of water-loving and alpine plants. The extent of the water gardens only becomes clear as you move along the grass paths between small, sometimes overgrown and abandoned plant 'tanks'. The large ponds and lakes, of which there is a considerable number, have been dug out from the clay-pit of an abandoned brickworks. Some are new, with brilliant lilies establishing themselves. Older ones are lined by marginal plants and the largest lake is now a wildlife area.

BOVERIDGE FARM 4
Cranborne, Dorset. Tel: (07254) 241
Mr D.J. Dampney

Nr Cranborne on Martin Road (unclassified). Take 2nd turn on right ● Open 22nd April, 13th May, 17th June, 2.00 – 5.30 p.m. ● Best season: April – June ● Entrance: 75p, children free ● Parking ● Teas ● Toilet facilities ● Plants for sale ● Grade IV

The house lies on a steep north-facing slope, and the garden has been laid out below it, to the west of it and above. The plants and shrubs on the lower side are on chalk, whilst the fern bank and shrubbery above is on neutral clay. There is a fine view across the rooftops and along the valley, which is largely arable with wooded hilltops. As a busy farmer, Mr Dampney has had to fit his enthusiasm for uncommon plants around his working life. It has taken some 35 years to create the garden as it is today, a colourful and interesting collection much of which he has himself grown from seed or cuttings.

BROADLANDS 5
Hazelbury Bryan, Nr Sturminster Newton, Dorset.
Tel: (0258) 817374
Mr and Mrs M.J. Smith

4m S of Sturminster Newton off A357 Blandford – Sherbourne road at signpost ½ beyond Antelope pub ● Open by appointment and 8th April, 6th May, 3rd June, 5th Aug and every Wed in July and Aug, 2.00 – 5.30 p.m. ● Entrance: £1.00, accompanied children free ● Parking ● Teas ● Toilet facilities ● Suitable for wheelchairs ● Plants for sale ● Grade III

This is a one and a half-acre garden in which the design and planting have the curious effect of obscuring the full size of the area while at the same time extending the apparent distance the visitor covers in walking round it. This is achieved by the clever siting of island beds, with grass walkways leading to features such as ponds, rockeries and paved seating areas. There are screening hedges to enhance the surprise of discovering the greenhouse, the vegetables, the ornamental woodland. Round every corner the visitor comes upon some new feature of interest and delight, and everywhere there are uncommon plants to give pleasure in all seasons. Begun in 1975, this is a most successful layout, excellently labelled and refreshingly imaginative, which should inspire gardeners of all levels of competence.

CANNINGS COURT 6
Pulham, Nr Sherborne, Dorset. Tel: (0258) 817210
Mr and Mrs J.D. Dennison

13m N of Dorchester, 8m SE of Sherborne. Turn E at crossroads in Pulham ● Open 20th May, 8th July, 2.00 – 6.00 p.m. ● Entrance: 75p, children free ● Parking ● Refreshments ● Toilet facilities ● Suitable for wheelchairs ● Plants for sale ● Grade IV

Twenty years of loving labour have gone into this farmhouse garden, developed virtually from scratch at the same time as the owners were busy with the rescue of the farm itself. The bare walls of the Georgian facade have been clothed with thriving creepers, the open land behind is sheltered by tree screens and contains colourful borders and shrubberies, a pond, an arboretum and – new this year – the framework for a *potager* (for the design of which the owners paid a special visit to the Chateau at Villandry). Not content, they have plans for a woodland walk, more tree screens and arbours – probably enough to occupy the next 20 years. Do not leave without looking in the tool store-cum-workshop which is entered through a huge Elizabethan fireplace rising 20 feet up a blackened chimney. The farm name is a corruption of 'Canon's Court' and it has probably been in continuous occupation for over 1000 years, as the surrounding buildings could testify.

CHARLTON COTTAGE 7
Tarrant Rushton, Nr Blandford, Dorset. Tel: (0258) 452072
The Hon. Penelope Piercy

3m SE of Blandford on B3082. Fork left at top of hill, right at T-junction, first left to village ● *Open 27th May, 10th June, 2.00 – 5.30 p.m.* ● *Entrance: £1.00, children 25p* ● *Parking in road* ● *Partly suitable for wheelchairs*
● *Grade IV*

Charlton Cottage lies at the end of the village where the garden surrounds what used to be two terraced cottages, now all one property. In place of the long narrow cottage strips, the back garden has two lawn areas separated by colourful borders and leading up a gentle slope among shrubs and trees to a vegetable area. In front of the house the road from the village peters out into a narrow track, so the owner has acquired land on the other side where there are further borders through which the visitor descends to a shady water garden and wild area. Other Tarrant Rushton gardens are also open (see page 120).

CHETTLE HOUSE 8
Blandford Forum, Dorset. Tel: (025889) 209
Mr and Mrs P. Bourke

6m NE of Blandford on A354, turn left to Chettle ● *Open April – 29th Oct, daily, except Tues* ● *Entrance: £1.00, children free* ● *Parking*
● *Refreshments at weekend* ● *Toilet facilities* ● *Suitable for wheelchairs*
● *Plants for sale* ● *Art gallery* ● *House open* ● *Grade III*

The wide lawns frame the attractive Queen Anne house with many chalk-loving varieties of shrubs and herbaceous plants (some quite rare) in the borders. Visitors can experience a very peaceful and relaxing atmosphere in this garden, and if interested can purchase plants raised from garden stock in the good small nursery not far from the house.

CHILCOMBE HOUSE 9
Chilcombe, Nr Bridport, Dorset. Tel: (03083) 234
Mr and Mrs J. Hubbard

5m E of Bridport off A35 ● *Open 24th June, 1st July, 2.00 – 6.30 p.m.*
● *Entrance: £1.00, children 50p* ● *Parking* ● *Teas for NGS* ● *Plants for sale* ● *Grade III*

There are wild areas, courtyards and a walled garden divided into smaller sections. Mixed plantings of shrubs, flowers and herbs cover every inch of ground to great advantage, and there is also a bank of mixed heather, angelica plants, fruit trees and vegetables with good clematis and many old roses. This garden is a marvellous creation in a beautiful setting.

COMPTON ACRES   10
Canford Cliffs, Poole, Dorset.   Tel: (0202) 700778
Mr and Mrs L. Green

From Poole/Bournemouth road onto Canford Cliffs road (near Sandbanks)
● *Open 24th March – Oct, daily, 10.30 a.m. – 6.30 p.m.*   ● *Entrance: £2.70, OAP £1.70, children 85p* ● *Parking* ● *Refreshments* ● *Toilet facilities* ● *Suitable for wheelchairs (can be supplied)* ● *Guide dogs only* ● *Plants for sale* ● *Shop* ● *Grade II*

Keen gardeners might be put off by the huge coach park, the frankly commercial and rather down-market approach. They should persevere, because the gardens themselves are well-designed, immaculately kept and stocked with many interesting and well-labelled plants, trees and shrubs. Water abounds in streams, waterfalls, ponds and formal lakes, the home of fat, multi-coloured carp. An enterprise aimed obviously (and very accurately) at the tourist, Compton Acres has the feel of a very opulent public park.

COPSE CORNER   11
Warden Hill, Dorchester, Dorset.
Mrs C. Angel

9m N of Dorchester off A37, turning to Batcombe ● *Open for NGS. Dates N.A.* ● *Entrance: 60p, children 20p* ● *Parking in road* ● *Partly suitable for wheelchairs* ● *Dogs on lead* ● *Plants for sale* ● *Grade IV*

Much time and effort (and obviously considerable expense) over the past seven years have created a large garden around a stone-built split-level bungalow. It has three large ponds and extensive rockery and border areas. As yet, it still looks raw and will need time to mature and meld together but those who are developing their own gardens from scratch will be interested in following its development. Proximity to a main road, a kart track and some light industry will be hard to overcome if this is to become a peaceful garden.

CRANBORNE MANOR GARDENS   12
Cranborne, Dorset.   Tel: (07254) 248
The Viscount and Viscountess Cranborne

10m N of Wimborne on B3078 ● *Open April – Sept, Wed, 9.00 a.m. - 5.00 p.m.* ● *Entrance: £1.30, OAP £1.00* ● *Parking* ● *Refreshments* ● *Toilet facilities* ● *Partly suitable wheelchairs* ● *Plants for sale* ● *Shop* ● *Grade II*

Tradescant established the basic framework in the early seventeenth century, but little is left of the original plan. Neglected for a long period, the garden has been revived in the last three generations and now includes several smaller areas surrounded by tall clipped yew hedges, a walled white garden at its best in midsummer, wide lawns (again yew-lined) and extensive woodland and wild areas. Best of all is the high-walled entrance courtyard to the south which is approached through an arch between the two Jacobean gate houses. Here the plant selection along the lengthy borders is delightfully imaginative, providing the perfect introduction to what has been called 'the most magical house in Dorset' (not least for the garden which surrounds it). The excellent nursery garden specializes in traditional rose varieties, but also carries a wide selection of other plants. Italian statuary and stone ornaments are also featured, together with very high quality garden furniture.

CULEAZE 13

Bere Regis, Dorset. Tel: (0929) 471058 and 471209
Col. and Mrs A.M. Barne

1½m S of Bere Regis on the road to Wool. Take 2nd left (signposted) then right
● *Open 6th, 7th May, 2.00 – 6.00 p.m.* ● *Entrance: 50p, children free*
● *Parking* ● *Refreshments in Bere Regis* ● *Toilet facilities* ● *Suitable for wheelchairs* ● *Dogs on lead* ● *Plants for sale* ● *Farm shop* ● ***Grade IV***

Most of the trees and plants in this well-established garden have been grown from seeds or cuttings raised by the owners. They include some rare and unusual specimens successfully reared despite the warning advice of experts – always ready to say it couldn't be done. There is a rhododendron-lined drive, a large lawn bordered by interesting trees, and a good-sized walled area with many more special and often sought-after plants, not to mention an extensive cut flower and Christmas tree plantation. This is a very large enterprise to be attempted with only part-time staff and the visitor will readily appreciate the effort required to maintain it.

DEAN'S COURT 14

Wimborne Minster, Dorset.
Sir Michael and Lady Hanham

In the centre of Wimborne off B3073 ● *Open April – Sept, except Aug, Thurs, 2.00 – 6.00 p.m.* ● *Entrance: £1.00, children 50p* ● *Parking nearby*
● *Refreshments (but not April/May or Sept)* ● *Toilet facilities* ● *Suitable for wheelchairs* ● *Shop for vegetables* ● ***Grade III***

A mellow brick house set in 13 acres of parkland containing a number of interesting and very large trees. A swamp cypress towers near the house, and a 92 foot tulip tree covers one wall. The many fine specimens include Lucombe oak, Wellingtonias, Caucasian wing nut, Chilean fire bush, Japanese pagoda tree, blue cedars and horse chestnuts. There are few formal beds, but a courtyard contains an unusually comprehensive herb garden with almost 100 different plants. The walled kitchen garden, in which many of the old varieties of vegetable are grown by organic production methods, is extensive and obviously successful. A peaceful haven from the busy town just a few yards away, and well worth a visit.

DOMINEY'S YARD   15
Buckland Newton, Dorset.   Tel: (03005) 295
Captain and Mrs W. Gueterbock

11m from both Dorchester and Sherborne, 2m E of A352 or take B3143 from Sturminster Newton. Take 'no through road' between church and pub next to phone box ● Open 6th May, 19th Aug, 2.00 – 6.00 p.m. ● Entrance: £1.00, children 25p ● Parking in lane ● Refreshments ● Toilet facilities ● Partly suitable for wheelchairs ● Grade III

An inviting swimming pool and an immaculate lawn tennis court are features of this attractive family garden; they are so placed that they neither dominate nor detract from the borders and shrubberies which will interest and delight amateurs and plantsmen alike. Blessed with three different soil types within two acres, the owners have been able to grow a wide variety of unusual plants during the 25 years they have lived here. Shrubs and trees provide year round colour to enhance their lovely seventeenth-century cottage.

EDMONDSHAM HOUSE   16
Edmondsham, Nr Cranborne, Dorset.   Tel: (07254) 207
Mrs J. Smith

2m S of Cranbourne. From the A354 turn at Sixpenny Handley crossroads to Ringwood and Cranborne ● Open by appointment and April – June and Oct, Wed – Sat, 10.00 a.m. – 12 noon ● Best season: spring ● Entrance: 75p, children 30p (£1.50, children 60p house and garden) ● Parking ● Refreshments on open days ● Toilet facilities ● Suitable for wheelchairs ● Plants and vegetables for sale ● House open 15th April, all Bank Holiday Mons, Weds in April and Oct, 2.00 – 5.00 p.m. ● Grade III

A vast, walled kitchen garden in which only organic methods are used provides the major interest here. This is very much a Victorian kitchen garden in origin, having been intensively cultivated since the mid-nineteenth century, but several modern and interesting vegetable variants are grown for sale. Herbaceous borders line the walls. Wide lawns surround the house, bordered by many fine and rare trees growing to a good height. An unusual circular grass hollow is said to be a cockpit, one of only a very few 'naturalised' areas of the sort in the country. The massed spring bulbs together with the many spring-flowering shrubs make this the best season to visit, but the peaceful, mellow atmosphere pervades the garden at all seasons. The house is of Tudor origin and the church nearby is also of historic interest.

FRANKHAM FARM 17
Ryme Intrinseca, Nr Sherborne, Dorset. Tel: (0935) 872304
Mr and Mrs R.G. Earle

3m S of Yeovil, turning off A37 at crossroads with garage. Long drive ¼m on left ● Open 15th April, 27th May, 2.00 – 5.30 p.m. ● Best season: spring/summer ● Entrance: 75p, children free ● Parking ● Partly suitable for wheelchairs ● Grade III

Approached by an impressive tree-lined drive the entrance yard has colourful climbing plants clinging to its grey walls. There is more colour and greenery in the beds and screening hedges that help to distance the farm house itself from the working buildings behind. To the south of the house, a lawn has curving borders on each side framing a low wall and leading the eye on to the fields beyond. The variety and success of the planting in the borders is evidence of the owners' flair for colour and form as well as their knowledge of unusual and interesting plants. From the end wall the visitor can begin to see the extent of the tree-screening which protects the garden on either side. This is a very exposed site around which shelter belts of quick-growing species have gradually been extended to allow replacement by a variety of plantings that should interest keen tree-lovers. On the west side, beyond the drive, a small orchard has been enlarged by the same means into a delightful arboretum, underplanted with spring bulbs, camellias and other shrubs. There is much to learn here for all gardeners facing the problems of an exposed position.

HARDY'S COTTAGE 18
Higher Bockhampton, Dorchester, Dorset. Tel: (0305) 62366
The National Trust

3m NE of Dorchester, ½m S of A35 ● Open April – 4th Nov, daily except Tues, 11.00 a.m. – 6.00 p.m. or dusk if earlier ● Best season: spring/early summer ● Entrance: free (£1.70 house) ● Parking in woods, 10 minute walk ● Toilet facilities (house only) ● Partly suitable for wheelchairs, but woodland walk not recommended and special parking arrangements for disabled can be made with the custodian ● House open ● Grade IV

A charming cottage garden in front of the small thatched house – in a peaceful and secluded woodland setting. Neat and well-tended with suitable herbaceous and climbing plants – roses, pansies, cherry pie, montbretias, stocks, etc.

HIGHBURY 19
West Moors, Dorset. Tel: (0202) 874372
Mr and Mrs S. Cherry

8m N of Bournemouth off B3072. Woodside Road is the last road at the N end of West Moors village ● Open by appointment for parties and on Suns and Bank Holidays, from 1st Sun in April to 1st Sun in Sept, 2.00 – 6.00 p.m.

● *Entrance: 65p, OAP and parties 45p, children 25p* ● *Parking in road*
● *Refreshments* ● *Toilet facilities* ● *Suitable for wheelchairs* ● *Plants for sale*
● *Grade III*

Mr and Mrs Cherry have amassed in their small botanical garden a fascinating collection of unusual specimens which will interest plantsmen and keen amateurs alike. With excellent labelling and much other general information available, this is a garden which delivers more to the enthusiast than is conveyed by the initial impression. It must be admitted that the average gardener might find the closely surrounding trees and the emphasis on rarity as against form and colour rather less than exciting.

IVY COTTAGE 20
Aller Lane, Ansty, Dorset. Tel: (0258) 880053
Mr and Mrs A. Stevens

8m W of Blandford, 12m N of Dorchester. Take A354 Puddletown/ Blandford road, turn first left after Blue Vinney, through Cheselbourne ● *Open April – Oct, Thurs, 10.00 a.m. – 5.00 p.m. and on 15th April, 27th May, 26th Aug, 23rd Sept, 2.00 – 5.30 p.m.* ● *Entrance on Thurs, April – Oct, £1.00, on Sun, £1.50 (combined with Aller Green – see below)* ● *Parking in road* ● *Teas*
● *Partly suitable for wheelchairs* ● *Plants for sale* ● *Grade II*

Mrs Stevens trained and worked as a professional gardener before coming to her cottage 27 years ago. Although chalk underlies the surrounding land, this garden is actually on greensand; it has springs and a stream that keep it well watered, and is therefore an ideal home for plants such as primulas, irises, gunneras, and in particular trollius and moisture-loving lobelias, for both of which this is the NCCPG National collection. A thriving and ordered vegetable garden (which never needs a hose), large herbaceous borders giving colour all year round, drifts of bulbs and other spring plants surrounding specimen trees and shrubs and two most interesting raised beds for alpines. This garden has been justifiably featured in print and on television, and merits a wide detour. Just up the road is Aller Green, a typical peaceful Dorset cottage garden of approximately one acre in an old orchard setting. The two share NGS opening days with a combined admission charge.

KESWORTH 21
Kesworth Farm House, Sandford, Wareham, Dorset.
Tel: (09295) 51577
Mr H.J.S. Clarke

1½m N of Wareham off A351 opposite Sandford School (Keysworth Drive)
● *Open 13th, 20th May, 12.30 – 7.00 p.m.* ● *Entrance: £1.00, children free*
● *Parking* ● *Toilet facilities* ● *Suitable for wheelchairs* ● *Dogs* ● *Grade III*

Kesworth is a twentieth-century park and garden scheme conceived on the scale of 'Capability' Brown, but carried out under unfavourable conditions.

Bordered on the south side by the marshy edge of Poole Harbour, to the north by a busy road and railway line, and with industrial estates, both active and derelict formerly in full view, it is hardly surprising that Mr Clark's friends feared for his sanity when he acquired Kesworth. His intention of revitalising the farmland and building his own residence there was to prove even more difficult than he imagined. Poor soil, voracious wildlife, wind and fire took constant toll of his plantings. Twenty-five years of effort and 40,000 trees have gone into the project, with the result that Kesworth farmhouse (a modern evocation of the mid-eighteenth century) now stands fronted by a wide yew-lined lawn, with flagged courts and borders to the rear linking it with the original farm outbuildings. On all sides are graduated screens of trees set in broad grassland. The eyesores have been successfully obliterated, the land revived. Kesworth may not stand among the foremost as a gardener's treasure trove, but with its avenue, groves and marshland scenery and wildlife it provides a wonderful example of conservation started 20 years before the concept became generally fashionable.

KINGSTON LACEY 22
Wimborne, Dorset.   Tel: (0202) 853402
The National Trust

1½m W of Wimborne on B3082   ● Open April – 4th Nov, daily except Thurs and Fri, 12 noon – 6.00 p.m.   ● Best season: spring   ● Entrance: £1.20   ● Parking 100 yards   ● Refreshments   ● Toilet facilities   ● Suitable for wheelchairs   ● Dogs on lead and in car park and N Park only   ● Shop   ● House open 12 noon – 5.30 p.m. Last admission 5.00 p.m. (£4.00)   ● Grade III

The terrace, modelled by Barry on the Queen's House at Greenwich, displays urns, vases and lions in bronze and marble. There are six interesting marble wellheads or tubs for bay trees, also an Egyptian obelisk and a sarcophagus. The small informal 'Dutch Garden' was laid out in 1899 for Mrs Bankes in memory of her husband and is still planted in the seasonal schemes designed for her. The restored Victorian fernery leads to the fine Cedar Walk where one of the trees was planted by the Duke of Wellington in 1827, others by visiting royalty and family members. New shrub areas, rhododendrons, azaleas, magnolias, etc. are in process of establishment. There is a laurel walk, an ancient lime avenue, and many areas of spring bulbs in the 400-acre park.

KINGSTON MAURWARD 23
Dorset College of Agriculture, Dorchester, Dorset.
Tel: (0305) 64738
Dorset County Council

E of Dorchester off A35. Turn off at roundabout at end of bypass   ● Open 16th, 22nd, 25th June, 6th July, 11.00 a.m. – 5.00 p.m. Parties by appointment   ● Best season: March, May and summer   ● Entrance fee donated to charity

● *Parking*   ● *Refreshments*   ● *Toilet facilities*   ● *Partly suitable for wheelchairs*
● *Plants for sale*   ● *Grade III*

As might be expected, the requirements of a busy agricultural and horticultural teaching centre have inevitably altered the character of what was for many generations an impressive private mansion. The garden, with its splendid stone terraces, balustrades and steps, was laid out to the west of the house during and soon after World War I and the hedges and topiary of box and yew which form such a feature also date from this period. From 1939 to 1947 the property suffered misuse and total neglect, and it has taken many years of dedicated work by staff and students to restore it to something of its former glory. Sadly, features such as statuary and a Grecian temple have gone for good, with the result that recesses in the hedges stand empty, carefully planned vistas lead to nothing. Nevertheless, the planting is colourful and interesting (the National Collection of penstemons and salvias is held here); drifts of bulbs in spring, mainly crocus and anemone species and later cyclamen and autumn crocus surround some fine specimen trees. The large lake below the wide, sloping lawn dates back to the late eighteenth century and provides shady walks around its margin, with the remains of what was once a Japanese garden, and a graceful folly and pond. The former walled kitchen garden provides a demonstration and practical working area for students. Much good restoration work is still being done, but to return it to its former status this garden needs the sort of lavish resources which are not available to a local authority in these times.

KNOLL GARDENS   24
(formerly Wimborne Botanic Gardens)
Stape Hill Road, Wimborne, Dorset.   Tel: (0202) 873931
Mr K. Martin

Off A31 Wimborne-Ferndown old road   ● *Open all year*   ● *Entrance: £1.95, OAP £1.50, children 95p*   ● *Parking*   ● *Refreshments*   ● *Toilet facilities*
● *Suitable for wheelchairs*   ● *Plants for sale*   ● *Shop*   ● *Grade IV*

The gardens cover some six acres and contain 3000 different, named plants. An ambitious rock terrace frames a waterfall and ponds (all new for 1989) currently set out with colourful bedding plants until newly-planted shrubs mature. A new herbaceous border is growing well and displays excellent colour and variety of form, while interesting trees and shrubs (particularly the Australian section) are grouped on pleasant lawns. All looks rather new (summer 1989) but should soon mellow and grow together. There is much to be learned here about what can be done in a short space of time to redesign and rebuild a garden.

THE MANOR HOUSE 25
Hinton St Mary, Sturminster Newton, Dorset. Tel: (0258) 72519
Mr and Mrs A. Pitt-Rivers

1m NW of Sturminster Newton on B3092 ● *Open 23rd, 24th June, 2.00 - 6.00
p.m.* ● *Entrance: £1.50, children 20p* ● *Parking* ● *Refreshments* ● *Toilet
facilities* ● *Suitable for wheelchairs* ● **Grade III**

The Manor House lies in the Blackmore Vale and has splendid vie˜ 's. There is
a pleasant sunken pond with fountains, an interesting arboretum to the side of
the house, a further sunken rose garden, again with statuary and fountains
screened by yew trees, a lime tree walk and an unusual stone gazebo as part of
a walled garden by the barn. Individually each part of this garden has interest
and attraction for the visitor, but taken together the result is somehow rather
disappointing. Perhaps the loss of some fine elm trees which used to surround
the garden has something to do with it; perhaps it may need the application of
an overall design to link the various sections. Plans are in hand to replant in
some areas, and hopefully the opportunity can be taken to provide the
coherence and 'heart' which currently this garden seems to lack. Events are
held from time to time in the large restored barn.

MAPPERTON 26
Beaminster, Dorset. Tel: (0308) 862645
The Montagu family

6m E of Bridport, 2m SE of Beaminster ● *Open March - Oct, daily except Sat,
2.00 - 6.00 p.m.* ● *Entrance: £1.20, children 60p (honesty box)* ● *Parking*
● *Toilet facilities* ● *House open to parties by appointment* ● **Grade II**

A garden with a difference, Mapperton runs down a gradually steepening
valley dominated by the delightful sixteenth-seventeenth-century manor
house. Terraces in brick and concrete descend through formal Italian-style
borders towards the summer house, which itself stands high above two huge
fish tanks (how have they resisted turning them into an Olympic-length
swimming pool?) On all sides there is topiary in yew and box. Beyond the
tanks, the valley becomes a shrubbery and arboretum, much of it recently
planted by the present owners. Many of the concrete features depicting
animals and birds, both natural and stylistic, are in need of attention, but in
general the numerous ornaments provide interest and surprise.

MINTERNE 27
Minterne Magna, Dorchester, Dorset. Tel: (03003) 370
Lord and Lady Digby

8m N of Dorchester on A352 ● *Open April - Oct, daily, 10.00 a.m. - 7.00
p.m.* ● *Entrance: £1.00 (honesty box), children (accompanied only) free*
● *Parking* ● *Toilet facilities* ● *Partly suitable for wheelchairs (but fairly steep
rough paths)* ● *Dogs on lead* ● **Grade III**

An interesting collection of Himalayan rhododendrons and azaleas, spring bulbs, cherries and maples. Many rare trees. One and a half miles of walks with palm trees, cedar, beech, etc. Alas no labelling to help the amateur. The first half of the walk is disappointing in midsummer although evidence remains of some spectacular spring colour. At the lower end of the valley the stream with its lakes and waterfalls is surrounded by splendid tall trees among which the paths wind back towards the house. A very restful and attractive atmosphere, but both lakes and undergrowth could do with attention. Tree colour in autumn should be special.

MOULIN HUET   28
15 Heatherdown Road, West Moors, Dorset. Tel: (0202) 875760
Mr H. Judd

8m N of Bournemouth. Look for cul-de-sac off the road ● Open by appointment for parties and on 13th, 20th May, 2.00 - 5.00 p.m. ● Entrance: 50p, children free ● Parking in road ● Grade IV

Mr Judd (now 85 years old) and his late wife built their garden from open heath over 20 years. Although only a third of an acre and triangular in shape, it seems to stretch and enlarge as the visitor is conducted from area to area through archways and along winding paths. All the plants, some of them quite rare, have been grown from seed or cuttings. There is also a fine collection of bonsai, grown by Mr Judd's own unique method which apparently defies all the rules.

NORTH LEIGH HOUSE   29
Colehill, Wimborne, Dorset. Tel: (0202) 882592
Mr and Mrs S. Walker

1m NE of Wimborne. Turn off B3073 by Sir Winston Churchill pub into North Leigh Lane (¾m) ● Open 8th April, 6th May, 5th Aug, 2.00 - 6.00 p.m. ● Entrance: 50p, children 20p ● Parking ● Refreshments ● Toilet facilities ● Suitable for wheelchairs ● Dogs on lead ● House open by appointment ● Grade III

The restoration of this delightful house and its once impenetrable grounds has taken 22 years to achieve, and the work continues. There are five acres of informal parkland, with mature trees, a small lake and grassy banks covered in drifts of wild orchids and naturalised spring bulbs. The Victorian features include a balustraded terrace, a fountain, a small walled garden and a magnificent conservatory in which a heavy-fruiting vine flourishes alongside other interesting specimens. There is a strong sense of the past being recaptured here; it is not difficult to imagine in such surroundings the tennis or croquet parties of 100 years ago, and the urbane butler bringing forth cooling drinks on a long-distant summer afternoon. Today figs from the tree may be taken with afternoon tea.

THE OLD RECTORY 30
Litton Cheney, Nr Bridport, Dorset.   Tel: (03083) 383
Mr and Mrs H. Lindsay

*1m S of A35, beside the village church ● Open 15th April, 27th May, and possibly 3rd June, 2.00 – 5.30 p.m. ● Best season: spring ● Entrance: 80p, children 10p ● Limited parking in centre of village ● Toilet facilities ● Dogs on lead ● Plants for sale when available ● **Grade III***

The Rectory rests comfortably below the church and is approached by a gravel drive which circles a small lawn. The thatched summer house stands to one side, like a massive beehive. The smallish walled garden has outhouses on two sides and borders around three, prolifically stocked with well-chosen and favourite plants in specific colour bands. A steep path leads into the four acres of natural woodland, a surprisingly extensive area of mature trees with many springs, streams and ponds – never a water shortage here, even in the driest of summers. This area was 'rescued' by the current owners, who are adding new young trees and shrubs as well as successfully encouraging many spring-flowering plant colonies. Climbing back up to the house, the visitor arrives at the terrace – a belvedere giving views over the trees to open farmland on the other side of the valley. Spring and autumn are the best times to see this garden, from which Reynolds Stone the engraver drew the inspiration for much of his best work.

THE OLD RECTORY 31
Pulham, Nr Sherborne, Dorset.   Tel: (0258817) 595
Rear Admiral and Mrs J. Garnier

*13m N of Dorchester, 8m SE of Sherborne on B3143. Turn E at crossroads in Pulham ● Open 20th May, 10th June, 8th July, 2.00 - 6.00 p.m. ● Entrance: £1.00, children free ● Parking ● Refreshments ● Toilet facilities ● Suitable for wheelchairs ● Dogs on lead ● Plants for sale ● **Grade III***

A wide lawn runs away southward from this delightful Georgian building, leading to a ha-ha and a really spectacular view over open countryside to distant hills. The main part of the three-acre garden is set to the west and includes some fine mature trees as well as interesting younger ones, a fenced pond, a rose arbour containing many varieties of bush, shrub and climbing plants, and a pleasant vista down a yew-lined lawn, back towards the west front. This is a lovely, peaceful, mature garden which fully compensates for the somewhat startling castellated Gothic facade of the north front.

PARNHAM HOUSE 32
Beaminster, Dorset.   Tel: (0308) 862204
Mr and Mrs J. Makepeace

¾m S of Beaminster on A3066 ● Open 24th March – 29th Oct, Wed, Sun and Bank Holidays, 10.00 a.m. – 5.00 p.m. ● Entrance: £2.50, children 10 – 15

£1.20, under 10 free (house and garden) • *Parking* • *Refreshments: licensed buttery* • *Toilet facilities* • *Partly suitable for wheelchairs* • *Dogs on lead* • *Shop* • *House open* • **Grade II**

The imposing stone terracing to the west of the house frames the many large clipped yews through which descend spring-fed water channels. A wide lawn leads to a balustrade and a small lake (under reconstruction – July 1989). There are large woodland and wild areas to the north and east, and sheltered borders along the brick wall of the old kitchen garden – the earliest part. Here Mrs Makepeace has used her gift for colour and form to create some splendid displays, notable as much for their shape and texture as for the well-chosen colour schemes. There are also delightful small and large courtyards to the south of the house with interesting plantings. Because the house is regularly open to the public in connection with John Makepeace's furniture design and workshops, there are asphalted drives and parking areas near the house, as well as a large grassed car park. This together with the proximity of the southern fencing to the house itself creates a somewhat disturbed and truncated effect which tends to take away from the overall excellence. Mr Makepeace, as well as being a designer with an international reputation, has recently taken an interest in the design of timber buildings.

RUSSETS   33
Rectory Lane, Child Okeford, Nr Blandford, Dorset.
Tel: (0258) 860703
Mr and Mrs G.D. Harthan

6m NW of Blandford off A357. Turn N after Shillingstone • *Open by appointment and on 6th May, 15th July, 26th, 27th Aug, and one other day in June, 2.30 – 5.30 p.m.* • *Entrance: 80p, children free* • *Parking in Rectory Lane* • *Teas* • *Suitable for wheelchairs* • *Dogs on lead* • *Plants for sale* • *Grade III*

This property, which used to be part of an old orchard, was acquired as a building plot in the early seventies. The garden has been more than 16 years in the making, and under the care of compulsive plant lovers now surrounds the house in a delightful variety of colour and shape. Although described as a 'plantsman's garden' this is much more than just a collector's display, and should give pleasure to any gardener who, like the owners, cannot resist acquiring plants simply for the love of their infinite variety.

SANDFORD ORCAS MANOR   34
Nr Sherborne, Dorset.   Tel: (096322) 206
Sir Merryn Medleycott, Bt.

2½m N of Sherborne, turning off B3148, next to village church • *Open Easter Mon, 10.00 a.m. - 6.00 p.m., then May – Sept, Sun, 2.00 - 6.00 p.m. and Mon, 10.00 a.m. - 6.00 p.m.* • *Entrance: £1.20, children 60p (house and garden). Pre-booked parties of 10 or more at reduced rates on other days if preferred* • *Parking* • *Toilet facilities* • *Suitable for wheelchairs* • *Dogs on lead* • *House open* • ***Grade III***

Looked at purely as a garden, Sandford Orcas is not exceptional. An old, flagged path slopes up between bordered lawns towards an open field. The stone walls at either side are attractive enough, but they stop suddenly at the wire fence and the view lacks a frame and a focal point. There is a herb garden with small box-bordered beds and a pleasant view across a lower lawn along the south side of the house. At the end of this lawn another viewpoint back towards the south front allows the attractive planting below the herb garden to show at its best. Roses and other climbing plants clinging to the honey-grey walls harmonize well with this gracious setting. It is the house, ancient and redolent of its long history, which permeates the scene and transforms the garden. On its own the visitor might enjoy but remain unmoved by the garden; but to see house and garden in perfect harmony on a warm summer's day is a pleasure not to be lightly forgone.

SHEPHERD'S COTTAGE 35
Whatcombe, Nr Blandford, Dorset. Tel: (0258) 880190
Rev. and Mrs R. East

5m SW of Blandford. Take A354 to Winterborne Whitchurch, at the bottom of the hill take the road to Winterborne Stickland. After 1m, take sharp left on bend, then immediately right along Forestry Commission road • *Open 28th, 29th July, 2.00 – 5.00 p.m.* • *Entrance: 50p, children 25p* • *Parking* • *Cream teas on 29th July only* • *Toilet facilities* • *Suitable for wheelchairs* • *Dogs* • *Plants for sale* • ***Grade IV***

This is a tiny jewel of a garden decorating a 300 year-old thatched cottage which nestles into a green parkland valley. Seen on a sunny autumn afternoon, this colourful plot is radiant with the care and interest that have been lavished upon it. Informal beds of shrubs, herbaceous plants, winter heathers and foliage plants.

SHUTE HOUSE 36
Donhead St Mary, Shaftesbury, Dorset. Tel: (0747) 88253
Lady Anne Tree

4m E of Shaftesbury, N off A30 on far side of village • *Open 26th May, and possibly twice later in the summer, 2.30 – 5.30 p.m.* • *Entrance: £2.00, OAP £1.00, children 50p* • *Parking on road* • *Partly suitable for wheelchairs* • ***Grade II***

Designed by Sir Geoffrey Jellicoe in the 1960s the beauty of Shute House garden depends entirely upon the water supplied by a bountiful spring. It is used throughout, in streams, in formal and informal pools, and above all in the 'Kashmiri' garden – the centrepiece of the design – where it falls from level to level over cascades arranged to vary the sound it makes; it runs through channels between octagonal pools, each with its own source so that the surface is never still; framed by grass and trees, reflecting and refracting the sunlight and culminating in a statue, beyond which are the fields and hills of open countryside. Vistas abound in this garden. There are statues to draw and satisfy the eye, varied and interesting trees to frame the view. Although there is colour particularly in spring, form is the key, in timberwork, in stone, in plant-entwined arches, in box-bordered flower beds, shaped pools and twisting paths. This theme is still being developed in a new area, where tall metal frames are to support ivy and other climbing plants in geometrical patterns. Even in the bog garden, perhaps the least ordered area, a primitive African figure enigmatically presides, and near to the house is an amusing 'bedroom' of clipped box, furnished with a dressing table and a four poster bed framed with climbing vines. Conceived with skill and wit, this is a garden not to be missed.

SMEDMORE HOUSE 37
Kimmeridge, Nr Wareham, Dorset. Tel: (0929) 480717
Major and Mrs J. Mansel

7m S of Wareham. Left off A351 at sign to Kimmeridge ● Open 7th June - 13th Sept, Wed, 2.15 - 5.30 p.m. ● Best season: June - July ● Entrance: 75p, children free (£1.50, children 75p house and garden) ● Parking ● Refreshments at post office in Kimmeridge ● Toilet facilities ● Suitable for wheelchairs ● Dogs on lead ● Plants for sale ● House open ● Grade III

The gardens at Smedmore are of necessity either surrounded by walls or protected by screens of trees in order to mitigate the damage from sea winds. The mellow walls are admirably used to display many attractive and interesting climbing plants, including fine double mauve and white wisterias and the tender *Cheiranthus punicens*, while among the trees are some splendid mature and unusual specimens. The large kitchen garden is now being prepared for use as a nursery. There are three very pretty small walled gardens as well, but the main pleasure at Smedmore is derived from the colourful principal garden with its air of age and tranquillity.

STICKY WICKET 38
Buckland Newton, Dorset. Tel: (03005) 476
Peter and Pam Lewis

11m from Dorchester and Sherborne, 2m E of A352 or take B3143 from Sturminster Newton. At T-junction midway between church and school ● Open by appointment and 13th May, 10th June, 15th July, 19th Aug, 16th Sept, 2.00 - 6.00 p.m. and every Thurs from 17th May - 20th Sept, 10.00 a.m. - 6.00 p.m. ● Entrance: 75p, children 30p ● Parking in road ● Refreshments ● Toilet facilities ● Partly suitable for wheelchairs ● Grade III

A design of concentric circles and radiating paths has enabled the creation of many separate beds showing different planting styles. A very fragrant and colourful display is enhanced by many unusual and/or variegated plants and bordered by species roses. The garden is designed to attract birds, butterflies and bees and to provide spectacular flowerheads for drying. There is a small pond and a wet area which is also attractive to wildlife. This is very much the garden of conservationist-minded plantlovers; plans are afoot to develop a white woodland area to carry the idea further. If the progress of the last two years is maintained this garden is destined to become outstanding.

STOUR HOUSE 39
East Street, Blandford, Dorset.   Tel: (0258) 452914
Mr T.S.B. Card

In Blandford, 100 yards from Market Place on the one-way system ● *Open 8th April, 15th July, 12th Aug, 2.00 – 6.00 p.m.* ● *Entrance: 50p, children 20p* ● *Parking in town* ● *Toilet facilities* ● *Suitable for wheelchairs* ● ***Grade III***

A wooden bridge of unusual design leads onto a long island set in the River Stour at the end of this garden. Mature trees and shrubs flourish on a lush green sward underplanted with massed spring bulbs. Walk westwards to the end of the island to enjoy a perfect view of the weir below a distant, graceful bridge. It is easy to imagine the romantic picnic parties that must have been held here in the past. The main garden has wide-bordered lawns with some interesting plants and shrubs, and an orchard and vegetable area. It might perhaps benefit by offering more interesting focal points, and needs some further screening from the presence of a supermarket and car park alongside, but the surprise and pleasure afforded by discovering such a pleasing, tranquil area in the heart of a busy market town makes this hidden garden well worth a visit.

TARRANT RUSHTON GARDENS
Nr Blandford, Dorset.

TARRANT RUSHTON HOUSE 40
Tel: (0258) 452256
Col. B.K. Blount

RIVER HOUSE 41
Tel: (0258) 452403
Drs A. and P. Swan

3m SE of Blandford on B3082. Fork left at top of hill, right at T-junction, first left to village ● *Open 10th June, 2.00 – 5.30 p.m.* ● *Entrance: £1.00, children 50p (combined admission)* ● *Parking in road* ● *Partly suitable for wheelchairs* ● ***Grade IV***

Two very different gardens, each of interest in its own way.

Tarrant Rushton House has its kitchen garden, its walled and bordered lawn (once an orchard) and a further tree-lined lawn all running down a slope to the stream at the bottom. The borders contain some interesting plants, including highly combustible fire bush and euphorbia reputed to repel moles.

River House next door is in a lower position so that the garden actually bestrides the stream. There are bridges, tributaries, a small weir and many interesting shrubs and plants – particularly shrub roses. The high hedge beyond the stream is somewhat claustrophobic, but a colourful herbaceous border on the other side of the house is backed most effectively by a tall screen of trees. Charlton Cottage at the end of the village is also open on an additional day (see page 106).

WINCOMBE PARK   42
Shaftesbury, Dorset.   Tel: (0747) 52161
The Hon Martin and Mrs Fortescue

2m N of Shaftesbury off A350 signed to Wincombe ● Open 10th June, 2.00 – 6.00 p.m., and possibly one day in autumn ● Best season: summer ● Entrance: £1.00, children 25p ● Parking ● Refreshments ● Toilet facilities ● Partly suitable for wheelchairs ● Dogs on lead ● Plants occasionally for sale ● Grade III

The former house of the historian Sir Arthur Bryant, this is essentially a beautifully landscaped park. The house is set upon the side of a valley, screened behind tall trees and approached by a winding drive. There is a high bank beside the drive containing an interesting and well-judged selection of shrubs and small trees. Below and to the side of the house are small lawns and a walled kitchen-garden (about to be developed as a flower garden). But the real pleasure for the visitor lies in the wide, sloping lawn below the lake, and then up the steep wooded valley side beyond. In addition to the new walled garden, the owners have plans to continue tree-planting around the valley. The garden alone would not justify a long detour but the whole ensemble is memorable.

DURHAM

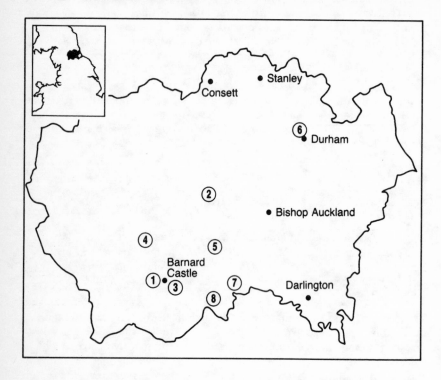

BARNINGHAM PARK

1

Barningham, Barnard Castle, Co. Durham. Tel: (0833) 21202
Sir Anthony Milbank

10m NW of Richmond off A66 at Smallways Garage ● Open 27th May, 3rd,
10th June, 1st July, 12th, 19th Aug, 16th, 23rd Sept, 1.00 - 5.00 p.m.
● Entrance: 85p, children free ● Parking ● Teas ● Partly suitable for
*wheelchairs ● Annual spring sale from the nurseries ● **Grade IV***

Predominantly a woodland garden, continuing to be developed by the present
owner, this has interesting walks and good stands of specimen trees. A garden
for recreation rather than serious horticultural study.

BEDBURN HALL GARDENS

2

Hamsterley, Bishop Auckland, Co. Durham. Tel: (038888) 231
Mr I. Bonas

9m NW of Bishop Auckland. W off A68 at Witton-le-Wear. 3m SE of
Wolsingham off B6293 ● Open by appointment and on 20th May, 17th June,

22nd July, 26th Aug, 1.00 – 6.00 p.m. • *Entrance: 75p, children 25p*
• *Parking* • *Teas* • *Partly suitable for wheelchairs* • *Plants for sale*
• **Grade IV**

A medium-sized terraced garden, largely developed by the present owner, it is beautifully situated by Hamsterley Forest. The garden is dominated by a lake with associated rhododendrons and bamboos. A new conservatory contains figs, bougainvilleas, passion flowers and other exotics. Woodland.

BOWES MUSEUM GARDENS 3
Barnard Castle, Co. Durham.   Tel: (0833) 690606
Durham County Council

From Barnard Castle E on the road towards Westwick • *Open daily* • *Best season: spring/summer* • *Entrance: free* • *Parking* • *Refreshments: coffee, lunch, teas in museum restaurant during summer* • *Toilet facilities* • *Suitable for wheelchairs* • *Shop in museum* • **Grade II**

The formal gardens reflect the grandeur of the museum buildings (built in the 1870s) which are like a large French chateau. The parterre has been recut in the style of the seventeenth century using elaborate shapes formed by box hedges and coloured gravels. The nineteenth-century tradition is continued by planting a succession of flowers during the spring and summer months and the whole impression is of a period-piece.

EGGLESTON HALL GARDENS 4
Eggleston, Barnard Castle, Co. Durham.   Tel: (0833) 50378
Mrs W.T. Gray

5m NW of Barnard Castle on B6278 • *Open daily, 10.00 a.m. – 5.00 p.m.* • *Entrance: £1.00, children 30p* • *Parking* • *Teas* • *Partly suitable for wheelchairs* • *Plants for sale* • *Shop at house* • **Grade III**

The current garden was developed by the present owner within the framework of an older garden that, apart from mature trees and an original walled garden, retains little of its early identity. It is largely informal with an excellent collection of unusual plants and flowers suitable for floral art. Extensive lawns and a kitchen garden run on organic lines.

RABY CASTLE GARDENS 5
Staindrop, Co. Durham.   Tel: (0833) 60202
The Rt Hon. The Lord Barnard

1m N of Staindrop on A688 Barnard Castle – Bishop Auckland road • *Open 30th April – June, Sat – Wed. July – Sept, daily except Sat. Bank Holiday weekends, 11.00 a.m. – 5.30 p.m.* • *Entrance: 80p, OAP and children 60p*

123

● *Parking* ● *Teas* ● *Toilet facilities* ● *Partly suitable for wheelchairs* ● *House open (extra charge)* ● *Grade III*

This formal garden dating from the mid-eighteenth century was designed by Thomas White, 2nd Earl of Darlington, and has a wide array of trees, shrubs and herbaceous plants. The garden walls are locally hand-made bricks with flues which used to enable sub-tropical fruits to be grown on the south terrace. The famous white Ischia fig tree brought to Raby in 1768 still survives. Rose garden, shrub borders, original yew hedges and ornamental pond.

UNIVERSITY OF DURHAM
BOTANIC GARDEN   6
Hollingside Lane, Durham, Co. Durham. Tel: (091) 3742670
Durham University

1m from centre of Durham City. Turn off A167 at Cock O' The North roundabout towards the city for 1m, garden off Hollingside Lane ● *Open all year except Christmas week, 10.00 a.m. – 5.00 p.m. and for NGS* ● *Entrance: free* ● *Parking* ● *Toilet facilities* ● *Partly suitable for wheelchairs* ● *Grade II*

Established in 1970 as a centre for botanical study, this is now one of the few botanical gardens in the north of England. It contains a fine labelled collection, especially of trees and shrubs, and conducts basic research into many aspects of the plant kingdom. There are demonstrations of major forest systems and cactus and tropical greenhouses. A garden for the keen plant lover rather than the landscape designer. On economic grounds, some of its previous collections and features have been rationalized.

WESTHOLME HALL   7
Winston, Co. Durham. Tel: (0325) 730442
Captain and Mrs J.H. McBain

10m W of Darlington. Turn N off A67 to B6274 ● *Open 3rd, 24th June, 8th, 29th July, 9th Sept, 1.00 – 6.00 p.m.* ● *Entrance: 75p, children 20p* ● *Parking* ● *Teas* ● *Partly suitable for wheelchairs* ● *Plants for sale* ● *Grade III*

The current garden has been developed from that started by the family in 1935. Mixed informal plantings with good collections of rhododendrons, lilac and roses. Extensive bulb plantings provide interest in spring.

WYCLIFFE HALL BOTANICAL GARDENS   8
Wycliffe Hall, Barnard Castle, Co. Durham. Tel: (0423) 771026
Wycliffe Horticultural Trust

10m W of Scotch Corner off A66, signposted Wycliffe ● *Open by arrangement with the director and on 15th July, 5th Aug, 2nd, 30th Sept, 2.00 – 6.00 p.m.*

● *Entrance: £1.00* ● *Parking* ● *Toilet facilities* ● *Partly suitable for wheelchairs* ● *Grade III*

The original layout in the 1770s was by Marmaduke Tunstall and includes his collection of forest trees. The current garden, being developed as a botanical collection by the Trust, was established as a centre for horticultural and botanical studies in 1988. Architectural features are being lovingly restored and Wycliffe is host for the National hyacinth and water lily collections. This was one of Turner's four landscapes on the Tees.

OPENING DATES AND TIMES

Times of access given are the best available at the moment of going to press, but some may have been changed subsequently. In the entries, the times given are inclusive – that is, an entry such as May-Sept means that the garden is open from 1st May to 30th Sept inclusive and 2 p.m. – 5 p.m. also means that entry will be effective during that period. Please note that many owners will open their gardens to visitors by appointment. They will often arrange to give a personally-conducted tour on these occasions. A few owners of gardens open under the NGS scheme have not been able to advise their opening times before the *Guide* went to press and in such cases the note N.A. (not available) indicates that so far as we know the garden will be open in 1990 but entry times must be checked.

TELEPHONE NUMBERS

Except where specifically requested to be excluded, telephone numbers to which enquiries may be directed are given for each property. To maintain the support and cooperation of private owners it is suggested that the telephone be used with discretion. Where visits are by appointment, the telephone can of course be used except where written application, particularly for parties, is specifically requested. Code numbers are given in brackets. For the Republic of Ireland when phoning from the United Kingdom dial 353 plus area code plus number (except Dublin numbers which are 0001 plus number). In all cases where visits by parties are proposed, owners should be advised in advance and arrangements preferably confirmed in writing.

London Telephone Codes: From May 1990 all London telephone numbers with the prefix 01 will be changed. The new prefix will be either 071 or 081. Details of these new numbers are available from British Telecom. During the changeover period in 1990 all London telephone numbers dialled with their 01 prefix will be redirected.

ESSEX

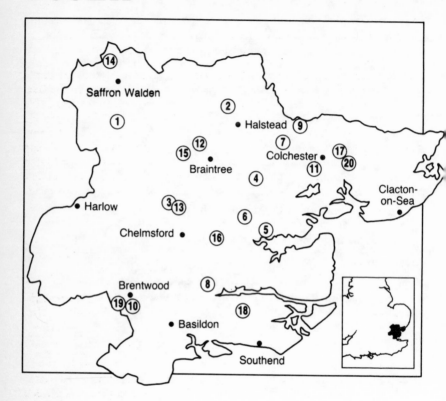

AMBERDEN HALL

Widdington, Nr Saffron Walden, Essex.   Tel: (0799) 40402
Mr and Mrs D. Lloyd

1

6m from Saffron Walden. E off B1383 near Newport, follow signs to Mole Hall
Wildlife Park, ½m past park on right ● Open 24th June, 2.00 – 6.00 p.m.
● Entrance: £1.00, children free ● Parking ● Teas ● Toilet facilities
● Suitable for wheelchairs ● Grade III

Some lovely old walls enclose this medium-sized garden set at one side of a fine
house. A pair of life-sized lead giraffes greet you as you step through the gate.
The borders are well designed, so that not all the garden is visible at once. All
are planted in specific colours – the red border being the newest with roses,
dahlias, hemerocallis, etc. The walls are covered in a variety of climbers, many
rare, like *Trachelospermum jasminoides* 'Variegatum'. To hide a barn roof, a
Leylandii hedge has been clipped with a crenellated top. Good vegetable
garden. Mrs Lloyd has plans to extend the garden beyond the walls with an
avenue of different ivies grown up stakes.

CRACKNELLS 2
Great Yeldham, Essex. Tel: (0787) 237370
Mr and Mrs T. Chamberlain

Off A604 between Halstead and Haverhill • *Open by appointment*
• *Parking* • *Suitable for wheelchairs* • *Grade III*

Mr Chamberlain started contouring this large garden even before he started
building his house. The garden rolls away from the house down to the lake,
also excavated at the start. This is not a garden in the accepted sense but 'a
garden picture painted with trees', to use Mr Chamberlain's own words. He
has collected trees from all over the country and has an impressive collection.
Here is the rare cut-leaved beech, *Fagus sylvatica heterophylla* and its purple and
pink-leaved forms, 'Rohanii' amd 'Roseomarginata' as well as the variegated
tulip tree *Liriodendron tulipifera* 'Aureomarginatum'. There are also collections of birches, acers, sorbus and oaks. If you are a lover of trees, make your
pilgrimage.

FANNERS GREEN 3
Great Waltham, Nr Chelmsford, Essex. Tel: (0245) 360035
Dr and Mrs T.M. Pickard

*4m N of Chelmsford. Take A130 from Chelmsford to Great Waltham, turn left
into South St, opposite Six Bells pub. Drive 1¼m* • *Open 13th, 14th, 20th, 21st
May, 10th, 11th, 24th, 25th June, 2.00 – 6.00 p.m.* • *Entrance: 50p, children
25p* • *Parking* • *Plants sometimes for sale* • *Grade III*

Mrs Pickard is a garden designer and it certainly shows in this small country
garden. Here are compartments in miniature with hedges of thuja and beech,
each compartment having a different theme. The vegetable garden is divided
by paths into tiny squares with vegetables grown for their decorative qualities
as well as their culinary uses. There is a large range of plants and shrubs,
including a half-standard purple-leaved sambucus, a herb garden and a well-
kept conservatory.

FEERINGBURY MANOR 4
Coggeshall Road, Feering, Essex. Tel: (0376) 561946
Mr and Mrs Giles Coode-Adams

On B1024 between Coggeshall and Feering • *Open 30th April – 29th May,
weekdays, 10.00 a.m. – 1.00 p.m., weekends and Bank Holidays, 2.00 – 6.00
p.m.* • *Best season: May – June* • *Entrance: £1.00, children 50p* • *Parking*
• *Teas on Suns* • *Toilet facilities* • *Suitable for wheelchairs* • *Grade III*

For all its size (seven acres) and variety this is a peaceful garden. The large
natural ponds are well planted with rare and unusual bog plants – gunneras
and primulas, blue and yellow meconopsis, kirengeshomas and a pale yellow
annual buttercup given to Mrs Coode-Adams by Christopher Lloyd. There

are fine trees, shrub borders and a long 'old rose' border backed by a wall with clematis and honeysuckles growing up it. Clematis are Mr Coode-Adams' speciality. Here are many exciting plants tucked into corners, by walls or on the terrace.

FOLLY FAUNTS HOUSE 5
Goldhanger, Colchester, Essex. Tel: (0621) 88213
Mr and Mrs J.C. Jenkinson

On B1026 between Maldon and Colchester • Open 25th June, 2.00 – 6.00 p.m. • Entrance: £1.00, children 40p • Teas • Toilet facilities • Suitable for wheelchairs • Dogs on lead • Plants for sale • Grade IV

A large five-acre garden, created by the owner in the last 17 years, divided into compartments each with a different theme. A hedge of *Hypericum* 'Hidcote' makes a splash of colour next to the large pond planted with primulas, hostas and a huge gunnera. Mr Jenkinson is fond of the Japanese wineberry which is planted or has seeded in different parts of the garden. Its red prickly stems and edible fruit make an unusual feature. The latest venture has been the planting of avenues of trees radiating from the drive – here, in contrast, is a purple-leaved acer and *Betula albo sinensis*.

GLEN CHANTRY 6
Wickham Bishop, Nr Chelmsford, Essex. Tel: (062189) 1342
Mr and Mrs W.G. Staines

SE of Witham on B1018 from Witham to Wickham Bishops. Cross bridge, turn left up track by Blue Mills • Open 22nd April, 6th, 20th May, 3rd June, 1st, 29th July, 9th Sept, 2.00 – 5.00 p.m. • Entrance: 60p, children 30p • Parking • Teas • Toilet facilities • Suitable for wheelchairs • Plants for sale • Grade III

This large undulating garden has been created by its owners in the last 12 years. The huge informally-shaped borders are jammed with a variety of plants and colours. The kniphofia 'Little Maid' was looking pretty, mixed with monardas, eryngiums, roses and hemerocallis. The unusual *Stokesia laevis* 'Blue Star' was particularly noticeable. A large rock garden with waterfalls and a stream running through it is being planted up. Heather and conifer borders and a very wide selection of herbaceous plants.

HILL HOUSE 7
Chappel, Nr Colchester, Essex. Tel: (0787) 222428
Mr and Mrs R. Mason

On A604 between Colchester and Earl's Colne • Open by appointment • Limited parking • Plants for sale occasionally • Grade III

This is a large garden at the beginning of its life. It has been designed by the owners on formal lines using yew hedging and walls to create vistas. A mixed planting of tough native trees, sorbus and hawthorn, etc. has been established as a windbreak. A new lime avenue is the latest addition – sited to lead the eye out into the country. The pond area will be planted next. The bones of the garden are now in place including urns, statues and seats. All the colour and secondary planting will come next. In a small courtyard, reminiscent of a London garden, is a raised pool planted only with green-leaved plants and white flowers.

HYDE HALL GARDEN 8
Rettendon, Nr Chelmsford, Essex. Tel: (0245) 400256
Hyde Hall Garden Trust

7m SE of Chelmsford, signposted from A130 and A132 ● *Open every Sun, Wed and Bank Holidays, 11.00 a.m. – 6.00 p.m. Open at other times by appointment* ● *Entrance: £1.00, OAP 85p, children 25p* ● *Parking* ● *Toilet facilities* ● *Suitable for wheelchairs* ● *Plants for sale* ● ***Grade II***

This is a huge garden containing many different collections of plants. There is a comprehensive rose garden showing both bedding roses and climbers. There are large borders filled with a variety of shrubs including collections of magnolias and viburnums. The greenhouses are well kept and colourful. Near them are containers, urns, pots and troughs planted with pelargoniums and helichrysum, also great mounds of *Chrysanthemum frutescens* now called *Argyranthemum frutescens*, phormiums and felicias. There is a newly-planted area, in hedge 'bays', in specific colour schemes. Good ponds and trees.

LOWER DAIRY HOUSE 9
Little Horkesley, Colchester, Essex. Tel: (0206262) 220
Mr and Mrs D.J. Burnett

7m N of Colchester off A134. Left at bottom of hill before Nayland Village, into Water Lane. Garden ½m on left after farm buildings ● *Open by appointment and 15th, 16th April, 5th, 6th, 7th, 26th, 27th, 28th May, 16th, 17th, 23rd, 24th, 30th June, 1st July, 2.00 – 6.00 p.m.* ● *Entrance: £1.00, children 50p* ● *Parking limited* ● *Teas* ● *Toilet facilities* ● *Plants for sale* ● ***Grade III***

This immaculately-kept garden of one and a half acres is a riot of colour. Mrs Burnett fills any spaces in between the perennials with annuals – marigolds and larkspur and geraniums – all old-fashioned plants. There is a newly-created stream that crosses the garden and runs into the existing stream; here the thick planting consists of primulas, hostas and mimulus. A bridge crosses the stream to a path which runs along the bank, much loved by the children who visit the garden.

THE MAGNOLIAS 10
18 St Johns Avenue, Brentwood, Essex. Tel: (0277) 220019
Mr and Mrs R.A. Hammond

*From A1023 turn S to A128. After 300 yards turn right at traffic lights, over
railway bridge. St Johns Avenue is third on right* ● *Open April – June, Weds,
2.00 – 5.00 p.m. Certain other days and parties by appointment* ● *Entrance:
70p, children 30p* ● *Restricted parking* ● *Teas* ● *Plants for sale* ● **Grade III**

This fascinating half-acre plantsman's garden illustrates what can be achieved
in a small space. Lawns are minimal. Paths wind through jungle-like borders
filled with acers, camellias and magnolias underplanted with smaller shrubs
and ground-cover plants. There is a large collection of hostas and unusual and
rare bamboos. Mr Hammond also keeps the National collection of Arisaemas.
Some huge koi live in raised pools and turtles swim happily in their
greenhouse. Something of interest here at any time of the year.

OLIVERS 11
Olivers Lane, Colchester, Essex. Tel: (0206) 330575
Mr and Mrs David Edwards

*3m SW of Colchester. From Colchester via B1022 Maldon Rd at Leather Bottle
pub, turn left into Gosbeck's Road, right into Olivers Lane* ● *Open all year,
Wed only and 2nd – 5th May. Other times by appointment* ● *Best season: spring
and early summer* ● *Entrance: £1.00, children 50p* ● *Parking* ● *Teas*
● *Toilet facilities* ● *Suitable for wheelchairs* ● *Plants for sale* ● **Grade II**

The moment you drive down to the attractive Georgian-fronted house and
step on to the large York paved terrace, beautifully planted in soft sympathetic
colours, you are entranced. Around you is 20 acres of garden and woodland
in fine condition. From the terrace you look down over lawn, pools and woods
to a natural meadow (cut only to encourage wild flowers and grasses) and to
trees bordering the river. A 'willow pattern' bridge crosses the first of a
succession of pools which drop down to an ancient fish pond. *Taxodium
distichum*, metasequoia and ginkgo flourish by the pools. There are yew
hedges and the delightful woodland walk. Here mature native trees shelter
rhododendrons, azaleas and shrub roses in the rides.

PANFIELD HALL 12
Nr Braintree, Essex. Tel: (0376) 24512
Mr and Mrs R. Newman

*2m from Braintree. N off A120 through Great Saline, right to Panfield,
through village and right into Hall Road* ● *Open 1st July, 2.00 – 6.00 p.m.*
● *Entrance: £1.00, OAP and children 50p* ● *Parking* ● *Teas* ● *Toilet
facilities* ● *Suitable for wheelchairs* ● *Dogs on lead* ● *Plants for sale
occasionally* ● **Grade III**

This four-acre garden surrounding an old house (1520) has been restored in the last six years. There are plans for further development. The rose garden is completed. Leading from there is a pergola with laburnum, wisterias and clematis already looking established. Crossing the bridge over the ponds is a sunken garden near the house, box-edged, with rose 'Little White Pet' and bonica planted with soft-coloured ground-cover. There is a box and topiary maze here too. The long formal canal-like pool and statue are in memory of Mr Newman's parents. The clipped box crowns add to the formality.

PARK FARM 13
Chatham Hall Lane, Great Waltham, Chelmsford, Essex.
Tel: (0245) 360871
Mr D. Bracey and Mrs J.E.M. Cowley

5m N of Chelmsford. Take A130 towards Braintree, on Little Waltham bypass left into Chatham Hall Lane ● *Open May – July, Sun, 2.00 – 6.00 p.m.* ● *Entrance: 60p, children 30p* ● *Parking* ● *Teas* ● *Toilet facilities* ● *Plants for sale* ● *Grade III*

Mrs Cowley immediately infects the visitor by her enthusiasm and energy. She is still creating her two-acre garden on the site of an old farmyard. Each part of her garden is different. A small copse by the drive leads to raised borders for plants that like hot dry conditions, which in turn lead back to the house. The garden surrounds the house and is divided up by hedges. Climbing roses cover the trees. The difficult *Romneya coulteri* mingles happily with other herbaceous plants. Shrub roses abound as they are special favourites. There are vistas and cross vistas all cleverly combined to lead you on. After visiting China and getting some cuttings (legally) Mrs Cowley has made her own Chinese garden. Giant hogweed and *Crambe cordifolia* fight over the pool.

REED HOUSE 14
Great Chesterford, Saffron Walden, Essex.   Tel: (0799) 30312
Mrs Felicity Mason

11m S of Cambridge in the village of Great Chesterford, E of the M11, S of the A11 ● *Open by appointment only* ● *Grade III*

Mrs Mason moved to her present house only four and a half years ago, leaving a large garden crammed with treasures that used to be open to the public four times a year. Her new garden is a revelation as to what can be achieved in a short time. She designed the garden and planted everything herself. Features include sink gardens, koi carp in the pool, bulbs everywhere, clematis, a greenhouse bursting at the seams, and a new conservatory rapidly filling up with rare plants.

SALING HALL

Great Saling, Nr Braintree, Essex. Tel: (0371) 850141/850243
Mr and Mrs Hugh Johnson

15

6m NW of Braintree, halfway between Braintree and Dunmow on A120 turn N at the Sailing Oak ● *Open for NGS, dates N.A.* ● *Entrance: £1.00, children free* ● *Parking* ● *Suitable for wheelchairs* ● **Grade II**

The extensive planting of trees will interest any gardener. It includes oaks, pines, prunus, willows, birches, junipers, maples and other species suited to the chalky boulder clays and gravels. But there is much to admire besides the trees. A row of tall Lombardy poplars leads up to the seventeenth-century manor house. The old walled garden facing the new conservatory is exuberantly planted with shrubs, bulbs and herbaceous plants bordered by clipped juniper, cypress and box. There is a vegetable garden, a Japanese garden, a water garden (recently planted with gunnera, primulas, irises, etc.), a valley garden and a rose glade. This last is mainly dedicated to pink shrub roses, including *Rosa* 'Complicata', *R. soulieana* and *R. glauca* (*rubrifolia*).

STONE PINES

Hyde Lane, Danbury, Chelmsford, Essex. Tel: (0245) 413252
Mr and Mrs David Barker

16

W of Chelmsford on A414 ● *Open by appointment* ● *Best season: spring, June and July* ● *Limited parking* ● *Plants for sale* ● **Grade II**

This small plantsman's garden is owned by the Vice President of the Hardy Plant Society. Mr Barker has filled it with choice and unusual plants. The area of grass is minimal and paths wind around borders crammed with trees, acers being particularly popular, and shrubs. Surprising plants appear around each corner like the rarely-seen *Paris quadrifolia*. Mr Barker is also an expert on lilies, hemerocallis, hostas and grasses of all kinds.

TYE FARM

Elmstead Market, Colchester, Essex. Tel: (0206) 222400
Mr and Mrs C. Gooch

17

2m from Colchester on A133, ½m before Elmstead Market ● *Open 23rd, 24th June, 2.00 – 6.00 p.m.* ● *Entrance: £1.00, children 50p* ● *Parking* ● **Grade III**

This one-acre garden is cleverly planted with hedges to make compartments and break the prevailing wind. There is a neat vegetable garden with newly-planted espalier peach trees. Mrs Gooch is thinking of adding some colour to her white garden where she has a collection of grey-leaved plants including a *Pyrus salicifolia* 'Pendula'. Outside her conservatory is a formally- planted area for herbs, box-edged. The conservatory has many unusual plants including a lemon tree and a pale apricot-coloured hibiscus. Mrs Gooch also has a collection of Chinese pots.

VOLPAIA 18
54 Woodlands Road, Hockley, Essex. Tel: (0702203) 761
Mr and Mrs D. Fox

2¾m NE of Rayleigh. On B1013 Rayleigh-Rochford road, turn S from Spa Hotel into Woodlands Road ● *Open April – June, Thurs and Sun, 2.30 – 5.30 p.m.* ● *Entrance: 70p, children 30p* ● *Limited parking* ● *Teas* ● *Toilet facilities* ● *Grade II*

Here is a garden for plant lovers – not a garden for lovers of massed colour. From the lawn at the rear of the house, paths lead into natural woodland of mature oak, hornbeam and birch where all kinds of rhododendron, camellia and magnolia have been planted and now flourish. *Davidia involucrata*, cornus and eucryphia flower in turn. Woodland plants seldom seen elsewhere are at home here: trilliums, uvularias, disporums, erythroniums and Solomon's seal. Corners have been cut back to allow lilies to flower in summer and the willow gentian in autumn. There is a bog garden where primulas, gunnera, ferns, and hostas and the skunk cabbage find the moisture they love.

WARLEY PLACE RESERVE 19
Great Warley, Essex. Tel: (0708) 754391.
Essex Naturalists Trust (Warden Mr P. Butler)

2m S of Brentwood in centre of Great Warley village, facing village green, opposite pub ● *Open by prior appointment or at open weekend 31st March – 1st April* ● *Parking* ● *Entrance: donations to Trust welcomed* ● *Grade III*

Ellen Willmott made her garden here at the beginning of the century and described it in a popular book *Warley Place in Spring and Summer* in 1909. Her garden and her patronage of plant collectors, particularly E.H. Wilson, made her name a famous one in botanical history. In 1978 part of her garden became the property of the Essex Naturalists Trust and it is still open to non-members by prior appointmant who wish to see the remnants of Willmottism. Lilies, daffodils and *Crocus vernus* grew wild in large drifts and these, particularly the daffodils, can still be seen. Visitors who wish to study the Willmott hybrids can either make a special appointment with the warden or attend the spring open weekend.

WHITE BARNS HOUSE 20
Elmstead Market, Colchester, Essex. Tel: (020622) 2007
Mrs Beth Chatto

¼m E of Elmstead Market off A133 ● *Open March – Oct, Mon – Sat, 9.00 a.m. – 5.00 p.m., Nov – Feb, Mon – Fri, 9.00 a.m. – 4.00 p.m. Closed Bank Holidays. Parties by arrangement* ● *Entrance: £1.00, children free* ● *Parking* ● *Toilet facilities* ● *Suitable for wheelchairs* ● *Plants for sale* ● *Grade II*

Beth Chatto, the Gertrude Jekyll of today, designed this garden in the 1960s from a neglected hollow which was either boggy and soggy or exceedingly dry. She more than anyone else has influenced gardeners by her choice of plants for any situation – dry, wet or shady – and her ability to show them off to perfection. The planting of her garden is a lesson to every gardener on how to use both leaf and flower to best advantage.

THE GRADING SYSTEM

This is the most subjective aspect of the *Guide* and one which may cause some disagreement on the part of owners as well as visitors. We stress that its purpose is to serve as an indication to visitors in order to give them some advance information about the status of the garden as viewed by our inspectors and editors. Readers will appreciate that direct comparisons cannot be made between a huge estate like Chatsworth with its staff of professional experts and a tiny plantsman's garden in a terraced house, tended with dedication by a single owner. This being said, both may be excellent of their kind and therefore be worthy of consideration for a visit, and considered by the *Guide* to be at the top of their class. Conversely a lesser grading does not imply any criticism of a garden but is an attempt to guide the potential reader as to its relative merits if a choice has to be made between several gardens. Broadly speaking the intention of the four grades is as follows:

Grade I Amongst the best gardens in the world in terms of design and content. Many are of historic importance, but some are of recent origin. Overseas visitors to Britain or Ireland are recommended to include them in their itinerary.

Grade II Gardens of high quality, though not perhaps as unique as Grade I, and worth travelling a considerable distance to visit. Sometimes the property as a whole, and the general ambience, make the visit particularly rewarding.

Grade III These are gardens which our inspectors suggest it would be worth driving fifty miles or more to visit. They may have some special feature of design or plant content while not being considered as justifying a higher grade overall.

Grade IV Gardens of considerable merit and well worth visiting when in the region.

GLOUCESTERSHIRE

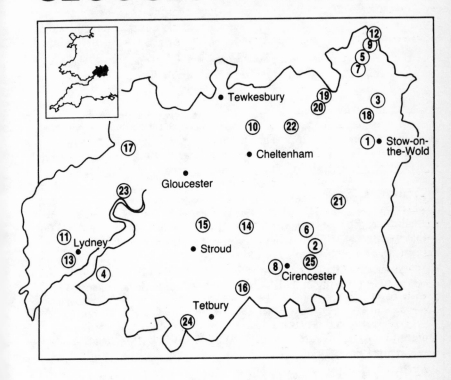

ABBOTSWOOD
Stow-on-the-Wold, Gloucestershire.   Tel: (0451) 30366
Dikler Farming Co

*1m W of Stow-on-the-Wold on B4077   ● Open 15th, 29th April, 13th May, 3rd June, 2.00 – 6.00 p.m.   ● Best season: spring   ● Entrance: £1.00, children 50p ● Parking free in grounds but no coaches   ● Teas   ● Toilet facilities   ● Partly suitable for wheelchairs   ● **Grade II***

The house is in one of the most beautiful of Cotswold settings. From the car park it is approached up a descending stream and pools, the woodland carpeted with spring flowers and bulbs, including one of the country's largest displays of fritillaries. The woods continue above and beyond the house and have been planted with rhododendrons, flowering shrubs and specimen trees. Near the house are formal gardens and terraces including a box-edged rose garden and a water garden. Extensive heather plantings. The house (not open) was formerly owned by Harry Ferguson, inventor of the modern tractor, who spent part of his considerable fortune developing the estate which has a somewhat park-like character.

BARNSLEY HOUSE 2
Barnsley, Gloucestershire.   Tel: (028574) 281
Mrs Rosemary Verey

3m N of Cirencester on A433 in village of Barnsley ● Open daily except Tues and Sun, 10.00 a.m. – 6.00 p.m. ● Entrance: £1.50, OAP £1.00, children free. Dec – Feb no charge. Parties by appointment ● Parking, not suitable for coaches ● Toilet facilities ● Suitable for wheelchairs ● Plants for sale ● Grade II

A splendid small garden under three acres, but comprising many garden styles from the past, carefully blended by the Vereys since they acquired the house and garden in the early 1960s. The Queen Anne stone house is set in an array of small gardens and vistas that blend perfectly to give a harmonious overall effect. The standard of horticulture and maintenance is very high. Great attention has been given to colour and texture. The kitchen garden is a particular delight with numerous small beds, ornate paths, box hedges, trained fruit trees etc. This garden was the recipient of the Christie's Award for the Best Garden in 1988. In 1989 other gardens in Barnsley were open for a July Festival weekend, including not only Mrs Verey's garden but also the fine Barnsley Park, owned by Lord Faringdon. At the time of going to press, no decision was available about when the next July Festival would be held, and it will be worth making enquiries, particularly if the Park can be seen.

BATSFORD ARBORETUM 3
Moreton-in-Marsh, Gloucestershire.   Tel: (0386) 700409/(0608) 50722
The Batsford Foundation

1½m NW of Moreton-in-Marsh on A44 to Evesham. Opposite the entrance to Sezincote (see entry) ● Open April to Oct, daily, 10.00 a.m. – 5.00 p.m. ● Best season: spring and autumn ● Entrance: £1.50, OAP and children 75p ● Parking ● Refreshments: coffees, light lunches and teas except Mons ● Toilet facilities ● Suitable for wheelchairs ● Plants for sale at garden centre open all year weekdays, 9.00 a.m. – 5.30 p.m., Sun, 10.00 a.m. – 5.00 p.m. ● Grade II

Over 1000 species of different trees in 50 acres of typical Cotswold countryside plus an unusual collection of exotic shrubs and bronze statues from the Far East, created from the garden laid out by Lord Redesdale. It was expanded into an arboretum by Lord Dulverton in the 1960s. For students, a guidebook gives the details, but everyone will enjoy the effects, particularly the autumn colours.

BERKELEY CASTLE 4
Berkeley, Gloucestershire.   Tel: (0453) 810332
Mr R.J.E. Berkeley

W of M5 between junctions 13 and 14 on B4066 ● Open April and Sept, daily except Mon, 2.00 – 5.00 p.m., May – Aug, Tues – Sat, 11.00 a.m. – 5.00 p.m.,

*Sun, 2.00 - 5.00 p.m., Oct, Sun, 2.00 - 4.30 p.m., Bank Holiday Mon, 11.00
a.m. - 4.30 p.m.* ● *Entrance: £2.90, OAP £2.60, children £1.45. Special
prices for parties* ● *Parking* ● *Refreshments and picnic area* ● *Toilet
facilities* ● *Shop* ● *House open* ● **Grade IV**

This is a most depressing castle, where dirty deeds were done, but it is
wonderful to have the soul uplifted by the beauty of the sheltered gardens and
lily pool. It originated in the 1920s and 1930s, much influenced by the aunt
of the owner, well-known gardener and rose enthusiast, Ellen Willmott of
Warley Place, Essex. *Magnolia grandiflora* and *M. delavayi* flourish here, as do
roses and clematis. The wisteria clings to the old walls and the herbaceous
plants and shrubs have been chosen with care.

BURNT NORTON 5
Nr Chipping Campden, Gloucestershire. Tel: (0386) 840359
The Earl of Harrowby

*1½m N of Chipping Campden on road to Mickleton, left into farm lane as road
goes downhill, then through wood for ½m* ● *Open for NGS, dates N.A.*
● *Parking* ● *Teas* ● *Suitable for wheelchairs* ● *Plants for sale* ● **Grade IV**

This is included specifically for those who like their gardens to have literary
associations. The owner somewhat misleadingly calls it, 'the subject of T.S.
Eliot's quartet' but those who have their copy of the *Four Quartets* handy will
probably agree that the subject is less likely the garden than a study of the
metaphysical opening 'Time present and time past/ Are both perhaps present
in time future/ And time future contained in time past.' Those who visit Burnt
Norton without their copy of T.S. Eliot may find the following quotations
evocative. 'Through the first gate/ Into our first world, shall we follow/ The
deception of the thrush?' ... 'The unheard music hidden in the shrubbery' ...
'The roses/ Had the look of flowers that are looked at' ... 'The pool was filled
with water out of sunlight' ... 'The leaves were full of children/ Hidden
excitedly, containing laughter' ... 'The moment in the rose-garden/ The
moment in the arbour where the rain beat' ... 'Will the clematis/Stray down,
bend to us; tendril and spray/Clutch and cling?' It would be wrong to
describe this rather grand park/garden in detail here and, by so doing, spoil
its connection with what many consider to be one of the most influential
poems of the twentieth century.

CHERRY ORCHARD 6
Foss Cross, Gloucestershire. Tel: (028572) 258
Mrs S. Michael

*Turning off A429 Cirencester - Northleach road, next to Hare and Hounds
pub* ● *Open 28th May and by appointment* ● *Entrance: £1.00, children 50p*
● *Parking* ● *Cream teas* ● *Suitable for wheelchairs* ● *Plants for sale*
● **Grade III**

The interest in this garden, created six years ago from a disused kennels, is in the arboretum. A large number of trees, shrubs and roses have recently been planted in a well-planned scheme. Arrangements of acers, sorbus, salix, prunus, etc. give spring and autumn colour. A small garden, using Cotswold stone walls as background, with different colour-theme beds, is in front of the house. Twin curved yew hedges form a backdrop behind the garden, in front of the back wall and fields beyond. The small garden is being replanted.

CHIPPING CAMPDEN GARDENS 7
Chipping Campden, Gloucestershire.

N of A44 between Evesham and Stow-on-the-Wold and S of Stratford- upon-Avon off A46 E of Broadway ● *Parking* ● *Refreshments: facilities in town* ● *Toilet facilities* ● *Suitable for wheelchairs* ● *Dogs* ● *Grade IV*

Because of its position near Hidcote, Kiftsgate and Stratford the town is a popular holiday stopping-off point for garden visitors, so it is fortuitous that it has two small gardens frequently open. Mr and Mrs Lusty's is entered through their house in the main street which is itself next door to Mrs Lusty's interior decorating shop The Green Dragon. It is a long, narrow town garden, with houses and a drive on one side, which has triumphed over its location by being cleverly designed to give surprises, informality, shelter and a wide variety of plants. Visitors are invited to contribute to an autistic charity, and the garden is open in the summer 'when it looks good' and is closed when it rains so check with the shop (0386) 840379. Another town garden normally open during the year is the Ernest Wilson Memorial Garden, also in the High Street. It was opened in 1984 in memory of 'Chinese' Wilson, who was born in Chipping Campden in 1876. The famous collector is estimated to have introduced 1200 species of trees and shrubs during his career and the garden includes several of his finds including *Acer griseum*, the paperbark maple, *Davidia involucrata*, the handkerchief tree, and the plant for which he wished to be remembered, the *Lilium regale*.

Other gardens in Campden and neighbouring Broad Campden are open under the NGS scheme and for the past three years another charity has arranged for 30 gardens to open over a June weekend. This will probably become an annual event. The choice of gardens appears to have been dictated by a desire for quantity rather than quality, and in general their appeal will be to those who like what is now called the traditional Cotswold style.

One of the pleasantest hotel gardens is to be found in the centre of the town, behind the King's Arms, where food and drink is served in the summer.

CIRENCESTER GARDENS 8
Cecily Hill, Cirencester, Gloucestershire.

On W side of Cirencester, near entrance to Cirencester Park ● *Open: see below* ● *Entrance: for NGS* ● *Parking* ● *Teas* ● *Toilet facilities* ● *Partly suitable for wheelchairs* ● *Plants for sale* ● *Grade IV*

The grandest garden in the town, Cirencester Park, is only open once a year in aid of charity but the park is open all the year round, courtesy of Earl Bathurst. Three gardens in Cecily Hill are open under the NGS on 15th July and one of them, the most publicised in the media, is at No 38. For those who like to see a garden full of flowers and colour this could be their Mecca, although another name would be more appropriate as it is owned by the Rev and Mrs John Beck. Entered through the house is a small square garden of great interest, but beyond this and concealed from view is a long low flower garden. Mrs Beck will open the garden by appointment. (0285) 653778. One of the other gardens open on NGS days, Cecily Hill House, has a small ornamental kitchen garden of original design and unusual vegetables. At the opposite end of the town is a tiny 70 foot garden entirely without grass and of considerable interest to anyone having to design for such a small space. Meg and Jeff Blumson open by appointment as well as on NGS (0285) 657696.

HIDCOTE MANOR GARDEN 9
Hidcote Bartrim, Chipping Campden, Gloucestershire.
Tel: (0386) 438333
The National Trust

Follow signposts from Chipping Campden or Mickleton near Stratford-on-Avon
● Open April – Oct, daily except Tues and Fri, 11.00 a.m. – 8.00 p.m. Last admission 7.00 p.m. or 1 hour before sunset if earlier ● Entrance: £3.50
● Parking but coaches by prior arrangement ● Refreshments: café for morning coffee, light lunches, teas 11.00 a.m. – 5.00 p.m. Party bookings. No picnics
● Toilet facilities ● Partly suitable for wheelchairs ● Plants for sale ● Shop
● Grade I

It is unnecessary to describe this garden in detail, one of the most famous in Britain and an essential visit for garden lovers of every persuasion. Created by Lawrence Johnston in the early years of the twentieth century, the original condition of the site may be judged from the early photographs in the entrance area. Johnston had a strong sense of design and great skill in planting, using mainly nineteenth-century specimens. Many varieties now bear the name Hidcote. Given to the National Trust in 1948, its splendid architectural effects and bold plantings have been retained, although these days some visitors are offended by the use of annuals. Johnston's achievement is all the more remarkable because of the isolation of the hill-top site whose scale can be appreciated by the view from the entrance to Kiftsgate garden which is within walking distance (see entry).

8 HYATT'S WAY 10
Bishops Cleeve, Cheltenham, Gloucestershire. Tel: (024267) 3503
Mr and Mrs P. Herbert

4m N of Cheltenham. Take A435 towards Evesham. At Bishops Cleeve turn right past Esso garage then 2nd right ● Open by appointment only from mid-

April to mid-August ● *Entrance: 50p, children 25p* ● *Parking very limited*
● *Plants for sale* ● *Grade IV*

A tiny plantsman's garden but with some very rare plants and all-year-round interest. The 500 varieties include 20 salvias and eight different digitalis. Friends have brought back seeds from the Himalayas from which the Herberts have grown alpines. Their back and front garden has received much tending and loving care over the past dozen years and the result will keep a plantsperson occupied for an hour or so.

JASMINE HOUSE 11
Bream, Nr Lydney, Gloucestershire. Tel: (0594) 563688
Mr V.M. Bond

W of the Severn estuary, 3m N of Lydney. At Bream Maypole Garage turn right to Park End. Immediately after crossroads, turn right by insurance office. House is 200 yards on left ● *Open all year round by appointment. Easter – Sept, Thurs, 2.00 – 5.00 p.m.* ● *Best season: summer* ● *Entrance: 50p, children free* ● *Parking in village only* ● *Plants for sale* ● *Grade IV*

A plantsman's garden developed over the last few years, virtually from scratch, on a ¾-acre cottage garden. Naturally there are cottage plants but the main interest is the alpines, heathers and fuchsias. There are many species of herbaceous plants. Among the fruit trees in the orchard are 'beds' – small wild gardens of differing types. Not far away is Lydney Park, a rather grand garden at its most spectacular in spring (see page 141).

KIFTSGATE COURT 12
Chipping Campden, Gloucestershire. Tel: (0386) 438777
Mr and Mrs A.H. Chambers

3m NE of Chipping Campden and near Mickleton. Kiftsgate is next to Hidcote Manor which is signposted ● *Open 30th March – Sept, Wed, Thurs, Sun, 2.00 – 6.00 p.m. Also Bank Holiday Mons (NB not identical opening times with Hidcote)* ● *Entrance: £2.60, children 60p* ● *Parking* ● *Plants for sale*
● *Grade I*

The house was built mid-nineteenth century on this magnificent site surrounded by three steep banks. The garden was largely created by the present owner's grandmother who with her husband moved there after World War I. Her work was continued by her daughter, Diana Binny, who made a few alterations but continued the colour schemes of the borders. In spring, the white sunken garden is covered with bulbs and there is s fine show of daffodils along the drive. June and July are the peak months for colour and scent but the magnificent old and species roses are the glory of this garden, home of *Rosa* 'Kiftsgate'. Other features are perennial geraniums, a large wisteria and many species of hydrangea, some very large. In autumn, Japanese maples glow in the bluebell wood. This garden should not be missed, not only because of its proximity to Hidcote, but because of its profusion of colour and apparent informality. Unusual plants are sometimes amongst those available for sale.

LYDNEY PARK 13
Lydney, Gloucestershire.   Tel: (0594) 42844
Lord Bledisloe

20m SW of Gloucester. N of A48 between Lydney and Aylburton ● *Open Easter Sun and Mon. Every Sun, Bank Holiday and Wed from 22nd April – 10th June and daily, 28th May – 3rd June, 11.00 a.m. – 6.00 p.m. Parties by appointment in season* ● *Entrance: £1.50 except Wed when £1.00. Car and accompanied children free* ● *Parking* ● *Refreshments: teas. Picnics in deer park* ● *Toilet facilities* ● *Partly suitable for wheelchairs* ● *Dogs on lead* ● *Shrubs for sale* ● *Shop* ● *Roman site and museum open* ● ***Grade III***

The park dates back to the seventeenth century and although it has been in the hands of one family since 1723, a new house was built in 1875 and the old one demolished. A new start was made on the garden in 1950 when the terrace was paved and a line of cupressus 'Kilmacurragh' planted to frame the view. An area near the house has an interesting collection of magnolias but the most picturesque sight is the bank of daffodils and cherries, splendid in season. From 1957, a determined attempt has been made to plant rhododendrons and azaleas in the wooded valley, behind and below the house, with the aim of achieving bold colour at different times between March and June. Near the entrance to the main part of the gardens there is a small pool surrounded by azaleas and a collection of acers. From here the route passes through carefully-planted groups of rhododendron and by a folly, brought from Venice as recently as 1961. This overlooks a valley and bog garden. Criss-crossing the hillside, there are rare and fine rhododendrons and azaleas, including an area planted with un-named seedlings. Enormous effort has gone into the plant design, colour combination and general landscaping, and those who are enthusiastic about rhododendrons, azaleas and camellias will find enough to enjoy for a whole day. Another interest for visitors is the Roman camp, excavated by Sir Mortimer Wheeler, and the museum which contains the famous bronze Lydney Dog, one of the finest pieces of Romano-British sculpture. Guide book with map available.

MISARDEN PARK GARDENS 14
Miserden, Stroud, Gloucestershire.   Tel: (028582) 309
Major M.T.N.H. Wills

7m SE from Gloucester, 3m from A417. Signposted ● *Open late April – Sept, Wed and Thurs, 10.00 a.m. – 4.30 p.m.* ● *Entrance: £1.50. Reduction for booked parties* ● *Parking* ● *Teas in village* ● *Toilet facilities* ● *Suitable for wheelchairs* ● *Nursery adjacent to garden open all year* ● ***Grade II***

This lovely, timeless English garden has most features that one comes to expect of a garden of the early twentieth century. There are extensive yew hedges, a York stone terrace, a loggia overhung with wisteria, a fine specimen of *Magnolia* x *soulangiana*. The south lawn sports very fine grass stairs. The west of the house descends to the nursery in a series of fine grassed terraces. There are two very good herbaceous borders leading to a traditional rose garden beyond. The grounds are planted with many fine specimen trees. The spring show of blossom and bulbs is particularly good. The gardens command excellent views over the famous Golden Valley.

PAINSWICK ROCOCO GARDEN   15
The Stables, Painswick House, Painswick.   Tel: (0452) 813204
Lord and Lady Dickinson

*½m from Painswick on B4073. Signposted ● Open Feb – mid-Dec, Wed – Fri and on Bank Holiday Mons, 11.00 a.m. – 5.00 p.m. and 1st, 8th April ● Best season: spring ● Entrance: £2.00, OAP £1.75, children £1.00 ● Parking ● Refreshments: teas and lunches ● Toilet facilities ● Suitable for wheelchairs ● Plants for sale ● Shop ● **Grade III***

A great deal of time, money and effort is going into the restoration (almost complete redevelopment) of this rare Rococo survival. Most of the work is new, plantings are incomplete and very young. Whole sections are yet to be restored. But, given time, it will be splendid. At present, the best features are the eighteenth-century garden buildings, the views into especially beautiful surrounding countryside, and the marvellous snowdrop wood spanning a stream that flows from a pond at the lower end. This must be one of the best displays of naturalized snowdrops in England. There are some splendid beech woods and older specimen trees. Wildflowers are allowed complete freedom. Rococo gardening was an eighteenth-century combination of formal geometric features with winding woodland paths, revealing sudden incidents and vistas. It was, in essence, a softening of the formal French style, apparent from about 1715 onwards in all forms of art. A painting by Thomas Robins (1716-1778) is the basis for Painswick's restoration.

RODMARTON MANOR   16
Rodmarton, Gloucestershire. Tel: (028584) 219
Mrs Anthony Biddulph

*6m SW of Cirencester, 4m NE of Tetbury off A433 ● Open by appointment ● Best season: May/June ● Entrance: £1.00, children free ● Refreshments: by prior arrangement ● Suitable for wheelchairs ● Plants for sale ● **Grade II***

This much praised garden has been featured in numerous books and magazines over the years. It is a good example of an 'English' garden in the classical sense, but firmly of this century. The garden is famous for its fine hedges of yew, hornbeam, beech and holly. The drive to the manor house, designed by Ernest Barnsley, lies between two immaculately clipped tall beech hedges. There are many good topiaries, a lovely hornbeam avenue and many fine vistas. The herbaceous borders, terrace and leisure gardens are of particular interest. The overall maintenace may have seen better days but as in so many large gardens, great emphasis has had to be placed on labour-saving schemes. This garden will appeal to those who like their design strong and undiluted.

RYELANDS HOUSE 17
Taynton, Gloucestershire. Tel: (045279) 251
Captain and Mrs E. Wilson

8m W of Gloucester, midway betwen Huntley (A40) and Newent (B4215)
● Open by appointment for parties and on 8th, 15th, 16th, 22nd, 29th April, 6th, 7th May, 3rd, 10th June, 26th, 27th Aug, 2.00 - 6.00 p.m. ● Best season: spring ● Entrance: £1.25, children free ● Parking ● Refreshments ● Toilet facilities ● Suitable for wheelchairs in dry weather ● Dogs allowed on the field walk only ● Plants for sale ● Grade III

An unusual combination of plantsman's garden with great charm and naturalness, created over the past 25 years from an unpromising rubbish tip and junk yard. Herbaceous borders are backed by a cherry hedge, there is a good sunken garden and a south-facing herb border, and unusual collections of alpines and species and old roses. The woodland area contains wild daffodils (the daffodil is said to have originated in Gloucestershire), anemones, bluebells, cowslips and primroses. Streams with waterside plants and a two-acre lake in a beautiful setting. Those who visit the garden at other times will, however, wish to return in the spring to see the poplar-lined drive which has been underplanted with thousands of bulbs and to see the display in the woods.

SEZINCOTE 18
Bourton-on-the-Hill, Nr Moreton-in-Marsh, Gloucestershire.
Mr and Mrs D. Peake

1½m from Moreton-in-Marsh on A44 just before reaching Bourton-on-the-Hill
● Open Jan – Nov, Thurs, Fri and Bank Holiday Mon, 2.00 - 6.00 p.m. Also for NGS. Closed Dec ● Entrance: £1.60, children 50p ● Parking ● Teas on one NGS day ● Toilet facilities ● Suitable for wheelchairs ● Dogs on lead ● House open May – July and Sept, Thurs, Fri, 2.30 - 6.00 p.m. ● Grade II

The estate, acquired in the early nineteenth century, was developed in the Indian style by the architect, Thomas Daniell, who combined this with Palladian motifs. In the twentieth century a canal pool, a curving conservatory and a little pavilion also in Indian style have been added. The garden reflects what the *Oxford Companion* calls its architectural dichotomy, and, despite some work by Repton, the mixture of traditional landscape with eastern ornamentation, such as the Indian bridge, is not one which every visitor finds satisfactory. However it is certainly unique, although there are echoes of Brighton Pavilion, for which Repton drew designs of an oriental nature.

SNOWSHILL MANOR 19
Nr Broadway, Gloucestershire. Tel: (038685) 2410
The National Trust

3m S of Broadway off A44 and off A424 between Broadway and Stow-on-the-Wold. 4m W of junction of A44/A424 ● *Open April and Oct, Sat, Sun, 11.00 a.m. - 1.00 p.m. and 2.00 - 5.00 p.m. Easter Sat, Sun and Mon, 11.00 a.m. - 1.00 p.m. and 2.00 - 6.00 p.m. May - Sept, Wed - Sun and Bank Holiday Mon, 11.00 a.m. - 1.00 p.m. and 2.00 - 6.00 p.m. Last admission ½ hour before closing* ● *Entrance: £3.20. Parties by written appointment only and no concessions* ● *Parking* ● *No refreshments but nearby pub serves morning coffee and lunches* ● *Partly suitable for wheelchairs* ● ***Grade II***

From a design by MH Baillie-Scott, the owner Charles Wade transformed a 'wilderness of chaos' on a Cotswold hillside into an interconnecting series of outdoor 'rooms' in Hidcote style from the 1920s onwards. Wade was, according to the *Oxford Companion*, a believer in the arts and crafts rustic ideal and the garden, like the house, expresses his eccentricities. Seats and woodwork are painted 'Wade' blue, a powdery dark blue with touches of turquoise which goes well with the Cotswold stone walls. The simple cottage style conceals careful planting with blue, mauve and purple as the motif. Organic gardening is employed here. The visitor may care to contrast Wade's success with some of the less happy attempts at the Cotswold garden style by others in this picture-postcard village no longer inhabited by traditional villagers.

STANWAY HOUSE 20
Winchcombe, Gloucestershire. Tel: (038673) 469
Lord Neidpath

1m E of A46 Cheltenham to Broadway road on B4077, 4m from Winchcombe ● *Open 29th April, 17th June, 2.00 - 5.00 p.m., June - Aug, Tues and Thurs, 2.00 - 5.00 p.m. Other times by appointment* ● *Entrance: £1.75, OAP £1.50, children 75p (house and garden)* ● *Parking* ● *Refreshments: coffee and tea, Bakehouse tea rooms in village. Picnics permitted in park* ● *Toilet facilities* ● *Partly suitable for wheelchairs* ● *Dogs* ● *House open* ● ***Grade III***

Stanway is a honey-coloured Cotswold village with its Jacobean 'great house' which has been in the hands of only two families since it was built. It was much frequented by Arthur Balfour and 'The Souls' in the latter years of the last century. More recently, the garden was used to film part of *The Draughtsman's Contract* so one need to say no more to those who favour grand design and effects. Contrariwise it offers nothing to the plantsperson as there is hardly a flower in sight. Behind the house, the garden rises in a series of dramatic lawns and a (rare) formal terraced mound to the pyramid folly which, in the eighteenth century was the pivot of the vast cascade descending to a lake by the house. The present owner plans to restore this with its 170m-long waterfall, its canal 35m wide, and to extend the lime avenue and vista. Alas the estimated cost is £¼ million. Other features include the fourteenth-century tithe barn, church and a dog cemetery whose inmates go back to 1700.

STOWELL PARK   21
Nr Northleach, Gloucestershire.
Lord and Lady Vestey

Off A429 • Open 24th June, 12th Aug, 2.00 – 6.00 p.m. • Entrance: £1.50, children free • Parking • Teas • Toilet facilities • Suitable for wheelchairs • Grade II

Stowell Park is a large garden of some age. There are fine terraced lawns, a very good collection of climbing roses, a pleached lime avenue (new). Perhaps the best feature is the old kitchen garden complete with glasshouses, where a wide range of fruits and flowers are grown for the big house. The views from the terraced lawns are particularly lovely. For those interested in ecclesiastical architecture, the nearby church has excellent wall paintings dating from the late twelfth century, as does most of the building itself.

SUDELEY CASTLE   22
Winchcombe, Gloucestershire.   Tel: (0242) 604357/8
Lord and Lady Ashcombe

6m N of Cheltenham Spa on A46. Entry through the town of Winchcombe • Open Easter – Oct, 11.00 a.m. – 5.30 p.m. • Entrance: £2.00 (castle extra) • Parking • Meals and refreshments. Picnic facilities in play area only • Toilet facilities • Suitable for wheelchairs • A good selection of plants for sale • Shop • House open 12 noon – 5.00 p.m. • Grade II

There has been a house on this magnificent site for over 1000 years and today the emphasis is on tourism with pleasant facilities, craft and other exhibitions such as falconry. The main attraction of the extensive grounds are the clipped yews by the park balustrade and the sculptural yew hedges with openings and tunnel walks round the so-called Queen's garden. This imitation of a medieval knot garden, made in the nineteenth century by an ancestor of the owners, has well-clipped rosemary, lavender and other herbs. Otherwise, the planting is rather patchy. The owners are renovating the Queen's garden under the guidance of Jane Fernley Whittingstall to 'become one of the major rose gardens of England'.

WESTBURY COURT GARDEN 23
Westbury-on-Severn, Gloucestershire. Tel: (045276) 461
The National Trust

9m SW of Gloucester on A48, close to the church ● Open April - Oct, Wed – Sun (except Good Friday) and Bank Holiday Mon, 11.00 a.m. – 6.00 p.m. Other months by appointment only ● Entrance: £1.50. Groups by prior arrangement ● Parking ● Picnic area ● Toilet facilities ● Suitable for wheelchairs ● Grade I

A unique and excellent example, in Britain, of a late seventeenth-century formal water garden featuring canals, 'Dutch' pavilions, yew hedges, and topiary. In the walled garden a special feature is made of over 100 species of plants grown in England before 1700.

WESTONBIRT ARBORETUM 24
Westonbirt, Gloucestershire. Tel: (066688) 220
The Forestry Commission

On A433, 5m NE of junction with A6 ● Open all year, 10.00 a.m. – 8.00 p.m. or dusk ● Best season: autumn ● Entrance: £1.50, OAP and children 50p ● Parking ● Light refreshments at café (closed late Nov – Easter). Picnic area ● Toilet facilities ● Suitable for wheelchairs ● Dogs ● Shop (closed late Nov - Easter ● Grade I

This is perhaps the finest arboretum in Britain. Started in 1829 by R. Staynor-Holford, Westonbirt was expanded and improved by successive generations of the same family until it was taken over by the Forestry Commission in 1956. Numerous grass rides divide the trees into roughly rectangular blocks, within which are various open spaces and glades used for special plantings such as the famous Japanese maple collection. Westonbirt is noted for its vast range of notable mature specimen trees. Colour is best in spring (rhododendron, magnolias etc) and autumn (Japanese maples, fothergilla) The Forestry Commission is continuing with new planting, for example the Hillier Glade with ornamental cherries. Across the valley from the original arboretum is Silk Valley with collections of native and American species that in spring are carpeted with primroses, wood anemones and bluebells.

YEW TREE COTTAGE 25
Ampney St Mary, Gloucestershire. Tel: (028585) 333
Mrs Shuker, Mr and Mrs Pollit

On A417 turn left at Red Lion. Take first left to Ampney St Mary, turn right in village and follow lane to house ● Open 25th March, 4th, 15th, 16th April, 2nd, 6th May, 3rd, 6th June, 4th July, 1st, 26th Aug, 5th Sept and by appointment for parties ● Best season: June/July ● Parking ● Teas ● Suitable for wheelchairs ● Plants for sale on occasions ● Grade IV

A carefully-planted, garden, making good use of all available space. Roses and clematis tumble over low front walls onto vergeside beds. Small front garden with interesting low-growing plants around lawn and abundant climbers on surrounding walls. Vegetable and alpine area behind house with further vegetable and orchard beyond. Good display of autumn cyclamen. Barnsley House (see page 136) is nearby.

HOW TO FIND THE GARDENS

Directions to each garden are included in each entry. This information has been supplied by the garden inspectors and is aimed to be the best available to those travelling by car. However, it has been compiled to be used in conjunction with a road atlas.

The unreliability of train and bus services makes it unrewarding to include details, particularly as many garden visits are made on Sundays. However, many properties can be reached by public transport and National Trust guides and the Yellow Book [NGS] give details. Future editions of the *Guide* may include a special list of gardens easily reached by public transport if readers indicate that this would be helpful.

The Maps: The numbers on the maps correspond to the numbers of the gardens in each county. The maps show the proximity of one garden to another so that visits to several gardens can be planned for the same day. It is worthwhile referring to the maps of bordering counties to see if another garden visit can be included in your itinerary. The maps should be used in conjunction with a road atlas.

TELEPHONE NUMBERS

Except where specifically requested to be excluded, telephone numbers to which enquiries may be directed are given for each property. To maintain the support and cooperation of private owners it is suggested that the telephone be used with discretion. Where visits are by appointment, the telephone can of course be used except where written application, particularly for parties, is specifically requested. Code numbers are given in brackets. For the Republic of Ireland when phoning from the United Kingdom dial 353 plus area code plus number (except Dublin numbers which are 0001 plus number). In all cases where visits by parties are proposed, owners should be advised in advance and arrangements preferably confirmed in writing.

London Telephone Codes: From May 1990 all London telephone numbers with the prefix 01 will be changed. The new prefix will be either 071 or 081. Details of these new numbers are available from British Telecom. During the changeover period in 1990 all London telephone numbers dialled with their 01 prefix will be redirected.

HAMPSHIRE
& ISLE OF WIGHT

BARTON MANOR 1
Whippingham, Cowes, Isle of Wight. Tel: (0983) 292835
Mr and Mrs A. Goddard

From E. Cowes A3021, 50 yards beyond Osborne House on left ● *Open Easter –
2nd Sun in Oct* ● *Best season: mid-May/June* ● *Entrance: £2.50, children
under 15 free* ● *Parking* ● *Refreshments: cafeteria and wine bar – all day
licence* ● *Toilet facilities* ● *Suitable for wheelchairs* ● *Plants for sale* ● *Shop*
● ***Grade II***

Prince Albert's original design included fine trees and the cork grove. The
grand terraces were added by Edward VII, sloping down towards Osborne
Bay. In 1924 no less than 225,000 daffodils were planted around the lake,
which give a fine display in spring. There is also a secret garden planted with
azaleas and roses, impressive herbaceous borders and a productive vineyard,
wine from which is on sale. In 1968 Hilliers laid out an intriguing water
garden on the far side of the lake, on what was originally Queen Victoria's
skating rink. The present owners, running the garden and vineyard as a
commercial operation, have spared no effort in restoring and maintaining the
estate to an immaculate standard. The NCCPG's National collection of red
hot pokers (kniphofia) is here.

BRAMDEAN HOUSE 2
Bramdean, Nr Alresford, Hampshire. Tel: (096279) 214
Mr and Mrs H. Wakefield

10m E of Winchester on A272 at W end of Bramdean ● *Open by appointment
and 18th March, 15th, 16th April, 20th May, 16th, 17th June (with other
gardens in Bramdean), 15th July, 19th Aug, 2.00 - 5.00 p.m.* ● *Best season:
summer* ● *Entrance: £1.00, children free* ● *Parking* ● *Refreshments*
● *Toilet facilities* ● *Plants for sale* ● ***Grade II***

A bumbling hedge of yew and box swelling out between a pair of armorial
gates lends a slightly eccentric air to the south front of the eighteenth-century
house and effectively conceals the fine country house garden to the north. A
grass path rises steadily from the centre of the garden front forming a vista
through the three main sections. The first is dominated by the famous double
herbaceous border, lawns and mature trees; a walled kitchen garden defines
the second and an orchard watched over by a cupola'ed gazebo the last. The
careful composition of colours, foliage and views is a continuous and
successful feature of those 'gardens', from *Crambe cordifolia* and onopordums,
the spreading *Prunus subhirtella*, yew topiary and huge beeches to the classical
and meticulously maintained kitchen garden. The view from the orchard
through the wrought iron gates of the walled garden with sundial to the
herbaceous borders and lily pond in midsummer is much admired.

BROADHATCH HOUSE 3
Bentley, Nr Alton, Hampshire. Tel: (0420) 23185
Mr Powell and Mrs Bruce

4m NE of Alton on A31. Turn right at pond ½m up School Lane, bear right at fork ● Open 24th June, 2.00 - 6.00 p.m., 25th June, 10.00 a.m. - 5.00 p.m. ● Entrance: £1.00, children free ● Parking ● Suitable for wheelchairs ● Dogs on lead ● Plants for sale ● Grade III

Spreading from the east, south and west of the house the three and a half acres are divided into a series of garden rooms which, although extremely well laid out are sometimes let down by the absence of a strong feature. However the view through the sunken rose garden with its 'Peace' and hybrid musks to the double herbaceous borders will be sufficient reward for any visitor. The kitchen garden is well-maintained by the present owners who have created the whole estate over the past 30 years.

BROADLANDS 4
Romsey, Hampshire. Tel: (0794) 516878
Lord Romsey

S of Romsey on A31. Signposted ● Open March – Oct, 10.00 a.m. - 5.30 p.m. Closed Mon except Aug, Sept and Bank Holidays ● Entrance: £3.95, OAP £2.95, children £2.25, children under 12 free ● Parking ● Refreshments and picnic site ● Toilet facilities ● Suitable for wheelchairs ● Shop ● Grade II

This former home of Lord Louis Mountbatten has a smooth lawn running from the steps of the porticoed west front to the River Test and spreading parkland trees of beech and cedar come together in a composition that epitomises the eighteenth-century English Landscape School. The elegant Palladianism of Broadlands could only be the work of 'Capability' Brown. To the south of the house a large circular pool and fountain hold centre stage within an enclosure of topiary yew hedges and, to the north and east a series of disappointing walled gardens. In addition to the house, arguably the finest in Hampshire, a classical orangery, ice house and a small garden are perfectly-sited in the immaculate lawns amongst noteworthy specimens of magnolias, taxodiums, limes and huge plane trees. It is for these overall impressions rather than details that Broadlands has gained its popularity.

BROCKENHURST PARK 5
Brockenhurst, New Forest, Hampshire.
Mr and Mrs R. Berry

S of the village on A337. Turn E to the old church. The drive is across lane to E ● Open for NGS ● Entrance: 80p, OAP and children 40p ● Parking ● Refreshments at Brockenhurst ● Suitable for wheelchairs ● Dogs on lead ● Grade II

Though altered considerably in some respects since its much vaunted days early this century when it was featured in *Country Life*, volumes by Gertrude Jekyll and C. Holmes, and painted by C.S. Elgood, Brockenhurst retains much of the sense of theatre in its Italianate-style gardens. Sentinel Irish junipers, clipped arches of *Quercus ilex* and statues of Dorothea and Venus reinforce ideas of Palladian stage sets. A modern brick house replaced the Victorian pile in 1960 and now sits disconcertingly at one end of a broad canal with a Palladian double stairway leading to a circular fountain pool at the other. Topiary yews along the length backed by *Sequoia sempervirens*, *Pinus sylvestris* and *Quercus* 'Lucombeana'. Elsewhere a cucumber tree, *Magnolia acuminata*, female ginkgo, *Kalopanax pictus* and Deodar and Lebanon cedars complete a remarkable collection of parkland trees in a unique setting.

COMPTON END 6
Compton Street, Compton, Nr Winchester, Hampshire.
Captain and Mrs G.A. Kitchin   Tel: (0962) 713342

3m S of Winchester at end of Compton village ● Open 6th, 7th May, 8th, 9th July, 26th, 27th Aug, 12 noon – 6.00 p.m. ● Entrance: 75p, children 10p ● Parking, unofficial, along road ● Partly suitable for wheelchairs ● Dogs on lead ● Grade III

Designed and laid out by George Herbert Kitchin from 1895 onwards. That he was a successful architect practised in the Arts and Crafts tradition is obvious in the confident manner of the layout and the assuredness behind the unity of the formal garden with the cottage garden. The garden can be divided into principally three levels, a series of 'rooms' on the upper, croquet/tennis lawn at the mid-point and vegetable/orchard to the SW. The garden is in the style of Hidcote with yew, box hedges and topiary, herbaceous borders and will not fail to delight every garden lover as well as historical enthusiasts.

EXBURY GARDENS 7
Exbury, Nr Southampton, Hampshire. Tel: (0703) 891203
Mr E.L. de Rothschild

2½m SE of Beaulieu, 15m SW of Southampton, via B3054 SE of Beaulieu after 1m turn right for Exbury ● Open mid-March – mid-July/Sept – late Oct, 10.00 a.m. – 5.30 p.m. ● Best season: spring/autumn ● Entrance: spring £2.20, OAP/children £1.70 (children under 12 free), Bank Holiday weekends and May weekends 50p extra, autumn £1.50, OAPs £1.00 ● Parking ● Refreshments ● Toilet facilities ● Suitable for wheelchairs ● Dogs on lead ● Plants for sale ● Shop ● Grade I

Established in the 1920s and 1930s these outstanding gardens are synonymous with the name of Rothschild and with the development of new hybrid rhododendrons and azaleas over the last 70 years or so. Work on this most beautifully tended woodland garden is continuing and the 200 acres provide aspects of planting from early nineteenth-century cedars and *Sequoiadendron giganteum* (Wellingtonias) to huge swathes of colour such as the apricot or the spectacular 'Lady Chamberlain's Walk' beneath the high canopy of oak and pine. In compositional terms it would be hard to better the layout of the area around the high and low ponds where Japanese maples, cercidiphyllum, *Salix fargesii* and primulas are the pick of the plants and the glimpsed views across the Beaulieu river refreshing. Three separate walks amongst conifers, camellias, wisteria, rock gardens, winter gardens and pools demand that nothing less than a day is spent here.

FAIRFIELD HOUSE 8
East Street, Hambledon, Nr Portsmouth, Hampshire.
Tel: (070132) 431
Mr and Mrs P. Wake

10m SW of Peterfield on B2150 • *Open by appointment and 17th, 24th June, 2.00 – 6.00 p.m.* • *Best season: summer* • *Entrance: £1.00, children 50p (suitable for groups)* • *Parking* • *Refreshments* • *Toilet facilities* • *Suitable for wheelchairs* • *Dogs on lead* • *Plants for sale* • *Grade II*

There can be little doubt that Lanning Roper, who assisted in the establishment of this excellent garden, would approve of the continuing development of the planting at Fairfield, particularly the climbing, shrub and bush roses around and on the elegant white Regency 'colonial' house set on a south-facing slope beneath chalk down and sheltered by hedges, walls and a legacy of fine trees, cedars of Lebanon and a stooled lime tree worthy of note, this largely informal garden has been skilfully shaped by the Wakes. The four acres not only hosts an impressive range of roses, of which there are over 160 in number, but mixed borders of choice specimens, clematis and solanum are very successful, and in spring drifts of bulbs.

FURZEY GARDENS 9
Minstead, Nr Lyndhurst, Hampshire. Tel: (0703) 812464
Mrs M.A. Selwood (Manager)

8m SW of Southampton, 1m S of A31, 2m W of Cadnam and the end of M27, 3½m NW of Lyndhurst • *Open daily except 25th and 26th Dec, 10.30 a.m. – 5.00 p.m. Dusk in winter* • *Best season: spring* • *Entrance: £1.75, children 90p, winter £1.00, children 50p* • *Parking* • *Refreshments at Honey Pot café ¼m away* • *Toilet facilities* • *Suitable for wheelchairs* • *Plants for sale* • *Shop* • *Sixteenth-century cottage open daily in summer, weekends in winter* • *Grade II*

This eight-acre garden was laid out by Hew Dalrymple in the early 1920s using plants from the nursery at nearby Bartley. The range of plants particularly those of Australasian descent make this garden a must for horticulturalists and plant historians. Situated on a south-facing slope, winding paths lead to many noteworthy and surprisingly large specimens. There is relatively little herbaceous planting but this is more than compensated for by the boldness and density of some of the most colourful planting schemes with the vermilion of Chilean Fire trees in May/June outstanding. Recent replanting has left some gaps in the borders but there does not seem to be anything from lawns to the shaded plants of the water garden that will not flourish here.

THE GILBERT WHITE MUSEUM 10
The Wakes, Selbourne, Alton, Hampshire. Tel: (042050) 275
Oates Memorial Trust

4½m S of Alton, 8m N of Petersfield on B3006 • Open March – Oct, Tues – Sun and Bank Holidays, 11.00 a.m. – 5.30 p.m., last admission 5.00 p.m. • Best season: spring • Entrance: £1.25, OAP/student £1.00, children 50p • Parking: public car park behind Selbourne Arms • Toilet facilities • Suitable for wheelchairs • Plants for sale • Shop • House open • Grade III

'The Wakes' through the great naturalist Gilbert White's *Garden Kalender* is probably one of the best documented gardens of the eighteenth century. Since their purchase in 1954 the gardens have been steadily restored to period form and now show many of the flowers described in White's journals. Of the many interesting and period features, the yew topiary, laburnum arbour, herb garden and rose garden should be noted. An original brick path may be followed past an ancient yew and out into the 'Great Mead' where from the shelter of an arbour Selbourne Hanger, the parkland trees and the early ha-ha can be enjoyed. Visitors may ponder on the fact that it was at 'The Wakes' that White made the first observations of the value of the earthworm to gardens and farms.

GREATHAM MILL 11
Greatham, Nr Liss, Hampshire. Tel: (04207) 219
Mrs E.N. Pumphrey

7m SE of Alton on B3006 turn off at Hawkley, 5m N of Petersfield, from A325 at Greatham turn onto B3006 towards Alton. After 600 yards left into No Through yard • Open mid-April – Sept, Sun and Bank Holiday, 2.00 – 7.00 p.m. Also by appointment • Entrance: £1.00, children free • Parking • Refreshments: picnic area • Toilet facilities • Plants for sale • Grade II

Seemingly protected by the moat-like River Rother and a mill race the 'cottage-style' garden of Greatham Mill harbours a wide-ranging collection of many unusual varieties as well as attractive planting associations of the more usual kind. The seventeenth-century mill half hidden by wisteria provides a romantic backdrop to a water garden at the front where large leaves and luxuriance of hostas, royal ferns, rodgersias and gunnera dominate more sensitive planting. Passing beside and behind the house the full extent of the Pumphreys' achievements since their arrival here in 1949 can be appreciated. Alpines, in spreading middle age, grasses and herbaceous plants provide constant ground cover interest amongst carefully laid out grass paths enticed by groupings of choice foliage shrubs, including a curious pencil-thin hedge, and trees.

HACKWOOD PARK (The 'Spring Wood') 12
Basingstoke, Hampshire. Tel: (0256) 23107
The Viscount and Viscountess Camrose

1m S of Basingstoke. The entrance is off Tunworth Road. Signposted ● *Open 8th April, 13th May, 14th Oct, 2.00 – 6.00 p.m.* ● *Best season: spring/ autumn* ● *Entrance: £1.00, children 50p* ● *Parking* ● *Refreshments* ● *Toilet facilities* ● *Suitable for wheelchairs* ● *Grade III*

Furnished with follies to the design of James Gibbs, architect of St Martin-in-the-Fields, and almost certainly laid out under the direction of the same hand, 'Spring Wood' is the only complete example in England of a garden wood in the French manner. Eight Le Nôtre-styled avenues radiate from a central round point leading the visitor beneath an impressive canopy of specimen and forest trees and revealing in turn the surprisingly subdued follies by Gibbs and others, the impressive earthworks of the woodland boundary and amphitheatre and distant prospects of the south and east fronts of Hackwood House. The nation probably has Lord Curzon to thank for the preservation of the house, which he leased after his return from India, much depressed by his treatment by the wretched Kitchener and the death of his wife.

HIGHCLERE CASTLE 13
Highclere, Nr Newbury, Hampshire. Tel: (0635) 253210
Lord and Lady Carnarvon

4½m S of Newbury on W side of A34 ● *Open July – Sept, Wed – Sun, 2.00 – 6.00 p.m.* ● *Entrance: £3.00, OAP, disabled, children under 16, £2.00* ● *Parking* ● *Refreshments* ● *Toilet facilities* ● *Suitable for wheelchairs* ● *Shop* ● *House open* ● *Grade III*

Though much altered by 'Capability' Brown in the 1770s, Highclere Park will still reward students of the earlier Rococo style with a rare and fine collection of early eighteenth-century follies. Around Charles Barry's huge battlemented house an equally fine collection of cedars – North Indian Deodar, Mount Atlas and Lebanon – may be identified, the near horizontal branches of the latter framing views to first of the house and then seemingly of all the district. Relegated to the slopes away from the house, the walled and secret garden is planted, for Highclere, in an uncharacteristically cautious manner and saved only by James Russell's eye for good spring and summer colour. It was on Lord Carnarvon's estate here that in 1909 the young Geoffrey de Havilland

made some of the early powered tests in his wood and fabric flying machine.
See also Hollington Herb Garden (page 156).

THE HILLIER GARDEN AND ARBORETUM   14
Jermyns Lane, Ampfield, Nr Romsey, Hampshire.
Tel: (0794) 68787
Hampshire County Council

*3m NE of Romsey, 9m SW of Winchester, ¼m W of A31 along Jermyns Lane.
Signposted from A31 and A3057* ● *Open all year Mon – Fri, 10.00 a.m. –
5.00 p.m., weekends and Bank Holidays (March - 2nd Sun in Nov) 1.00 – 6.00
p.m.; Brentry Woodland open late spring only* ● *Entrance: £1.50, OAP £1.20,
children under 15, 50p at weekends and Bank Holidays, free on weekdays. Season
tickets £7.50. For parties exceeding 30 adults, £1.20 per head* ● *Parking*
● *Toilet facilities* ● *Suitable for wheelchairs* ● *Dogs in car parks only* ● *Plants
for sale at Hilliers Nursery/Garden Centre* ● ***Grade I***

Administered by Hampshire County Council since 1977 this enormous
collection of trees and shrubs was begun by the late Sir Harold Hillier using
his house and garden as a starting point in 1953. Extends to 160 acres and
includes approximately 14,000 different species and cultivars, with many
rarities. With a total of 36,000 plants it is impossible not to be impressed or
to learn something about how, what and where to plant. Seasonal interest
maps and labelling will lead the visitor to herbaceous, scree, heather and bog
gardens. Amongst the trees and shrubs *Eucalyptus nitens* and *niphophila*,
Magnolia cylindrica and the acers are worthy of note. Much more than an
arboretum this attractively laid-out garden can be enjoyed at many levels and
can only increase in interest as the immense collection of young trees gains in
maturity. Keen gardeners should partake little and often and always be armed
with a notebook.

HINTON AMPNER   15
Hinton Ampner, Bramdean, Nr Winchester, Hampshire.
Tel: (096279) 361
The National Trust

1m W of Bramdean village, 8m E of Winchester on A272 ● *Open April – Sept,
Sat – Wed and Good Friday, 1.30 – 5.30 p.m. Last admission 5.00 p.m.*
● *Entrance: £1.50. Parties must book* ● *Parking. Special entrance for coaches
through village* ● *Homemade teas* ● *Toilet facilities* ● *Partly suitable for
wheelchairs* ● *Dogs in car park only* ● *House open Tues and Wed, 1.30 – 5.30
p.m. Last admission 5.00 p.m. Also Sat and Sun in Aug. £1.00 extra*
● *Grade II*

Located on the shoulder of a ridge, the ascent to the house through almost
routine parkland in no way prepares the visitor for the view to the south of
classic English downland scenery over a series of descending terraces laid out

in the Hidcote style. From his inheritance of the estate in 1935 onwards Ralph Dutton, later Lord Sherborne, set about transforming the remnants of a Victorian/Edwardian park into a series of gardens on different levels linked by the 'Long Walk' and the 'main terrace'. The skill with which features such as the temple, obelisk and statue of Diana are sited and with which many surprise vistas were created is testimony to Lord Sherborne's knowledge of garden history. Although areas of the garden are in the process of restoration and some large shrubs need to be rescued, both from rampant climbers, Russian vine and Kiftsgate roses and undisciplined pruning, the masterly design of this garden and the elegance of its topiary, yew and box hedges deserve wide recognition.

HOLLINGTON HERB GARDEN 16
Wootton Hill, Nr Newbury, Hampshire. Tel: (0635) 263908
Mr and Mrs S.G. Hopkinson

4m S of Newbury off A343. Follow signs to Herb Garden ● *Open March – Sept, daily, 10.00 a.m. – 5.30 p.m., Oct – Feb, Mon – Fri, 10.00 a.m. – 5.00 p.m., Sun and Bank Holidays, 11.00 a.m. - 5.00 p.m.* ● *Best season: summer* ● *Entrance: free. Collecting box on NGS days* ● *Parking* ● *Refreshments* ● *Toilet facilities* ● *Suitable for wheelchairs* ● *Plants for sale* ● *Shop* ● *Grade IV*

Interestingly laid out, this small garden modestly but successfully combines the function of a sales pitch for its specimen plants with the art of garden design. Set within an old walled garden a small fountain, knot garden and rampant hop climbing over gnarled espalier provide the visual treats, but it is the pot-pourri of aromas that distinguishes this garden and nursery. It could be combined with a visit to Highclere Castle nearby (see entry).

HOUGHTON LODGE 17
Stockbridge, Hampshire. Tel: (0264) 810646
Captain and Mrs M. Busk

6m S of Andover, 1½m S of Stockbridge on minor road signposted Houghton ● *Open March – Aug, Wed – Thurs, 2.00 – 5.00 p.m., Easter, May and Spring Bank Holiday Mon and Sun preceeding, 2.00 – 6.00 p.m.* ● *Best season: spring* ● *Entrance: £1.00, children 50p* ● *Parking* ● *Refreshments on Sun and Mon only. Picnic area* ● *Suitable for wheelchairs* ● *Dogs on lead* ● *Plants for sale* ● *House open by appointment only* ● *Grade II*

Built shortly before 1801 Houghton Lodge is probably among the most 'picturesque' of Gothic cottage ornés both in its architectural fantasy and its perfect garden setting alongside the River Test. Marie Antoinette would certainly have approved of this idyll. A succession of snowdrops and massed daffodils beneath fine parkland specimens of plane, oaks and horse chestnuts clothe the ridge beyond the lawns from where a unique rustic flint grotto can be reached; in autumn the colours of Indian gums and maples can be observed reflected in the river. A well-maintained walled garden with espalier fruit trees and glasshouses stocked with vines seems to be able to pass without comment in a garden such as this but needless to say it is quite as excellent as the rest.

JENKYN PLACE   18
Bentley, Nr Alton, Hampshire.   Tel: (0420) 23118
Mr and Mrs G.E. Coke

4m SW of Farnham on A31, signposted 400 yards N of Bentley crossroads
● Open mid-April – mid-Sept, Thurs – Sun and Bank Holiday Mons, 2.00 –
6.00 p.m.   ● Entrance: £1.50, children 75p   ● Parking   ● Toilet facilities
● Suitable for wheelchairs   ● Plants for sale   ● Grade II

Since their arrival just after World War II Mr and Mrs Coke have created a remarkable garden that is somewhat reminiscent of Hidcote, both in spirit and structure. Falling steadily to the south-east the high ground of this garden is dominated by a series of formal rooms arranged on terraces of which the sundial garden, an elegant rose garden (note the *Caesalpinia japonica* and loquat shrub), and a scented Dutch garden are the pick. A classically-perfect double herbaceous border backed by high hedges ends the sequence of walled and hedged enclosures and leads by way of cross axis to a succession of less intensively and informally planted areas which do tend to be less successful in design. A long sloping lawn returns to the house revealing the handsome seventeenth-century facade and a superb Cedar of Lebanon planted in 1828. This is a garden to be visited more than once.

LONGSTOCK PARK GARDENS   19
Longstock, Nr Stockbridge, Hampshire.   Tel: (0264) 810894
John Lewis Partnership (Leckford Estates Ltd)

2m N of Stockbridge. From A30 turn N on A3057. Signposted   ● Open
occasionally for charities. April – Sept on 3rd Sun in each month, 2.00 – 4.30
p.m.   ● Entrance: £1.00, children 50p   ● Parking   ● Refreshments at
Leckford   ● Toilet facilities   ● Suitable for wheelchairs   ● Plants for sale
● Grade II

The huge leaves of gunnera, the stilts (pneumatophores) of *Taxodium distichum*, varied nymphaeas and a giant white lily *Cardiocrinum giganteum* are just a few of the many interesting features and unusual plants to be found in this most immaculate and loveliest of water gardens. Developed between 1946 and 1953 the garden is fed by the River Test and is located some way from the house. Approached with an air of increasing expectation between a high hedge and old oak trees the garden reveals itself all at once as a veritable archipelago connected by narrow bridges and causeways beneath which clear waters and golden carp slowly move. The background is formed by woodland trees into which a variety of acid-loving trees and shrubs and wild flowers have been introduced as a contrast to the sometimes over-disciplined planting of this successful garden.

THE MANOR HOUSE 20
Upton Grey, Nr Basingstoke, Hampshire. Tel: (0256) 862827
Mr and Mrs J. Wallinger

6m SE of Basingstoke in Upton Grey village on hill immediately behind church
• *Open by appointment and 27th May, 3rd June and 1st July, 2.00 – 5.00 p.m.*
• *Best season: May – Aug* • *Entrance: £1.00, children under 10 free*
• *Parking. Coaches by appointment only* • *Suitable for wheelchairs* • *Dogs on lead* • *Grade IV*

Here are formal gardens and terraces with excellent herbaceous borders and dry-stone walling. They have been meticulously restored by the present owners over the past four years to the original plans prepared by Gertrude Jekyll in 1908 – 1910 and this garden illustrates many of the designer's favourite herbaceous planting combinations. The yew hedging in the formal garden is far from maturity and consequently deprives the scene of much needed structure but the colour and shape are clearly evident. To the south-west is an informal wild garden and pool. The house was designed by Ernest Newton for Charles Holmes, editor of *The Studio* magazine.

MERDON MANOR 21
Hursley, Nr Winchester, Hampshire. Tel: (0962) 75215
Mr and Mrs J.C. Smith

4m SW of Winchester. From the A3090 Winchester – Romsey road at Standon turn onto Slackstead Road and continue for 2m • *Open by appointment and 27th May, 2.00 – 6.00 p.m.* • *Entrance: 80p, children 20p* • *Parking* • *Refreshments on NGS days* • *Plants for sale* • *Grade III*

It is difficult to imagine a more surprising feature for this or any other garden than the enclosed pool garden that is revealed only by opening a heavy door in a barn wall. The sheltered microclimate protects many tender plants grown in raised troughs and a myriad of pots and urns surround two formal pools. The whole effect is quite extravagant and a marvellous foil to the sophistication of the rest of the garden, which has been created by the present owners over the last 30 years. There is a large area of parkland.

MORTON MANOR 22
Brading, Sandown, Isle of Wight. Tel: (0983) 406168
J.B., J. and J.A. Trzebski

3m from Ryde on A3055, turn right at Brading traffic lights, signposted 100 yards up hill • *Open 1st Sun in April – Oct, daily except Sat, 10.00 a.m. – 5.30 p.m.* • *Best season: April – June* • *Entrance: £1.75, OAP £1.50,*

children 80p (house and garden) • *Parking* • *Refreshments: morning coffee,
lunch, cream teas. Fully licensed* • *Toilet facilities* • *Suitable for wheelchairs*
• *Dogs on lead* • *Home-grown plants and vines for sale* • *Shop* • *House open*
• *Grade III*

The history of Morton dates back to the thirteenth century. The Elizabethan
sunken garden is surrounded by a 400 year old box hedge and old-fashioned
roses and shaded by a magnificent *Magnolia grandiflora*. The terraces are
nineteenth-century with extensive herbaceous borders and a huge London
plane. Masses of spring bulbs are followed by rhododendrons and traditional
herbaceous displays. Among the wide range of fine trees is an Indian Bean
(*Catalpa bignonioides*). Little remains of the old walled garden but in the
corner behind the herbs are the restored bee boles; also a turf maze has been
made for children and there is a vineyard.

MOTTISFONT ABBEY 23
Mottisfont, Nr Romsey, Hampshire. Tel: (0794) 40757
The National Trust

4½m NW of Romsey, ¾m W of A3057 • *Open April – Sept, daily except Fri
and Sat, 2.00 - 6.00 p.m., last admission 5.00 p.m. Evening opening of rose
garden Tues, Wed, Thurs and Sun, 7.00 - 9.00 p.m. during rose season only.
Last admission 8.30 p.m.* • *Best season: midsummer* • *Entrance: April/May
£1.50, Aug/Sept £1.00, children half price* • *Parking* • *Refreshments at local
post office* • *Toilet facilities* • *Suitable for wheelchairs* • *Shop* • *House open
Wed afternoons only but numbers restricted* • *Grade I*

Established in only 1972, the walled rose garden designed by Mr Graham
Stuart Thomas is already famous and deservedly so. Between the gravel paths,
meeting at a small pool and fountain, is assembled one of the most
comprehensive collections of old French roses of the nineteenth century, seen
and smelt at its best in midsummer when the scent is trapped within its walls.
Broad herbaceous borders containing pinks, aubretias, saponaria and much
else ensure that from very early in the season there is always something to
enjoy. It is to be hoped that the visitor will not miss, if it is possible to miss,
the enormous London plane trees, *Platanus* x *hybrida (acerfolia)* (the largest in
the country) that occupy parkland sweeping down to the River Test. Pockets
of formal gardens can be found around the house created by such accomplished designers as Geoffrey Jellicoe (the pleached lime walk underplanted
with *Chionodoxa luciliae*) and Norah Lindsay.

MOTTISTONE MANOR 24
Mottistone, Newport, Isle of Wight. Tel: (0983) 740946
The National Trust

SW of Newport on B3399 between Brighstone and Brook • *Open 4th April –
26th Sept, Wed only and Bank Holiday Mon, 2.00 - 5.30 p.m. Last admission*

5.00 p.m. ● *Best season: May/June* ● *Entrance: 70p, children 35p* ● *Parking on village green when garden open* ● *House open 27th Aug only* ● *Grade III*

A terraced garden, best seen in spring for a glorious display of irises, laid out to gain maximum effect from the views over the Needles, Channel and south-west coast of the island. Not so much a plantsman's garden as an impressive frame for the Manor.

MOUNDSMERE MANOR 25
Preston Candover, Nr Basingstoke, Hampshire. Tel: (025687) 207
Mr and Mrs Andreae

6m S of Basingstoke on B3046. Drive gates on left just after Preston Candover sign ● *Open 8th July, 2.00 – 6.00 p.m.* ● *Entrance: £1.00, children 50p* ● *Parking. Coaches by appointment* ● *Suitable for wheelchairs* ● *Dogs on lead* ● *Grade III*

Inspired by Hampton Court and designed in 1908, the pleasing relationship of house to garden to landscape marks Moundsmere Manor as one of Sir Reginald Blomfield's (1856-1942) best surviving gardens. To the south of the 'Wrenaissance' house the principal formal garden descends in terraces framed by clipped yews with deep herbaceous borders. This is Edwardian gardening on a grand scale, characteristically architectural and will not disappoint students of Blomfield's *The Formal Garden in England* in which he attacked the informal style of gardening supported by William Robinson. For Blomfield, gardens were primarily works of art. Other examples of his work are found at Godington Park (see page 191) and Athelhampton (see page 104). There is a pinetum to the north.

MOUNTBATTEN HOUSE 26
(formerly Gateway House)
Basing View, PO Box 117, Basingstoke, Hampshire.
Tel: (0256) 56144
IBM plc

In central Basingstoke, just off A339, adjacent to AA HQ ● *Open by written application only to Mr K. Reed but excellent views can be gained from the nearby park* ● *Parking by prior arrangement* ● *Grade IV*

Designed by Arup Associates and James Russell in 1976 for Wiggins Teape, this is one of the foremost roof gardens in Britain and illustrates what can be achieved when landscape design is given proper consideration at the design stage of a modern building. Essentially a ziggurat-building, access to six levels can be gained directly from the offices to terraces which by their luxuriance of planting, cascading foliage and climbing wisteria belie the fact that you are all the time standing on the roof of an office or car park. Romantic combination of building and planting.

THE NEW FOREST BUTTERFLY FARM 27
Longdown, Ashurst, Nr Southampton, Hampshire.
Tel: (042129) 2166/3367
New Forest Butterfly Farm Ltd

From M27 take M271 to Redbridge then A35 to Lyndhurst. Left to Longdown.
Farm signposted ● *Open 7th April – 28th Oct, 10.00 a.m. – 5.00 p.m.*
● *Entrance: £2.95, OAP £2.75, children 5 – 16 £1.95* ● *Parking*
● *Refreshments* ● *Toilet facilities* ● *Suitable for wheelchairs* ● *Dogs on lead,*
but not allowed in glasshouses ● *Plants for sale* ● *Shop* ● *Grade IV*

This covered tropical garden with free-flying butterflies and dragonfly pond
is perhaps one of the more unusual gardens of Hampshire. Certainly it has
been designed and has evolved as the most exotic. After the vivid colours of the
glasshouses, the 'cottage garden' filled with more recognizable blooms and
the woodland glades seem pale but will prove no less interesting for the
naturalist and plantsman alike.

NINGWOOD MANOR 28
Ningwood, Newport, Isle of Wight.   Tel: (0983) 407240
Lt. Col. and Mrs K.J. Shapland

3m E of Yarmouth. Take A3054 Newport – Yarmouth road, at Horse and
Groom 1m W of Shalfleet turn left and continue ½m ● *Open 24th June, 2.00 –*
5.00 p.m. ● *Entrance: 75p, children free* ● *Parking* ● *Suitable for*
wheelchairs ● *Plants for sale* ● *Grade III*

This is a two-acre formal garden of a seventeenth-century manor house. The
lawn is surrounded by trees, shrubs and herbaceous plants including the
yellow garden round the sundial. The rose garden is a recent addition laid out
in the Victorian style and leads to the white garden which Mrs Shapland has
made from the old kitchen garden.

NORTHCOURT 29
Shorwell, Newport, Isle of Wight.   Tel: (0983) 740415
Mr and Mrs J. Harrison

4m S of Newport on B3323. Entrance on right after rustic bridge, opposite
thatched cottage ● *Open 13th May, 23rd June and 24th June* ● *Best season:*
May/June ● *Entrance: approx. £1.00 (varies according to charity)*
● *Parking* ● *Refreshments* ● *Partly suitable for wheelchairs* ● *Dogs on lead*
(under sufferance) ● *Plants for sale* ● *Grade II*

Twelve acres of wooded grounds surround a Jacobean manor house. There are
three varied gardens (divided between members of the Harrison family)
consisting of landscaped terraces leading down to the stream and water
gardens; herbaceous borders, woodland walks, walled rose garden and walled
kitchen garden containing over 50 varieties of apples. The more interesting

plants include *Echium pininana* (biennial from the Canaries) on the top terrace by the pond; eucryphias; and the dainty little daisy *Erigeron mucronatus* in the rose garden that may have been inspired by Gertrude Jekyll. Northcourt offers bed and breakfast accomodation and could be the ideal spot for a gardener's tour of the Isle of Wight.

NUNWELL HOUSE   30
Coach Lane, Brading, Ryde, Isle of Wight.   Tel: (0983) 407240
Col. and Mrs J.A. Aylmer

3m S of Ryde, signed off the A3055 in Brading into Coach Lane   ● Open July – 27th Sept, daily except Fri and Sat, 10.00 a.m. – 5.00 p.m.   ● Best season: June and September   ● Entrance: £1.80, children 60p (house and garden)   ● Parking   ● Toilet facilities   ● Shop   ● House open   ● Grade III

Nunwell House stands in six acres of gardens with wonderful views across the park to Spithead. The rose garden (originally a bowling green in the seventeenth century) is set at the top of a slope, in front of the walled garden (not open), which leads down the Long Walk past the side of the house, where stand two very handsome paulownias, to the front. The fountain came from the Crystal Palace and below the balustrade is a lily pond, formerly a swimming pool. Among the varied plants in the borders there is the pretty mallow 'Barnsley' and on the front of the house are two large myrtles. A steep flight of steps bordered by lavender leads up to the woods. To the rear of the house is an arboretum laid out by Russel Vernon Smith in 1963. The Aylmers are gradually restoring the gardens to their former glory.

OWL COTTAGE   31
Hoxall Lane, Mottistone, Newport, Isle of Wight.
Tel: (0983) 740433
Mrs A.L. Hutchinson, Miss S.L. Leaning

From B3399 turn down Hoxall Lane by Mottistone green. Owl Cottage is 200 yards on right   ● Open May – Sept, 2.00 – 6.00 p.m., by appointment for parties of 10   ● Best season: late June/early July   ● Entrance: £1.00   ● Refreshments: homemade teas by appointment   ● Toilet facilities   ● Suitable for wheelchairs   ● Dogs   ● Grade II

A brilliant cottage garden with sea views (the thatched cottage is sixteenth-century), planted to give year round colour. There are 26 flowering cherries and over 50 varieties of clematis, including the *balearica* flowering from January to October and the *armandii*. In addition to a large herbaceous section there are colourful bulbs and flowering shrubs, euphorbias, amaryllis lilies, agapanthus and delphiniums. This lovely garden is the creation of the present owners.

QUEEN ELEANOR'S GARDEN   32
Great Hall, Winchester, Hampshire. Tel: (0962) 841841
Hampshire County Council (sponsored by Hampshire Gardens Trust)

*Through the Great Hall, central Winchester ● Open Mar – Oct, daily inc.
Bank Holidays, 10.00 a.m. – 5.00 p.m., Nov – Feb, Sat and Sun, 10.00 a.m. –
4.00 p.m. ● Entrance: free ● Suitable for wheelchairs ● Shop ● Grade IV*

Faced with a wedge of land 90 x 30 feet and bounded by buildings, the
designer, Dr Sylvia Landsberg, has achieved the only authentic recreation of
its type in Britain of a thirteenth-century medieval pleasure garden. When
viewed against the neighbouring wall of the Great Hall the maturing Queen's
herber, tunnel arbour and the detailed research behind the rill and fountain
make it just possible to forget that this is a garden of so recent creation.

SPINNERS   33
School Lane, Boldre, Nr Lymington, Hampshire.
Tel: (0590) 73347
Mr and Mrs P.G.G. Chappell

*1½m N of Lymington. From A337 Brockenhurst – Lymington road, turn E for
Boldre. RAC signposted through village ● Open April - Aug, daily, 10.00 a.m.
– 6.00 p.m. Other times by appointment ● Entrance: 75p ● Parking
● Suitable for wheelchairs ● Plants for sale ● Grade II*

Created and developed by the Chappells on a wooded slope falling westwards
towards the Lymington river it is not difficult to understand why Roy
Lancaster and many other plantsmen have so highly praised this garden. The
spirit of the nearby New Forest has been carefully maintained and shade and
acid-loving plants flourish beneath a canopy of indigenous and specimen
shrubs and trees. *Cornus kousa chinensis*, a grove of eucalyptus and unusual
magnolias catch the eye amongst many other specimens that are improved by
good plant associations. Cyclamen, erythroniums, trillium and hellebores in
spring; lush hostas, primulas, ferns and rodgersias in the bog garden;
magnolias in summer and the autumn colours of *Nyssa sinensis* and many
maples ensure that wherever the meandering paths lead in this excellent
informal garden there is always something of interest and apparently
something of everything.

STANSTEAD PARK   34
Rowlands Castle, Hampshire. Tel: (0705) 412265
The Earl and Countess of Bessborough

*1m N of Emsworth, just off the B2149 ● Open end March – Sept, Sun – Tues,
2.00 – 5.30 p.m. ● Best season: early summer ● Entrance: £2.00, OAP £1.40,
children 80p ● Parking ● Refreshments ● Toilet facilities ● Plants for sale
● Shop ● House open ● Grade III*

A woodland walk with fine spring bulbs encloses walled gardens with good greenhouses with muscat vines and other organically-grown produce. There is an elegant Dutch-style rose garden, which is set off beautifully by the mellow red brick eighteenth-century house, and a fine arboretum which is quickly recovering from the gale damage of 1987. There is also a prettily set cricket ground with cricket every Sunday, taking place in view of the tea room.

THE TUDOR HOUSE MUSEUM 35
Tudor House, Bugle Street, Southampton, Hampshire.
Tel: (0703) 332513
Southampton City Council

A36 to West Quay Road or Western Esplanade or A33, follow signs to Docks and Town Quay • *Open daily except Mon; Tues – Fri, 10.00 a.m. – 5.00 p.m., Sat, 10.00 a.m. – 4.00 p.m., Sun, 2.00 – 5.00 p.m.* • *Entrance: free* • *Parking by public swimming pool* • *Toilet facilities* • *Suitable for wheelchairs* • *Shop* • *Museum open* • *Grade III*

This must be many people's favourite museum, not particularly for its collection although it is good, but for its timber-framed building and garden setting. Designed by Dr Sylvia Landsberg and completed in 1982 the garden is a convincing distillation of ornamental gardens of the Tudor period. Packed with authentic details such as heraldic beasts, a camomile lawn, a knot garden and many old English flowers and sixteenth-century roses, this is a surprisingly peaceful place.

VENTNOR BOTANIC GARDEN 36
The Undercliffe Drive, Ventnor, Isle of Wight.
Tel: (0983) 855397
South Wight Borough Council

Follow signs from A3055 • *Open all year* • *Entrance: free (35p for Temperate House)* • *Paying car park* • *Refreshments: restaurant/café, licensed bar* • *Toilet facilities* • *Suitable for wheelchairs* • *Dogs* • *Limited plants for sale* • *Shop* • *Temperate House open daily* • *Grade I*

Twenty-two acres, sheltered from north and east and planted with *Quercus ilex*, *Pinus nigra* and cypresses interspersed with escallonia, griselinia and viburnums to give shelter from sea winds to the south. Many tender plants (including olives; *Berberis asiatica* and *Acer sikkimensis* from the Himalayas; *Cestrum elegans* from Mexico; *Pittosporum daphniphylloides* from China all of which flourish in the mild climate). The rose garden has over 700 hybrid teas and floribundas also modern shrub, Banksian, climbing, rambler, rugosa, etc. The pinetum has many exotic species from the Canary Islands, New Zealand and China and in the palm garden banana plants from Japan and *Citrus ichangensis* are but a few of the rare plants displayed to maximum effect in surroundings designed by Geoffrey Hillier. There is also a magnificent temperate house with a worldwide collection of plants from the warmest zones of the world, together with impressive written and pictorial displays. There is an Australian section, a central bed of flowers from southern Africa, an island section with palms from Crete and a unique collection from St Helena.

THE VYNE   37
Sherborne St John, Nr Basingstoke, Hampshire.
Tel: (0256) 881337
The National Trust

4m N of Basingstoke between Sherborne St John and Bramley on A340, turn E at NT signs • *Open April – 21st Oct, daily except Mon and Fri, 12.30 – 5.30 p.m. Open Good Friday. Bank Holiday Mon, 11.00 a.m. – 5.30 p.m., closed Tues following* • *Entrance: £2.60 (£3.00 on Sun and Bank Holiday Mon); Garden only £1.30, (£1.50 on Sun and Bank Holidays)* • *Parking* • *Refreshments: light lunches, homemade teas, 12.30 – 5.00 p.m.* • *Toilet facilities* • *Suitable for wheelchairs* • *Shop* • *House open* • **Grade III**

This example of the English School was landscaped by John Chute between 1755 and 1776 to complement the early classical portico and garden houses designed by John Webb, disciple of Inigo Jones. Though not as grand or extensive as many country houses in the ownership of The National Trust this early sixteenth-century house provides to the west of its modest entrance one of the best, though small, herbaceous borders of such properties and to the north broad lawns and fine trees that perfectly match the famous Corinthian portico. The framed views to the house from across the lake will amply reward those who venture the woodland walk. Other features include stone seats in architectural yews, great oaks, the Garden House lake and *Phillyrea latifolia* specimens.

WEST GREEN HOUSE   38
Hartley Wintney, Basingstoke, Hampshire.   Tel: 01 837 3377
The National Trust (Lord McAlpine)

7m SW of Camberley on A30, turn W at Hartley Wintney for 1m • *Open April – Sept, Wed, Thurs and Sun, 2.00 – 6.00 p.m.* • *Entrance: £1.30* • *Parking* • *Partly suitable for wheelchairs* • *House open on Wed, 2.00 – 6.00 p.m. by written appointment only (minimum notice 7 days) to Lord McAlpine of West Green, 40 Bernard St, London WC1N 1LG* • **Grade IV**

The surrounds to this notable eighteenth-century house offer studies in three distinct aspects of garden design each contained within a walled or hedged enclosure – Formality, Jardin Potager and Wilderness. Formality is given reign immediately around the house so that a terrace lawn with its yew allée, connecting orangery and 'monkey' house, extends from the famous West front and a parterre with its box balls and spirals lies to the south. The secret garden atmosphere of the walled kitchen garden is lightened by some of the best romantic planting combinations, the rambling musk roses through and in old apple trees and the glimpsed views of a Greek urn. Lavender, peonies and phlox seem to mingle with rhubarb and currant bushes in this classic *jardin potager*. Through the Moon gate, to the west, are the Wilderness garden and the Nymphaeum designed by Quinlan Terry, the classical revivalist architect, and to the south the lake and parkland. Lord McAlpine, the tenant, had he lived in the eighteenth century might have been described as an eccentric and examples of his individual taste, such as in sculpture, are frequently apparent.

YAFFLES 39
Bonchurch, Ventnor, Isle of Wight. Tel: (0983) 852193
Mrs Wolfenden

Immediately above St Boniface Church in Bonchurch ● *Open 6th May, 10th June, 2.30 – 5.00 p.m.* ● *Best season: April/May* ● *Entrance: probably £1.00, children free* ● *Parking difficult* ● *Refreshments: home-made teas* ● *Dogs on lead* ● *Plants for sale* ● *Shop* ● ***Grade III***

A quarter of an acre of sheltered cliff garden with spectacular sea views, sculpted by Mrs Wolfenden from a precipice overgrown with weeds and scrub. Years of very hard work have made this garden of ledges and glades, with a variety of flowering shrubs, spring bulbs and plants of botanical interest. Taking advantage of the mild climate of the island's undercliff the owner has succeeded in creating a sheet of colour all the year round.

HOW TO FIND THE GARDENS

Directions to each garden are included in each entry. This information has been supplied by the garden inspectors and is aimed to be the best available to those travelling by car. However, it has been compiled to be used in conjunction with a road atlas.

The unreliability of train and bus services makes it unrewarding to include details, particularly as many garden visits are made on Sundays. However, many properties can be reached by public transport and National Trust guides and the Yellow Book [NGS] give details. Future editions of the *Guide* may include a special list of gardens easily reached by public transport if readers indicate that this would be helpful.

The Maps: The numbers on the maps correspond to the numbers of the gardens in each county. The maps show the proximity of one garden to another so that visits to several gardens can be planned for the same day. It is worthwhile referring to the maps of bordering counties to see if another garden visit can be included in your itinerary. The maps should be used in conjunction with a road atlas.

HEREFORD & WORCESTER

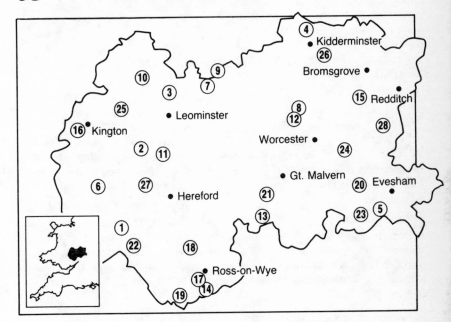

ABBEY DORE COURT   1
Pontrilas, Hereford, Hereford & Worcester. Tel: (0981) 240419
Mrs C.L. Ward

*11m SW of Hereford ●Open mid-March – mid-Oct, daily except Wed, 11.00
a.m. - 6.00 p.m. ●Entrance: £1.00, children 50p ●Parking
●Refreshments: tearoom ●Toilet facilities ●Partly suitable for wheelchairs
●Plants for sale ●Shop ●Grade III*

An interesting collection of plants in a garden created by the present owners
and their family 20 years ago. Formal/informal water and woodland
situations. Unusual plants for sale.

ARROW COTTAGE GARDEN   2
Ledgemoor, Weobley, Hereford & Worcester. Tel: (0544) 318468
Mr and Mrs L. Hattatt

*10m NW of Hereford ●Open May – Aug, Sun, 2.00 - 6.00 p.m. At other
times by appointment ●Best season: June ●Entrance: £1.00, children free
●Parking on roadside ●Grade IV*

Designed as a series of small gardens by the present owner and his family since 1972. Some of the more mature areas have lost form and scale and would benefit from replanting, and the new areas need time to mature. However the one and a half acres contain some interesting flowers, trees and shrubs and everything is well-maintained.

BERRINGTON HALL   3
Leominster, Hereford & Worcester.   Tel: (0568) 5721
The National Trust

3m N of Leominster on W side of A49 ● *Open April, Sat, Sun and Easter Mon, 1.30 – 5.30 p.m. May – Sept, Wed – Sun and Bank Holiday Mon, 1.30 – 5.30 p.m. Oct, Sat and Sun, 1.30 – 4.30 p.m. Grounds open from 12.30 p.m.* ● *Entrance: £1.50 (grounds only)* ● *Parking* ● *Refreshments: lunches and teas (opening 12.30 p.m.) Picnic tables in car park* ● *Toilet facilities* ● *Suitable for wheelchairs* ● *National Trust shop* ● *House open but last admission ½ hour before closing* ● ***Grade III***

This late eighteenth-century house designed by Henry Holland is set in mature grounds landscaped by 'Capability' Brown. The gardens have seen better times but are well-maintained. The new woodland area needs time to mature and a new orchard planting scheme has been undertaken in the walled garden. There is a joint entry ticket with Croft Castle (see page 170) nearby and the two gardens have enough of interest to fill a day.

BODENHAM ARBORETUM   4
Bodenham, Wolverley, Nr Kidderminster, Hereford & Worcester.
Tel: (0562) 850382
Mr and Mrs J.D. Binnian

2m N of Wolverley at roundabout take Bridgnorth Road. In ½m turn right into Sladd Lane and follow signs to Kingsford, then left and go up 'no through road' ● *Open 3rd June, 2.00 – 6.00 p.m. and by appointment* ● *Entrance: £1.00, children free* ● *Parking. No coaches* ● *Teas* ● *Toilet facilities* ● ***Grade IV***

This 128-acre valley has been developed by the owners since 1973 into a landscaped arboretum and one needs to be a really keen tree and shrub enthusiast to obtain the full pleasure of this wonderful collection of over 1000 different varieties planted in beautiful countryside. Great thought has gone into the planting of different areas and the creation of many pools. A Poplar Dingle is underplanted with silver firs and flowering crabs and 10 incense cedars at the top to symbolise the Ten Commandments. There are great collections of acers, Spanish chestnuts, rowans, oaks and beech, and *Taxodium distichum* in the pools along with masses of bulrushes and willows. Wellingtonia and *Pinus aristata* will provide joy for generations to come. For the keen enthusiast there is accommodation for a group of six to stay. For the non expert it would be nice to have more labelling.

BREDON SPRINGS   5
Ashton-under-Hill, Evesham, Hereford & Worcester.
Tel: (0386) 881328
Mr R. Sidwell

6m SW of Evesham • *Open April – Oct, Sat, Sun, Wed, Thurs, also Bank Holiday Mons and following Tues, 10.00 a.m. – dusk* • *Best season: summer* • *Entrance: 50p, children free* • *Small free car park 300 yards from garden* • *Dogs* • *Grade III*

A plantsman's garden created by the owner over the last 40 years with a diverse collection of material, carefully arranged and planted in an old cottage garden. Areas of woodland have been added to increase the range of growing conditions.

BROBURY GARDENS AND GALLERY   6
Brobury, Hereford & Worcester.   Tel: (09817) 229
Mr E. Okarma

11m NW of Hereford • *Open June – Sept, Mon – Sat, 9.00 a.m. – 4.30 p.m.* • *Entrance: £1.00, children 50p* • *Parking* • *Toilet facilities* • *Art Gallery open* • *Grade IV*

Seven acres of mature garden developed in the 1930s and 1940s along the banks of the Wye. There are some fine old trees, particularly conifers. Shrubs and herbaceous borders, also rhododendrons. It is beautifully maintained, has fine views but not much to interest the plantsperson.

BURFORD HOUSE GARDENS   7
Tenbury Wells, Hereford & Worcester.   Tel: (0584) 810777
Mr J. Treasure

1m W of Tenbury Wells on A456 • *Open 17th March – 21st Oct, Mon – Sat, 11.00 a.m. – 5.00 p.m., Sun, 2.00 – 5.00 p.m.* • *Best season: summer* • *Entrance: £1.95, children 80p. Parties 25 and over £1.60 per person* • *Parking close to garden* • *Refreshments: tea room* • *Toilet facilities* • *Suitable for wheelchairs* • *Plants for sale in nursery open Mon – Sat, 9.00 a.m. – 5.00 p.m., Sun, 2.00 – 5.00 p.m.* • *Bookshop in tea room* • *Grade II*

The Georgian house dates from 1728 but the gardens today from only 1954 when the present owners took over. The garden and adjoining nursery is best known for its collection of clematis. However it is very diverse in its plants and plantings. Formal water gardens at the rear of the house give way to a variety of informal shrub and herbaceous borders. Good autumn colour is provided by the woodland planting. A garden that cannot fail to please throughout the growing season.

CLACKS FARM   8
Boreley, Ombersley, Hereford & Worcester.   Tel: (0905) 620250
Mr and Mrs A. Billitt

1m N of Ombersley on A449 • Open 12th, 13th May, 9th, 10th, 23rd, 24th June, 7th, 8th, 28th, 29th July, 11th, 12th Aug, 8th, 9th Sept • Entrance: 50p, children 25p • Teas • Toilet facilities • Suitable for wheelchairs • Dogs on lead • Plants for sale • Grade III

This garden was created by the Billitts with T.V. demonstrations in mind. There are eight glasshouses, a large fruit and vegetable garden. Ornamental and water gardens. It is very much a learning garden and planted to teach the amateur. It has been featured many times on *Gardener's World*.

THE COTTAGE HERBERY   9
Boraston, Tenbury Wells, Hereford & Worcester.
Tel: (0584) 79575
Mr and Mrs R.E. Hurst

1m W of Tenbury off A456 • Open end April – Sept, 10.00 a.m. - 6.00 p.m. • Best season: May – July • Entrance: 60p, children 20p • Limited parking • Teas at cottage • Toilet facilities • Partly suitable for wheelchairs • Plants for sale • Shop • Grade IV

A half-acre garden created by the owner since 1986 specialising in herbs and being extended annually. The extensive range of herbs is planted on a cottage-garden theme and includes beds of unusual hardy perennials and variegated plants. Nursery sells plants and horticultural products.

CROFT CASTLE   10
Leominster, Hereford & Worcester.   Tel: (056885) 246
The National Trust

5m NW of Leominster off B4362 • Open Easter Sat, Sun, Mon, 2.00 – 6.00 p.m., April and Oct, Sat, Sun, 2.00 – 5.00 p.m., May – Sept, Wed – Sun and Bank Holiday Mon, 2.00 – 6.00 p.m. Last admission ½ hour before closing • Entrance: £2.20 • Parking • Refreshments: light lunches and teas • Toilet facilities • Partly suitable for wheelchairs • Dogs in park only on lead • Plants for sale • House open • Grade III

This is a traditional estate garden with formal beds around the house which dates from the fourteenth century. It is well-kept and pleasant to walk through but lacks specific interest for the plantsperson except perhaps for the walled garden which is in good condition and the fine avenue of Spanish chestnuts. There are charming walks in the Fishpool valley.

DINMORE MANOR 11
Dinmore, Leominster, Hereford & Worcester.   Tel: (043271) 240
Mr R.G. Murray

*6m N of Hereford on A49. 1m driveway signposted ● Open daily 10.00 a.m. –
5.00 p.m. ● Best season: summer ● Entrance: £2.00, OAP £1.00,
accompanied children under 14 free ● Parking ● Toilet facilities ● Suitable
for wheelchairs ● Grade III*

The site was originally the twelfth/fourteenth-century church of the Knights
Hospitaller. An unusual garden centred around the small church, its
outstanding feature is the rock garden with some excellent specimens of *Acer
palmatum*. This part of the garden is bordered on two sides by cloisters which
adjoin the main house and contain the grotto. The house and garden are built
on high ground with surrounding stone wall and some outstanding views.

EASTGROVE COTTAGE GARDEN 12
Sankyns Green, Little Witley, Hereford & Worcester.
Tel: (0299) 896389
Mr and Mrs J. Malcolm Skinner

*8m NW of Worcester between Shrawley (B4196) and Great Witley (A443)
● Open April – Oct but closed Aug, daily except Tues and Wed, 2.00 – 5.00
p.m. ● Best season: June/July ● Entrance: 80p, children 20p ● Parking.
Coaches by appointment ● Toilet facilities ● Suitable for wheelchairs ● Plants
for sale ● Grade II*

This delightful cottage garden with a superb range of hardy plants has been
created and maintained by the present owners since 1970. The garden is full
of colour, spring to autumn. It has the benefit of being connected with a
commercial nursery developed by the owners and is highly recommended.

EASTNOR CASTLE 13
Eastnor, Ledbury, Hereford & Worcester.   Tel: (0531) 2304/5
Eastnor Estates

*2m E of Ledbury on A438 ● Open Easter – Aug, Mon, end May – Sept, Sun,
July – Aug, Wed and Thurs, 2.15 – 5.30 p.m. Parties by appointment at other
times ● Best season: spring ● Entrance: 50p (house and garden £1.50)
● Parking ● Refreshments on Castle open days ● Toilet facilities ● Dogs on
lead ● Shop ● Castle open selected days for collections of armour etc. Parties by
appointment any day ● Grade III*

Essentially an arboretum, Eastnor is one of the best nineteenth-century
plantings in the country with many mature specimens. It is worth visiting early
in the year for the display of spring bulbs. The house is an early nineteenth-
century castle in medieval style surrounded by a deer park and overlooking the
Malvern Hills.

GLEN WYE   14
Courtfield, Ross-on-Wye, Hereford & Worcester.

5m S of Ross-on-Wye, 2m from Goodrich along a no through road • *Open for NGS* • *Best season: summer* • *Entrance: £1.00, children 50p* • *Limited parking* • *Teas* • *Toilet facilities* • ***Grade III***

Formerly the dower house to Courtfield, where Henry V was brought up, this garden was created by the late Mrs J.H. Vaughan from 1955. An interesting Italianate style-garden, it lends itself well to the differing levels. Rockeries, herbaceous borders, a water garden, a herb garden, terrace walks, statuary and view points across the Wye Valley create great diversity within the main theme over two and a half acres.

HANBURY HALL   15
**Droitwich, Hereford & Worcester.   Tel: (052784) 214
The National Trust**

4½m E of Droitwich • *Open Easter Sat, Sun, Mon, 2.00 – 6.00 p.m. Easter Tues – Fri, 2.00 – 5.00 p.m., May – Sept, Wed – Sun and Bank Holiday Mon, 2.00 – 6.00 p.m.* • *Entrance: £2.20* • *Parking* • *Refreshments: tea room in house* • *Toilet facilities* • *Partly suitable for wheelchairs* • *Dogs on lead in park only* • *National Trust shop* • *House open* • ***Grade III***

This is a pleasant garden to visit with very good examples of an ice-house and eighteenth-century orangery. The overall design is formal but there is more of interest here for the visitor who will wish to see the Wren-type house with murals by Thornhill than for the garden connoisseur.

HERGEST CROFT GARDEN   16
**Kington, Hereford & Worcester.   Tel: (0544) 230160
W.L. Banks and R.A. Banks**

½m W of Kington off A44 • *Open end April – Oct, daily* • *Entrance: £1.30, children 60p, season ticket £4.00* • *Parking* • *Teas* • *Toilet facilities* • *Partly suitable for wheelchairs* • *Dogs on lead* • *Plants for sale* • *Shop* • ***Grade II***

This has been the family home of the Banks family since 1896, and the garden design was much influenced by the writings of William Robinson and Gertrude Jekyll. There is an interesting collection of plants including huge rhododendrons in delightful woodland setting which extends to 50 acres and has general appeal as well as to the plantsperson. Formal garden. Half a mile through the park is a wood containing the National collection of birches and maples.

HILL COURT 17
Hom Green, Ross-on-Wye, Hereford & Worcester.
Tel: (0989) 62413
Mr C. Rowley

2¾m SW of Ross-on-Wye. Take B4228 towards Walford, after ½m bear right and follow garden signs for 1½m to lodge gates on right ● *Walled garden open daily, and 6th May, 8th July, 26th Aug, 2.00 – 6.00 p.m.* ● *Best season: summer* ● *Entrance: £1.50, OAP and children 75p* ● *Parking* ● *Refreshments: tearoom open daily* ● *Toilet facilities* ● *Suitable for wheelchairs* ● *Dogs on lead* ● *Plants for sale at garden centre open daily* ● ***Grade II***

An eighteenth-century Grade I listed house (not open) with a well-preserved and well-maintained traditional estate garden, incorporating a well-stocked garden centre. The walled garden and yew walk are excellent examples of their type. Also original glasshouses. Herbaceous borders and woodland garden. Extensive private gardens, in which are incorporated a bronze and silver fountain garden, are open to the public only on NGS days.

HOW CAPLE COURT 18
How Caple, Ross-on-Wye, Hereford & Worcester.
Tel: (098986) 626
Mr and Mrs P. Lee

10m S of Hereford on B4224, turn right at How Caple crossroads ● *Open April – Oct, Mon – Sat, 9.00 a.m. – 4.30 p.m., also April – Sept, Sun, 10.00 a.m. – 5.00 p.m.* ● *Best season: summer* ● *Entrance: £1.50, children free* ● *Parking* ● *Refreshments on Sun and Bank Holidays. Parties by appointment* ● *Toilet facilities* ● *Partly suitable for wheelchairs* ● *Dogs* ● *Plants for sale* ● *Shop* ● ***Grade III***

House and garden overlook the River Wye. The steep ground lends itself to terracing, together with formal gardens and a valley of informal planting which includes a herbaceous border. When restored, the Florentine garden will add a new dimension.

THE JUBILEE MAZE 19
Wye Valley Visitor Centre, Whitchurch, Ross-on-Wye,
Hereford & Worcester. Tel: (0600) 890360
Mr L. Heyes and E. Heyes

Midway between Ross-on-Wye and Monmouth just off the A40 ● *Open Good Friday – Oct, daily, 11.00 a.m. – 5.30 p.m.* ● *Entrance: £1.00* ● *Parking* ● *Refreshments: restaurant* ● *Toilet facilities* ● *Suitable for wheelchairs* ● *Plants for sale at garden centre* ● *Shop* ● ***Grade IV***

A 'garden' for the maze enthusiast or for those who wish to be entertained. The maze, built to celebrate the Queen's Silver Jubilee in 1977, is explained to you by the owner before entry, and if you are shorter than his trousers you don't have to pay!

PERSHORE COLLEGE OF HORTICULTURE 20
Pershore, Hereford & Worcester. Tel: (0386) 552443
Hereford & Worcester County Council/Royal Horticultural Society

1m S of Pershore on A44. 7m from M5 junction 7 • Open all year for parties and every Thurs for retail plant sales, 2.00 – 4.30 p.m. and for NGS, dates N.A. • Best season: summer • Entrance: 50p • Parking • Toilet facilities • Suitable for wheelchairs • Dogs on lead • Plants for sale • Grade IV

The gardens are designed with a definite bias towards education so although not picturesque they are worth visiting. Extensive ornamental grounds include an arboretum, orchard, vegetables, automated glasshouses and a large commercial nursery. Pershore is now a satellite RHS centre.

THE PICTON GARDEN 21
Old Court Nurseries, Colwell, Malvern, Hereford & Worcester.
Tel: (0684) 40416
Mr and Mrs P. Picton

3m W of Malvern on B4218 • Open July – Oct, most Sats and Suns, 10.00 a.m. – 1.00 p.m., 2.15 – 5.30 p.m. • Best season: Sept/Oct • Entrance by collecting box • Limited parking • Suitable for wheelchairs • Plants for sale • Grade IV

This small garden has been created on the site of the Old Court Nurseries. It retains a nursery atmosphere (old frames now contain alpine beds) and plants for sale in neat rows. Herbaceous borders and shrubs create diversity. Holds the NCCPG Michaelmas daisy collection.

PONTRILAS COURT 22
Pontrilas, Hereford & Worcester. Tel: (0981) 240220
Mr and Mrs D.A. Keown-Boyd

11m S of Hereford on B4347 just off A465 • Open weekends by appointment and 11th/12th Aug • Entrance: £1.00 • Parking • Wonderful teas by arrangement • Suitable for wheelchairs • Plants for sale • Grade IV

Stretching away from this wisteria-clad seventeenth-century house are lawns backed by fine high trees, some of them planted by George Bentham, with a clear break southward to the Dawn of Day hill. Another stretch, punctuated by young crab apple trees, leads to the banks of the River Dore where there are riverside walks. Mrs Keown-Boyd apologises for the lack of rare specimen plants but is rightly proud of, for example, an immense Tulip Tree. She especially recommends April (for the daffodils) and September. The place is 'worst in June but always tidy'. Her husband's pride lies most in the walled vegetable garden, and keen eaters and growers will find some unusual kinds such as a Greek white bean called Elephant. Otherwise speciality hunters may have a thin time, but those seeking a place of quiet grace set in a sublimely pastoral landscape will be enchanted. Moreover, not far away is Kilpeck, perhaps the first Romanesque church in England: a jewel.

THE PRIORY 23
Kemerton, Tewkesbury, Hereford & Worcester.
Tel: (038689) 258
Mr and the Hon. Mrs Peter Healing

5m NE of Tewkesbury off B4080 ● *Open 20th May, 17th June, 8th July, 5th, 26th Aug, 9th Sept* ● *Parking* ● *Suitable for wheelchairs* ● *Dogs on lead* ● *Plants for sale at small nursery* ● *Grade III*

A garden of herbaceous borders, planted in colour groups with many unusual trees and shrubs. A stream garden, sunken garden and fern garden add diversity. There is also a small nursery. However it is the herbaceous borders that really make this garden. The careful choice of colours and textures often using tender plants make the borders unusual and outstanding.

SPETCHLEY PARK 24
Spetchley, Nr Worcester, Hereford & Worcester.
Tel: (090565) 224/213
Mr J. Berkeley

3m E of Worcester on A422 ● *Open April – Sept, daily except Sat, 11.00 a.m. – 5.00 p.m. Sun, 2.00 – 5.00 p.m., Bank Holidays 11.00 a.m. – 5.00 p.m.* ● *Entrance: £1.50, children 80p* ● *Parking* ● *Refreshments on Sun and Bank Holidays* ● *Toilet facilities* ● *Suitable for wheelchairs* ● *Plant centre* ● *Grade II*

Rose Berkeley was sister of the great Ellen Willmott and in her day the garden was one of the wonders of England. Now, this formal garden provides many vistas along borders and walls, through clipped yew hedges and open arches. Combined with the successive planning and planting it has a rich and abundant feel. The old kitchen garden is now surrounded by splendid borders. The fountain gardens, rose lawn and other planted areas are all worth careful study and there are pleasant walks to the lake and woods.

STAUNTON PARK 25
Staunton-on-Arrow, Leominster, Hereford & Worcester.
Tel: (05447) 474
Mr E.J.L. and Miss A. Savage

3m from Pembridge, 6m from Kington on the Titley road. Signposted ● *Open April – mid-Oct, Tues, Wed and Sun, 2.00 – 6.00 p.m.* ● *Best season: spring/*

summer • *Entrance: £1.00, children 50p* • *Parking inside garden* • *Teas*
• *Toilet facilities* • *Suitable for wheelchairs* • *Dogs on lead* • *Plants for sale*
• *Shop* • *Norman church adjoining open* • ***Grade III***

This 14-acre landscaped park contains many classical features and some
excellent specimen trees. There is a large lawn (covering the site of previous
manor house), lake, dovecote, ha-ha, ice-house, rockery with fountain and
clipped yews. Recent planting includes a herb garden, herbaceous borders and
a hosta collection. This garden has only been open to the public for one year
and is worth seeing for the classical architectural features.

STONE HOUSE COTTAGE GARDEN   26
Stone, Kidderminster, Hereford & Worcester.   Tel: (0562) 69902
Major and the Hon. Mrs Arbuthnott

2m SE of Kidderminster via A448 • *Open March – Nov, Wed – Sat, 10.00
a.m. – 6.00 p.m. Certain Sundays between April and Aug* • *Entrance: £1.00,
children free* • *Parking* • *Toilet facilities* • *Suitable for wheelchairs* • *Plants
for sale* • ***Grade III***

This sheltered walled garden is an absolute delight for plantsman and amateur
alike. Not only for the rare herbaceous plants, shrubs and climbers but for the
overall picture they create. There is also a nursery adjacent to the garden with
a large selection of plants for sale, emphasis being on the less hardy. One
evening a year the owners throw their garden open to picnicking parties and
invite an orchestra to play – a kind of Glyndebourne but at a much more
approachable price.

THE WEIR GARDEN   27
Swainshill, Hereford & Worcester.
The National Trust

5m W of Hereford on A438 • *Open 14th Feb – Oct, Wed – Sun and Bank
Holiday Mon, 11.00 a.m. – 6.00 p.m. Closed on Good Friday* • *Best season:
spring* • *Entrance: £1.00* • *Parking. No coaches* • ***Grade IV***

This garden offers a pleasant walk along the banks of the Wye and is at its best
in the spring. It is terraced in an informal way on a cliffside and would be
improved by extensive re-planting. Includes a small Japanese-style garden.

WHITE COTTAGE   28
Earls Common Road, Stock Green, Hereford & Worcester.
Tel: (0386) 792414
Mr and Mrs S.M. Bates

7m E of Worcester off A422 • *Open Easter to Oct. Daily in early months except
Thurs, 10.00 a.m. – 5.00 p.m. but by appointment only in Aug and Oct* • *Best*

season: May/June • *Entrance: 75p, children free* • *Limited parking* • *Teas at Jenny Ring Craft Centre, Hanbury (approx 6m)* • *Toilet facilities* • *Suitable for wheelchairs* • *Plants for sale* • ***Grade III***

A two-acre garden with large lawns and shrub and herbaceous borders created by the owner over the last 8 years. Artificial stream and soil type creates good conditions for primula collection. Extensive collection of hardy geraniums. Part of the garden has been set aside for a small nursery selling many of the plants featured in the garden.

THE GRADING SYSTEM

This is the most subjective aspect of the *Guide* and one which may cause some disagreement on the part of owners as well as visitors. We stress that its purpose is to serve as an indication to visitors in order to give them some advance information about the status of the garden as viewed by our inspectors and editors. Readers will appreciate that direct comparisons cannot be made between a huge estate like Chatsworth with its staff of professional experts and a tiny plantsman's garden in a terraced house, tended with dedication by a single owner. This being said, both may be excellent of their kind and therefore be worthy of consideration for a visit, and considered by the *Guide* to be at the top of their class. Conversely a lesser grading does not imply any criticism of a garden but is an attempt to guide the potential reader as to its relative merits if a choice has to be made between several gardens. Broadly speaking the intention of the four grades is as follows:

Grade I Amongst the best gardens in the world in terms of design and content. Many are of historic importance, but some are of recent origin. Overseas visitors to Britain or Ireland are recommended to include them in their itinerary.

Grade II Gardens of high quality, though not perhaps as unique as Grade I, and worth travelling a considerable distance to visit. Sometimes the property as a whole, and the general ambience, make the visit particularly rewarding.

Grade III These are gardens which our inspectors suggest it would be worth driving fifty miles or more to visit. They may have some special feature of design or plant content while not being considered as justifying a higher grade overall.

Grade IV Gardens of considerable merit and well worth visiting when in the region.

HERTFORDSHIRE

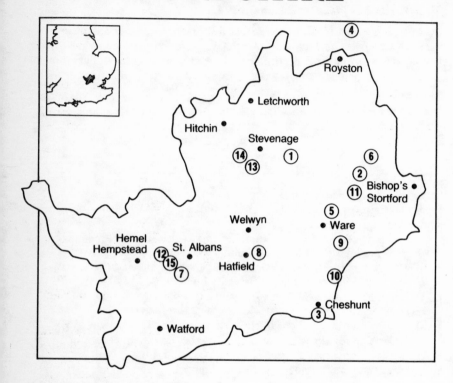

BENINGTON LORDSHIP

1

Benington, Nr Stevenage, Hertfordshire. Tel: (043885) 668
Mr and Mrs C.H.A. Bott

*5m E of Stevenage • Open Bank Holiday Mons, 12 noon – 5.00 p.m., Sun, 7th,
14th, and 21st May, June – 6th Aug, 2.00 – 5.00 p.m., Wed, May – Oct, 11.00
a.m. – 5.00 p.m., Sat, Sun, 24th and 25th June, 12 noon – 6 p.m. • Entrance:
£1.50, children free • Parking • Refreshments on Sun only • Toilet
facilities • Suitable for wheelchairs • Dogs on lead • Plants for sale
• Grade II*

Here is a garden that has almost everything: wonderful views, lakes to wander
round, a Victorian folly and a Norman keep and moat, as well as a colourful
rockery and big double herbaceous borders. Borders in the kitchen garden are
in the process of being made – one in shades of gold and silver, another full of
penstemons.

BROMLEY HALL   2
Standon, Ware, Hertfordshire.
Mr and Mrs A.J. Robarts

6m W of Bishop's Stortford near A120 and A10 on Standon – Much Hadham road ● *Open 3rd, 10th June, 2.30 – 5.30 p.m.* ● *Parking* ● *Suitable for wheelchairs* ● ***Grade III***

Mrs Robarts has created this garden entirely herself over the last 20 years. Improvements and alterations are going on all the time so there is always something new to see. It is both an architectural garden making good use of walls and hedges, statuary and seats, and also a plantsman's garden. Mr Robarts does the vegetable garden himself and it is immaculate.

CAPEL MANOR
(Horticultural and Environmental Centre)   3
Bullsmoor Lane, Waltham Cross, Hertfordshire.   Tel: (0992) 763849
London Borough of Enfield

From the M25 junction with the A10, it is AA signposted via Turkey Street/ Bullsmoor Lane ● *Open April – Sept, weekdays, 10.00 a.m. – 4.30 p.m., weekends, 10.00 a.m. – 5.30 p.m., Oct – March, weekdays, 10.00 a.m. – 4.30 p.m.* ● *Entrance: £1.25, OAP and children 60p* ● *Parking* ● *Teas* ● *Toilet facilities* ● *Suitable for wheelchairs* ● *Dogs on lead* ● ***Grade III***

For a teaching establishment this garden is a real eye-opener. It already had good bones and beautiful ancient trees. The clever use of plants and designs in an instructive and practical way include a garden for the partially-sighted. Extensive rock gardens and many other imaginative schemes are under way. Interesting ornamental features include a seventeenth-century type knot garden and a collection of medicinal plants.

DOCWRA'S MANOR   4
Shepreth, Nr Royston, Hertfordshire.   Tel: (0763) 60235/61473
Mrs John Raven

8m SW of Cambridge, ½m W of A10. Turn off road opposite war memorial ● *Open 15th March – 18th Oct, Sun, Mon, Wed and Fri, 10.00 a.m. – 5.00 p.m. Also by appointment* ● *Best season: May – July* ● *Entrance: £1.00, children free* ● *Parking in street* ● *Teas* ● *Toilet facilities* ● *Suitable for wheelchairs* ● *Plants for sale* ● ***Grade III***

This two and a half-acre garden round a Queen Anne house has been created by the owner since 1954. It is divided into different areas by using buildings, hedges and walls, thus enabling choice and tender plants to be protected from winds. Collections of euphorbias and clematis species. The garden has been encouraged to develop jungle-like and seedlings grow where they will unless they are near something too small. Many bulbs and unusual plants.

FANHAMS HALL 5
Ware, Hertfordshire. Tel: (0820) 60511
J Sainsbury plc

1m NE of Ware on road to Much Hadham ● *This garden was open when the inspector called but may be closed in 1990* ● **Grade II**

The gardens near the Hall are typically English in character, featuring a rose garden, a lily pond and a croquet lawn with shrub borders. Indeed, shrubs are the main beauty of this garden. There is a *Magnolia grandiflora* against the house and island beds of stellata magnolias. Also a wonderful wisteria pergola with tree peonies planted down the outside. The grounds abound with fine old trees, among them cedars, beech, catalpa and Japanese maples. Beyond the sweeping lawns is the Japanese garden, designed by Mr Inaka and laid out by Professor Suzuki. Until World War I, Japanese gardeners came every year to work on the ornamental lakes and the artificial hill known as Little Fuji-Jama. Nearby is a Japanese tea house. There is a most interesting water garden planted in 1959 with rodgersias, gunneras and metasequoia. You will also find masses of *Helleborus orientalis*, many viburnums and *Magnolia* x *soulangiana*.

FURNEAUX PELHAM HALL 6
Buntingford, Hertfordshire. Tel: (027978) 224
Mrs Peter Hughes

2m N of Little Hadham off A120 at traffic lights; E of A10 ● *Open 22 April, 17 June, 2.00 – 6.00 p.m.* ● *Best season: spring* ● *Entrance: £1.00, children 20p* ● *Parking* ● *Teas* ● *Toilet facilities* ● *Suitable for wheelchairs* ● *Dogs on lead* ● *Farm shop where venison is sold* ● **Grade III**

The house has connections with the Gunpowder Plot, but today all is peaceful. The superb Elizabethan house dominates a wide lawn with peacocks, sweeping down to a lake with waterfowl, spring bulbs and cherry trees. Old red brick walls. Huge clipped yew hedges. A cherry orchard with masses of spring bulbs. Borders beneath the walls with *Arum dracunculus* and a great patch of petasites outside the entrance gate with majestic and invasive giant hemlock. A wild garden with cyclamen and primulas round a bog with a resident heron. Deer park with the largest herd of red deer in England.

GARDENS OF THE ROSE 7
Chigwell Green, St Albans, Hertfordshire. Tel: (0727) 50461
Royal National Rose Society

2m S of St Albans on B4630 (signposted) ● *Open mid-June – Oct, Mon – Sat, 9.00 a.m. – 5.00 p.m., Suns and Bank Holidays, 10.00 a.m. – 6.00 p.m.* ● *Entrance: £2.00, OAP and disabled £1.00, groups £1.50* ● *Parking* ● *Refreshments: licensed cafeteria* ● *Toilet facilities* ● *Suitable for wheelchairs with good facilities for disabled* ● *Dogs on lead* ● *Miniature rose plants for sale, growers' catalogues available* ● **Grade III**

The Royal National Rose Gardens provide a wonderful display of one of the best and most important collections of roses in the world. There are some 30,000 rose trees and at least 1700 varieties including hybrid teas, floribundas and climbing roses of every kind, miniature roses and ground-cover roses. Some of the roses are thought to differ little from the roses admired in the classical world. Part of the gardens is the trial grounds for roses from all over the world. The Society is now trying to introduce other plants which harmonize with roses and enhance the planting schemes to give a more natural effect. Already there is a touch of blue from a bank of geraniums and an edging of golden *Alchemilla mollis*. H.M. The Queen Mother is particularly fond of old roses and the garden named for her contains a fascinating collection of Gallicas, Albas, Damasks, Centifolias, Portlands and Moss roses. Here can be seen what is thought to be the original red rose of Lancaster and white rose of York. Among the Gallicas is the 'Rosa Mundi' said to have been named for Fair Rosamond, the mistress of Henry II. This is an historic wonderland which could be explored indefinitely by rose lovers and will have interest for all gardeners. (Note: for those who wish to be up-to-date, hybrid teas and floribundas are now known as large-flowered and cluster-flowered roses respectively.)

HATFIELD HOUSE 8
Hatfield, Hertfordshire. Tel: (07072) 62823
The Marquess and Marchioness of Salisbury

Opposite Hatfield railway station on A1000 ● *Open daily except Mon and Good Friday, Tues – Sat, 12 noon – 5.30 p.m., Sun, 11.00 a.m. – 6.00 p.m. Open Bank Holiday Mons* ● *Parking* ● *Refreshments: light meals and teas, 12 noon – 5.30 p.m.* ● *Toilet facilities* ● *Suitable for wheelchairs* ● *Plants for sale* ● *Shop* ● *House open* ● ***Grade I***

Originally laid out in the early seventeenth century by Robert Cecil and planted by John Tradescant the Elder. Nothing new can be written about this fascinating garden with its presiding genius the Marchioness of Salisbury except to say do visit it. Try to choose a time when the private gardens in front of the house are open for it is here that some of the most beautiful plants are to be seen. See the mop-headed *Quercus ilex* imported especially for the garden and the great double anemone said to have been given to Tradescant, now re-introduced and growing. Amongst the many features are the varied knot gardens, the wilderness and the scented gardens.

HILL HOUSE 9
Stanstead Abbotts, Ware, Hertfordshire. Tel: (0920) 870013
Mr and Mrs R. Pilkington

Halfway between Hertford and Harlow. From A10 turn E on to A414, left at end of High Street, 1st right past church ● *Open 3rd June, 2.00 – 6.00 p.m., possibly also on spring Bank Holiday and on other days* ● *Entrance: £1.00, OAP and children 50p* ● *Parking* ● *Teas* ● *Toilet facilities* ● *Suitable for wheelchairs* ● *Dogs on lead* ● *Plants for sale* ● **Grade III**

Six acres of very varied garden including woodland, a bog garden, a fine herbaceous border and a highly recommended conservatory. The owners tend the immaculate borders themselves and employ help to mow the extensive lawns. The position is an interesting one, on a south-facing slope overlooking Stanstead Abbotts and as a bonus, ospreys have been seen in the valley.

HIPKINS   10
Broxbourne, Hertfordshire.
Mr Stuart Douglas Hamilton and Mr Michael Goulding

1m from Broxbourne. From A10 to Broxbourne turn up Bell or Park Lane to Baas Lane ● *Open 20th May, 2.30 - 6.00 p.m.* ● *Entrance 80p, children 20p* ● *Parking* ● *Teas* ● *Toilet facilities* ● *Suitable for wheelchairs* ● *Dogs on lead* ● *Plants for sale* ● **Grade III**

Mr Goulding is a famous flower arranger and lecturer and grows much of his material in this charming oasis in Hoddesden. The three-acre garden is in a delightful setting with azaleas and rhododendrons and a bog garden with *Lysichiton americanus*. Good and unusual herbaceous borders. Well-kept kitchen garden. Slightly disappointing for the plantsman but the garden claims highest attendance in any one day in Hertfordshire.

HOPLEYS   11
Much Hadham, Ware, Hertfordshire.   Tel: (027984) 2509
Dr and Mrs David Barker, Mr A. Barker

50 yards N of Bull public house in centre of Much Hadham ● *Open by appointment, and all year except Jan and Aug; open Sun, 2.00 - 5.00 p.m., Mon, Wed - Sat, 9.00 a.m. - 5.00 p.m. and on special days for charities* ● *Entrance: between 80p and £1.50, children 40p* ● *Parking* ● *Teas* ● *Toilet facilities* ● *Suitable for wheelchairs* ● *Dogs on lead* ● *Plants for sale* ● **Grade III**

The owners have been working on this garden for many years and it has been expanding yearly. The relatively new pool and bog area look well established. There are numerous borders filled with shrubs and hardy plants, most of which are for sale in the nursery. The long-established conifer bed illustrates the different sizes and shapes of mature conifers. There is also a border for tender plants which have come through the last two winters well. Shrub seed seems to germinate well in the fertile soil and Dr and Mrs Barker have found self-seeded gems.

KING CHARLES II COTTAGE 12
Leverstock Green, Hemel Hempstead, Hertfordshire.
Tel: (0442) 64233
Mr and Mrs F.S. Cadman

Via A4147, midway between Hemel Hempstead and St Albans ● *Open 1st July,*
11.00 a.m. – 5.00 p.m. ● *Entrance: £2.00 (for all NGS gardens in group)*
● *Parking* ● *Teas at two other cottages in NGS group* ● *Suitable for*
wheelchairs ● *Plants for sale elsewhere in village on NGS* ● *Grade III*

This one-acre garden has evolved over 30 years from an overgrown orchard. A
huge gnarled apple tree and a yew hedge are survivors from a former garden.
The roses are a special feature, planted in long beds and following the curve
of the drive, with some splendid shrub roses in island beds. One remembers
especially a rock pool beneath the willows planted with foliage plants; the
terrace with cushions of pinks and small bedding plants between the York
paving stones; climbers on the black and white cottage walls, mainly roses and
clematis; and a vista across the lawn through the beech hedge to a mixed
border beyond planted with a successful mixture of unusual shrubs, herbaceous plants, azaleas in late spring, providing a succession of good colour and
foliage. Other gardens in this village and Gorhambury also open, including
Westwick Cottage (see page 184).

KNEBWORTH HOUSE 13
Knebworth, Nr Stevenage, Hertfordshire.   Tel: (0438) 812661
The Lord Cobbold

28m N of London, 3m from Stevenage. Direct access from A1 ● *Open April*
and May, weekends, Bank Holidays, school holidays, 11.00 a.m. – 5.30 p.m.,
June – mid-Sept, daily, 11.00 a.m. – 5.30 p.m. ● *Entrance: £3.00, OAP*
£2.50 (house and garden) ● *Parking* ● *Refreshments: in sixteenth-century*
tithe barn ● *Toilet facilities* ● *Suitable for wheelchairs* ● *Grade III*

As the historic home of the Lytton family, the garden evolved from a simple
Tudor green and orchard to Sir Edward Bulwer Lytton's elaborate Victorian
design. After his marriage into the family, Edwin Lutyens made alterations
and simplified the main central area. In 1980 a programme of restoration was
started with the aim of reinstating as much as possible of the original Lutyens
designs. The twin pleached lime avenues planted by Lutyens lead to an upper
lawn of rose beds and herbaceous borders with tall yew hedges behind. These
are mixed borders of blue, pink, silver, mauve and white. Clematis 'Perle
d'Azur' and rose 'New Dawn' are grown on iron frames. The 'Wilderness' is a
mass of daffodils in spring. Other features are a vast 300-year-old oak tree, a
small pinetum of exotic pines and a large leaning Wellingtonia. *Clematis*
montana and the 'Garland' rose are draped over Lutyens' garden bothy.

ST PAUL'S WALDEN BURY   14
Whitwell, Nr Hitchin, Hertfordshire.   Tel: (043887) 218
The Hon. Lady Bowes Lyon and Mr and Mrs Simon Bowes Lyon

5m S of Hitchin, ½m N of Whitwell on B651 ● *Open by appointment and 22nd April, 13th May, 10th June, 15th July, 2.00 – 7.00 p.m.* ● *Best season: spring* ● *Entrance: 80p* ● *Parking* ● *Teas* ● *Suitable for wheelchairs* ● *Dogs on lead* ● ***Grade III***

This garden is a fine example of a formal landscape garden influenced by the French taste. Symmetrically arranged patterns and rides lead to temples, statues and ponds. Interesting plants in flower gardens made more recently. The original design is 40 acres. Fine mature trees and a woodland garden made in 1960 and planted with rhododendrons, azaleas, pieris and many other lime-haters. The landscape is incorporated into the garden planning, the church being included. A vast undertaking but extremely interesting as a rare example of a formal eighteenth-century garden.

WESTWICK COTTAGE   15
Leverstock Green, Hemel Hempstead, Hertfordshire.
Tel: (0442) 521291
Mrs Sheila MacQueen

On A4147, midway between Hemel Hempstead and St Albans ● *Open 1st July, 11.00 a.m. – 5.00 p.m.* ● *Entrance: £2.00, children free* ● *Parking* ● *Teas* ● *Suitable for wheelchairs* ● *Plants for sale* ● ***Grade III***

Created by the owner 40 years ago, and planted with the idea of picking for flower arranging. A large border designed to be viewed end on from the house is full of colour and interest, with mixed perennials and annuals, white delphiniums, *Alchemilla mollis*, phlox and interesting shrubs to give it body and texture. Staddle stones under a big flowering cherry *Prunus* 'Kanzan' catch the eye, as does a stone trough in front of the house. A stone urn filled with nicotiana, pelargoniums, etc. shows Mrs MacQueen's skills as a flower arranger. Other Leverstock Green gardens are open on the same day.

HUMBERSIDE

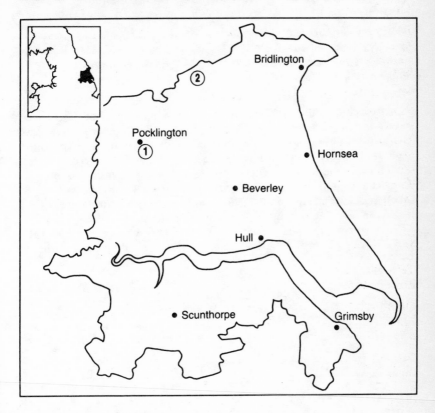

BURNBY HALL
Pocklington, Humberside.   Tel: (0759) 302068
Stewart's Burnby Hall Gardens and Museum Trust

1

13m E of York on B1247 on the outskirts of Pocklington ● Open Easter – mid-Oct, daily, 10.00 a.m. – 6.00 p.m. ● Best season: summer ● Entrance: 80p, OAP 60p, children 5 – 16 30p, under 5 free. Parties 60p per person ● Parking ● Refreshments: cafeteria for teas in garden ● Toilet facilities ● Suitable for wheelchairs ● Shop ● Grade II

The gardens were established on open farmland in 1904 by Major Stewart the original ponds being constructed for fishing and swimming, but in 1935 they were converted to water lily cultivation. They are now one of the finest water gardens in Europe. A large collection of water lilies forms a subsidiary of the National collection. Lilies may be seen from May to mid-September in a normal year and in July there are some 5000 blooms.

SLEDMERE HOUSE 2
Sledmere, Great Driffield, Humberside. Tel: (0377) 36208
Sir Tatton Sykes, Bt

9m NW of Great Driffield, signposted off A166 ● *Open May Bank Holiday –*
Sept, daily except Mon and Fri, 1.30 – 5.00 p.m. Open Bank Holidays
● *Entrance: £1.00, children 60p* ● *Parking* ● *Teas* ● *Toilet facilities*
● *Suitable for wheelchairs* ● *Plants for sale* ● *Shop* ● *House open as above,*
price inclusive ● **Grade III**

A listed garden, Sledmere is among the most well-preserved of 'Capability' Brown's landscape schemes. Dating from the 1770s it clearly reveals his characteristic belting and clumping of trees and carefully controlled diagonal vistas to distant 'eye-catchers'. His use of a ha-ha allows the park to flow up to the windows of the house (whence it is best seen) across extensive tree-planted lawns. To the rear of the house are a well-stocked herbaceous border, a newly planted knot garden and an interesting Italian paved sculpture court (1911) which is undergoing restoration. The eighteenth-century walled gardens are now grassed over and planted with mainly spring-flowering shrubs and are entered through a small but attractive rose garden set off by garden urns.

HOW TO FIND THE GARDENS
Directions to each garden are included in each entry. This information has been supplied by the garden inspectors and is aimed to be the best available to those travelling by car. However, it has been compiled to be used in conjunction with a road atlas.

The unreliability of train and bus services makes it unrewarding to include details, particularly as many garden visits are made on Sundays. However, many properties can be reached by public transport and National Trust guides and the Yellow Book [NGS] give details. Future editions of the *Guide* may include a special list of gardens easily reached by public transport if readers indicate that this would be helpful.

The Maps: The numbers on the maps correspond to the numbers of the gardens in each county. The maps show the proximity of one garden to another so that visits to several gardens can be planned for the same day. It is worthwhile referring to the maps of bordering counties to see if another garden visit can be included in your itinerary. The maps should be used in conjunction with a road atlas.

KENT

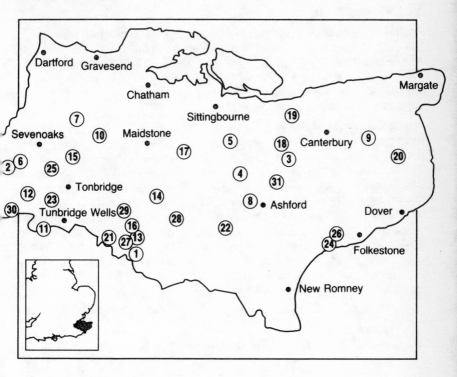

BEDGEBURY NATIONAL PINETUM 1
Nr Goudhurst, Cranbrook, Kent.   Tel: (058087) 377
Forestry Commission (Head Forester)

*On B2079 Goudhurst to Flimwell road off the A21   ● Open daily, 10.00 a.m. –
8.00 p.m. or sunset, whichever is earlier   ● Entrance: £1.00, children 50p
● Parking. Disabled persons may be brought to and collected from lake
● Refreshments: light refreshments in car park at weekends only   ● Toilet
facilities   ● Suitable for wheelchairs   ● Dogs on lead   ● Shop   ● Grade II*

The Pinetum lies on sandy soil too infertile for sustained agriculture, being
silty, very acid and deficient in phosphates. Specimen trees were initially
cultivated with the addition of essential nutrients. However, although the size
of some of the conifers is inevitably limited, the variety of species is not, and
the Pinetum offers a comprehensive collection of the conifers that can be
grown in Britain. It has been planted so that the form, colour and texture of
the mature trees can readily be seen. As well as being a valuable educational
resource for schools and students of forestry and related subjects, it is also a
place for quiet enjoyment.

CHARTWELL   2
Westerham, Kent.   Tel: (0732) 866368
The National Trust

*2m S of Westerham off B2026 ● Open April – Oct, Tues, Wed and Thurs, 12
noon – 5.30 p.m., Sat, Sun and Bank Holiday Mon, 11.00 a.m. – 5.30 p.m.
Closed Good Friday and Tues following Bank Holiday Mon ● Entrance: £1.30
(garden only) ● Parking ● Refreshments: licensed self-service restaurant
● Toilet facilities ● Partly suitable for wheelchairs ● Dogs on lead ● Shop
● House open extra charge ● Grade III*

The effect of the 1989 drought on the lawns and shrubs is evident as is that of
the 1987 gales which devastated the wooded combe surrounding the grounds
– now extensively replanted. The lawns to the front of the house slope down
to two large lakes and a swimming pool (constructed by Sir Winston
Churchill). A walled rose garden at the side of the house leads to a loggia, with
grapevine, adjoining the Marlborough Pavilion which contains bas reliefs of
the Battle of Marlborough. Another main feature, adjoining an orchard, is the
Golden Rose Garden and Walk – extending to the kitchen garden, where Sir
Winston built the summer house and part of the brick wall. Lady Churchill
had a good deal to do with the original design of the garden. This is a garden
worth exploring and for enjoying the sense of space and history but it is not
of particular interest to the plantsperson.

CHILHAM CASTLE   3
Chilham, Nr Canterbury, Kent.   Tel: (0227) 730319
The Viscount Massereene and Ferrard

*S side of A252, just W Chilham village ● Open week before Easter – mid-Oct,
daily, 11.00 a.m. – 5.00 p.m. ● Best season: spring, summer ● Entrance:
Mon – Fri, £1.80, other weekdays with wild bird display £2.00, Sun with
jousting £3.00 ● Parking ● Occasional refreshments ● Toilet facilities
● Suitable for wheelchairs ● Dogs on lead ● Shop ● House possibly open
● Grade III*

This garden (12 acres) has no current horticultural merit as such but views
from the top terrace and the history of the garden amply compensate for the
general air of neglect. One visits Chilham to see the outstanding view down to
the Stour Valley and the terracing supposedly designed by John Tradescant.
This was later destroyed by 'Capability' Brown in the interests of naturalism,
then restored in the 1920s. All the elements of garden history are here –
Jacobean terracing, mid-eighteenth-century deer park, viewing mound,
formal Victorian garden, lake garden. Old trees that survived the hurricane
include a fine *Quercus ilex* planted to mark the completion of the house, and a
splendid cedar of Lebanon. Use your imagination and think of Old England
while others in your party enjoy the tourist attractions at the side.

CHURCH HILL COTTAGE GARDENS   4
Charing Heath, Ashford, Kent.   Tel: (023371) 2522
Mr and Mrs M. Metianu

Follow sign S from dual-carriageway section of A20, ½m W of Charing, to Charing Heath and Egerton. Fork right at Red Lion pub after 1 mile, take next right and 250 yards on right ● Garden open by appointment except Mon and Tues, and on 8th, 15th, 16th, 22nd April, 2nd, 6th, 7th, 13th, 16th, 27th, 28th May, 6th, 10th, 13th, 17th June, 8th, 11th, 15th, 18th, 25th July, 1st, 8th, 12th, 15th, 19th, 22nd, 29th Aug, 2.00 – 5.00 p.m. Nursery open all year, Wed – Sun ● Best season: end June ● Entrance: £1.00, children 50p. Collecting box for visits by appointment ● Parking ● Refreshments ● Toilet facilities ● Suitable for wheelchairs ● Plants for sale ● Grade III

In spite of current works for the M20 in the vicinity, Church Hill Cottage Gardens have an air of peace and tranquillity rarely equalled in much larger gardens. There is a strong sense of design in the curves of borders and island beds but these are so well matched by the fine and well-developed planting that the whole seems natural and much more established than one normally expects after only eight years. Established birches form a central point. Beds are varied, some with colour themes, others with shrubs heavily underplanted with a wide range of unusual hardy plants, bulbs in season, foliage plants, etc. One point of plantsman's interest is the large collection of dianthus, which includes between 30 and 40 types of old forms dating from the sixteenth to eighteenth centuries. This garden is always evolving and will soon feature a new woodland area.

DODDINGTON PLACE   5
Doddington, Nr Sittingbourne, Kent.   Tel: (079586) 385
Mr R. and the Hon. Mrs Oldfield

6m S of Sittingbourne. From A20 turn N at Lenham. From A2 turn S at Teynham. Signposted ● Open May – Sept, Wed and Bank Holidays, 11.00 a.m. – 6.00 p.m. ● Best season: May/June ● Entrance: £1.50, children 25p ● Parking ● Refreshments: morning coffee, light lunch, afternoon tea ● Toilet facilities ● Suitable for wheelchairs ● Dogs on lead ● Plants for sale when available ● Shop ● Grade III

Created in the nineteenth century by Nesfield and developed in the 1910s with woodland garden added in the 1960s by Mr and Mrs Oldfield, the gardens are set in open countryside in 10 acres of landscaped grounds surrounding a Victorian country house. They include lawns with established oaks, a Wellingtonia walk, a sunken garden, rock garden and much fine yew hedging. The main feature for the plantsman is the well-designed woodland garden set, in the 1960s, on acid soil to the side of the main garden. Here are rhododendrons and azaleas, numerous acers and a variety of other trees and shrubs, some rare. The ideal time for this is spring and early summer, but there is year round interest.

EMMETTS GARDEN 381
Ide Hill, Sevenoaks, Kent.   Tel: (073275) 429
The National Trust

1½m S of A25 on Sundridge to Ide Hill road. 1½m N of Ide Hill off B2042
● Open April – Oct, Wed – Sun and Bank Holiday Mon, 2.00 – 6.00 p.m. Last
admission 5.00 p.m.   ● Best season: spring to midsummer   ● Entrance: £1.70,
children 90p   ● Parking   ● Teas   ● Partly suitable for wheelchairs   ● Dogs on
lead   ● Grade II

Set on the top of Ide Hill, Emmetts Garden gives a superb view over the Weald
of Kent and provides an impressive setting for this plantsman's collection of
trees and shrubs. This is a garden to visit at any time of the year but is
particularly fine in spring, with its bluebell woods and flowering shrubs. First
planted by Frederick Lubbock, the owner, from about 1890 until his death in
1926, it is specially noted for its rhododendrons and azaleas. It follows the late
nineteenth-century style of combining exotics with conifers to provide a 'wild'
garden, all well listed in the Trust guide. Recent additions to extend the
interest throughout the season include a rose garden, a rock garden and
extensive planting of acers for autumn colour. The enforced clearance of some
trees and shrubs after the gales of 1987 has enabled new planting to keep the
traditions of the garden but also to develop it.

FAIRSEAT RECTORY 7
The Rectory, Vigo Lane, Fairseat, Sevenoaks, Kent.
Tel: (0732) 822494
The Reverend and Mrs David Clark

½m W A227 at the Vigo pub, 1½m N of Wrotham   ● Open 17th June, 22nd
July, 25th July 1989, 2.00 – 5.00 p.m.   ● Entrance: 80p   ● Parking in village
● Refreshments   ● Toilet facilities   ● Suitable for wheelchairs   ● Plants for sale
● Grade IV

This is a delightful garden in the grounds of the only weather-boarded rectory
in Kent. Though still on the North Downs, there is a good layer of soil
(Bagshot clay) over the chalk, permitting pieris and magnolia to flourish. The
present incumbent and his wife have created the garden over the last 20 years.
With 14 island beds set in and around a large lawn, the plant succession is
excellent giving colour in all seasons. Individual beds have different colour
themes, combining shrubs and herbaceous plants. It is worth visiting to see
how to bring a sense of garden design into a relatively small space. The garden
is only open three days a year, in its best seasons, thus enabling the owners to
have ready a plant description written for each occasion in minute detail.

GODINTON PARK 8
Ashford, Kent. Tel: (0233) 620773
Mr Alan Wyndham Green

*1½m W of Ashford on A20 at Potter's Corner ● Open June – Sept, Sun, 2.00 –
5.00 and parties by appointment ● Best season: summer ● Entrance: 70p
(£1.50, children 30p house and garden) ● Parking ● Toilet facilities ● Partly
suitable for wheelchairs ● Dogs on lead ● Plants for sale sometimes ● House
open ● Grade II*

The key features of the formal areas are the water garden, well stocked with
lilies and surrounded by shrubs and beds, and the small enclosed Italian
garden; two statues, draped in wisteria, guard the entrance to this peaceful
spot with its cruciform pool, statuary, loggia and summerhouse. There are
also several shrubbed areas, a rose garden with triangular beds of annuals, and
much statuary, reflecting the architectural interest of the designer. The layout
was developed by Sir Reginald Blomfield when remodelling the house
between 1902-6, and he used yew hedges to separate the gardens from the
park, marking the different areas with lesser hedges and level changes,
evolving a happy mix of balance and order. Much of the topiary reflects the
outlines of the Jacobean house, although some of the symmetry has been lost
with time. The garden is important evidence of Blomfield's formal style which
was so much at variance with Robinson's. Surrounding the house and gardens
is an ancient park, of some 240 acres, containing some of the oldest trees in
England.

GOODNESTONE PARK 9
Nr Wingham, Canterbury, Kent. Tel: (0304) 840218
The Lord and Lady Fitzwalter

*5m E of Canterbury on A257 turn S onto B2045, after 1m turn E ● Open 9th
April – 28th Sept, Mon – Fri, 11.00 a.m. – 5.00 p.m. inc. Bank Holidays, Sun,
15th and 22nd April, 20th and 27th May, 3rd, 10th, 17th and 24th June, 1st
and 8th July, 26th Aug, 2nd, 9th, 16th, 23rd and 30th Sept, 2.00 p.m. – 6.00
p.m. Closed Sat ● Entrance: £1.30, OAP £1.10, Disabled in wheelchairs 90p,
children 20p, parties over 25 £1.20 per person ● Parking ● Refreshments: Teas
on Sun except April and Sept, by arrangement for parties in week ● Toilet
facilities ● Suitable for wheelchairs ● Plants for sale ● Shop ● Grade II*

Goodnestone (pronounced Gunston) Park is a 14-acre garden in rural setting
round the eighteenth-century house. First built in 1700 by Brook Bridges, this
Palladian-style house was rebuilt and enlarged by his great-grandson, Sir
Brook Bridges, 3rd Bart. whose daughter Elizabeth, married Jane Austen's
brother, Edward. Jane Austen refers frequently to Goodnestone and her
Bridges cousins in her letters. There are pleasant vistas within the garden and
good views out to open countryside. The garden ranges in planting from the
mid-eighteenth-century parkland with fine trees and cedars to the walled area
behind the house designed since the early 1970s by the present Lady

Fitzwalter. The garden tour leads along a broad terrace in front of the house, planted with an abundance of roses and mixed shrubs. Behind the house a small woodland garden, laid out in the 1920s gives pleasant walks and welcome shade. Here are rhododendrons, camellias, magnolias and hydrangeas among many others. A cedar walk leads between spring borders on the left and more roses on the right, to a new walled garden overlooked by the church tower. Old roses mingle with mixed underplanting. Walls bear clematis, jasmine, climbing roses. This is a good example of a garden continuously evolving.

GREAT COMP   10
Borough Green, Sevenoaks, Kent.   Tel: (0732) 882669
Great Comp Charitable Trust

2m E of Borough Green. Take B2016 S from A20 at Wrotham Heath, right at first crossroads, then ½m ahead on left ● *Open April – October, 11.00 a.m. – 6.00 p.m.* ● *All seasons, especially spring and autumn colour* ● *Entrance: £1.50, children 70p* ● *Parking* ● *Teas every Sun p.m.* ● *Toilet facilities, but not adapted for wheelchairs* ● *Suitable for wheelchairs* ● *Plants for sale* ● *Grade II*

Great Comp consists of seven acres of mature gardens round a seventeenth-century house and an original Edwardian-style garden created by Mr and Mrs Roderick Cameron since 1957. This is a delightful garden with semi-woodland walks, changing vistas and plantsman's interest. Extended from an original four and a half acres of garden, rough woodland and paddock, Great Comp now contains 3000 named plants. Each area or walk makes a separate entity yet is designed to lead on to another part. Some stonework gives added interest as focal points. Carefully mixed deciduous and evergreen planting provides all-year round variety, including magnolias, rhododendrons, azaleas, maples, underplanted with heathers, hostas and geraniums. A guide book is available at the gate.

GROOMBRIDGE PLACE   11
Groombridge, Kent.   Tel: (0892) 864226
Mrs R. Newton

5m SW of Tunbridge Wells on B2110 ● *Open 1st July, 2.00 – 6.30 p.m.* ● *Entrance: £1.00, children 50p* ● *Parking* ● *Refreshments* ● *Toilet facilities* ● *Partly suitable for wheelchairs* ● *Grade III*

Peacocks roam amongst the yews and along the terraces. Swans and mallards enjoy the lake by the drive. The herbaceous borders are well kept, neat and tidy. Wild mimulus can be seen in the damper areas, with hostas and primulas. The greenhouses, vegetable and flower areas for the house are orderly and altogether the gardens enhance this mid-seventeenth-century listed moated manor house set in a typical and attractive Kent village.

HEVER CASTLE   12
Hever, Edenbridge, Kent.   Tel: (0732) 865224
Broadlands Properties Ltd

3m SE of Edenbridge, midway between Sevenoaks and East Grinstead between B2026 and B2027 ● *Open throughout year* ● *Entrance: £2.50, OAP £2.20, children £1.50 (castle and gardens, £3.70, OAP £3.40, children £1.90)* ● *Refreshments* ● *Toilet facilities* ● *Suitable for wheelchairs* ● *Plants for sale* ● *Shop* ● *House open* ● *Grade I*

The gardens were laid out between 1904-8 to William Waldorf Astor's designs. One thousand men were employed, 800 of whom dug out the 35-acre lake; steam engines moved rock and soil to create apparently natural new features and teams of horses moved mature trees from the Ashdown forest. Today the gardens have reached their maturity and are teeming with colour and interest throughout the year. Amongst the many superb features is an outstanding four-acre Italian garden, the setting for a large collection of classical statuary. Opposite, there is a magnificent pergola, supporting camellias, wisteria, crab apple, Virginia creeper and roses. It fuses into the hillside beyond which has shaded grottos of cool damp-loving species such as hostas, astilbes and polygonum. Less formal areas include the rhododendron walks, Anne Boleyn's orchard and her walk, which extends along the full length of the grounds and is particularly attractive in autumn.

HUSH HEATH MANOR   13
Hush Heath Manor, Goudhurst, Kent.   Tel: (0580) 211312
Mr Richard Balfour-Lynn

From Goudhurst on B2079 follow Heart of Kent Country Tour signs. Turn right at sign for Colliers Green 2m ● *Open for NGS weekends and Mons, dates N.A.* ● *Entrance: £1.00, children 50p* ● *Parking* ● *Arrangements available for wheelchairs* ● *Grade III*

The four-acre gardens have many well planned and maintained hedges, making perfect settings for the many statues and stone ornaments. Extensive replanting of the wonderful displays of azalea and rhododendron bushes may be necessary due to damage during the 1989 drought. The many flower borders and rose bushes also suffered. The well-stocked kitchen garden is worth a study.

IDEN CROFT HERBS LTD   14
Frittenden Road, Staplehurst, Kent.   Tel: (0580) 891432
Rosemary and David Titterington

Sign from A229 S of Staplehurst. Turn down Frittenden Road at Amoco garage and follow signposts ● *Open Mon – Sat, 9.00 a.m. – 5.00 p.m., and April – Sept only Sun and Bank Holidays, 11.00 a.m. – 5.00 p.m.* ● *Entrance: free*

- *Parking* - *Light refreshments* - *Toilet facilities* - *Suitable for wheelchairs*
- *Plants for sale* - *Shop* - *Grade IV*

Gardens situated in quiet backwater near Staplehurst. There are acres of herbs bordered by grass paths and a large walled garden. A variety of demonstration gardens help the garden planner and over 600 varieties of herbs are available in pots for planting according to seasonal variations. The origanums here were designated as The National collection in 1983. The latest garden is specially designed for the enjoyment of blind and disabled visitors.

IGHTHAM MOTE GARDEN   15
Ivy Hatch, Nr Borough Green, Kent. Tel: (0732) 810378
The National Trust

6m E of Sevenoaks, off A25 and 2½m S of Ightham off A227 - *Open April –
Oct, Mon, Wed – Fri, 12 noon – 5.30 p.m., Sun and Bank Holiday Mon, 11.00
a.m. – 5.30 p.m. Last admission 5.00 p.m.* - *Entrance: £2.80, children £1.20*
- *Parking* - *Tea Bar open from 11.30 a.m. weekdays, 10.30 a.m. Sun and
Bank Holidays* - *Toilet facilities inc. disabled* - *Suitable for wheelchairs with
special parking available* - *Shop* - *House open* - *Grade II*

Situated in a wooded cleft of the Kentish Weald, this medieval and Tudor manor house lies in the valley of Dinas Dene, where a stream has been dammed to form small lakes and the moat which surrounds the house. The medieval design of the gardens has evolved over several centuries. The present lawn replaces the stew pond, which was used for breeding fish for the table. Further household needs were satisfied with vegetables and herbs for culinary and medicinal purposes, and flowers for decorating and scenting the house were also prevalent. During the nineteenth century the garden emerged as an excellent example of the ideal 'old English' garden, and The National Trust is gradually restoring this with extensive replanting. Six acres of woodland walks with fine rhododendrons are re-established and the long border has returned to its former glory.

LADHAM HOUSE   16
Goudhurst, Kent. Tel: (0580) 211203
Lady Betty Jessel

NE of village off A262 - *Open 6th, 13th May, 24th June, 11.00 a.m. – 6.00
p.m.* - *Entrance: £1.00, children 50p* - *Parking* - *Toilet facilities*
- *Suitable for wheelchairs* - *Dogs on lead* - *Grade III*

This Georgian farmhouse with additional French features has been in the family for over 100 years and the garden developed over that period. Interesting features are the newly-planted bog garden, replacing a leaking pond, and the arboretum, in an early stage of development, with the outlines of the old kitchen garden still much in evidence. The mixed shrub borders are attractive; notable are the magnolias – two *watsonii* over 30ft and a deep red flowering 'Betty Jessel'. Amongst the other rarer trees and shrubs are American oaks, *Aesculus parviflora* and *Carpenteria californica*. The newly-planted arboretum replaces over 250 trees and shrubs lost in the 1987 storm.

LEEDS CASTLE AND CULPEPER GARDENS 17
Maidstone, Kent. Tel: (0622) 65400
Leeds Castle Foundation

On B2163 off junction 8 of M20 ● *Open 24th March – 31st Oct, 11.00 a.m. – 5.00 p.m., weekends in winter, 12 noon – 4.00 p.m.* ● *Best season: Culpeper Gardens in spring, rose season and high summer, Castle grounds, spring and autumn* ● *Entrance: £4.80 inc. car park and Castle, OAP and students £3.80, children £3.30, family ticket £14.50* ● *Refreshments* ● *Toilet facilities* ● *Suitable for wheelchairs with transport from car park to castle* ● *Dogs in car park only* ● *Shop* ● *House open* ● ***Grade III***

Visit Leeds Castle and grounds for its romantic, wooded setting, designed by 'Capability' Brown. The woodland walk with old and new plantings of shrubs is especially beautiful in daffodil time. The atmosphere is also much enhanced by wildfowl. The Culpeper Garden alone, in a secluded area beyond the Castle, provides the main interest for the keen gardener. This is not the herb garden as often thought, though a small area does include some herbs, but is named after a seventeenth-century owner of Leeds Castle, distantly related to the herbalist. Started in 1980 by Russell Page on a slope overlooking the River Len, and surrounded by high brick walls of stabling and old cottages, the garden already gives an established feel of old world charm. A simple pattern of paths lined with box contains areas full of old roses (40 varieties), riotously underplanted with herbaceous perennials. The National collection of bergamots (nepetas and monardas) is situated in one corner. The new grotto has been much publicised.

LONGACRE 18
Perry Wood, Selling, Kent. Tel: (0227) 752254
Dr and Mrs G. Thomas

5m SE of Faversham. From A2 (M2) take A251 S then follow signs for Selling. Pass White Lion on left, 2nd right, then left, continue for ¼m. From A252 at Chilham, take road to Selling at Badgers Hill Fruit Farm, turn left at 2nd crossroads, first right, next left, then right. ● *Open by appointment and 6th, 7th, 27th, 28th May, 10th, 17th, 24th June, 8th, 22nd July, 5th, 26th Aug, 9th Sept, 2.00 – 5.00 p.m.* ● *Best season: spring and summer* ● *Entrance: 75p* ● *Parking* ● *Teas* ● *Suitable for wheelchairs* ● *Plants for sale* ● ***Grade III***

This is a delightful, secluded small garden set beside Perry Woods, then open country. Created entirely by the present owners, it provides year-round plantsman's interest with a wide variety of unusual hardy plants. Woodland section, alpine section and pleasantly designed beds stand out for their colour themes with attractive foliage base. Numerous spring bulbs and flowers give way to summer herbaceous plants. Nearby woods give good opportunity for walking dogs and children.

MOUNT EPHRAIM 19
Hernhill, Nr Faversham, Kent. Tel: (0227) 751496
Mrs M.N. Dawes and Mr and Mrs E.S. Dawes

Take A299 N from A2/M2, then right to Hernhill at Duke of York pub, through village on left ● *Open May – Sept, Suns and Bank Holiday Mons, 2.00 – 6.00 p.m.* ● *Entrance: £1.25* ● *Parking* ● *Refreshments* ● *Toilet facilities* ● *Partly suitable for wheelchairs* ● *Dogs on lead* ● *Shop* ● *Grade III*

Mount Ephraim is remarkable for its variety on seven sloping acres with distant views of the Thames Estuary, surrounding fruit orchards and new vineyard. With a backdrop of trees of outstanding shapes and contrasts, it includes rose gardens, rock garden, a small Japanese garden and a lake. Restored, from 1950 onwards after years of neglect, it retains much of the original design of the 1800s, laid out again in 1912 by William Dawes, including topiary effects and the original rock garden. It has continuously evolved and a new water garden will soon extend the range and diversity even further. Spring bulbs, prunus in blossom, and rhododendrons make spring to early June an ideal time to visit but herbaceous borders and shrubs extend the interest through the season. A ¾m orchard walk on Sundays provides further interest, explaining growth, development and types of fruit farming.

NORTHBOURNE COURT 20
Northbourne, Deal, Kent. Tel: (0304) 3608113
The Hon. Charles James

1½m W of Deal. From A258 at W of Deal take turning W towards Great Mongeham and Northbourne ● *Open Suns 6th and 27th May, 10th and 24th June, 8th and 22nd July, 12th and 26th Aug, 16th Sept, 2.00 – 6.00 p.m. Weds, 30th May – 29th Aug, 2.00 - 5.00 p.m.* ● *Best season: June and July* ● *Entrance: £1.50, children 50p* ● *Parking* ● *Refreshments sometimes* ● *Toilet facilities: unisex* ● *Partly suitable for wheelchairs* ● *Dogs on lead* ● *Plants for sale when available* ● *Grade III*

Originally created in Tudor times, with Jacobean structure providing the basis, the garden in its present form was the creation of the father of the present Lord Northbourne. The main feature of this delightful garden, set within high walls to protect it from easterly winds, is the series of small and enclosed gardens with profuse and colourful, cottage-style planting. The old tiered terraces give further character and a distinctive setting for chalk-loving plants. Specially noticeable are grey-foliage plants, including lavender and dianthus. Also distinctive fuchsias and geraniums. Numerous pots and urns.

OWL HOUSE 21
Mount Pleasant, Lamberhurst, Kent. Tel: (0892) 890230
Marchioness of Dufferin and Ava

*Off A21 in Lamberhurst ● Open daily except 25th Dec and 1st Jan, 10.00 a.m.
– 6.00 p.m. ● Best season: spring and early summer ● Entrance: £1.50,
children 75p ● Parking ● Toilet facilities ● Dogs on lead ● Plants for sale
● Shop ● Grade III*

During the sixteenth century the house (with the crookedest chimney in Kent)
was the hiding place for wool smugglers known as owlers (they hooted by way
of warning). The present owner planted prunus, malus and particularly roses
along the many walks with their ample seats and sculptured owls. One water
garden is attractively surrounded with azaleas and lilies; the other is wilder
and danker. It is altogether a garden of great peace which has been open to the
public since 1960.

PEDDAR'S WOOD 22
14 Orchard Road, St Michael's, Tenterden, Kent.
Tel: (05806) 3994
Mr and Mrs B.J. Honeysett

*From A28 1m N of Tenterden turn W to Grange Road at Crown Hotel, 2nd
right Orchard Road ● Open by appointment ● Entrance: 75p, children 20p
● Refreshments ● Grade III*

This plantsman's garden of exceptional opulence and interest is approximately 80 x 30 feet behind a typical small town semi-detached house. Great
imagination and expertise have been used to develop it over the last five years
into a garden of many delights. Other than potash only the usual organic
composts are used but a two inch mulch of peat has been laid over the loamy
soil. Amongst the clematis which trail rampantly are 'Gypsy Queen' and 'Belle
of Woking'. Pink abutilon, solanum, vines, wisterias and roses vie for space
while specimens such as cannas, the almost black viola 'Molly Sanderson' and
impatiens 'Congo Cockatoo' are evident. A small damp area is equally vibrant
and there is colour throughout the year.

PENSHURST PLACE 23
Penshurst, Tonbridge, Kent. Tel: (0892) 870307
Lord De L'Isle

*S of Tonbridge on B2176, N of Tunbridge Wells on A267 ● Open April – 1st
Sun in Oct, daily except Mon, 12.30 – 6.00 p.m. Open Bank Holidays
● Entrance: £2.00, OAP £1.50, children under 16 £1.00, inc. entrance to toy
museum, venture playground and nature trail ● Parking ● Refreshments:
12.30 – 5.00 p.m. ● Toilet facilities ● Suitable for wheelchairs in grounds
● Guide dogs only ● Shop ● House open ● Grade II*

The 600-year-old gardens, contemporary with the house, reflect their development under their Tudor owner Sir Henry Sidney and the restoration by the present owner and his grandfather Lord De L'Isle. The many separate enclosures, surrounded by trim tall yew hedges, offer a wide variety of interesting planting, with continuous displays from spring to early autumn. The Italian garden with its oval fountain and century-old gingko dominates the front of the magnificent house. The herbaceous border is teeming with colour from irises, phlox, anemones, anchusa, coreopsis and yuccas amongst others. Contrast is made by the nut trees and over a dozen different crab apples underplanted with daffodils, myosotis, tulips, bluebells, Lenten lilies and a magnificent bed of peonies which borders the orchard. Even in late summer the rose garden is colourful with 'King Arthur' and 'Elizabeth Glamis' and their perfumes mingle with that from mature lavender bushes. A new lake and nature trail are being developed so that the style of design so much enjoyed here by Gertrude Jekyll and Beatrix Farrand is fully epitomised. Numerous seats make it easy to enjoy the garden and the views.

PORT LYMPNE   24
Nr Hythe, Kent.   Tel: (0303) 264646
Mr J. Aspinall

3m W of Hythe ● *Open daily except 25th Dec, 10.00 a.m. – 5.00 p.m.
(summer) and to 1 hour before dusk (winter)* ● *Entrance: £4.00, children
£2.00* ● *Parking* ● *House open. A Lutyens-style house with Rex Whistler
mural* ● *Grade III*

This is one of those gardens which some people enjoy very much and leaves others pretty cold. It stands in a 300-acre park with views across the Channel. Before World War I Sir Philip Sassoon began building a new house and garden with the help of Sir Herbert Baker and Ernest Willmote and, after the war, with much assistance from the architect Philip Tilden. After a period of distinction in the 1920s and 30s it fell into decay until it was rescued in the 1970s by John Aspinall who wanted the surrounding land for his private zoo. He has reconstructed the 15-acre garden to something like its original design with advice from experts like the late Russell Page. Visitors enter down a great stone stairway of 125 steps, flanked by clipped Leyland cypress, to the paved West Court with lily pool. Beyond is the Magnolia Walk and a series of terraces planted with standard fig trees and vines. Everywhere there is fine stone paving and walls with appropriately-placed urns, caryatids etc. There is extensive bedding and use of bedding-out. Arthur Hellyer admits that 'for years it has been fashionable to denigrate Port Lympne' but he admires. Others however feel it lacks 'soul' that vital element every great garden must have, however extensive the resources that have been poured into it.

RIVERHILL GARDENS 25
Sevenoaks, Kent. Tel: (0732) 452557
Mr John Rogers (correspondence to Mrs David Rogers)

On A225 left-hand side of road, 2m S of Sevenoaks ● *Open April - June, every Sun and all Bank Holidays, 12 noon – 6.00 p.m.* ● *Entrance: 80p, children 40p* ● *Parking* ● *Refreshments on Bank Holidays only* ● *Toilet facilities* ● *Plants for sale* ● *Shop* ● *House open only to bona fide booked charities* ● *Grade III*

This was originally one of the great smaller country-house gardens, housing a plantsman's collection of trees and species shrubs as introduced by John Rogers, a keen horticulturist, in the mid-1800s. The twin stresses of the 1987 hurricane, when Riverhill received the full force of the winds, and the 1989 drought have taken their toll. However, massive rhododendrons, many of them species, topped by cedar of Lebanon planted in 1815, also azaleas, and outstanding underplanting of bulbs still make Riverhill a fine sight in early summer. Other features include wood garden, rose walk and old orchard with Wellingtonia (planted in 1815), magnolias etc. Work continues to restore and develop the gardens and undoubtedly the immense care lavished on it will enable it in time to be restored to its rightful Grade II.

SANDLING PARK 26
Nr Hythe, Kent. Tel: (0303) 66516
Captain G.A. Hardy

Just S of A20, ¼m to E of junction 11 on M20 ● *Open 13th, 20th, 27th May* ● *Entrance: £1.50* ● *Parking* ● *Refreshments* ● *Toilet facilities* ● *Suitable for wheelchairs in upper areas* ● *Grade III*

Sandling Park stands in an exceptional position close to the South Downs but on rich, acidic soil. Planted originally by the present owner's grandfather, its 30 acres include upper lawns and terraces, a fine, large, walled vegetable garden with flowers. A woodland garden of exceptional interest with long walks through azaleas and rhododendrons in season. The collections of these, which include many species as well as hybrids, are among the most comprehensive in the country. There is also a good variety of other trees and shrubs, including viburnums and sorbus. Most of the replanting and development necessary after the 1987 gales has already been done, with plants often restocked from material originally propagated at Sandling.

SCOTNEY CASTLE 27
Lamberhurst, Tunbridge Wells, Kent. Tel: (0892) 890651
The National Trust

1½m S of Lamberhurst on E side of A21, 8m SE of Tunbridge Wells ● *Open April - 11th November, Wed - Fri, 11 a.m. - 6.00 p.m., Sat, Sun and Bank Holidays, 2.00 - 6.00 p.m. or sunset if earlier. Closed Good Friday* ● *Best season: spring and autumn* ● *Entrance: £2.00. Wed – Fri, Sun and Bank Holidays £2.50. Pre-booked parties, £1.60, children £1.00* ● *Parking* ● *Refreshments* ● *Toilet facilities* ● *Partly suitable for wheelchairs* ● *Plants for sale* ● *Shop* ● *Castle open May – Aug Bank Holiday Mon same times* ● **Grade II**

This is an unusual garden designed in the romantic manner by the Hussey family following the tradition established by William Kent. The sloping grounds include many smaller garden layouts in the overall area. A formal garden overlooks a quarry garden. The grounds of the old castle enclose a rose garden. Lakeside planting adds an air of informality. Evergreens and deciduous trees provide the mature planting. They link shrubs and plants to give something in flower at every season. Daffodils, magnolias, rhododendrons and azaleas are the most spectacular. Also notable are the kalmias and hydrangeas. In a good autumn, the colours are spectacular. In some ways the planting seems occasional and haphazard, but visit this garden for its setting on a slope that gives fine views of open countryside, and for the romantic eighteenth- to nineteenth-century theme uniting it. The old castle beside the lake gives added interest.

SISSINGHURST CASTLE 28
Sissinghurst, Nr Cranbrook, Kent. Tel: (0580) 712850
The National Trust

2m NE of Cranbrook, 1m E of Sissinghurst on A262, 13m S of Maidstone ● *Open April – 14th Oct, Tues – Fri, 1.00 – 6.30 p.m., Sat – Sun, 10.00 a.m. – 6.30 p.m. Closed every Mon inc. Bank Holidays. Last admission 6.00 p.m.* ● *Entrance: Tues – Sat, £3.50, children £1.80. Sun, £4.00* ● *Parking but parties by appointment only and no coaches at weekends* ● *Refreshments* ● *Toilet facilities* ● *Wheelchairs restricted to two chairs at one time because of narrow uneven paths* ● *Limited choice of plants for sale* ● *Shop* ● *Tower and library open* ● **Grade I**

'Profusion, even extravagance and exuberance within the confines of the utmost linear severity' is Vita Sackville-West's description of her design when creating Sissinghurst with her husband Harold Nicolson. It is a romantic garden with seasonal features throughout the year. Certain colour schemes have been followed, as in the purple border, the orange and yellow cottage garden, and the white garden, which is probably the most beautiful garden at Sissinghurst, itself one of the outstanding gardens in the world. The Nicolsons added little to, but saved much of, the Elizabethan mansion. The site was first occupied in the twelfth century, when a moated manor was built where the orchard now stands. The library and tower are open and the latter is well worth climbing in order to see the perspective of the whole garden and surrounding area. The garden is in immaculate condition, well-labelled, well-restored after the gales of 1987, with changing vistas at every turn of the winding paths or more formal walks. The rose garden contains many old-fashioned roses as well as flowering shrubs such as *Ceanothus impressus,*

Hydrangea villosa which together with yuccas, clematis and pansies fill the area. There is a thyme lawn leading to the herb garden filled with fragrance and charm. It is a truly magnificent example of Englishness and has had immense influence on garden design because of its structure of separate 'gardens' within the garden – but it is liable to be very crowded at weekends.

SPRIVERS GARDEN 29
Sprivers Estate, Lamberhurst Road, Horsmonden, Kent.
Tel: (089272) 3266
Chilstone Garden Ornaments

From A21 nr Lamberhurst turn onto B2167 and Sprivers is signposted on the left opposite the turning to Horsmonden church ● *Open daily except Sat*
● *Entrance: 70p* ● *Parking* ● *Teas* ● *Toilet facilities* ● *Suitable for wheelchairs* ● *Shop with Chilstone garden ornaments on sale* ● ***Grade IV***

A decorative garden, consisting of small gardens divided by old brick walls and yew hedges surrounding an early seventeenth-century house. There is a water garden which, like the rest of the area, is laid out to display garden statuary and ornaments to their best advantage.

WAYSTRODE MANOR 30
Cowden, Kent. Tel: (0342) 850695
Mr and Mrs Peter Wright

4½m S of Edenbridge, off B2026 Edenbridge Hartfield road ● *Open by appointment and 27th May, 2.00 – 6.00 p.m., 13th, 20th June, 1.30 – 5.30 p.m. and 24th June, 2.00 – 6.00 p.m.* ● *Entrance: £1.20, children 50p*
● *Parking, disabled drivers allowed into drive, otherwise on roadside* ● *Teas and picnics allowed* ● *Toilet facilities* ● *Partly suitable for wheelchairs* ● ***Grade III***

The half-timbered sixteenth-century house and its surrounding gardens, developed by the present owners over the past 25 years, are set deep in the wooded Kentish countryside on Wealden clay. Plants tumble over the paving stones in front of the house and borders of shrubs and perennials, the wisteria walk and the laburnum tunnel all make more formal contrasts. Clipped yew hedges surround the island beds which are arranged in varying colour schemes; for example the oranges and reds of dahlias and roses in one and grey-foliage plants in another. The plants are well-labelled and there is also an interesting small collection of garden statuary.

WITHERSDANE GARDENS 31
Wye, Nr Ashford, Kent. Tel: (0233) 812401
Wye College, University of London

5m NE of Ashford. Turn E from A28 3m NE of Ashford, take road through Wye to Withersdane Hall ● *Open by appointment and for NGS, some Suns May*

– Sept, dates N.A. ● *Best season: June to Sept* ● *Entrance: 80p, children 30p* ● *Parking* ● *Refreshments on NGS days* ● *Toilet facilities* ● *Suitable for wheelchairs* ● *Dogs on lead* ● ***Grade II***

Withersdane Gardens, part of the University of London's Wye College, offer a series of immaculately kept small gardens of botanical and plantsman's interest. These are well laid-out according to themes with plants labelled for education and interest. Of special note are the herbaceous borders, spring bulbs, herb garden and a good variety of hardy plants, specimen trees and early-flowering shrubs. The gardens are of particular interest to those gardening on chalk soil.

THE GRADING SYSTEM

This is the most subjective aspect of the *Guide* and one which may cause some disagreement on the part of owners as well as visitors. We stress that its purpose is to serve as an indication to visitors in order to give them some advance information about the status of the garden as viewed by our inspectors and editors. Readers will appreciate that direct comparisons cannot be made between a huge estate like Chatsworth with its staff of professional experts and a tiny plantsman's garden in a terraced house, tended with dedication by a single owner. This being said, both may be excellent of their kind and therefore be worthy of consideration for a visit, and considered by the *Guide* to be at the top of their class. Conversely a lesser grading does not imply any criticism of a garden but is an attempt to guide the potential reader as to its relative merits if a choice has to be made between several gardens. Broadly speaking the intention of the four grades is as follows:

Grade I Amongst the best gardens in the world in terms of design and content. Many are of historic importance, but some are of recent origin. Overseas visitors to Britain or Ireland are recommended to include them in their itinerary.

Grade II Gardens of high quality, though not perhaps as unique as Grade I, and worth travelling a considerable distance to visit. Sometimes the property as a whole, and the general ambience, make the visit particularly rewarding.

Grade III These are gardens which our inspectors suggest it would be worth driving fifty miles or more to visit. They may have some special feature of design or plant content while not being considered as justifying a higher grade overall.

Grade IV Gardens of considerable merit and well worth visiting when in the region.

LANCASHIRE

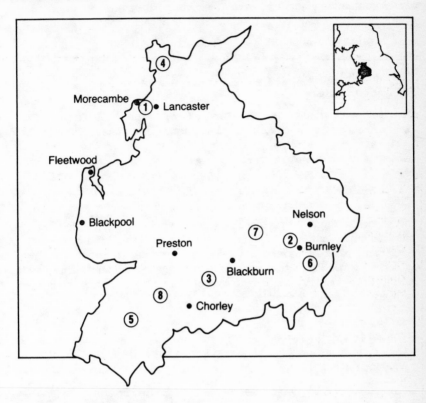

ASHTON MEMORIAL
Williamson Park, Lancaster, Lancashire.   Tel: (0524) 33318
Lancashire County Council

E of Lancaster town centre. Signposted   ● Open daily except 25th, 26th Dec and 1st Jan, summer 10.00 a.m. – 5.00 p.m., winter 10.00 a.m. – 3.00 p.m.   ● Best season: spring   ● Entrance: free to gardens   ● Parking   ● Refreshments: tea shop   ● Toilet facilities inc. disabled   ● Suitable for wheelchairs   ● Dogs ● Shop   ● Memorial open. Entrance to viewing gallery 40p, ground floor with exhibition free. Butterfly house £1.75   ● Grade III

Ashton Memorial was described by Pevsner as 'the grandest monument in England'. It stands at the highest point of Williamson Park looking down on the town of Lancaster. There are many views of the surrounding country from various points in the superbly landscaped park. Broad paths run through the grounds much of which is woodland with an underplanting of rhododendrons and other shrubs. There is a small lake spanned by a stone bridge, and from near here is a large stairway that leads to the huge domed monument.

Behind the monument across a cobbled area and mosaic is the palm house which now houses a collection of tropical butterflies. To the rear is a small garden containing plants attractive to local butterflies. Both monument and palm house were designed in 1906 in the style of the Baroque revival.

GAWTHORPE HALL 2
Padiham, Nr Burnley, Lancashire. Tel: (0282) 78511
The National Trust

N of A671 just E of Padiham town centre ● *Open all year 10.00 a.m. – 6.00 p.m.* ● *Best season: spring* ● *No charge for gardens (house and gardens £1.80)* ● *Parking* ● *Refreshments when hall is open* ● *Toilet facilities inc. disabled* ● *Partly suitable for wheelchairs* ● *Dogs on lead* ● *Craft gallery and shop* ● *House open April – Oct, daily except Mon and Fri but open Good Friday and Bank Holiday Mon, 1.00 – 5.00 p.m. Last admission 4.30 p.m.* ● *Grade III*

This garden, though not particularly special in botanical terms, does set off the Elizabethan Hall. To the front is a formal layout of lawns and gravel paths, to the rear a parterre by Barry in the form of a sunburst overlooks the River Calder. The woodlands that surround the formal garden are planted with rhododendrons and azaleas. Through them are many walks with views back to the house and across the valley.

HOGHTON TOWER 3
Hoghton, Nr Preston, Lancashire. Tel: (025485) 2986
Sir Bernard de Hoghton

5m SE of Preston N of A675 midway between Preston and Blackburn ● *Open Easter – Oct, Sun, also July and Aug, Sat and all Bank Holidays, 2.00 – 5.00 p.m.* ● *Best season: Summer* ● *Entrance: £2.50, children £1.00 (house and gardens)* ● *Parking* ● *Refreshments: tearooms* ● *Toilet facilities* ● *Partly suitable for wheelchairs* ● *Dogs on lead in grounds but not garden* ● *Shop* ● *House open* ● *Grade III*

Hoghton Tower, a sixteenth-century house built of stone, occupies a hilltop position with good views to all sides. The house and outbuildings are built around two courtyards which although not qualifying as gardens are fine areas. Surrounding the house are three walled gardens; the first contains a large lawn and herbaceous borders. The second has a smaller rectangular lawn at the centre of which is a raised square pond with an elaborate stone fountain; to one end is a statue and at the other a sundial on a stone pedestal; clipped yews flank two sides of the lawn. The third is mainly lawn with access to the tops of two small crenellated towers. Around the walled gardens runs 'the long walk' which passes under some large beech trees and is newly planted with shrubs, mainly rhododendrons and azaleas. Good views of the surrounding countryside.

LANCASHIRE

LEIGHTON HALL 4
Carnforth, Lancashire. Tel: (0524) 734474
Mr R.G. Reynolds

*2m W of Yealand Conyers, signposted from M6 junction 35 ● Open May –
Sept, daily except Sat and Mon, 2.00 - 5.00 p.m. ● Best season: summer
● Entrance: £2.20, children £1.20 (house and grounds). Special rates for parties
over 25 ● Parking ● Teas ● Toilet facilities ● Suitable for wheelchairs
● Shop ● House open ● Grade III*

Very striking when first seen from the entrance gates, the white stone facade
(*c.* 1800) shines out in its parkland setting with the hills of the Lake District
visible beyond. The most interesting area of the gardens, which lie to the west
of the house, is the walled garden with its unusual labyrinth in the form of a
gravel path that runs under an old cherry orchard. Opposite is a vegetable
garden made in a geometric design with grass paths. There are also
herbaceous borders and a very aromatic herb garden containing a wide variety
of perennials with climbing roses on the wall behind.

RUFFORD OLD HALL 5
Rufford, Nr Ormskirk, Lancashire. Tel: (0704) 821254
The National Trust

*7m N of Ormskirk, N of Rufford village on E of A59 ● Open April – 4th Nov,
daily except Fri (closed Good Friday), 12 noon - 5.30 p.m., Sun, 1.00 – 5.30
p.m. ● Best season: spring ● Entrance: £1.00 (house and garden £2.00)
● Parking ● Refreshments: lunches and teas, teas only on Sun ● Toilet
facilities ● Suitable for wheelchairs ● Dogs on lead ● Shop ● House open
1.00 – 5.00 p.m., extra charge ● Grade III*

Rufford Old Hall is an exceptional fifteenth-century timber-framed house
whose gardens complement it perfectly, having been laid out by the Trust in
the style of the 1820 period. On the south are lawns and gravel paths laid out
in a formal manner. The many island beds are formal in layout, too, but the
shrubs, small trees and herbaceous plants they contain are planted in a more
relaxed way. In the centre a path leads from two large topiary squirrels to a
beech avenue that goes beyond the garden towards Rufford. There are many
mature trees and rhododendrons in this area. To the east of the house by the
stables is an attractive cobbled area with climbing plants on the surrounding
walls. Look for the gardener's own garden to the north side of the house, in
which grow many old-fashioned plants enclosed by a rustic wooden fence.

TOWNELEY PARK 6
Todmorden Road, Burnley, Lancashire. Tel: (0282) 24213
Burnley Corporation

*1½m SE of Burnley town centre on A671 ● Open all year during daylight
hours ● Best season: spring ● Entrance: free ● Refreshments: cafeteria*

205

- *Toilet facilities* • *Suitable for wheelchairs* • *Dogs on lead* • *Gift shop in Hall* • *Hall open daily except Sat, weekdays 10.00 a.m. – 5.00 p.m., Sun, 12 noon - 5.00 p.m. Closed Christmas week* • *Grade III*

The Hall dates from 1500 but its exterior is largely the work of 1816–20. The gardens are not its main attraction but are pleasantly grassed and contain many mature trees. Parkland laid out in the late eighteenth century forms the basis of today's gardens. The front of the house looks out over a pond and beyond across a ha-ha to open parkland. There are some formal beds to the east of the house planted with bright arrangements of annuals. Further to the east as well as to the south and west are extensive woodlands containing many large rhododendrons and long walks. There is also a craft museum and a nature centre.

WHALLEY ABBEY 7
Whalley, Blackburn, Lancashire. Tel: (025482) 2268
Diocese of Blackburn

8m NNW of Burnley, Whalley is S of A59 between Clitheroe and Blackburn • *Open all year dawn – dusk* • *Best season: summer* • *Entrance: 75p, OAP 40p* • *Refreshments: small selection of drinks and ices* • *Toilet facilities* • *Partly suitable for wheelchairs* • *Dogs on lead* • *Shop* • *Grade IV*

Whalley Abbey is visited mainly by those wishing to see the ruins of the fourteenth-century abbey, and the gardens run round their periphery. These gardens are of recent creation and consist mainly of herbaceous borders and shrubs; in one area there are conifers and heathers. The stone terraces that have been made against the north outer wall of the garden are perhaps its most attractive feature. To the south of the ruins is an avenue of mixed trees flanking the River Calder that runs behind them. Development of the gardens is continuing.

WORDEN PARK 8
Arts and Crafts Centre, Leyland, Lancashire.
Tel: (0772) 455908/421109
Borough of South Ribble

Take B5248 S from Leyland and at Leyland Cross follow signs to Worden Park • *Open daily, 8.00 a.m. - sunset* • *Entrance: free, except one day in the year when a charge is made* • *Parking* • *Refreshments: coffee shop and snacks at Craft Centre* • *Toilet facilities* • *Partly suitable for wheelchairs* • *Dogs* • *Craft centre open all year* • *Grade III*

These gardens are set around part of an old house and a stable block that now contains a craft workshop (the rest of the house was burnt down in the 1950s). There are formal gardens with brightly planted beds amongst cobbled paths and a garden for the blind with scented plants grown in raised beds. The maze is quite unusual being made of hornbeam hedges in a circular pattern. A little distance away is a large conservatory with a rockery to one side and a herbaceous border to the other. They face a formal lawned area that is enclosed by a low balustrade and some fine ironwork gates. On occasions a walled garden can be entered; this has a mulberry tree and a greenhouse with a vine. Large areas of open parkland surround the gardens.

OPENING DATES AND TIMES

Times of access given are the best available at the moment of going to press, but some may have been changed subsequently. In the entries, the times given are inclusive – that is, an entry such as May-Sept means that the garden is open from 1st May to 30th Sept inclusive and 2 p.m. – 5 p.m. also means that entry will be effective during that period. Please note that many owners will open their gardens to visitors by appointment. They will often arrange to give a personally-conducted tour on these occasions. A few owners of gardens open under the NGS scheme have not been able to advise their opening times before the *Guide* went to press and in such cases the note N.A. (not available) indicates that so far as we know the garden will be open in 1990 but entry times must be checked.

TELEPHONE NUMBERS

Except where specifically requested to be excluded, telephone numbers to which enquiries may be directed are given for each property. To maintain the support and cooperation of private owners it is suggested that the telephone be used with discretion. Where visits are by appointment, the telephone can of course be used except where written application, particularly for parties, is specifically requested. Code numbers are given in brackets. For the Republic of Ireland when phoning from the United Kingdom dial 353 plus area code plus number (except Dublin numbers which are 0001 plus number). In all cases where visits by parties are proposed, owners should be advised in advance and arrangements preferably confirmed in writing.

London Telephone Codes: From May 1990 all London telephone numbers with the prefix 01 will be changed. The new prefix will be either 071 or 081. Details of these new numbers are available from British Telecom. During the changeover period in 1990 all London telephone numbers dialled with their 01 prefix will be redirected.

LEICESTERSHIRE

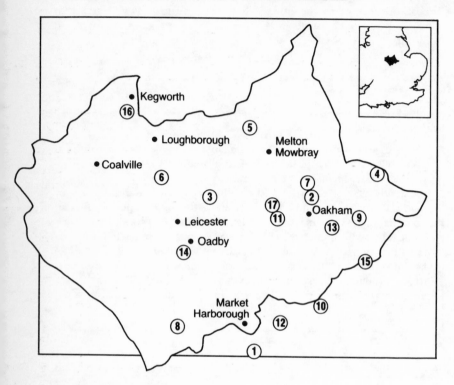

ARTHINGWORTH MANOR 1
Arthingworth, Nr Market Harborough, Leicestershire.
Tel: (085886) 219
Mr and Mrs W. Guinness

5m S of Market Harborough. Turn left off A508 to Arthingworth, fork right past the church, left by the white cottage over a cattle grid ● Open 17th June, 2.00 – 6.00 p.m., 7th July (for village fête), 2.00 – 5.00 p.m. ● Entrance: £1.00, children 20p (25p on July 7th) ● Parking in field ● Teas ● Toilet facilities inc. disabled ● Suitable for wheelchairs ● Plants for sale ● Grade III

A six and a half-acre garden designed by John Codrington 20 years ago. Shrub borders contain interesting colour combinations, there are walls with roses, clematis and wisteria, a herb garden, delphinium border, many old trees and greenhouses with vines, corn and tomatoes, and a special one with orchids, ferns, azaleas, abutilon, clivia, plumbago and house plants. Beside the ruined manor house is a walled garden with white specimens. Great splashes of colour are provided by beds of dahlias, chrysanthemums and annuals.

ASHWELL LODGE   2
Ashwell, Nr Oakham, Leicestershire. Tel: (0572) 722825
Mrs B.V. Eve

*3m N of Oakham between A606 to Melton Mowbray and B668 Oakham –
Cottesmore road ● Open 29th April and possibly 17th June, 2.30 - 6.00 p.m.
● Entrance: £1.00 ● Parking in street ● Teas ● Toilet facilities ● Suitable
for wheelchairs ● Plants for sale ● Grade IV*

A one and a half-acre garden redesigned by Percy Cane about 1973 and
divided up into little gardens by hedges of beech and yew. A paved rose garden
with shrub and pillar roses and a crown-shaped trellis with roses, as well as
clematis with roses on arches provide masses of colour. A border of peony. A
good range of cottage-garden plants in the herbaceous borders and also
shrubs and acers. Water and a greenhouse are other features in this very
pleasant garden which in spring is colourful with bulbs. There are fruit trees,
and smaller plants on the patio.

BARKBY HALL   3
Barkby, Nr Syston, Leicestershire.
Mr J. Pochin

*5m NE of Leicester off the A46 ● Open 1st July, 3.00 - 6.00 p.m. or by
appointment ● Entrance: £1.00, children 30p ● Parking ● Suitable for
wheelchairs ● Grade III*

An eight-acre garden on heavy clay in a cold situation developed by the family
particularly since 1973. The large and rare trees both in the garden and
surrounding parkland form the framework for this lovely garden which has a
wide range of features and unusual plants. The woodland garden contains
rhododendrons and azaleas along with ferns, hellebores, hepatica, erythroniums and trilliums. The rose garden has beds and arches with clematis and
roses and there are areas of shrub roses and patio roses in a raised bed. Peat
beds have been made for a heather collection and these are in island beds with
a range of conifers. The newly-planted scented garden is a beautiful memorial
to the late owner and has a small pool. Walled gardens contain a vast fruit
orchard, masses of flowers for cutting, and greenhouses. Under glass are
cymbidiums, fuchsias, plumbago and fremontodendron. The herbaceous and
shrub borders are packed with a wide range of plants and there are many
different climbers on the walls.

CLIPSHAM HOUSE   4
Clipsham, Leicestershire. Tel: (0780) 410238
Mr and Mrs R. Wheatley

*2m N of Oakham, E of A1 on B668 ● Open 24th June, 2.00 – 6.00 p.m.
● Entrance: £1.00 ● Parking in grounds or nearby lane ● Teas ● Toilet
facilities ● Suitable for wheelchairs ● Dogs on lead ● Grade III*

This garden is set in parkland with some good trees and various conifers and acers. There is a lovely walled garden with island beds and grass paths and a pool and fountain. Herbaceous borders contain a wide range of shrubs, ground-cover plants and roses, and on the walls are climbers and fruit trees. A conservatory houses more tender plants and there is a vegetable garden and orchard. Designed to give pleasure and colour throughout the summer.

FRIARS WELL   5
Wartnaby, Nr Melton Mowbray, Leicestershire.
Lord and Lady King

4m NW of Melton Mowbray. From A606 turn W in Ab Kettleby for Wartnaby • *Open by appointment on weekdays. Telephone ex- directory so write* • *Best season: end May – mid-Aug* • *Entrance: £1.00, children 25p* • *Parking* • *Refreshments* • *Toilet facilities* • *Partly suitable for wheelchairs* • *Dogs on lead* • *Plants for sale* • *Grade III*

This garden has delightful little gardens within it, including a grey garden, a sunken garden and a purple border of shrubs and roses, and there are good herbaceous borders, climbers and old-fashioned roses. A large pool has an adjacent bog garden with primulas, ferns and astilbe and several varieties of willow. There is an arboretum with a good collection of trees and shrub roses, and alongside the drive is a beech hedge in a Grecian pattern. Greenhouses contain peaches, orchids and a vine and there is a new fruit garden with fruit arches and cordon trees. Fine views.

LONG CLOSE   6
Main Street, Woodhouse Eaves, Leicestershire.   Tel: (0509) 890376
Mrs Marian Johnson

S of Loughborough off B591 between the A6 and M1 junctions 22 and 23 • *Open 27th May, 2.00 – 6.00 p.m. Parties by prior arrangement* • *Entrance: £1.00, children 20p* • *Parking in street or village car park* • *Refreshments: tea and cakes for parties* • *Toilet facilities* • *Partly suitable for wheelchairs* • *Dogs on lead* • *Plants for sale* • *Grade III*

A typical woodland garden with 150 types of rhododendron, 16 of magnolia and 40 different camellias. Pools with lilies, herb garden, superb *Magnolia grandiflora* on the house. Herbaceous borders and shrub roses, hydrangeas, *Paulownia tomentosa*, viburnums, good colour combinations and plenty of rare specimens for the keen gardener. Somewhat overgrown in parts, but one can still see beauty. One of the interesting features is a courtyard with *Sophora tetraptera* and *Crinodendron hookerianum*.

THE OLD RECTORY 7
Teigh, Nr Oakham, Leicestershire. Tel: (057284) 681
Mr and Mrs D.B. Owen

5m N of Oakham between Wymondham and Ashwell ● Open 10th June, 2.00 –
6.00 p.m. ● Best season: mid-June ● Entrance (combined with Netherfield)
£1.00, children under 12 free ● Parking around the village ● Teas ● Toilet
facilities ● Suitable for wheelchairs ● Plants for sale ● Grade IV

This old walled garden of medium size is maintained by the owners and
contains a variety of climbers including clematis. There is a small pool, raised
beds with iris, geraniums, rock roses and hebe and borders with a range of
shrubs. An old orchard has climbers and shrub roses, and elsewhere are grey-
foliage plants and ground-cover specimens.

ORCHARDS 8
Hall Lane, Walton, Nr Lutterworth, Leicestershire.
Tel: (0455) 556958
Mr and Mrs G. Cousins

8m S of Leicester. Take A50, turn right for Bruntingthorpe then follow signs for
Walton ● Open for parties by appointment and on 5th Aug, 2.00 – 5.00 p.m.
● Best season: summer ● Entrance: 90p, children free ● Parking in nearby
roads ● Teas for NGS ● Toilet facilities ● Suitable for wheelchairs ● Dogs on
lead ● Plants for sale ● Grade III

A fine example of how to create variety in a small area round a village
bungalow. The courtyard has many unusual plants on the walls. There are
raised beds around a pool, old brick paths, troughs with alpines, island beds,
a cottage garden with shrub roses, lavender, verbascum and geraniums. Full of
ideas and original plant combinations in foliage and colour.

PREBENDAL HOUSE 9
Empingham, Nr Stamford, Leicestershire. Tel: (078086) 234
Mr and Mrs J. Partridge

4m from Stamford, just off the A606 in Empingham behind the church ● Open
3rd June, 2.00 – 6.00 p.m. ● Entrance: £1.00, children free ● Parking
● Teas ● Toilet facilities ● Suitable for wheelchairs ● Grade III

The medium-sized garden of the old bishop's palace has yew hedges dividing
the garden into smaller areas and forming backing to herbaceous borders. The
walled kitchen garden has a wide range of vegetables, fruit trees and bushes as
well as herbaceous borders with masses of dahlias and peonies. Also in this
area are greenhouses and a fig on the wall. The sunken garden contains three
pools with fish and water lilies and a beautiful beech tree. There are several
large trees in the garden and drive which blend the garden into the adjacent
parkland. Many shrub roses along with cottage-garden plants and this gives
the garden a great feeling of peace. The yews are an attractive feature.

ROCKINGHAM CASTLE GARDENS 10
Market Harborough, Leicestershire. Tel: (0536) 770240
Commander Michael Saunders Watson and family

2m N of Corby on A6003 ● Open Easter Sun – Sept, Sun and Thurs, Bank Holiday Mons and the Tues following, also Tues in Aug, 1.30 – 5.30 p.m. Groups by appointment ● Best season: June ● Entrance: £1.30 ● Parking ● Refreshments ● Toilet facilities ● Dogs on lead ● Shop ● House open ● Grade III

Rockingham sits on a hilltop fortress site with stunning views of three counties. Features remain from all periods of its 800-year history. The garden's major features range from formal seventeenth-century terraces and yew hedges to the romantic wild garden of the nineteenth century. The wild garden was replanted with advice from Kew Gardens in the late 1960s and it includes over 200 species of trees and shrubs. The result is a delightful blend of form, colour, light and shade. Recommended for group/family outings and for those who combine interest in horticulture with history.

ROSE COTTAGE 11
Owston, Nr Oakham, Leicestershire. Tel: (066477) 545
Mr and Mrs J.D. Buchanan

6m W of Oakham via Knossington, 3m S of Somerby ● Open 22nd April, 10th June, 2.00 – 6.00 p.m. ● Entrance: 80p, children 25p ● Parking outside village hall ● Refreshments: tea and biscuits ● Toilet facilities ● Suitable for wheelchairs ● Plants for sale ● Grade III

This one and three quarter-acre garden made from an old sand quarry over the past 12 years on clay and lime conditions has a wide range of plants and the design features are very good. There is a beautiful hedge of *Rosa rugosa*, island beds, a raised bed with conifers and heathers, ground-cover plants, collection of hollies, roses, hardy geraniums, hebes, ferns, alpines and potentillas. In addition a peat bed, scree border and a good vegetable garden. Pool. A garden full of interesting ideas.

STOKE ALBANY HOUSE 12
Stoke Albany, Nr Market Harborough, Leicestershire.
Tel: (085885) 227
Mr and Mrs A.M. Vinton

4m E of Market Harborough off A427 to Corby. Turn to Stoke Albany, right at White Horse on B669. The garden is ½m on the left ● Open 15th July, 2.00 – 6.00 p.m. ● Entrance: £1.00, children 20p ● Parking ● Teas ● Toilet facilities ● Suitable for wheelchairs ● Grade III

Vast oaks and beeches form a backcloth to this garden in its country setting. The herbaceous borders have a wide range of perennials and shrubs to give colour over the summer months. A delightful grey garden formed by five circular beds with a conifer or *Pyrus salicifolia* as the central feature. Pergola walk of vines and roses underplanted with mauve campanulas. The large walled garden contains iris and rose beds as well as annuals. A small arboretum has apple trees, *Fagus sylvatica*, potentillas and malus. Children's garden with plenty of space for them to play.

STONE COTTAGE   13
Hambleton, Oakham, Leicestershire.   Tel: (0572) 722156
Mr J. Codrington

3m E of Oakham, turn S off A606 for Hambleton   ● Open by appointment April – Oct. Also 6th May, 17th June, 2.30 – 6.00 p.m.   ● Entrance: £1.00, children 50p   ● Parking   ● Suitable for wheelchairs   ● Plants for sale
● Grade II

John Codrington has been one of the most influential of designers over the post-war years and his small garden is essential viewing for all who are interested in the subtleties of planting. The garden is also notable for the clever way in which the designer has divided his plot – linking the separate areas by cross walks which make the garden seem much larger than it is.

UNIVERSITY OF LEICESTER
BOTANIC GARDEN   14
Stoughton Drive South, Oadby, Leicestershire.
Tel: (0533) 717725
Leicester University

3m SE of city centre, just off the A6 opposite Oadby race course   ● Open all year, Mon – Fri, 10.00 a.m. – 5.00 p.m. or dusk   ● Entrance: free   ● Parking in nearby roads   ● Toilet facilities   ● Suitable for wheelchairs   ● Plants for sale during the summer   ● Grade II

A 16-acre garden founded in the early 1900s incorporating the gardens of four large houses with many interesting features ranging from the large trees of *Pinus nigra*, *Sequoiadendron giganteum*, *Fraxinus excelsior* and *Juglans regia* to the alpine houses' lewisias and drabas. A cactus house, shrub borders with a wide range of acers and conifers, a fern house, fuchsias and herbaceous borders. Borders of ericas, climbers on the wall and on a stone pergola, a formal pool and a raised-bed garden. National collections of aubretias and hardy fuchsias. A typical Leicestershire meadow has been recreated. Visitors can learn much botanically.

WAKERLEY MANOR   15
Wakerley, Nr Uppingham, Leicestershire.   Tel: (057287) 511
Mr and Mrs A.D.A.W. Forbes

6m from Uppingham. Turn right off A47 through Barrowden to Wakerley
● Open by appointment and 1st July, 2.00 – 6.00 p.m. For weekdays March –
Nov, telephone Stuart Baines on the above number evenings only ● Best season:
July ● Entrance: £1.00, OAP 50p, children 10p ● Parking ● Refreshments
● Suitable for wheelchairs ● Dogs on lead ● Plants for sale when available
● Grade III

A four and a half-acre garden landscaped 15 years ago and being developed by
the present owners with large areas of lawn and mature trees – weeping ash,
Cedrus atlantica and sequoiadendron. Autumn colour is provided by several
acers, sorbus and fagus and new trees and shrubs are being planted to provide
shelter. Herbaceous borders with perennials, shrubs and shrub roses provide
summer colour. Climbers adorn the house walls and there is a pool with fish
and plants. A hedge of lavatera gives a splash of colour and in the greenhouses
are a range of good pot plants. Vegetable garden.

WHATTON HOUSE   16
Nr Kegworth, Leicestershire.   Tel: (0509) 842268
Lord Crawshaw

4m NE of Loughborough on A6 between Kegworth and Hathern. 1m from M1
junction 24 ● Open Easter – Sept, Sun and Bank Holidays, 2.00 – 6.00 p.m.
● Best season: spring ● Entrance: £1.00, OAP 50p, children 40p ● Parking in
grounds ● Refreshments in tea room ● Toilet facilities ● Partly suitable for
wheelchairs ● Dogs on lead ● Plants for sale ● Grade II

This 15-acre garden created by Lord Crawshaw and developed over the years
contains wide interest with the lovely herbaceous border, the unusual Chinese
garden and the many large trees and more recently-planted arboretum. There
is an ice-house, a dog cemetery, rose garden, woodland garden and the
Canyon garden. Water adds to the beauty with pools and there are brick
channels that can be filled with water. There is a large walled kitchen garden
and in the early part of the year masses of wild flowers. Some areas are
somewhat overgrown but an air of peace surrounds the whole property.

WILDWOOD   17
Somerby, Nr Oakham, Leicestershire.   Tel: (066477) 336
Mrs Stella Arnison Nugas

5m W of Oakham. Turn off A606 to Somerby. The garden is by the village
pond ● Open by appointment ● Best season: June ● Entrance: £1.00
● Parking in village or driveway ● Teas ● Partly suitable for wheelchairs
● Plants for sale when available ● Grade IV

This three quarter-acre garden developed by the owner over the past 11 years is of special interest to the keen plantsperson with many unusual specimens raised from seed and cuttings brought from abroad. Pool in the patio and a range of climbers on the house together with an archway of clematis. A herbaceous border surrounds the vegetable garden. There are hellebores, roses, hostas, iris and trillium and many good shrubs along with a raised bed for species rhododendrons.

HOW TO FIND THE GARDENS

Directions to each garden are included in each entry. This information has been supplied by the garden inspectors and is aimed to be the best available to those travelling by car. However, it has been compiled to be used in conjunction with a road atlas.

The unreliability of train and bus services makes it unrewarding to include details, particularly as many garden visits are made on Sundays. However, many properties can be reached by public transport and National Trust guides and the Yellow Book [NGS] give details. Future editions of the *Guide* may include a special list of gardens easily reached by public transport if readers indicate that this would be helpful.

The Maps: The numbers on the maps correspond to the numbers of the gardens in each county. The maps show the proximity of one garden to another so that visits to several gardens can be planned for the same day. It is worthwhile referring to the maps of bordering counties to see if another garden visit can be included in your itinerary. The maps should be used in conjunction with a road atlas.

TELEPHONE NUMBERS

Except where specifically requested to be excluded, telephone numbers to which enquiries may be directed are given for each property. To maintain the support and cooperation of private owners it is suggested that the telephone be used with discretion. Where visits are by appointment, the telephone can of course be used except where written application, particularly for parties, is specifically requested. Code numbers are given in brackets. For the Republic of Ireland when phoning from the United Kingdom dial 353 plus area code plus number (except Dublin numbers which are 0001 plus number). In all cases where visits by parties are proposed, owners should be advised in advance and arrangements preferably confirmed in writing.

London Telephone Codes: From May 1990 all London telephone numbers with the prefix 01 will be changed. The new prefix will be either 071 or 081. Details of these new numbers are available from British Telecom. During the changeover period in 1990 all London telephone numbers dialled with their 01 prefix will be redirected.

LINCOLNSHIRE

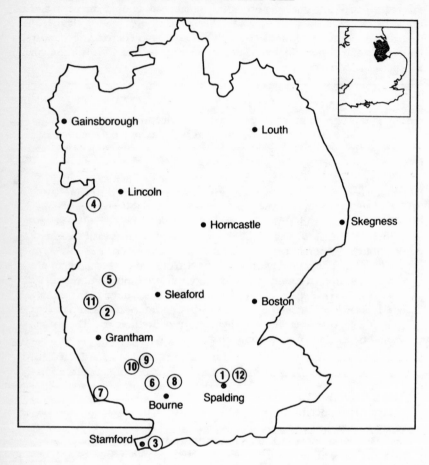

AYSCOUGH FEE HALL AND GARDENS   1
Churchgate, Spalding, Lincolnshire. Tel: (0775) 5468
South Holland District Council

Centre of Spalding ● Open daily, Mon – Sat, 8.00 a.m. – 5.00 p.m. or ½ hour after sunset, Sun, 10.00 a.m. – 5.00 p.m. or ½ hour after sunset. Closed Christmas Day ● Entrance: free ● Parking on Churchgate ● Refreshments: café open seasonally ● Toilet facilities inc. disabled ● Suitable for wheelchairs ● Dogs on lead ● House open: Mon – Thurs, 10.00 a.m. – 5.00 p.m., Fri, 10.00 a.m. – 4.30 p.m., Sat, Mar – Oct, 10.00 a.m. – 5.00 p.m., Sun, 11.00 a.m. – 5.00 p.m. ● Grade IV

Next to the River Welland the gardens of this public park are in a beautiful setting. Entirely enclosed by lovely old walls, they are worth visiting for the bizarrely-shaped, clipped yew walks, its old rectangular fish pond with fountains and the fascinating medieval red-brick hall now housing the museum of South Holland. In addition there are good bedding displays, lawns, formal rose garden, pergola, and wall shrubs including a fruiting vine.

BELTON HOUSE 2
Belton, Nr Grantham, Lincolnshire. Tel: (0476) 66116
The National Trust

4m N of Grantham off A607 ● Open April – Oct, Wed – Sun, 11.00 a.m. – 5.30 p.m., Nov – 23rd Dec, Sat and Sun, 12 noon – 4.00 p.m. Open Bank Holiday Mons, but closed Good Friday. Free access to park on foot from Lion Lodge gates all year but this does not give admittance to house, garden or adventure playground ● Entrance: £3.20. Parties of 15 or more, rates on request ● Parking ● Refreshments: light lunches, teas, etc., 12 noon - 5.30 p.m . ● Toilet facilities inc. disabled ● Suitable for wheelchairs ● Dogs on lead ● Gift shop ● House open, April – Oct, Wed – Sun, 1.00 – 5.00 p.m. Open Bank Holiday Mons, but closed Good Friday ● Grade II

The gardens at Belton are large and impressive. The extensive woodland area has two lakes, a small canal and good cedars; a childrens' adventure playground makes it ideal for families. However, it is the formal area to the north of the house, completed by the superbly restored and replanted Jeffrey Wyatville orangery, that makes the garden memorable. The 'Dutch garden' has clipped yew hedging, formal beds with lavender edging, standard 'Iceberg' roses and well-planted stone urns. The earlier Italian garden has a large central pond with fountain, a lion-headed exhedra, lawns and clipped yews. The gradual but extensive restoration of the garden, including the reforming of herbaceous borders and the old statue walk, ensures a garden of great merit and authenticity.

BURGHLEY HOUSE 3
Stamford, Lincolnshire. Tel: (0780) 52451
Burghley House Preservation Trust
Custodian: Lady Victoria Leatham (née Cecil)

½m E of Stamford on Barnock Road, close to A1. Well signposted ● Open Easter – Sept, daily, 11.00 a.m. – 5.00 p.m. Avoid Burghley Horse Trials, 6 – 9th Sept 1990, when it is closed Sat, 8th Sept ● Entrance: £3.00, £1.70 children inc. guided tour of house and entrance to special exhibition ● Parking ● Refreshments ● Toilet facilities ● Limited access for wheelchairs ● Dogs on lead in park only ● Shop ● House open ● Grade IV

The main attraction at Burghley is the magnificent Elizabethan house with its immense collection of art treasures, built by Richard Cecil, created Lord

Burghley by his Queen. Both the house and its custodian, Lady Victoria Leatham, have appeared on many television antiques programmes. The parkland, landscaped by 'Capability' Brown, is delightful and extensive. There is only a small area of formal rose garden with oval pond, lavender, fountain and urns so Burghley is of limited interest to visitors with more botanical leanings. In addition to creating a large serpentine lake, Brown built a new stable block, an orangery, a gamekeeper's lodge, a dairy and an ice-house. The finest surviving small building is a lakeside summer house.

DODDINGTON HALL   4
Doddington, Nr Lincoln, Lincolnshire.   Tel: (0522) 694308
Mr and Mrs A.G. Jarvis

5m W of Lincoln on B1190 ● Open Easter Mon and May – Sept, Wed and Sun inc. Bank Holidays, 2.00 – 6.00 p.m. Parties at other times by arrangement ● Entrance: £1.35, children 70p (house and garden £2.70, children £1.35) ● Parking ● Refreshment: restaurant ● Toilet facilities inc. disabled ● Suitable for wheelchairs ● Dogs on lead ● Shop ● House open ● Grade III

The romantic gardens of the Elizabethan house successfully combine many different styles and moods. The simplicity of the gravel, box and lawned courtyard, the formal croquet lawn and the gravel walk along the kitchen garden wall contrasts with the walled west garden with its elaborate parterres of roses, iris and clipped box edging with borders of herbaceous plants and old roses. (The parterres were restored in Elizabethan style in 1900.) Fine eighteenth-century Italian gates open from here on to a formal yew alley, more old roses and a good wild garden. Here the meandering walks take in a turf maze, stream, ancient specimens of sweet chestnut, cedar, yew and holly, and the Temple of the Winds built by the present owner. The more recently-planted herb garden, pleached hornbeams and dwarf box-edging continue to harmonize the different areas and create more interest in this peaceful garden.

FULBECK HALL   5
Fulbeck, Nr Grantham, Lincolnshire.   Tel: (0400) 72205
Mr and Mrs Fry

On A607 Lincoln – Grantham road ● Open 3rd – 29th Aug, Easter and May Bank Holiday Mons, 2.00 – 5.00 p.m. ● Entrance: £1.10, OAP 75p, children 50p (house and garden £2.20, OAP £1.50, children 50p) ● Parking ● Toilet facilities ● Suitable for wheelchairs ● Dogs on lead ● Plants for sale ● House open ● Grade IV

The 11-acre garden at Fulbeck is varied and interesting with newly-planted informal areas together with a formal Victorian terrace. Many of the trees here are as old as the house (1733). The top terrace with a gravel walk is backed by a superbly-shaped clipped yew hedge. The bottom lawn has shrubs, roses, unusual clematis and ramblers climbing into the surrounding trees. Against a limestone wall at the south of the house is a herbaceous border with many choice plants. Beyond the immediate garden is a pleasant wild garden and nature trail.

GRIMSTHORPE CASTLE 6
Grimsthorpe, Nr Bourne, Lincolnshire. Tel: (0778) 32205
Grimsthorpe and Drummond Castle Trust Ltd

4m NW of Bourne on A151 Colsterworth – Bourne road ● Open 3rd June – 2nd Sept, Sun and Bank Holidays, 2.00 – 6.00 p.m. Other dates to be advertised locally or on application to Estate Office ● Parking ● Teas ● Toilet facilities inc. disabled ● Suitable for wheelchairs ● House open ● Grade III

The impressive house, part-medieval, part-Tudor and part-eighteenth-century, of Vanburgh design, is surrounded on three sides by good pleasure gardens in which 'Capability' Brown had a hand. The Victorian knot garden to the east of the house has beds of lavender, roses and catmint with edges of clipped box. To the south are two yew-hedged rose gardens with topiary, a yew 'broad walk' and a retreat. Leading to the west terrace is a double yew walk with classic herbaceous borders and beyond a shrub rose border and row of 70-year-old cedars. The yew hedging throughout the garden is superbly maintained and differs in design from one area to another. Beyond the pleasure gardens are the arboretum, wild garden, an unusual geometrically-designed kitchen garden with clipped box and bean pergola, and extensive parkland. Views of the old oak and chestnut avenues and the parkland with its lake and Vanbrugh summer house are provided by cleverly positioned vistas and terraces.

GUNBY HALL 7
Gunby, Nr Spilsby, Lincolnshire.
The National Trust (Mr and Mrs Wrisdale)

2½m NW of Burgh-le-Marsh on S of A158 ● Open April – Sept, Wed and Thurs, 2.00 – 6.00 p.m. Tues and Fri by written appointment ● Entrance: £1.00 garden (house and garden £1.50) ● Parking ● Toilet facilities ● Suitable for wheelchairs ● Dogs on lead ● Plants for sale ● House open April – Sept, Wed, 2.00 – 6.00 p.m. Other weekdays by written appointment as above ● Grade II

The early eighteenth-century house, with its walls smothered in fine plants, is set in parkland with avenues of lime and horse chestnut. The shrub borders, wild garden, lawns with old cedars and the restrained formal front garden of catmint and lavender beds backed by clipped yew provide a startling contrast to the main attraction of Gunby – its walled gardens. The dazzling pergola garden with its apple-tree walkway has a maze of paths leading to beds of old roses, herb garden and brimming herbaceous and annual borders. The second walled area houses an impressive kitchen garden reached after passing more borders of perfectly-arranged herbaceous plants and hybrid musk roses. Backing on to its wall is another wonderfully classic herbaceous border and beyond an early nineteenth-century long fish pond and orchard completing an altogether enchanting garden. It is fitting that it was the subject of Tennyson's 'Haunt of Ancient Peace'.

32 MAIN STREET 8
Ouke, Nr Bourne, Lincolnshire. Tel: (0778) 422241
Mr and Mrs D. Sellars

1m N of Bourne, off A15 ● Open April and August, certain Suns to be advertised. Also by appointment ● Entrance: 70p, children 25p ● Parking ● Teas ● Toilet facilities at nearby village hall ● Dogs on lead ● Plants for sale ● Grade IV

This small area of 100 x 50 feet is subdivided into tiny compartments allowing an astonishing number of planting schemes. Every available space is crammed with a choice plant, ornament, trough or architectural feature and by careful planning and underplanting, overflows with a continuous display of colour. Such is the enthusiasm of the owner that the garden is constantly changing and may well vary significantly from year to year; it is daunting to recall that it has been developed over a period of only five years.

MANOR FARM 9
Keisby, Nr Lenton, Bourne, Lincolnshire. Tel: (047685) 607
Mr and Mrs C.A. Richardson

9m NW of Bourne, N of A151 ● Open 1st July, 2.00 – 6.00 p.m. ● Entrance: 75p, children free ● Parking ● Teas ● Toilet facilities on ground floor ● Suitable for wheelchairs ● Dogs on lead ● Plants for sale ● Grade IV

This pretty, informal garden is a delight with its artistic planning and colour harmonization. The tiny paths to the vegetable plot, pergola and stream meander through the beds and so allow close inspection of the many choice plants, including shrub roses, ramblers and clematis.

MANOR HOUSE 10
Bitchfield, Grantham, Lincolnshire. Tel: (047685) 261
Mr John Richardson

Centre of Bitchfield village on B1176 south-east of Grantham ● Open by appointment ● Best season: June and July ● Entrance: Donations to charity ● Parking ● Toilet facilities ● Grade III

A one and a half-acre garden with a delightful atmosphere created and tended by the owner. A successful blend of the traditional – mature apple trees, small formal garden and bronze sundial – and the contemporary – terrace with urns, informal mixed rose, shrub and herbaceous borders. Good show from bulbs in spring. Pond. Much recommended for lovers of shrub roses and those planning or dreaming about creating a medium-sized garden, with 86 varieties of roses to be seen.

MARSTON HALL 11
Marston, Nr Grantham, Lincolnshire.   Tel: (0400) 50225
Reverend Henry Thorold

*6m NW of Grantham, 1½m off A1   ● Open 10th, 17th and 24th June, 1st, 15th and 22nd July, 2.00 – 6.00 p.m. Other times by appointment   ● Entrance: £1.50, children 75p   ● Teas   ● Toilet facilities   ● Suitable for wheelchairs ● Dogs on lead   ● Plants for sale when available   ● House open   ● **Grade IV***

The gardens reflect the intimate nature of the beautiful and ancient Ancaster stone house. A series of small, walled and high-hedged gardens, courtyards and walks house formal rose beds, cottage garden, knot garden planted with herbs, and vegetables screened by herbaceous borders and trellising. To the south of the house are lawns, clipped yews and walks through the newly-planted laburnum avenue and ancient trees including an enormous laburnum and a 400-year-old wych elm. The Lancing avenue of Lombardy poplars stretches from the orchard to the nearby River Witham and perfectly unites the garden with the parkland beyond.

SPRINGFIELDS GARDENS 12
Springfield, Spalding, Lincolnshire.   Tel: (0775) 4843
Springfields Horticultural Society

*1½m from Spalding on A151   ● Open 30th March – Sept, daily, 10.00 a.m. – 6.00 p.m.   ● Best season: mid-April and mid-August   ● Entrance: £2.00, children free. £2.50 special events   ● Parking   ● Refreshments: café, tea shop and licensed restaurant   ● Toilet facilities   ● Suitable for wheelchairs   ● Plants for sale   ● Shop   ● **Grade IV***

The 25 acres of gardens have been designed to maximize areas of show bedding – whether of the colourful spring displays of thousands of bulb varieties or of the later roses and annuals. Subdivided into smaller areas by shrub borders and small copses, the garden boasts many different features all easily accessible for wheelchairs. However, with the exception of an excellent herbaceous border, with its bold plantings, the gardens and glasshouses can be monotonous. The colour schemes are dazzling but wearing and the gardens themselves – the lake, the pergolas and the architecture – are all somewhat dated.

LONDON (Greater)

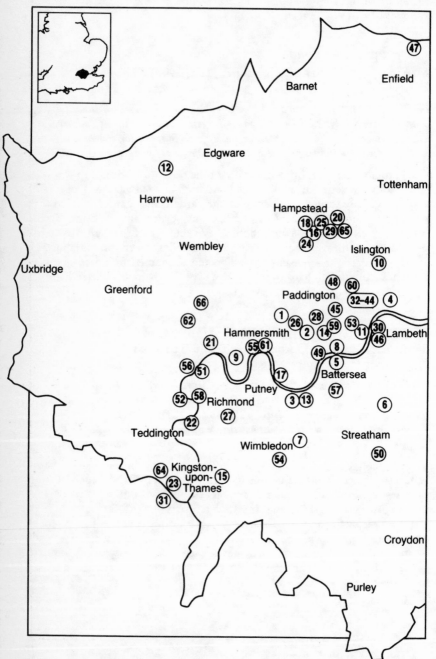

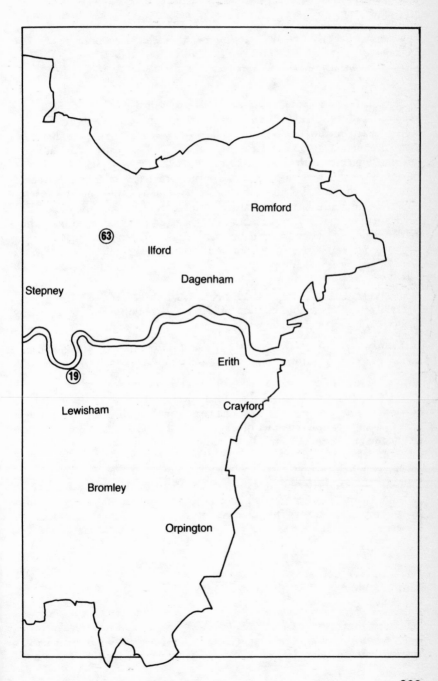

29 ADDISON AVENUE 1
London W11. Tel: (01) 603 2450
Mrs Shirley Nicholson (Mr and Mrs D.B. Nicholson)

Off Holland Park Avenue, W of tube station. Cars must enter via Norland Square and Queensdale Road • *Open 22nd July, 2.00 – 6.00 p.m.*
• *Entrance: probably 80p* • *Parking* • *Plants for sale, cuttings on request*
• *Grade III*

Meticulously kept and well-designed small town walled garden (about 30 x 40 feet) with a profusion of plants on every surface. It makes the best use of every inch of space. A tiny lawn is dominated by two venerable pear trees. Beyond them are perennial borders, slightly raised, and formally laid out but informally planted with an emphasis on phlox and hardy geraniums. To one side of the studio workshop at the end of the garden is a small shade garden, complete with statue. In late summer *Solanum jasminoides* blossoms profusely on one of the walls, filling the garden with scent. The colour themes of the borders (pink, blue and white) and the variegated foliage help to unify the garden, which is an excellent balance between design and planting. Interestingly 'everything is used to being moved and hardly ever sulks'.

ASSOCIATED NEWSPAPERS OFFICE GARDEN 2
Derry Street, Kensington, London SW7. Tel: (01) 938 6000
Associated Newspapers Group

Nr Kensington High St tube, down the W side of Barkers store. Take escalator to reception desk • *Open during office hours* • *Parking difficult* • *Grade IV*

Said to be the biggest atrium in Europe, 115 feet high with waterfalls and fully-grown trees, this is the most splendid example of the passion which developers and their patrons have displayed for the obligatory new green-filled space in the modern office block. The word atrium originally meant the open courtyard of the Roman villa but now it is applied to any glass-enclosed office/hotel entrance. At present the planting is a little sparse, but will doubtless improve with time. For connoisseurs of the atrium, more flamboyant examples can be found in Wilton Road, Victoria (near the station) and Triton Court on Fisbury Square in the City, which has been described as 'an air-conditioned Majorca'. There is also a much-praised atrium at the offices of Robert Fleming Holdings Ltd, 25 Copthall Avenue, EC2.

32 ATNEY ROAD 3
Putney, London SW15. Tel: (01) 785 9355
Mrs Sally Tamplin

Off Putney Bridge Rd • *Open 20th May, 17th June, 16th Sept, 2.00 – 6.00 p.m.* • *Entrance: 80p* • *Parking in street* • *Refreshments* • *Partly suitable for wheelchairs* • *Grade III*

The garden has been designed to give the owner plenty of room for her collection of perennials and shrubs. A rose-covered pergola divides the garden into two compartments, each comprising a lawn surrounded by flower beds. At the furthest end from the house Mrs Tamplin is planning a scree garden. Shrub roses, philadelphus, iris, lavatera and climbing roses predominate.

BARBICAN CONSERVATORY 4
The Barbican, London EC2. Tel: (01) 638 4141
City of London

In the Barbican Centre, on the 8th floor • *Open daily, Mon – Fri, 10.00 a.m. – 6.00 p.m., Sat, Sun, 12 noon – 6 p.m.* • *Entrance: 60p, OAP and children 40p* • *Parking* • *Refreshments at waterside café in Barbican centre* • *Toilet facilities* • *Partly suitable for wheelchairs* • *Grade II*

Hidden amongst the concrete towers of the Barbican complex (on the 8th floor) is an amazingly lush mini-jungle of temperate and sub-tropical plants, opened to the public within the last five years. The conservatory was created around the theatre's fly tower, and plants familiar as house-plants can be seen growing here to about 20 times their usual size, in an attractive layout that includes several levels, half-hidden corners, an arid house and fish ponds housing giant koi carp, golden orfe, roach, shubunkins and terrapins. A massive date palm (*Phoenix dactylifera*) that grew too large for St Paul's School is housed here, as are many giant-sized *Ficus benjamina*, rubber and banyan trees. An alpine bed is currently being created outside the conservatory. The arid house, opened in 1986, houses a fascinating display of cacti, including the largest *Carnegiea gigantea* (now an endangered species) in Europe, donated by the Mayor of Salt Lake City, as well as American chameleons (rather successful ones, as they were invisible) and more terrapins. At the time of visiting, lime deposits from the watering system were making unsightly blotches on the plants, but a new system is being installed which will, hopefully, return the plants to their former glossy, unblemished condition.

BATTERSEA PARK 5
Battersea, London SW11. Tel: (01) 871 6347
Wandsworth Borough Council

S side of Thames, from Chelsea Bridge to Albert Bridge • *Open daily* • *Entrance: free* • *Parking free in car park* • *Refreshments* • *Toilet facilities* • *Suitable for wheelchairs* • *Dogs* • *Grade III*

Laid out 1852-8 on Battersea Fields, an old duelling rendezvous. It has been much improved by the late-lamented GLC and contains many interesting features such as the Bhuddist temple, zoo, aviary, sculptures, large boating lake and also frequent entertainments in tented accommodation. The plantsperson should make a point of visiting the glasshouses near Albert Bridge. Sub-tropical garden, water garden and modern wooden arbourwork.

BROCKWELL PARK 6
Tulse Hill, London SE24.   Tel: (01) 674 6141
Lambeth Council

Take A205 then A215, entrances at Herne Hill Gate, Norwood Road, Brockwell Gardens Road etc. ● *Open daily, 9.00 a.m. – dusk* ● *Best season: summer (July)* ● *Entrance: free* ● *Parking: Herne Hill Gate, Norwood Road, Brockwell Gardens Road* ● *Refreshments* ● *Toilet facilities inc. disabled* ● *Partly suitable for wheelchairs* ● *Dogs, except in walled garden* ● *Grade III*

A peaceful and attractive refuge from nearby Brixton shopping centre, within a surprisingly large park, Brockwell has both a pretty and secluded old English walled garden, with rose beds, and a delightful mixture of herbaceous bedding, providing almost year-round interest. (Radios, cassettes, and dogs are banned from the walled garden – and children under 14 have to be accompanied by an adult.) On the hilltop surrounding the clock-tower are a variety of shrubs and trees and formal bedding. Both park and gardens are very well-maintained, apart from the small aviary. The parkland is well provided with benches. Ground staff are helpful and informative. There are three ponds.

CANNIZARO PARK 7
Westside, Wimbledon, London SW19.   Tel: (01) 946 7349
Merton Council

Westside, Wimbledon ● *Open daily, Mon – Fri, 8.00 a.m. – sunset, Sat, Sun and Bank Holidays, 9.00 a.m. – sunset* ● *Best season: May* ● *Entrance: free* ● *Parking: Westside and surrounding side roads* ● *Teas Sun only, 2.00 p.m. – 5.00 p.m., provided by Wimbledon Guides and Brownies* ● *Toilet facilities* ● *Wheelchairs have reasonable access for top gardens* ● *Dogs on lead* ● *Grade III*

Formerly the grounds of Cannizaro House, the approach is through imposing gates and a formal drive, lined with beautifully-kept seasonal bedding. Cannizaro's trees are its principal attraction: cork oaks, mulberry and sassafras (until a few years ago it had the oldest sassafras in England). Some enormous and beautiful beeches have been slightly damaged. In the midst of the trees a secluded picnic area, set with tables, contains – somewhat unexpectedly – a bust of the Emperor Haile Selassie of Ethiopia, who sought refuge in Wimbledon. There is a small aviary, a pretty walled rose garden, an azalea and rhododendron collection and a heather garden. The old garden, the rather disappointing formal Italian garden and the pool are found down a steep slope directly in front of Cannizaro House. A wild garden is being created here. Sculpture exhibitions are sometimes held in the park.

CHELSEA PHYSIC GARDEN 8
66 Royal Hospital Road, Chelsea, London SW3. Tel: (01) 352 5646
Trustees of Chelsea Physic Garden

One entrance in Swan Walk, off Chelsea Embankment and another in Royal Hospital Road ● Open 2nd April - 22nd Oct, Wed, Sun, 2.00 - 5.00 p.m., also during Chelsea Flower Show, 12 noon - 5.00 p.m. Entrance: £2.00, students, children and unemployed £1.00 ● Parking: meters in side street ● Teas on Sun ● Toilet facilities ● Partly suitable for wheelchairs ● Plants for sale ● Grade II

Founded to train London's apothecaries in herbal medicine in the seventeenth century, the Chelsea Physic Garden is still actively involved in research into herbal medicine, as well as playing an important botanical role. Its three and a half acres, tucked between Cheyne Walk and Swan Walk, are well worth visiting, not only for the fascinating range of medicinal plants grown there, but also for their rare and interesting ones, including beautiful trees like the magnificent golden rain tree (*Koelreuteria paniculata*). The gardens also house the earliest rock garden in Europe, created on basaltic lava brought back by the botanist, Joseph Banks, from Iceland in 1772. The main part of the garden is devoted to systematic-order beds of plants, but there are also displays associated with the plant hunters and botanists who have played their part in the development of the garden, including Banks, Philip Miller, William Hudson and Robert Fortune, as well as an attractive woodland garden. You can become a Friend of the Chelsea Physic Garden for a smallish sum, entitling you and a guest to free entry on all public open days.

CHISWICK HOUSE 9
Burlington Lane, Chiswick, London W4. Tel: (01) 994 2861
Department of the Environment

5m W of central London, just off A4, fork left at Cherry Blossom roundabout ● Open daily dawn - dusk ● Entrance: free ● Parking in side roads off Burlington Lane ● Refreshments ● Toilet facilities ● Suitable for wheelchairs ● Dogs on lead, not admitted in Italian garden ● House open ● Grade I

Handsome, semi-classical gardens, stretching over many acres, with lakes, statues, monuments and magnificent trees. Created by William Kent to complement the Palladian villa built by Lord Burlington in 1729, the gardens are full of splendid vistas, avenues and changes of contour. There is a formal Italian garden with parterres filled with technicolour bedding plants in front of the handsome conservatory (both introduced after Kent's day) and a large canal-shaped lake, with informal woodland planting around it. The gardens are well worth visiting at any time of the year, but particularly in autumn and winter when many other gardens have lost their charm.

53 CLOUDESLEY ROAD   10
London N1. Tel: (01) 278 3170
Dr and Mrs N. Milward

Off Barnsbury Street, Islington • Open by appointment • Best season:
*summer • Parking in street • Plants for sale • **Grade III***

The tiny patio garden behind the attractive Georgian house has been extended
into an L-shape with the acquisition of a plot of land about 30 x 40 feet. The
garden is on several levels. The patio near the house is paved with containers
of plants for summer colour. The remainder of the garden consists of a small
lawn with granite setts and with perennial and shrub borders, enclosed by
high walls in attractive London brick. There is a surprising variety of plants
considering the size of the garden; an attractive yellow shrub and perennial
border, masses of climbers on the walls including the golden-leaved *Hedera
helix* 'Buttercup', *Solanum jasminoides* and several different, not commonly
seen, clematis. Two small hornbeam hedges have been made to divide the
garden into compartments, and there is also a small pond, surrounded with
granite setts.

COLLEGE GARDEN AND LITTLE CLOISTER   11
Westminster Abbey, London SW1. Tel: (01) 222 5152
Dean and Chapter of Westminster Abbey

Off Dean's Yard, next to Abbey shop • Open April – Sept, Thurs, 10.00 a.m. –
5.00 p.m., Oct – March, Thurs, 10.00 a.m. - 4.00 p.m. • Entrance: free
*• Suitable for wheelchairs • Shop • Abbey open • **Grade III***

The eleventh-century college garden, the oldest garden in England, is mildly
disappointing, largely laid to lawn with two formal grey borders. The Little
Cloister is, however, an enchanting oasis, with a fountain making echoes
round the stone walls, surrounded by a herb garden laid out exactly as it might
have been by the monks five hundred years ago. The gardens offer an ideal
rendezvous for any gardener whose companions are more eager to visit the
Abbey or Houses of Parliament. Next door are the Victoria Tower gardens, a
pleasant grass-lined space which has one of the finest pieces of sculpture in
London, a replica of Rodin's *Burghers of Calais*. Lovers of sculpture should
also cross the road to look at Henry Moore's bronze *Knife Edge*.

98 COLLEGE HILL ROAD   12
Harrow, Wealdstone, Middlesex. Tel: (01) 954 2893
Mr F. Bowles

Turn off A409, 1¼m N of Harrow/Wealdstone BR station • Open April -
Sept, 1st Sun in month, 2.00 p.m. – 5.00 p.m. • Best season: April
• Entrance: 50p • Parking in road • Teas and ice creams • Dogs • Plants
*for sale • **Grade IV***

The owner, resident here for 18 years, has made an interesting experiment in combining contrived waterways with wild flower laissez-faire gardening in a very limited space (80 x 30 feet). A self-sown Himalayan honeysuckle flourishes a few yards from a miniature bog garden. Flowering pond plants provide the main bog feature in April.

28 DEODAR ROAD
London SW15. Tel: (01) 788 7976
Mrs M. Assinder

13

S bank of Thames, off Putney Bridge Rd • Open by appointment and 29th April, 20th May, 17th June, 2.00 – 5.00 p.m. • Best season: spring and early summer • Entrance: 80p, children 40p • Parking in street • Teas • Plants, cuttings by arrangement • Grade III

Developed over the past 30 years, this is a long narrow garden running down to the Thames, currently shaded by a large mulberry tree about to be removed by the owners to give them more planting scope. It is essentially an informal plantsperson's garden – for example there is a vast collection of more than 70 camellias and also hardy geraniums. The owners encourage wild flowers. Three small ponds. Plant list available.

DERRY AND TOMS' ROOF GARDEN
99 High St, Kensington, London W8. Tel: (01) 937 7994
Mr Richard Branson

14

In Derry St off Kensington High Street • Open daily, best to check first as sometimes closed for private functions and times alter • Entrance free • Toilet facilities • Grade II

Fantasy garden 100 feet above the ground with magnificent views over London's skyline, designed in three compartments including a splendid Moorish garden, with formal water canals and exotic plants – including palms, figs and vines. Ducks swim about in their high-rise ponds and the garden is a delightful maze of small paths, bridges and walkways, with peepholes in the outer walls giving fascinating glimpses across the city. Ralph Hancock's design also includes a Tudor garden and a woodland garden. More than 500 varieties of trees and shrubs introduced by him flourish in soil that is nowhere thicker than three feet. The garden surrounds what was once Derry and Toms' restaurant; it is still a restaurant, now owned by Richard Branson, but caters only for private functions – a pity, since taking tea in this high-level oasis was once a delightful experience. There are, however, plenty of seats if you wish to take your own.

THE ELMS 15
13 Wolverton Avenue, Kingston-on-Thames.
Tel: (01) 546 7624
Dr and Mrs R. Rawlings

1m E of Kingston on A308, 100 yards from Norbiton station • Open 24th, 25th, 30th, 31st March, 20th, 21st April, 11th, 12th May, 15th, 16th June, 2.00- 5.00 p.m. • Entrance: 60p • Parking in street • Teas by Home Farm Trust • Grade III

Recently re-designed by the owners (Mrs Rawlings is a professional landscape gardener) this is a true collector's garden with some rare and unusual plants, featuring rhododendrons, magnolias, camellias, dwarf conifers and a wide range of evergreen and deciduous shrubs. Small trees, ground cover (herbaceous) a two-level pool with geyser and well planted margins, also interesting alpine trays featured. This very small garden (only 55 x 25 feet) even has fruit, plum, pears and soft fruit.

FENTON HOUSE 16
Hampstead Grove, London NW3. Tel: (01) 435 3471
The National Trust

Centre of Hampstead in area known as Holly Hill behind Heath Street • Open March, Sat and Sun, 2.00 – 6.00 p.m., April - Oct, Sat – Wed, 11.00 a.m. – 6.00 p.m. Last admission 5.00 p.m. Parties on weekdays by appointment • Entrance: free • Parking difficult • Toilet facilities • Partly suitable for wheelchairs • House open • Grade III

Handsome seventeenth-century house and walled garden (about half an acre). The entrance garden (not open) is through an impressive wrought-iron gate with a formal layout. The entrance to the house is via the side door. Behind the house, enclosed by high brick walls, is a terraced, formal garden with elegant standard *Prunus lusitanica* in tubs, gravel walks, herbaceous borders edged with neatly-clipped box. Further from the house, the garden becomes less formal with a sunken rose garden. In fact, many of the perennials and herbs in the borders are scented – lavender, santolina, rosemary and dianthus among them. Steps down from the terrace past the rose garden lead to an orchard of mature fruit trees and a small kitchen-cum-cottage garden. The garden is surprisingly peaceful and the scented plants seem to attract lots of bees.

FULHAM PALACE 17
Fulham Palace Road, London SW6. Tel: (01) 736 5821
London Borough of Hammersmith and Fulham

Fulham Palace Road and Bishop's Avenue to the N • Open all year round • Entrance: free • Parking • Suitable for wheelchairs • Dogs • Plants for sale. Nursery nearby • Grade III

The palace, surrounded by a moat in its prime, was the former home of the Bishops of London where in the eighteenth century Bishop Compton used his missionaries to help him establish here a collection of shrubs and trees sent back from America. Today it is rather sad in a faded way, like an overgrown country house garden, but it is a charming place for a peaceful walk, far superior to many other open spaces in London, and the two gardeners are doing their best in the impossible position in which they are placed by the Borough Council's financial position. The 37-acre area to wander round is seldom crowded. The south front of the house looks over lawns with enormous cedars and other trees. The remains of the old walled garden contains a very long ruined glasshouse built along a curved wall and a box-edged herb garden. Another part has order beds. A large rough area with beech hedges. The small courtyard at the front of the house (part Henry VII, part Victorian) has euphorbias, some climbers and other plants and a fountain. It must be said that some visitors find the overall atmosphere depressing but that is not the general view. Do not mistake this for Bishop's Park which extends to the south as far as the river. There are rumours that this garden, which is of great historical importance, will shortly be refurbished.

GOLDERS HILL PARK 18
North End Road, Hampstead, London NW3.   Tel: (01) 455 5183
London Borough of Barnet

From Hampstead, past Jack Straw's Castle on Golders Green Road, opposite Bull and Bush pub. The flower garden is on right of park, past café ● Open daily, 7.30 a.m. - dusk ● Best season: spring, summer, autumn ● Entrance: free ● Refreshments: North End Road entrance, not in winter ● Toilet facilities ● Partly suitable for wheelchairs ● Dogs on lead ● Greenhouses open weekends, 2.00 p.m. - 4.00 p.m. ● Grade III

The manicured 39-acre park was created in 1899 in the grounds of a manor house (bombed in World War II). The two-acre dazzling flower garden on the north side is designed in a series of garden rooms, with a mixture of perennial and bedding plants. It has an almost Victorian feel with its neat, brilliantly coloured displays of flowers, although the colour scheme can appear on the vulgar. On a less strident note is the canal feature planted with water-loving and woodland plants, leading down to the ornamental pool with its ducks and flamboyant flamingos. Plenty of seats at strategic points ensure that the garden is much used by elderly local residents. (The park itself has a large menagerie with deer, goats, wallabies, oryx and many birds.)

GREENWICH PARK 19
Greenwich, London SE10.   Tel: (01) 858 2608
Department of the Environment

Entrances in Greenwich (Romney Road) and in Blackheath (Chorlton Way) ● Open dawn - dusk ● Entrance: free ● Parking easier at Blackheath entrance • Refreshments • Toilet facilities • Suitable for wheelchairs but quite steep in places • Dogs • Observatory and Maritime Museum. Ships at Greenwich pier • *Grade III*

The design dates from the seventeenth century when André le Nôtre is purported to have been involved at the behest of Charles II. Splendid sloping site, crowned by the observatory (with wonderful views from the top of the hill) with magnificent avenues of chestnuts, and scatterings of ornamental cherries and magnolias. There are large Victorian-style flower beds in one area of the park and, in another part, a lake with an island attracts plenty of wildlife. Behind the Ranger's House is a large rose garden. Greenwich Park is beautifully kept, offers lots of variety and has the bonus of the Observatory and the Maritime Museum, plus the Naval College buildings, some by Wren and Hawksmoor. Music recitals are held in the Ranger's House. On the south side of the park is Blackheath, a common of over 250 acres.

7 THE GROVE   20
Highgate, London N6. Tel: (01) 340 7205
The Hon. Mrs Judith Lyttelton

In Highgate village • Open 13th May, 2.00 – 5.00 p.m. • Best season: summer • Entrance: £1.00 • Parking • Refreshments • Toilet facilities • Suitable for wheelchairs • Shop • House open • Grade II

A huge half-acre London walled town garden behind a very handsome Georgian house c.1815, splendidly designed by the owner for low-maintenance, but with bags of interest. Tunnels, arbours, screens abound. A series of brick built arches across the width of the garden separate it into two compartments. The area near the house is formal with a lawn, the area beyond the screen much less so, with many fine compartments and features. Full of secret paths and unexpected views. A magic garden for children. Much use is made of evergreens and there are some exquisite shrubs, including a row of camellias down one wall and a massive *Hydrangea petiolaris* with a trunk as thick as a boxer's biceps! There are many species and varieties of a particular genus – five varieties of box and even more of ivies for example. The owner describes it as a gold, green and red garden. The canal feature, planted with yellow irises, has become very overgrown, as have some of the allées and tunnels, but the layout and choice of planting is still sufficiently restrained to provide inspiration for busy garden-owners who would still like to have an interesting garden. Several other gardens in The Grove are open on NGS days.

GUNNERSBURY PARK   21
London W3. Tel: (01) 992 1612
London Borough of Ealing and Hounslow

½m N of Chiswick roundabout turn left off A406 • Open daily 7.30 a.m. – dusk • Entrance: free • Parking: entrance from Popes Lane, no coaches

● *Refreshments* ● *Toilet facilities* ● *Suitable for wheelchairs* ● *Dogs*
● *Museum open Mon – Fri, 1.00 – 5.00 p.m., winter, 1.00 – 4.00 p.m., Bank
Holidays, March and Sept, 2.00 – 6.00 p.m. Closed Christmas* ● **Grade III**

Little remains of the grandiose gardens of the Rothschild days except the rose
gardens in the traditional 'Clock' pattern. Formal flower beds near the
museum are well kept and colourfully planted, with a background of parkland.
Beyond the trees the sports grounds, golf course and tennis courts are hidden
from view from the terrace where it is difficult to realize one is only a few miles
from Marble Arch. Amongst the gardeners who have toiled here are William
Kent and J.C. Loudon. For children, there is a boating pool.

HAM HOUSE   22
Ham Street, Richmond, Surrey.   Tel: (01) 940 1950
The National Trust

On S bank of Thames, W of A307 at Petersham ● *Open daily except Fri, 11.00
a.m. – 5.30 p.m.* ● *Entrance: gardens free, 50p from April 1990* ● *Parking
400 yards by river, disabled in courtyard* ● *Refreshments: teas, light lunches by
arrangement with manager* ● *Toilet facilities inc. disabled* ● *Partly suitable
for wheelchairs* ● *National Trust Shop* ● *House open daily except Mon and Fri
different times, £2.00. Pre-booked parties £1.00 per person* ● **Grade I**

Relatively recently restored by the National Trust, the gardens at Ham House
now retain their seventeenth-century appearance in which formality predominates. In the south garden, below a wide gravel terrace, are eight square lawns
divided by paths. The strong architectural nature of the hornbeam avenues,
gravel terraces and parterres of box and cotton lavender mean that the garden
looks good in any season, and the authenticity of the restoration, down to
replicas of the seventeenth-century garden furniture, adds to its charm. Even
the tea room, in part of the old orangery, with tables and chairs on the lawns
in summer, has a stately elegance.

HAMPTON COURT   23
Hampton Court Road, Surrey.   Tel: (01) 977 1328
Department of the Environment

On A308 at junction of A309 on N side of Kingston bridge over Thames
● *Open daily, dawn – dusk* ● *Entrance: free* ● *Parking difficult* ● *Toilet
facilities* ● *Mostly suitable for wheelchairs* ● *Dogs on lead* ● *Shop* ● *House
open (extra charge)* ● **Grade I**

Hampton Court itself is worth a visit to study the activities of British
monarchs from Henry VIII onwards, and the gardens are an exciting and
eclectic mixture of styles and taste, with many different areas of interest. Most
famous for its Great Vine, planted in 1796, which still produces hundreds of
'Black Hamburgh' grapes each year (on sale to the public when harvested in

September or October) and its maze, planted in the reign of Queen Anne, with half-a-mile of densely hedged paths. The pond gardens offer a magnificent display of bedding plants (best seen in summer), and there is a Tudor knot garden with interlocking bands of dwarf box, thyme, lavender and cotton lavender, infilled with bedding plants. On a truly grand scale, the great fountain gardens, an immense semi-circle of grass and flower beds with a central fountain, is probably the most impressive element, but the wilderness garden in spring, with its mass of daffodils and spring-flowering trees – principally cherry and crab – has the most charm. The laburnum walk off the wilderness garden – a tunnel of trained trees with butter-coloured rivulets of flowers in May – is another great attraction. The former kitchen garden now houses a rose garden, mainly comprising old-fashioned roses. The 40p guide book gives an excellent potted history of the gardens and a much-needed map. There is too much to see in one day – plan at least two trips; one in spring and one in summer.

37 HEATH DRIVE   24
London NW3. Tel: (01) 435 2419
Mr and Mrs C. Caplin

Off Finchley Road • Open 13 May, 2.30 – 6.00 p.m. • Best season: late spring and summer • Parking • Refreshments • Suitable for wheelchairs • Plants for sale • Grade III

Largish, square garden (about one fifth of an acre) with a vast number of plants packed into it. There is an elegant pergola walk and unusual and interesting plants, including a wisteria grown as a standard (now 30 years old and about 20 feet tall) which makes an attractive small tree. Lots of lavatera – several species and varieties, tree peonies, rhododendrons (including a climbing form), palms (trachycarpus), a fig and a mulberry tree. The large pool was well stocked with fish until a heron had them. Now there are only black ones (the heron can't see these apparently!). Other features of the garden include a fruit tree tunnel (apple and pears), raised beds and a greenhouse and conservatory for exotics. The garden boasts a very well-hidden compost heap behind a hedge of attractive cut-leaved alder. In the front garden there is a particularly good semi-evergreen *Buddleia colvillei* with magenta hanging flower heads in June and July. The Caplins have won the Frankland Moore Trophy (for gardens with help) six times.

THE HILL   25
Inverforth Close, North End Way, London NW3.
Tel: (01) 455 5183
London Borough of Barnet

From Hampstead past Jack Straw's Castle on Golders Green Road, on left hand side • Open daily, 9.00 a.m. – dusk • Entrance: free • Partly suitable for wheelchairs • Dogs on lead • Grade III

Created by Lord Leverhulme in the 1920s, the garden was designed by Thomas Mawson, an architect. Overgrown in parts, its chief charm lies in its secluded setting and the romantic pergola walk, festooned in unchecked climbers. Wonderful views across the heath from many points in the garden. There is a large formal lily pond (slightly unkempt) as well as herbaceous borders, undulating lawns, and many shrubs and trees.

HOLLAND PARK 26
Kensington, London W8. Tel: (01) 602 9483
Royal Borough of Kensington and Chelsea

Between Kensington High Street A31 and Holland Park Avenue, with several entrances ● Open daily, 8.00 a.m. - sunset ● Entrance: free ● Parking from Abbotsbury Road entrance ● Refreshments: light lunches etc. Restaurant (rather expensive) ● Toilet facilities ● Dogs on lead ● Grade III

Most of the famous Holland House was destroyed by bombs in World War II. The formal gardens, created in 1812 by Lord Holland, have been maintained. The small park contains some rare (unlabelled) trees such as Pyraenean oak, Chinese sweet gum, Himalayan birch, violet willow and the snowdrop tree which flowers in May. The rose walk is in the process of being replanted but the formal Italian-style gardens are always colourfully bedded out. There is a small iris garden round a fountain. Peacocks strut the lawns and drape the walls with their tail feathers and in the woodland section birds and squirrels find sanctuary from London's noise and traffic. There is a children's play area. One of the nicest small London parks. Next to the entrance in Kensington Road/High Street, opposite the cinema, is the Commonwealth Institute, whose gardens have seen better days.

ISABELLA PLANTATION 27
Richmond Park, Richmond, Surrey. Tel: (01) 948 3209
Department of the Environment

Richmond Park, Broomfield Hill ● Open daily, dawn - dusk ● Best season: late spring ● Entrance: free ● Parking: Broomfield Hill car park, Pembroke Lodge (Roehampton Gate), disabled at north entrance by way of Ham Gate ● Refreshments ● Toilet facilities ● Suitable for wheelchairs ● Dogs on lead ● Grade II

A wooded enclosure, this features many fine indigenous forest trees – oaks, beeches and birch – as well as more exotic specimens like the pocket handkerchief tree (*Davidia involucrata*) and many species of magnolia. The principal glory, however, is the collection of rhododendrons and azaleas, the earliest rhodendron 'Christmas Cheer' blossoming in the New Year, but the garden is at its best from April until June, when the dwarf azaleas and the waterside primulas around the pond are also in flower. The garden is a notable bird sanctuary – nuthatches, treecreepers, kingfishers, woodpeckers and owls have all been spotted here, and badgers have their own entrance to the gardens. The Waterhouse Plantations in neighbouring Bushy Park are also very fine (see page 249).

KENSINGTON GARDENS   28
London SW7. Tel: (01) 723 3509
Royal Parks

Nearest entrance for gardens is Bayswater Road ● Open daily 8.00 a.m. – dusk ● Best season: spring and summer ● Entrance: free ● Refreshments ● Toilet facilities ● Suitable for wheelchairs ● Dogs ● Palace Museum open Mon – Sat, 9.00 a.m. – 5.00 p.m., Sun, 1.00 p.m. – 5.00 p.m. ● Grade III

This 274 acres of the finest park, adjoining Hyde Park, have their own pleasures, including sculpture by Henry Moore and G.F. Watts and, for children and older enthusiasts, the Peter Pan statue. The orangery probably by Hawksmoor, with decoration by Grinling Gibbons, is well worth a visit. So, too, is the sunken water garden surrounded by beds of bright seasonal flowers which can be viewed from 'windows' in a beech walk. From the Broad Walk south to the Albert Memorial, semi-circular flower beds are kept planted against a background of flowering shrubs. Nannies and prams are much in evidence along the Flower Walk at the South side near the Albert Memorial.

KENWOOD   29
Hampstead Lane, London NW3. Tel: (01) 340 5303
London Heritage

N side of Hampstead Heath, on Highgate to Hampstead Road ● Open daily, dawn – dusk ● Entrance: free ● Parking at Hampstead Lane entrance ● Refreshments until 6.00 p.m. ● Toilet facilities ● Suitable for wheelchairs ● Dogs on lead ● House open ● Grade III

Vistas, sweeping lawns from the terrace of Kenwood House and views over Hampstead Heath (and London) predominate. Magnificent mature trees, mainly oak and beech. Large-scale shrubberies, dominated by rhododendrons – among which nestles Dr Johnson's summer house (used by the great man on visits to his friends, the Thrales, in Streatham). There is also some magnificent modern sculpture including a Henry Moore. The garden slopes down towards two large lakes known as the Lily pond (the largest) and the Concert pond (where open air concerts are held in summer). Woods fringe the heath side of the gardens, with several gates onto the heath itself. A good place to walk at any season, but particularly when the trees are turning in autumn.

LAMBETH PALACE GARDENS 30
Lambeth Palace Road, London SE1. Tel: (01) 928 8282
Church of England

S side of the Thames, next to Lambeth Bridge ● *Open 31st March, 8th Sept,*
2.00 - 5.30 p.m. ● *Best season: spring and summer* ● *Entrance: £2.00, OAP*
and children 10 - 16 £1.00, children under 10 free ● *Suitable for wheelchairs*
● *Grade IV*

Only Buckingham Palace, apparently, has bigger grounds in central London.
Lambeth Palace stands in 10½ acres, roughly nine of them devoted to the
gardens. There is a magnificent fig tree in the entrance garden to the palace.
Behind the palace, and facing it, is a restored rose terrace, fronted by a
perennial border designed by Beth Chatto. Beyond, more or less around the
walled perimeter of the garden, is a woodland walkway that encompasses at
various points a scented garden, a wild garden (with lily pond) and a Chinese
garden. Close to the house is a relatively newly commissioned herb garden (by
Faith and Geoff Whitten) the design of which, though attractive, seems at
odds with the nearby rose terrace. Mrs Runcie, wife of the Archbishop of
Canterbury, whose London residence this is, has undertaken a great deal of
restoration work in the garden over the last few years and over 2000 trees and
shrubs have been planted. Despite the attractive setting, the gardens have a
curiously bitty and disconnected feel to them, although some of that may be
due to the newness of a lot of the planting which needs a good five or six years
before its impact begins to be felt. Not far from Lambeth Palace, towards
Waterloo is St Thomas's Hospital. Inside one of the large courtyards is a
pleasant garden, abutting the foot of Westminster Bridge, which contains one
of the most spectacular modern sculpture water fountains in the world. This
is the stainless steel *Revolving Torsion* by Naum Gabo.

LITTLE LODGE 31
Watts Road, Thames Ditton, Surrey. Tel: (01) 398 5550
Mr and Mrs P. Hickman

Opposite the library in Watts Road which leads into Giggshill Road (off A307
between Esher and Kingston) ● *Open for NGS* ● *Best season: May - July*
● *Entrance: 70p, children 30p* ● *Parking* ● *Refreshments on NGS day*
● *Suitable for wheelchairs* ● *Plants for sale* ● *Grade III*

A half-acre country-cottage garden, deep in suburbia, reclaimed from
wilderness in the last 10 years. Curved beds and borders crammed full with
plants of many varieties. Big climbers, roses, wisterias, clematis, solanums,
etc. Kitchen garden with brick paths and box-edged beds. Courtyard with pots
and some tender plants. Small pond with water plants. Many self-seeded and
native plants encouraged alongside rarer specimens.

LONDON SQUARES

Many other cities have squares but probably none has more than London. They were built in the eighteenth and nineteenth centuries to provide an outlook for the fashionable houses which surrounded them and in not so fashionable areas like Pimlico so that the lesser classes could imitate the behaviour of their betters. A few squares still remain the joint property of the owners of houses (and today, flats) round them, the grandest being Belgrave Square built by Basevi in 1825, Eaton Square and Cadogan Square. Other private squares, hardly less grand, include Montpelier, Brompton, Carlyle, Lowndes, Onslow and others to the west of Hyde Park Corner. Since they so rarely appear to be occupied by the residents, particularly at weekends when they have gone to their houses in the country, it is surprising that there has been no movement to agitate for their occasional unlocking to admit the public at large. However some squares (and 'gardens' as other areas are called) have over the years become places where the public may be admitted and these include the following:

CENTRAL AREA

BERKELEY SQUARE W1   32
North of Piccadilly via Berkeley Street

Plane trees were planted here at the end of the eighteenth century replacing the previous yew and fir. There is pleasant statuary and an agreeable copy of an early pavilion. Alas the buildings surrounding the square get worse and worse.

CAVENDISH SQUARE W1   33
North of Oxford Street, behind John Lewis

Rather noisy, with a car park beneath.

GROSVENOR SQUARE W1   34
South of Oxford Street via Duke Street

A six-acre garden designed by William Kent but nothing of his Italian concept remains. The memorial to President Roosevelt includes rose beds, pools and fountains.

ST JAMES'S SQUARE SW1   35
South of Piccadilly behind St James's Church

The nicest, quietest and most private of the squares, it is also the earliest, begun in 1665.

EASTERN AREA
GRAY'S INN WC1   36
Enter from Holborn just N of Grays Inn Road

More Oxbridge atmosphere, particularly with the narrow seventeenth-century gatehouse entrance off Holborn. These are plain gardens but, here and there, colourful planting of a conventional kind. A statue of Francis Bacon is inscribed with his quotation 'God Almighty first planted a garden. And indeed it is the purest of human pleasures.' Bacon would have wanted the lawyers to do better here, and perhaps they may to the north, where further building development is planned. Field Court is open to the public during weekday lunchtimes in the summer.

INNER & MIDDLE TEMPLE GARDENS EC4   37
(The Temple)
Entrance in Fleet Street, but southern part visible from Embankment

Charming – reminiscent of an Oxbridge College or as Boswell with his usual flair described it, 'a pleasant academical retreat'. The large gardens to the south are not open but the smaller such as Fountain's Court are, with its mulberry tree. Take a copy of Shakespeare's *Twelfth Night* with you as it is said to have been first performed here in the Temple.

KING'S CROSS/ST PANCRAS WC1   38
This is a wasteland at present, but square watchers should keep their eyes on the plan to rejuvenate this Victorian wilderness north of the two stations. A recent development scheme showed a 34-acre pear-shaped park here, but will it be for the residents or the public?

LINCOLN'S INN WC2   39
W off Chancery Lane to the N near Holborn

An interesting hotch-potch of buildings and open areas again reminiscent of Oxbridge. The central garden in New Square is Victorian, with a pool, roses and trees. Two adjacent houses have old trees, one a fig, the other a wisteria. North of New Hall is a garden which the public may use between 12 noon and 1.30 p.m. Mon – Fri only. Lincoln's Inn Fields, a large square to the W, has some of the largest plane trees in London which make it popular for office workers having a green thought in a green shade in summer. Games and café society also flourish here. There is an interesting Flanagan sculpture at one corner and the fascinating Sir John Soane Museum on the north side. At the time of writing the gardens, usually bedded out, are being extensively replanted.

NORTHERN AREA

FITZROY SQUARE W1   40
West of Tottenham Court Road via Grafton Way

One of the few London squares to be the work of a distinguished landscape
architect, Jellicoe. It is also one of the few London squares to be round. It has
a sculpture called 'View' at one corner and a wide paved area outside the
railings. Usually quiet. The actual garden itself is private but it can be enjoyed
from seats outside and no residents ever seem to bother to enter it. Famous
members of the Bloomsbury group lived here.

GORDON SQUARE WC1   41
W of Gower Street via Torrington Place

A quiet spot, with roses, but closed to the public at weekends. Tavistock
Square to the E nearby is not so placid.

RUSSELL SQUARE WC1   42
At the joining of Southampton Row and Woburn Place

One of the largest and most run-down of London's squares, old timers still
remember its days of glory. If Grosvenor Square can be kept neat and tidy why
must this be so tatty? Now it is a repository for black plastic bags but at least
it is possible to enjoy a cup of coffee from the small café, a rare treat in
London's open spaces.

SOHO SQUARE W1   43
South of Oxford Street, near the junction with Charing Cross Road

Rather a hotch-potch but with some fine plane trees. In the square is a curious
Walt Disney-like building perhaps erected here because it is the centre of the
film industry.

SOUTHERN AREA

DOLPHIN SQUARE SW1   44
Vauxhall Embankment, halfway between Vauxhall and Chelsea bridges

Although a private block of flats, the gardens appear to be open to the public
and are an interesting example of 1930s architectural gardening with some
stone and wooden features.

WESTERN AREA
Despite all the many private Kensington and Chelsea squares none is open
to the public, but fortunately the parks are not far to walk, and there are
Ranelagh and the Physic Garden – almost larger squares.

MOUNT STREET GARDENS   45
Mount Street, London W1. Tel: (01) 828 8070
Westminster Borough Council

Two entrances on the S side of Mount Street, one from W off South Audley Street
near the Public Library and a fourth to the S from South Street, Mayfair.
● Open weekdays, 8.00 a.m. – up to 9.30 p.m. spring and summer. Autumn and
winter, 8.00 a.m. – 4.30 p.m., Sun and Public Holidays, open from 9.00 a.m.
Closed from end of BST to 15th Feb ● Entrance: free ● Dogs on lead
● Grade IV

One of the most private gardens in London open to the public. Immensely
popular with those that know it – witness the dozens of wooden benches
donated by habituées to its charms. Mostly grass and hardly at all disfigured
by bedding-out. Not far away is the so-called 'secret garden' which can be only
glimpsed over walls between Green Street, Dunraven Street, Woods Mews
and Park Street.

MUSEUM OF GARDEN HISTORY   46
St Mary-at-Lambeth, Lambeth Palace Road, London SE1.
Tel: (01) 373 4030 (before 9.00 a.m.), (01) 261 1891
(11.00 a.m. – 3.00 p.m.)
The Tradescant Trust

Lambeth Palace Road, parallel to River Thames on S bank, hard by Lambeth
Bridge ● Open Mon – Fri, 11.00 a.m. – 3.00 p.m., Sun, 10.30 a.m. – 5.00
p.m. ● Best season: spring and summer ● Entrance: free, donations welcomed
● Refreshments in church ● Toilet facilities ● Suitable for wheelchairs
● Limited selection of plants for sale ● Shop ● Church open with Museum of
Garden History, inc. garden tools and artefacts and Gertrude Jekyll's desk
● Grade III

A small formal knot garden in the churchyard of St Mary-at-Lambeth features
the plants originally collected by the John Tradescants (Elder and Younger)
on their plant-hunting trips to America and Asia in the sixteenth and
seventeenth centuries, many of them now so familiar we think of them as
indigenous to this country. The knot garden designed by Lady Salisbury has
32 compartments of dwarf box, densely infilled with herbs and perennials.
The centrepiece of the knot is a handsome clipped holly, *Ilex* 'Silver King'. A
detailed planting plan of the knot is available (price 25p) in the museum shop,
and some of the plants featured in the knot are on sale as well.

MYDDLETON HOUSE   47
Bulls Cross, Enfield, Middlesex. Tel: (0992) 717711
Lea Valley Regional Park Authority

Turn W from A10 down Carterhatch Lane, Myddleton House is on the left
shortly after Jesus Church ● Open daily, 10.00 a.m. – 3.30 p.m. Closed Bank

Holidays ● *Entrance: 75p* ● *Parking* ● *Toilet facilities* ● *Suitable for wheelchairs* ● *Plants for sale occasionally* ● *Grade II*

A magnificent diverse plant collection set in four acres built up by the famous E.A. Bowles and now restored and maintained by Geoff Stebbings. Splendid spring bulbs, followed by iris, followed by autumn crocus and impressive varieties of autumn remontant iris make this garden a joy all year round. Zephyranthus, nerines, belladonna lilies, acidantheras are but a few of the autumn bulbs and there is a fine *Crinum moorei* near the conservatory. This is by no means a municipal garden and the impressive plant collection is displayed attractively, in a well-designed garden surrounding the impressive Regency house of mellow golden brick.

QUEEN MARY'S ROSE GARDEN   48
Inner Circle, Regent's Park, London NW1. Tel: (01) 486 7905
Department of the Environment

Approach via York Gate, off Marylebone High Street. Many other entrances to the park ● *Open daily, dawn – dusk* ● *Best season: June and July* ● *Entrance: free* ● *Parking: Inner Circle, weekdays, from 11.00 a.m., Sat and Sun, all day* ● *Refreshments* ● *Toilet facilities* ● *Suitable for wheelchairs* ● *Grade II*

These sedate, well-laid out and beautifully manicured gardens are justly famous. Playing host to more than 60,000 roses – old-fashioned, species and modern varieties – the sight and scent of the gardens in high summer is a magnet for thousands of visitors. The roses are grown with almost military precision and are in perfect condition. Swagged and garlanded climbers surround the circular rose garden, but the herbaceous borders are also worth visiting, as is the large ornamental lake with its central island. It attracts many varieties of water fowl, including herons which nest on the island. The Broad Walk (five minutes from the Rose Gardens) between the Inner and Outer circle towards Cambridge Gate is another exquisitely-maintained Victorian-style area of planting. St John's Lodge, on the north side of the Inner Circle and now part of what was Bedford College, has a secluded garden including a rose garden. The park as a whole is one of the most pleasant in London.

RANELAGH GARDENS   49
Royal Hospital Road, London SW3. Tel: (01) 730 0161
Royal Hospital Chelsea

Chelsea Bridge Road. Through Chelsea Hospital main gate in Royal Hospital Road, then small gate on left. Also gates in Lower Sloane Street, Chelsea Embankment ● *Open 10.00 a.m. – 1.00 p.m., 2.00 p.m. – dusk* ● *Entrance: free* ● *Parking difficult in street* ● *Suitable for wheelchairs* ● *Grade II*

Elegant and attractive gardens with over a mile of wide walkways through undulating park-like grass and handsome tree and shrub planting, with a few perennial and shrub borders. Formerly the pleasure grounds of Ranelagh, complete with a large rotunda (now demolished) and laid out in formal style, they were redesigned by Gibson in the nineteenth century, but turned into allotments for pensioners between the World Wars. They were later reconstructed according to Gibson's plan. A summerhouse by Sir John Soane, near the entrance to the garden houses several seats plus glass cases with a history and a map of the gardens with the major trees marked on it. These include many species of poplar, birch, beech, holly, cherry, chestnuts, lime, oak and so on, with a couple of more exotic ones – the tree of Heaven and the maidenhair tree. The serenity of the gardens is slightly marred by traffic in Chelsea Bridge Road. To one side of the park is the area used to house the Chelsea Flower Show. A long avenue of plane trees marks the western edge of the gardens.

THE ROOKERY 50
Streatham Common South, London SW16. Tel: (01) 764 5478
Lambeth Council

Streatham High Road, then Streatham Common South ● *Open daily, 10.00 a.m. – dusk. Closed 25th Dec* ● *Best season: July* ● *Parking top of Streatham High Road* ● *Light Refreshments* ● *Toilet facilities* ● *Partly suitable for wheelchairs* ● *Dogs on lead on top terrace only* ● ***Grade II***

A secluded and beautifully kept mixed garden – formerly the walled garden of a private house and the surrounding hillside – with sloping lawns and terraces. Views over Streatham Vale. Walled garden, the beautiful white garden best seen in July, extensive rock garden with a small stream and goldfish pond. Orchard. The entire garden, shrubbery, and herbaceous borders are very well stocked and carefully tended. Delightful old English garden, beautifully scented, with large variety of annual and perennial plants. An orchard picnic area with tables. Abundance of benches donated by grateful Streatham residents for this peaceful and pretty garden a quarter of a mile (uphill) off the busy High Road. Plenty of litter bins. Children enjoy the orchard area (no ball games), the dense shrubbery and hidden, winding paths leading up through the rock garden area and stream.

ROYAL BOTANIC GARDENS 51
Kew Green, Kew, Richmond, Surrey. Tel: (01) 940 1171
Trustees and the Department of the Environment

Kew Green, S of Kew Bridge ● *Open daily, 9.30 a.m. – 4.00 /6.00 p.m. depending on season, glasshouses, 10.00 a.m. – 2.00 /4.00 p.m.* ● *Entrance: £1.00, OAP, children and wheelchair visitors 50p* ● *Parking Kew Green/Queen Elizabeth's Lawn car park (Brentford Gate)* ● *Refreshments: Orangery restaurant, pavilion and tea bar* ● *Toilet facilities inc. disabled* ● *Suitable for wheelchairs which may be hired in advance for 50p* ● *Shop* ● *Kew Palace open summer, Queen Charlotte's cottage open summer weekends and public holidays (April – Sept)* ● ***Grade I***

Internationally renowned, and primarily a botanic institution, collecting, conserving and exchanging plants from all over the world, Kew's delightful and varied gardens and grounds of more than 300 acres have something for everyone. In spring, the flowering cherries, crocuses, daffodils, and tulips and the lovely rock garden, in May and June, the bluebell wood, its lilacs (made famous by the song) and the water-lily house, in summer the herbaceous garden, the rose and cottage gardens, in the autumn bulbs and trees, and in the winter, the heath garden, the winter flowering cherries and (indoors) the alpine house, as well as the year-round pleasure of Decimus Burton's Palm house, the temperate and arid houses, and the recently opened Princess Diana Conservatory with its computer-controlled micro-climates.

Kew's grounds also contain four temples, the famous Pagoda, Japanese Gateway, a campanile, the wood museum, the Marianne North gallery, (filled with 832 oil paintings of plants) besides Kew Palace itself, and the charming Queen Charlotte's cottage. The grass garden has over 600 grasses – besides those of the bamboo garden. About fifty per cent of the herbaceous garden's 2000 species are of wild origin. There is a somewhat formal rose garden, a delightful rock garden – originally of limestone, but completely replaced by sandstone. The Cambridge cottage gardens, the Queen's garden (in the style of a seventeenth-century garden) and the heather garden should not be missed.

The huge glasshouses, which are kept at tropical temperatures, are well worth visiting in winter, with their unique collections of exotic and unusual plants, ranging from banana-trees to giant water lilies. In the Princess Diana Conservatory are imaginative mangrove swamps and deserts, carnivorous plants and orchids.

The trees range from ash and birch collections, through conifers, eucalyptus and mulberry to walnut. The wood museum contains not only specimens of different woods but also inlay work, a history of the manufacture of paper, etc. The lake, once a disused gravel pit, has an abundance of wildfowl. The orangery does not contain oranges – which are to be found in the Citrus Walk (the orangery now has a bookshop, exhibition area and waiter-service restaurant).

It is well worth buying the souvenir guide (price £1.35) and planning a route for the elderly or unenergetic. The disabled will find most parts of Kew very accessible. Children will particularly enjoy the Princess Diana Conservatory, with its Namib deserts and carnivorous plants, as well as the Palm House to see 'real' bananas. Tree-climbing, ball-games, and other sports are not allowed. Neither are radios, cassettes, etc.

7 ST GEORGE'S ROAD   52
St Margaret's, Twickenham, Middlesex.   Tel: (01) 982 3713
Mr and Mrs R. Raworth

Off A316 between Twickenham Bridge and St Margaret's roundabout ● *Open by appointment and Sun 17th June, 2.00 – 6.00 p.m.* ● *Best season: May –*

July • *Entrance: 60p, children 20p* • *Parking in road* • *Teas on open day and by arrangement* • *Plants for sale* • *Grade II*

A most successful result of garden design inspired by Hidcote and Tintinhull, on a miniature scale, seventeen years ago. Mature garden of grace and peacefulness only yards from one of London's main routes to the west. The various 'rooms', Italianate patio, herb garden and knot garden lead through to an emerald carpet of grass and flower borders backing onto old trees in a private park. There are honeysuckles, old roses and many rare shrubs to interest the plantsperson and also the contents of a large elegant greenhouse on the north-facing wall of the wisteria-covered house.

ST JAMES'S PARK 53
The Mall, London SW1. Tel: (01) 930 1793
Department of the Environment

From Buckingham Palace on the W to Horse Guards Parade on the E, the Mall on the N and on the S by Birdcage Walk • *Open daily* • *Entrance: free* • *Parking difficult* • *Refreshments in park* • *Toilet facilities* • *Suitable for wheelchairs* • *Grade I*

Nearly 100 acres, this was the first of the Royal parks in London, originally laid out for Henry VIII. After the Restoration the famous French designer Le Nôtre was employed to make 'great and very noble alterations' and he united the ponds to form what is now one of the finest lakes in London. Charles II opened the park to the public, although the king continued to use it, and it had the advantage, which it still retains, of being relatively unenclosed by railings. Nash altered the form of the lake in 1827-9. Birdcage Walk is so named because it was a Royal aviary. Today the park is perhaps the favourite of Londoners and visitors to the city, not least to civil servants and politicians who can be seen walking across it while ruminating what to do about the Bank Rate. It can be enjoyed at all seasons.

11 SPENCER HILL 54
Wimbledon SW19.
Mr and Mrs B. Willmott

Between The Ridgeway and Worple Road • *Open 20th May, 2.00 - 6.00 p.m.* • *Entrance: £1.50 (combined entry with two other NGS gardens)* • *Parking in street* • *Refreshments: tea and biscuits* • *Toilet facilities* • *Grade III*

The 100 x 50 feet garden of extremely busy owners. The almost dazzling effect of light and colour is achieved entirely by trees, flowering and variegated shrubs. There is scarcely a herbaceous plant or an annual in the place. Apart from one or two trees, everything else has been planted since 1981 but has grown so well that it looks mature and settled. Very large climbers on the house (particularly roses), a pergola planted with old-fashioned roses and clematis, curved beds containing a very wide selection of shrubs, both usual and unusual, planted with particular attention to their association with each other. Also a small vegetable plot and a fruit cage.

STRAWBERRY HOUSE 55
Chiswick Mall, London W4. Tel: (01) 994 3052
Beryl, Countess of Rothes

On River S of Great West Road between Hammersmith flyover and Hogarth roundabout • Open for NGS, parties by appointment • Entrance: 80p, children 20p • Parking in adjacent roads difficult • Grade II

Medium-sized walled London garden with fine mature flowering shrubs and trees; magnolias, camellias, etc. The area near the house paved with old York stone, gives a theatrical effect. A long canal along one side of garden with water plants and sheltered area with tender plants. Furthest third of garden a shaded, woodland area. Tubs of hostas, enormous *Hydrangea petiolaris*. A shaded and slightly shaggy garden with interesting plants and design.

SYON PARK 56
Brentford, Middlesex. Tel: (01) 560 0881/3
His Grace the Duke of Northumberland

2m W of Kew Bridge, road marked from A315/310 at Busch Corner • Open daily 10.00 a.m. – dusk • Entrance: £1.50, OAP and children £1.00 (house and gardens £3.00, OAP and children £2.00) • Parking • Refreshments • Toilet facilities • Suitable for wheelchairs • Plants for sale • Shop • House open, Easter – Sept, 12 noon – 5.00 p.m. • Grade I

The house, built by Robert Adam *c.*1760 was the seat of the Northumberland family who also employed 'Capability' Brown. From woodland garden to Charles Fowler's Great Conservatory (1830) Syon Park shows British gardening on a grand scale. The lakeside walk is of great interest; specimen trees planted in the eighteenth century by Brown still survive, supplemented by irises, day lilies and clumps of Chilian rhubarb. The six-acre rose garden, separated from the park (entrance 10p coin) created on the raised terrace that was constructed by the Protector Duke of Somerset in the sixteenth century, is well worth the extra effort of visiting, especially in June.

TRINITY HOSPICE 57
30 Clapham Common North Side, London SW4.
Tel: (01) 622 9481
Trustees of the Hospice

Off N side of the common • Open 21st, 22nd April, 2nd, 3rd June, 21st, 22nd July, 22nd, 23rd Sept, 2.00 – 5.00 p.m. • Best season: spring, mid-summer • Entrance: 50p, children free • Parking on common • Refreshments • Toilet facilities • Suitable for wheelchairs • Grade II

The gardens at Trinity Hospice were designed primarily for the benefit of patients, their families and their staff. Stretching over nearly two acres, the gardens are set out on slightly rolling park-like terrain and designed by John Medhurst and David Foreman of London Landscape Consortium on the principles adhered to by Lanning Roper. The latter had originally been asked by the Sainsbury Family Charity Trust to design these gardens on a dilapidated site but his illness caught up with him before he could do much. The gardens were finished because of donations made by his friends and called the Lanning Roper Memorial Garden. Perennials and shrubs predominate but there is also a wild garden at one end and a large pool with a modern nubile sculpture and a duck house as slightly incongruous company.

TRUMPETER'S HOUSE AND LODGE GARDEN   58
Old Palace Yard, Richmond, Surrey. Tel: (01) 948 5858
Enquiries to the Environment Trust for Richmond-upon-Thames
Mrs Pamela and Miss Sarah Franklyn

On Richmond Green ● *Open occasionally for charity* ● *Best season: summer* ● *Entrance: £1.50* ● *Parking* ● *Refreshments* ● *Toilet facilities* ● *Suitable for wheelchairs* ● *Plants for sale* ● **Grade II**

Three acres of garden stand on the site of the former Richmond Palace. The gardens feature ponds, many varieties of roses, Judas and mulberry trees and extensive lawns. Behind ironwork gates lies a 'secret garden' where Queen Elizabeth I walked and where a raised Georgian gazebo overlooks one of the loveliest stretches of the river. Here the garden has been laid out with plants of the Elizabethan period and the eye is drawn to a fine white aviary housing white doves. Very well maintained, this is one of the most interesting middle-sized gardens in the London region.

VICTORIA AND ALBERT MUSEUM   59
Cromwell Road, London SW7. Tel: (01) 938 8500
Trustees and Department of the Environment

Cromwell Road, close to South Kensington tube and in walking distance of Harrods ● *Open daily* ● *Entrance: voluntary donation* ● *Parking difficult* ● *Toilet facilities* ● *Suitable for wheelchairs* ● **Grade IV**

Only rarely does the owner of a run-down garden find himself in the position of being offered vast sums by a sponsor who will foot the bill for a complete redesign. This was the case with Sir Roy Strong, former director of the V & A, and his benefactor Pirelli. It is strange that Sir Roy, who is a distinguished writer on gardening and has developed a beautiful garden of his own, should have approved a scheme which is so dessicated, although perhaps he was influenced by the desire to acknowledge his debt to the Italians by making this large open space at the heart of the museum a classic geometry which would shine under a blue Roman sky of the kind rarely prevailing in South Kensington. Whatever the reason, what was done was done with elegance and is maintained to a high standard. Perhaps it would look at its best on one of those V & A club evenings if members were permitted to sip their wine in its calm atmosphere.

WALLACE COLLECTION 60
Manchester Square, London W1. Tel: (01) 935 0687
Trustees of the Wallace Collection

N of Wigmore Street, behind Selfridges • Open daily, weekdays, 10.00 a.m. – 5.00 p.m., Sun, 2.00 – 5.00 p.m. Closed Good Friday, 24th and 25th Dec • Entrance: free • Parking difficult • Toilet facilities (most elegantly tiled in London) • Suitable for wheelchairs • Shop • Gallery open • Grade IV

In the centre of what was the privately-owned Hertford House is one of the most peaceful and secluded courtyard gardens in London. Apart from some clipped box, there is little vegetation, but a French serenity and stylishness are evident in the four pairs of bronze vases, formerly in Lord Hertford's chateau and now flowing with variegated ivy. A fine place to sit and survey the elegant fountain before or after viewing some of the best oil paintings in the world.

WALPOLE HOUSE 61
Chiswick Mall, London W4. Tel: (01) 994 1611
Mr and Mrs Jeremy Benson

S of Great West Road (M4) between Hammersmith flyover and Hogarth roundabout • Open for parties by appointment and 22nd April, 2.00 – 6.00 p.m., 20th May, 2.00 – 7.00 p.m. • Entrance: £1.00, children 20p • Parking in adjacent roads difficult • Refreshments • Toilet facilities • Partly suitable for wheelchairs • Seeds for sale from excellent lists, packed with information and from 10p a packet • Grade II

Two thirds of an acre of formally-designed and informally-planted garden whose sheer size (for London) takes your breath away as you come out into it from the house. A large paved area leading up steps to wide lawns with mature and handsome trees. Beyond a yew hedge is a woodland area, heavily shaded, and intersected with old brick paths. Statues and old garden seat. A formal lily pond (larger than many town gardens) is surrounded by borders and a fence covered with climbers. Many varieties of peonies, irises, climbing roses, clematis, etc. Other borders and further small pool. Much self-seeding in the borders which accounts for the informality within the mostly formal lay-out. The 'front' gardens across the road are regularly flooded by the river.

WALPOLE PARK 62
Ealing, London W5. Tel: (01) 579 2424
London Borough of Ealing

*Centre of Ealing, access from Uxbridge Road and High Street ● Open daily, 8.00 a.m. – dusk ● Parking in surrounding residential roads ● Toilet facilities ● Suitable for wheelchairs ● Dogs on lead ● **Grade III***

The gardens were acquired by the Council and opened to the public in 1901. Large walled rose garden with a pergola. Formal beds set in lawn framed by old cedar trees. Centrepiece of topiary in the shape of a peacock but its tail is a bed of suitably-coloured flowering plants. There is also a water garden in Oriental style.

WANSTEAD PARK 63
Wanstead, London E11. Tel: (01) 530 4594
Corporation of London

*Its western boundary is close to Leytonstone High Road, and its southern boundary to Manor Park ● Open at all times ● Entrance: free ● Parking at any of the several entrances ● Refreshments ● Toilet facilities ● Suitable for wheelchairs ● Dogs ● **Grade IV***

Once the landscaped parkland of the former eighteenth-century Wanstead House, Wanstead Park is now part of Epping Forest. It has minor appeal for gardeners although it forms a major nature reserve with plenty of wildlife, including herons on the large lakes. It is, though, interesting to compare the park today with the map provided by the Corporation of the layout of the original parkland and to trace the relics of the former avenues. With the resurgence of the Docklands, perhaps London Corporation will recreate the park to its former magnificence. The area would be greatly improved by a truly handsome park.

WATERHOUSE PLANTATION 64
(also known as Woodland Garden)
Bushy Park, Hampton, London. Tel: (01) 977 1328
Department of the Environment

*On A308 Hampton Court road, ¼m W of Hampton Court roundabout. Short walk from car park, gate on main road alongside ● Open daily, 9.00 a.m. – dusk ● Best season: spring ● Entrance: free ● Parking ● Suitable for wheelchairs ● **Grade II***

There are two Plantations, both in Bushy Park, adjoining Hampton Court. Planting similar to the Isabella Plantation in Richmond Park (see entry) concentrating on masses of shrubs – rhododendrons, azaleas and camellias. The artificial river, the Longford, is a dramatic feature with many small bridges. Waterhouse suffered in the 1987 gales but has recovered well and there is something to see at all times of the year, such as a heather garden and wild flowers in season.

WATERLOW PARK 65
Highgate High Street, London N6. Tel: (01) 272 2825

Entrance off Highgate Hill and Dartmouth Park, next to Highgate Cemetery
● *Open 7.30 a.m. – dusk* ● *Entrance: free* ● *Parking* ● *Refreshments: café/ restaurant in Lauderdale House* ● *Toilet facilities* ● *Suitable for wheelchairs* ● *Dogs on lead* ● *House open* ● *Grade III*

Roughly 20 acres of woodland shrubberies, lakes, and grassland, plus herbaceous borders and bedding schemes at the Dartmouth Park end of Waterlow Park, it was presented to the public by Sir Sydney Waterlow as 'a garden for the gardenless' in 1891. One of its assets is its size and the varied nature from a formal bedding scheme in one part to wild lakeside planting in another. The excellent views and the sloping nature of the site are also attractive. The café is deservedly popular, particularly in summer, when visitors can sit out on the terrace, actually the back of Lauderdale House. The attractive Highgate Cemetery holding Karl Marx's mortal remains is adjacent.

42 WOODVILLE GARDENS 66
London W5. Tel: (01) 998 4134
Mrs J. Welfare

Off Hanger Lane (off A40) ● *Open by appointment only* ● *Best season: summer* ● *Entrance: free* ● *Parking in street* ● *Suitable for wheelchairs* ● *Grade IV*

Larger than average town garden laid out predominantly to accommodate the owner's love of plants. The beds surrounding the lawn have grown in size as the need for more plant space demanded. There are a number of interesting and unusual ones, including a *Cestrum parqui* on the house wall, a small bed under an apple tree with four different pulmonarias and a large number of silver-leaved and variegated perennials and shrubs. The small raised terrace by the house is interplanted with low-growing silver-foliage plants and geraniums. Below it is a densely planted bed of dwarf alpines. At the bottom is a small bog garden.

A few gardens with Surrey addresses are included in the Greater London section for convenience, but check the Surrey section as another beautiful garden may be nearby.

When telephoning London telephone numbers please note that from May 1990 the 01 prefix will be changed to either 071 or 081. Details from British Telecom.

MANCHESTER (Greater)

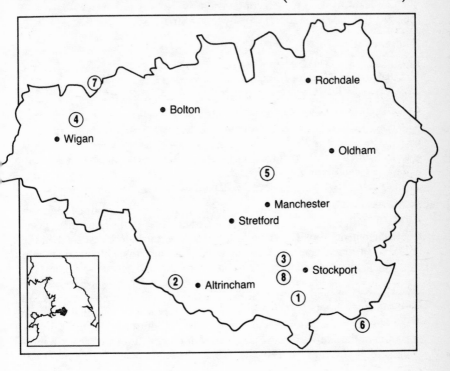

BRAMALL HALL

1

Bramhall Park, Bramhall, Stockport, Greater Manchester.
Tel: (061) 485 3708
Stockport Metropolitan Borough Council

2m S of Stockport on A5102 between Bramhall and Stockport, follow signposts
● *Open daily all day* ● *Best season: late spring/early summer* ● *Entrance: free*
(gardens) ● *Parking* ● *Refreshments in tea shop in converted stables* ● *Toilet*
facilities ● *Partly suitable for wheelchairs* ● *Dogs* ● *Shop in Hall* ● *House*
open April – Sept, daily, 1.00 – 5.00 p.m., Oct – Dec, Feb – March, daily except
Mon, 1.00 – 4.00 p.m. Closed January, 25th, 26th Dec. Entrance £1.50, OAP
and children 75p ● ***Grade IV***

The gardens of Bramall Hall are a missed opportunity. At the front of this
magnificent black and white timber-framed house is a courtyard covered in
tarmac. To the back a slope down from the house has been terraced using brick
retaining walls. These are in bad repair and of an unfortunate choice of brick.
The best parts of the gardens are a little distance to the front of the house
where, in a narrow strip of land, are some formal beds containing bright

annuals and a herbaceous border enclosed by a hedge. The parkland is another matter. In the valley of a small river are broad areas of grassland and a number of small lakes. Woods, which contain some very large beech trees, surround the park and hide all sign of the suburbs of Stockport.

DUNHAM MASSEY   2
Nr Altrincham, Greater Manchester.   Tel: (061) 941 1025
The National Trust

*3m SW of Altrincham off A56 ● Open 31st March – Oct, daily, 12 noon –
5.30 p.m., Sun and Bank Holiday Mons, 11.00 a.m. - 5.30 p.m. ● Entrance:
£1.00 garden only ● Parking ● Refreshments: licensed self-service restaurant
● Toilet facilities ● Suitable for wheelchairs ● Dogs on lead in park only
● Shop ● House open 31st March – Oct, daily except Fri, 1.00 – 5.00 p.m., Sun
and Bank Holiday Mons, 12 noon - 5.00 p.m. ● Grade II*

Dunham Massey has extensive parkland with much of its layout dating from the eighteenth century and earlier. The gardens close to the house have many historic elements too. The lake that borders the north and west sides of the house was formerly part of a moat and overlooking it is a mount that dates from the Tudor period, now grassed over and planted with false acacias. On the north side of the house, in front of the lake, is an Edwardian parterre planted in purple and gold; to the east is a large lawn bordered by shrubs and trees where there is an eighteenth-century orangery and an old well house. The Trust has carried out much replanting with the aim of restoring it 'in the character of the late-Victorian Pleasure Ground'. The result appears extremely successful. Some engravings in the stables show Dunham Massey as it was.

FLETCHER MOSS BOTANICAL GARDENS
and PARSONAGE GARDENS   3
Mill Gate Lane, Didsbury, Greater Manchester.
Tel: (061) 434 1877
Manchester City Council (Recreational Services)

*5m S of Manchester city centre on Mill Gate Lane which runs S of the A5145
close to the centre of the village of Didsbury ● Open all year, 9.00 a.m. - dusk
● Entrance: free ● Limited parking ● Refreshments: in small café (the
building where the first meeting of the RSPB took place) but opening times
uncertain ● Toilet facilities inc. disabled ● Partly suitable for wheelchairs
● Dogs allowed in certain areas only ● House open. The Fletcher Moss Museum
and Art Gallery, in the Parsonage Gardens on Stenner Lane on the N side of
Fletcher Moss Gardens, open daily except Tues, 10.00 a.m. – 6.00 p.m., Sun 2.00
– 6.00 p.m. ● Grade II*

Much of this garden is set on a steep south-facing bank that is planted with a great variety of shrubs, heathers, bulbs, alpines, azaleas and small trees. Amongst them are rocky streams running down to a water garden and lawned area where there are moisture-loving plants including a large clump of gunnera. Across some tennis courts is a large grassed area containing specimen trees. Within a short walking distance are the Parsonage Gardens which are the grounds of the Fletcher Moss Museum. They were laid out in Victorian times and are more formal, containing lawns, good herbaceous borders, camellias and rhododendrons. There are also some fine trees notably a swamp cypress and a mulberry. Excellent well-maintained gardens.

HAIGH HALL GARDENS 4

Haigh Country Park, Haigh, Nr Wigan, Greater Manchester.
Tel: (0942) 832895
Metropolitan Borough of Wigan (Department of Leisure)

2m NE of Wigan on N side of B5238. Signposted ● Parkland open all year, daily during daylight hours. Zoo open, daily, Easter - Sept ● Entrance: mainly free, but some areas of the gardens are entered through the zoo for which there is a charge ● Parking (50p on Sun and Bank Holidays) ● Refreshments: café ● Toilet facilities ● Suitable for wheelchairs which are available from the information centre ● Dogs on lead ● Shop ● Grade III

Haigh Hall is surrounded by mature parkland, and a short distance to the east of the hall are some formal gardens probably of Victorian and Edwardian origin. In an open area of lawn there is an oval pool around which are rose beds and specimen shrubs. Close by are three adjoining walled gardens, the middle one containing a good herbaceous border and a well-stocked shrub border. The second, to the south, has shrubs around the walls and young specimen trees planted in a lawn in the centre; the wall to the south is low and gives a view across a wild garden with a pond. The third walled garden at the northen end can only be entered from the zoo and here against the south facing wall is a cactus house and a butterfly house. On the west side is a landscaped area with heathers and conifers. The rest is a formal layout with roses, yew hedges and lawns and, against the east wall, a border of shrub roses.

HEATON HALL 5

Heaton Park, Prestwich, Greater Manchester.
Tel: (061) 773 1231
Manchester City Council

4m N of the city centre on A576 just S of junction with M66 ● Open all year during daylight hours ● Best season: spring ● Entrance: free ● Parking ● Refreshments: café ● Toilet facilities ● Some areas suitable for wheelchairs, but ring for advice before visiting ● Dogs ● Shop ● House open April - Sept, daily except Tues, weekdays, 10.00 a.m. - 6.00 p.m., Sun, 2.00 - 6.00 p.m. entrance free ● Grade III

Heaton Hall, built in 1772 by Wyatt, was described by Pevsner as 'the finest house of its period in Lancashire'. To the front of the lovely Hall is an area of formal, brightly planted gardens that would perhaps go better in front of a Victorian house. To the rear are some stables, with a small heather garden at their front and behind a large formal rose garden. A path leads through a tunnel to an attractive dell planted with a variety of mature trees and many rhododendrons. From here a path follows a stream through a series of pools and waterfalls with many new plantings on its surrounding banks leading to a large boating lake. On the Prestwich side of the park is an old walled garden where small demonstration gardens have been created including a low-maintenance garden, a cottage garden and an alpine garden. A large greenhouse is also open to view.

LYME PARK   6
Disley, Stockport, Greater Manchester.   Tel: (0663) 62023
The National Trust

6m SE of Stockport just W of Disley on A6   ● Open all year, daily except 25th and 26th Dec. Summer 11.00 a.m. – 6.00 p.m. Winter 11.00 a.m. – 4.00 p.m. Guided tours at special times   ● Entrance: pedestrians free, car £2.50 to include occupants   ● Parking   ● Refreshments: teas sometimes available in hall, kiosk in car park   ● Toilet facilities   ● Special help is available with wheelchairs. Phone in advance   ● Dogs on leads   ● Shop   ● House open at different times and at extra charge   ● Grade II

Lyme Park has immense character and the gardens contrast well within the rugged hills (and usually clouds) that surround it. A lawn at the front of the house leads down to a lake beyond which is a woodland garden underplanted with rhododendrons and other shade-loving plants. To the east is a fine orangery and below the terrace to the west is a well-kept geometric Dutch garden.

RIVINGTON TERRACED GARDENS   7
Rivington, Greater Manchester.   Tel: (061) 477 1100
North West Water Authority

2m NW of Horwich. Follow the signposts to Rivington from the A673 in Horwich or in Grimeford village. The gardens are reached by a 10-minute walk from Rivington Hall and Hall Barn   ● Open at all times   ● Best season: June   ● Entrance: free   ● Parking, refreshments, toilet facilities and shop at Hall Barn   ● Dogs   ● Grade IV

These are not gardens as such but the remains of gardens that were built by Lord Leverhulme in the early part of this century. They are set mainly in woodland on a steep west-facing hillside and have fine views across Rivington reservoirs. It is worth buying the guide which leads the visitor round and explains the various features. Particularly impressive is a rocky ravine, the remains of a Japanese garden and the restored pigeon tower. There are a variety of mature trees and many rhododendrons and once this must have been a very grand estate. When visiting be prepared for a stiff walk and beware of the paths which can be slippery in some areas.

WYTHENSHAWE HORTICULTURAL CENTRE 8
Wythenshawe Park, Wythenshawe Road, Greater Manchester.
Tel: (061) 945 1768
Manchester City Council

7m S of Manchester city centre, ¼m from M63 junction 9, ½m from M56 junction 3, S of B5167 ● *Open daily, 10.00 a.m. – 4.00 p.m.* ● *Parking* ● *Refreshments: cafeteria at hall, April – Sept. Closed Tues* ● *Toilet facilities inc. disabled in park* ● *Partly suitable for wheelchairs* ● *House open April – Sept, weekdays except Tues, 10.00 a.m. – 6.00 p.m., Sun, 2.00 - 6.00 p.m.* ● *Grade III*

Set on the site of an old vegetable garden, this centre is now the nursery that provides most of the bedding stock for the city's parks. It also houses many surprisingly large collections of plants. Outside are herbaceous beds, vegetable plots, heather beds and an area of small trees and conifers. Among the many greenhouses is a cactus house containing many large specimens, a temperate house, a fern and orchid house, an alpine house and a chrysanthemum house. There is also a Visitors' Centre where the staff are always willing to help with advice. To the east of the Centre is the Hall, with some formal gardens, including a large bed devoted to spiraeas.

HOW TO FIND THE GARDENS

Directions to each garden are included in each entry. This information has been supplied by the garden inspectors and is aimed to be the best available to those travelling by car. However, it has been compiled to be used in conjunction with a road atlas.

The unreliability of train and bus services makes it unrewarding to include details, particularly as many garden visits are made on Sundays. However, many properties can be reached by public transport and National Trust guides and the Yellow Book [NGS] give details. Future editions of the *Guide* may include a special list of gardens easily reached by public transport if readers indicate that this would be helpful.

The Maps: The numbers on the maps correspond to the numbers of the gardens in each county. The maps show the proximity of one garden to another so that visits to several gardens can be planned for the same day. It is worthwhile referring to the maps of bordering counties to see if another garden visit can be included in your itinerary. The maps should be used in conjunction with a road atlas.

MERSEYSIDE

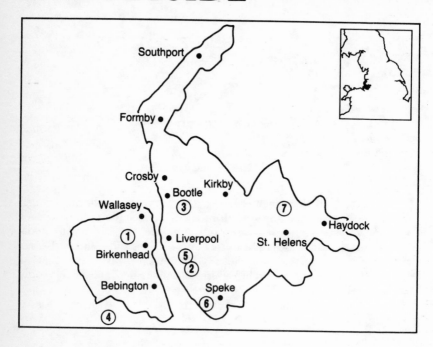

BIRKENHEAD PARK 1
Birkenhead, Wirral, Merseyside. Tel: (051) 647 2366
Metropolitan Borough of Wirral

1m from the centre of Birkenhead on S of A553 ● *Open during daylight hours*
● *Best season: autumn* ● *Entrance: free* ● *Parking around park*
● *Refreshments: tea kiosk sometimes open* ● *Partly suitable for wheelchairs*
● *Dogs in some areas only* ● *Grade II*

Birkenhead Park is rich in history. Opened in 1847, it was the world's first
park to be built at public expense. Joseph Paxton produced its design which
was highly influential in the creation of New York's Central Park. It is split
into two by a road; on the eastern side is a lake with well-landscaped banks
planted with trees and shrubs. A Swiss-style bridge links two islands and to
one end is a fine stone boathouse, soon to be the subject of a restoration
project. In the west part is another lake with weeping willows and rhododendrons planted round its edge. There is also an enclosed area of more
ornamental plants. This park is so well landscaped and planted that it is
possible to overlook the litter and vandalism from which it suffers.

CALDERSTONE PARK 2
Liverpool, Merseyside. Tel: (051) 724 2371
Liverpool City Council, Environmental Services

4m SE of Liverpool city centre, S of A562 ● Park open at all times. Old English Garden and Japanese Garden open April - Sept, 8.00 a.m. - 7.30 p.m., Oct - March, 8.00 a.m. - 4.00 p.m. Closed 25th Dec ● Entrance: free ● Parking ● Refreshments in teashop ● Toilet facilities ● Suitable for wheelchairs ● Dogs in park only ● Grade II

This is a large landscaped park with mature trees, shrubs, a lake and rhododendron walk. In its centre are three gardens set around an old walled garden which are a credit to the city council gardener here. The first is a flower garden which has semiformal beds of perennials and grasses, formal beds of annuals and a long greenhouse. Next is the Old English garden, where amongst a formal layout of paths are beds containing a huge range of perennials, bulbs and shrubs. There is a circular pond at the centre and pergolas carrying clematis, vines and other climbers cross the paths at various points. Finally the Japanese garden has a chain of rocky streams and pools around which are pines, acers and clumps of bamboo. A greenhouse contains the National Collection of the genus *Aechmea*. Altogether this must be one of the best 'free' gardens in the country. Unfortunately the park itself is badly affected by litter.

CROXTETH HALL AND COUNTRY PARK 3
Liverpool, Merseyside. Tel: (051) 228 5311
Liverpool City Council

Turn N off A5058 Liverpool ring road into Muirhead Avenue on NE side of city. Croxteth Park is well signposted ● Open 16th April - 24th Sept, daily, 11.00 a.m. - 5.00 p.m., Easter and winter times on request ● Best season: summer ● Entrance: 50p for walled garden ● Parking ● Refreshments in cafeteria ● Toilet facilities ● Partly suitable for wheelchairs ● Dogs in park only ● Shop in house ● House open, entrance 90p ● Grade III

Croxteth Hall stands in 500 acres of parkland in which there are large areas of woodland and many rhododendrons. The centre of interest to gardeners is the large walled garden to the north of the house. Divided up by gravel paths, this garden contains areas growing a great variety of fruit, vegetables and decorative plants; fruit espaliers are grown against the walls and trained on wire fences and the south-facing wall has a broad herbaceous border containing a good variety of perennials and ornamental grasses. In the north east corner are several greenhouses and a mushroom house surrounded by herb beds, and, close by, some working beehives.

NESS GARDENS 4
University of Liverpool Botanic Gardens, Ness, Weston, South Wirral, Merseyside. Tel: (051) 336 2135
University of Liverpool

2m off A540 on Neston Road between Ness and Burton ● Open daily except 25th Dec, 9.00 a.m. – sunset ● Entrance: £1.80, OAP and children 8 – 18 years £1.00, family ticket £4.00 ● Parking ● Refreshments available Easter – Sept ● Toilet facilities ● Suitable for wheelchairs ● Dogs on lead ● Plants for sale ● Shop ● Grade I

A Mr Bulley began gardening on this site in 1898 using plants collected for him by George Forrest, the noted plant hunter. His daughter gave the gardens to the University in 1948. They extend to over 60 acres. Those who have experience of the north west winds blowing off the Irish Sea will marvel at the variety and exotic nature of the plant life. The secret is in the Lombardy poplars, holm oaks and Scots pines which have been planted as shelter belts shielding the specialist areas. The aim has been to provide all-year round interest from the spring, through the herbaceous and rose gardens of the summer to the heather and sorbus collections of the autumn. There are in addition areas of specialist interest such as the Nature Plant Garden which houses plants raised from seed or cuttings from wild plants and used for propagation or the re-stocking of natural habitats. For all its specialist and academic background we found the labelling of plants somewhat inadequate and though there are a number of signed 'walks' (including one suitable for wheelchairs) here again the signs could be clearer without being obtrusive. The coloured illustrated guide (at £1.00) is therefore a must.

SEFTON PARK 5
Liverpool, Merseyside. Tel: (051) 724 2371
Liverpool City Council (controlled by Environmental Services, Calderstone Park)

3m SE of Liverpool city centre, N of A561 ● Open at all times ● Best season: spring ● Entrance: free ● Parking at various points around park ● Refreshments at café in centre of park ● Suitable for wheelchairs ● Dogs ● Grade III

Although this large park suffers badly from litter and vandalism it remains an extremely fine Victorian park, with many of its monuments, gateways and shelters as well as the large houses surrounding it built in the Gothic style of the late 1800s. A large serpentine boating lake has two small streams entering at its northern end. One stream flows from the east through a lightly wooded valley that has been landscaped with large rocks and planted with rhododendrons. The other flows from the north through a series of small lakes passing a replica of Piccadilly's Eros, a statue of Peter Pan and an ornate bandstand. In the centre of the park is a magnificent palm house now in bad repair but a restoration scheme is soon to be undertaken.

SPEKE HALL 6
The Walk, Liverpool, Merseyside.   Tel: (051) 427 7231
The National Trust

8m SE of Liverpool city centre, S of A561. Signposted ● Open April – Oct, daily except Mon, weekdays, 1.00 – 5.30 p.m., 3rd Nov – 16th Dec, Sat and Sun, 1.00 – 4.30 p.m. Closed Good Friday ● Best season: spring ● Entrance: 50p ● Parking 50p ● Refreshments in teashop ● Toilet facilities inc. disabled ● Partly suitable for wheelchairs ● Shop ● House open £2.20. Reductions for parties ● Grade III

The gardens at Speke are neither as old nor as impressive as the Elizabethan hall. They are remarkable however for although they are situated amidst the industrial areas of south Liverpool they seem to be set in the heart of the countryside, despite their proximity to Liverpool airport. In front of the house is a large lawn with shrub borders to the sides containing mainly rhododendrons and hollies. On the side opposite the house is a ha-ha allowing views to the fields and woodland. A stone bridge leads over a drained moat to the ornate stone entrance of the hall. The moat continues to the west where there is a herbaceous border with a variety of perennials; a large holm oak stands opposite. To the south is a formal rose garden containing fragrant varieties of old-fashioned roses. In the centre of the house is a large cobbled courtyard in which grow two enormous yews.

WINDLE HALL 7
St Helens, Merseyside.
The Lady Pilkington

1½m NE of St Helens, N of A570 ● Open 1st July, 2nd Sept, 2.00 – 5.00 p.m. ● Entrance: 60p ● Parking ● Refreshments ● Toilet facilities ● Partly suitable for wheelchairs ● Dogs on leads ● Grade III

A large part of these gardens is set in a 200-year old walled garden where there is a complex layout of well-tended lawns, paths and flower beds. The latter contain many bright annuals and modern roses. There are also herbaceous borders, rose trellises and fruit trees. At one end is a small greenhouse and close by a pool with a fountain. To the east of the walled garden in an area that is mainly lawned is a small rock garden, water garden and stone grotto. The east front of the hall looks down on a pool that is surrounded by azaleas and backed by high conifers. In an area of woodland around the garden are spring-flowering plants.

MIDLANDS (West)

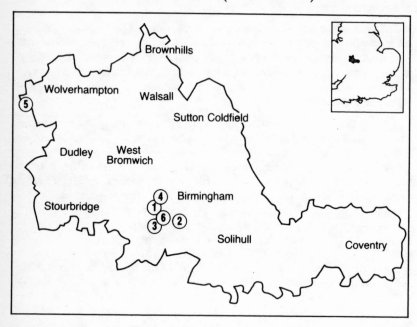

BIRMINGHAM BOTANICAL GARDENS 1
Westbourne Road, Edgbaston, Birmingham, West Midlands.
Tel: (021) 454 1860

2m from city centre. Approach from Hagley Road or Calthorpe Road ● *Open summer, Mon – Sat, 9.00 a.m. – 7.30 p.m., Sun, 10.00 a.m. – 7.30 p.m., winter closes at 6.00 p.m. or dusk* ● *Entrance: £2.00, OAP and children £1.00* ● *Parking* ● *Refreshments: restaurant. Picnics allowed* ● *Toilet facilities* ● *Suitable for wheelchairs. Two chairs available for use free of charge* ● *Plants for sale* ● *Shop* ● **Grade II**

This garden will appeal to the keen plantsperson and also to the everyday gardener. In addition to the unusual plants in the Tropical house and the orangery, there is a cactus and succulent house, and cages with parrots and also guinea fowl, ducks, peacocks, geese and other birds. Some beautiful old trees, a border for E.H. Wilson plants, a raised alpine bed and a raised garden area to give ideas and enjoyment to disabled visitors. Good colour foliage contrasts and a small area laid out with model domestic gardens. The rock garden contains rhododendrons, primulas, astilbes and azaleas and there are also herbaceous borders and a rose garden. A children's playground makes the garden a pleasant place for a family outing.

CANNON HILL PARK 2
Moseley, Birmingham, West Midlands.   Tel: (021) 449 0238
Birmingham City Council

2m from Birmingham city centre opposite Edgbaston Cricket Ground   ● Open daily, 8.00 a.m. - dusk   ● Best season: spring/ summer   ● Entrance: free ● Parking   ● Refreshments: lunches and snacks in park restaurant. Picnic area ● Toilet facilities in Midlands Art Centre open 9.00 a.m. - 9.00 p.m. ● Suitable for wheelchairs   ● Dogs   ● Art Centre in park, bookshop, gallery and restaurant   ● Grade III

Eighty acres of park with formal beds, wide range of herbaceous plants, shrubs and trees. Glasshouse with collection of tropical and sub-tropical plants open 10.00 a.m. - 4.00 p.m. Nature trails. Children's area.

MARTINEAU ENVIRONMENTAL
STUDIES CENTRE 3
Priory Road, Edgbaston, Birmingham, West Midlands.
Tel: (021) 4404883
City of Birmingham Education Department

Turn off A38 road into Priory Road and entrance is 100 yards on right opposite Priory Hospital   ● Open 15th July and weekdays by arrangement, 10.00 a.m. - 6.00 p.m.   ● Best season: July   ● Entrance: £1.00, children 50p   ● Parking ● Tea on open day   ● Toilet facilities   ● Suitable for wheelchairs   ● Plants for sale   ● Grade III

This is a two-acre educational garden designed for teachers and children but the wide range of features make it interesting for all, and a good place for the family with children interested in gardening. There are annuals, herbaceous and shrub borders, roses, raised beds, herbs, alpines, bulbs, miscanthus and the greenhouse with a collection of cactus, tomatoes and peppers along with tropical crops such as a banana, fig and coffee plant. In the woodland area there are native plants and a pool with plenty of wildlife. The vegetable plots contain brassicas, root crops and legumes and the fruit trees and soft fruit include a medlar, greengage, apricot, blueberry and tayberry. School children work on some of the plots – so the weeds prosper during school holidays.

8 VICARAGE ROAD 4
Edgbaston, Birmingham, West Midlands.
Tel: (021) 455 0902
Mr and Mrs C.R. King-Farlow

1½ W of city centre off A456 Hagley road. Turn left from city into Vicarage Road   ● Open 17th June and by appointment   ● Best season: May/June and early July   ● Entrance: 50p, children 20p   ● Parking in local roads   ● Teas ● Suitable for wheelchairs   ● Plants for sale at certain times   ● Grade III

A visit to this garden should give pleasure to most gardeners as there is a sense of mystery as one moves from one area to the next. Plenty of good planting ideas can be seen with the clever use of colour and foliage combinations – a range of grey and variegated foliage. Roses and clematis scramble through old fruit trees and other shrubs. There is a bank of shrub roses, and the herbaceous border consists of three tiers and contains a wide range and some rare plants. There is a conservatory, pool and 1920s rock garden providing year-round colour. The walled kitchen garden has fruit and vegetables. It is hard to believe that one is walking through a garden so near the centre of a large city.

WIGHTWICK MANOR 5
Wightwick Bank, Wolverhampton, West Midlands.
Tel: (0902) 761108
The National Trust

3m W of Wolverhampton off A454. Turn by the Mermaid Inn up Wightwick Bank ● *Open all year, except Feb, Thurs and Sat, Bank Holiday Sun and Mon, 2.00 – 6.00 p.m. Closed 25th, 26th Dec and 1st, 2nd Jan. Parties by arrangement* ● *Entrance: £1.00* ● *Parking* ● *Minimal refreshments* ● *Toilet facilities* ● *Suitable for wheelchairs* ● *Dogs on lead* ● *Shop* ● *House open at extra charge* ● ***Grade III***

This 10-acre garden, designed by Alfred Parsons, surrounds an 1887 house strongly influenced in its design by William Morris and his movement; it contains a collection of pre-Raphaelite paintings. Large trees form a delightful framework to the garden with a central octagonal arbour with climbing roses and clematis. Moving through an old orchard one reaches a less formal area with pools surrounded by shrubs and rhododendrons. There are herbaceous borders, two rows of barrel-shaped yews and beds containing plants from gardens of famous men. As a surprise round a corner one comes across a line of boulders from Scotland and the Lake District which were left when the great glaciers melted in the last Ice Age.

WINTERBOURNE 6
Edgbaston Park Road, Edgbaston, Birmingham.   Tel: (021) 414 5613
(Warden: D.C. Barre – Friends of Winterbourne)
University of Birmingham School of Continuing Studies

Off A38 Bristol Road leading out of the city, adjacent to the University campus ● *Open for parties by arrangement* ● *Parking* ● *Toilet facilities* ● *Suitable for wheelchairs* ● *Plants sometimes for sale* ● ***Grade III***

About nine acres of garden originally belonging to a large house, this is of interest to the botanist and the ordinary gardener as it contains so many different features and a wide range of plants. There is a large collection of trees – acers, conifers, giant oaks, *Gingko biloba*, and hedges of yew, *Taxus baccata* and newly planted copper beech. The pergola is covered with clematis and roses, there are herbaceous borders backed by brick walls covered with climbers, beds of berberis and a wide selection of heathers and rhododendrons. The range of plants continues with the rock and water gardens, troughs and raised beds with alpines. The labels with details of country of origin and family are especially good and the walled garden is laid out with beds of roses depicting the origin of rose varieties from 1750-1986. Elsewhere is a more recent planting of roses.

THE GRADING SYSTEM

This is the most subjective aspect of the *Guide* and one which may cause some disagreement on the part of owners as well as visitors. We stress that its purpose is to serve as an indication to visitors in order to give them some advance information about the status of the garden as viewed by our inspectors and editors. Readers will appreciate that direct comparisons cannot be made between a huge estate like Chatsworth with its staff of professional experts and a tiny plantsman's garden in a terraced house, tended with dedication by a single owner. This being said, both may be excellent of their kind and therefore be worthy of consideration for a visit, and considered by the *Guide* to be at the top of their class. Conversely a lesser grading does not imply any criticism of a garden but is an attempt to guide the potential reader as to its relative merits if a choice has to be made between several gardens. Broadly speaking the intention of the four grades is as follows:

Grade I Amongst the best gardens in the world in terms of design and content. Many are of historic importance, but some are of recent origin. Overseas visitors to Britain or Ireland are recommended to include them in their itinerary.

Grade II Gardens of high quality, though not perhaps as unique as Grade I, and worth travelling a considerable distance to visit. Sometimes the property as a whole, and the general ambience, make the visit particularly rewarding.

Grade III These are gardens which our inspectors suggest it would be worth driving fifty miles or more to visit. They may have some special feature of design or plant content while not being considered as justifying a higher grade overall.

Grade IV Gardens of considerable merit and well worth visiting when in the region.

NORFOLK

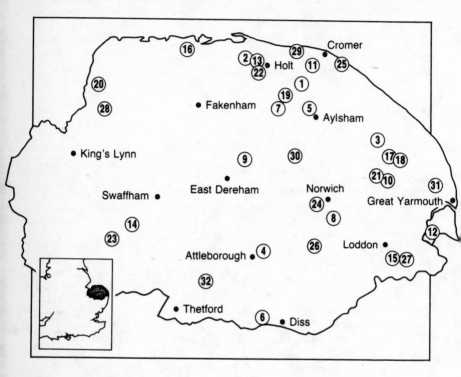

BARNINGHAM HALL

1

Little Barningham, Matlaske, Norfolk. Tel: (026377) 250
Sir Charles and Lady Mott-Radclyffe

18m NW of Norwich, 3m N of B1149 and B1354 junction at Saxthorpe
● Open 26th Aug, 2.00 – 6.30 p.m. ● Entrance: 50p ● Parking
● Refreshments ● Partly suitable for wheelchairs ● Grade III

An Elizabethan house surrounded by mature parkland across which there is a
fine prospect of the lake, the work of Repton who also redesigned the east
facade and added a terrace which has herbaceous beds. There is a walled
garden with herbaceous plants as well as trained fruit trees.

BAYFIELD HALL

2

Nr Holt, Norfolk. Tel: (026371) 2219
Mr and Mrs R.H. Combe

3m NW of Holt off B1156 ● Open for NGS ● Best season: June – Aug
● Entrance: £1.00, children 50p ● Parking ● Refreshments ● Grade III

The house commands one of the most beautiful views in Norfolk. The grounds are thought to have been landscaped by Repton. The wooded valley of the Glaven has been dammed to form a lake. A formal garden designed by Lanning Roper was established in the mid-twentieth century with borders containing a good selection of shrubs and herbaceous plants and sited on rising ground at one side, it does not interfere with the relationship of the house with its landscape. A ruined church forms another pleasing feature.

BEESTON HALL 3
Beeston St Lawrence, Wroxham, Norfolk. Tel: (0692) 630771
Sir Ronald and Lady Preston

2¼m NE of Wroxham off A1151 ● *Open April – Sept, Fri, Sun, Bank Holiday Mon, also Wed in Aug, 2.00 – 5.30 p.m.* ● *Best season: early summer*
● *Entrance: £1.50, OAP £1.20, children 60p, grounds only 60p* ● *Parking*
● *Toilet facilities* ● *Suitable for wheelchairs* ● *Shop* ● *House open*
● *Grade III*

The Gothic house of 1786 stands on rising ground overlooking a long serpentine lake. The gardens to the south of the house are pretty although not extensive. There is a brick orangery, herbaceous and shrub borders, and some mature trees of early nineteenth-century planting. The park originally laid out by Richmond (a contemporary of 'Capability' Brown) is now largely given over to farming and a broad path winds down through corn fields to woodland where there is an ice-house and a lakeside walk.

BESTHORPE HALL 4
Besthorpe, Attleborough, Norfolk. Tel: (0953) 452138
Mr J.A. Alston

1m E of Attleborough on Bunwell Road. Entrance on right, past church ● *Open by appointment and 17th June, 2.00 – 5.30 p.m., 15th July, 2.00 – 5.00 p.m.*
● *Best season: June* ● *Entrance: £1.00* ● *Parking* ● *Refreshments* ● *Toilet facilities* ● *Suitable for wheelchairs* ● *Plants for sale* ● *Grade II*

A pool and fountain occupy the centre of the entrance forecourt. Beyond the house, more pools and fountains are set among lawns skirted by high clematis-hung walls of Tudor brick which form a backdrop to long herbaceous borders. The largest lawn, believed to have once been a tilt yard, has developing topiary, while on another is an enormous and shapely Wellingtonia. There are many other fine trees among which are paulownia, and a variety of birches, acers and magnolias including the sumptuous *M. delavayi*. There are walled kitchen gardens, a nuttery, a herb garden, and a small lake with wildfowl. On another lushly planted pool live a pair of black swans.

BLICKLING HALL 5
Aylsham, Norfolk. Tel: (0263) 733084
The National Trust

1½m NW of Aylsham on N side of B1354 ● Open March – Oct, daily except Mon and Thurs, 1.00 – 5.00 p.m. and in July and Aug, 12 noon – 5.00 p.m. Open Bank Holiday Mons, closed Good Friday ● Entrance: £2.00 ● Parking ● Refreshments ● Toilet facilities ● Suitable for wheelchairs ● Plants for sale ● Shop ● House open £4.00 inc. garden ● Grade II

Although a garden for over 300 years the formal area was only designed in 1872 by W.A. Nesfield. It was given its present shape by Norah Lindsay in the 1930s. The main garden is in keeping with the Jacobean house with topiary features and well-planted beds and walls. Beyond it lies the park with radiating vistas through mature woodland though much of this was severely damaged in the October 1987 gale. There are still good specimen trees. Close to the house the moat contains plants which appreciate shade and shelter.

BRESSINGHAM GARDENS 6
Bressingham, Diss, Norfolk. Tel: (037988) 386/382
Mr Alan Bloom

3m W of Diss on A1066 ● Open Thurs and Sun, May – Sept and Wed in Aug, also Bank Holiday Mons, 10.00 a.m. – 5.30 p.m. ● Best season: all spring and summer ● Entrance: £2.00, OAP £1.75, children £1.00 ● Parking ● Refreshments ● Toilet facilities ● Suitable for wheelchairs ● Plants for sale ● Shop ● Grade II

The six acres of this garden are chiefly occupied by island beds, a scheme which, if it lacks variety, allows for the display of over 5000 kinds of hardy perennials, and the beds are full of colours and interest throughout the spring, summer and autumn. Unfortunately, Bressingham's importance as a garden is seriously compromised by the associated steam museum through which it is necessary to pass and no attempt has been made to keep the two competing attractions apart. On the contrary, a railway runs through the garden and the potentially very beautiful lakeside area in particular has been spoilt by trampling feet and railway paraphernalia. The large plant centre, although adding to the general feeling of commercialisation, does offer a wide variety of trees, shrubs and herbaceous plants. The adjoining garden of Adrian Bloom, with a large collection of conifers and heathers, is open on three days during the year and offers the chance to see many rare conifers becoming well established.

CORPUSTY MILL GARDENS 7
Corpusty, Norfolk.   Tel: (026387) 223
Mrs H.M. Last

*15m NW of Norwich on B1149   ● Usually open first Sun in July but enquire. At
other times by appointment   ● Best season: May – July   ● Entrance: £1.00,
children 50p   ● Dogs on lead   ● Grade II*

By the River Bure is a series of linked lawns, glades, and enclosures with open
and shady spaces among a rich variety of trees, shrubs and herbaceous plants.
A stream runs through the garden supporting luxuriant growth. Garden
buildings in the form of Gothic ruins, a classical pavilion and a grotto, provide
a series of incidents along a meandering route, taking in a kitchen garden. By
fully utilising every corner, these make the garden seem much larger than its
present one acre. A riverside extension of two acres is being developed. This
is one of Britain's most stylish and interesting recently-created gardens.

CROWN POINT 8
Whitlingham Hospital, Whitlingham, Norwich, Norfolk.
Tel: (0603) 628521
Norwich Health Authority

*2m SE of Norwich. Fork left off A146 at Trowse   ● Open by appointment
● Entrance: donations invited to help with upkeep   ● Parking   ● Toilet facilities
● Suitable for wheelchairs   ● Grade III*

An elaborate formal garden was established after 1866 around a new mansion
built in eighteenth-century parkland. The great iron-frame conservatory,
probably designed by H.E. Coe, remained unglazed until 1900-1905 when
Edward Boardman completed it for J.J. Coleman, adding the marble floor and
mosaic-lined basin. Recently threatened with demolition, this splendid aisled
structure, 76 x 44 x 34 feet in height, has now been saved and restored to its
former grandeur. Some of the Edwardian plants remain including palms,
hibiscus, orange, *Acacia dealbata* and *baillyana* and *Cupressus cashmeriana*. The
Victorian bedding- out was replaced by an 'Arts and Crafts' garden of yew
topiary and a large pool replaced by a croquet lawn. Much has been lost since
the conversion of the house to a hospital for the elderly but the remaining
gardens are cared for and with change of use likely in the near future,
opportunities for further restoration may arise.

ELSING HALL 9
Elsing, Nr Dereham, Norfolk.   Tel: (0362) 83224
Mr and Mrs D.H. Cargill

*5m NE of East Dereham. Elsing signposted off A47 and B1067   ● Open 24th
June, 1st July, 2.00 - 6.00 p.m.   ● Entrance: £1.00, children free   ● Parking
● Refreshments   ● Dogs on lead   ● House open by appointment   ● Grade II*

Notwithstanding the claims of Mannington Hall or nearby Swannington Manor, this is probably the most romantic garden in Norfolk. It surrounds a moated flint and chalk timbered manor house. The garden, although mostly of recent planting, is rich, lush, and wild, and if rather too overgrown for those with more manicured tastes, perfectly complements the beautiful manor house. The lawn between the house and the moat has been abandoned to wild orchids; wildfowl nest in the reedy water. A walled kitchen garden contains many old varieties of fruit trees. Old roses everywhere. A perfect setting for Tennyson's 'Mariana'.

FAIRHAVEN GARDEN TRUST 10
South Walsham, Norwich, Norfolk.
Fairhaven Garden Trust

9m NE of Norwich off B1140 • *Open April, Sun and Bank Holidays, May – Sept, Wed – Sun and Bank Holiday Mons, 2.00 – 6.00 p.m.* • *Best season: May/June* • *Entrance: £1.50, OAP £1.00, children 70p* • *Parking* • *Refreshments* • *Toilet facilities* • *Suitable for wheelchairs* • *Dogs on lead* • *Plants for sale* • ***Grade II***

A garden created in natural woods of oak and alder extending to about 230 acres surrounding the unspoiled South Walsham Broad. Paths wind among banks of azaleas and large-leaved rhododendrons and lead to the edge of the broad itself. Much of the area is wet and supports a rich variety of primulas with lysichitons, astilbes, ligularias and gunneras of exceptional size, merging into the natural vegetation among which are many Royal ferns and some majestic oaks. Although particularly colourful during the flowering of the azaleas in the spring, this garden gives pleasure at all times of the year when natural beauty is preferred to man-made sophistication.

FELBRIGG HALL 11
Felbrigg, Cromer, Norfolk. Tel: (026375) 444
The National Trust

3m SW of Cromer off A148. Main entrance on B1436 • *Open 31st March – 28th Oct, daily except Tues and Fri, 11.00 a.m. - 5.30 p.m. Closed Good Friday. Woodland walks all year except 25th Dec, dawn – dusk* • *Best season: summer* • *Entrance: £1.00 (house and gardens £3.50)* • *Parking* • *Refreshments* • *Toilet facilities* • *Suitable for wheelchairs* • *Plants for sale* • *Shop* • *House open* • ***Grade II***

The house faces south across the park which is notable for its fine woods and lakeside walk. A ha-ha separates the park from the lawns of the house where there is an orangery planted with camellias. To the north the ground rises and are specimen trees and shrubs. At some distance to the east there is a large walled kitchen garden now richly planted with a combination of fruit, vegetables and flowers in a formal design behind clipped hedges. There is also a vine house and a great brick dovecote. In early autumn there is a display of many varieties of colchicums: the National Collection is kept here. The gardens are kept in immaculate order.

FRITTON LAKE 12
Fritton, Great Yarmouth, Norfolk. Tel: (0493) 79208
Lord and Lady Somerleyton

5m SW of Great Yarmouth off the A143 ● *Open daily Good Friday - 1st Oct* ● *Best season: summer* ● *Entrance: £2.00, OAP/ children £1.50* ● *Parking* ● *Refreshments* ● *Toilet facilities* ● *Suitable for wheelchairs* ● *Shop* ● *Grade III*

Visitors should not be put off at the entrance by the paraphernalia associated with the development of Fritton Lake as a country park. The large lake remains almost unspoilt and separate from the tea rooms and other commercial attractions. An unusual feature is a Victorian garden of about half an acre in the gardenesque style with irregular beds surrounded by clipped box hedges and filled with shrubs and herbaceous perennials that give a colourful display in the summer. The gardens were pleasantly uncrowded on a hot July afternoon.

GLAVENSIDE 13
Letheringsett, Nr Holt, Norfolk. Tel: (0263) 713181
Mr J Cozens-Hardy

1m W of Holt on A148 ● *Open daily, 10.00 a.m. - sunset* ● *Best season: summer* ● *Entrance: 50p, children 20p* ● *Parking* ● *Refreshments* ● *Toilet facilities* ● *Suitable for wheelchairs* ● *Mill shop* ● *Working water mill overlooking the garden is open* ● *Grade III*

A three-acre garden on the banks of the River Glaven which is crossed by a high arched bridge. Sloping lawns flank the river and there are further streams and pools, a small rock garden, rose garden and kitchen garden. In spite of the number of recently established trees and shrubs, this could not be described as a plantsman's garden but the flower beds are colourful and well-maintained. Five other gardens are open in Letheringsett usually for one day in April.

GOODERSTONE WATER GARDENS 14
Crow Hall, Gooderstone, King's Lynn, Norfolk. Tel: (0366) 21208
Mr and Mrs W.H. Knights

4m SW of Swaffham. E of Gooderstone village ● *Open weekdays 10.30 a.m. - 6.00 p.m., Sun 1.30 - 6.00 p.m.* ● *Best season: summer* ● *Entrance: £1.00, children 30p* ● *Parking* ● *Tea and biscuits* ● *Toilet facilities* ● *Suitable for wheelchairs* ● *Grade IV*

A very colourful garden which makes use of the excavated waterways which are planted with chiefly herbaceous plants but also shrubs and trees along their margins. No outstanding design features.

HALES HALL   15
Hales, Loddon, Norfolk.   Tel: (050846) 395
Mr and Mrs T.E. Read

*14m SE of Norwich, signposted off A146   ● Open July and Aug, Wed, 2.00 –
5.00 p.m. Party visits at other times by arrangement   ● Entrance: collection
box   ● Parking   ● Plants for sale   ● Grade III*

A moat surrounds the remaining wing of a vast house of the early sixteenth century and a central lawn with well-planted borders backed by high brick walls. Work is continuing on the restoration of the garden after centuries of neglect. The garden specialises in the growing of rare and unusual perennial plants, and houses the National Collection of citrus, figs and greenhouse grapes. The associated nurseries offer an extensive range of conservatory plants, vines, figs and mulberries.

HOLKHAM HALL   16
Holkham, Wells-next-the-Sea, Norfolk.
Tel: (0328) 710374 (garden centre number)
The Viscount Coke

*2m W of Wells on A149   ● Open May – Sept, daily except Fri and Sat, 1.30 –
5.00 p.m. Garden Centre open Mon – Sat 10.00 a.m. – 5.00 p.m., Sun 2.00 –
5.00 p.m.   ● Entrance: £1.70, OAP £1.30, children 50p   ● Parking
● Refreshments   ● Toilet facilities   ● Suitable for wheelchairs   ● Plants for sale
● Shop   ● House open   ● Grade II*

The vast park at Holkham was laid out originally by William Kent and later worked on by both Brown and Repton. The park is famous for its holm oaks and contains an arboretum with many rare trees and shrubs. On the west side of the house, lawns sweep down to the great lake. The terrace which fronts the south facade was added in 1854 but the scale of the house and park is so large that, from a distance at least, this does not seriously disrupt the vision of the two, in spite of the garish and inappropriate beds of polyantha roses. These formal beds flank a great fountain representing Perseus and Andromeda. There is a walled garden in the grounds extending to over six acres, subdivided into six areas with perennial borders and the original greenhouses. Holkham also has a garden centre with a wide range of plants.

HOW HILL FARM 17
Ludham, Norfolk. Tel: (069262) 558
Mr P.D.S. Boardman

2m W of Ludham. Follow signs to How Hill, Farm Garden S of How Hill
• *Open the Sun 2 weeks before Spring Bank Holiday, 2.00 – 5.00 p.m., and by
appointment* • *Best season: May* • *Entrance: £1.00, children 50p* • *Parking*
• *Refreshments* • *Toilet facilities* • *Partly suitable for wheelchairs* • ***Grade** II*

This garden adjoins that of the How Hill Trust but is not open at the same
time for fear of being overwhelmed. The garden around the farm is
comparatively conventional except for a large Chusan palm planted in a dog
cage from which it threatens to escape. Here too is a collection of over 50
varieties of *Ilex aquifolium* as well as many rare species of the same holly genus.
Over the road in the river valley is a rich combination of exotics mingled with
native vegetation. Around a series of pools, banks of azaleas merge into reed
beds, rhododendron species rise over thickets of fern and bramble, wild
grasses skirt groves of the giant *Arundo donax*, with birches and conifers
against a background of a recently-created three-acre broad, thick with water
lilies. The soil is exceptionally acid, as low as ph 2.5, but supports a wide
variety of trees and shrubs.

HOW HILL GARDEN 18
Ludham, Norwich, Norfolk. Tel: (069262) 555
How Hill Trust

2m W of Ludham, signposted from village • *Open Spring Bank Holiday Sun
and the Suns before and after, 2.00 – 6.00 p.m.* • *Best season: May/June*
• *Entrance: £1.50, children 50p* • *Parking* • *Refreshments* • *Toilet
facilities* • *Suitable for wheelchairs* • *Shop* • *House open* • ***Grade** II*

There are two gardens here, a formal Edwardian garden terraced into rising
ground overlooking the valley of the River Ant, and a separate water and
woodland garden. The formal garden has herbaceous borders surrounded by
high yew hedges forming a series of linked enclosures and backed by a great
brick wall above which rises the dramatically-positioned house. Unfortunately
the borders have lost much of their Edwardian character and a white border
has gone entirely. Some informal planting leads towards the woodland in
which the water garden is set, where quiet waterways, crossed by wooden
bridges, are lined with native and exotic aquatic plants. This area is thickly
planted with azaleas, highly colourful at the time of the spring open days.

MANNINGTON HALL 19
Nr Saxthorpe, Norfolk. Tel: (026387) 284
Lord and Lady Walpole

18m NW of Norwich, signposted at Saxthorpe off B1149 • *Open Easter Sun,
then April – Dec, Sun 12 noon – 5.00 p.m. or dusk, also June – Aug, Wed – Fri,*

11.00 a.m. – 6.00 p.m. ● *Best season: June/July* ● *Entrance: £1.50, OAP £1.00, children free* ● *Parking* ● *Refreshments* ● *Toilet facilities* ● *Suitable for wheelchairs* ● *Plants for sale* ● *Shop* ● **Grade II**

The romantic appearance of this garden of 20 acres is only matched in Norfolk by Elsing Hall where the house is also of the fifteenth century. Lawns run down to the moat which is crossed by a drawbridge to herbaceous borders backed by high walls of brick and flint. The moat also encloses a secret, scented garden in a design derived from one of the ceilings of the house. Outside the moat are borders of flowering shrubs flanking a Doric temple, and beyond are woodlands containing the ruins of a Saxon church. Within the walls of the former kitchen garden, a series of rose gardens has been planted following the design of gardens from medieval to modern times and featuring roses popular at each period. Also a lake, woods and meadowland with extensive walls.

NORFOLK LAVENDER LTD 20
Caley Mill, Heacham, King's Lynn, Norfolk. Tel: (0485) 70384
Norfolk Lavender Ltd

13m N of King's Lynn on A149 ● *Open daily, April – Sept, 10.00 a.m. – 5.30 p.m.* ● *Best season: July/Aug* ● *Entrance: collecting box* ● *Parking* ● *Refreshments* ● *Toilet facilities* ● *Suitable for wheelchairs* ● *Plants for sale* ● *Shop* ● **Grade III**

Here is the National collection of lavenders, displaying all the species and varieties which can be grown in this country, set in two acres around a Gothic watermill on the banks of the Heacham river. The fields of lavender are a fine sight in July and August, and there is also a rose garden and a herb garden.

THE OLD HOUSE 21
Ranworth, Norwich, Norfolk. Tel: (0605) 49300
The Hon Mrs Cator

9m NE of Norwich, turn L off B1140 at Panxworth ● *Open on two Suns in April and occasionally in the summer. Enquire for dates* ● *Best season: spring* ● *Entrance: £1.00, children 50p* ● *Parking* ● *Refreshments* ● *Toilet facilities* ● **Grade III**

Lush natural vegetation half conceals the garden from unspoilt Ranworth Inner Broad. Moist green lawns run up to the house where there are some enclosed gardens with borders of perennials and a formal pool. Rising ground behind is planted with a variety of trees and shrubs. Beyond the kitchen garden is a half mile grassy walk leading through woodlands along the side of the broad. The garden is particularly attractive in the spring with enormous displays of daffodils.

THE OLD RECTORY 22
Holt, Norfolk. Tel: (026371) 2204
Lady Harrod

½m W of Holt on A148 ● *Open 6th, 13th March, 10.00 a.m. – 12 noon*
● *Entrance: £1.00 (inc. coffee)* ● *Parking* ● *Refreshments* ● *Partly suitable*
for wheelchairs ● *Plants for sale* ● ***Grade III***

Steep wooded banks display a mass of snowdrops in the early spring. A stream
rises from a pool to cross the garden through lush borders. There is a meadow
filled in early summer with wild orchids. The walled kitchen garden is well
stocked with fruit, vegetables, and old roses but is not always open to the
public. Historians will be interested to know that a concealed moat indicates
this was a medieval site.

OXBURGH HALL 23
Oxborough, Swaffham, Norfolk. Tel: (036621) 258
The National Trust

7m SW of Swaffham off A134 ● *Open 31st March – Oct, daily except Thurs*
and Fri, 12 noon – 5.30 p.m. ● *Entrance: £3.00* ● *Parking* ● *Refreshments*
● *Toilet facilities* ● *Suitable for wheelchairs* ● *Plants for sale* ● *Shop* ● *House*
open different times ● ***Grade III***

The neat gardens of this fine moated house, carefully tended by the National
Trust, lack the romantic appeal of Elsing or Rainthorpe. There are some good
trees, pleasant lawns, and well-stocked herbaceous borders. On the north side
of the house is a parterre with bedding plants in colour masses, said to be of
French design but somewhat modest by French standards and, while worth
inspecting, somehow seeming inappropriate here.

THE PLANTATION GARDEN 24
Earlham Road, Norwich, Norfolk.
Tel: (0603) 713174 (Mr John Watson)
Plantation Garden Preservation Trust

Entrance off Earlham Road, shared with hotel immediately to W of R.C.
cathedral ● *Open by appointment* ● *Best season: summer* ● *Entrance:*
donations welcome ● *Suitable for wheelchairs* ● ***Grade III***

Designed by the architect Edward Boardman in the 1850s this garden shows
the possible influence of Sir Charles Barry's 'Shrublands' near Ipswich. It was
formed in a narrow steep-sided chalk quarry not far from the centre of
Norwich. Now crowded around with mature trees, lawns cover the quarry
floor reached by an extraordinary series of terraces constructed of a jumble of
architectural fragments and slag, and other industrial waste. The centre piece
is a tall, multi-tiered fountain. Flower beds with typical Victorian bedding
have been reinstated although more, now covered by grass, have yet to be

recovered. Dedicated volunteers have made themselves responsible for restoration and although there is still much to do, this has been revealed as a most remarkable garden.

THE PLEASAUNCE   25
Harboard Road, Overstrand, Norfolk. Tel: (026378) 212
Christian Endeavour Holiday Homes Ltd

3m E of Cromer off B1159 ● Open end May – Oct, Mon, Wed and Thurs, 2.00 – 5.00 p.m. ● Entrance: £1.00 ● Limited parking in grounds ● Light tea inc. in entrance fee ● Toilet facilities, inc. disabled ● Suitable for wheelchairs ● House open ● Grade IV

Of limited interest except for the Lutyens house, sunken Italian garden, walls and paving. Nothing of the original Jekyll planting survives although an attempt is being made to restore this.

RAINTHORPE HALL GARDENS   26
Tasburgh, Norwich, Norfolk. Tel: (0508) 470618
Mr G.F. Hastings

8m S of Norwich off A140. At Newton Flotman fork right by garage, on 1m to red brick gates on left ● Open May – Sept, Sun p.m. ● Best season: June/July ● Entrance: £1.00, OAP and children 50p ● Parking ● Refreshments ● Toilet facilities ● Suitable for wheelchairs ● Plants for sale ● House open by appointment only ● Grade II

The gardens at Rainthorpe Hall, which is one of the most beautiful houses in Norfolk, extend to five acres. Of the sixteenth-century garden there are some remains in the knot garden, the nuttery, and an ancient yew tree. The lawn runs down to the River Tas and there is a recently developed conservation lake. There are many fine and rare trees and a collection of bamboos. What this garden lacks in overall cohesion of design, it makes up for in the peace and beauty of its setting.

RAVENINGHAM HALL   27
Raveningham, Norwich, Norfolk. Tel: (050846) 206/222
Sir Nicholas Bacon

14m SE of Norwich off A140, left at Hales on B1136, then 1st right ● Open April – Sept, Sun, 2.00 – 5.00 p.m. Nursery open daily, 9.00 a.m. – 3.00 p.m. ● Entrance: £1.00 ● Parking ● Refreshments ● Toilet facilities ● Suitable for wheelchairs ● Plants for sale ● Grade II

This garden, in a fine landscaped park, has a rich variety of trees, shrubs and herbaceous plants dating from the eighteenth century to the present day. There is a large collection of galanthus species and varieties. The walled kitchen garden and greenhouses are still in use, and the associated nurseries offer an exceptional range of shrubs, climbers and herbaceous plants. Many rarely available elsewhere. A new arboretum is currently being developed.

SANDRINGHAM HOUSE   28
Sandringham, King's Lynn, Norfolk.   Tel: (0553) 772675
H.M. The Queen

9m NE of King's Lynn on B1440 near Wolferton ● Open Easter Sun to last Sun in Sept except when royalty are present ● Best season: May/June ● Entrance: £1.50, OAP £1.10, children 80p ● Parking ● Refreshments ● Toilet facilities ● Suitable for wheelchairs ● Plants for sale ● Shop ● House open ● Grade III

Created in 1880, the grounds contain a fine woodland garden featuring magnolias, camellias and rhododendrons in spring. Interest is carried through summer with fuchsias, hydrangeas, etc but these are not outstanding. An interesting rock-work feature by the lake was designed in the 1960s and planted with heathers and conifers and good damp borders around the lake. Particularly worth seeing in late spring.

SHERINGHAM PARK   29
Upper Sheringham, Norfolk.   Tel: (0263) 823778
The National Trust

4m NE of Holt off A148 ● Open daily, sunrise – sunset ● Best season: May/ June ● Entrance: free ● Parking: £1.50 per car to include all occupants ● Partly suitable for wheelchairs ● Grade II

Sheringham Park stands in a secluded valley at the edge of the Cromer/Holt ridge, close to the sea but protected from its winds by steep wooded hills. Both house and park are now the property of the National Trust although the house remains in private occupation. The park is remarkable not only for its great beauty and spectacular views but also for an extensive collection of rhododendrons which thrive in the acid soil. Crowning an eminence is a classical temple based on a design by Humphrey Repton and erected to mark the 60th birthday of Mr Thomas Upcher, the last descendant of the original owner to live at Sheringham. The Trust has now begun to remove some inappropriate twentieth-century planting and to restore the original form of the garden, the favourite and best-preserved work of Repton.

SWANNINGTON MANOR 30
Swannington, Norwich, Norfolk. Tel: (0603) 860700
Mr and Mrs R. Winch

10m NW of Norwich turning off A1067 at Attlebridge ● *Open Easter – Sept,*
Wed and Bank Holiday Mons, 11.00 a.m. – 6.00 p.m. ● *Entrance: £1.50,*
children 50p ● *Parking* ● *Refreshments* ● *Toilet facilities* ● *Partly suitable*
for wheelchairs ● *Plants for sale* ● *Shop* ● *Grade III*

An informal garden within a curiously cut (cloud-shaped) 300-year old yew
barrier. Modern topiary, a small formal herb garden, mixed borders, orchid
house. Good planting. House for sale at time of going to press.

THRIGBY WILDLIFE GARDENS 31
Thrigby Hall, Filby, Great Yarmouth, Norfolk. Tel: (049377) 477
Mr K.J. Sims

6m NW of Great Yarmouth, signposted at Filby on A1064 ● *Open daily, 10.00*
a.m. – 5.00 p.m. or dusk ● *Best season: summer* ● *Entrance: £2.50, children*
£1.30 ● *Parking* ● *Refreshments* ● *Toilet facilities* ● *Suitable for*
wheelchairs ● *Shop* ● *Grade III*

The chief attraction of these gardens is a collection of Chinese plants arranged
to form the landscape of the Willow Pattern plate, complete with pagodas and
bridges across a small lake. Complementing a collection of Asiatic animals,
the plants include *Gingko biloba, Pinus parviflora, Paeonia suffruticosa,*
Nandina domestica and *Chimonobambusa quadrangularis,* against a background of willows. Planted in 1989 but interesting even in an immature state.

WRETHAM LODGE 32
East Wretham, Thetford, Norfolk. Tel: (095382) 366
Mrs A. Hoellering

5m NE of Thetford. Left by village sign, right at crossroads then bear left
● *Open 6th, 13th May, 24th June, 1st July, 2.30 - 5.30 p.m. and by*
appointment ● *Best season: May – July* ● *Entrance: £1.00, children 50p*
● *Parking* ● *Refreshments* ● *Toilet facilities* ● *Suitable for wheelchairs*
● *Plants for sale* ● *Grade II*

Extensive lawns surround the handsome flint-faced former rectory set in its
own walled park. There are herbaceous borders and hundreds of old, species
and climbing roses massed in informal beds or covering high flint walls. Walls
surround the kitchen garden supporting espalier and fan-trained fruit trees –
pears, cherries and apricots. There is a vine house and a variety of figs. Roses
and herbaceous plants are mixed with the vegetables and in the spring there is
a display of many species of tulip. A wide grassy walk runs round the park
through a range of mature and recently established trees where spring-
flowering bulbs are naturalised with a mass display of bluebells in May.

NORTHAMPTONSHIRE

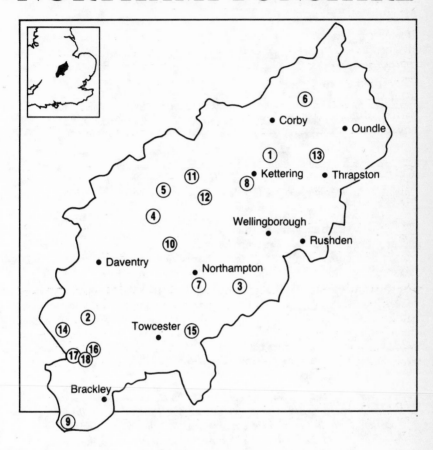

BOUGHTON HOUSE GARDEN 1
Kettering, Northamptonshire. Tel: (0536) 515731
The Duke and Duchess of Buccleuch and Queensberry

On A43, N of Kettering, between Weekley and Geddington ● *Open 29th April*
– Sept, daily except Fri, 2.00 – 5.00 p.m. ● *Entrance: £1.00, children 50p*
● *Parking* ● *Refreshments weekends and Aug* ● *Toilet facilities* ● *Partly*
suitable for wheelchairs ● *Dogs on lead* ● *Plants for sale* ● *Shop* ● *House open*
(times differ from grounds) ● ***Grade IV***

Magnificent and extensive sixteenth/seventeenth-century manor house with
collections of paintings, tapestries, furniture, porcelain, etc., and with
grounds laid out by Bridgeman. Lakes, nature walks and woodland adventure
play area in working estate. Excellent selection of pot, herbaceous and shrub

plants at nursery garden. Good choice for a family visit with historic house, walks, play area and plants for sale. No formal gardens.

CANONS ASHBY HOUSE 2
Woodford Halse, Nr Daventry, Northamptonshire.
Tel: (0327) 860044
The National Trust

B4525 Northampton to Banbury road near Daventry ● *Open April – Oct, Wed – Sun and Bank Holiday Mon, 1.00 – 5.30 p.m. or dusk if earlier. Closed Good Friday* ● *Best season: summer* ● *Entrance: £2.50, children £1.20 (house and gardens)* ● *Parking 200 yards from house. Disabled ring in advance and park near house* ● *Refreshments* ● *Toilet facilities* ● *Suitable for wheelchairs, two wheelchairs available. Taped guide for blind visitors* ● *Dogs on lead in Home Paddock only* ● *House open* ● ***Grade II***

This well-maintained garden is being extensively restored by the National Trust. Formal with axial arrangements of paths and terraces, high stone walls and gateways, it dates almost entirely from the beginning of the eighteenth century. Yew court with fine topiary. Old varieties of pear, apple, plum trees and soft fruit. Cedar planted in 1715 and espaliers grown from the original stock planted by Edward Dryden, whose family has owned the house since the sixteenth century.

CASTLE ASHBY GARDENS 3
Castle Ashby, Northamptonshire. Tel: (060129) 234
The Marquess of Northampton

5m E of Northampton, between A45 Northampton to Wellingborough road and A428 Northampton to Bedford road ● *Open daily, 10.00 a.m. - 6.00 p.m., with occasional closures for events* ● *Best season: March – May* ● *Entrance: £1.00, children 50p* ● *Parking* ● *Teas at farm shop in village, 400 yards* ● *Suitable for wheelchairs, paths not very smooth* ● *Dogs on lead* ● *Plants rarely for sale* ● *Farm shop in village* ● *House open during 'Country Fair', 1st week July, check by phone* ● ***Grade I***

Originally Elizabethan, then a park landscaped by 'Capability' Brown, then a Matthew Digby Wyatt Terrace, Italian garden and arboretum, Castle Ashby is now primarily an 'all function centre' for company and private events. There is public access to most of the gardens (except East terrace) which present a glorious combination of a fine and well kept Italian garden, leading off to lakes, ponds, and 'Capability' Brown landscapes. An outstanding nature walk past well-labelled trees over the terracotta bridge and to the 'knucklebone arbour', a summerhouse with what are probably sheep or deer knuckles set in the floor. Among the wild and naturalised plants are carpets of aconites and snowdrops, winter heliotrope, butterbur, daffodils, bluebells, wood anemones, celandines, bush vetch, wood buttercups and a wide selection of lake and pondside plants. Features include an orangery and archway greenhouses, topiary and terracotta vases.

COTON MANOR GARDENS   4
Ravensthorpe, Northamptonshire. Tel: (0604) 740219
Cdr and Mrs H. Pasley-Tyler

*10m N of Northampton, signs A428 and A50 ● Open Easter – Sept, Sun, July
– Aug, Wed, also Bank Holiday Mon ● Entrance: £2.00, OAP £1.50, children
50p ● Parking ● Home-made teas ● Toilet facilities ● Suitable for
wheelchairs ● Dogs on lead ● Unusual plants and shrubs for sale ● Shop
● Grade III*

A carefully planned and tended garden on several sloped acres which provide colour and interest throughout the year. There is an excellent variety of foliage plants, herbaceous borders, lawns and hedges plus lakes with ornamental waterfowl. It is a garden which will appeal most to those seeking inspiration for their own medium-sized gardens, and those who enjoy waterfowl.

COTTESBROOKE HALL   5
Cottesbrooke, Northampton, Northamptonshire.
Tel: (060124) 717
Captain and Mrs J. McDonald-Buchanan

*10m N of Northampton between A50 and A508 ● Open 20th May, 24th June,
2nd Sept, 2.00 – 6.00 p.m. ● Entrance: £1.00, children 50p ● Parking
● Teas ● Toilet facilities ● Suitable for wheelchairs ● Dogs on lead ● Plants
for sale ● Grade II*

An excellently maintained formal garden in a superb park setting. Areas to suit every taste and interest, and being improved yet further for planned greater public opening of house and gardens. Design work here by Edward Schultz, Geoffrey Jellicoe and Lady McDonald-Buchanan. Hall, garden and grounds complemented by gamekeeper's cottage, garden of head gardener, Mrs D Daw, featuring unusual herbaceous plants, flowers for drying, fruit and vegetables; and the Old Bothy heather garden's collections of callunas and ericas. This last started in 1982 and still being developed. Cottesbrooke Hall stands on the threshold of the highest rank of gardens with public access. It also has the reputation for being the model for Jane Austen's 'Mansfield Park'.

DEENE PARK   6
Corby, Northamptonshire. Tel: (078085) 278/223
Mr Edmund Brudenell

*6m N of Corby off A43 Kettering to Stamford road ● Open June – Aug, Sun,
1.00 – 5.00 p.m. and Bank Holiday weekends, Easter – Aug. Groups by
appointment ● Entrance: £3.00, children £1.00, inc. house ● Parking*

● *Teas* ● *Toilet facilities* ● *Partly suitable for wheelchairs* ● *Dogs in car park only* ● *Shop* ● *House open* ● *Grade III*

The glory of Deene, which was created by generations of the Brudenell family, is its trees. Fine mature specimens and groups fringe the formal areas and frame tranquil and enchanting views of the parkland and countryside. A main feature of its garden are the long borders, old-fashioned roses and the lake. The gardens, parkland, church and house together provide a delightful, interesting and relaxing afternoon for visitors in what was the home of the Earl of Cardigan who led the Charge of the Light Brigade in 1854.

DELAPRE ABBEY 7
London Road, Northampton, Northamptonshire.
Tel: (0604) 762129
Northamptonshire County Council

1m S of Northampton on A508 ● *Open daily, kitchen garden only early May – Sept* ● *Best season: summer* ● *Parking* ● *Toilet facilities* ● *Suitable for wheelchairs* ● *Dogs on lead* ● *House is County Record Office, open to researchers, readers and students. Parts of building shown on Thurs throughout year, 2.30 – 4.00 p.m.* ● *Grade IV*

In need of tender loving care but it is still possible to glimpse the hey-day of a lovely garden. Excellent walks through wilderness garden with fine trees and shrubbery, a good walled kitchen garden and lily ponds.

31 DERWENT CRESCENT 8
Kettering, Northamptonshire. Tel: (0536) 520070
Mr and Mrs B.J. Mitchell

W side of Kettering, off A43 to Northampton. Take right along Bowhill after going under railway bridge, then 1st right, 1st right, 1st left or phone for instructions ● *Open any time by appointment* ● *Entrance: 50p, children 20p* ● *Parking on street* ● *Teas, proceeds to charity* ● *Toilet facilities* ● *Plants for sale occasionally, proceeds to charity* ● *Grade III*

Strictly for the plantsperson, but an absolute jewel for herbaceous, bulb, alpine and fern enthusiasts. Owners' knowledge of their plants and propagation methods (over 33 years experience here) is enormous and enthusiastically passed on to satisfy the curiosity of visitors.

FRIARS WELL 9
(formerly The Dower House)
Aynho, Northamptonshire. Tel: (0869) 810284
Mr and Mrs T.R. Sermon

6m SE of Banbury, turn E off A423 Oxford – Banbury road at Adderbury. The village is shortly to adjoin the M40 extension ● *Open 1st July, 2.30 – 6.00 p.m.* ● *Entrance: £1.50, children 20p* ● *Parking in village* ● *Teas* ● *Suitable for wheelchairs* ● ***Grade III***

Friars Well (formerly The Dower House) of Aynhoe Park was converted into a separate private residence in the early 1960s by Mrs Peggy Ward (Munster), a well-known gardener. Just as the large house had attracted a great designer in the eighteenth century, the new offspring attracted two of the twentieth century's most distinguished men, Lanning Roper and John Fowler. Because the main garden had to be at the front of the house, the plan was to fill the space with a series of small 'rooms' walled by high hedges, mostly of beech. These contain mini-gardens, tiny orchards, etc. and another area has the swimming pool and tennis court. The influence of Hidcote is very evident. Other village gardens are usually open at the same time as Friars Well to benefit NGS.

HOLDENBY HOUSE GARDENS 10
Holdenby, Northampton, Northamptonshire. Tel: (0604) 770241
Mr and Mrs James Lowther

7m N of Northampton, signposted A50 and A428 ● *Open June – Aug, Thurs, 2.00 – 6.00 p.m., Sun, Bank Holidays, Easter – Sept, 2.00 – 6.00 p.m. Groups by appointment* ● *Entrance: £2.75, children £1.00* ● *Parking* ● *Refreshments: meals by appointment* ● *Toilet facilities* ● *Partly suitable for wheelchairs* ● *Dogs on lead* ● *Plants and herbs for sale* ● *Shop inc. croquet mallet hire* ● ***Grade IV***

House and gardens used for events, conferences and school visits, and so more suited to family visitors and outings than garden enthusiasts but a superb setting and with many features of interest including impressive remains of an Elizabethan terrace garden and scented Victorian borders.

KELMARSH HALL 11
Kelmarsh, Northampton, Northamptonshire. Tel: (060128) 276
Miss C.V. Lancaster

On A508 5m S of Market Harborough, 11m N of Northampton ● *Open Easter – Aug, Sun and Bank Holidays, 2.00 – 5.00 p.m., April and Sept, by appointment (minimum 12 persons)* ● *Best season: spring* ● *Entrance £1.00, children free* ● *Parking* ● *Refreshments* ● *Toilet facilities* ● *Dogs* ● *Plants and produce for sale occasionally* ● *James Gibbs 'Palladian House' open with escorted visits* ● ***Grade III***

The drive is an avenue of lime trees bordering the park of 20 acres where a herd of rare British white cattle graze. Close-clipped yew hedges and colonnades lead to secret and quiet gardens with views of a lake. There are fine herbaceous borders and a rose garden. Seats are provided at vantage points and spring flowers and rhododendrons are special features.

LAMPORT HALL GARDEN 12
Lamport Hall, Northampton, Northamptonshire.
Tel: (060128) 272
Lamport Hall Trust

8m N of Northampton on A508 • *Open Easter – Sept, Sun and Bank Holidays, July and Aug, Thurs, 2.15 – 5.15 p.m.* • *Entrance: free, donations welcome* • *Parking* • *Refreshments* • *Toilet facilities* • *Suitable for wheelchairs* • *Dogs on lead* • *Shop* • *House open* • *Grade IV*

Lamport Hall is now essentially an event (dog shows, antique fairs) and school study centre. Grounds initially laid out by Gilbert Clarke in 1655 are in the process of restoration and provide a pleasant setting, but at this stage will mainly interest those who want to follow the progress of restoration. Ultimately the local ironstone rock garden and the refurbished nineteenth-century Italian garden with its fine urns should be most attractive.

THE OLD RECTORY 13
Sudborough, Northamptonshire. Tel: (08012) 3247
Mr and Mrs Anthony Huntington

Off A6116 Corby – Thrapston road • *Open by appointment and 1 day in June for NGS* • *Best season: July* • *Entrance: £1.00* • *Teas by prior request* • *Toilet facilities* • *Suitable for wheelchairs* • *Plants for sale occasionally* • *Grade III*

Delightful three-acre rectory garden in beautiful stone and thatch village. Much has been accomplished in last five years to develop a garden of interest to all. Copious planting in the mixed borders, around the pond and with climbers. Vegetable garden fascinating, small beds with brick paths leading to a central wrought-iron arbour. Standard roses and gooseberries and tents of runner beans provide vertical features.

THE SPRING HOUSE 14
Mill Lane, Chipping Warden, Northamptonshire.
Tel: (0295) 86261
Mr and Mrs C. Shepley-Cuthbert

At Chipping Warden, NNE of Banbury, follow 'village only' signs into Mill Lane. Last house on left • *Open by appointment and on limited days to public*

(check first) ● *Best season: early July* ● *Entrance: contributions for charity appreciated* ● *Parking* ● *Refreshments: on public open days and by arrangement* ● *Toilet facilities* ● *Suitable for wheelchairs* ● *Dogs*
● *Grade III*

This splendid English village-garden designed by Kitty Lloyd-Jhones in the 1920s has an outstanding bog garden with primulas, hostas, rhododendrons, azaleas and rare species. Trees include American red oak, Mitchell's white-beam, weeping silver lime. Also statues and urns and magnificent hedge of beech, copper beech and lime. Chipping Warden Manor open on NGS days.

STOKE PARK   15
Stoke Bruerne, Towcester, Northampton, Northamptonshire.
Tel: (0604) 862172
Mr R.E. Chancellor

Clearly signposted from A5, N of Milton Keynes ● *Open June – Aug, weekends and Bank Holidays, 2.00 – 6.00 p.m., rest of year by appointment* ● *Best season: summer* ● *Entrance: £1.00* ● *Parking* ● *Suitable for wheelchairs* ● *Dogs on lead* ● *Pavilion open* ● *Grade IV*

Stoke Park was the first house to display the Palladian plan in Britain but now (due to a fire) only the splendid pavilion with colonnaded walls remain. The outline of the original Italianate garden by Inigo Jones can be seen below the lawn so the site is of particular interest to students of historical gardens. However, the svelte lawns, herbaceous borders and a large fountain basin with water lilies are now the features at Stoke Park which will be enjoyed by all who visit.

SULGRAVE MANOR   16
Sulgrave, Northamptonshire. Tel: (029576) 205
Trustees, endowed by Colonial Dames of America

7m NE of Banbury, 1m off B4525 ● *Open Feb only to pre-booked parties of 12 or more, March, daily except Wed, 10.30 a.m. – 1.00 p.m., 2.00 – 4.00 p.m., April – Sept, daily except Wed, 10.30 a.m. – 5.30 p.m., Oct – Dec, daily, 10.30 a.m. – 4.00 p.m. Closed 25th and 26th Dec* ● *Entrance: £2.00, children £1.00 (house and garden)* ● *Parking* ● *Light refreshments at Thatched House Hotel opposite* ● *Toilet facilities* ● *Suitable for wheelchairs* ● *House open*
● *Grade II*

American visitors are in the majority here, as the house was built in 1560 by a distant ancestor of George Washington. It was acquired in 1914 and restored after World War I, with the benefit of U.S. generosity. The gardens, like the house, bear little relation to their sixteenth-century condition, but the rose garden, herb garden and kitchen garden are attractive examples of their kind. Many bags of lavender from the garden have by now crossed the Atlantic.

THORPE MANDEVILLE COURT 17
Thorpe Mandeville, Northamptonshire. Tel: (0295) 711586
Mr B.G. Tyrell

4m NE of Banbury on B4525 ● *Open 22nd July, 2.30 – 6.00 p.m.* ● *Best season: summer* ● *Parking* ● *Plants for sale* ● ***Grade IV***

Paved walks lead to several different types of garden created on a naturally sloping site. Formal rose gardens with urns and statues close to the house give way to woodland walks with fine specimen trees and lead to a water garden on two separate levels with a diversity of aquatic plants. In need of some tender loving care but new owner intends to restore the garden to its former glory.

THORPE MANDEVILLE MANOR 18
Thorpe Mandeville, Northamptonshire. Tel: (0295) 711006
Mr and Mrs D. Ancil

4m NE of Banbury on B4525 ● *Open 22nd July, 2.30 – 6.00 p.m.*
● *Entrance: £1.00* ● *Parking* ● *Refreshments* ● *Toilet facilities* ● ***Grade IV***

Four acres of gardens slope away from the seventeenth-century house forming a natural site for a succession of terraced gardens. Formal paved walk and patterned beds in foreground close to house, intriguing circular design of shallow steps leading to second lawn and enchanting garden house. Sunken rose garden, enclosed by dry-stone walls, tennis pavilion with an ellipse of brick tiles in foreground; beyond is the lake and fish ponds.

HOW TO FIND THE GARDENS
Directions to each garden are included in each entry. This information has been supplied by the garden inspectors and is aimed to be the best available to those travelling by car. However, it has been compiled to be used in conjunction with a road atlas.

The unreliability of train and bus services makes it unrewarding to include details, particularly as many garden visits are made on Sundays. However, many properties can be reached by public transport and National Trust guides and the Yellow Book [NGS] give details. Future editions of the *Guide* may include a special list of gardens easily reached by public transport if readers indicate that this would be helpful.

The Maps: The numbers on the maps correspond to the numbers of the gardens in each county. The maps show the proximity of one garden to another so that visits to several gardens can be planned for the same day. It is worthwhile referring to the maps of bordering counties to see if another garden visit can be included in your itinerary. The maps should be used in conjunction with a road atlas.

NORTHUMBERLAND

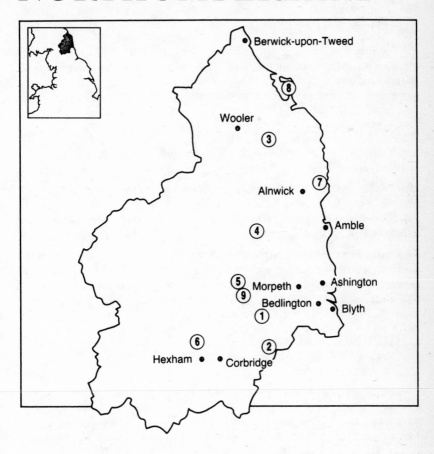

BELSAY HALL
Belsay, Nr Newcastle-upon-Tyne, Northumberland.
Tel: (066181) 636
Sir Stephen Middleton

14m NW of Newcastle on A696 ● *Open Good Friday – Sept, daily except Mon,
10.00 a.m. – 6.00 p.m., Oct – Easter, daily except Mon, 10.00 a.m. – 4.00
p.m.* ● *Entrance: £1.50, concessions £1.10, children 75p* ● *Parking. Coaches
please notify in advance* ● *Refreshments: drinks machine, picnic area* ● *Toilet
facilities inc. disabled* ● *Suitable for wheelchairs (available on loan)* ● *Dogs on
lead* ● *Shop* ● *House open* ● ***Grade II***

The gardens are the creation of two men who between them owned the Hall
in succession from 1795 to 1933. Sir Charles Monck built a severe neo-

classical mansion with formal terraces leading through woods to a 'garden' inside the quarry from which the house was built. His grandson took over in 1867, adding Victorian features. Both were discerning plantsmen. The result is a collection of rare, mature and exotic specimens in a fascinating sequence. The terrace looks across to massed early rhododendrons. Other areas (rose garden, magnolia terrace, winter-flowering heathers) lead to woods, a wild meadow and the quarry garden itself. Reminiscent of the ancient Greek quarries in Syracuse, it was carefully contrived and stocked to achieve a wild romantic effect and give shelter to some remarkable specimens.

BRADLEY HERB GARDEN 2
Sled Lane, Wylam, Northumberland. Tel: (0661) 852176
Bradley Herb Garden

10m W of Newcastle off A695 at Crawcrook (well signposted) ● *Open Easter - mid-Oct, daily, 9.00 a.m. - 5.00 p.m.* ● *Entrance: free* ● *Parking* ● *Refreshments starting in 1990* ● *Toilet facilities* ● *Suitable for wheelchairs* ● *Dogs on lead* ● *Plants for sale* ● *Shop* ● *Grade IV*

This garden has particular appeal for a plantsperson. It is stocked at present with a variety of Victorian apple trees, lavenders and an extensive collection of herbs. Fresh cut herbs are sold to both public and catering trade. There are also some Victorian cottage-garden plants such as aquilegias.

CHILLINGHAM CASTLE 3
Chillingham, Northumberland. Tel: (06685) 359/390
Sir Humphrey Wakefield

12m NNW of Alnwick between A1 (signed), A697, B6346 and B6348 ● *Gardens open April and Oct, Sat and Sun, 1.30 - 5.00 p.m., May - Sept, daily except Tues, 1.30 - 5.00 p.m.* ● *Best season: spring, midsummer* ● *Entrance: £1.90, concessions £1.75, children £1.25* ● *Parking* ● *Teas* ● *Toilet facilities* ● *Shop* ● *House open May - Sept* ● *Grade III*

Not easy to find but well worth an effort, this one-time home of the Grey family is being vigorously restored along with the grounds landscaped by Wyatville (of Hampton Court fame). The Elizabethan walled garden has been virtually excavated by Isobel Murray to expose its intricate pattern of clipped yew and box (enlivened by scarlet tropaeolum), a central avenue and flourishing borders around the walls. Outside are lawns and a rock garden, delightful woodland and lakeside walks through drifts of snowdrops and spring displays of daffodils, bluebells and later, rhododendrons.

CRAGSIDE 4
Rothbury, Morpeth, Northumberland. Tel: (0669) 20333
The National Trust

14m SW of Alnwick off A697 between B6341 and B6344 ● Open April - Oct, daily except Mon, 10.30 a.m. – 7.00 p.m., Nov – Mar, Sat and Sun, 10.30 a.m. – 4.00 p.m. ● Best season: early summer ● Entrance: £2.00. Groups by appointment £1.50 per person ● Parking ● Refreshments: light lunches 11.00 a.m. – 5.30 p.m. ● Toilet facilities inc. disabled ● Partly suitable for wheelchairs ● Dogs in grounds only ● House open April – Oct, daily except Mon but inc. Bank Holidays, 1.00 – 5.30 p.m. Last admission 5.00 p.m. £3.50 ● Grade III

Lord Armstrong, the greatest of Victorian engineers, clothed this hillside above the Coquet Valley with millions of trees and shrubs as the setting for a house (the first ever lit by hydro- electricity) that was then the wonder of the world. Now properly managed, the 900-acre park with its 40 miles of driveways and rambling paths is a mass of rhododendrons in June. Higher up there are enclaves of bare rock and heather, a reminder of the original state of the land, with lovely views over wooded valleys under broad Northumbrian skies. The man-made lakes, hydro-electric and hydraulic systems (also on view) add another dimension and a tribute to Victorian vigour and ingenuity at its peak.

HERTERTON HOUSE 5
Hartington, Cambo, Morpeth, Northumberland.
Tel: (067074) 278
Frank and Marjorie Lawley

2m N of Cambo on B6342 ● Open April – Oct, daily except Tues and Thurs, 1.30 – 5.30 p.m. ● Best season: high summer ● Entrance: 50p ● Parking ● Toilet facilities ● Plants for sale ● Grade III

The Lawleys took over this land and near-derelict Elizabethan building, with commanding views over picturesque upland Northumberland, in 1976. With vision and skill they have created three distinct areas. In front, a winter garden with tranquil vistas; alongside, a cloistered 'monastic' knot garden of mainly medicinal, occult and dye-producing herbs; and to the rear, their most impressive achievement, a flower garden. This is a carefully designed Persian carpet, with perceptively mingled hardy flowers chosen with an artist's eye. Many are unusual traditional plants (including 58 species from the wild) that flourish within the newly-built sheltering walls. A gem of a place, of great interest to the plantsperson.

HEXHAM HERBS 6
The Chesters Walled Garden, Humshaugh,
Nr Hexham, Northumberland.
Kim and Susie White

5m N of Hexham, ½m W of Chollerford on B6318 ● *Open March – Nov, daily,*
10.00 a.m. – 5.00 p.m., Dec – Feb, weekends by appointment ● *Best season:*
March – Sept ● *Entrance: 50p* ● *Parking* ● *Refreshments: planned* ● *Toilet*
facilities: planned ● *Suitable for wheelchairs* ● *Plants for sale* ● *Shop*
● *Grade III*

The tall brick walls of the old kitchen garden slope gently south from the very
line of Hadrian's Wall, echoing the Roman forts that lie to east and west.
Within these ramparts, still with vestiges of the Victorian glasshouses and
heating system, the Whites have fashioned a superb herb collection, including
most fittingly a unique Roman garden with plants (myrtle, etc.) identified by
archaeologists through pollen analysis. A major feature is the national
NCCPG thyme bank. A rose garden (over 60 species), extensive herbaceous
sections (some 800 varieties) and terraced lawns against an architectural
backdrop (Norman Shaw's Chesters mansion) fill out this splendid 'fort'.

HOWICK HALL 7
Howick, Northumberland. Tel: (066577) 285
Sir Charles Baring (Howick Hall Trust)

5m NE of Alnwick off B1339 ● *Open Easter – Oct, 2.00 – 7.00 p.m.* ● *Best*
season: spring/summer ● *Entrance: £1.00, children and concessions 50p*
● *Parking* ● *Toilet facilities* ● *Partly suitable for wheelchairs* ● *Dogs on lead*
● *Grade II*

The accident of woodland which sheltered this site from the blasts of the
North Sea enabled Lord and Lady Grey to come here during World War I and
start building an amazing collection of tender plants which would do credit to
a Scottish west coast garden. The central terrace has a pool and excellent
borders and the lawns run down through feature shrubs to a stream. Winding
paths lead through shrubbery or parkland to the 'silver wood', under whose
magnificent trees one passes among numerous fine shrubs and woodland
flowers given to Earl and Lady Grey for their silver wedding in the 1930s.
There are good varieties of rhododendron and azalea, and outstanding species
hydrangea (*H. villosa*) apart from unusual flower varieties. A large pond-side
garden is developing and an arboretum. Labelling is scarce but a catalogue is
in preparation. This is a plantsperson's garden but there are many delights for
the aesthete such as the agapanthus of varying blues on the terrace.

LINDISFARNE CASTLE 8
Holy Island, Berwick-upon-Tweed, Northumberland.
Tel: (0289) 89244
The National Trust

On Holy Island, 6m E of A1 across a causeway at low tide only. Tide tables printed in local papers and displayed at causeway. Access to garden on foot only, ½m from parking area • *Open April – Sept, daily except Fri but open Good Friday, 1.00 – 5.30 p.m. Last admission 5.00 p.m. Oct, Wed, Sat and Sun, 1.00 – 5.30 p.m. Last admission 5.00 p.m.* • *Entrance: June – Aug £2.50, other months £1.50 (castle and garden)* • *Parking by castle ½m from garden* • *Refreshments in village* • *Dogs on lead as far as Lower Battery only* • *National Trust shop in village* • *Castle open. Visitors must leave bulky objects inc. back-packs in entrance* • ***Grade IV***

This garden must be unique both in design and setting. Its existence on Holy Island off the coast of Northumberland came about like this: in 1901 Edward Hudson owner and founder of *Country Life*, on holiday, saw the ruins of the castle, rapidly purchased them from their owner the Crown and invited the young architect Lutyens to rebuild. Lutyens had been introduced to Hudson by his friend Gertrude Jekyll. The latter advised Hudson to have a low walled garden built to the north of the castle approached by a walk across the fields. This was done in 1911. In the patterned paving, a selection of Jekyll's favourite plants were planted in gradations of colour. The original plans were recently discovered in a Californian collection and recreated by the Trust and the University of Durham. The garden is at its best in summer.

WALLINGTON 9
Cambo, Morpeth, Northumberland. Tel: (067074) 283
The National Trust

20m W of Newcastle off A696 (signed on B6342) • *Open: walled garden April – Oct, daily, 10.00 a.m. – 7.00 p.m., Nov – Mar, daily, 10.00 a.m. – dusk. Grounds open all year round during daylight hours* • *Best season: spring – autumn* • *Entrance: £1.00, children 50p* • *Parking* • *Refreshments: coffee, lunch and teas in Clock Tower Restaurant (067074) 274. Picnics in car park* • *Toilet facilities inc. disabled* • *Suitable for wheelchairs* • *Dogs on lead in garden, free in grounds* • *Shop* • *House and museum open April – Oct, daily, except Tues, 1.00 – 5.30 p.m. Entrance: £3.00, children £1.50* • ***Grade II***

The superb house in a 100-acre landscape of lawns, terraces and flower beds has an excellent walled garden, with a great variety of climbers and an impressive summer house designed in Tuscan style by 'Capability' Brown who was a local man. The conservatory plants include a great tree fuchsia. Outside, the walks step down from a classical fountain past beds re-designed by Lady Trevelyan in the 1930s, including notable heathers and many herbaceous varieties, through to the water meadow. Trees include two larches by the China Pond planted by the Duke of Argyll in 1738. New circular walk.

NOTTINGHAMSHIRE

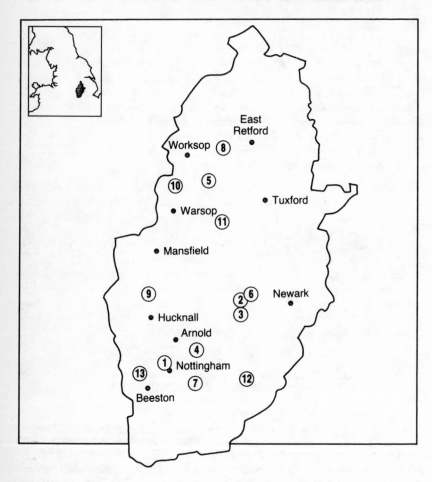

THE ARBORETUM

1

Waverley Street, Nottingham.
Nottingham City Council

Located a short walk from the Victoria shopping centre along Shakespeare Street to Waverley Street entrance ● Open daily, 8.00 a.m., Sat and Sun, 9.00 a.m. – 9.30 p.m. (or dusk if earlier) ● Entrance: free ● Light refreshments at kiosk near entrance, 10.00 a.m. – 5.00 p.m. ● Toilet facilities ● Suitable for wheelchairs (note arboretum is on hillside) ● Dogs (fouling not allowed) ● Grade III

This is an arboretum within a city park, unusually sited on a hillside. The Royal National Rose Society's display garden within the arboretum is at its best late June/early July – almost a total lack of labels unfortunately. This quiet, mature park, close to the city centre with aviaries and large lake and lawns is particularly suitable for children. Another spectacular feature is a 170-yard dahlia border.

BISHOP'S MANOR 2
Bishop's Drive, Southwell, Nottinghamshire. Tel: (0636) 812112
The Rt Rev. the Lord Bishop of Southwell and Mrs Harris

12m NE of Nottingham on A612. Situated at the end of Bishop's Drive on the S side of the Minster ● *Open 19th Aug, 2.00 – 6.00 p.m.* ● *Parking in village car parks* ● *Refreshments: tea and biscuits* ● *Suitable for wheelchairs* ● *Grade IV*

The charm of this garden is its unusual setting. Part of it is enclosed in the ruins of the medieval palace providing a sheltered area for the plants to flourish. The present gardener has been there four years and has created a well-maintained garden of over three acres, with rose beds and borders as well as informal areas.

BRACKENHURST COLLEGE 3
Southwell, Nottinghamshire. Tel: (0636) 812252
Nottinghamshire Education Committee

1m S of Southwell on A612 ● *Occasional open days and NGS. Open for parties by arrangement and on 1st July 2.00 – 6.00 p.m.* ● *Entrance: 70p, children free. Parties by prior arrangement at other times £1.20 per head* ● *Parking by arrangement* ● *Toilet facilities* ● *Partly suitable for wheelchairs* ● *Dogs* ● *Farm museum open* ● *Grade II*

This was once a wealthy estate with gardens to match and fine views of the surrounding countryside. Ornamental shrubs, rose and sunken gardens, walled garden, glasshouses, mature trees, especially fine cedars of Lebanon, experimental trial beds. The artificial lake constructed on the dewpond principle is carefully managed with wildlife in mind. The garden is in the process of being rehabilitated so some areas are now less impressive and more labelling would be helpful. A farm museum is open, and a farm institute is established on the estate.

17 BRIDLE ROAD 4
Burton Joyce, Nottinghamshire. Tel: (0602) 313725
Mr and Mrs Bates

Turn N off A612 Nottingham to Southwell Road up Lambley Lane. After ½m fork right down impassable-looking Bridle Road, and the property is on the left

● *Open by appointment and on 22nd July, 2.00 – 6.00 p.m.* ● *Best season: spring/summer* ● *Entrance: 75p, children 40p* ● *Parking very restricted in lane by the gates to the house* ● *Teas in the village* ● *Partly suitable for wheelchairs* ● **Grade III**

The one-acre garden is situated on a slope, mainly facing south and west. The mixed border is of the highest standard combining extremely well a variety of plants including dahlias and grasses. Worth looking at is the way the very steep slope on the garden's southern border has been utilized with zigzagging gravel paths. Common and unusual bulbous plants abound – those such as acidanthera and nerines are in the hot, sunny spots near the house, others in the grass, woodland and mixed border. There is a stream with naturalized ferns, primulas and the like.

CLUMBER PARK   5
Clumber Estate Office, Clumber Park, Worksop, Nottinghamshire.
Tel: (0909) 476592
The National Trust

4½m SE of Worksop off A1 and A57, 11m from junction 30 off M1 ● *Always open* ● *Entrance: pedestrians free, cars £2.00, cars with caravan £3.00, coaches midweek £5.00, weekends and Bank Holidays £10.00* ● *Parking*
● *Refreshments: cafeteria and restaurant, daily, 10.30 a.m. – 5.00 p.m.*
● *Toilet facilities* ● *Partly suitable for wheelchairs (wheelchairs inc. those for children available)* ● *Dogs* ● *National Trust shop* ● *Chapel open except 25th Dec, 10.00 a.m. – 5.00 p.m.* ● **Grade III**

In 1707 the Park was enclosed from Sherwood Forest and the Dukes of Newcastle had their seat here. Only the stable block, chapel and entrance gates remain as the great house was demolished in 1938. The National Trust purchased the park in 1946. The Lincoln terrace and pleasure gardens were laid out by William Sawrey Gilpin in the early nineteenth century. Twenty-five acres out of the 3800 acres of parkland are managed by just two gardeners. The vinery and palm house survive (being restocked) and the extensive glass houses (450 feet) are the best and longest in the National Trust's properties. The kitchen garden exhibition of late nineteenth-century and early twentieth-century tools is fascinating and reminds us that modern powered-garden tools have taken much of the heavy work out of gardening. The walled kitchen garden has some fruit bushes, a herb garden in the making and a few young fruit trees in the grassy centre but is otherwise a disappointment. The Lincoln terrace reached its height of excellence in the 1920s and after years of neglect is being restored. The cedar avenue has cedars and sweet chestnut trees of breath-taking size.

CLYDE HOUSE 6
Westgate, Southwell, Nottinghamshire. Tel: (0636) 812634
Mr and Mrs G. Edwards

In Southwell on A612 a few hundred yards before the Minster on the right
● *Open 19th Aug, 2.00 – 6.00 p.m.* ● *Entrance: 75p* ● *Restricted roadside parking* ● *Toilet facilities* ● *Suitable for wheelchairs* ● *Plants for sale*
● *Grade IV*

Totally organically-managed private gardens are regrettably rare but this example will convince visitors that it is possible to 'go organic' and still have a beautifully healthy garden – only the rose against the wall of the house looked the worse for black spot but that was the only obvious sign of disease anywhere. The immaculate green lawn on closer inspection was full of clover – but so what if it looked and felt luxurious underfoot? The composting area (the secret of success?) is an education in itself and Mr Edwards will explain its workings.

HOLME PIERREPONT HALL 7
Radcliffe-on-Trent, Nottinghamshire. Tel: (0602) 332371
Mr and Mrs R. Brackenbury

5m SE of Nottingham off A52. Approach past the National Water Sports Centre and continue for 1½m ● *Open Easter Sun, Mon, Tues, May Bank Holiday, Spring and Summer Bank Holidays, June - Aug, Sun, Tues, Thurs, Fri, 2.00 – 6.00 p.m.* ● *Entrance: £1.80, children 75p* ● *Parking* ● *Teas. Other refreshments by prior arrangement* ● *Toilet facilities* ● *Suitable for wheelchairs* ● *Dogs on lead* ● *Shop* ● *House open* ● *Grade IV*

The Hall is a medieval brick manor house but the garden and parterre have been restored by the present owners. The box parterre is the outstanding feature of the gardens and the newly created herbaceous borders next to the York stone path (replacing old rose beds) once matured will enhance the courtyard garden further. (The Jacob sheep are very friendly lawnmowers.) Mr and Mrs Brackenbury work hard with improvements to this peaceful house and garden and willingly provide ample information. Their improvements include a winter garden.

MORTON HALL 8
Ranby, Retford, Nottinghamshire. Tel: (0777) 702530
Lady Mason

4m W of Retford. Entrance on link road from A620 to southbound A1 ● *Open 13th, 20th, 27th May, 7th Oct, 2.00 – 6.00 p.m.* ● *Best season: spring and autumn* ● *Entrance: £1.25 per car or 65p per person whichever is least* ● *Teas* ● *Toilet facilities* ● *Partly suitable for wheelchairs* ● *Dogs* ● *Morton Hall Gardens nurseries adjacent to garden* ● *Grade II*

'The gardens are celebrated' wrote Henry Thorold in his *Shell Guide to Nottinghamshire*. It is not surprising for there are a large number of mature and rare specimen trees and shrubs in a relatively small park. They were planted over 100 years ago by one of the Mason family, the botanist William Mason, and a Mason now runs a well-stocked nursery beside the garden. The soil is sandy and poor but obviously suits the slightly more tender shrubs – romneyas thrive next to the house. Enjoy the rare and unusual and the colours in spring and autumn in this peaceful garden but do not expect immaculate lawns and flower beds.

NEWSTEAD ABBEY 9
Linby, Nottinghamshire. Tel: (0623) 793557
Nottingham City Council

11m N of Nottingham on A60 ● *Open daily, 10.00 a.m. – dusk* ● *Entrance: 85p, children 40p* ● *Parking* ● *Refreshments: tea room in grounds open Good Friday – Sept* ● *Toilet facilities* ● *Partly suitable for wheelchairs* ● *Dogs on lead* ● *Shop* ● *House open at extra charge, Good Friday to Sept, 11.30 a.m. – 6.00 p.m. Last admission 5.00 p.m. Contains Byron memorabilia* ● ***Grade II***

Water predominates in this estate that the poet Byron inherited but could rarely afford to live in. In most of the extensive and immaculate gardens there is much of interest. The Japanese gardens are justly famous and the rock and fern gardens worth visiting. Indeed the waterfalls, wildfowl, passageways, grottos and bridges provide plenty of fun for children, but in addition there is an excellent, imaginatively-equipped play area with plenty of bark mulch for safety. The tropical garden and the monks' stew pond are visually uninteresting but they are of laudable age. It is a pity that the large walled kitchen garden is now a rose garden – rose gardens however pretty are commonplace but large kitchen gardens to the great houses are rare now and of more interest. The old rose garden is now the iris garden – an insipid area with gladioli planted in the regular plots in an effort to liven up the place.

OLD MILL HOUSE 10
Cuckney, Nottinghamshire. Tel: (0623) 842696
Dr and Mrs E.A. Nicoll

6m N of Mansfield on A60 in middle of Cuckney ● *Open 6th May, 2.00 – 6.00 p.m.* ● *Best season: late spring and summer* ● *Entrance: 60p, children 20p* ● *Parking on open days* ● *Refreshments: teas on NGS* ● *Toilet facilities* ● *Partly suitable for wheelchairs* ● *Dogs on lead* ● ***Grade III***

This private garden has been built by the present owners who have capitalized on the inherent water features. A 50p booklet sold at the entrance gives all the information needed about the garden as well as the mill's history and Cuckney itself. The butterfly meadow is a good 20 minutes' walk – read the notice with the description of it before starting. The ancient woodland is being restored.

RUFFORD COUNTRY PARK 11
Nottinghamshire. Tel: (0623) 824153
Nottinghamshire County Council

*2m S of Ollerton on A614 ● Open daily, dawn - dusk ● Entrance: free
● Parking ● Refreshments: main meals - the Buttery, Mon - Sat, 12 noon -
2.30 p.m., Sun, 12 noon - 3.30 p.m., snacks at the Coach House daily, 10.00
a.m. - 5.00 p.m. ● Partly suitable for wheelchairs, two available which can be
booked in advance ● Dogs (guide dogs only in shops and restaurants) ● Shops
● Rufford Abbey closed for repairs and restoration ● Grade III*

Rufford Country Park contains almost everything that might be expected of
an important country park e.g. lakes, lime avenues, mature cedars, etc.
Recently the gardeners have created eight theme gardens including herb and
scented plants, all within a larger sculpture garden. These promise to be worth
another visit when established. Large areas are managed with wildlife in mind
hence plenty of birdlife. Ball games are allowed on the lawns beneath cut-
leaved beeches and cedars. Ample picnic areas. Conducted walks arranged
during the week and weekends; telephone for dates and times.

THE WILLOWS 12
5 Rockley Avenue, Radcliffe-on-Trent, Nottinghamshire.
Tel: (06073) 3621
Mr and Mrs R.A. Grout

*6m E of Nottingham N of A52. From Radcliffe-on-Trent High Street P.O. turn
into Shelford Road, over railway bridge, 300 yards opposite bus shelter turn left
into Cliff Way, then 2nd right ● Open for parties by appointment, and 1st Wed
in every month April - Sept, 2.00 - 6.00 p.m. ● Entrance: 75p, OAP, children
50p ● Parking on street ● Teas on NGS days ● Not very suitable for
wheelchairs ● Grade III*

This small private garden, designed by the owners in 1982, is of greatest
appeal to those interested in rare hardy herbaceous plants. Because of its size,
trees and shrubs are limited but are unusual or handled in such a way as to fit
the area e.g. pollarding. Excellent labelling. Collections of hostas, hellebores,
pulmonarias and snowdrops.

WOLLATON HALL 13
Nottingham. Tel: (0602) 281333
Nottingham City Council

*2½m from the city centre on A609. From M1 junction 25 take A52, turn left
onto A614 and left onto A609 ● Open daily all year ● Entrance: free
● Parking ● Refreshments: snacks near Wollaton Road car park ● Toilet
facilities ● Partly suitable for wheelchairs ● Dogs on lead because of deer
● Shop ● House open April - Sept, Mon - Sat, 10.00 a.m. - 7.00 p.m., Sun,*

2.00 – 5.00 p.m., Oct – March, Mon – Sat, 10.00 a.m. – dusk, Sun, 1.30 – 4.30 p.m. Closed 25th Dec. Free except small charge on Sun ● *Grade III*

This large park and garden is surrounded by the city but because of its size the visitor feels deep in the country – unfortunately near the park periphery the roar of traffic dispels that illusion. The polyanthus in spring are spectacular as is the summer bedding where castor-oil plants and ornamental cabbages have their place in the schemes. The formal gardens at the top of the hill give onto views of huge cedars and holm oaks and thence on to the lime avenues and the deer in the park.

THE GRADING SYSTEM

This is the most subjective aspect of the *Guide* and one which may cause some disagreement on the part of owners as well as visitors. We stress that its purpose is to serve as an indication to visitors in order to give them some advance information about the status of the garden as viewed by our inspectors and editors. Readers will appreciate that direct comparisons cannot be made between a huge estate like Chatsworth with its staff of professional experts and a tiny plantsman's garden in a terraced house, tended with dedication by a single owner. This being said, both may be excellent of their kind and therefore be worthy of consideration for a visit, and considered by the *Guide* to be at the top of their class. Conversely a lesser grading does not imply any criticism of a garden but is an attempt to guide the potential reader as to its relative merits if a choice has to be made between several gardens. Broadly speaking the intention of the four grades is as follows:

Grade I Amongst the best gardens in the world in terms of design and content. Many are of historic importance, but some are of recent origin. Overseas visitors to Britain or Ireland are recommended to include them in their itinerary.

Grade II Gardens of high quality, though not perhaps as unique as Grade I, and worth travelling a considerable distance to visit. Sometimes the property as a whole, and the general ambience, make the visit particularly rewarding.

Grade III These are gardens which our inspectors suggest it would be worth driving fifty miles or more to visit. They may have some special feature of design or plant content while not being considered as justifying a higher grade overall.

Grade IV Gardens of considerable merit and well worth visiting when in the region.

OXFORDSHIRE

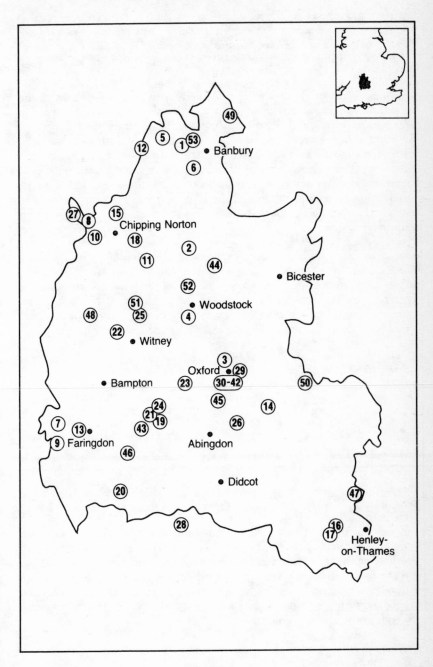

BALSCOTE GARDENS 1
Balscote, Nr Banbury, Oxfordshire.

5m W of Banbury S of A422 ● *Two Balscote gardens open on 27th May, 2.00 –*
6.00 p.m. (80p for combined entrance). Two Balscote and two Shutford gardens
(Shutford Manor and Five Ways Cottage) open on 8th July, 2.00 – 6.00 p.m.
(£1.50 for combined entrance to all four) ● *Parking* ● *Teas* ● *Plants for sale*
● *Grade IV*

Balscote is a remote hilltop village, formerly with several farms which the
present residents have developed into a kind of public garden that will please
everyone. They have done this by ensuring that the frontages which abut on to
the steep village streets and lanes are well-decorated with plants and by
cultivating almost every inch of their gardens, most of which can be seen over
the stone walls and hedges by strollers. Home Farm, designed since 1984/5,
has sought all-year interest by growing heathers and alpines in addition to the
visual variety of trees, plants and shrubs, all packed into a sloping half acre. In
addition the owner has collected together all the farmyard archaeology dug up
while making the garden – old-fashioned tools, horse paraphernalia, etc,
which is displayed in the small cow-byre. Next door at Homeland, another
plantsman's garden with a very wide range grown on sloping ground includes
a rock garden and a terraced vegetable plot. A field with new trees leads to the
interesting church with its tiny tower built over the porch. Notice also the
terraced stonework recently completed at another house with an apparently
impossibly steep garden. As in so many villages, the main environmental
eyesores are those perpetrated by the electricity and telephone engineers.

BARTON ABBEY 2
Middle Barton, Oxfordshire.   Tel: (0869) 40227
Mr and Mrs J.C. Fleming

10m S of Banbury, turn W off A423 on the B4030 for 1m ● *Open 6th May,*
8th July, 5th Aug, 2nd Sept, 2.00 – 5.30 p.m. ● *Entrance: 80p, children 30p*
● *Parking* ● *Teas* ● *Toilet facilities* ● *Suitable for wheelchairs* ● *Dogs*
● *Grade III*

This is an object lesson in what to do if a place designed to be staffed by ten
gardeners is reduced to having to make do with two. The Flemings have
eliminated the vast beds, let the rock garden grow over and concentrated on
the grandeur of the setting of the Abbey in its hollow in the hills with fine
lawns running down to the lake. Two trees have been bent into a 'whalebone'
arch leading to the wild garden. One economy the Flemings have not made is
to reduce work on the vast Victorian walled kitchen garden. This is a model of
its kind, with a large rose arch at the centre. In the unheated greenhouses
beyond, nectarines and vines flourish. Note also the thatched early version of
a Wendy house and the lavender walk.

23 BEECH CROFT ROAD 3
Summertown, Oxford. Tel: (0865) 56020
Mrs A. Dexter

Summertown, 2m from centre of Oxford. Beech Croft Road runs between the
Banbury and Woodstock roads which connect Oxford centre to ring road ● *Open*
by appointment only from June – Sept. Proceeds to NGS ● *Entrance: £1.00*
● *Parking* ● *Grade I*

This small paved garden only 23 x 7 yards is a plantsperson's delight.
Although at a terraced house, Mrs Dexter has achieved seclusion by evergreen
shrubs, climbing roses and clematis. Unusual plants in shady beds and
troughs include alpines and ferns. (See also Silver Trees, page 315.)

BLENHEIM PALACE 4
Woodstock, Oxfordshire. Tel: (0993) 811325
The Duke of Marlborough

8m NW of Oxford on A34 at Woodstock. Entrance in town to W of A34 ● *Park*
open daily except 25th Dec, 9.00 a.m. – 9.00 p.m. ● *Entrance: park only,*
pedestrians 50p, children 25p, cars £2.50 ● *Parking* ● *Refreshments: cafeteria,*
Orangerie restaurant ● *Toilet facilities inc. disabled* ● *Partly suitable for*
wheelchairs ● *Dogs on lead* ● *Good garden centre open daily, 9.30 a.m. – 5.30*
p.m., with refund on entrance charge for purchases ● *House open, mid-March –*
Oct, 10.30 a.m. – 5.30 p.m. (last admission 4.45 p.m.) £4.50, OAP £3.20,
children £2.20 ● *Grade I*

The visitor who walks through Hawksmoor's Triumphal Arch into Blenheim
Park sees one of the greatest contrived landscapes in Britain. The architect
Vanbrugh employed Bridgeman and Henry Wise, Queen Anne's master
gardener and the last of the British formalists, to contrast a bastion-walled
'military' garden and kitchen gardens. Wise also planted immense elm
avenues, and linked Vanburgh's bridge to the sides of the valley. However the
garden was far from ready when the first Duke of Marlborough moved into
the palace in 1719. Major alterations were made by the 4th, 5th and 9th
Dukes, one of the earliest of which was the grassing over of Wise's formal
gardens by 'Capability' Brown after 1764. Brown also developed the two huge
lakes. It is possible to spend several hours walking through the grounds, for
which no charge is made. The gardens (entrance only with paid palace ticket)
include formal areas restored by Achille Duchêne in the 1920s from those
grassed by Brown in the North forecourt. He made formal gardens on the east
and west, the latter two water terraces in the Versailles style. To the east of the
elaborate Italian garden is a sunken garden of patterned box and golden yew,
interspersed with various seasonal plantings. To the west from the terraces are
the rose garden and arboretum (1984). From the vast south lawn 'one passes
through a magnificent grove of cedars and on towards Wise's walled garden,
past shrubberies of laurel and an Exedra of box and yew, the whole
exemplifying the Victorian pleasure grounds' (*Oxford Companion*).

BROOK COTTAGE 5
Alkerton, Nr Banbury, Oxfordshire. Tel: (029587) 303/590
Mr and Mrs D. Hodges

6m W of Banbury. From A422 Banbury – Stratford road, turn W at sign for Alkerton. Soon after entering village, small war memorial on right. Turn left and right at fork ● Open April – Oct, Mon – Fri, 9.00 a.m. – 6.00 p.m. and 9th, 10th June, 29th, 30th Sept, 2.00 – 7.00 p.m. Other weekends, evenings and all group visits by appointment ● Entrance: £1.00, children free ● Partly suitable for wheelchairs ● Grade II

This garden, designed and planted since 1964, is on a steeply-sloping, west-facing site of four acres much of which is mown grass and lawn. The owners have used the natural features in an interesting way. For example by planting large species, old- fashioned and modern shrub roses in the grass on a steep slope. Good use is made of water and there is a large unusual-shaped pond. Indeed shape is a feature of the overall effect, such as in a sweeping crimson copper beech hedge and the maze-like series of beds and paths which hide a tennis court. There is something here for everyone in all seasons, from the alpine scree to the small 'cottage' and vegetable gardens above the house. Most plants are labelled. On NGS days, the owner next door at Alkerton House opens the connecting gate to show off his two and a half acres of trees, shrubs and conifers. Upton House (see page 400) nearby shows an earlier and more formal use of slopes.

BROUGHTON CASTLE 6
Broughton, Nr Banbury, Oxfordshire. Tel: (0295) 62624
The Lord Saye and Sele

2½m SW of Banbury on B4035 ● Open 18th May – 14th September, Wed and Sun, also Thurs in July and Aug and Bank Holiday Sun and Mon, inc. Easter, 2.00 – 5.00 p.m. Also by appointment for groups throughout year ● Entrance: £2.00, children £1.00 ● Parking ● Teas on open days, refreshments for parties by arrangement ● Toilet facilities ● Suitable for wheelchairs ● House open ● Grade II

More of a house than a castle, the gardens are unexpectedly domestic within the confines of the moat. In 1900 there were 14 gardeners but the present owner and his inspired gardener have reduced the workload somewhat while retaining the overall splendour. The most important changes were made after 1969 following a visit from Lanning Roper who suggested opening up the views across the park. There are now two magnificent borders. The west-facing one, backed by the battlement wall, has a colour scheme of blues and yellows, greys and whites. The other long border is based on reds, mauves and blues. Great planting skill is evident in the serpentine flows of colour. On the south side is the walled 'ladies garden' with box-edged fleur-de-lys-shaped beds holding floribunda roses. Another wonderful border rises up to the house wall. Everywhere is a profusion of old-fashioned roses and original planting. Visitors who are members of a group may also like to see one of the more interesting small gardens in the area. This is Mrs Pedder's 'Yeomans' at Tadmarton which is only open to groups in the summer by appointment.

BUSCOT PARK 7
Faringdon, Oxfordshire.   Tel: (0367) 20786 (not weekends)
The National Trust

On A417 between Lechlade and Faringdon ● Open 4th April – Sept, Wed – Fri (inc. Good Friday), and every 2nd and 4th Sat and Sun immediately following, also Easter Sat and Sun, 2.00 – 6.00 p.m. Closed Bank Holiday Mon. Last admission 5.30 p.m. ● Entrance: £2.00, (house and garden £3.00) ● Parking ● Refreshments: teas and light refreshments ● Toilet facilities ● Plants for sale ● House open ● Grade II

Although the house was built in 1780, this garden has been developed during the twentieth century. The water garden was created by Harold Peto in 1912, although the avenues linking lake to house were added later using a goose-foot plan from the house, with fastigiate and weeping varieties of oak, beech and lime. The Egyptian avenue created by Lord Faringdon in 1969 is guarded by sphinxes and embellished with Coade stone statues copied from an original from Hadrian's Villa. The large walled kitchen garden was redesigned by Tim Rees using pleached hedges of Judas trees (which should grow into a tunnel) and hornbeam underplanted with hemerocallis. Deep borders under walls with unusual, and skilful mixture of old roses and vegetables (gourds, marrows, red chard, parsley, etc.) Walkway outside kitchen garden between two wide borders using exterior wall and trellis as screens. Exceptionally effective planting by Peter Coats three years ago and, over the years, imaginative development by Lord Faringdon.

CHASTLETON HOUSE 8
Chastleton, Oxfordshire.   Tel: (060874) 355
Mrs Clutton-Brock

3m SE of Moreton-in-Marsh, 5m N of Chipping Norton off A44 ● Open Good Friday – last Sun in Sept, weekdays, 10.30 a.m. – 1 p.m., 2.00 – 5.30 p.m., Sun, 2.00 – 5.00 p.m. Will open at other times for parties of 20 or more by appointment ● Entrance: £2.50, children £1.25 inc. house. Garden only free ● Parking ● Toilet facilities in house ● Suitable for wheelchairs ● House open (as above) ● Grade IV

This small and rather unkempt garden is well worth a visit because it can be combined with a tour of the 'unaltered' early seventeenth Jacobean mansion, charming especially because of its lack of National Trust restoration. It is a simple grass affair leading to a surreal box garden dating from 1700. When last visited by this writer on a sunny February day a large male fox was moving stealthily through the box features to avoid the attentions of the Heythrop Hunt whose members surrounded the grounds.

CLOCK HOUSE 9
Coleshill, Faringdon, Oxfordshire. Tel: (079376) 2476
Michael and Denny Wickham

*3½m SW of Faringdon on B4019 ● Open by appointment and 18th June, 15th Oct, 2.00 – 6.00 p.m. ● Best season: June/July ● Entrance: 50p, children free ● Parking ● Teas in courtyard in fine weather ● Toilet facilities ● Suitable for wheelchairs ● Dogs on lead ● Plants for sale ● **Grade II***

Situated on a hillside overlooking the Vale of the White Horse, this exuberant, delightful garden was created by the present owners in the last forty years in the grounds of Coleshill House, burned, then demolished in the 1950s. Courtyard with collection of plants in pots. Sunny walled garden in old laundry-drying area with herbs, roses and variety of mixed plants. Lawns in front of the house with lime avenue to the right, leading away from house. Vegetable gardens bordered by tall hedge of old roses; sweeping views over the Vale. Pond and terrace enclosed by arches and tall hedges; many mixed herbaceous borders. The ground plan of the original house is now being planted out in box of different shades to show layout of walls and windows. This is an original garden, designed by an artist with a large collection of plants in imaginative settings, the atmosphere being prolific rather than tidy.

CORNWELL MANOR 10
Cornwell, Nr Kingham, Oxfordshire. Tel: (060871) 605
The Hon Mrs Peter Ward

*2m from Chipping Norton, S off A44 ● Open for parties by appointment in June and July at £1.00 per person. Tel: (060871) 671 also 6th May, 2.00 – 6.00 p.m., 24th June, 11.00 a.m. – 5.00 p.m. when entrance: £1.50 ● Parking ● Teas on NGS days ● Toilet facilities ● Not very suitable for wheelchairs ● Plants for sale ● **Grade I***

Looking at this house and garden through the wrought-iron gates on the road frontage, it seems all-year-round the quintessence of seventeenth-century gracious living. Inside, the garden has been modernised without losing any of its charm. Begin by standing on the south-facing terrace in front of the house and looking down over the croquet lawn and up to the roadside gates and the view beyond; it is as good as anything in Italy. To the east is the spring garden and a formal garden on three levels with interesting plantings such as box-edged beds of peonies. Everywhere there are trained trees and clever plantings to emphasise leaf colouring. On the other side of the house is the original one and a quarter-acre walled kitchen garden, organically cultivated and, in the owner's words 'maintained in the traditional manner, now rarely seen.' Note also the children's garden, with an early form of Wendy house, and peek in the indoor games-room window to see the mass of amazing trophies of the chase. Returning to the main house, the visitor descends the south terraces to the water pools below and turns east along the woodland walk, passing on the way the rock and bog gardens. The wild garden surrounds vast and unspoilt lakes.

Everywhere there is evidence of sensitive new planting. The plant sales are amongst the best. The small village nearby was refurbished by the architect of Portmeirion, Sir Clough Williams Ellis (see page 487).

DITCHLEY PARK 11
Enstone, Oxfordshire. Tel: (060872) 346
Ditchley Foundation

1½m W of A34 at Kiddington, N of Woodstock, 2m from Charlbury • *Open by appointment until early July, Mon – Thurs p.m.* • *Parking* • *Toilet facilities* • *Suitable for wheelchairs* • *House open by appointment £15.00 per couple then £2.50 per head, reduced rate for OAP and children* • *Grade III*

Variously attributed to Kent and Brown, this small landscape garden is probably an early nineteenth-century work by the gardenesque exponent J.C. Loudon. Attractive walks around his small lake through woodland recently planted with flowering trees passes Leadbetter's earlier Ionic Rotunda. Formal parterres and pleached lime walks in a characteristically architectural setting are the work of Geoffrey Jellicoe in the 1930s, a small part of a much larger plan which would have destroyed the balance of this fine site.

EPWELL MILL 12
Epwell, Nr Banbury, Oxfordshire. Tel: (029578) 327
Mr R.A. Withers

Epwell lies off the A4035, 7m W of Banbury. The Mill is about 1m after leaving the village • *Open 8th April, 20th May, 23rd Sept, 2.00 – 6.00 p.m.* • *Entrance: £1.00, children free* • *Parking outside and along drive* • *Partly suitable for wheelchairs* • *Grade III*

The owners designed this garden, with its interesting water and water garden features, on the site of a disused mill in attractive countryside. It is open three times a year (NGS), once in April when the drive should be lined with daffodils, again in late May/early June for the azaleas, and then in September.

FARINGDON HOUSE 13
Faringdon, Oxfordshire. Tel: (0367) 20145
Miss S. Zinovieff

Entered from centre of town which is off the A420 between Oxford and Swindon • *Open by appointment and 14th, 15th April, 23rd Sept, 2.00 – 6.00 p.m.* • *Entrance: £1.00, accompanied children free* • *Parking* • *Teas on NGS days* • *Partly suitable for wheelchairs* • *Grade III*

Medium-sized apparently conventional park with fine terrace and trees. Its main charm lies in its eccentric features such as the coloured doves introduced by a previous owner the dilettanti musician Lord Berners and continued by his disciple and successor, the late Robert Heber-Percy and, another oddity, the orangery pool in whose centre is a bust of some long-forgotten ancestor apparently sinking to his doom; and most impressive of all, the splendid swimming pool, designed by Heber-Percy, with a medieval motif.

GARSINGTON MANOR 14
Garsington, Oxfordshire. Tel: (086736) 234
Mr and Mrs L. Ingrams

SE of Oxford, N of B480 or via A40, S of Wheatley turn off ● *Open 8th May, 30th Sept, 2.00 – 6.00 p.m.* ● *Entrance: £1.50, accompanied children under 16 free* ● *Parking* ● *Teas for NGS* ● *Partly suitable for wheelchairs* ● *Dogs* ● *Grade III*

Visitors interested in the Bloomsbury Group can people this garden with the ghosts of those to whom the former owners Philip and Lady Ottoline Morrell offered regular hospitality. The latter also laid out the flower and box parterre and the Italian garden in the grounds of their Elizabethan house which slope down to a large pool, formerly monastic fish-ponds. Below the house is a large croquet lawn and the seventeenth-century dovecote alongside steps leading down to an orchard, halfway down is the Italian garden and a pool. At the north front of house are said to be the tallest pair of yews in the country. Fine views to the south but the approaches are disfigured by electricity pylons.

GREAT ROLLRIGHT 15
Nr Chipping Norton, Oxfordshire.

3m N of Chipping Norton off A34 or A361 ● *Open for NGS* ● *Parking* ● *Teas* ● *Toilet facilities* ● *Suitable for wheelchairs* ● *Dogs* ● *Grade IV*

A number of gardens in this heavily developed village on the edge of the Cotswolds show what can be done in the Midlands climate if a dedicated professional gardener not only puts his back into it but is backed by considerable financial resources. Of the smaller residences, The Old Beer House is interesting because its mature effect has been created in a mere 15 years. A few more conventional cottage gardens which are not open to the public can be studied by looking over low stone walls. This is a colourful, well-maintained garden.

GREYS COURT 16
Rotherfield Greys, Henley-on-Thames, Oxfordshire.
Tel: (04917) 529
The National Trust

3m W of Henley-on-Thames on A423 Peppard road ● *Open April – Sept, Mon – Sat, 2.00 – 6.00 p.m. Last admission 5.30 p.m. Closed Good Friday*

● *Best season: April – June* ● *Entrance: £2.00 (garden)* ● *Parking* ● *Teas*
● *Toilet facilities* ● *Suitable for wheelchairs* ● *House open Mon, Wed, Fri,*
£3.00 ● **Grade II**

A small park with walled gardens and maze surrounds this Jacobean house
with Georgian additions. The gardens have been re-created in the ruins of the
fourteenth-century fortified house; they form a series of walled gardens, some
fairly small, enclosing old roses, white flowers and shrubs; cistus, rosemary
and lavender borders and a circular walled area surrounding ancient wisterias.
The kitchen garden was replanted in 1980s; avenues of morello cherries,
espaliered apples and a border of peonies. Water tanks, lily pond. Fine 'Rosa
Mundi' border round statue of St Fiacre, patron saint of gardeners. Beyond
kitchen garden, across the nut avenue, is the maze.

GREYSTONE COTTAGE 17
Colmore Lane, Kingwood Common, Henley-on-Thames,
Oxfordshire. Tel: (04917) 559
Mr and Mrs W. Roxburgh

5m N of Reading between B481 Nettlebed – Reading road, and Sonning
Common – Stoke Row road. ½m down Colmore Lane, next to Unicorn pub
● *Open by appointment April – Sept and 13th May, 10th June, 2.00 – 6.00*
p.m. ● *Best season: spring/early summer* ● *Entrance: 70p, children free*
● *Parking in lane and field* ● *Refreshments on special opening days* ● *Suitable*
for wheelchairs ● *Plants for sale* ● **Grade II**

The owners have created this garden over the past 15 years. Sunny courtyard
in front of house with planting betwen stones: dry, Mediterranean area and
small beds of mixed blue, white and yellow (nicotiana, feverfew, etc),
vegetables in large pots. Pear-tree alleyway leading away from house, with
vegetable garden to right, hedges of beech beyond; lawns and woodland with
long border to the left. Woodland with primroses, primulas and fritillaries,
hellebores, azaleas, bilberries and blueberries. Golden garden behind house
with wildlife pond.

HEYTHROP HOUSE TRAINING CENTRE 18
Heythrop, Oxfordshire. Tel: (060872) 721
National Westminster Bank

W off A34 near Enstone. Only the road marked 'Training Centre' leads to
entrance ● *An open day every other year, inc. 1990, usually Sept. Information*
and special arrangements from the Bursar ● *Parking* ● *Suitable for*
wheelchairs ● *Dogs* ● **Grade III**

In 1705, after making the Grand Tour, the 1st and only Duke of Shrewsbury
returned to his newly-acquired estate and Italianate house and now developed
extensive gardens including wildernesses, a walled garden and a classical

grove which contained a rill and a cold bath. The River Glyme was dammed to create eight cascades. Today, the Bank keeps the grounds in good order and the walled kitchen garden is retained, but while many traces of the Baroque remain, the overall effect is rather institutional.

KINGSTON HOUSE 19
Kingston Bagpuize, Oxfordshire. Tel: (0865) 820259
Lord and Lady Tweedsmuir

5½m W of Abingdon at entry to Kingston Bagpuize where the A415 meets the A420 ● *Open May, June and Sept, and May and Aug Bank Holidays, Wed and Sun, 2.30 – 5.30 p.m.* ● *Entrance: garden only 50p, children under 5 free but not admitted to house. Group rates on request in writing* ● *Parking* ● *Teas* ● *Toilet facilities* ● *Suitable for wheelchairs* ● *Plants for sale* ● *House open* ● *Grade II*

This Charles II manor house was owned in the pre-war years by Miss Marlie Raphael, a friend of Sir Harold Hillier, the great tree and shrub plantsman; accordingly she planted a woodland garden crossed by narrow curving earth paths and featuring plants from all over the world. This can be reached by an original green walk, which is to the left of the entrance. Miss Raphael's niece, Lady Tweedsmuir, continued the good work by planting the so-called Leap Wood begun on 29 February 1984. It has many rare and interesting plants although their arrangement is in some cases incongruous. The formal garden lawns and beds near the house are in need of attention. A useful notated map can be purchased at the gate.

KINGSTON LISLE PARK 20
Wantage, Oxfordshire. Tel: (036782) 223
Mrs Leopold Lonsdale

4m W of Wantage on B4507 ● *Open Easter – Aug, Thurs, Bank Holiday weekends, Sat, Sun, Mon, 2.00 – 5.00 p.m. Parties at other times* ● *Best season: June/July* ● *Entrance: £2.20* ● *Parking* ● *Teas* ● *Toilet facilities* ● *Suitable for wheelchairs* ● *Dogs on lead* ● *Plants for sale* ● *House open* ● *Grade II*

The house, built in 1677, and extended early in the nineteenth century, is in a park setting of great tranquillity. The gardens have been restored by the present owners. Clipped yew trees surround the terrace next to the house; lawns lead to wrought-iron gates and an avenue of limes. Rose garden to the right of the lawn, a replica of Queen Mary's garden in Regent's Park, has climbing roses growing up poles and along encircling chains. Large trees at edge of lawns, mainly beech, with standard trees and shrubs. Greenhouse and vegetable gardens in walled garden with herbaceous border.

LONGWORTH MANOR 21
Longworth, Abingdon, Oxfordshire. Tel: (0865) 820223
Lieutenant-Colonel and Mrs J Walton

8m W of Abingdon and 2m NW of Kingston Bagpuize, N off A420. House near church ● Open 13th May, 2.00 – 6.00 p.m. ● Entrance: £1.00 for combined admission with Haugh House, Longworth ● Parking ● Teas ● Suitable for wheelchairs ● Grade IV

This medium-sized garden has fine red roses, tulips, borders and ornamental ponds. From the terrace there are good views over the Thames. It is a pity that its NGS opening times do not coincide with that of Marten's Hall Farm in the same village (see entry). However Kingston House, nearby in Kingston Bagpuize, is open on Sundays in May (see entry).

MANOR FARM 22
Minster Lovell, Nr Witney, Oxfordshire.
Sir Peter and Lady Parker

1½m NW of Witney off B4074. Follow signs to Old Minster Lovell and Leafield, cross Windrush bridge, turn right at the Old Swan ● Open 24th June, 2.00 – 6.00 p.m. ● Best season: June ● Entrance: £1.00, children free ● Parking ● Teas ● Toilet facilities ● Suitable for wheelchairs ● Dogs on lead ● Plants for sale ● Grade III

The garden is planted next to the ruins of the medieval Minster around a farmhouse and barns. There is a sunken garden next to the house with hellebores, hostas, epimediums, etc. There is a circle of old-fashioned roses, informal borders, natural-stone paths planted with herbs and creepers. Two pools, one formal – surrounded with trellised vines, hops, alchemillas and hellebores; the other informal, in shape and planting. A spacious and varied garden, well-planted in a successful, informal style.

MANOR HOUSE 23
Stanton Harcourt, Oxfordshire. Tel: (0865) 881928
Mr and The Hon Mrs Gascoigne

9m W of Oxford, 5m SE of Witney on B4449 ● Open 15th, 16th, 26th, 28th April; 3rd, 6th, 7th, 17th, 20th, 24th, 27th, 28th May; 7th, 10th, 21st, 24th June; 5th, 8th, 19th, 22nd July; 3rd, 5th, 23rd, 26th, 27th Aug; 6th, 9th, 20th, 23rd Sept, 2.00 – 6.00 p.m. ● Best season: late spring/early summer ● Entrance: £1.00 (£2.00 house and garden) ● Parking ● Toilet facilities ● Suitable for wheelchairs ● Dogs on lead ● Plants for sale ● House open ● Grade II

Twelve acres of gardens incorporated in and around ruins of a fourteenth and fifteenth-century manor house. Entrance through courtyard into large, walled garden with yew-bush avenue leading from house to chapel. Herbaceous borders and crimson plants to right, and mixed colours on left. Old roses, viburnum, clematis and hydrangeas on walls of chapel and medieval kitchen. Alpines in troughs, geraniums in urns. Paths lead through nut-tree vistas, past shrubs round ancient stew ponds (sadly low in water after gravel-work drainage nearby). Hedges of lavender in walled garden. Rotunda in hedge gives views from garden to fields beyond.

MARTEN'S HALL FARM 24
Longworth, Abingdon, Oxfordshire.
Tel: (0865) 820376
Mrs J. Parker-Jervis

8m W of Abingdon, 2m NW of Kingston Bagpuize. Longworth is 1m N of A420 • *Open six times for NGS and other days by appointment. Attached is a professional nursery run by the owners, open Wed – Sat, 9.00 a.m. – 5.00 p.m.* • *Entrance: NGS* • *Parking* • *Teas on Sun only* • *Suitable for wheelchairs* • *Plants for sale* • *Grade II*

Longworth village is near the River Thames which can be reached by footpath or by car to Folly Bridge by the Rose Revived Inn. It has long been a centre for professional nurserymen, particularly rose growers but now only two remain in the village although there are many in the surrounding country. The Parker-Jervis garden is, like their nursery, a haven for the plantsperson, particularly those interested in old-fashioned plants such as pinks. Their love of white flowers is evident (they take up one sixth of the catalogue). It is also a haven for flower arrangers in search of new ideas. The other, less specialized nursery in the village is Woodbridge's in Rectory Lane.

MOUNT SKIPPET 25
Ramsden, Oxfordshire. Tel: (099386) 253
Dr and Mrs M.A.T. Rogers

4m N of Witney off B4022 to Charlbury. At crossroads marked to Finstock turn E and almost immediately turn right. Then after 400 yards turn left up No Through Way Lane • *Open April to Sept by appointment* • *Entrance: 70p for NGS* • *Parking* • *Refreshments by arrangement. Picnic area available* • *Suitable for wheelchairs* • *Plants for sale* • *Grade II*

Dr Rogers, now retired after a career as a research chemist, is a dedicated plantsman, preferring to grow everything from seeds or cuttings. He took over this family house of two acres and has developed a very attractive garden in a beautiful Cotswold setting. Plants are his love and there are many rare ones, including several that Wisley cannot identify. He has two rock gardens, an alpine house, interesting shrubs and trees and a bog garden adjoining the village pond. Everywhere there are collections of pots with his well-beloved plants (almost everything in the garden is labelled) some of which are sometimes for sale. Long may this garden continue.

NUNEHAM COURTENAY ARBORETUM 26
Nuneham Courtenay, Nr Oxford, Oxfordshire.
Oxford University

S of Oxford on A423 • *Open May – Oct, Mon – Sat, 9.00 a.m. – 5.00 p.m.,*
Sun, 2.00 – 6.00 p.m. • *Best season: mid-June – early Oct* • *Entrance: free*
• *Parking* • *Suitable for wheelchairs* • *Grade IV*

Originally designed by the Rev. William Sawrey Gilpin, nephew of the pioneer
of the Picturesque Theory, Rev. William Gilpin and son of the water-colourist
Rev. Sawrey Gilpin, the arboretum at Nuneham was an attempt to recreate the
characteristic scenery of Claudean paintings as part of 'Capability' Brown's
neighbouring parkland. Much later planting has obscured the original
intention. However, the arboretum now has fine collections of pines, acers
and rhododendrons and is a pleasant place to wander for an hour or so. Sadly
the neighbouring park and Rev. William Mason's flower garden will not be
open in 1990.

THE OLD POST OFFICE 27
Chastleton, Oxfordshire. Tel: (060874) 242
Mrs Penelope Mortimer

3m SE of Moreton-in-Marsh off A44 • *Open 23rd June, 22nd Sept*
• *Entrance: for NGS* • *Plants for sale* • *Parking in village street* • *Grade IV*

The former gardener's cottage for Chastleton House, now called The Old
Post Office, is described by the owner as 'a garden of ideas – some more
successful than others' and amongst many worth looking at are the swing
overlooking the view, the long arch of mixed climbers, the standard-
gooseberry fruit bed and the various statues. For plantspersons, there are
interesting things to see and a list of roses is provided; a varied selection of
plants is available for sale. Another garden, Chastleton Glebe, is also open one
Sunday under the NGS scheme.

THE OLD RECTORY 28
Farnborough, Wantage, Oxfordshire. Tel: (04882) 298
Mrs Michael Todhunter

4m SE of Wantage off B4494 • *Open 13th May, 1st, 8th July, 2.00 – 6.00 p.m.*
and by written appointment • *Best season: June/July* • *Entrance: £1.00,*
children free • *Parking* • *Teas sometimes* • *Suitable for wheelchairs* • *Plants*
for sale • *Grade II*

Outstanding four-acre garden created over 25 years on good original
structure of large trees and hedges with magnificent views over the Downs.
Deep, parallel herbaceous borders, backed by yew hedges; Subtle and effective
planting next to the front of the house; smaller areas laid out for sun or shade-
loving plants; woodland and shrubs lawns; swimming pool surrounded by

large *Hydrangea sargentiana*, potted lilies, agapanthus, with mixed roses around outside walls. Collection of old roses and small-flowered clematis. Wild flowers at edge of front lawn by ha-ha. Those who like John Betjeman's poetry will be interested to know that he lived here 1945-50 and can look for the ghost of Miss Joan Hunter Dunn in the shrubberies. One of Oxfordshire's highest gardens, 600 feet, prey to winds from the Downs.

OXFORD BOTANIC GARDEN 29
Oxford. Tel: (0865) 276920
University of Oxford

In centre of Oxford opposite Magdalen College near bridge ● Open 9.00 a.m. - 5.00 p.m. (4.15 p.m. during GMT). Last admission 4.45 p.m. Daily except Sun when 2.00 - 6.00 p.m. Greenhouses 2.00 - 4.00 p.m. Closed 25th Dec and Good Friday ● Entrance: free ● Parking difficult ● Picnics, while not specifically authorised, could be taken overlooking river ● Suitable for wheelchairs ● Plants for sale at arboretum (see below) on NGS days only when staff available to answer queries ● Photography and music prohibited ● Grade I

This is the oldest Botanic garden in Britain and one of the most attractive to the general visitor. Founded in 1621, it is surrounded by a high wall and entered through a splendid gateway by Inigo Jones's master mason. Two yews survive from the early plantings and there are a series of beds containing herbaceous plants in systematic and labelled groups. The old walls back beds with tender plants including roses and clematis. To the left is the greenhouse area, modern ones replacing those built in 1670. There is also a rock garden. Outside the front entrance is a large rose garden donated by Americans in memory of those university staff who developed penicillin. Several miles away (south of the A423) is Nuneham Courtenay Arboretum opened in 1968 (see page 309).

OXFORD COLLEGE GARDENS
Most colleges are helpful about free access to their gardens although the more private ones, such as the Master's or Fellows', are rarely open. Specific viewing times are difficult to rely on because some colleges prefer not to have visitors in term time or on days when a function is taking place. The best course is to ask at the Porter's Lodge or to telephone ahead of visit. However, it is fair to say that some Oxford college gardens will always be open to the visitor, by arrangement with porters, even if others are closed on that particular day. There are also NGS openings at some colleges, when a charge is made; Master's and Fellows' gardens may also be open then.

Parking is difficult in term time and the park-and-ride from the ring road is easier ● Refreshments in the town ● All gardens suitable for wheelchairs ● Access to college buildings, such as chapels, is often possible by permission of porters and charges are now being made at some for this privilege.

CHRIST CHURCH   30
St Aldates. Tel: (0865) 276150

*Memorial garden open winter 9.30 a.m. – 4.30 p.m., summer 9.30 a.m. – 5.30
p.m. The Deanery and Master's Garden are only open to the public once or twice a
year for NGS.*

In the Deanery garden, Lewis Carroll's Alice played in the Cheshire Cat's
chestnut tree; there is the Oriental plane planted in 1636. The Master's garden
created in 1926 has good herbaceous borders. The Memorial garden on St
Aldates (which is free) will please some people. Visitors in May should make
a point of seeing Christ Church Meadow, an old pasture, where a vast area of
fritillaries will be in flower. (Do not miss the art gallery.)

CORPUS CHRISTI   31
Merton Street. Tel: (0865) 276700

Open term 1.30 – 4.00 p.m., vacation 10.00 a.m. – 4.00 p.m.

The smallest college in Oxford with pleasant gardens, worth a visit, although
the eighteenth-century Topiary Garden shaped like a sundial is now no more.

GREEN COLLEGE   32
Woodstock Road. Tel: (0865) 274770

Open by appointment

The Radcliffe Observatory's Tower of the Seven Winds is worth a long
journey in order to see Oxford from the air. Green College is entered through
an old cobbled yard filled with geraniums leading to the garden and the new
building, which looks like an eighteenth-century house. The medicinal bed is
well-labelled and the rest of the small garden is devoted to lawns and shrubs
with some herbaceous borders.

HOLYWELL MANOR   33
Manor Road. Tel: (0865) 277777

Open 10.30 a.m. – 6.30 p.m.

A garden of about one acre, made round an old horse chestnut. Both formal
and informal areas – a sunken lawn flanked by four well-grown gingkos, a
spinney with spring flowers, and a small cottage garden, all restful and well-
maintained.

LADY MARGARET HALL   34
Norham Gardens. Tel: (0865) 274300

Open 9.00 a.m. – 6.00 p.m. or dusk if earlier

Built in 1896 by Blomfield in Queen Anne style this is a good example of his theory that the architect should be responsible for the design of the garden, not the gardener. Eight acres of formal and informal gardens, water meadows with daffodils by the Cherwell. Some interesting plants and trees.

NEW COLLEGE 35
Holywell Street. Tel: (0865) 279555

Open term 2.00 – 5.00., vacation 11.00 a.m. – 5.00 p.m.

Admiring readers of Robin Lane Fox will want to visit this garden over which he exercises a Fellow's influence. The main garden is approached through large gates in a wrought-iron screen. Well-planted, deep border over 100 feet long, against the magnificent thirteenth-century city walls. Rose border, group of chestnut trees behind 'mound' – a landscape feature built in 1529 now rather neglected – but still dominating the lawns and borders. The Warden's garden is a small enclosed area across the street from the main college buildings.

NUFFIELD COLLEGE 36
New Road. Tel: (0865) 278500

Open daily, 9.00 a.m. – 7.00 p.m.

A pleasant formal garden in a new building, mainly lawns and roses, with two interesting water features. One of these is a fine sculpture which spouts water, but the head porter, fountain of all knowledge in most such establishments, did not know the name of the sculptor. Note also the remarkable hedge of Russian vine outside the building on the street.

QUEEN'S COLLEGE 37
High Street. Tel: (0865) 279121

Open 2.00 – 5.00 p.m.

In 1358 John Godspeede was ortulanus, growing vegetables and saffron to sell. Today, the front quad is a dramatic green lawn edged by a pink, white and blue border with, through the archway, a vast lead vase filled with red geraniums. The Fellows' garden has good herbaceous borders, and the Provost's fourteenth-century garden has interesting shrubs and trees and good statues.

REWLEY HOUSE 38
Wellington Square, St John's Street. Tel: (0865) 270360

Open by appointment

This interesting building, opened in 1986, has a roof garden 60 x 26 feet and courtyard gardens with an automatic watering system and clever mobile boxes on wheels – a good start for a roof garden. Once the deciduous shrubs have been replaced by evergreens there should be a good show most of the year round.

ST HUGH'S COLLEGE
St Margaret's Road. Tel: (0865) 274900

39

Open by appointment

Largely created by Annie Rogers, Fellow of St Hugh's, this is a terraced area behind the college with predominantly grey plants growing between paving stones and in small beds and borders. Steps lead down to large lawns, many old trees, island beds of peonies, dahlias, a fern 'dell', rose tunnel and allée of apple trees. More formal beds with Victorian planting near to buildings with dianthus, nicotiana, dahlias, etc. In all about 10 acres.

WADHAM COLLEGE
Parks Road. Tel: (0865) 277900

40

Open 1.00 – 4.30 p.m.

The main feature of the Wadham gardens is the fine old trees: purple beech, gingko, *Magnolia acuminata*, *Tilia tomentosa*, etc in a classic college setting. The herbaceous borders are not noteworthy.

WOLFSON COLLEGE
Linton Road. Tel: (0865) 274100

41

Open by appointment

A nine-acre garden, backing onto the River Cherwell, designed around modern college buildings built by Powell and Moya. Lawns surrounded by borders: raised, herbaceous, shrub and silver. A further garden behind with rectangular island beds, and pergola with wisteria and incarvillea. Woodland paths between shade-loving plants lead down to river. Bridge over Cherwell leads to water meadows on far bank.

WORCESTER COLLEGE
Worcester Street. Tel: (0865) 278300

42

Open term 9.00 a.m. – 12 noon, vacation 9.00 a.m. – 12 noon, 2.00 – 6.00 p.m.

This is the only true landscaped garden in Oxford, having its own designed lake, which was made from a swampy area in 1817. The three acres were laid out by the bursar, Richard Gresswell. The banks in the front quad are variously said to have been made from excrement of the monks' longroom latrine, or stones and rubble of the dissolved monastery, or the earth from the swamp. Whichever it may have been, the grass is green and well kept as are the terraces and sunken lawn. The flower beds in this quad are the best of any of the colleges and a good example of Edwardian planting, although some may find them garish in colouring.

PUSEY HOUSE   43
Pusey, Faringdon, Oxfordshire.   Tel: (036787) 222

*½m S of A420. 12m W of Oxford, 5m from Faringdon ● Best season: June/ July ● Parking ● Teas ● Toilet facilities ● Suitable for wheelchairs ● Dogs on lead ● Plants for sale ● **Grade II***

House built in 1748 with original park probably early eighteenth century. Geoffrey Jellicoe was commissioned by Mr and Mrs Michael Hornby in 1935 to redesign the terrace. Large garden in park setting, with lake in front of house and many fine trees. Terrace below house with steps leading down to long herbaceous border backed by stone wall with climbing clematis, vines, abutilons, roses, etc. Water gardens by lakeside; shrubberies and more mixed planting on either side of lawns. Walled garden enclosing fine old roses, clematis, hydrangeas and ceanothus. Entrance to garden between herbaceous borders. House for sale at time of going to press.

ROUSHAM HOUSE   44
Steeple Aston, Oxfordshire.   Tel: (0869) 47110
Mr C. Cottrell-Dormer

*Not in Steeple Aston but 2m W off A423 Oxford – Banbury road or E off A43 Oxford – Brackley road ● Open all year, daily, 10.00 a.m. – 4.30 p.m. ● Entrance: £1.50, no children under 15 ● Parking ● Toilet facilities ● Suitable for wheelchairs ● House open ● **Grade I***

This is much admired because William Kent's design of 1738 is effectively frozen in time. Historical enlightenment can be combined with the enchantment of the setting and the use he made of it. In fact, before Kent, it was already a famous garden described by the poet Pope as 'the prettiest place for water-falls, jetts, ponds, inclosed with beautiful scenes of green and hanging wood, that ever I saw.' Kent's design, influenced perhaps by stage scenery, created a series of effects, and the best way to view the garden is to follow these one by one, rather than to attempt to grasp the design as a whole.

SILVER TREES   45
Bagley Wood Road, Kennington, Oxford.   Tel: (0865) 735232
Dr and Mrs P.F. Barwood

Avoid approach through Kennington which is 3m from the centre of Oxford.
Preferably enter from the Oxford – Abingdon road, via Hinksey Hill, taking
turning marked Kennington and stop at third house on left. Other approaches
difficult • Open by appointment • Entrance: £1.00 to charity • Parking
*• Suitable for wheelchairs • Plants for sale on NGS days • **Grade II***

The owners, who developed this garden over the past 30 years, have
reluctantly decided to leave it but may not have done so by the 1990 season.
On a three-acre site in Bagley Wood they have created a plantsperson's
paradise in very natural surroundings. It is impossible to list all the varieties,
but suffice it to say that a few of Mrs Barwood's specialities are geraniums,
ferns, hostas and small conifers. There are also fine old roses and it is
interesting that no chemical sprays are used here. Fine old trees in the wood
to the south, part of which has been planted with interesting varieties by the
Barwoods. If they do sell the house, it is to be hoped that the new owners will
insist on inheriting a list of plants and notated map.

STANSFIELD   46
49 High Street, Stanford-in-the-Vale, Oxfordshire.
Tel: (03677) 710340
Mr and Mrs D. Keeble

3½m SE of Faringdon, turn off A417 opposite Vale Garage • Open by
appointment and 10th June, 12th Aug, 2.00 – 6.00 p.m. • Best season: June –
Aug • Parking in street • Suitable for wheelchairs by consultation with
*owners • Plants for sale • **Grade II***

A one-acre plus plantsman's garden, not yet finished, with many island beds
and borders. Large collection of plants, both for damp and dry conditions.
All-year round interest in wide use of foliage and seasonal flowers, starting
with species spring bulbs. Many shrubs interplanted and a new woodland area
is planned. Alpines in sinks and troughs. Attention is focused on number and
variety of plants rather than layout and design.

STONOR PARK   47
Henley-on-Thames, Oxfordshire.   Tel: (049163) 587
Lord Camoys

4m NW of Henley-on-Thames on B480 • Open April – Sept • Best season:
June/July • Entrance: £2.00, OAP £1.70, children in family parties free
• Parking • Teas. Party lunches by arrangement • Toilet facilities • Suitable
for wheelchairs by special arrangement • Dogs on leads • Shop • House open
*• **Grade III***

The house, a red-brick Tudor E-shaped building in a bowl of hills, is the main attraction at Stonor Park. It is set on the side of a hill with open parkland and large trees in front, and with flower and vegetable garden behind and to the side sheltered against the hill. Lawns behind the house lead up to a hill terrace, pools, stone urns and planting along the steps. Orchard with cypresses and espaliered fruit trees, lavender hedges.

SWINBROOK HOUSE 48
Swinbrook, Nr Burford, Oxfordshire.
Mr J.D. Mackinnon

2m N of Burford on road between Swinbrook and Shipton-under- Wychwood
● *Open 1st July, 2.00 – 6.30 p.m.* ● *Entrance: 60p, children free* ● *Parking*
● *Suitable for wheelchairs* ● ***Grade III***

Here on the edge of the Wychwood Forest is a beautifully-preserved example of how the other half lived in the years between the wars. Old-fashioned shrub roses in immaculate beds, greenhouses full of peaches and vast beds of asparagus presumably reigned over by 'Uncle Matthew' with his entrenching tools. It was to Swinbrook House that the Mitfords moved after leaving Batsford. A substantial area is put over to breeding pheasants for the shoot. There is a fine walled garden and pleached fruit trees alongside the croquet lawn and everywhere ancient trees, presumably from the forest, as the house was not built until the late 1920s. A mile or two nearer Burford is Fulbrook, probably opening its smaller 'village' gardens on the same day and providing tea for visitors.

WARDINGTON MANOR 49
Wardington, Nr Banbury, Oxfordshire.
Tel: (0295) 750202/758481
The Lord Wardington

5m NE of Banbury of A361 ● *Open 29th April, 3rd June, 12th Aug, 2.00 –
5.30 p.m.* ● *Entrance: £1.00, children free* ● *Parking* ● *Teas* ● *Toilet
facilities* ● *Suitable for wheelchairs* ● *Plants for sale* ● ***Grade IV***

One of the great lawns of England spreads itself in front of this Jacobean manor house with its wisteria-covered walls. The topiary is impeccable too, and there are attractive borders. Away from the house, the owners have created a flowering shrub walk leading down to a pond.

WATERPERRY GARDENS 50
Nr Wheatley, Oxfordshire.   Tel: (08447) 226/254
School of Economic Science

8m E of Oxford, 2m N of Wheatley. Turn off M40/A40 and follow signs
● *Open daily, April – Sept, 10.00 a.m. – 5.30 p.m. or 6.00 p.m. at weekends;*

Oct – March, 10.00 a.m. – 4.30 p.m. Closed Christmas and New Year holidays
● *Entrance: Nov – Feb, no charge. March – Oct, £1.20, OAP 90p, children 60p,*
coach parties by appointment only ● *Parking* ● *Refreshments: Tea shop open*
10.00 a.m. to ½ hour before closing. Light lunches, wine licence ● *Toilet*
facilities ● *Suitable for wheelchairs* ● *Plants for sale in large nursery* ● *In*
July during a 3-day event called 'Art in Action' which has a strong craft bias,
increased entrance fees are charged and normal garden entry arrangements are
suspended. Church open (Saxon origins) all year round ● ***Grade II***

Waterperry has to be included in this guide but its 20 acres are difficult to
categorize. There is a strong institutionalised/education atmosphere going
back to the 1930s when a Miss Havergal opened up a small horticultural
school. There is also a commercial garden centre which occupies large areas of
the so-called garden, with row upon row of flowers and shrubs being grown
for seeds or cuttings. Intermixed with all this are major features of the old
garden, lawns and a substantial herbaceous border; also new beds containing
collections of alpines, dwarf conifers and other shrubs. The South Field is a
growing area for soft fruit. The Clay Bank is planted with shade lovers. Almost
all the plants are labelled and the owners describe the place as one where 'the
ornamental and the utilitarian live side by side'. Several hours need to be spent
here to do it justice and if the visitor is overpowered by the 'utilitarian' aspect,
he or she can stroll down the shady path by the little River Thame. A guide is
sold at the shop. Several Wheatley gardens are also open in May under the
NGS, together with Shotover House.

WILCOTE HOUSE 51
Wilcote, Finstock, Oxfordshire. Tel: (099386) 606
The Hon. C.E. Cecil

3m S of Charlbury E off B4022 ● *By appointment and 4 times for NGS* ● *Best*
season: early summer ● *Parking* ● *Teas* ● *Poor toilet facilities* ● *Suitable for*
wheelchairs ● *Plants for sale* ● ***Grade II***

It is worth visiting this garden in May/June in order to walk down the
laburnum tunnel planted as recently as 1984. The house is a splendid
eighteenth/nineteenth-century copy in Cotswold stone of earlier periods and
the large garden is also a period piece with extensive beds of old-fashioned
roses and mixed borders. An unusual feature is the vast wild garden planted
with an interesting selection of trees and intersected by grass paths. Very fine
setting in this beautiful part of England.

WOOTTON PLACE 52
Wootton, Nr Woodstock, Oxfordshire. Tel: (0993) 811485
Jasper Clutterbuck

3m N of Woodstock, turn E off the A34 ● *Opening dates uncertain at present*
owing to family circumstances ● *Parking* ● *Teas* ● *Suitable for wheelchairs*
● ***Grade III***

This garden has an atmosphere not easy to define but probably related to nostalgia. There are fine trees including a huge walnut and, within the stone-walled garden, a somewhat wild effect perhaps connected with the claim that the grounds were laid out by 'Capability' Brown. The owners say there are 150 varieties of daffodil.

WROXTON ABBEY   53
Wroxton, Nr Banbury, Oxfordshire.   Tel: (0295) 730551
Wroxton College of Fairleigh Dickinson University of New Jersey USA

3m W of Banbury off A422 ● *Open all year* ● *Entrance: free* ● *Parking in village* ● *Suitable for wheelchairs* ● *Dogs on lead* ● *Grade II*

The historical interest of this garden and park is that in 1727 Tilleman Bobart (a pupil of Wise) was commissioned to construct a Renaissance-style garden with canals by the owners of the large Jacobean manor house, the 2nd Baron of Guildford. But by the late 1730s his son had this grassed over to convert it to the then fashionable landscape-style. Sanderson Miller designed some of the garden buildings *c.* 1740. The present American owners have restored much of this early landscape garden since 1978. On entering the long drive up to the house, it appears to be a conventional park, but beyond are interesting features including a serpentine river, lake, cascade which can be seen from a viewing mount, Chinese bridge, Doric temple, Gothic dovecote, obelisk, ruined arch and ice-house all restored from their derelict state. There is a rose garden and a newly-created knot garden. In all, the grounds cover 56 acres and offer many hours of pleasant walks. Unfortunately there is no map readily available and sign-posting is minimal.

TELEPHONE NUMBERS

Except where specifically requested to be excluded, telephone numbers to which enquiries may be directed are given for each property. To maintain the support and cooperation of private owners it is suggested that the telephone be used with discretion. Where visits are by appointment, the telephone can of course be used except where written application, particularly for parties, is specifically requested. Code numbers are given in brackets. For the Republic of Ireland when phoning from the United Kingdom dial 353 plus area code plus number (except Dublin numbers which are 0001 plus number). In all cases where visits by parties are proposed, owners should be advised in advance and arrangements preferably confirmed in writing.

London Telephone Codes: From May 1990 all London telephone numbers with the prefix 01 will be changed. The new prefix will be either 071 or 081. Details of these new numbers are available from British Telecom. During the changeover period in 1990 all London telephone numbers dialled with their 01 prefix will be redirected.

SHROPSHIRE

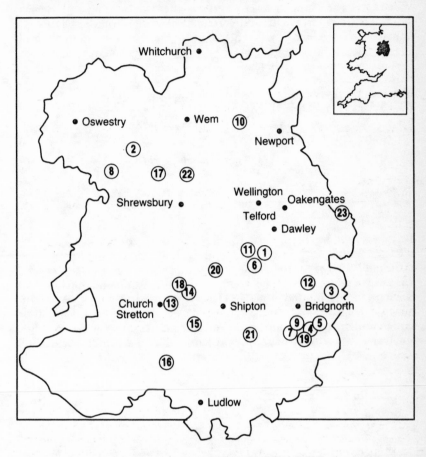

BENTHALL HALL   1
Broseley, Shropshire.   Tel: (0952) 882159
The National Trust

1m SW of Broseley off B4375, 4m NE of Much Wenlock, 8m S of Wellington
● Open April – Sept, Wed, Sun and Bank Holiday Mon, 1.30 – 5.30 p.m. Last
admission 5.00 p.m. Parties at other times by arrangement   ● Best season: spring
and summer   ● Entrance: £1.00 (£1.80 house and gardens)   ● Parking 150
yards down road   ● Toilet facilities   ● Partly suitable for wheelchairs   ● Part of
*house open   ● **Grade III***

A small garden containing some interesting plants and features and some nice
topiary. George Maw and Robert Bateman both lived in the house and
contributed to the garden design and plant collection. Graham Stuart Thomas

was involved in the restoration work. The rose garden has some lovely plants and a small pool and there is a delightful raised scree bed. A good collection of geraniums and ground-cover plants together with a peony bed, clematis and roses through trees and shrubs create a pleasant garden to stroll through. The crocus introduced by George Maw and daffodils in spring provide interest and the many large trees of Scots pine, beech and oak are stunning features. A monument to botanical history.

BROWNHILL HOUSE   2
Ruyton XI Towns, Shropshire.   Tel: (0939) 260626
Roger and Yolande Brown

10m NW of Shrewsbury on B4397 just through the village ● *Open 26th – 28th May, 7th, 8th July, 2.00 – 6.00 p.m. and by appointment May – Aug* ● *Best season: end May/mid-July* ● *Entrance: 80p, children free* ● *Parking at the Bridge Inn 100 yards away* ● *Teas* ● *Toilet facilities* ● *Plants for sale*
● *Grade III*

This garden is a great credit to the owners who have incorporated a wide range of design features in a most difficult sloping site of one and a half acres. There are about 300 steps through the garden which includes a laburnum walk, patio with a pond, riverside beds with polygonum, astilbe and wild flowers, a bog garden with iris and primulas. Herbaceous borders, a rock garden with shrubs, a range of shrubs and conifers and a good vegetable garden and soft fruit as well as 16 different types of fruit and nut trees; also grape vines and a peach tree. The variety of features is remarkable in a garden started from scratch in 1972.

THE DAIRY HOUSE   3
Ludstone, Nr Claverley, Shropshire.   Tel: (07466) 237
Miss N.E. Wood

7m W of Wolverhampton and S of the A454 ● *Open by appointment and for Claverley Flower Festival from 15th – 21st July, 2.00 – 6.00 p.m.* ● *Best season: spring and mid-July* ● *Entrance: £1.00* ● *Parking* ● *Teas* ● *Toilet facilities*
● *Plants for sale* ● *Grade III*

An interesting three-acre garden with a waterside setting, its banks and island beds have been cleverly planted to overcome the low pH and dry areas. It is simple but has a wide variety of plants with roses and heathers used largely for ground cover. A golden border and the use of colour combinations together with trees – including sorbus, golden elm, junipers and cypresses, Scots pine and birch along with rhododendrons and hostas – provide a pleasant garden in a lovely setting. Some areas of the garden are now slightly weedy.

DINGLE BANK   4
Chelmarsh Common, Nr Bridgnorth, Shropshire.
Tel: (0746) 861418
Mr and Mrs Trevor Ford

*3m S of Bridgnorth on Highley Road ● Open certain Sundays through the
summer or by appointment ● Best season: summer ● Entrance: 80p, children
20p (covers this garden and The Paddocks) ● Parking 300 yards away at The
Bull's Head, Chelmarsh ● Partly suitable for wheelchairs ● Plants for sale at
nursery ● Grade IV*

A pleasant garden developed by the owners with a wide range of conifers,
perennials, grasses, lilies and shrubs. Roses and clematis climb through trees.
The keen gardener can compare the plants growing here with those available
at the nursery. One can then walk through the gate to the cottage-style garden
next door (see The Paddocks, page 326).

DUDMASTON   5
Quatt, Nr Bridgnorth, Shropshire.   Tel: (0746) 780866
The National Trust

*4m SE of Bridgnorth on A442 ● Open April – Sept, Wed and Sun, 2.30 – 6.00
p.m. Last admission 5.30 p.m. Special opening for pre-booked parties only Thurs
p.m. ● Best season: late May but planted for spring, summer and autumn
colour ● Entrance: £1.00 (garden only) ● Parking ● Teas ● Toilet facilities
 ● Partly suitable for wheelchairs ● Dogs on lead ● Plants for sale ● Shop
● House open £2.40 ● Grade III*

An eight-acre garden of appeal and interest with its large pool and bog garden
and the associated plants along with island beds with shrubs, azaleas,
rhododendrons, viburnum and lovely old roses. Some large specimen trees
bring an air of peacefulness to the garden, and there are old fruit trees
including mulberry and medlars to add to the interest of old shrubs.

FARLEY HOUSE   6
Nr Much Wenlock, Shropshire.   Tel: (0952) 727017
Mr and Mrs R.W. Collingwood

*In Much Wenlock on the A458, turn left by garage on to A4169 signed
Ironbridge, garden is 1m on left ● Open by arrangement April – Oct ● Best
season: spring/summer ● Entrance: 60p ● Parking very limited on main road
 ● Toilet facilities ● Plants for sale ● Grade III*

This one-acre garden has been created on a hillside since 1980 by the present
owners and it is interesting to see how they have gradually cleared land to
create island beds containing a wide variety of plants. The garden is not yet
finished. It has a cottage-garden feel and this is reflected in the plants. Paved
area with alpines and raised beds and a peat bed. Small vegetable garden. Nice

troughs and range of conifers. There is something of interest in this garden over many months.

GLAZELEY OLD RECTORY 7
Glazeley, Nr Bridgnorth, Shropshire. Tel: (074635) 221
Mr and Mrs J.A. Goodall

3½m S of Bridgnorth on B4363 ● *Open for parties by appointment and 15th July, 2.00 – 6.00 p.m.* ● *Best season: spring and July* ● *Entrance: £1.00, children 25p* ● *Parking by church* ● *Teas. Teas and lunch for parties by arrangement* ● *Toilet facilities* ● *Suitable for wheelchairs* ● *Plants for sale* ● *Grade III*

This two-acre garden was for many years a nursery and is well designed, leading from one interesting area to another, with a wonderful collection of plants. There is a heather border, paved garden, bed of potentillas, a glade garden with hellebores, hostas, alliums and agapanthus, scree bed, a bog area with primulas and rodgersias, a fern collection and several good herbaceous borders. There are imaginative colour and foliage combinations and many unusual plants; in spring masses of bulbs.

THE GROVE 8
Kinton, Nr Nesscliff, Shropshire. Tel: (074381) 263
Mr and Mrs P. Radcliffe Evans

10m NW of Shrewsbury. Travelling towards Shrewsbury on A5, turn right at Nesscliff, following sign to Kinton. Pass through the village ● *Open for NGS and by appointment for parties April – July* ● *Entrance: 70p, children 10p* ● *Parking on road* ● *Teas* ● *Toilet facilities* ● *Suitable for wheelchairs* ● *Plants for sale* ● *Grade III*

This is a plantsperson's garden created by the owners since 1972 and set in beautiful countryside. It is designed in 'rooms'. Clematis climb through rose trees. There are other climbers on the house, a good collection of hardy geraniums, many ground-cover plants, and also potentillas. The vegetable garden is screened by a box hedge over which climbs a tropaeolum. Design features include a blue, pink and purple border, roses, honeysuckles and gentians growing in the base of an old greenhouse and trees providing good colour and foliage combinations. Many 'cottagey' plants to be enjoyed.

HAYE HOUSE 9
Eardington, Nr. Bridgnorth, Shropshire. Tel: (07462) 4884
Mrs Eileen Paradise

2m S of Bridgnorth. Take B4363 road to Cleobury Mortimer and go through village of Eardington, then 1 mile on left ● *Open by arrangement* ● *Best season: July • Entrance: 65p • Parking in field • Teas with home-made cakes • Toilet facilities • Partly suitable for wheelchairs • Plants possibly for sale • Grade IV*

The owner is a National Flower Demonstrator and accepts parties for demonstrations. The garden is planned to provide appropriate material and specimens. Half the vegetable garden contains foliage material. The old tennis court is being planted up on the outskirts with trailing plants and the whole garden has a sense of peacefulness. Of particular interest to flower arrangers but also to keen gardeners.

HODNET HALL 10
Hodnet, Shropshire. Tel: (063084) 202
Mr A.E.H. and The Hon. Mrs Heber-Percy

5½m SW of Market Drayton, 12m NE of Shrewsbury at junction of A53 and A442 • Open Good Friday – Sept, daily, 2.00 – 5.00 p.m., Sun and Bank Holidays, 12 noon – 5.30 p.m. • Best season: early June • Entrance: £1.80, OAP £1.25, children £1.00 • Parking for cars and coaches • Refreshments: snacks and teas • Toilet facilities • Partly suitable for wheelchairs • Dogs on lead • Plants for sale • Shop • Grade I

This garden has been superbly planted to give interest through the seasons – daffodils and blossom in spring, then primulas, rhododendrons, azaleas, laburnums and lilacs, followed by roses, peonies and astilbes merging in summer with the hydrangeas and shrubs that continue until the autumn foliage and berries round off the year. There are great trees on the estate and a magnolia walk along with many unusual plants. One of the oak trees is mentioned in the Domesday Book. Arranged around a chain of lakes which comprise one of the largest water gardens in England it is the home of a romantic bevy of black swans. A garden which needs to be visited many times to see its magnificence at all seasons, and one can visit the walled kitchen garden to purchase shrubs, fruit, flowers and vegetables.

LIMEBURNERS 11
Lincoln Hill, Ironbridge, Shropshire. Tel: (095245) 3715
Mr and Mrs J.E. Derry

Turn off B4380 W of Ironbridge up Lincoln Hill and garden is on left at top • Open April – Sept by appointment • Entrance: 75p, children 25p • Toilet facilities • Partly suitable for wheelchairs • Grade II

Walking round this delightful garden there are always surprises in store and a wealth of interesting plants to see. The wildlife-garden has a wide range of trees and shrubs and the use of ground-cover plants must help to reduce maintenance. Nice to see roses climbing through shrubs and the planting combinations throughout the garden are excellent. The owners have even managed to provide colour on a limestone bank. Further developments keep taking place including a new lilium area.

LOWER HALL 12
Worfield, Nr Bridgnorth, Shropshire. Tel: (07464) 607
Mr and Mrs C.F. Dumbell

A454 Wolverhampton/Bridgnorth road, turn right to Worfield and after passing village stores and pub turn right • *Open by arrangement* • *Best season: May – July* • *Entrance: £1.20, OAP £1.00, children free* • *Parking in driveway or nearby roads and in school grounds* • *Tea and biscuits for parties* • *Toilet facilities* • *Suitable for wheelchairs* • *Dogs on leads* • *Plants for sale* • *Grade II*

This modern plantsman's garden has been created by the present owners since 1964 with help from the designer Lanning Roper. The walled garden has old brick paths and fruit trees through which climb roses and clematis; over the walls the village cottages and the Tudor house provide a fine backcloth to the garden. Everywhere the use of colour combinations and plant associations is good – a red border, another of white and green, giving a cool effect. The water garden contains two weirs and the woodland garden includes rare magnolias, a collection of birch to provide bark interest, conifers, acers, amelanchiers – everything to provide all-year variety and colour.

MALLARDS KEEP 13
13 Allison Road, Church Stretton, Shropshire.
Tel: (0694) 722558
Mr and Mrs Franklin Barrett

From Church Stretton take B4371 to Much Wenlock. 1st left up Watling Street to Helmuth Road – Alison Road • *Open by arrangement and 15th, 16th April, 6th, 7th, 10th, 27th, 28th, 31st May, 2.00 – 6.00 p.m.* • *Best season: May/ June until end of August* • *Entrance: 60p, children free* • *Parking in street* • *Toilet facilities* • *Suitable for wheelchairs* • *Dogs on lead* • *Plants for sale* • *Grade III*

The owners have created a beautiful effect in this sixth of an acre garden of shrubs, roses, climbers and alpines. It also includes 100 rhododendrons, 40 clematis and 300 orchids in their own special house. This is a plantsman's garden with lovely colour and foliage combinations.

THE MORLEYS 14
Wallsbank, Church Stretton, Shropshire. Tel: (06943) 276
Mr and Mrs J. Knight

Off B4371 Church Stretton/Much Wenlock road. 3½m E of Church Stretton fork left for Stone Acton and Cardington, garden 200 yards on right • *Open by arrangement* ● *Best season: April – Sept, but best from late May* ● *Entrance: by arrangement* ● *Parking in field* ● *Refreshments: provided by WI in village hall for parties by arrangement* ● *Toilet facilities* ● *Partly suitable for wheelchairs* ● ***Grade III***

This four-acre garden created and maintained by the owners will appeal both to the plantsperson and to those perhaps starting a garden from scratch. It contains a wide variety of alpines, small plants, trees and shrubs and the island beds have good foliage and colour combinations of herbaceous material. The vegetable garden provides a constant supply for the owners. The bog garden and stream give an added dimension as does the woodland area with its collection of conifers, sorbus, beech and rhododendrons. The owners maintain it superbly for a long period of the year by planting for ease of maintenance.

NEW HALL 15
Eaton-under-Heywood, Nr Church Stretton, Shropshire.
Tel: (0694) 722226
Mrs R.H. Treasure

4m SE of Church Stretton between B4368 and B4371 ● *Open by appointment and in April, dates N.A.* ● *Best season: April/May* ● *Entrance: 70p, children 10p* ● *Parking in drive, along road or in field* ● *Picnics allowed* ● *Dogs on lead* ● ***Grade IV***

A 10-acre woodland garden with a difference and probably mainly of interest to those wishing to spend several hours walking through the woods enjoying the collection of wild flowers and conifers and the very peaceful situation. Insects and birds abound among the conifers and in the pools and streams. A good spot for a family outing taking a picnic.

OLDFIELD 16
Nr Long Meadow End, Craven Arms, Shropshire.
Tel: (0588) 672733
Mr and Mrs P. Housden

From Craven Arms take B4368 towards Clun. After 1½m turn right at telephone box, after 200 yards, turn left over cattle grid then on ¾m ● *Open 1st July, 2.00 – 6.00 p.m. and by appointment* ● *Best season: July – Oct* ● *Entrance: £1.00, children 50p* ● *Parking* ● *Teas for NGS* ● *Toilet facilities* ● *Partly suitable for wheelchairs* ● ***Grade III***

The owners have worked hard since 1980 to create this three-acre garden with its pool and bog garden and are still working on it. Roses surround the house and are also used for ground cover. A range of soft fruits and fan and espalier-trained trees, a vegetable garden and old and new woodland areas. Other attractions include bee hives and bonsai trees.

THE OLD RECTORY   17
Fitz, Shrewsbury, Shropshire. Tel: (0743) 850555
Mrs J.H.M. Stafford

5m NW of Shrewsbury. From A5 turn off at Montford Bridge, take 2nd turn to Fitz. The house is just past a farm ● Open for NGS ● Best season: June ● Entrance: 75p, children 10p ● Parking ● Teas ● Toilet facilities ● Suitable for wheelchairs ● Grade III

This botanist's garden should give pleasure to the keen plantsperson with its wide range of shrubs and plants. The water garden contains primulas, gunnera musk and rhus. There is a rose hedge, a collection of ferns and hellebores, many clematis scrambling through trees and shrubs, a raised peat bed and collections of geranium and euphorbias. A vegetable garden and fruit trees.

THE OLD VICARAGE   18
Cardington, Shropshire. Tel: (0694) 3354
Mr W.B. Hutchinson

3m N off B4371 Church Stretton/Much Wenlock road ● Open 2nd June, 15th July, 2.00 – 5.30 p.m. ● Entrance: £1.00, children 10p ● Parking in field adjoining ● Teas. Picnics allowed ● Toilet facilities ● Partly suitable for wheelchairs ● Dogs on lead ● Grade III

This two and a half-acre garden contains some beautiful old trees including a 175 year-old Spanish chestnut, and a copper beech. The owner has planted a good collection of conifers, shrub roses, sorbus, a peat bed with heathers, made a limestone pavement, a gravel bed for conifers, hebes and berberis, a rose border and a collection of Japanese azaleas. Although some areas are slightly untidy there is an air of peace, particularly around the pool. An alpine greenhouse and collection of primulas.

THE PADDOCKS   19
Chelmarsh Common, Chelmarsh, Nr Bridgnorth, Shropshire.
Tel: (0746) 861271
Mr and Mrs P. Hales

3m S of Bridgnorth on Highley Road ● Open by prior appointment and certain Sundays through the summer ● Best season: summer ● Entrance: 80p, children 20p to cover this garden and Dingle Bank on NGS ● Parking 300 yards away at The Bulls Head, Chelmarsh ● Partly suitable for wheelchairs ● Grade IV

A contrast to the more formal garden next door, with good use of old materials to make paths, pergolas and a rockery. Typical cottage plants have been used and the garden is divided into 'room' areas. There is a stream garden with a bog area with good ideas for the amateur gardener and a nursery attached to Dingle Bank next door (see page 321).

PREEN MANOR 662
Church Preen, Nr Church Stretton, Shropshire.
Tel: (06943) 207
Mr and Mrs P. Trevor-Jones

5m SW of Much Wenlock on B4371, 3m turn right for Church Preen and Hughley and after 1½m turn left for Church Preen, over crossroads and drive ½m on right ● *Open by appointment and NGS June/July* ● *Entrance: £1.00, children 25p* ● *Parking* ● *Teas* ● *Toilet facilities* ● *Plants for sale if available* ● **Grade II**

An exceptional garden designed by Norman Shaw with many features, and set in a park and with lovely old trees. The present owners have restored and replanted it and round every corner or through a gateway there is always a surprise. The gravel garden has a yellow and white border and elsewhere is a silver border. The chess garden has replaced the swimming pool and there is a pot garden filling a corner. The vegetable garden has a parterre design and each bed has variety. The bog garden is attractive and the unusual fernery is sited amongst some ruins. One could spend a day here trying to absorb the design features and superb planting and enjoying the peaceful setting.

RUTHALL MANOR 21
Ditton Priors, Bridgnorth, Shropshire. Tel: (074634) 608
Mr and Mrs G.T. Clarke

From Morville take B4368 and turn off for Ditton Priors. Weston Road from village church and take 2nd left road ● *Open to parties by arrangement* ● *Best season: Easter – Oct* ● *Entrance: £1.00* ● *Parking in adjacent field* ● *Tea shop in village from 11.00 a.m. – 5.00 p.m.* ● *Toilet facilities* ● *Suitable for wheelchairs* ● *Plants possibly for sale* ● **Grade II**

This one-acre garden has been cleverly designed since 1972 for ease of maintenance and planted to give pleasure to keen plant lovers. There are some unusual specimens and a collection of daphnes and birch and a group of sorbus, ilex, robinia and willows. By the pool is a collection of primulas, astilbes and iris. Good foliage and contrasting colours provide something of interest all through the year. There is also a small vegetable garden and a good collection of ferns.

SWALLOW HAYES 22
Rectory Road, Albrighton, Shropshire. Tel: (0907) 222624
Mrs Michael Edwards

7m NW of Wolverhampton. Turn off A41 into Rectory Road ● *Open 29th April, 10th, 17th, 20th May, 3rd, 7th June, 2.00 – 6.00 p.m. and for parties by arrangement* ● *Best season: May/June and autumn* ● *Entrance: 80p, children 10p* ● *Parking in drive and nearby road* ● *Teas on open days* ● *Toilet facilities* ● *Suitable for wheelchairs* ● *Dogs on lead* ● **Grade II**

A delightful two-acre modern garden with masses of design features and a beautiful display of plants, shrubs and trees. Although planted for easy maintenance, it contains 2000 different types of plants and provides all-year interest. Alpine border divided into various soil conditions, Mediterranean wall with tender plants. Small pools, herbs, a woodland area, colour and foliage contrasts. The National Collection of witch hazels and lupins and an interesting area of small gardens for one to copy at home. Vegetable and fruit trees; further developments in hand.

WESTON PARK 23
Weston-under-Lizard, Nr Shifnal, Shropshire. Tel: (095276) 207
The Earl and Countess of Bradford

On A5 7m W of junction 12 on M6 and 3m N of junction 3 on M54 ● Open April/May weekends and Bank Holidays, June/July daily except Mon and Fri, Aug/Sept weekends only, 11.00 a.m. – 7.00 p.m. ● Best season: May/June ● Entrance: £2.00, OAP, children £1.50 ● Parking ● Cafeteria in old stables providing home baking and estate produce. Also picnic teas ● Toilet facilities ● Partly suitable for wheelchairs ● Dogs ● Shop ● House open on certain occasions at additional entrance fee ● Grade II

A distinctive 'Capability' Brown creation covering almost 1000 acres of delightful woodland planted with rhododendrons and azaleas, together with beautiful pools. Some magnificent trees form a handsome backcloth to many shrubs. A rose walk leads to the deer park and there is a walled garden. There are many architectural features – The Temple of Diana, Roman bridge and the orangery all designed by James Paine. For children of all ages there is an adventure playground, the Weston Park Railway, a pets corner, pottery, aquarium and museum.

OPENING DATES AND TIMES
Times of access given are the best available at the moment of going to press, but some may have been changed subsequently. In the entries, the times given are inclusive – that is, an entry such as May-Sept means that the garden is open from 1st May to 30th Sept inclusive and 2 p.m. – 5 p.m. also means that entry will be effective during that period. Please note that many owners will open their gardens to visitors by appointment. They will often arrange to give a personally-conducted tour on these occasions. A few owners of gardens open under the NGS scheme have not been able to advise their opening times before the *Guide* went to press and in such cases the note N.A. (not available) indicates that so far as we know the garden will be open in 1990 but entry times must be checked.

SOMERSET

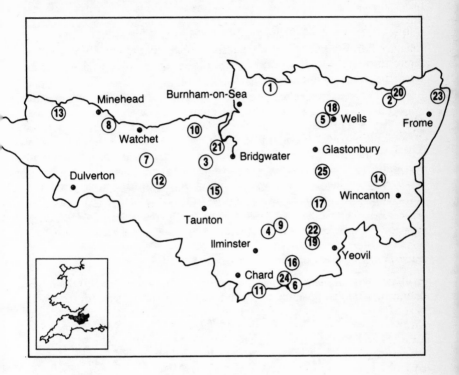

AMBLESIDE AVIARIES AND GARDENS 1
Lower Weare, Nr Axbridge, Somerset. Tel: (0934) 732362
Mrs T.K. Pickford

1½m SW of Axbridge on A38 ● *Open all year except 25th Dec – 16th Jan,*
10.00 a.m. – 5.00 p.m. ● *Best season: May* ● *Entrance: £1.00, OAP 90p,*
children 2 – 14 60p ● *Parking* ● *Coaches by appointment* ● *Refreshments:*
restaurant, cream teas, ice-creams ● *Toilet facilities* ● *Suitable for wheelchairs*
● *Grade IV*

The trees around the large pool, which is bisected by a bridge, are really all
that remain of the original plan by the owner of some 40 years ago who
conceived the idea of a water garden as depicted on the 'Willow Pattern' plate.
The cherry blossom reflected in the lily pond, silhouetted by willow of
different varieties, give an oriental effect. The aviaries do not intrude on the
water garden and the variety of ducks adds to the atmosphere of rural peace in
spite of the busy road running alongside a high hedge.

AMMERDOWN HOUSE 2
Kilmersdon, Radstock, Somerset.
Lord Hilton

On the B3139, ½m off A362 Radstock to Frome road ● *Open Bank Holidays only* ● *Best season: summer* ● *Entrance: £1.40* ● *Parking* ● *Toilet facilities* ● *Suitable for wheelchairs* ● ***Grade II***

A Bath-stone house perched on the crest of a hill with panoramic views on one side and a Lutyens garden on the other. This garden was a brilliant conception by Lutyens who wanted to link the house with the orangery. When one walks through the Italianate 'rooms' of yew and sculpture and parterre, one is unaware of the tricks of space that are being played. Massive yew planting now mature and fully 12 foot high creates enclosed formal areas which lead irresistably one from another – the awkward-shaped spaces between being almost entirely filled with hedging. Upkeep seems to have been pared to a minimum but the originality and grandeur remain as do some particularly nice details such as the clipped Portuguese laurels, honeysuckles trained over wire umbrellas and ancient lemon verbenas in pots in the orangery.

BARFORD PARK 3
Enmore, Nr Bridgwater, Somerset. Tel: (0278) 67269
Mr and Mrs M. Stancombe

5m W of Bridgwater. Turn right to Spaxton off the Enmore Road from Bridgwater ● *Open May – Sept, Wed, Thurs and Bank Holidays* ● *Best season: June/July* ● *Entrance: £1.50, children 50p* ● *Parking* ● *Teas by arrangement* ● *Partly suitable for wheelchairs* ● *Dogs on lead* ● *Primulas for sale in season* ● *House open* ● ***Grade II***

This is a garden in the eighteenth-century style developed over the last 32 years. Set in parkland and protected by a ha-ha on three sides, it has many features. After watching the golden orfe darting around the lily pond, stroll down a sweep of lawn to a stand of tall trees. There, in the woodland glade is a carpet of many shades of primulas. A lawn on two levels with herbaceous borders provides the view from the terrace.

BARRINGTON COURT 4
Barrington, Ilminster, Somerset. Tel: (0460) 52242/40601
The National Trust under the management of the Lyle family

3m NE of Ilminster on B3168 ● *Open April – 14th Oct, Sat – Wed (inc. Good Friday), 11.00 a.m. – 5.30 p.m.* ● *Best season: spring/summer* ● *Entrance: £2.80* ● *Parking* ● *Refreshments: morning coffee, light lunches, cream teas. Licensed* ● *Toilet facilities* ● *Suitable for wheelchairs* ● *Shop* ● ***Grade III***

The house, farm and derelict gardens were converted to a model estate by Col. Lyle in the 1920s using plans provided by Gertrude Jekyll. The flower gardens reflect the priorities of a working estate in that basic cultivation is carried out but without a manicured finish. On the other hand, the magnificent kitchen garden, without a weed in sight, is an education in planning to produce a great variety of fruit and vegetables with the maximum use of every inch of ground and wall space.

THE BISHOP'S PALACE 5
Wells, Somerset. Tel: (0749) 78691
The Church Commissioners

In centre of Wells ● Open Easter – Oct, Sun, Thurs and Bank Holidays, 2.00 – 6.00 p.m. ● Entrance: £1.50, children 80p ● Public parking in city car parks nearby ● Light refreshments from cathedral cloisters ● Toilet facilities ● Grade II

The ruins of the banqueting hall have been 'room scaped' with shrubs and herbaceous plants. A shrub rose garden has been planted near the water (from the wells). An unusual garden ornament has been carved from the root of a very old yew tree, depicting Adam and Eve being expelled from the Garden of Eden by an angel with a flaming sword. Since World War II the old allotment has been planted as an arboretum which is now well-established.

CLAPTON COURT 6
Clapton, Crewkerne, Somerset. Tel: (0460) 73220/72200
Captain S.J. Loder

3m S of Crewkerne on B3165 ● Open April – Oct, Mon – Fri, also Easter Sat and Sats in May, 10.30 a.m. – 5.00 p.m., Sun, 2.00 – 5.00 p.m. ● Entrance: £2.00, OAP £1.60, children under 14, 30p ● Parking ● Coaches and private parties by arrangement ● Refreshments: light lunches and teas for parties by arrangement ● Toilet facilities ● Partly suitable for wheelchairs ● Plants for sale Feb – Nov ● Grade II

A very well-kept formal garden, with rare plants and shrubs clearly labelled, rubbing shoulders with some homely indigenous varieties. The woodland garden developed by the present owner on a steep slope set amongst some mature trees has a stream controlled by a series of small brooks that provides the conditions required for rarer wild plants. Many of the plants are 'Loderi' varieties and hybrids of rhododendrons which were introduced by Captain Loder's relation who developed the famous Leonardslee garden in Sussex.

COMBE SYDENHAM HALL 7
Monksilver, Taunton, Somerset. Tel: (0984) 56284
Mr and Mrs W. Theed

5m S of Watchet on B3188 between Monksilver and Elworthy ● Open Easter – Oct, Mon – Fri, 11.00 a.m. – 5.00 p.m. ● Best season: May – Sept.

• *Entrance: £2.50, OAP/children £1.80 (house, garden & country park)*
• *Parking inc. coaches* • *Light refreshments, home-made teas* • *Toilet facilities* • *Plants for sale* • *Shop (inc. trout from estate)* • *House open*
• **Grade III**

Set in a deer park, the small formal Elizabethan parterre-garden is being restored and restocked with old types of roses. The pink lavender is a source of pride to Mrs Theed who also cultivates the old herb garden. Quince trees and a peacock house help to create the atmosphere of a domestic garden in Tudor times.

DUNSTER CASTLE   8
Dunster, Nr Minehead, Somerset. Tel: (0643) 821314
The National Trust

3m SE of Minehead on A39 • *Open April – Sept, daily except Fri and Sat, but open Fri and Sat in June – Aug, 11.00 a.m. - 5.00 p.m., Oct – 4th Nov, daily except Fri and Sat, 2.00 - 4.00 p.m.* • *Best season: May/June* • *Entrance: £1.70, children 70p (£3.50, children £1.50 house and gardens)* • *Parking*
• *Refreshments in Dunster* • *Toilet facilities* • *Dogs in park only* • *National Trust shop* • *Castle open* • **Grade II**

The family which had lived here since the fourteenth century gave it to the National Trust in 1976. A very fine herbaceous border backed by rare shrubs surrounds a lawn by the keep and is well worth the steep climb to view. On the formal terraces below thrives a variety of sub-tropical plants, camellias and azaleas. There are views across to Exmoor, the Quantocks and the Bristol Channel. The park totals 28 acres in all.

EAST LAMBROOK MANOR   9
Nr South Petherton, Somerset. Tel: (0460) 40328
Mr and Mrs A. Norton

2m NE of South Petherton off A303 • *Open all year except Christmas and New Year, Mon – Sat, 9.00 a.m. – 5.00 p.m.* • *Entrance: £1.20, small children free* • *Parking* • *No coaches* • *Refreshments: coffee and biscuits only but parties by arrangement* • *Toilet facilities* • *Plants for sale (mailing list)*
• *Shop for Margery Fish publications* • **Grade II**

Margery Fish established these gardens for endangered species and the present owners have carried on her tradition. The result is an impression of luxuriant growth. The garden's ring paths are half-hidden by the profusion of plants and its controlled wilderness of colour and scent give the discerning a chance to find rare plants and shrubs.

FAIRFIELD 10
Stogursey, Somerset. Tel: (0278) 733251
Lady Gass

11m NW of Bridgwater. Turn off A39 at Nether Stowey. House is 1½m W of Stogursey ● Open Easter Sun, for NGS and Red Cross. Parties at other times by arrangement ● Best season: spring/summer ● Entrance: £1.00, children 50p ● Parking ● Teas for NGS and Red Cross ● Suitable for wheelchairs ● Dogs on lead in park only ● Grade III

A magnolia grows against the wall of the Elizabethan house, with views over the Quantocks and the sea. Having a neutral soil, a wide variety of shrubs flourishes including shrub roses, camellias and azaleas. The woodland garden has many bulbs, from snowdrops to cyclamen. Strutting peacocks add to the interest of this garden. Eighteenth-century walled kitchen garden.

FORDE ABBEY 11
Chard, Somerset. Tel: (0460) 21366
Mr M. Roper

7m W of Crewkerne, 4m SE of Chard off A30 ● Open all year, daily, 10.30 a.m. - 4.30 p.m. ● Entrance: £2.00, OAP £1.80, children free ● Parking ● Refreshments ● Toilet facilities ● Suitable for wheelchairs ● Dogs ● Plants for sale ● House open ● Grade I

This unique and fascinating former Cistercian abbey, inhabited as a private house since 1649, is set in a varied and pleasing garden. Old walls and colourful borders, wide sloping lawns, lush ponds and cascades, graceful statuary and huge mature trees combine to create an atmosphere of timeless elegance. There is something here for every gardener to appreciate; the bog garden displays a large collection of primulas and other Asiatic plants; the shrubbery contains a variety of magnolias, rhododendrons and other delightful specimens. There is a rock garden and a very fine arboretum built up since 1947; at the back of the abbey is an extensive kitchen garden and a nursery selling rare and unusual plants which look in fine health.

GAULDEN MANOR 12
Tolland, Nr Lydeard St Lawrence, Somerset. Tel: (09847) 213
Mr J.H.N. Starkie

9m NW of Taunton off A358 ● Open May - mid-Sept, Sun, Thurs and Bank Holidays, 2.00 - 5.30 p.m. ● Entrance: 80p (house and gardens £2.00, children 80p) ● Parking ● Teas by arrangement for parties ● Toilet facilities ● Shop ● House open ● Grade II

Garden seats at vantage points give the visitor a chance to appreciate the many different vistas provided in this country garden which includes a bog garden, herb garden, butterfly garden and herbaceous borders of selected colour. A short walk through a woodland glade leads to a secret garden of white flowering plants. Visitors should not miss the small duck garden near the tea house with carvings on the fence posts.

GREENCOMBE   13
Porlock, Somerset. Tel: (0643) 862363
Greencombe Garden Trust (Miss Joan Loraine)

*½m W of Porlock off B3226 • Open 3rd weekend of April to 2nd weekend of July, Sat – Mon, 2.00 – 6.00 p.m. or by appointment • Entrance: £1.50, children 50p • Parking • Coaches by arrangement • Partly suitable for wheelchairs • Plants for sale • **Grade II***

Created in 1946 by Horace Stroud, this garden was extended by the present owner over the last 21 years. Overlooking the Severn, on a hillside where the sun cannot penetrate for nearly three months in the winter, it glows with colour. The formal lawns and beds round the house are immaculate and by contrast the woodland area, terraced on the hillside, provides a nature walk of great interest. A wide variety of rhododendrons and azaleas flowers in the shadow of mature trees, where ferns and woodland plants flourish. No sprays or chemicals are used in the cultivation of this completely 'organic' garden which contains the National collection of polystichum.

HADSPEN HOUSE   14
Castle Cary, Somerset. Tel: (0963) 50939
Mr N.A. Hobhouse

*2m SE of Castle Cary on A371 • Open March – Oct, daily except Mon but open Bank Holiday Mon, 9.00 a.m. – 6.00 p.m. • Entrance: £1.00, children 50p • Parking • Coaches by arrangement • Teas on Sun and Bank Holidays • Toilet facilities • Partly suitable for wheelchairs • Plants for sale • **Grade II***

This family garden, developed over the last 200 years, was reclaimed by Penelope Hobhouse after the last war. A large curved wall encloses a garden, sectioned by paved paths, which offers vistas of individual interest including herbaceous plants, old-fashioned roses and vegetables. A wild-flower meadow set in parkland contrasts with the ornamental garden near the house.

HESTERCOMBE HOUSE GARDENS   15
Cheddon Fitzpaine, Taunton, Somerset. Tel: (0823) 333451
Somerset County Council

*2m NE of Taunton off A358 • Open all year, Mon – Fri • Best season: midsummer • Entrance: donation of £1.00 for garden plan • Parking • No coaches • **Grade I***

This is a superb product of the collaboration between Edwin Lutyens and Gertrude Jekyll, blending the formal art of architecture with the art of plants. On a limited budget the Somerset County Council has endeavoured to maintain the gardens, respecting the colour groupings of the original designs and keeping the water courses flowing as they would have in Edwardian days. The *Oxford Companion* describes this as Lutyens at his best in the detailed design of steps, pools, walls, paving and seating. The canal, pergola and orangery are fine examples of his work.

LOWER SEVERALLS 16
Haselbury Road, Crewkerne, Somerset. Tel: (0460) 73234
Audrey and Mary Pring

1½m NE of Crewkerne off B3165 ● Open Mar – Oct, weekdays except Thurs, 10.00 a.m. - 5.00 p.m., Sun, 2.00 - 5.00 p.m. ● Entrance: by collecting box, 50p for NGS ● Parking on road ● Teas for NGS ● Suitable for wheelchairs ● Plants for sale ● Grade III

A typical cottage garden with herbaceous border against stone-walled house and vista through stone pillars to valley beyond a wild-flower area. Specialists in herbaceous geraniums and fuchsias. Also an interesting herb garden.

LYTES CARY MANOR 17
Nr Somerton, Somerset. Tel: (045822) 3297
The National Trust

2½m NE of Ilchester, signposted from A303 ● Open 2nd April – 3rd Nov, Mon, Wed and Sat, 2.00 - 6.00 p.m. or dusk if earlier. Last admission 5.30 p.m. ● Best season: late May/early June ● Entrance: £2.20, children £1.00 ● Parking (¼m walk) ● No coaches ● Plants for sale inc. good selection of perennials ● Grade III

This garden was revived by its former owner with advice from Graham Stuart Thomas. Pleasing lawns with hedges in Elizabethan style and some topiary. A wide herbaceous border along the length of a stone wall. A large orchard with naturalized bulbs and mown walks adds to the peaceful ambience. Regretfully there is no trace of the original herb garden for which Lytes Cary was famed in the sixteenth century but a border along the south front is stocked with species of plants cultivated in those days.

MILTON LODGE 18
Wells, Somerset. Tel: (0749) 72168
Mr D.C. Tudway-Quilter

½m N of Wells. From A39 to Bristol turn N up Old Bristol Road ● Open May - July, Wed, 2.00 - 5.00 p.m., Sun, 2.00 - 6.00 p.m. ● Best season:

midsummer ● Entrance: £1.00, children 50p. Special parties £2.00 per person ● Car park on left before reaching drive to house ● No coaches ● Teas on Sun ● Toilet facilities ● Grade II

The garden, replanted by the present owners in the 1960s, is cultivated down the side of a hill overlooking the Vale of Avalon, affording a magnificent view of Wells Cathedral. A wide variety of plants all suitable for the alkaline soil provides a succession of colours and interest during the summer season, interspersed with ancient oak, cedar and established gingko trees. The adjacent seven-acre arboretum is included in the admission fee.

MONTACUTE HOUSE   19
Montacute, Yeovil, Somerset.   Tel: (0935) 823289
The National Trust

4m W of Yeovil. NT signs off A3088 and A303 near Ilchester ● Open all year except Tues, 12.30 – 5.30 p.m. or dusk if earlier ● Best season: June – Sept ● Entrance: £1.00 (Oct - May 60p), children 50p (Oct – May 30p) (£3.00 house and garden) ● Parking ● Refreshments: light lunches and teas ● Toilet facilities ● Suitable for wheelchairs ● Dogs on lead. Special walks in park ● Plants for sale March – mid-Dec ● National Trust shop ● House open April – 4th Nov, daily except Tues, 12.30 – 5.00 p.m. Closed Good Friday ● Grade I

This Elizabethan garden of grass lawns surrounded by clipped yews set in terraces is a triumph of formality. Colours are provided by herbaceous borders from mid-summer. The arboretum of rare trees is so far not labelled. The gardens are surrounded by graceful parklands giving vistas and an impression of space. The house is interesting as a venue for George Curzon's affair with Elinor Glyn.

R.T. HERBS AND GARDEN   20
Kilmersdon, Radstock, Somerset.   Tel: (0761) 35470
Mr and Mrs R. Taylor

6m NE of Shepton Mallet on B3139 ● Open daily, 9.00 a.m. – 6.00 p.m. or dusk ● Best season: spring/summer ● Entrance: donation box for NGS ● Public car park adjacent ● Refreshments in local pub ● Plants for sale ● Grade IV

This is a working garden far removed from the gracious lawns of a stately home but demonstrating the potential of a narrow plot to become a graceful and attractive garden. The wide variety of herbs mingled with herbaceous plants and wild flowers attracts bees, butterflies and insects during the summer and provides feeding grounds for wildlife during the winter months.

SOMERSET COLLEGE OF AGRICULTURE AND HORTICULTURE   21
Cannington, Somerset. Tel: (0278) 652226
Somerset County Council

*3m NW of Bridgwater on A39 ● Open all year, Mon – Fri, 10.00 a.m. – 6.00 p.m. or dusk in winter, Sat/Sun, 9.00 a.m. – 5.00 p.m. ● Entrance: £1.00, children free ● Parking ● Teas for parties by arrangement ● Toilet facilities ● Suitable for wheelchairs ● Plants for sale from April 1990 ● **Grade II***

The College was founded in 1922 in the grounds of an old Benedictine priory. Plant specialists may find here the fulfillment of their wildest expectations: the National collection of ceanothus, fremontias, wisteria, osteospermum, abutilon, phormium, cordyline and yucca. Various greenhouses reproduce the conditions – Mediterranean, alpine etc. – for house plants of a different clime. Younger gardeners will be interested in the documented development over the last few years of a butterfly garden. On the other side of the A39 from the College buildings an open area has been landscaped to include a nine hole golf course and a putting green as well as science plots.

TINTINHULL HOUSE GARDEN   22
Tintinhull, Yeovil, Somerset. Tel: (0935) 76233
The National Trust

*5m NW of Yeovil, ½m S of A303 ● Open April – 29th Sept, Wed, Thurs, Sat and Bank Holiday Mons, 2.00 – 6.00 p.m. ● Entrance: £2.20 ● Parking ● Teas ● Suitable for wheelchairs ● **Grade II***

A relatively small modern garden, barely one acre, which achieves an impression of greater size which is being developed by Penelope Hobhouse. The wide variety of plants are not labelled in order to retain the charm of a private garden but an inventory is available for interested visitors.

THE TROPICAL BIRD GARDENS   23
Rode, Nr Bath, Somerset. Tel: (0373) 830326
Mr and Mrs D. Risdon

*5m NE of Frome, signed off A361 ● Open all year except 25th Dec, summer 10.30 a.m. – 7.00 p.m., winter 10.30 a.m. – sunset ● Entrance: £2.50, children £1.30 ● Parking ● Refreshments: licensed cafeteria in summer, light refreshments in winter ● Toilet facilities ● Suitable for wheelchairs ● Clematis for sale in season ● Shop ● **Grade III***

The gardens have been developed to provide the background and natural habitat, as far as possible, for the birds. The clematis collection was started in 1985 and is now established. The wide variety of trees on the tree trail are not all labelled but a detailed guide is available to aid identification of the many rare varieties.

337

WAYFORD MANOR 24
Clapton, Crewkerne, Somerset. Tel: (0460) 73253
Mr R.L. Goffe

3m SW of Crewkerne off B3165 at Clapton ● Open 22nd April, 13th May, 3rd June, 2.00 – 6.00 p.m. Parties by appointment ● Best season: spring/early summer ● Entrance: £1.00, children 30p ● Limited parking ● Teas for parties ● Partly suitable for wheelchairs ● Dogs on lead ● Plants for sale ● Grade II

A very well-maintained garden of flowering shrubs and trees, rhododendrons and spring bulbs, against the stonework of an Elizabethan house. This is a fine example of the work of Harold Peto who redesigned the garden in 1902.

WOOTTON HOUSE 25
Butleigh Wootton, Nr Glastonbury, Somerset. Tel: (0458) 42348
The Hon. Mrs J. Acland-Hood

3m S of Glastonbury. Minor road to Butleigh from Glastonbury, turn right to Butleigh Wootton. Continue through the village to house ● Open by appointment and 6th May, 2.00 – 5.30 p.m. and 1 other day during summer ● Entrance: £1.00 ● Parking in road ● Teas on NGS days ● Suitable for wheelchairs ● Dogs on lead ● Grade II

The present garden design has been developed since 1900. It is a beautiful example of a private country-house garden. A terrace with a view to the Beacon Hill in the Mendips framed by herbaceous beds set in a sweep of lawn. The old-fashioned rose garden against a stone wall leads to the woodland area where anemones and fritillaries grow as well as cyclamen. In the park is a monument to Admiral Hood, a family ancestor.

OPENING DATES AND TIMES
Times of access given are the best available at the moment of going to press, but some may have been changed subsequently. In the entries, the times given are inclusive – that is, an entry such as May-Sept means that the garden is open from 1st May to 30th Sept inclusive and 2 p.m. – 5 p.m. also means that entry will be effective during that period. Please note that many owners will open their gardens to visitors by appointment. They will often arrange to give a personally-conducted tour on these occasions. A few owners of gardens open under the NGS scheme have not been able to advise their opening times before the *Guide* went to press and in such cases the note N.A. (not available) indicates that so far as we know the garden will be open in 1990 but entry times must be checked.

STAFFORDSHIRE

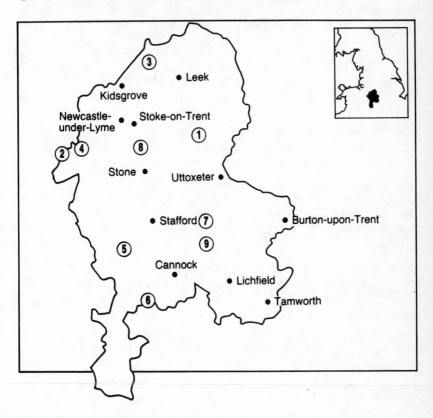

ALTON TOWERS 1
Alton, Staffordshire.   Tel: (0538) 702200
Alton Towers Ltd

From N take M6 junction 16 or M1 junction 28, from S take M6 junction 15 or M1 junction 24. Signposted ● Open all year ● Best season: spring/summer ● Entrance: £1.50, OAP £1.00 ● Parking ● Refreshments: restaurants, kiosks, picnic areas ● Toilet facilities ● Suitable for wheelchairs ● Dogs on lead ● Shop ● Ruin open. Pleasure park open at additional cost, Easter – early Nov ● Grade II

This fantastic garden of ornamental garden architecture was one of the last great follies, created in the early nineteenth century. It contains many beautiful and unusual features including the Chinese Pagoda fountain, a copy of the To Ho pagoda in Canton. The enormous rock garden is planted with a range of conifers, acers and sedums. The fine conservatory houses geraniums and other colour according to the season and the terraces have rose and herbaceous borders. There is a Dutch garden, Her Ladyship's Garden featuring yew and rose beds, the Italian garden, a yew arch walkway and woodland walks. There is water to add further beauty and interest. In addition, there are all the attractions of the pleasure park in season.

ARBOUR COTTAGE 2
Napley, Norton in Hales, Staffordshire. Tel: (063087) 2852
Mr and Mrs D.K. Hewitt

4m N of Market Drayton. Take A53 then B5415 signed Woore, after 1¾m turn left ● *Garden may not open in 1990* ● *Best season: summer* ● *Entrance: £1.00, children 50p* ● *Parking* ● *Teas on NGS open days* ● *Toilet facilities* ● *Suitable for wheelchairs* ● *Plants for sale* ● **Grade III**

The owners created this garden from a 1¾-acre field and it should appeal equally to those interested in design and to plant lovers. There is an excellent collection of plants and young trees and some rare and tender specimens as well as some unusual plant and colour combinations.

BIDDULPH GRANGE GARDEN 3
Biddulph Grange, Biddulph, Stoke-on-Trent, Staffordshire.
Tel: (074377) 649/343
The National Trust

10m N of Stoke-on-Trent off A527 and 4m from Kidsgrove and Congleton. Open to the public for the first time in 1991, this little known Victorian garden may be seen in 1990 while restoration work is in progress by applying to the Heart of England Appeal Office, PO Box 144, Shrewsbury (phone above). An admission donation of £5.00 is required for these special admissions.

Described by George Plumptre as a Victorian *pot-pourri* combining fantastic and picturesque elements, Biddulph Grange was divided into distinct areas by its owner/designer James Bateman (d. 1897). Some are Chinese and Egyptian, and others very English.

THE DOROTHY CLIVE GARDEN 4
Elds Wood, Willoughbridge, Staffordshire. Tel: (063081) 237
Willoughbridge Garden Trust

7m N of Market Drayton, 1m E of Woore on A51 between Nantwich and Stone ● *Open Good Friday – Nov, weekdays, 2.00 – 5.30 p.m., Sun, 12 noon – 5.30 p.m.* ● *Entrance: £1.00, children 25p* ● *Parking inc. car park for disabled persons* ● *Refreshments in tea room* ● *Toilet facilities* ● *Partly suitable for wheelchairs* ● *Plants for sale in certain seasons* ● **Grade II**

Created by the late Colonel Clive in memory of his wife with the help of distinguished gardeners including John Codrington, this garden has wide appeal because of both its design and inspired planting. The coloured guide identifies the highlights season by season. These include the rhododendrons and azaleas in the quarry garden and the pool with the scree garden rising on the hillside above it. In spring there are unusual bulbs and primulas, in summer colourful shrubs, unusual perennials and many conifers; other trees provide autumn colour. The scree garden must give gardeners many good ideas. A garden of great peace and pleasure.

LITTLE ONN HALL   5
Church Eaton, Near Stafford, Staffordshire.   Tel: (0785) 840154
Mr and Mrs I.H. Kidson

6m SW of Stafford, 2m S of Church Eaton, midway between the A5 and A518
● Open 20th May, 10th June, 2.00 – 6.00 p.m.   ● Entrance: £1.25, children
*50p ● Parking ● Teas ● Partly suitable for wheelchairs ● **Grade III***

Entering this six-acre garden the driveway is flanked with long herbaceous borders backed by yew hedges and elsewhere are more herbaceous borders. The large rose garden has standards, shrub and hybrid teas. An unusual-shaped pool known as the 'Dog Bone' has water lilies and elsewhere in the garden are bog plants. Since 1971 the present owners have been planting new trees and are trying to maintain the original design by Thomas H. Mawson of Windermere. There are many rhododendrons, spring bulbs and large beeches and conifers thus ensuring colour for quite a long season. Some areas are somewhat overgrown, but the moat garden gives a sense of mystery and charm.

MOSELEY OLD HALL   6
Moseley Old Hall Lane, Fordhouses, Wolverhampton, Staffordshire.
Tel: (0902) 782802
The National Trust

*4m N of Wolverhampton. Traffic from S on M6 and M54 take junction 1 to Wolverhampton. Traffic from N on M6 leave motorway at Shareshill then take A460. Coaches must go on A460 ● Open 17th March – Oct, Wed, Sat, Sun and Bank Holiday Mon, also Tues in July and Aug only, 2.00 – 5.30 p.m. Closed Good Friday. Pre-booked parties at other times inc. evening tours ● Best season: June/July ● Entrance: £2.00, family £5.50 ● Refreshments: teas and lunches for parties ● Toilet facilities ● Suitable for wheelchairs ● Shop ● House open (Elizabethan house where Charles II hid after the Battle of Worcester) ● **Grade IV***

A garden mainly for the specialist interested in old plants as all specimens are seventeenth-century except for a few fruit trees. The knot garden is from a design of 1640 by the Reverend Walter Stonehouse. A wooden arbour is covered with clematis and *Vitis vinifera* 'Purpurea'. The fruit trees include a mulberry, medlars and morello cherry. The walled garden has some topiary and herbaceous borders and the nut walk has fritillarias. There is a small herb garden and boles for bees. A nice change to see some interesting old plants which were grown in former times to provide dyes and for cleansing and medicinal purposes.

SHUGBOROUGH 7
Great Haywood, Milford, Staffordshire.   Tel: (0889) 881388
The National Trust

6m E of Stafford on A513   ● Open 31st March – 28th Oct, daily, 11.00 a.m. – 5.00 p.m. 29th Oct – 22nd Dec, 11.00 a.m. – 4.00 p.m. 2nd Jan – 28th March 1991, 10.30 a.m. – 4.00 p.m. for pre-booked parties only. Also open for pre-booked parties all year round from 10.30 a.m.   ● Best season: spring/summer ● Entrance: £1.00   ● Parking   ● Refreshments: lunches and snacks in tea room, also picnic area   ● Toilet facilities   ● Suitable for wheelchairs   ● Dogs on lead ● Shop   ● House open and also museum and adjacent farm at extra charge ● Note: Times and admission charges subject to change   ● Grade II

Of interest to garden historians as there are many buildings and monuments in neo-Grecian style ascribed to James 'Athenian' Stuart and built for Admiral Anson from the 1740s onwards. These are some of the earliest examples of English neo-classicism and there is also an early example of chinoiserie based on a sketch made by one of the officers on Admiral Anson's voyage round the world. However the buildings are 'somewhat randomly scattered rather than sited according to a programme' as at Stourhead, according to the *Oxford Companion*. As for the garden, the Victorian layout was revitalized for the Trust in the mid-1960s by Graham Stuart Thomas who designed a rose garden with various elements in the French style, with roses appropriate to the period. There is also a woodland walk.

TRENTHAM PARK GARDENS 8
Trentham, Stoke-on-Trent, Staffordshire.   Tel: (0782) 657341
National Coal Board

On A34 S of Stoke-on-Trent. 2m from M6 junction 15   ● Open all year 9.00 a.m. – dusk   ● Best season: summer   ● Entrance: £2.00, OAP and children £1.00   ● Parking   ● Refreshments   ● Toilet facilities   ● Suitable for wheelchairs   ● Dogs on lead   ● Garden centre and conference centre with restaurant facilities adjacent   ● Grade III

These 400 acres of parkland were designed by 'Capability' Brown. Nesfield added a large Italian garden and Sir Charles Barry laid out formal gardens for the Duke of Sutherland. The gardens have been greatly simplified under the Coal Board ownership but still retain many features such as Brown's large lake on which one can now water sport or go boating. Rose garden and displays of bedding plants, a good selection of shrubs including hebes, potentillas and buddleias. Magnificent trees both alongside the River Trent, which flows through the gardens, and in the woodland area by the lake. The Italian garden has masses of colour from annuals and also some yew trees. A clematis walk has been replanted, but the rock garden needs some attention. A good place for a family day-out as there are picnic areas, a riding school with pony rides, a children's play area, wildfowl pens and a Shire and Craft Centre.

WOLSELEY GARDEN PARK   9
Wolseley Bridge, Stafford, Staffordshire.   Tel: (0889) 576366
Sir Charles and Lady Wolseley

At junction of A51 with A513 between Rugeley and Stafford ● *Open daily. Times vary seasonally but 10.00 a.m. – 6.00 p.m. in summer* ● *Entrance: charges seasonally variable, advertised* ● *Parking* ● *Refreshments* ● *Toilet facilities* ● *Suitable for wheelchairs* ● *Plants for sale at Cramphorn garden centre in park* ● *Shop* ● ***Grade II***

An outstanding new 50-acre garden development as part of the owners' plan to make the site a major leisure and educational centre. Features include a two-acre walled rose garden, a water bog garden with broad walk, rockery, a large collection of willows, a large new lake set in a water meadow, a woodland spring garden with flowering shrubs and bulbs. There is a scented garden for the particular enjoyment of the blind and partially sighted and a winter garden aimed at giving colour Nov – March. Similar 'theme' gardens are being developed by the team of designers. Summer visitors will also be intrigued by the sight of the archaeologists excavating the remains of the twelfth-century castle.

HOW TO FIND THE GARDENS

Directions to each garden are included in each entry. This information has been supplied by the garden inspectors and is aimed to be the best available to those travelling by car. However, it has been compiled to be used in conjunction with a road atlas.

The unreliability of train and bus services makes it unrewarding to include details, particularly as many garden visits are made on Sundays. However, many properties can be reached by public transport and National Trust guides and the Yellow Book [NGS] give details. Future editions of the *Guide* may include a special list of gardens easily reached by public transport if readers indicate that this would be helpful.

The Maps: The numbers on the maps correspond to the numbers of the gardens in each county. The maps show the proximity of one garden to another so that visits to several gardens can be planned for the same day. It is worthwhile referring to the maps of bordering counties to see if another garden visit can be included in your itinerary. The maps should be used in conjunction with a road atlas.

SUFFOLK

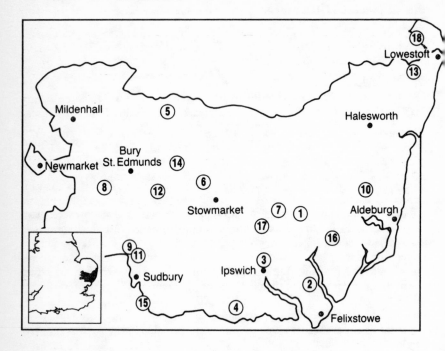

AKENFIELD 1
1 Park Lane, Charsfield, Woodbridge, Suffolk. Tel: (047337) 402
Mrs Peggy Cole

3m W of Wickham Market on B1078 ● *Open end May – Sept, daily, 10.30*
a.m. – 7.00 p.m. ● *Entrance: 75p* ● *Plants for sale* ● ***Grade IV***

Akenfield, formerly a council house, has a quarter of an acre cottage garden
full of charm, and overflowing with flowers and vegetables. To one side the
front garden is planted with roses and bedding plants, to the other a small
honeysuckle arch leads to a patio with containers of flowers, hanging baskets
– and a shed full of home-made wines which is an irresistible attraction to
robins who nest among the bottles. Opposite the patio is a tiny water garden
complete with waterfall and wishing well. The back garden is divided in two;
to one side is a vegetable garden with about thirty different kinds of vegetables
and a hen house at the far end. On the other side there are two large
greenhouses, overflowing with pot plants, tomatoes and cucumbers. Beyond
are small gardens connected by archways, apple trees and a grape vine;
hanging baskets and even bottles hold more plants.

BUCKLESHAM HALL 2
Bucklesham, Ipswich, Suffolk. Tel: (047388) 263
Mr and Mrs P.A. Ravenshear

6m E of Ipswich, ½m E of Bucklesham village. Entrance opposite and just N of Bucklesham primary school ● *Open by appointment* ● *Entrance: £1.50, OAP and children £1.00* ● *Parking. Coaches by appointment* ● *Refreshments by special arrangement* ● *Plants for sale* ● *Shop* ● ***Grade III***

The great interest of Bucklesham is how these five acres of interlocking gardens, terraces and lakes have been created from scratch by the present owners since 1973. Round the house are secret gardens so packed with flowers that no weed could survive; a courtyard garden has been created almost instantly with the use of every kind of container. Descending terraces of lawns, ponds and streams lead to the woodland and beyond; round each corner is a new vista. Skill, wide horticultural knowledge and imagination have enabled Mr and Mrs Ravenshear to achieve their aim of displaying plants, shrubs and trees of interest to the plantsman in tranquil surroundings appealing to the layman, all with minimum maintenance, although some may be put off by all those containers.

CHRISTCHURCH PARK 3
Ipswich, Suffolk. Tel: (0473) 262626
Ipswich Borough Council

In Ipswich, just N of town centre. Main entrance in Soane Street ● *Open daily, Mon - Sat, 7.30 a.m. - dusk, Sun, 9.00 a.m. - dusk. Times shown on signs at park entrance* ● *Entrance: free* ● *Parking in surrounding roads* ● *Suitable for wheelchairs* ● *House open different times* ● ***Grade IV***

Christchurch Mansion was built in a large park on the north side of Ipswich on the site of an Augustinian priory and dates from 1548. In 1894 Mr Felix Cobbold bought the house and gardens and presented them to the Borough, on condition they purchased the park, together with the contents. This magnificent gift has given Ipswich one of the finest Tudor houses, as well as municipal parks, in the country. Ancient oak and other mature trees are interspersed with new planting, gardens and borders with beautifully kept flower beds, a lake and even a bowling green.

EAST BERGHOLT LODGE 4
Via Colchester, Suffolk. Tel: (0206) 298278
Captain C. Wake-Walker RN

Halfway between Colchester and Ipswich on A12. Take B1070, first right and through white gate at crossroads ● *Open by appointment and some Suns in May and June, 2.00 - 6.00 p.m. or as arranged* ● *Entrance: £1.00, OAP 50p, children under 12 free* ● *Parking* ● *Teas and picnic area* ● *Toilet facilities* ● *Partly suitable for wheelchairs* ● *Dogs on lead* ● *Plants for sale* ● ***Grade IV***

The gardens at East Bergholt are rather wild and informal but beautiful, with terraced, semi-formal areas developed by the family since 1912, full of old-fashioned roses. Snowdrops, daffodils, bluebells and many wild flowers lead to woodland where damage by the 1987 gales is still being cleared. Walking is quite an adventure but the paths and rides lead the visitor to discover over 350 varieties of trees and shrubs grown in a natural setting teeming with wildlife.

EUSTON HALL 5
Euston, Thetford, Suffolk. Tel: (0842) 766366
The Duke and Duchess of Grafton

3m S of Thetford on A1088 ● *Open 7th June – 27th Sept, Thur, 2.30 – 5.30 p.m., Suns, 24th June and 2nd Sept, 2.30 – 5.30 p.m.* ● *Best season: June and July* ● *Entrance: £2.00, OAP £1.60, children 50p, parties of 12 or more £1.50* ● *Parking* ● *Refreshments* ● *Toilet facilities* ● *Suitable for wheelchairs* ● *Plants for sale* ● *Shop* ● *House open* ● **Grade II**

Fronted by terraces, the Hall stands among extensive lawns and parkland along a winding river, the work of William Kent in the 1740s, (followed by 'Capability' Brown) as is the splendid domed temple isolated on an eminence to the east, and also the pretty garden house in the formal garden by the house, developed by the present Duke. The pleasure grounds laid out in the seventeenth century by John Evelyn have grown into a forest of yew but straight rides trace out the original formal layout. Also from this period are the stone gate piers which, together with the remnants of a great avenue, mark the original approach to the house. A small lake reflects the house across the park, and there are many fine specimen trees and a wealth of shrub roses.

HAUGHLEY PARK 6
Nr Stowmarket, Suffolk. Tel: (0359) 40205
Mr A.J. Williams

4m NW of Stowmarket, signposted Haughley Park off A45 ● *Open May – Sept, Tues, 3.00 – 6.00 p.m.* ● *Entrance: £1.50, children 50p* ● *Parking. Coaches by appointment* ● *Picnics in grounds* ● *Toilet facilities inc. disabled* ● *Suitable for wheelchairs* ● *Dogs on lead* ● *House open* ● **Grade II**

A hundred acres of rolling parkland edged by 50 more acres of woodland surround the seventeenth-century Jacobean mansion. Unexpected secret gardens edged by clipped hedges or flint and brick walls hide their immaculate flower beds, climbers and flowering shrubs; each garden has its own character. The main lawn is surrounded by herbaceous borders, with, at the end, a splendid lime avenue drawing the eye across many miles of open countryside. Rhododendrons, azaleas and camellias grow on soil which is, unexpectedly for Suffolk, lime-free. The trees include a splendid *Davidia involucrata*, a 40 foot-wide magnolia and a flourishing oak, over 30 foot in girth, reputed to be 1000 years old. Beyond is the walled kitchen garden, the greenhouses and the shrubbery. In spring the broad rides and walks through the ancient woodland reveal not only the newly planted trees, specimen rhododendrons and other ornamental shrubs but 10 acres of bluebells and, more remarkably, two acres of lilies-of-the-valley.

HELMINGHAM HALL 7
Stowmarket, Suffolk.
Tel: (047339) 217/363 (Contact Mrs McGregor)
Lord Tollemache

9m NE of Ipswich on B1077. 6m E of A45 on B1078 then signposted ● *Open May – Oct, Sun, 2.00 – 6.00 p.m.* ● *Entrance: £1.50, OAP and children reduced charge* ● *Parking* ● *Teas in coach house, picnic facilities* ● *Toilet facilities* ● *Suitable for wheelchairs* ● *Dogs on lead* ● *Plants for sale* ● *Gift shop. Safari rides to see deer, Highland cattle and Soay sheep* ● ***Grade I***

The double-moated Tudor mansion house of great splendour and charm, built of warm red brick, stands in a 400-acre deer park. A nineteenth-century parterre, edged with a magnificent spring border, leads to the Elizabethan kitchen garden which is surrounded by the Saxon moat with banks covered in daffodils. Within the walls the kitchen garden has been transformed into an enchanting garden most subtly planted; the meticulously maintained herbaceous borders and old-fashioned roses surround beds of vegetables separated by arched tunnels of sweet peas and runner beans. Beyond is a meadow garden with, leading from it, a yew walk with philadelphus and shade-loving plants. On the other side of the Hall is a newly created garden dating from 1982. Designed by Lady Salisbury and planted by the Tollemaches, it is an historical knot garden and herb garden, with a magnificent collection of shrub roses underplanted with campanulas and geraniums, framed by a yew hedge. All the plants are chosen to be contemporary with the house.

ICKWORTH 8
The Rotunda, Horringer, Bury St Edmunds, Suffolk.
Tel: (028488) 270/288
The National Trust

3m SW of Bury St Edmunds, W of A143 ● *Open 31st March – April, Sat, Sun and Bank Holiday Mon, 1.30 – 5.30 p.m. May – Sept, daily except Mon, 1.30 – 5.30 p.m. Oct, Sat and Sun, 1.30 – 5.30 p.m. Park all year, daily, dawn – dusk* ● *Entrance: £1.00 (house and garden £3.50)* ● *Parking inc. disabled near house* ● *Refreshments: restaurant in house when open* ● *Toilet facilities in house* ● *Suitable for wheelchairs but paths are gravel* ● *Shop* ● *House open* ● ***Grade II***

Until recently the gardens at Ickworth were disappointing but over the last few years there have been some exciting changes. Research has shown that the earliest plantings appear to have been an unusual attempt to re-create a realistic Italian landscape to complement the emphatically Italian building. Much of what the visitor sees today is the recent restoration of this theme. Cypress and other sharp Mediterranean trees punctuate secret gardens surrounded by newly planted hedges and the main path to the south terrace is bordered with the evergreen shrub phillyrea, which will be clipped to window height. The south garden is further enclosed by a fine terrace which has a wonderful view of the garden and surrounding parkland. The north gardens, to the front of the house as you drive up, were largely planted in the 1870s and have now been considerably re-planted following general neglect and the 1987 gales. Although many of the great trees still remain, there has been an impressive planting of cedars to restore a unique feature – the cedar woodland as well as a small arboretum. The north gardens are at their best in the spring months with lawns of spring bulbs and wild flowers.

KENTWELL 9
Long Melford, Suffolk. Tel: (0787) 310207
Mr P. Phillips

On A134 just N of the green in Long Melford ● *Open April – mid-June, Bank Holiday weekends and Sun, mid-July – Sept, daily except Mon and Tues, 1.00 – 5.30 p.m. (11.00 a.m. – 5.30 p.m. on Bank Holiday weekends)* ● *Entrance: £1.75, OAP £1.45, children £1.15 (House, gardens and farm £2.75, OAP £2.40, children £1.60)* ● *Parking* ● *Refreshments: light lunches and teas. Picnics in avenue only* ● *House open* ● *Grade II*

The gardens at Kentwell have evolved over the centuries, and part of the pleasure of a visit is to see the works currently being undertaken. The garden is in transition, the walled garden retaining its seventeenth-century design but now being laid out as a pleasure garden. The walls are lined with espaliered apple and pear trees of which over 40 varieties have so far been identified. A formal herb garden is being created and so far over 160 different varieties of herbs have been planted; curiously the paths between them have yet to be built. Much of the work in the garden is being built on the foundations of the 1920s and 30s but concentrating on lawns, allées and avenues which take full advantage of Kentwell's lovely situation. The overall impression is of peace and tranquillity created by several moats, the ancient yews and cedars and mellow red brick.

MAGNOLIA HOUSE 10
Yoxford, Suffolk. Tel: (072877) 321
Mr M. Rumary

4m N of Saxmundham on A12, turn W on to A120 ● *Open 17th June, 2.30 – 6.00 p.m.* ● *Best season: spring and summer* ● *Entrance: £1.00* ● *Grade III*

A walled garden of only one-third of an acre but seeming larger with its division by hedges, walls and arches into a series of smaller enclosures. There is a central lawn at one side of which grows an ancient mulberry tree. In a secluded corner is a raised pool of Moorish inspiration, rich with lilies and exotic fish. Tubs of oleanders, agaves and other tender plants add to the Mediterranean feel of this area. The whole garden is filled with a wealth of fine herbaceous plants. There are many flowering trees and shrubs, including a variety of magnolias.

MELFORD HALL 11
Long Melford, Sudbury, Suffolk. Tel: (0787) 880286
The National Trust. Sir Richard Hyde Parker Bt

E side of A134, 14m S of Bury St Edmunds, 3m N of Sudbury ● *Open Easter or beginning April, weekends only and Bank Holiday Mons. Closed Good Friday. May – Sept, Wed, Thurs, Sat, Sun, Bank Holiday Mon, 2.00 – 6.00 p.m. Oct, Sat and Sun, 2.00 – 5.00 p.m. Pre-booked parties Wed and Thurs. Last admission 5.00 p.m.* ● *Entrance: £2.00, children £1.00* ● *Parking* ● *Refreshments in Long Melford, picnics in car park* ● *Toilet facilities by main entrance* ● *Mostly suitable for wheelchairs, one wheelchair provided. Disabled driven to Hall* ● *House open with special Beatrix Potter exhibition* ● ***Grade II***

This magnificent sixteenth-century Hall of mellow red brick is set in a park and formal gardens. A plan by Samuel Pierse of 1613 shows that the park was separated from the Hall by a walled enclosure outside which was the moat. Part of this is now the sunken garden. The avenue in front of the house is currently being replanted with oak grown from acorns taken from the existing trees. The octagonal brick pavilion, a rare and beautiful example of Tudor architecture, on the north side of the park overlooks the village green and the herbaceous borders inside the garden which are being restored to their original Victorian and Edwardian design and planting. Outside the pavilion are clipped box hedges and a bowling green terrace which lead past dense shrubbery. The garden has many good specimen trees including the rare Oriental tree *Xanthoceras sorbifolium*. Great domes of box punctuate the lawns and an interesting detail is the arrangement of yew hedges and golden yew to the north of the house. Outside the walls are topiary figures. Round the pond and fountain are beds originally planted with herbs in 1937 and now being gradually improved.

NETHERFIELD HERBS 12
37 Nether Street, Rougham, Nr Bury St Edmunds, Suffolk.
Tel: (0359) 70452
Mr L. Bremuess

Extremely difficult to find. 4m SE of Bury St Edmunds between the A45 and the A134. Aim for Rougham Green and ask for directions ● *Open daily, 10.30 a.m. – 5.30 p.m.* ● *Entrance: free* ● *Parking. No coaches* ● *Plants for sale* ● ***Grade IV***

Twisting lanes through beautiful unspoilt countryside eventually bring the visitor to a small, early cottage, charmingly restored, buried in a garden full of specialist herbs. Box hedges outline the beds in which culinary, medicinal, cosmetic, aromatic and decorative herbs and perennials grow in exotic confusion. Over 100 varieties of herb plants are for sale – as well as books on how to use and grow them; herb pillows, sachets and pot pourri, essential oils and herbal teas.

NORTH COVE HALL 13
North Cove, Beccles, Suffolk. Tel: (050276) 631
Mr and Mrs B. Blower

3½m E of Beccles, 50 yards off A146 Lowestoft road ● Open 1st Sun in July, 2.30 – 6.00 p.m. ● Best season: summer ● Entrance: £1.00, OAP 70p, children free ● Parking ● Refreshments ● Toilet facilities ● Suitable for wheelchairs ● Dogs on lead ● Plants for sale ● Grade III

Climbing roses adorn the eighteenth-century house which is set in lawns with parkland beyond. Belts of trees and shrubs, including shrub roses, hide a large deep pool with steeply-sloping grassy banks. There are many conifers here, ranging from a border of dwarf forms to ancient yews and cedars. Beyond the pool are herbaceous borders and kitchen garden, backed by high brick walls. A woodland walk runs outside the walls – a mature davidia is among the trees to be seen here.

NORTON BIRD GARDENS 14
Norton, Bury St Edmunds, Suffolk. Tel: (0359) 30957
Mr and Mrs D.W.G. Frost

5m E of Bury St Edmunds. Signposted off A45 and A143 and close to A1089 ● Open daily, 11.00 a.m. – 6.00 p.m. or dusk in winter ● Entrance: £2.25, OAP £1.75, children £1.00, under 5 free. Reduction for parties of 20 or more. ● Refreshments. Picnics allowed ● Toilet facilities inc. disabled ● Suitable for wheelchairs ● Shop ● Grade IV

Among beds of roses and perennials, ornamental trees and shrubs wander peacocks and other exotic birds. Huge aviaries are planted with more shrubs and even small trees, giving a special charm to the wonderful collection of over 100 species of tropical and European birds. Black swans and many different kinds of ornamental duck swim in the ponds, flamingos adding a very exotic touch. The tropical house has not only sugar birds, tanagers, hummingbirds and many other species, but tropical plants which help create a familiar atmosphere for the birds to breed and raise their young. The charm of the bird garden lies not only in its many exotic birds, lovingly cared for, but in the wonderful collection of more familiar owls, bantams, pheasants – and even guinea pigs, who rush round their own garden plot and in and out of an amazing Wendy house.

PARADISE CENTRE   15
Lamarsh Bures, Suffolk.   Tel: (078729) 449
Hedy and Cees Stapel-Jack

Through village of Lamarsh, lane opposite white Georgian house, on right up
lane ● *Open Bank Holidays, Sat and Sun or by appointment, 10.00 a.m. –*
5.00 p.m. ● *Entrance: free* ● *Parking* ● *Refreshments and picnic area*
● *Toilet facilities* ● *Plants for sale* ● *A paddock with unusual pets will amuse*
the children ● *Grade IV*

The Paradise Centre is a nursery specialising in unusual plants and bulbs,
especially those which are shade-loving, naturalizing in a sloping five-acre
garden, attractively laid out amongst the trees and hills of the lovely Stour
Valley. In autumn the garden is carpeted with autumn crocus, including the
double variety and sweeps of cyclamen leading down to three ponds full of
golden orfe and koi carp. The banks are edged with bog plants and giant
gunnera. Children will particularly enjoy the many ornamental duck, the
African pygmy goats and other wildlife.

THE ROOKERY   16
Eyke, Woodbridge, Suffolk.   Tel: (0294) 460226
Captain and Mrs R. Sheepshanks

5m E of Woodbridge. Turn N off B1084 Woodbridge – Orford road when sign
says Rendlesham 2 ● *Open by appointment and charity days, 2.00 – 6.00 p.m.*
● *Entrance: £1.00, OAP and children 50p* ● *Parking* ● *Refreshments on*
charity days ● *Suitable for wheelchairs* ● *Plants for sale on charity days*
● *Grade IV*

The 1987 gale which devastated so many fine gardens had occasionally the
unexpected advantage of opening up large areas which were subsequently, as
at the Rookery, planted as an arboretum with many rare specimen trees.
Captain and Mrs Sheepshanks have designed a garden which is landscaped on
differing levels, providing views and vistas; the visitors' curiosity is constantly
aroused as to what is round the next corner. A small pond, a bog garden,
shrubbery and evergreen walk, spring bulbs and large collection of cornus add
to the general interest. The old vegetable garden is now a flourishing vineyard
of one acre.

SHRUBLAND HALL   17
Coddenham, Suffolk.   Tel: (0473) 830404
Lord de Saumarez

4m N of Ipswich. Turn off A45 to B1113 at Claydon ● *Open 2nd Sun in July*
(if mid-month), 2.00 – 6.00 p.m. ● *Entrance: £1.50* ● *Parking*
● *Refreshments and picnic area in car park* ● *Toilet facilities* ● *Suitable for*
wheelchairs ● *Plants for sale* ● *Grade I*

The magnificence of Shrubland Hall is reflected in the Victorian gardens, laid out by Sir Charles Barry and later modified by William Robinson. They are amongst the most important of their type remaining in England. From the upper terrace outside the house one descends by a stunning cascade of a hundred steps and descending terraces to a garden of formal beds, fountain and eye-catching arch. Beyond is the wild garden which merges into the woods and is bordered by the park with its many fine trees, some reputed to be 800 years old. The gardens are punctuated by a series of enchanting follies ranging from a Swiss cottage to an alpine garden and magnificent conservatory. Lord and Lady de Saumarez have an extensive programme of restoration which includes the box maze and the old dell garden. Many trees blown down in the gales are being cleared and replaced.

SOMERLEYTON HALL 18
Nr Lowestoft, Suffolk.   Tel: (0502) 730224/730308
Lord and Lady Somerleyton

8m from Yarmouth, 6m NW of Lowestoft off B1074 signposted   ● Open Easter Sun – June 1st, Thurs, Sun and Bank Holidays, June – 1st Oct, Mon – Thurs, 2.00 – 5.30 p.m.   ● Entrance: £2.50, children £1.20   ● Parking   ● Teas and picnics   ● Toilet facilities inc. disabled   ● Suitable for wheelchairs   ● Gift shop   ● House open. On certain days the miniature railway runs   ● Grade I

An Elizabethan house extensively rebuilt in the mid-nineteenth century as a grand Italianate palace and the gardens splendidly reflect this magnificence with 12 acres of formal gardens, a beautiful walled garden, an aviary and a loggia surrounding a sunken garden displaying statues from the old, now demolished, winter garden. A major programme of replanting and restoration has included replacing many of the great trees in the park which were lost in the gales and cutting back the overgrown yews of the maze, originally laid out by William Nesfield in 1846. Not to be missed are the extraordinary peach cases and the ridge-and-furrow greenhouse designed by Sir Joseph Paxton, now containing peaches, grapes and a rich variety of other tender plants. In 1990 the Victorian kitchen garden will be open, and, hopefully by Easter, a museum of gardening.

SURREY

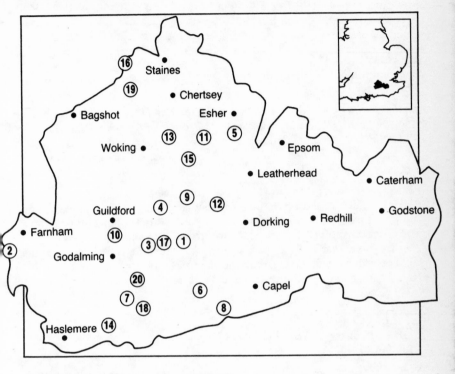

ALBURY PARK MANSION 1
Albury, Guildford, Surrey. Tel: (048641) 2964 (Administrator)
Country Houses Association Ltd

*Turn off A25 onto A248 (signposted Albury). Turn left just before village and
entrance is immediately left* ● *Open May – Sept, Wed and Thurs, 2.00 – 5.00
p.m.* ● *Best season: spring, early summer* ● *Entrance: £1.00* ● *Parking*
● *Toilet facilities* ● *House open (Pugin) also old Saxon church* ● **Grade IV**

The gardens remaining around the house are mainly under grass with gravel
walks, a ha-ha and stream providing the boundaries. A small formal rose
garden, azaleas and rhododendrons are to be seen and an herbaceous border.
However it is the trees that are most impressive – several oaks, a tulip tree and
a very old London plane amongst them. There is a tree chart of the estate in the
house. Although not open to visitors the azaleas and rhododendrons on the
estate are visible from the garden in spring and are a beautiful sight when in
bloom. The pleasure grounds which lie north of the Tillingbourne remain in
the ownership of the Trustees of the Albury Estate and are not open to the
public. This is unfortunate as the layout owes much to the assistance given by
John Evelyn to his neighbour, later 6th Duke of Norfolk, in or before the

1660s. These included the terraces, one in the style of a Roman bath, a tunnel, now walled in at one end, and a canal. In 1882 William Cobbett on one of his rural rides described them as 'without exception the prettiest in England; that is to say, that I ever saw in England.'

BIRDWORLD 2
Holt Pound, Nr Farnham, Surrey. Tel: (0420) 22140
The Harvey family

3m S of Farnham on A325 ● *Open daily except 25th Dec, summer 9.30 a.m. – 6.00 p.m., winter 9.30 a.m. – 3.30 p.m.* ● *Best season: Sept* ● *Entrance: £2.60, children £1.40* ● *Parking* ● *Refreshments: cafe for light lunches, coffee and teas* ● *Toilet facilities* ● *Suitable for wheelchairs. Wheelchairs available for hire* ● *Shop* ● *Grade III*

First-time visitors to Birdworld will be surprised by the extensive gardens which provide a backdrop to the bird sanctuary. With its wide flat paths and ample seating there is plenty of space to enjoy the variety of planting on show. The variety ensures that the gardens are attractive and colourful on all of the 364 days a year that they are open. Features include summer bedding, hanging baskets, wall baskets, rose garden, heather bed, ornamental grasses border, pergola and climbing roses, pond and white garden.

CHILWORTH MANOR 3
Chilworth, Surrey. Tel: (0483) 61414
Lady Heald

3½m SE of Guildford off A248. In the centre of Chilworth village on right up Blacksmiths Lane ● *Open 7th, 8th, 9th, 10th, 11th April, 12th, 13th, 14th, 15th, 16th May, 16th, 17th, 18th, 19th, 20th June, 21st, 22nd, 23rd, 24th, 25th July, 4th, 5th, 6th, 7th, 8th Aug, 2.00 – 6.00 p.m. (house and garden open on Sat & Sun, garden only open Mon, Tues, Wed)* ● *Best season: spring and June* ● *Entrance: £1.00 house, £1.00 garden, children free* ● *Parking* ● *Refreshments: teas in house on Sat and Sun. Picnicking from 12.30 p.m.* ● *Toilet facilities* ● *Partly suitable for wheelchairs* ● *Dogs on lead* ● *House open Sat and Sun* ● *Grade III*

A lovely old garden, particularly in spring and autumn, but something to see all the year round. Laid out in the seventeenth century, a walled garden was carved in three tiers out of the side of the hill early in the next century by Sarah, Duchess of Marlborough before she moved to Blenheim. The high walls, backed by wisteria, shelter many fine plants, a herbaceous border, lavender walks and shrubs. There is also a rock garden and a woodland area with magnolias, rhododendrons, azaleas, an oak tree reputed to be 400 years old and a Judas tree. Our visitor, there in spring, was impressed by the candelabra primulas along the stream and golden carp in the monastic stewponds. At weekends, the house is decorated by various Surrey flower clubs in turn.

SURREY

CLANDON PARK 4
West Clandon, Guildford, Surrey.   Tel: (0483) 222482
The National Trust

3m E of Guildford. Take A247 or A3 to Ripley and join A247 via B2215
• Open April - Oct, daily except Thurs and Fri (open Good Friday), 1.30 - 5.30
p.m. Bank Holiday Mon and preceeding Sun, 11.00 a.m. - 5.30 p.m. Last
admission 5.00 p.m.   • Entrance: £2.60. Parties by prior arrangement
• Parking. Disabled drivers only near front of house   • Refreshments: licensed
restaurant when house is open, teas for visitors to the house only. Picnic area
• Toilet facilities inc. disabled   • Suitable for wheelchairs   • Dogs on lead in
picnic area and car park only   • Shop   • House open   • Grade III

Built by a Venetian architect in the early 1730s for the 2nd Lord Onslow,
whose family still owns the park, although the house and seven-acre garden are
owned by the Trust. It is a pleasant garden to visit and look around. An
interesting feature is the Maori meeting house, known as Hinemihi, brought
from New Zealand by Lord Onslow, which is said to be one of the oldest in
existence. The garden is on a hillside and gives a fine view of the lake which is
in the private part of the park.

CLAREMONT LANDSCAPE GARDEN 5
Portsmouth Road, Esher, Surrey.   Tel: (0372) 67806
The National Trust

E of A307, S of Esher just out of the town   • Open all year, daily, April - Oct,
9.00 a.m. - 7.00 p.m. (11th - 14th July garden closes 4.00 p.m.), Nov - March,
9.00 a.m. - 5.00 p.m. or sunset if earlier. Last admission ½ hour before closing.
Closed 25th Dec, 1st Jan and 14th July   • Entrance: Mon - Sat £1.20, Sun
and Bank Holiday Mon £1.70. No reduction for parties   • Parking
• Refreshments in tea room with hot lunch menu, March, Sat and Sun, April -
Oct, daily   • Toilet facilities   • Partly suitable for wheelchairs   • Dogs on lead
• Shop   • Grade II

The *Oxford Companion* describes this as one of the most significant historic
landscapes in the country. The 50 acres being restored by the Trust is only part
of the original estate which was broken up in 1922 and part became a school.
The great landscape designers of the eighteenth century each adapted it in
turn for the owner, the immensely wealthy man who eventually became Duke
of Newcastle. First he retained Vanburgh, then Bridgeman, then Kent. Later,
when Clive of India purchased the estate he brought in 'Capability' Brown
who also designed the house, now the school and, in typical form, diverted the
London–Portsmouth road to improve the viewpoints, the most striking of
which is the grass amphitheatre. In the nineteenth century it was a favourite
retreat of Queen Victoria and her younger son. A useful leaflet describes the
various contributions to the park, which will appeal to everyone by its sensitive
reconstruction of the eighteenth-century English style, even if it has nothing
specific to offer the plantsperson, except perhaps the magnolia walk.

355

COVERWOOD LAKES AND GARDEN 6
Peaslake Road, Ewhurst, Surrey. Tel: (0306) 731103
Mr and Mrs C.G. Metson

7m SW of Dorking. Off A25 ½m S of Peaslake ● *Open 7th, 13th, 20th, 27th, 30th May, 3rd, 10th June, 2.00 - 6.30 p.m.* ● *Best season: May and June* ● *Entrance: £1.00, £1.50 garden and farm, children 50p. Reductions for large parties by prior arrangement* ● *Parking* ● *Home-made teas* ● *Toilet facilities* ● *Suitable for wheelchairs* ● *Plants for sale* ● *Grade IV*

Despite obstacles such as the 1987 gales which brought down 3000 of their trees, a poor sandy soil and discouragements like voracious Surrey deer and rabbits which munch their way through any new plantings, the Metsons with the help of one full-time gardener, have succeeded in maintaining and improving their fine garden. Plans have been formulated for a new arboretum to be planted in 1990. In all, there are four lakes, 12 acres of garden devoted mainly to rhododendrons and azaleas, a stream and bog garden. The original gardens were designed in 1910 by the owner of 'Stephens' Ink'.

FEATHERCOMBE GARDENS 7
Feathercombe, Hambledon, Nr Godalming, Surrey.
Tel: (048632) 257
Miss Parker

5m S of Godalming, E of A283 between Hydestile and Hambledon ● *Open 6th, 7th, 27th, 28th May, 2.00 - 6.00 p.m.* ● *Entrance: £1.00, children 10p* ● *Parking* ● *Picnic area available* ● *Toilet facilities* ● *Partly suitable for wheelchairs* ● *Dogs on lead* ● *Plants for sale* ● *Grade IV*

Although mainly worth visiting for the good display of rhododendrons and azaleas, there are fine views across three counties framed by larches and some tree heaths which are now 20 to 30 feet high. Now that the garden is maintained solely by the family, some of the features in the original design of 1910 by Eric and Ruth Parker have had to be changed through lack of labour which is a great pity. Ruth Parker was one of Leonard Messel's daughters and there must have been strong connections between her garden at Feathercombe and his at Nymans (see page 381).

HANNAH PESCHAR GALLERY GARDEN 8
Black and White Cottage, Standon Lane, Ockley, Surrey.
Tel: (030679) 269
Hannah Peschar

1m SW of Ockley. Signposted from Cat Hill Lane onwards as Black and White Cottage ● *Open May - 24th Dec, Fri, Sat, 11.00 a.m. - 6.00 p.m., Sun, 2.00 - 5.00 p.m. Other days (except Mon) by private appointment.* ● *Entrance: £2.00, children £1.00. Guided tours for parties £5.00 per person inc. tea* ● *Parking*

● *Teas for parties by arrangement* ● *Toilet facilities* ● *Suitable for wheelchairs (but not gallery)* ● *Sculpture gallery open* ● **Grade IV**

This delightful Surrey woodland garden is of primary interest to those who enjoy contemporary outdoor sculpture, as Mrs Peschar represents a wide range of artists whose work is displayed in natural settings, including water. The exhibits change, of course, as they are sold, and anyone planning to place objects of art outdoors will find a study of the sculptures here a source of inspiration. Note too the way art contributes to function as in the bridge made by landscape designer Anthony Paul.

HATCHLANDS 9
East Clandon, Guildford, Surrey. Tel: (0483) 222787
The National Trust

E of East Clandon, N of A246 ● *Open April – 14th Oct, Tues, Wed, Thurs, Sun and Bank Holiday Mon, also Sat in Aug, 2.00 – 6.00 p.m. Last admission 5.30 p.m. Closed Good Friday* ● *Best season: spring and summer* ● *Entrance: £2.00, parties £1.50 per person (house and garden)* ● *Parking. Disabled visitors may be set down at house* ● *Home-made teas* ● *Toilet facilities* ● *Suitable for wheelchairs* ● *House open* ● **Grade III**

The main interest is in the Gertrude Jekyll garden which is being returned to its original dimensions and being replanted to her original plans (1914 revision). It will be two to three years before completion as plants are coming from abroad and some have to be propagated. There is a wild meadow featuring cowslips and many wild flowers. It is never cut until July. Mature London plane and cedar trees. Further improvements will include regrading to Humphrey Repton's original design.

LOSELEY PARK 10
Nr Guildford, Surrey. Tel: (0483) 66090
Mr and Mrs J. More-Molyneux

2m SE of Guildford off B3000 ● *Open Wed, Thurs, Fri, Sat from 2nd Bank Holiday in May – last Sat in Sept, 2.00 – 5.00 p.m.* ● *Entrance: free* ● *Parking* ● *Refreshments: wholefood restaurant offering organic lunches and teas* ● *Toilet facilities* ● *Shop selling own organic produce* ● *House open* ● **Grade IV**

Although Loseley has a fine reputation, this is due more to its overall appeal as a destination for a family outing than for the excellence of the garden. Seen in conjunction with the Elizabethan house, farm tours, trailer rides and delicious refreshments, the garden is an added bonus offering peace and tranquillity. Seen in isolation, the garden lacks interest but were the owners to re-instate the planting designs of Gertrude Jekyll, there would surely be an increase in the number of visits by garden enthusiasts.

PAINSHILL PARK 11
Portsmouth Road, Cobham, Surrey. Tel: (0932) 68113
Elmbridge Borough Council on lease to Painshill Park Trust

1m W of Cobham on A245. Entrance on right, 200 yards E of A3/A245
roundabout ● Open Sun, 2.00 – 6.00 p.m. Last admission 5.00 p.m. Also by
appointment ● Entrance: £2.00, OAP and children £1.50 ● Limited
parking ● Teas and light refreshments ● Toilet facilities inc. disabled
● Suitable for wheelchairs except for grotto island ● Shop in Visitor Centre
● Grade II

Painshill was developed by Charles Hamilton (1704 – 86) a great English
landscape designer who acquired the lease in 1738 and got severely into debt
by his ambitious plans. He should be better known and is described by the
Oxford Companion as 'a brilliant and subtle designer (who) could create
illusion and vary scene and mood. His work strikes a delicate balance between
art and nature, between the artist and the plantsman'. His work was nearly lost
to posterity but after 30 years of neglect and delay it was rescued at the
eleventh hour when it was bought by Elmbridge Borough Council and an
independent Trust was established in 1981. There are now 158 acres of which
14 are taken up by the lake. A great deal of work has already been done, and
Charles Hamilton's garden is coming to life again. There are about 100 trees
surviving at Painshill that were planted between 1738 – 1773 including the
great cedar of Lebanon, the largest in England (120 x 32 feet) and the pencil
cedar (*Juniperus virginiana*) approx 60 x 6½ feet – the tallest in England with
a mountain ash growing from the trunk seven feet from the ground. Another
unusual sight is a beech and London plane with branches apparently fused
together. Features include Gothic temple, water wheel, grotto island and
ruined abbey.

POLESDEN LACEY 12
Great Bookham, Nr Dorking, Surrey. Tel: (0372) 53401
The National Trust

3m W of Dorking off A246 ● Open all year, 11.00 a.m. – sunset ● Entrance:
April – Oct, £1.50, Nov – March, £1.20. Reduced rates for parties, Wed – Fri
by appointment ● Parking 150 yards away ● Refreshments: lunches, teas, etc.
in licensed restaurant ● Toilet facilities ● Partly suitable for wheelchairs
● Dogs on lead ● Shop ● House open special times and £2.00 extra ● Grade I

This 17-acre garden has grown up over several centuries. Richard Brinsley
Sheridan the dramatist who owned the house for over 20 years lengthened the
Long Walk before he died here in 1816. The present house was built a few
years later by Cubitt in the Greek classical manner for an owner who made
extensive alterations and planted over 20,000 trees. The garden was further
developed early this century and given to the Trust in 1944. The walled rose
garden is in four square areas divided by paths and covered by wooden
pergolas and the area is dominated by a well-head covered by an ancient

Chinese wisteria. There are small gardens of peonies, bearded irises, beds of different kinds of lavender. A winter garden overshadowed by four Iron trees. A long border of herbaceous plants is a colourful sight in summer. There is also a sunken garden. A fully detailed garden guide is available giving numbered lists of plants, shrubs and flowers.

PYRFORD COURT   13
Pyrford Common Road, Pyrford, Woking, Surrey.
Tel: (0483) 765880
Mr and Mrs C. Laikin

2m W of Woking. M25 Junction 10. B367 junction with Upshott Lane ● Open by appointment and 27th May, 3rd June, 2.00 – 6.30 p.m., 21st Oct, 12 noon – 4.00 p.m. ● Entrance: £1.25, children 50p ● Parking ● Teas ● Toilet facilities ● Suitable for wheelchairs ● Dogs on lead ● Grade III

Transformed at the turn of the century by Lord and Lady Iveagh with advice from Gertrude Jekyll, this varied garden covers about 20 acres, both formal and woodland. The wild garden to the South is a blaze of colour in the autumn, especially the Japanese maples. The north lawn of around four acres is bordered by a high brick wall with a pillared loggia and features several pear-shaped Irish yews. Noticeable on the wall is a loquat *Eriobotrya japonica*. The wisterias on the pergola walk are from Japanese raised seedlings imported about 70 years ago from Yokohama and are remarkable for their extremely long flower panicles. The ornamental grape *Vitis coignetiae* is a fine sight at the end of the pergola walk, brilliant when in autumn colours. By the stream is a rare flowering camellia (*C* x *williamsii* 'Hiracthlyn').

RAMSTER   14
Chiddingfold, Surrey.   Tel: (0428) 4422
Mr and Mrs P. Gunn

1½m S of Chiddingfold on A283 ● Open 21st April – 10th June, 2.00 – 6.00 p.m. and parties by appointment ● Best season: spring ● Entrance: £1.30, children free ● Parking ● Refreshments: teas on Sat, Sun and Bank Holiday Mon. Lunches for pre-booked coach parties ● Toilet facilities ● Suitable for wheelchairs ● Dogs on lead ● Plants for sale ● Grade III

Laid out in 1904 by Gauntlett Nurseries of Chiddingfold and owned by the same family for close to 70 years, this was one of the original gardens to open for the National Garden Scheme in 1927. Twenty acres of peaceful woodland with views of lakes and hillsides filled with colour and interest. Planting includes Californian redwoods, cedars, firs, camellias, rhododendrons and azaleas plus the rarer *Styrax obassia*, *Tetracentron sinense*, and *Kalopanax pictus*. A camellia garden, magnolia bed and widespread bluebells and daffodils ensure flowers are on view throughout the spring. Especially notable is an avenue of *Acer palmatum* 'Dissectum'.

ROYAL HORTICULTURAL SOCIETY'S GARDEN 15
Wisley, Woking, Surrey. Tel: (0483) 224234
Royal Horticultural Society

4m from Cobham, 1m from Ripley, W of London on A3 and M25 ● *Open
daily, 10.00 a.m. - 7.00 p.m. (Sun for RHS members only)* ● *Entrance: by
membership or £2.50, children 6 - 14 £1.00, under 6 free* ● *Parking*
● *Refreshments: licensed restaurant and self service cafeteria* ● *Toilet facilities
inc. disabled* ● *Suitable for wheelchairs* ● *Plants for sale* ● *Shop* ● *Grade I*

George Fox Wilson, a former treasurer of the RHS established a famous
woodland garden here *c.* 1880. After his death it was purchased by Sir Thomas
Hanbury (owner of the famous garden in Italy) and together with surrounding land became the site of the fourth RHS garden. The wild and woodland
areas remain and elsewhere the somewhat difficult growing conditions have
been overcome by planting a very wide range of ornamental plants.
Glasshouses were added in 1905, a pinetum in 1907 and a large rock garden
in 1911. There are several small, specialised gardens aimed at providing ideas
for owners of restricted areas – wild, rose, rock, heather and peat gardens for
example. The chief purpose of Wisley is instruction and the highly competent
staff will help visitors with their problems. The garden is also used for trials of
fruit and flowers and there is a model vegetable garden. In the 1960s the
designers Sir Geoffrey Jellicoe and Lanning Roper built a formal garden with
canals and walled area. Wisley was badly hit by the 1987 gales but it is hoped
that the pinetum will be fully reopened by 1990.

THE SAVILL GARDEN 16
Wick Lane, Englefield Green, Surrey. Tel: (0753) 860222
(and Windsor Great Park, Berkshire)
Administered by the Crown Estate Commissioners

*5m from Windsor. From A30, turn into Wick Road and follow signs, or follow
signs from Englefield Green* ● *Open daily, 10.00 a.m. - 6.00 p.m. (7.00 p.m.
at weekends) or sunset. Closed 25th - 28th Dec* ● *Entrance: £1.80, OAP
£1.80, accompanied children under 16 free. Special rates for parties* ● *Parking*
● *Refreshments: licensed self-service restaurant open Feb/mid-Dec (0784) 32326.
Picnics allowed in car park area* ● *Toilet facilities inc. disabled* ● *Suitable for
wheelchairs* ● *Plants for sale* ● *Shop* ● *Grade I*

Covering some 35 acres of woodland it contains a fine range of rhododendrons, camellias, magnolias, hydrangeas and a great variety of other trees and
shrubs producing a wealth of colour throughout the seasons, particularly in
spring and summer – meconopsis and primulas in June especially. A more
formal area is devoted to modern roses, herbaceous borders, a range of alpines
and a very interesting and attractive dry garden. Windsor Castle gardens
(admission free, 10.00 a.m. - 7.15 p.m., 4.15 p.m. in winter) retain the formal
gardens designed by W.J. Aiton for George IV.

VALE END 17
Albury, Surrey. Tel: (048641) 2594
Mr and Mrs J. Foulsham

4½m SE of Guildford. From Albury take A248 W for ½m • *Open 1st July and by appointment 2.00 - 6.00 p.m.* • *Best season: summer/autumn* • *Entrance: £1.00, children free* • *Limited parking* • *Refreshments* • *Toilet facilities* • *Dogs on lead* • *Plants for sale if available* • ***Grade IV***

A one-acre walled cottage garden surrounding an eighteenth- to twentieth-century house. Fine views from terrace across sloping lawns to mill pond and woodlands with a wide variety of herbaceous plants and roses, ornamental pond. This garden is entirely maintained by its owners and as well as being in a beautiful setting will interest plantsmen because on a light, well-watered soil, the owners have interspersed old favourites with 'little gems' such as diascia. There is a fine magnolia with a spread of over 40 feet and a small fruit and vegetable garden.

VANN 18
Hambledon, Surrey. Tel: (042879) 3413
Mr and Mrs M.B. Caröe

6m S of Godalming, E of A283 at Chiddingfold • *Open 16th April, 2.00 - 7.00 p.m., 17th - 21st April, 10.00 a.m. - 6.00 p.m., 7th May, 2.00 - 7.00 p.m., 8th - 12th May, 10.00 a.m. - 6.00 p.m., 17th June, 2.00 - 7.00 p.m., 18th - 23rd June, 10.00 a.m. - 6.00 p.m. and any time by appointment* • *Best season: spring* • *Entrance: £1.20, children 30p* • *Parking* • *Refreshments: teas in barn on Sun/Bank Holiday Mon. Lunches bookable for parties by arrangement* • *Limited toilet facilities* • *Limited access for wheelchairs* • *Dogs on lead* • *Plants for sale* • ***Grade III***

The six different areas within this garden will provide some interest for most types of gardener. From the student of garden design viewing the water garden still containing plants selected by Gertrude Jekyll, to the admirer of the formal garden complete with clipped yews and regular brick paths, there is something for everyone. The most disappointing aspect of this garden is the Yew Walk. Deer are apparently responsible for eating the shrubs and as the garden is maintained by the family with 10 hours' assistance per week, it is understandable that some things have to be neglected.

VIRGINIA WATER LAKE 19
London Road, Surrey. Tel: (0753) 853747
Crown Estate, Great Park, Windsor

Off A30, adjacent to junction with A329 • *Open all year* • *Entrance: free* • *Parking 60p* • *No refreshments, but picnics permitted* • *Toilet facilities* • *Suitable for wheelchairs* • *Dogs* • ***Grade III***

This was a grand eighteenth-century ornamental addition to Windsor Great Park by the Duke of Cumberland who became its ranger in 1746. It had dams, rockwork, a cascade and grotto. There was a fake 'Mandarin Yacht', a Chinese pavilion and a Gothic belvedere with a mighty single arch bridge spanning the water. Alas almost all have disappeared but the woodland and the lovely one and a half-mile lake, full of fish and wildfowl survive, and there is still a colonnade of pillars.

WINKWORTH ARBORETUM   20
Hascombe, Nr Godalming, Surrey.   Tel: (048632) 477
The National Trust

2m SE of Godalming, E of B2130 ● *Open all year, daily, dawn – dusk* ● *Best season: spring/autumn* ● *Entrance: free but donations appreciated* ● *Parking inc. disabled* ● *Refreshments: teashop open April – Oct, Tues – Sun, 2.00 – 6.00 p.m. (Sun, 12 noon – 6 p.m.) or dusk if earlier* ● *Toilet facilities* ● *Dogs* ● *Shop* ● ***Grade III***

The public footpath through Winkworth ensures access 365 days of the year, so it's a great place to take the family for a walk on Christmas Day or any other! The 60 plant families and 150 genera grown here provide variety and interest throughout the year. In the spring there are the azaleas, rhododendrons, cherries and maples and in the autumn sorbus, liquidambar, acers and *Cotinus coggygria*. Its hillside setting and two lakes give pleasing views from almost all of the site. Clearer labelling would help the enthusiast to identify the more unusual species. Contains the National whitebeam collection.

SURREY AND GREATER LONDON
We have included some gardens with Surrey postal addresses in the Greater London section for convenience. So before planning a day out in Surrey it is worthwhile consulting the Greater London section.

SUSSEX (East)

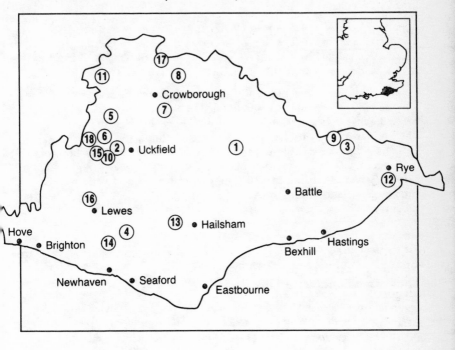

BATEMAN'S 1
Burwash, Etchingham, East Sussex. Tel: (0435) 882302
The National Trust

½m S of Burwash on A265 towards Lewes • *Open April – Oct, daily except Thurs and Fri but open Good Friday, 11.00 a.m. – 6.00 p.m. Last admission 5.00 p.m.* • *Entrance: £2.80, weekends, Good Friday and Bank Holidays £3.20. Pre-booked parties reduced rates. All prices inc. house and mill* • *Parking* • *Refreshments: light lunches, coffees, teas* • *Toilet facilities* • *Suitable for wheelchairs* • *Shop* • *House open and mill which grinds flour in season* • *Grade IV*

Kipling wrote one of the most-quoted poems about English gardening which is perhaps why Bateman's where he lived from 1902-36 is much visited. Not of great botanical interest, but it is well-kept and pleasant to sit in. Formal, with lawns, yew hedges, rose garden with pond, and wild garden, much of which was his doing, although the garden was laid out before he bought the house (built 1634).

BEECHES FARM   2
Buckham Hill, Nr Uckfield, East Sussex.   Tel: (0825) 2391
Mrs V. Thomas

1½m W of Uckfield on Isfield road off A2102 ● *Open all year, daily, 10.00 a.m. – 5.00 p.m. and for NGS* ● *Best season: autumn/winter* ● *Entrance: 50p, children 25p* ● *Parking* ● *Teas on NGS days* ● *Dogs on lead* ● *Plants for sale* ● *House open by appointment with seven days notice* ● *Grade IV*

One wall of this sixteenth-century tile-hung farmhouse is covered by a *Magnolia grandiflora* and it is surrounded by a dozen or more enormous and very attractive containers, once used for cooling the local smelted iron ore. The circular rose garden has mainly old French, musk and moss roses. There are beds of lilies near the house and various borders of annuals add colour to the lawned areas. There is a newly planted 'glade' and *Eucalyptus niphophila* and *dalrympleana* are settling in well. The garden has been cleverly planted for winter colour and is one of the few in Sussex open between October and February.

BRICKWALL   3
Northiam, East Sussex.   Tel: (0797) 223329
The Frewen Educational Trust

On B2088 Rye road ● *Open first Sat in April – last Sat in Sept, 2.00 – 5.00 p.m.* ● *Best season: July* ● *Entrance: £1.00, children under 10 free. Coach parties by arrangement* ● *Parking* ● *Suitable for wheelchairs* ● *Dogs on lead* ● *Shop with postcards and booklets* ● *House open* ● *Grade III*

Brickwall is an interesting example of a Stuart garden, and care has been taken to use the plants chosen by Jane Frewen when she was making and planting it between 1680–1720, such as day lilies, bergamot, *Lychnis chalcedonica*, Cheddar pinks and columbines. There are large lavender beds, a number of ancient mulberries, groups of clipped yew, and a superb pleached beech walk. A striking modern addition is the Chess Garden with green and golden yew chessmen in iron frames, set in squares of white and black pebbles. This garden is not far away from Great Dixter (see page 367) and a visit to both would make an excellent day out.

CHARLESTONE FARMHOUSE   4
Nr Firle, Lewes, East Sussex.   Tel: (0321) 83265
The Charleston Trust

6m E of Lewes on A27 ● *Open April – Oct, Wed, Thurs, Sat, Sun and Bank Holiday Mon, 2.00 – 6.00 p.m.* ● *Best season: spring and midsummer* ● *Entrance: £3.00, children £2.25 (house and garden)* ● *Parking 50p* ● *Refreshments* ● *Toilet facilities* ● *Partly suitable for wheelchairs* ● *Plants for sale* ● *Shop* ● *House open* ● *Grade II*

In terms of pure gardening this does not deserve a Grade II, but it is of national interest because it was created by leaders of the Bloomsbury movement. The walled garden has been meticulously restored through painstaking research and the memories of people who visited when Vanessa Bell and Duncan Grant lived at the farmhouse and those like Angelica Garnett and Quentin Bell, who spent their childhood there. It is a delightful example of a garden created during the 1920s by an idiosyncratic group of highly creative people, and might be called an artist's garden.

CHELWOOD VACHERY 5
Nutley, Nr Uckfield, East Sussex. Tel: (082571) 3404
BAT Industries

3m S of Forest Row on A22 ● *Open 20th May, 2.00 – 6.00 p.m. and by appointment for parties and small groups* ● *Best season: spring* ● *Entrance: £1.50, children 60p* ● *Parking* ● *Refreshments* ● *Toilet facilities* ● *Suitable for wheelchairs* ● *Dogs on lead* ● *Plants for sale* ● ***Grade II***

The house built in 1906 was bought by Mr Nettlefold in 1925 and bought by BAT as a conference centre in 1955. Nearly 130 acres of woodland and formal garden offer a wide variety of plantings and interest. Even the well-preserved tea room rewards careful inspection of its kingpost and mouldings. Over 280 varieties of heathers are to be found either in their own areas or as underplanting for acer, azalea or dwarf conifer collections. The rock garden is shingelled over polythene for practical purposes, and among the myriad plants are more than 20 varieties of gentians. A Zen garden by the wisteria walk is a simple yet dominant feature, as is the nearby grave of Mr Nettlefold's retriever. Ten varieties of magnolias mingle with rhododendrons. A substantial broad-leaved planting scheme is underway to replace the damage from the 1987 gales and wildlife conservation is much in mind, with bird and bat boxes and wild flowers. There are three large lakes, two smaller ones, bog gardens, and several small ponds and waterfalls. Amongst the variety of interesting species are *Stranvaesia davidiana* 'Palette', *Viburnum opulus* 'Fructuluteo', *Salix hyptilloides* 'Pink Tassel', *Populus* x *candicans* 'Aurora', *Magnolia* x *thompsoniana* (60 feet tall) and *Ceratostigma willmottianum*. The peacocks and guinea fowl roaming around, together with the careful, ample labelling, make this a garden for all to enjoy.

CLINTON LODGE 6
Fletching, Nr Uckfield, East Sussex. Tel: (0825) 722952
Mr and Mrs Cullum

4m W of Uckfield from A272. Turn N at Piltdown from Fletching, 1½m in main village street surrounded by a yew hedge ● *Open 16th/17th June, 2.00 – 6.00 p.m.* ● *Entrance: £1.00, children 40p* ● *Parking on street* ● *Refreshments* ● *Toilet facilities* ● *Suitable for wheelchairs* ● *Dogs on lead* ● *Grade II*

This Queen Anne house was built for the first Lord Sheffield's daughter who married Henry Clinton. The garden of about four acres of clay soil is basically divided into four areas by period. There is a seventeenth-century herb garden with well-tended camomile paths and turfed seats, a lawn and ha-ha at the rear of the house with views to distant woods, creating an eighteenth-century atmosphere, a white, yellow and blue Victorian herbaceous border with its 'hot' colours purposely absent, and a pre-Raphaelite alley of white roses, purple vines and lilies; the twentieth century is represented in the area surrounding the swimming pool. There are also walks of quince, vines and white cherry underplanted with white bluebells, and a rose garden of musk and English roses complete with fully-occupied dovecote. Pillars of ceanothus and roses cover the walls in early summer, and less formal areas of orchard and wild flowers complete a garden of outstanding imagination and charm.

COBBLERS 7
Mount Pleasant, Tollwood Road, Jarvis Brook, Crowborough, East Sussex. Tel: (0892) 655969
Martin and Barbara Furniss

On A26 at Crowborough Cross take B2100 to Crowborough Station. At the 2nd crossroads take Tollwood Road • Open 20th, 27th, 28th May, 10th, 17th June, 1st, 15th, 29th July, 5th, 12th Aug, 2.30 – 5.30 p.m. • Entrance: £1.00, children 50p • Parking • Teas • Toilet facilities • Suitable for wheelchairs but garden sloping • Plants for sale • Grade III

Martin Furniss, an architect, created the garden from old meadows over 20 years ago. He is fascinated by the architectural forms of plants, and this is reflected in inspired planting. Full of surprises and delights, an outstanding feature is the water garden. It is both a plantsman's and an artist's garden.

CROWN HOUSE 8
Eridge Green, Nr Tunbridge Wells, East Sussex. Tel: (0892) 864389
Major and Mrs L. Cave

3m SW of Tunbridge Wells. Take A26 Tunbridge Wells – Crowborough road. In Eridge take the Rotherfield turn S. House is first on the right • Open 14th/ 15th July, 2.00 – 6.00 p.m. • Entrance: 75p, children 30p • Parking on road • Teas • Toilet facilities • Suitable for wheelchairs • Plants for sale • Shop for home-made produce • Grade IV

This gently sloping one and a half-acre garden contains several different areas of interest. Dominating the side of the house is a colourful umbrella of old-fashioned musk roses, astilbes, golden flame spirea and catmint. At the front of the house the alpine garden is to be extended during winter 1989 and a further pond added. The rose garden is underplanted with cranesbill and is surrounded by a yew hedge and *Clematis montana* 'Rubens'. The heather bed, herb garden and herbaceous borders are all carefully tended, giving a great variety of colour and interest which extend to the aviary, containing budgerigars, cockatiels and green parrots.

GREAT DIXTER 9
Dixter Road, Northiam, East Sussex. Tel: (07974) 3160
The Lloyd family

½m N of Northiam. Turn off A28 at Northiam post office ● Open March – Oct, Tues – Sun ● Entrance: £1.50 (£2.25 house and garden), reduction for children ● Parking ● Refreshments ● Toilet facilities ● Suitable for wheelchairs (some steps) ● Plants for sale at nursery. Extensive choice of clematis ● Shop ● House open ● Grade I

Probably too well-known to need describing, Great Dixter was bought by Nathaniel Lloyd in 1910. The fifteenth-century house was restored by Lutyens. The sunken garden was designed and constructed by Nathaniel Lloyd. His son Christopher has continued his family's fine gardening tradition, striving to maintain the garden with a dwindling labour force. Composed of a series of gardens, these include fine topiary, a magnificent long mixed border, and enchanting rose garden, gardens where vegetables and flowers mingle, and throughout the complex of gardens are pockets of wild flowers. The spring at Great Dixter is famous for the huge drifts of naturalised bulbs. Truly a plantsman's garden, but a joy for anyone who enjoys gardening in the finest tradition.

KETCHES 10
Newick, Nr Uckfield, East Sussex. Tel: (082572) 2021
Mr David Manwaring Robertson

5m W of Uckfield on A272. Take Barcombe Road S out of Newick. House is on the right opposite the turning to Newick Church ● Open 27th May, 24th June, 2.00 – 6.00 p.m. ● Entrance: unavailable at time of going to press ● Parking on road or lower field if dry ● Teas ● Toilet facilities ● Suitable for wheelchairs ● Grade II

The three acres are mainly greensand with some clay patches, producing ideal growing conditions for the wide variety of plantings here. Roses, of which there must be more than 50 varieties, include 'Cerise Bouquet', 'Madame Isaac Pereire', 'Apricot Nectar', 'New Dawn' and 'Goldwings' and are often planted with *Geranium wallichianum* 'Buxton's Blue' or *Solanum crispum*. To the side of the house a wide lawn leads to a rougher grass area planted with spring bulbs, with views to newly planted American elm and distant woods. A 300-year-old oak and an aged Spanish chestnut dominate the various shrubbed areas, which include *Cotinus coggygria*, *Eleagnus* 'Dicksonii' and *Hydrangea villosa*. Among the other trees are *Catalpa orientalis*, *Malus tschonoskii* and *Arbutus andrachne*. The problems caused by the gales in 1987 are being overcome with philosphical optimism.

KIDBROOK PARK 11
Forest Row, East Sussex. Tel: (0342) 822275
Rudolph Steiner Trust

At Forest Row 1m W of A22 • *Open Aug, daily, 2.00 – 5.30 p.m.* • *Best season: summer* • *Entrance: £1.00, children 50p* • *Parking* • *Toilet facilities (not disabled)* • *Suitable for wheelchairs* • *Dogs on lead* • *Grade III*

A sandstone house built in 1725 now used as Michael Hall School. Its 125-acre park lies on the northern boundary of the Ashdown Forest. Work is in progress to restore the main elements of Repton's design, though this has been hampered by the loss of 1500 trees during the 1987 gales. 'Swallow' spring, cascades, stepping stones, a pond and a twentieth-century weir add interest, together with wild and bog gardens. The parkland is obviously a shadow of its former glory.

LAMB HOUSE 12
West Street, Rye, East Sussex.
The National Trust

In centre of Rye, in West Street, near the church • *Open April – Oct, Wed and Sat, 2.00 – 6.00 p.m. Last admission 5.30 p.m.* • *Entrance: £1.00 (house and garden) No reductions for children or parties* • *Parking difficult* • *House open. Home of Henry James, American novelist, 1898-1916. Later, the brothers Benson, now televised writers, lived there* • *Grade IV*

Americans are frequent visitors to this house where James wrote some of his best books and studied the English character including its passion for gardening. Although not of considerable botanic interest, this high-walled garden has great charm and it is surprising to find it so big – one acre in the middle of overcrowded Rye. It is well-maintained by the Trust's tenants who have done much in recent years. They have a good sense of design and colour – viz the wooden-painted furniture which is their own mixture.

MICHELHAM PRIORY 13
Upper Dicker, Hailsham, East Sussex. Tel: (0323) 844224
The Sussex Archaeological Society

10m N of Eastbourne off the A22 and A27. Signposted • *Open 25th March – Oct, daily, 11.00 a.m. – 4.00 p.m., Nov, Feb and March, Sun, 11.00 a.m. – 4.00 p.m.* • *Best season: spring/summer* • *Entrance: £2.50, OAP £2.30, children £1.50* • *Parking* • *Refreshments and picnic area* • *Toilet facilities inc. disabled* • *Suitable for wheelchairs* • *Dogs on lead in car park* • *Herbs and some herbaceous plants for sale* • *Shop* • *House and working watermill open* • *Grade III*

A major feature of the garden is the Physic Garden, a reconstruction of a monastic physic garden, based on that at ninth-century St Gall, which was regarded as the ideal. The 11 beds contain medicinal plants for specific complaints. Many of them are the herbs of the hedgerows. A serpentine moatside border has been planted and there are plans to extend it. The monastery stew ponds are also being planted up. A large herbaceous border, backed by a shrubbery, was designed and planted by local horticultural students. This was an Augustinian priory, founded in 1229.

MONK'S HOUSE   14
Rodmell, Lewes, East Sussex.
The National Trust

4m SE of Lewes off former A275 now C7. In Rodmell village follow signs to Church. Sign is 400 yards from the house • Open 24th March – April and Oct, Wed and Sat, 2.00 – 5.00 p.m., May – Sept, Wed and Sat, 2.00 – 6.00 p.m. Last admission ½ hour before closing • Entrance: £1.50. No reduction for children or parties • Parking further down narrow road • Toilet facilities • House open • Grade III

The cottage home of Virginia and Leonard Woolf from 1919 until his death in 1969. In autumn 1989 work commenced on redesigning the garden on the basis of the Woolf's notebooks and writings. Leonard Woolf had kept the village self-sufficient in vegetables, as well as showing them, and the original vegetable area is still thriving. There are two ponds, one in dewpond style. An orchard, underplanted with spring and autumn bulbs, contains a comprehensive collection of daffodils. These have suffered from over-cutting but are now reappearing and hopefully will soon be in full bloom. The 1¾-acre garden is a mixture of chalk and clay, nurturing a wide variety of species. Flint stone walls and yew hedges frame the more formal herbaceous areas, leading to a typical Sussex flint church at the bottom of the garden. Among the interesting specimen trees are *Salix hastata* 'Wehrhahnii', Chinese lantern (20 feet tall), *Magnolia liliflora*, walnut, mulberry, and *Catalpa bignonioides* (Indian Bean). Literary folk will want to compare and contrast this garden with the other Bloomsbury lot's house at Charlestone Farmhouse (see page 364).

NEWICK PARK   15
Newick, Nr Lewes, East Sussex.   Tel: (082572) 3633
Viscount Brentford

7m N of Lewes, 1m from A272. Also 7m SE of Haywards Heath, 1m from A275 • Open 15th March – Oct, 10.30 a.m. – 6.00 p.m. • Entrance: £1.00, OAP 75p, children 25p. Reductions for parties of 4 or more • Parking • Refreshments: teas, lunches by arrangement • Suitable for wheelchairs • Herbs for sale • House open for conferences, special parties, functions and promotional events • Grade III

Set in 240 acres of park and farm, this listed 12-acre garden is (surprisingly) built over Tudor mine workings as the now predominatly Georgian house was built around an Elizabethan ironmaster's house. Specimen ferns, trees and an extensive collection of camellias, azaleas and rhododendrons. Many of the spring flowers are over 100 years old. Walled garden with herb nursery, Elizabethan ponds and woodland walks. National collection of candelabra and Sikkimensis primulas.

OFFHAM HOUSE 16
Offham, Nr Lewes, East Sussex.   Tel: (0273) 474824
Mr and Mrs H.N.A. Goodman

2m N of Lewes on A275, ½m from Cooksbridge Station   ● Open 6th May, 1st July, 2.00 – 6.00 p.m.   ● Best season: late spring, high summer   ● Entrance: £1.00, children 25p   ● Limited parking on property, more on road   ● Refreshments   ● Toilet facilities   ● Suitable for wheelchairs   ● Dogs on lead   ● Plants for sale   ● Grade II

This garden offers a wide variety of interest and perspectives. Lawns sweep from the extremely attractive house (with its well- blended, lush conservatory) to a colourful shrubbery, which contains shrub roses and a variety of trees, including an evergreen or holm oak, a tulip tree underplanted with bulbs, and a weeping mulberry; beyond is an arboretum with a weeping elm and collections of acers and sorbus. The colourful well-stocked herbaceous borders contain a variety of penstemons, euphorbias and salvias as well as an unusual sundial, contemporary with the house. Other features include a spring path with early purple orchids and fritillaries, a collection of lilacs, a cherry orchard (with several Japanese varieties), and an unusually long bed of peonies and aquilegias. A fine new addition is the herb garden, which is bursting with life; bergamots, alpine strawberries and marjorams, mixed with *Tricyrtis stolonifera, Phygelius aequalis* 'Yellow Trumpet', euphorbias and verbenas, are framed by box, lavenders and thymes. At the front of the house is a fountain and a splendid example of davidia (pocket handkerchief tree). A particularly large and well-kept greenhouse is the backbone to this fine, well-tended garden.

PENNS IN THE ROCKS 17
Groombridge, East Sussex.   Tel: (0892) 864244
Lord and Lady Gibson

7m SW of Tunbridge Wells on Groombridge – Crowborough road just S of Plumeyfeather Corner   ● Open 1st April, 1st, 2nd July, 2.30 – 5.30 p.m.   ● Entrance: £1.00, first 2 children 50p, further children free   ● Parking   ● Refreshments   ● Toilet facilities   ● Suitable for wheelchairs   ● Dogs in park only   ● Grade II

The name comes from the distinguished American Quaker whose family owned the property from 1672 to 1762 and from the Tunbridge Wells rock formations in the garden. It has emerged over the years into a happy combination of formality and informality within a lovely setting. Lady Dorothy Wellesley developed it extensively and built the temple on the slope facing the Georgian house. The present owners have much developed the grounds since purchasing the house in 1956. It is approached by a long drive through parkland full of wild daffodils and other spring flowers. Pleached limes, a walled garden, a stream and pools, a clipped yew hedge, statuary, old roses and extensive borders provide more formal features, and many well-placed seats help visitors enjoy the beauties of this outstanding garden.

SHEFFIELD PARK GARDEN 18
Nr Uckfield, East Sussex. Tel: (0825) 790655
The National Trust

5m NW of Uckfield, midway between East Grinstead and Lewes on E of A275
● Open April – 10th Nov, Tues – Sat (closed Good Friday), 11.00 a.m. – 6.00
p.m. or sunset if earlier. Sun and Bank Holiday Mons, 2.00 – 6.00 p.m. or
sunset if earlier, Suns in Oct and Nov, 1.00 p.m. – sunset. Last admission 1 hour
before closing ● Entrance: £3.00 (April, June – Sept), £3.50 (May, Oct, Nov)
● Teas at Oak Hall (not National Trust) ● Toilet facilities ● Partly suitable
for wheelchairs. Wheelchairs available ● Shop ● House under separate
ownership and divided from garden by screen planting ● Grade I

One hundred-acre garden and arboretum with two lakes installed by 'Capability' Brown for the Earl of Sheffield in 1776. Repton also worked here in 1789 and was responsible for the string of lakes up to the mansion. Later still, the lakes were extended and cascades added. Between 1909 and 1934 a collection of trees and shrubs notable for their autumn colour was added, including many specimens of *Nyssa sylvatica*. These and other fine specimen trees particularly North American varieties provide good all-year-round interest. Features include good water lilies in the lakes, the Victorian Queen's Walk and, in autumn, two borders of the Chinese *Gentiana sino-ornata* of amazing colour. The Trust is continuing to open up new areas.

SUSSEX (West)

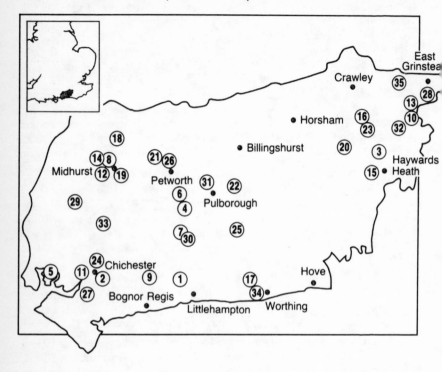

BERRI COURT
Yapton, Arundel, West Sussex.   Tel: (0243) 551663
Mr and Mrs J.C. Turner

1

*5m SW of Arundel, on A2024 Chichester/Littlehampton road in centre of village
between Black Dog pub and Post Office* ● *Open 8th, 9th April, 13th, 14th May,
24th, 25th June, 2.00 - 5.00 p.m., 21st, 22nd Oct, 12 noon – 4.00 p.m.*
● *Entrance: 80p, children 30p* ● *Parking by Baptist Church opposite* ● *Suitable
for wheelchairs* ● *Dogs on lead* ● ***Grade II***

A series of sheltered gardens within a three-acre garden of great interest to
plant enthusiasts created over a period of 20 years. There is a mass of daffodils
in spring with azaleas and rhododendrons. The borders have an impressive
display of shrubs and herbaceous plants and many varieties of shrub and
climbing roses. Around the house are magnificent *Magnolia grandiflora,
Drimys winteri* and *Clematis rehderiana*. Eucalyptus grove.

BISHOP'S PALACE 2
Chichester, West Sussex.
Diocese of Chichester

From South Street, turn into Canon Lane, left through the Palace Gatehouse • *Open daily, 8.00 a.m. to 9.00 p.m. or sunset* • *Entrance: free* • *Parking difficult* • *Refreshments: refectory in Cathedral cloisters* • *Toilet facilities in Cathedral cloisters* • *Suitable for wheelchairs* • *Cathedral shop* • **Grade IV**

After roaming the Cathedral pass down St Richard's Walk from the cloisters, turn right in the close, through the Palace gatehouse and follow the path to the gardens. These lie just within the city walls and have many tall ilex and bay trees. Well kept herbaceous borders and shrubs. A place to linger in the shadow of the Cathedral with a view of the medieval palace. On the way out along Canon Lane the houses and gardens of the close should not be passed by in a hurry.

BORDE HILL GARDEN 3
Haywards Heath, West Sussex.
Tel: (0444) 450326 or weekends (0444) 412151
Borde Hill Gardens Ltd

1½m N of Haywards Heath on Balcombe-Haywards Heath road • *Open Good Friday – last weekend in Oct, daily* • *Best season: March - May* • *Entrance: £1.50, OAP £1.00, children 50p, parties of 20 or more £1.00 per person, season tickets £6.00* • *Parking* • *Refreshments* • *Toilet facilities* • *Suitable for wheelchairs* • *Dogs on lead* • *Plants for sale* • *Shop* • **Grade II**

The garden was started by Col. Stephenson Clarke when he bought the Borde Hill property in 1893. Many of the trees, shrubs and particularly the rhododendrons were grown from seed collected by great plant hunters like Reginald Farrer, George Forrest, Frank Kingdon-Ward and Joseph Rock. There is a sad lack of labels on the plants, and parts of the garden, especially the bog and bamboo garden, show signs of neglect. However the garden is important for its collection of exotics.

CHAMPS HILL 4
Coldwaltham, Pulborough, West Sussex. Tel: (0798) 831868
Mr and Mrs D. Bowerman

From A29 at Coldwaltham turn W towards Coates/Fittleworth. Champs Hill is 300 yards up on right • *Open 24th, 25th March, 18th, 19th, 20th May, 2nd, 3rd June, 17th, 18th, 19th Aug, 11.00 a.m. - 5.00 p.m., Sun, 1.00 - 5.00 p.m.* • *Entrance: £1.00, children free* • *Limited parking* • *Teas in May, June, Aug but not in March* • *Dogs* • **Grade IV**

Champs Hill house is approached by a long drive through the 27-acre garden with one of the most interesting collections of heathers in the area. The current owners plan to plant parts of the garden with something different, but the sandy soil, and high woodland walks make this a pleasant place for a country walk with views over the Arun, while keeping the plantsman in the family occupied provided he likes heather.

CHIDMERE HOUSE 5
Chidham, Chichester, West Sussex. Tel: (0243) 572287
Mr T. Baxendale

E of Nutbourne, S off A27. Turn right at southern end of Chidham village
● *Open 15th, 16th April, 20th, 21st May, 24th, 25th June, 26th, 27th Aug,*
2.00 – 7.00 p.m. ● *Best season: spring* ● *Entrance: 80p, children 30p*
● *Parking in road* ● *Toilet facilities* ● *Dogs on lead* ● *Grade III*

Chidmere gardens were laid out in 1930-36 by the present owner's father on the site of a farm and orchard. Modelled on Hidcote they incorporate impressive allées bordered by tall yew and hornbeam hedges together with a sizeable lake. The house (not open) is medieval in origin and, together with the outbuildings, it has been blended into a setting which looks far older than the 1930s. Trees include a davidia, *Gingko biloba*, *Prunus serrula*. There is a good collection of flowering shrubs and interesting French statues of the nineteenth century. In spring the daffodils in the orchard and plantation make a spectacular display.

COATES MANOR 6
Fittleworth, Pulborough, West Sussex. Tel: (0798) 82356
Mrs G.H. Thorpe

½m S of Fittleworth off B2138 ● *Open 17th, 18th, 19th June, 11.00 a.m. –*
6.00 p.m. ● *Entrance: £1.00, children 20p* ● *Suitable for wheelchairs*
● *Plants for sale* ● *Grade II*

An unusual garden, which, Mrs Thorpe modestly explains, has been planned for ease of maintenance, using only plants which respond to local conditions. As an experienced flower arranger, she uses trees and shrubs which give long-term pleasure in the form of interesting foliage, berries and autumn colour. The front border running along the road blends a fine copper beech with *Elaeagnus pungens* and a purple-leaved *Cotinus coggygria*. The house is covered with a large-leaved variegated ivy and, particularly on the back lawn, there are some fine specimen trees, including a dramatically-sited *Liquidambar styraciflua* 'Warplesden', giving autumn colour. In addition to the two main gardens there is a delightful small walled garden to the side of the house with ceanothus, clematis and a host of scented honeysuckles and borders containing *Choisya ternata* and *Philadelphus coronarius*. This is a truly inspiring one-acre garden.

COKE'S BARN 7
West Burton, Pulborough, West Sussex. Tel: (0798) 831636
Mr and Mrs N. Azis

Turn W off A29 at foot of Bury Hill, first right at West Burton. Coke's Barn, a black barred barn conversion, is on the right ● *Open for NGS* ● *Entrance: 60p* ● *Parking in field opposite* ● *Suitable for wheelchairs* ● **Grade III**

A gravelled courtyard garden, surrounding a small impressively-stocked conservatory, gives useful inspiration to those with a small or perhaps urban site. This gives on to a charming mixed garden with a rose arbour covered with 'Kiftsgate', neat rose borders and penstemons and to two ponds (one new in 1989) surrounded by water plants. Old apple trees have been retained, giving the garden a pleasant feeling of old-fashioned space for what is in reality quite a small area.

COWDRAY PARK 8
Midhurst, West Sussex. Tel: (0730) 812423/(0730) 812215
Viscount Cowdray

N of Midhurst on A272 Petworth Road ● *Deer park open all year round but garden of new house only open on 3rd Sun in May* ● *Best season: May/June* ● *Entrance: 80p* ● *Parking* ● *Toilet facilities* ● *Suitable for wheelchairs* ● *Dogs on lead* ● **Grade III**

Fine hilly deer park enclosing the remains of the Tudor House, burned down in 1793. The gardens surrounding the present-day house include a fine collection of rhododendrons, interesting to compare with nearby Ramster Gardens, fine cedars and azaleas and a sunken garden.

DENMANS 9
Denmans Lane, Fontwell, West Sussex. Tel: (0243) 542808
Mrs J.H. Robinson/ Mr J. Brookes

5m W of Chichester. Turn S off A27, W of Fontwell racecourse ● *Open 5th March – 16 December, daily, 9.00 a.m. – 5.00 p.m.* ● *Best season: late May/ early June* ● *Entrance: £1.70, OAP £1.50, children £1.00, groups of 15 or more £1.40 per person* ● *Parking* ● *Refreshments: dairy tea shop offering coffee, light lunches and teas from 10.00 a.m. – 5.00 p.m.* ● *Toilet facilities* ● *Plants for sale* ● *Shop* ● *The Clock House is home to John Brookes' school of garden design running day courses on a variety of horticultural topics* ● **Grade II**

A small walled garden of approximately three and a half acres purchased originally as a vegetable garden by the Robinsons in 1946 and gradually extended and redesigned by Mrs Robinson who retired in 1984 when John Brookes took over. With so much colour and variety, one does not at first realize that there are relatively few flowers. Use is made of groups of trees and shrubs with matching foliage to provide background colour for low-growing and ground-cover plants of similar shades to self-seed and naturalize at the front of borders and through gravel paths. For example, *Robinia pseudoacacia* 'Frisia', a variegated holly, *Elaeagnus pungens* 'Maculata', marjoram 'Aureum' and *Alchemilla mollis* provide yellow accents in one border, whilst in another *Berberis thunbergii* 'Atropurpurea', *Cotinus coggygria* 'Foliis Purpureis', *Sedum spectabile* and *Anemone* x *hybrida* 'Max Vogel' are all toning shades of pink. The idea of growing in gravel beds came to Mrs Robinson when visiting Greece and has been skilfully extended by John Brookes to include a lake.

DUCKYLS   10
Sharpthorne, Nr East Grinstead, West Sussex.   Tel: (0342) 801352
Sir Michael and Lady Taylor

4m SW of East Grinstead, 6m E of Crawley. Take B2028 S at Turners Hill and fork left after 1m to W Hoathly. Left at sign to Gravetye Manor Garden on right ● *Open 24th, 29th, 30th April, 1st, 6th – 8th May, 5th June, 2nd, 16th Oct, 2.00 – 6.00. Parties by appointment* ● *Entrance: £1.00, children 25p* ● *Parking* ● *Toilet facilities* ● *Partly suitable for wheelchairs* ● *Dogs on lead* ● *Plants for sale if available* ● ***Grade III***

These 14 acres of terraced and hilly grounds, established with rhododendrons and azaleas, are gradually being developed into many interesting individual areas without any loss of the overall grandeur. The 1987 gales actually helped in thinning out some of the older, less vigorous trees and carpets of bluebells, daffodils, fritillaries, common primroses and violets burgeon. A *Clethara alnifolia* (sweet pepper bush) has reappeared from beneath brambles, and many of the old paths can now be taken, leading through colourful pink pearls, griersonianum and chaetomallum to two ponds and a bog garden. Dogwoods and *Kalmia latifolia* are benefitting from a hard cut-back. The orchard has several wild orchids – early purple, green-winged and common-spotted – and the undisturbed areas nurture a wide variety of butterflies and birds. The more formal areas reflect the present owners' keen interest in auriculas and double primroses, in particular Duckyls Red (which received the R.H.S. Award of Merit). Among other features, the restored rose garden and several newly planted alpine areas, rare poultry and magnificent views across to Wierwood Reservoir make this an ever-inviting garden.

FISHBOURNE ROMAN PALACE GARDEN   11
Salthill Road, Fishbourne, West Sussex.   Tel: (0243) 785859
Sussex Archaeological Society

1½m W of Chichester off A27 ● *Open March – Nov, daily. March, April and Oct, 10.00 a.m. – 5.00 p.m., May – Sept, 10.00 a.m. – 6.00 p.m., Nov, 10.00 a.m. – 4.00 p.m. Dec – Feb, Sun, 10.00 a.m. – 4.00 p.m.* ● *Entrance: £2.00, OAP and students £1.60, children £1.00, pre-booked parties of 20 or more adults £1.60 per person* • *Refreshments: cafeteria for light lunches, teas and coffees. Closed Dec – Feb* • *Toilet facilities inc. disabled* • *Suitable for wheelchairs* • *Guide dogs only* • *Plants and herbs which would have been in use in Roman times for sale* • *Roman remains open* • **Grade IV**

Definitely not a plantsman's garden (in fact there are very few plants in evidence), but one which will appeal to students of history and garden design. Fishbourne is the fascinating recreation of a Roman palace and garden probably built for the local King Tiberius Claudius Cogidubnus about AD 75-100. Visitors would be advised to look at the model of the palace in the museum before viewing the site itself in order to better appreciate the symmetry of the design, as only half of the garden has been excavated. Whilst there is evidence, from the trenches filled with loam that were discovered during excavation, of the layout of paths and surrounding hedges, the planting has been done by guesswork, being taken from descriptions found in contemporary writings.

FITZHALL 12
Iping, Nr Midhurst, West Sussex.   Tel: (073081) 3634
Mr and Mrs Bridger

W of Midhurst off A272. Turn S opposite Iping turnoff • *Open April – Sept, Sun 2.00 – 6.00 p.m.* • *Entrance: £1.00, children under 14, 50p* • *Parking* • *Teas* • *Toilet facilities* • *Partly suitable for wheelchairs* • *Dogs* • *Plants for sale* • *Shop* • **Grade III**

Three generations of the Bridger family work together to restore and maintain the nine-acre garden on a high South Down site. Surrounded by high rhododendron and yew hedges, the lawns east of the house include fine herbaceous borders, shrubs and heathers, but perhaps the best surpise is the hidden herb garden, enclosed by fine yew hedges. This in turn gives onto a flagstone walk between two gardens full of cyclamen, roses, herbaceous plants. A short woodland walk, carpeted in April with bulbs, leads to a highly productive vegetable garden with produce on sale. Children will be interested in the farm animals.

GRAVETYE MANOR 13
Vowels Lane, Nr East Grinstead, West Sussex.
Tel: (0342) 810567
Mr P. Herbert

4m from East Grinstead off M23 and A22, turn towards West Hoathly, but drive carefully as entrance somewhat concealed • *Open all year to hotel guests, perimeter footpath for public. Small groups by appointment* • *Best season: spring* • *Entrance: free* • *Parking in Vowels Lane car park* • *Refreshments at hotel and for country club members only* • *Toilet facilities for hotel guests and country club members only* • *Dogs on lead* • **Grade II**

This historically important garden has been carefully restored in the style set out by William Robinson. It has a wild meadow leading down to trout lakes from terraced formal gardens. The elliptical kitchen garden enclosed by Sussex sandstone walls is unique and is cultivated to produce fresh vegetables for the hotel kitchen. It is worth giving yourself a treat, either spending a weekend at Gravetye, or going for lunch but enquire about prices before making plans as this is an expensive as well as enjoyable experience. Either way you will be able to enjoy the garden, lakes and woods.

HAMMERWOOD HOUSE GARDEN   14
Iping, Midhurst, West Sussex. Tel: (073081) 3635
Mrs John Lakin

3m W of Midhurst, 1m N of A272 ● *Open for one day in May for NGS* ● *Best season: spring* ● *Entrance: £1.00, children 30p* ● *Parking* ● *Refreshments* ● *Toilet facilities* ● *Suitable for wheelchairs* ● *Dogs on lead* ● *Plants for sale* ● *Grade III*

This is a peaceful country garden formerly part of a Regency vicarage that has been planted with care and a fine eye for good plants. Although the rhododendrons and azaleas give it its most spectacular flowering season, there are some good seedling abutilons and specimen trees. Across a meadow from the main garden is the semi-wild garden set in a small wood.

HEASELANDS   15
Haywards Heath, West Sussex. Tel: (0444) 454181
Mrs Ernest Kleinwort

1m from Haywards Heath on A273 ● *Open 10th, 14th, 17th, 21st, 24th, 28th May, 23rd July, 2.00 – 6.00 p.m. Special arrangements on other days. Coaches/ parties by appointment* ● *Entrance: £1.20, children 30p* ● *Parking* ● *Teas* ● *Toilet facilities inc. disabled* ● *Suitable for wheelchairs* ● *Grade II*

Beautiful home and gardens created by owners from the original farmhouse, meadow and woodlands. Earliest work consisted of planting shelter belts, then the sunken garden, rock gardens, tennis court, swimming pool – the yew hedges for the enclosed gardens were constructed and planted before the war. Other garden features have been formed over the last 30 years. The guide book photographs of rhododendron and azalea displays promise worthwhile visits, there being 82 rhododendron hybrids. There are large duck ponds and a goose paddock, and the kitchen garden also contains aviaries where birds are bred. A visit in October on a mild, sunny afternoon to view the autumn colour is highly recommended.

THE HIGH BEECHES 16
Handcross, West Sussex. Tel: (0444) 400589
High Beeches Gardens Conservation Trust

1m E of Handcross, S of B2110 ● *Open Easter – June, Sept – Oct, daily except Sun and Wed, 1.00 – 5.00 p.m. Also Bank Holidays 10.00 a.m. – 5.00 p.m.* ● *Best season: spring and autumn* ● *Entrance: £1.50 (accompanied children under 14 free). Guided parties of 10 or more £3.00 per person, any day or time* ● *Parking* ● *Refreshments on Spring Bank Holidays and for autumn event on 21st Oct 1990 for RNLI* ● *Toilet facilities inc. disabled* ● **Grade I**

A garden bearing the mark of the Loder family, which is now being maintained by the Boscawen family as Col. Loder designed it in 1906. The early planting was influenced by John Millais, son of the pre-Raphaelite artist, Arthur Soames of Sheffield Park, Sussex, and William Robinson, whose philosophy of allowing plants to grow naturally has greatly influenced the development of the garden. A series of valleys or ghylls, the garden was badly damaged by the October 1987 gales, but skilful remedial work has removed the most harrowing scars. It has a superb collection of rhododendrons and specimen trees. Willow gentians grow wild, and the front meadow, which has not been ploughed in living memory, is filled with native grasses and wild flowers. The woodland garden is also a haven for wild flowers. Autumn colouring is outstanding.

HIGHDOWN 17
Littlehampton Road, Goring-by-Sea, West Sussex.
Tel: (0903) 48067
Worthing Borough Council

3m W of Worthing, N of A259 ● *Open April – Oct, Mon – Fri, 10.00 a.m. – 4.30 p.m., weekends and Bank Holidays, 10.00 a.m. – 8 p.m. or dusk* ● *Best season: April* ● *Entrance: by donation* ● *Parking* ● *Refreshments at peak times* ● *Toilet facilities inc. disabled* ● *Suitable for wheelchairs (1 available for hire on request)* ● **Grade III**

Created by Sir Frederick Stern from a bare chalk pit in 1910, Highdown was donated to Worthing Corporation in 1968. Without a rhododendron or camellia in sight, Highdown makes a refreshing change for those used to gardening on acid soil. From such an unpromising site a garden has been created illustrating the scope and possibilities of a garden of chalk-loving plants. These include buddleia, mahonia, paulownia, althaea and paeonia, as well as rarities such as *Itea ilicifolia* and *Clerodendrun trichotomum fargesii* which was in full flower and glorious scent when seen in early August.

KING EDWARD VII HOSPITAL 18
Midhurst, West Sussex. Tel: (0730) 812341
King Edward VII Hospital Trust

3m NW of Midhurst on A286. Well signed down a 1m drive ● *Open 19th May, all day* ● *Entrance: by collecting box* ● *Parking* ● *Refreshments* ● *Toilet facilities* ● *Suitable for wheelchairs* ● *Dogs on lead* ● *Shop* ● **Grade III**

Gertrude Jekyll laid out a series of fine herbaceous borders on terraces immediately south of the large hospital opened for officers after World War I. The terraces overlook extensive parkland and playing fields with an elevated view towards the South Downs Way. There are good woodland walks to the north of the hospital which stands in parkland of 152 acres. Also good beds of chrysanthemums etc. grown for the hospital shop.

LANE END 19
Sheep Lane, Midhurst, West Sussex. Tel: (0730) 813151
Mrs C.J. April

In centre of Midhurst ● *Open 19th, 20th, 21st, 26th, 27th, 28th May, 11.00 a.m. – 6.00 p.m.* ● *Best season: spring* ● *Entrance: 50p, children 25p* ● *Parking in town car parks* ● *Partly suitable for wheelchairs* ● **Grade III**

This garden is as packed with interest as it is with plants. Created since 1972 on a sharp bulldozed slope, great use is made of raised beds, rock garden feature, and a large heather bank, all leading down to a semi-wild garden of shrubs and fine specimen forest trees. It is hard to believe that the garden is in a busy rural town.

LEONARDSLEE GARDENS 20
Lower Beeding, Nr Horsham, West Sussex. Tel: (0403) 891212
The Loder family

3m SW of Handcross and M23 on the A279/A281 ● *Open mid-April – mid-June, daily, 10.00 a.m. – 6.00 p.m., July – Sept, weekends only, 12 noon – 6.00 p.m., Oct, weekends only, 10.00 a.m. – 5.00 p.m.* ● *Best season: mid-April – mid-June and autumn* ● *Entrance: £1.50 – £3.00 (depending on season), children £1.00 – £1.50* ● *Parking* ● *Refreshments* ● *Toilet facilities* ● *Large selection of plants, esp. rhododendrons, for sale* ● *Shop* ● **Grade I**

This famous garden was started by Sir Edmund Loder, a member of the family which has left its mark on a number of great gardens in West Sussex. Sir Edmund raised the famous Rhododendron Loderi hybrids, with their enormous scented flowers. The gardens, with their seven lakes, contain a superb collection of rhododendrons, azaleas, acers, two magnificent dawn redwoods (*Metasequoia glyptostroboides*), as well as a wide variety of shrubs. Far from being depressed by the hurricane damage of 1987, Mr Robin Loder, who runs the gardens, is using the natural clearance to develop and replant and eventually extend the gardens and parklands to 180 acres. A great deal of money and care has been expended on the excellent facilities for visitors.

THE MANOR OF DEAN 21
Tillingworth, Petworth, West Sussex.
Miss S.M. Mitford

Turn N from A272 ¼m W of Tillington ● *Open for NGS, dates N.A.* ● *Best season: spring* ● *Entrance: 50p* ● *Parking nearby* ● *Teas* ● *Shop for produce* ● *Grade III*

A charming garden, with old walls and terraces, some dating from the building of the house in 1615, also old sundial and other impressive stone ornaments. Some rare plants still survive from Captain Mitford's subscription to the Kingdon-Ward expeditions, the last of the great plant-hunting journeys. The one-acre walled kitchen garden is still used for growing vegetables and also houses a greenhouse containing a fine yellow rose, grown from a cutting from the wedding bouquet of the present owner's great-grandmother. Throughout the garden there are fine lilies and dense banks of the wild Swiss mauve crocus.

MILL HOUSE 22
Nutbourne, Nr Pulborough, West Sussex. Tel: (07983) 3314
Sir Francis and Lady Avery Jones

At far end of cul de sac immediately to the left of Nutbourne Manor Vineyard ● *Open by appointment and 1st, 2nd July, 2.00 – 6.00 p.m.* ● *Entrance: £1.00, combined with other Nutbourne gardens* ● *Refreshments* ● *Plants for sale* ● *Grade III*

Mill House garden slopes steeply to a fast-running stream surrounded by bamboo thickets and a water garden. The steep banks are a profusion of wild flowers in June/July and the house itself is surrounded by a cottage garden. There is a fine walled herb garden containing about 140 different species to the side. Other gardens open in the Nutbourne garden NGS scheme include Ebbsworth and Manor Farm and you can also visit the neighbouring Nutbourne Manor Vineyard, of 14 acres, which contains predominantly vines imported from Germany.

NYMANS 23
Handcross, Nr Haywards Heath, West Sussex. Tel: (0444) 400321
The National Trust

At the southern end of Handcross village, off M23 and A279. Well signposted ● *Open April – Oct, daily except Mon and Fri (but open Good Friday and Bank Holiday Mon), 11.00 a.m. – 7.00 p.m. or sunset if earlier. Last admission*

1 hour before closing • *Best season: spring and summer* • *Entrance: £2.50,
pre-booked parties £2.00 per person* • *Parking* • *Toilet facilities* • *Suitable for
wheelchairs* • *Plants for sale* • *Shop* • **Grade I**

For 100 years the Messel family have developed Nymans gardens to
accommodate a very wide collection of plants, of which rhododendrons,
magnolias, camellias and eucryphias are outstanding. The large circular rose
garden has been restored and replanted with the old-fashioned roses for which
the garden is also famous. Wild and woodland gardening, influenced by
William Robinson, dominate Nymans, but there are fine examples of more
formal gardening, such as the circular garden sheltered by camellias, and
planted with annuals, and the walled garden with its fine double borders of
perennial and annual herbaceous plants. Lord and Lady Rosse made a fine
decision when leaving the relics of a nineteenth-century Gothic portion of the
house standing after it was gutted by fire in the 1950s as it provides the garden
with a wonderfully romantic backdrop.

PALLANT HOUSE 24
North Pallant, Chichester, West Sussex. Tel: (0243) 774557
Pallant House Gallery Trust

Proceed from the station up South Street. Turn left in West Pallant • *Open all
year, Tues – Sat, 10.00 a.m. – 5.30 p.m. Last admission 5.00 p.m.* • *Entrance:
£1.00, OAP, students, children over 7, 60p* • *No parking* • *Toilet facilities*
• *House open* • **Grade III**

A small Dutch-style garden close to Pallant House, an interesting local
museum, lovingly restored in 1982 by Claud Phillimore, a well-known
architect and leading light of the Georgian group. The use of Versailles tubs
and eighteenth-century pots enables the tender exotics which were so new and
exciting to fashionable men of the eighteenth century to be changed
constantly to provide a succession of flowers. The sheltered site allows for
some unusual tender plants (e.g. *Syringa* x *persica*, *Punica granatum* and *Rosa
bracteata*) which were all introduced in the eighteenth century, while the small
square beds, box edgings, hoggin-covered paths, trellis work and ornaments
add to the effect of a strictly period but nevertheless charming town garden.

PARHAM HOUSE 25
Pulborough, West Sussex. Tel: (09066) 2021
Mrs P.A. Tritton

4m SE of Pulborough on A283 • *Open Easter Sun – 1st Sun in Oct, Wed,
Thurs, Sun and Bank Holidays, 1.00 – 6.00 p.m. Last admission 5.30 p.m.*
• *Entrance: £1.00, children 75p (house and garden £2.50, OAP £2.00,
children £1.50)* • *Parking* • *Refreshments in big kitchen from 3.00 p.m.*
• *Toilet facilities* • *Suitable for wheelchairs (garden only)* • *Dogs on lead*
• *Plants for sale* • *Shop* • *House open* • **Grade II**

The gardens of this Elizabethan house are approached through the Fountain Court. A broad gravelled path leads down a slope through a wrought-iron gate guarded by a pair of Istrian stone lions to the walled garden of about four acres. This retains its original quadrant layout divided by broad walks and includes an orchard. In 1982 it was redesigned retaining its character and atmosphere; the borders were replanted to give interest for many months, with shrubs as well as herbaceous plants. In one corner is the enchanting miniature house, a delight for both children and adults. The pleasure grounds of about seven acres provide lawns and walks under stately trees to the lake, with views over the cricket ground to the South Downs.

PETWORTH HOUSE   26
Petworth, West Sussex.   Tel: (0798) 42207
The National Trust

6½m E of Midhurst on A272 in the centre of Petworth ● Deer park open all year, daily, 9.00 a.m. – sunset. Gardens and car park open April – Oct, daily except Mon and Fri (but open Good Friday and Bank Holiday Mon. Closed Tues following), 12.30 – 5.00 p.m. ● Entrance: park free. House and gardens £3.00 ● Parking ½m N of Petworth on A283 ● Refreshments when house open ● Toilet facilities ● Suitable for wheelchairs ● Dogs on lead ● Shop ● House open dates as above, 1.00 – 5.00 p.m. Last admission 4.30 p.m. Entrance £2.70, children £1.35 ● Grade II

The park grew from a small enclosure for fruit and vegetables in the sixteenth century to its present size of 705 acres over centuries, and is enclosed by an impressive 14-mile-long stone wall. George London worked here as did 'Capability' Brown. The latter toiled from 1753-63 for the 2nd Lord Egremont modifying the contours of the ground, planting cedars and many other trees and constructing the serpentine lake in front of the house. It was one of Brown's earliest designs, planned while he was still at Stowe. Turner painted fine views of the park (as well as the interior of the house) and it is interesting to see these and have them in one's mind as one strolls around the park as he must have done many times while staying at Petworth. This is not a garden for the botanist, but it is a very splendid experience, all year round, for any lover of man's improvements over nature, and individual trees and shrubs, including Japanese maples and rhododendrons, deserve close study.

RYMANS   27
Apuldram, Chichester, West Sussex.   Tel: (0243) 783147
The Hon Claud and Mrs Phillimore

1½m SW of Chichester. Turn right off A286 signposted Apuldram and turn right again ● Open for NGS ● Best season: spring ● Entrance: 60p, children 20p ● Parking ● Partly suitable for wheelchairs ● House open for art exhibitions ● Grade III

Surrounding this fifteenth-century house are three pretty formal gardens laid out by the Phillimores, and containing ponds, rose borders and fine cherry trees; past a huge ilex is the orchard which is a mass of bulbs in spring. The tennis court has flowering shrub borders and the eighteenth-century walled garden contains herbaceous borders, fruit trees and vegetables. The poplar avenue leads to the church (not to be missed) and gives a good view towards Chichester and the Cathedral.

STANDEN 28
East Grinstead, West Sussex. Tel: (0342) 323029
The National Trust

2m S of East Grinstead signposted from A22 at Felbridge, and also B2110
- *Open April – Oct, Wed – Sun and Bank Holiday Mon, 1.00 – 5.30 p.m.*
- *Best season: May/June* • *Entrance: £1.40 (£2.80 house and garden)*
- *Parking* • *Refreshments* • *Toilet facilities* • *Partly suitable for wheelchairs*
- *Dogs in car park and woodland walks only* • *Shop* • *House open* • **Grade II**

The house and estate have close connections with William Morris, and the late Victorian garden reflects much of the romantic era of the latter part of the nineteenth century. It is made up of a succession of small, very English gardens. Perhaps the most outstanding is the little quarry, which has survived as a Victorian fernery. Good views from this hillside-garden across the Medway Valley. The house, designed by Philip Webb, will be of interest to architectural pundits.

TELEGRAPH HOUSE 29
North Marden, Chichester, West Sussex. Tel: (0730 825) 206
Mr and Mrs D. Gault

Turn N on B2141 Chichester/South Harting road opposite North Marden
- *Open by appointment May – Aug, 2.00 – 5.00 p.m. and last weekend in June/ July for NGS, times N.A.* • *Entrance: £1.00, children 40p* • *Parking* • *Teas for NGS* • *Toilet facilities* • *Suitable for wheelchairs* • **Grade III**

Originally a semaphore station used to convey news from Portsmouth to the Admiralty, Telegraph House is approached up a magnificent one-mile drive of copper beeches, and the gardens sit in a park which includes a yew wood with a 40-minute woodland walk. The views, as far as the Isle of Wight, are preserved while an impressive array of roses, autumn and spring crocuses, and herbaceous plants and shrubs are enclosed by immaculate yew and hornbeam hedges. It is very interesting to see what the owners have managed to develop from a chalky, windswept site, albeit in a magnificent setting, over a period of twenty years.

UPPER HOUSE 30
West Burton, Pulborough, West Sussex. Tel: (0798) 831604
Mr and Mrs C.M. Humber

5m SW of Pulborough. Turn right off A29 at Bury/West Burton crossroads
● Open 23rd, 24th, 25th June, 2.00 - 6.00 p.m., 26th - 29th June, 4.00 - 6.00
p.m. ● Entrance: 75p, children 25p ● Teas on 23rd – 25th June only ● Partly
suitable for wheelchairs ● Plants for sale ● Grade III

Upper House has a large garden that incorporates several different 'rooms'
each enclosed within yew hedges. One side of the house gives on to a paved
garden with a wide variety of herbs. By the front door is a large *Magnolia*
grandiflora and shrubs surrounding a gravelled drive. A large Victorian
greenhouse in an immaculate state of preservation, in front of which you can
see a rose garden which the owners are thinking of replanting. Beyond this is
a lawn enclosed by a close-clipped yew hedge. This is a generous country-
house garden, with a deceptive air of having happened by chance.

UPPER LODGE 31
Stopham, Pulborough, West Sussex. Tel: (0798) 82532
Mr J.W. Harrington

From Pulborough take A283 westwards towards Fittleworth. At Stopham, the
Lodge is on the left by the telephone box past the entrance to Stopham House
● Open 9th, 13th, 15th, 16th, 29th April, 2.00 - 5.00 p.m., 6th, 7th, 13th,
20th, 27th, 28th May, 2.00 - 6.00 p.m. ● Entrance: 50p, children 8 – 14, 20p,
children under 8 free ● Plants for sale ● Grade III

By no means the cottage garden that the name Lodge might suggest. The acid
soil has enabled Mr Harrington to concentrate on an impressive range of
azaleas and rhododendrons within a comparatively small area, raised from the
road and with views over the surrounding park and farmland. There is usually
a good range of shrubs for sale and it is a particularly useful garden to visit for
those with similar acid soil.

WAKEHURST PLACE GARDEN 32
Ardingley, Nr Haywards Heath, West Sussex. Tel: (0444) 892701
The National Trust

From London take A(M)23, A272, B2028 or A22, B2110, B2028 ● Open
daily, except 25th Dec and 1st Jan, 10.00 a.m. - 4.00 p.m. (Nov – Jan), 5.00
p.m. (Feb and Oct), 6.00 p.m. (March), 7.00 p.m. (April – Sept). Last
admission ½ hour before closing ● Entrance: £1.50, children 60p. Booked parties
of 12 or more adults £1.00, children 40p ● Parking ● Toilet facilities
● Suitable for wheelchairs ● Shop ● Part of house open ● Grade I

Dating from Norman times, the estate was bought by Gerald W.E. Loder
(Lord Wakehurst) in 1903. He spent 33 years developing the woodland and

formal gardens, a work carried on by Sir Henry Price. The gardens are used as an annexe of the Royal Botanic Gardens, Kew. It has a fine collection of rhododendrons, kalmias, camellias, corylopsis and viburnums. Unique is the Himalayan glade planted from species growing at 10,000 feet in the Himalayas. Many tender plants such as callistemon, olearias, crinodendron, leptospermums, mimosa and hoherias flourish. Wakehurst is a place for the botanist, plantsman and garden lover.

WEST DEAN GARDENS 33
West Dean College, Singleton, Chichester, West Sussex.
Tel: (0243) 63303
Edward James Foundation

5m N of Chichester on A286 ● *Open Easter – Sept, daily, 11.00 a.m. – 6.00 p.m. Last admission 5.00 p.m.* ● *Best season: spring/early summer* ● *Entrance: £1.40, OAP £1.20, children 65p. Parties by appointment £1.00 per person* ● *Parking* ● *Refreshments* ● *Toilet facilities* ● *Suitable for wheelchairs* ● *Dogs on lead* ● *Plants for sale* ● *Grade II*

This estate was acquired in 1891 by William James who planted fine trees in the 30 acres of informal nineteenth-century gardens which surround an impressive flint house by Wyatt. Range of plants slightly limited by alkaline soil and severe frost pockets. There is a sunken garden, with a deep pond; 300-foot pergola built in 1911 by Harold Peto, leads to a gazebo, surrounded by rare evergreens (*Clematis armandii, Cupressus goveniana, Cryptomeria japonica*) and fine fern-leafed beeches (*Fagus sylvatica heterophylla*). In addition to the romantic water garden (designed by Gertrude Jekyll) and wild garden there is a sizeable walled garden with lovingly restored greenhouses containing an amusing collection of antique lawnmowers. The garden borders the Weald and Downland Museum of traditional rural life from 1400 to 1900. The house is now a training college. The arboretum forms part of the gardens and, despite the depredations of the gales, is full of interest for the tree lover.

WORTHING BOROUGH COUNCIL NURSERIES 34
Titnore Way, Worthing, West Sussex.   Tel: (0903) 39630
Worthing Borough Council

1m N of Goring roundabout on A259 ● *Open for NGS* ● *Entrance: by collecting box* ● *Parking* ● *Suitable for wheelchairs* ● *Grade IV*

There are more than a dozen greenhouses here, the largest of which is the palm house. Worthing is noted for its public floral displays and many of those grown for arrangements in municipal buildings can be admired. In the palm house is a large selection of foliage plants.

YEW TREE COTTAGE 35
Crawley Down, Turners Hill, West Sussex. Tel: (0342) 714633
Mrs Hudson

1m S of A264. Down lane opposite Cretan Pottery shop on B2028, take right turn and the cottage is the second of semi-detached on left ● *Open 30th June and 1st July, 2.00 - 6.00 p.m. and by appointment for small groups* ● *Best season: spring/early summer* ● *Entrance: 50p, children 20p* ● *Parking* ● *Suitable for wheelchairs* ● *Plants for sale* ● *House open* ● ***Grade II***

A plantsman's delight and an encouragement to all with small gardens, it is not surprising that this third of an acre plot has been a prizewinner. Developments continue and the vegetable garden is now a small Jekyll-style masterpiece. The front garden is divided between a scree with alpines and herbs and a shrubbery with a golden area including *Hypericum frondosum*, physocarpus, forsythia and *Philadelphus coronarius* 'Aureus'. To the rear of the house a mature quince, underplanted with campanulas and rue, stands over a well, while the borders are bursting with colour and unusual plants. Ballerina and Felicia geraniums, *Mertensia sibinica*, pink phlomis, *Babtisia australis*, toad lilies, mutabilis and erysimum wallflowers, sweet rocket and *Rhododendron impeditum* are but a few of the interesting plants in this exceptional garden.

TELEPHONE NUMBERS
Except where specifically requested to be excluded, telephone numbers to which enquiries may be directed are given for each property. To maintain the support and cooperation of private owners it is suggested that the telephone be used with discretion. Where visits are by appointment, the telephone can of course be used except where written application, particularly for parties, is specifically requested. Code numbers are given in brackets. For the Republic of Ireland when phoning from the United Kingdom dial 353 plus area code plus number (except Dublin numbers which are 0001 plus number). In all cases where visits by parties are proposed, owners should be advised in advance and arrangements preferably confirmed in writing.

London Telephone Codes: From May 1990 all London telephone numbers with the prefix 01 will be changed. The new prefix will be either 071 or 081. Details of these new numbers are available from British Telecom. During the changeover period in 1990 all London telephone numbers dialled with their 01 prefix will be redirected.

TYNE & WEAR

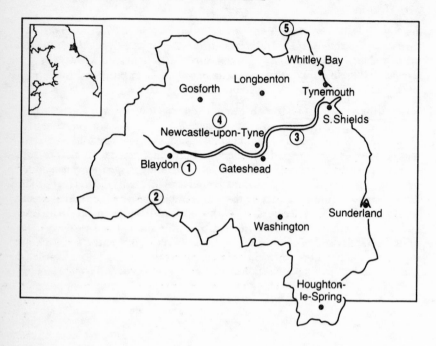

GATESHEAD NATIONAL FESTIVAL
GARDEN (1990)   1
Gateshead, Tyne & Wear. Tel: (091) 4821333
Gateshead Borough Council

*3m W of Gateshead (B6081) ● Open 18th May – 21st Oct, daily, 10.00 a.m. –
dusk ● Entrance: £6.00, children £3.00, concession £4.00, season £45.00
● Parking ● Refreshments ● Toilet facilities ● Suitable for wheelchairs
● Plants for sale ● Shop*

Whether British garden festivals are a good thing and whether they have a
future is open to question. There is no doubt though, that those held to date
have been enjoyed by very large numbers of visitors and Gateshead (planned
since 1985) promises to be no exception. The gardens run down either side of
the River Team, flowing northward into the Tyne. In addition to 25 planned
and designed horticultural shows there will be 'theme weeks' dedicated to
France, Italy, Japan, Australia, the USA, etc. An outstanding feature of the
Festival Gardens will be the Northern Landscapes' garden designed by that
imaginative trio George Carter, Raf Fulcher and Elizabeth Tate.

GIBSIDE CHAPEL 2
Burnopfield, Newcastle-upon-Tyne, Tyne & Wear.
Tel: (0207) 542255
The National Trust

6m SW of Gateshead, 20m NW of Durham from B6314, off A694 Rowlands Gill ● *Open April – Oct, Wed, Sat and Sun, 1.00 – 5.00 p.m. Open Good Friday and Bank Holidays, other times by appointment* ● *Entrance: £1.00, children 50p, parties 80p* ● *Light teas* ● *Dogs on lead* ● *Shop* ● *Chapel open and service 1st Sun each month, 3.00 p.m. Concerts and guided walks* ● *Grade III*

The chapel is an outstanding example of English Palladian architecture by James Paine. There is no 'real' garden but the fine avenue of Turkey oaks leading to the derelict Gibside Hall is memorable. The chapel is surrounded by woods managed by the Forestry Commission and has three Wellingtonia firs. There is a Victorian walled kitchen garden which is being reclaimed and returned to original use.

JARROW HALL HERB GARDEN 3
Bede Monastery Museum, Church Bank, Jarrow, Tyne & Wear.
Tel: (091) 4892106
English Heritage

6m E of Gateshead off A185 ● *Open April – Oct, daily except Mon, 10.00 a.m. – 5.30 p.m., Nov – Mar, 11.00 a.m. – 4.30 p.m., Suns, 2.30 – 5.30 p.m.* ● *Best season: summer* ● *Entrance: free* ● *Parking* ● *Refreshments* ● *Toilet facilities* ● *Suitable for wheelchairs* ● *Dogs on lead* ● *Plants for sale* ● *House open as garden. Entrance: 60p, student 40p, OAP and children 30p* ● *Grade IV*

A nicely planted small herb garden with a wide range in four sections: culinary, Anglo-Saxon medicinal, aromatic and medicinal. Currently in need of attention but interesting to the herbalist.

JESMOND DENE 4
Jesmond, Newcastle-upon-Tyne, Tyne & Wear.
Tel: (091) 2328520
Newcastle City Parks Department

1m W of city centre along Jesmond Road ● *Open all year* ● *Best season: summer* ● *Entrance: free* ● *Parking in Freeman Road* ● *Toilet facilities* ● *Partly suitable for wheelchairs* ● *Dogs on lead* ● *Grade III*

Presented to the city by Lord Armstrong, the famous engineer, in 1883 and only a mile from the city centre, this steep-sided thickly-wooded dene provides extensive walks in an entirely natural setting, complete with a waterfall, a ruined mill and some fine old buildings (and even a well-run pets corner).

From Freeman Road the upper park has a play pond and good bedding plants. Quite exceptional condition for a city park.

SEATON DELAVAL HALL   5
Seaton Sluice, Whitley Bay, Tyne & Wear.
Tel: (091) 2373040/2371493
Lord Hastings

10m NE of Newcastle, ½m inland from Seaton Sluice on A190 • *Open May – Sept, Wed, Sun and Bank Holidays, 2.00 – 6.00 p.m.* • *Best season: early summer* • *Entrance: £1.00, OAP and children 50p* • *Parking* • *Toilet facilities* • *Partly suitable for wheelchairs* • *Dogs on lead* • *Souvenir stall* • *House open* • ***Grade III***

The original grounds of this architectural masterpiece by Vanburgh no doubt matched its magnificence but little is known save for an early painting showing a swan lake. A notable weeping ash survives from that time, and there is a venerable rose garden. Since 1950 an excellent parterre has been laid out, soon to be embellished by a large Italianate pond and fountains. An attractive shrubbery (rhododendron, azalea, etc) and herbaceous borders have also been established on the south side towards the fine Norman chapel. Replanting continues and the garden is obviously in good hands.

HOW TO FIND THE GARDENS
Directions to each garden are included in each entry. This information has been supplied by the garden inspectors and is aimed to be the best available to those travelling by car. However, it has been compiled to be used in conjunction with a road atlas.

   The unreliability of train and bus services makes it unrewarding to include details, particularly as many garden visits are made on Sundays. However, many properties can be reached by public transport and National Trust guides and the Yellow Book [NGS] give details. Future editions of the *Guide* may include a special list of gardens easily reached by public transport if readers indicate that this would be helpful.

   The Maps: The numbers on the maps correspond to the numbers of the gardens in each county. The maps show the proximity of one garden to another so that visits to several gardens can be planned for the same day. It is worthwhile referring to the maps of bordering counties to see if another garden visit can be included in your itinerary. The maps should be used in conjunction with a road atlas.

WARWICKSHIRE

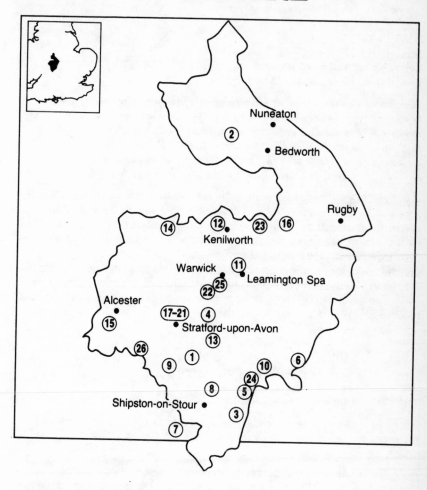

ALSCOT PARK

Alscot, Warwickshire. Tel: (078987) 451
Mrs James West

2½m S of Stratford-upon-Avon on A34 • *Open 10th June, 8th July, 2.00 –*
6.00 p.m. • *Entrance: £80p, children 20p* • *Parking* • *Teas* • *Toilet*
facilities • *Suitable for wheelchairs* • *Dogs* • *Plants for sale* • *Grade III*

A typical eighteenth-century park with one of the earliest mock-Gothic houses
(not open), this has all the requisite main features – extensive lawns, fine trees,
orangery, deer park, river and lakes. There is a small garden round the house
but the main interest lies in the new garden developed by Mrs West near the

orangery, now the site of a pool area. Around it a large semi-formal garden features old-fashioned roses, a mixed flower and vegetable garden and strong lines of hedging. Note the fine quality of the seats, urns, ornaments etc.

ARBURY HALL 2
Arley, Nr Nuneaton, Warwickshire. Tel: (0203) 382804
Viscount and Viscountess Daventry

10m from Coventry, 7m from Meriden off the Fillongley/Nuneaton road
● *Open Easter – Sept, Sun and Bank Holidays, also Tues and Wed in July/Aug,*
2.00 – 6.00 p.m. ● *Best season: spring/summer* ● *Entrance: £1.20, children*
60p (park and gardens), £2.50, children £1.20 (hall, park and gardens)
● *Parking in adjoining field* ● *Teas* ● *Toilet facilities* ● *Suitable for*
wheelchairs ● *Dogs on lead* ● *Shop* ● *House open* ● ***Grade II***

A delightful garden with a sense of peace. Bulbs at the start of the season followed by rhododendrons and azaleas, then roses in June and autumn colour from trees and shrubs. Formal rose garden and climbing roses. Lakes with wildfowl, parkland, the drive and bluebell woods. A canal system was installed years ago as a method of transport. Pleached limes and the old walled garden are some of the features of this pleasant garden, along with the beautiful old trees. There is a museum in the old stables containing a collection of veteran cycles, motor cycles, sewing machines and some old farm implements. Gift and craft shop in the Old Dairy.

BRAILES HOUSE AND STABLES 3
Lower Brailes, Nr Shipston-on-Stour, Warwickshire.
Tel: (060885) 400
Mrs P.M. Laing and Major and Mrs R.F. Birch Reynardson

4m E of Shipston-on-Stour on B4035 ● *Open 24th June, 2.30 – 5.00 p.m.*
● *Entrance: 50p, children 25p* ● *Parking* ● *Suitable for wheelchairs*
● ***Grade III***

A large garden surrounding two Georgian houses, one of which has been cleverly converted from a former stable block. There has been extensive planting of old-fashioned roses and while most were introduced by the present owners over the past 15 years, they give the impression of having grown up with the house. Other features include a bog garden and a delightful conservatory, full of geraniums. Brailes House has more interest for the visitor than others open under the NGS scheme at the height of summer, and it is to be hoped that the owners can be persuaded to open it during the spring months as well.

CHARLECOTE PARK 4
Charlecote, Warwickshire. Tel: (0789) 840277
The National Trust

1m W of Wellesbourne, 5m E of Stratford-upon-Avon on road immediately S of bridge • *Open April – Oct, daily except Mon and Thurs but open Bank Holiday Mon and closed Good Friday, 11.00 a.m. – 6.00 p.m. Evening tours for pre-booked parties 2nd Wed in each month inc. house 7.30 – 9.30 p.m.* • *Entrance: £3.00* • *Parking* • *Refreshments: morning coffee, light lunches, afternoon teas in orangery. Picnics in deer park* • *Toilet facilities* • *Partly suitable for wheelchairs* • *Large commercial plant nursery opposite main gate* • *Shop* • *House open* • *Grade III*

More of picturesque and historic than garden interest. Home of Lucy family since the thirteenth century. Shakespeare reputedly poached deer, which still populate the park alongside Jacob sheep. Park laid out by 'Capability' Brown who was directed not to destroy the avenues of elms, later eliminated by Dutch elm disease. Orangery and wild garden.

COMPTON WYNATES 5
Warwickshire. Tel: (029588) 229
The Marquess of Northampton

10m W of Banbury, 6m E of Shipston-on-Stour, turn N off B4035 • *Open only by special pre-arrangement, preferably in writing* • *Entrance: by arrangement* • *Parking* • *Partly suitable for wheelchairs* • *House open by special arrangement* • *Grade II*

Until 1980 this garden was one of the favourites of those fortunate enough to be able to visit it. Then it closed, when the owner returned to live in the house. However the owner is sometimes able to make special arrangements for garden enthusiasts, but casual callers are definitely not welcomed. The house is also sometimes open on a similar basis, and in both cases a charge may be made. The garden enjoys a perfect setting around the early sixteenth-century house, which itself nestles in a natural depression, beautifully treed, all of which can be glimpsed as the visitor descends the road towards the gates. The view from these entrance gates has been described as 'fairyland'. The prize exhibit in the gardens used to be a topiary area of such dazzling virtuosity and apparent maturity that most visitors thought that like the house it was contemporary with Henry VIII. Not so. It was begun in 1895 by the 5th Marquis who wanted to economise on the high cost of Victorian parterre. Less than 100 years later, alas, it was grubbed up to make way for roses. The moat which almost surrounds the house has been led off to form a small picturesque flower garden which admirably sets off the lawns and the mellow Tudor brick of the towering house, a miniature Hampton Court.

FARNBOROUGH HALL 6
Farnborough, Warwickshire. Tel: (029589) 202
The National Trust/Mr and Mrs Holbech

5m N of Banbury, ½m W off A423 or E off A41 ● *Open April – Sept, Wed and Sat, also 6th, 7th May, 2.00 – 6.00 p.m. Terrace walk only every Thurs and Fri, 2.00 – 6.00 p.m. Parties of 15 or more by prior arrangement at other times* ● *Entrance: £2.00 (house, grounds and terrace walk), £1.30 (gardens only), terrace walk only on Thurs and Fri 80p* ● *Suitable for wheelchairs (grounds only)* ● *Dogs on lead (grounds only)* ● **Grade II**

Grounds improved in the eighteenth century with aid of Sanderson Miller, an architect, landscape gardener and dilettante who lived at nearby Radway. The fine S-shaped terrace walk climbs gently along the ridge looking towards Edgehill. Legend has it that the owner, William Holbeck, built the walk in order to see, in the distance, another landowning friend. The *Oxford Companion* describes it as a majestic concept marking the movement towards the great landscaped parks at the end of the eighteenth century. Two temples along the walk and an obelisk at the end. The trees are beeches, sycamores and limes. To the north, part of the site of the former orangery and now a rose garden, is a yew walk ending where formerly a cascade linked the oval pond (now woodland) with the remaining long lake across the road from the house. The atmosphere will unfortunately be affected by the building of the M40 extension nearby.

FOXCOTE 7
Nr Shipston-on-Stour, Warwickshire. Tel: (060882) 240
Mr C.B. and the Hon Mrs Holman

4½m W of Shipston-on-Stour, 4m N of Moreton-in-Marsh. It can also be approached by forking left in Ilmington ● *Open 1st July, 2.00 – 6.00 p.m.* ● *Entrance: 80p, children free* ● *Parking* ● *Teas* ● *Toilet facilities* ● *Partly suitable for wheelchairs* ● *Dogs on lead* ● **Grade III**

When the owners came here nearly 30 years ago there were mature yew and beech hedges and from this basic structure they have created a strong design which takes advantage of the wonderful setting. The plantsperson would probably call this minimalist gardening although there are good borders on the terraces with roses, irises, lavender and selected annuals which contrast with the fifteenth-century monastery fish ponds below. The owners have rebuilt these, stocked them with trout and created a woodland walk around. Note also the walled kitchen garden, very orderly and highly productive.

HONINGTON HALL AND VILLAGE GARDENS 8
Honington, Nr Shipston-on-Stour, Warwickshire.
Tel: (0608) 61434
Sir John Wiggin Bt

1½m N of Shipston-on-Stour, ½m to E off A34 • Open June – Aug, Wed and Bank Holiday Mons, 2.30 – 5.00 p.m. Parties at other times by appointment. Also NGS • Entrance: £1.50, children 50p • Parking • Teas in Honington village hall • Toilet facilities • Suitable for wheelchairs • Dogs • Grade III

Honington is a well-kept village of up-market houses – some may think so well-kept as to have lost the village character. From the A34, the approach is over a charming eighteenth-century bridge from which the Carolingian house can be seen to the left. This is surrounded by extensive lawns and fine trees and, like most front gardens in the village, well-manicured flower beds.

ILMINGTON MANOR 9
Ilmington, Nr Shipston-on-Stour, Warwickshire.
Tel: (060882) 230
Mr D.L. Flower

4m NW of Shipston-on-Stour, 8m S of Stratford-upon-Avon • Open by appointment and 22nd, 29th April, 13th May, 1st July, 2.00 – 6.00 p.m. • Entrance: £1.00, children free except 29th April when £1.50 for combined admission for other village gardens • Parking • Teas for NGS • Toilet facilities • Suitable for wheelchairs • Plants for sale • Grade III

Created from an orchard in 1909 this is now a mature garden with strong formal design which is full of surprises. There is also much to interest the plantsperson. To the right of the drive is a paved pond, with thyme of many varieties ornamenting the stones. Scented and aromatic climbers surround this area. Next, a walk up the pillar border presents an unusual combination of shrubs and herbaceous plants in colour groups. Then, up stone steps, is the formal rose garden and the long double border planted with old and modern shrub roses. The so-called Dutch garden is really an informal cottage garden with a profuse mixture of colour. There is much more – a trough garden, iris and foliage beds, a rock garden and, in the spring, plenty of daffodils and crocus. New plants and trees are still being added. Cottage gardens in Ilmington are open on NGS days and Foxcote (see page 394) is nearby.

IVY LODGE 10
Radway, Warwickshire. Tel: (029587) 371
Mrs M.A. Willis

7m NW of Banbury via A41 and B4086. 14m SE of Stratford-upon-Avon via A422 • Open for NGS • Best season: spring, July and autumn • Parking in village • Refreshments: teas and, in Oct, soup • Suitable for wheelchairs • Grade IV

Radway nestles below Edgehill, and the garden of Ivy Lodge runs back across the former battlefield. Above on the skyline can be seen the mock castle, now a pub. In spring there is a profusion of bulbs and blossom; in summer a fine collection of roses. The village contains many cottages with interesting gardens and every other year (including 1990) about a dozen are open to the public. Their attractions range from a good collection of garden gnomes to grander efforts such as pleached limes. In 1988/9 the village achieved the 'Best Kept Village' award but despite this it retains a marked villagey character.

JEPHSON GARDENS   11
Leamington Spa, Warwickshire.
Leamington Borough Council

In centre of Leamington, main entrance opposite Pump Rooms ● *Open daily 8.00 a.m. (9.00 a.m. Sun and Bank Holidays) to ½ hour after dusk* ● *Entrance: free* ● *Parking* ● *Refreshments* ● *Toilet facilities* ● *Suitable for wheelchairs* ● *Dogs* ● **Grade IV**

This Spa town has always made a great effort in the floral decoration of its streets, and this activity can be enjoyed at its peak in the intensive bedding out of the principal formal public garden.

KENILWORTH CASTLE   12
Kenilworth, Warwickshire. Tel: (0926) 52078
Department of the Environment

On outskirts of town, alongside road to Tile Hill ● *Grounds open at all times* ● *Entrance: grounds free, small charge to castle ruin* ● *No refreshments but pub opposite and tea shop in High Street* ● *Partly suitable for wheelchairs* ● *Castle open Easter – Sept, daily, 10.00 a.m. – 6.00 p.m., Oct – Easter, weekdays, 9.30 a.m. – 4.00 p.m., Sun, 2.00 – 4.00 p.m.* ● **Grade IV**

It is worth a détour to see this ruin, now surrounded by grass, in order to imagine what it was like in its day as the earliest important Elizabethan garden. The twelfth-century keep with later great hall by John of Gaunt was modernised by Queen Elizabeth's courtier, Robert Dudley, Earl of Leicester. The format was a square area divided into quarters focusing on a heraldic fountain. An obelisk in each quarter was surrounded by fruit trees and herbs, and the whole was viewed from a terrace with aviary and balustrading.

LOXLEY HALL   13
Loxley, Nr Stratford-upon-Avon, Warwickshire. Tel: (0789) 840212
Col. A. Gregory-Hood

4m SE of Stratford-upon-Avon, N off A422 or W off A429 ● *Open 26th May, 30th June, 2.30 – 7.00 p.m.* ● *Entrance: £1.00, children 20p* ● *Parking in*

village • *Teas on NGS days* • *Suitable for wheelchairs* • *Dogs* • *House closed
but church open* • *Grade IV*

Two reasons for visiting this garden: first, the owner has designed it as a series
of 'rooms' in the Sissinghurst tradition and it is interesting to evaluate his
success; second, he has added to them examples of contemporary sculpture
from a London gallery. Some may find the result rather arid, with not much
of interest except large areas of grass; others will enjoy the sculpture. The
church next door is said to be one of the oldest in Britain, founded AD761.

MILL GARDEN
(see Warwick Castle, page 401)

PACKWOOD HOUSE   14
Lapworth, Solihull, Warwickshire.   Tel: (05643) 2024
The National Trust

2m E of Hockley Heath on A34, 11m SE of central Birmingham • *Open April
– Sept, Wed – Sun and Bank Holiday Mon (closed Good Friday), 2.00 – 6.00
p.m., Oct, Wed – Sun, 12.30 – 4.00 p.m.* • *Entrance: £1.50 (garden), £2.20
(house and garden). Reduced rates for parties by written arrangement*
• *Parking* • *Toilet facilities* • *Suitable for wheelchairs* • *Shop* • *House
open. Last admission ½ hour before closing* • *Grade II*

Hidden away from a rather suburban part of Warwickshire this garden is
notable for its intact layout with courtyards, terraces, brick gazebos and
mount of the sixteenth and seventeenth centuries when the house was built.
Even more remarkable is the almost surreal yew garden, unique in design.
Tradition claims that it represents the Sermon on the Mount but in fact the
'Apostles' were planted in the 1850s as a four-square pattern round an
orchard. Never mind, the result is now homogenous. There is a spiral 'mount'
in yew and box which is a delightful illusion. Note also the clever use made of
brick. G Baron Ash who gave the property to the Trust made a sunken garden
in the 1930s and restored earlier design features. He also introduced
colourful border planting, but the garden also looks splendid early and late in
the year when there is scarcely a flower to be seen.

RAGLEY HALL   15
Alcester, Warwickshire.   Tel: (0789) 762090
The Marquess of Hertford

1m from Alcester on A435 • *Open Easter – Oct, except Mon and Fri, 11.00
a.m. – 5.00 p.m.* • *Best season: spring* • *Parking* • *Refreshments: tearooms
and small café open from 11.00 a.m.* • *Toilet facilities inc. disabled* • *Partly
suitable for wheelchairs* • *Shop* • *House open* • *Grade III*

Not a well-cultivated garden and some areas weed-infested, but the climbers on the pillar by the house, the rose garden and some lovely old trees are (certainly for the family outing) worthy of a visit. There is also a beautiful lake surrounded by lawns with picnic tables, an adventure area with very good facilities and woodland walks and country trails.

RYTON GARDENS   16
(National Centre for Organic Gardening)
Ryton-on-Dunsmore, Coventry, Warwickshire.
Tel: (0203) 303517
The Henry Doubleday Research Association

5m SE of Coventry. Turn off A45 onto B4029 ● *Open April – Sept, daily, 9.00 a.m. – 6.00 p.m., Oct – Mar, daily except Christmas period, 10.00 a.m. – 4.00 p.m.* ● *Entrance: £2.00, OAPs, children under 18, students, unemployed, £1.00, family £4.50. Tickets last a year* ● *Parking* ● *Refreshments: café serving organic food* ● *Toilet facilities* ● *Suitable for wheelchairs* ● *Guide dogs only* ● *Plants for sale* ● *Shop* ● ***Grade III***

Six acres including conservation area with pond, native woodland, wild flower meadow, wildlife garden, bee garden, soft fruit garden and trained fruit trees, rose garden, herbaceous and shrub borders, herbs, large vegetable plots including old varieties together with examples of compost-making, raised beds, mulching, green manure crops, plants for drying, use of deep beds and methods of attracting beneficial wildlife into the garden. Also an alpine garden. A children's play area and picnic facilities make it somewhere for the family to visit and learn something for their own garden, even if not intending to use organic methods.

SHAKESPEARIAN GARDENS
Stratford-upon-Avon, Warwickshire.   Tel: (0789) 204016
Shakespeare Birthplace Trust & Stratford Council

Located in Stratford-upon-Avon and surrounding area ● *Open at individual times for properties, but others open daily, 9.00 a.m. – dusk. Closed 24th – 26th Dec and 1st Jan* ● *Entrance: to Trust properties by individual charge or £5, children £2.50 for all of them. Some free* ● *Toilet facilities in town* ● *Shops in properties*

If it is true that little is known about Shakespeare, less is known about his gardens. The Trustees have done their best to make them an interesting adjunct to the properties, mostly with tourists in mind.

BIRTHPLACE GARDEN   17
Described as an 'association' garden, this is an informal collection of trees, shrubs, herbs and flowers mentioned in the works of Shakespeare, over 100 varieties in all.

MARY ARDEN'S HOUSE   18

Where Shakespeare's mother lived when young. The front is a mélange of box, roses and flowers; the rear a stretch of lawn in the former farmyard and, through the archway beyond, a 'wild' garden.

ANN HATHAWAY'S HOUSE   19

Where Shakespeare's wife lived before their marriage. It has been turned into the accepted image of an old-fashioned cottage garden. The orchard beyond has trees and wild flowers.

NEW PLACE   20

To which Shakespeare retired, was burnt down and on the foundations is a garden around which the Trustees suggest his orchard and kitchen garden lay. This includes an ancient mulberry perhaps grown from a cutting from one planted by Shakespeare. Beyond this is a reconstruction of what an Elizabethan knot garden may have looked like. Note the oak palisade covered by crab apples as is also the 'tunnell' or 'pleached bower'.

HALL'S CROFT   21

Where Shakespeare's daughter and doctor son-in-law lived. Now a spacious walled garden it bears little resemblance to Shakespeare's time but has a pleasant lawn laid down in 1950 and an old mulberry tree. There are herbs such as Hall the doctor might have used. Some unfortunate cypress trees tend to spoil the view. *All the above are trust properties and fee charged.*

Beyond the knot garden is a large free garden with lawn and interesting topiary although some may not approve of the regimented bedding plants alongside. Also free are Bancroft Gardens in front of the Theatre and a smaller, more intimate garden behind the Theatre looking down along the Avon towards the church where Shakespeare is buried.

SHERBOURNE PARK   22
Sherbourne, Nr Warwick, Warwickshire.   Tel: (0926) 624255
Lady Smith-Ryland

½m N of Barford, 3m S of Warwick off A249, close to the junction of the A46 and the M40 extension ● Open 6th May with plant sale for NCCPG, 3rd, 17th June, 9th Sept. Also by appointment ● Entrance: £1.00, children free ● Parking ● Teas ● Suitable for wheelchairs ● Plants for sale and nursery open daily ● Grade II

A fine park surrounds the early Georgian house (1730), and adjacent Gilbert Scott church (1863), in which Lady Smith-Ryland has developed a series of imaginative smaller gardens characterized by inspired planting. In particular, the 'square' garden at an angle shows great originality. All the conventional features of the English garden – shrubs, herbaceous borders, roses, lilies and so on – are combined in most pleasing and sometimes surprising congruity.

There is a temple and a small lake beyond the church. More of the grounds are being developed, and this will ultimately be one of the most distinguished in an area full of gardens of distinction.

UNIVERSITY OF WARWICK 23
Coventry, Warwickshire. Tel: (0203) 523523
Warwick University

Nearer to Coventry than Warwick, the most direct access is off the A45 signed University/Stoneleigh just S of the Coventry city turn-off • *Open at all times* • *Parking difficult in term* • *Refreshments* • *Toilet facilities* • *Suitable for wheelchairs* • **Grade IV**

The Oxbridge college gardens are much-publicised so it is interesting to see what a new university makes of its campus in botanical terms. The buildings here have been the subject of some controversy but the landscaping of the surrounding area has done something to mellow their impact on the Warwickshire landscape. The work is continuing and those interested in landscaping in the larger areas will want to see the use of trees and the long lake and, in the smaller spaces, the wisteria-covered pergola in the Social Sciences block and the water features (cascading is planned). Formal gardens are being considered for some of the new residences.

UPTON HOUSE 24
Edgehill, Nr Banbury, Warwickshire.
Tel: (029587) 266
The National Trust

7m NW of Banbury on A422 • *Open April and Oct, Sat, Sun and Bank Holiday Mon (closed Good Friday), 2.00 – 6.00 p.m. May – Sept, Sat – Wed, 2.00 – 6.00 p.m. Parties of 15 or more by written permission of Estate Office at reduced rate* • *Entrance: £1.80 (garden only)* • *Parking. Coaches by arrangement with administrator* • *Teas by arrangement for parties only on Sat* • *Partly suitable for wheelchairs* • *Dogs* • *House open. Last admission ½ hour before closing. £1.00 extra* • **Grade II**

The house itself, which dates from 1695, contains a fine collection of paintings including two grand Stubbs. More interesting to the garden visitor is that it stands on sandstone, 700 feet above sea level, at the ridge of Edgehill, site of the famous battle. Below a great lawn, the garden descends in a series of long terraces, along one side of which is an impressive flight of stone steps, leading down to the large lake below. The grand scale of the plan is the main interest, but there are many unusual plants, particularly perennials and, along the lake, bog plants. About twice a year the Warwickshire Hunt meets at the house, and by following the hunt to the surrounding hills at the back, gardening enthusiasts who are also hunt supporters may enjoy a unique view of the descending terraces and lake.

WARWICK CASTLE 25
Warwick, Warwickshire. Tel: (0926) 49542
Pearsons plc

In the centre of Warwick, which is off the A46 bypass ● *Open all year round*
except 25th Dec ● *Entrance: April – Sept, £4.50, children £3.00, Oct – Mar,*
£4.00, children £2.00 (castle and grounds) ● *Parking* ● *Refreshments of all*
kinds in castle and town. Picnics in grounds ● *Toilet facilities* ● *Suitable for*
wheelchairs ● *Shop* ● *Castle open* ● ***Grade II***

Despite its commercial nature (the previous owner sold 63 acres to Madame
Tussauds and 1000 acres to a farmer) this is a pleasant place to visit. There is,
however, no reduction in the entrance price for visiting the grounds alone.
Some 30 acres of the medieval castle site were set out by 'Capability' Brown,
the first work commissioned after he set up on his own. He removed the old
formal garden outside the wall and shaped the grounds to frame a view, using
great trees, notably cedars of Lebanon. The courtyard was levelled and made
into lawns with Scots pines. It is worth climbing the eleventh-century mound
to gain a view of the site and country beyond the River Avon – Brown later
worked on Castle Park on the other side. The newly-restored conservatory
houses tender plants including the *Grevillea* species from Australia, named
after the family. From this conservatory, the vistor looks across the large
parterre, peopled by shrieking peacocks. This was laid out in the late
nineteenth century when the Pageant Field park beyond was also planted with
rhododendron which this visitor finds obtrusive. On the other side of the
castle entrance is a formal Victorian rose garden which has been recreated
from Robert Marnock's designs of 1868 and a rock garden and pool of *c.*1900.
The present owner's intention is to restore the whole to its appearance in
1901, the period of the main interior rooms, now peopled with waxworks of
former distinguished guests.

One interesting way to see the castle is to go first to the Mill Garden, in Mill
Street, Warwick, south of the town. From this excellent informal little place,
beside the river, planted by Mr A.B. Measures with a wide selection of unusual
plants, one can see the old bridge across which Shakespeare is said to have
ridden to London. There is also a herb garden and raised alpine beds, all
available most days of the year with a collecting box for charity. Later from the
castle grounds, the visitor can view this area from the riverside by crossing the
bridge near the boat house.

WOODPECKERS 26
The Bank, Marlcliff, Nr Bidford-on-Avon, Warwickshire.
Tel: (0789) 773416
Dr and Mrs A.J. Cox

7m SW of Stratford-upon-Avon on B4085 between Bidford and Cleeve Prior
● *Open various dates from April – July and by prior arrangement* ● *Best*
season: spring/summer ● *Entrance: £1.00* ● *Parking in road and nearby car*

park • *No refreshments but picnics allowed* • *Suitable for wheelchairs*
• *Plants for sale* • *Grade III*

This two and a half-acre garden contains many good ideas and blends in with the surrounding countryside. Island beds and the patio area with troughs provide all year round interest and colour and there are several borders of individual colours. There is a pool and bog garden, an ornamental vegetable garden or potager with standard currants and gooseberries, a knot garden and a round greenhouse containing tender plants.

THE GRADING SYSTEM

This is the most subjective aspect of the *Guide* and one which may cause some disagreement on the part of owners as well as visitors. We stress that its purpose is to serve as an indication to visitors in order to give them some advance information about the status of the garden as viewed by our inspectors and editors. Readers will appreciate that direct comparisons cannot be made between a huge estate like Chatsworth with its staff of professional experts and a tiny plantsman's garden in a terraced house, tended with dedication by a single owner. This being said, both may be excellent of their kind and therefore be worthy of consideration for a visit, and considered by the *Guide* to be at the top of their class. Conversely a lesser grading does not imply any criticism of a garden but is an attempt to guide the potential reader as to its relative merits if a choice has to be made between several gardens. Broadly speaking the intention of the four grades is as follows:

Grade I Amongst the best gardens in the world in terms of design and content. Many are of historic importance, but some are of recent origin. Overseas visitors to Britain or Ireland are recommended to include them in their itinerary.

Grade II Gardens of high quality, though not perhaps as unique as Grade I, and worth travelling a considerable distance to visit. Sometimes the property as a whole, and the general ambience, make the visit particularly rewarding.

Grade III These are gardens which our inspectors suggest it would be worth driving fifty miles or more to visit. They may have some special feature of design or plant content while not being considered as justifying a higher grade overall.

Grade IV Gardens of considerable merit and well worth visiting when in the region.

WILTSHIRE

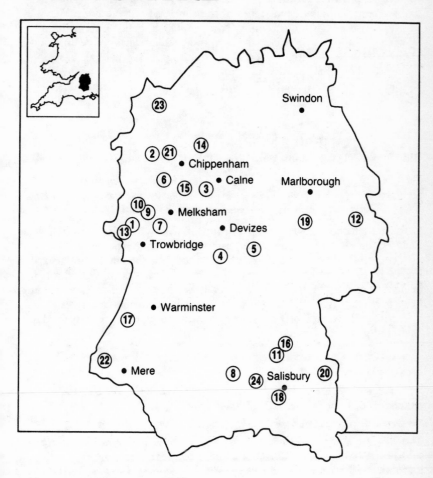

Swindon

(23)

(2) (21) (14)
• Chippenham
(6)
(15) (3) • Calne   Marlborough
(10)
(9) • Melksham
(13)(1) (7)   (19)   (12)
• Trowbridge • Devizes
(4) (5)

• Warminster

(17)

(16)
(11)
(22)   (8) (24) Salisbury (20)
• Mere   (18)

BELCOMBE COURT   1
Bradford-on-Avon, Wiltshire.   Tel: (02216) 2897
Mrs A.J. Woodruff

On Bradford-on-Avon – Turleigh road, entrance by derestriction speed sign
• Garden may not open in 1990   • Entrance: £1.00, children 10p   • Parking
• Teas   • Plants for sale   • Grade II

The house is for sale at time of going to press and it is not known if it will be
open for 1990. It is a fine one in a fine town, and was designed by John Wood
the Elder who, together with his son built a vast part of Bath. The centrepiece

of the two-acre garden is a Doric pavilion which Wood wrote 'wanted' the correct proportion, 'an error pardonable in a working mason'. The garden looks across to the wooded slopes of the south side of the Avon Valley. In addition to the charming pavilion/rotunda which stands on a little hill in front of a small lake, there is a large grotto which now has colourful modern planting. There are other interesting buildings, all providing a splendid background to the sensitive plantings of Mrs Woodruff who began her restoration work only in 1977. A garden described by Arthur Hellyer as having 'a touch of magic'.

BIDDESTONE MANOR 2
Biddestone, Nr Corsham, Wiltshire. Tel: (0249) 714520

5m W of Chippenham, 3m N of Corsham. On A4 between Chippenham and Corsham, turn N. Or from A240, 5m W of Chippenham, turn S ● *Open for NGS* ● *Entrance: for NGS* ● *Parking* ● *Teas* ● **Grade III**

Large garden and small lake behind beautiful stone walls with intriguing vista of lavender borders through gateposts to the manor front door. An early dovecote and outbuildings, recently restored like the seventeenth-century manor house, and beautifully set in fine spreading lawns with good topiary, ancient hedges and a splendid herbaceous border, the work of a new young head gardener. A small lake is planted with water plants and trees, and is attracting wild fowl. Don't miss the new swimming pool, properly sited in a sheltered position between the house and a barn.

BOWOOD 3
Bowood House, Derry Hill, Calne, Wiltshire. Tel: (0249) 812102
Marquess of Lansdowne, Earl of Shelburne

4½m W of Calne, 5m SE of Chippenham, 8m S of M4. On A342 ● *Open March – Oct, daily, 11.00 a.m. – 6.00 p.m.* ● *Best season: spring and autumn* ● *Entrance: £3.00, OAP £2.20, children £1.60 (house and garden)* ● *Parking* ● *Refreshments* ● *Toilet facilities* ● *Suitable for wheelchairs* ● *Plants for sale* ● *Shop* ● *House open* ● **Grade II**

Over 90 acres of 'Capability' Brown landscaped park with a very large lake. At the end of this are a cascade and grotto built by the Lane brothers (1785) and a classical temple. The arboretum is remarkable with more than 400 trees and 300 shrubs and climbers. Thousands of flowering bulbs cover the grass in spring. The Robert Adam orangery (converted into a picture gallery) is particularly fine and in front of it are formal Bath-stone terraces with rose beds, standard roses and fastigiate yews. *Magnolia grandiflora* flourishes on these hot Italianate terraces. Robert Adam's mausoleum is worth a walk, and from here one can move on down to the rhododendrons. A wide range of species and cultivars have been planted in chronological succession of flowering.

BROADLEAS   4
Broadleas, Devizes, Wiltshire.   Tel: (0380) 2035
Lady Anne Cowdray

5m S of Devizes on A360   ● Open 1st April – 30th Oct, Sun, Wed, Thurs, 2.00 – 6.00 p.m.   ● Best season: spring   ● Entrance: £1.00   ● Parking   ● Toilet facilities   ● Plants for sale   ● Grade III

This garden was bought just after World War II and started from nothing by Lady Anne Cowdray in a combe below Devizes. Semi-mature magnolias form a forest long and steeply dropping. As good as any Cornish garden, it is stuffed with fine things that one would think too tender for these parts. Large specimens of everything (much of it now forty years old) *Paulownia fargesii, Parrotia persica*, all manner of magnolias, azaleas, hydrangeas, hostas, lilies and trilliums of rare and notable species. It is a garden of tireless perfectionism at its most stunning in spring when sheets of bulbs stretch out beneath the flowering trees. Rarely seen in such quantities for instance are the erythroniums or dog-tooth violets. There is also a sunken rose garden and a silver border. This is serious plantsmanship and dendrology.

CONOCK MANOR   5
Devizes, Wiltshire.   Tel: (0380) 84227
Mr and Mrs Bonar Sykes

5m SE of Devizes off A342   ● Open 20th May, 2.00 – 6.00 p.m.   ● Entrance: £1.00, children 20p   ● Parking   ● Teas   ● Suitable for wheelchairs   ● Grade IV

Good Georgian house flanked by topiary in the front. The walled garden is to the east behind the stable block. The south face of the house provides a cosy border for abutilons, magnolias, roses, wisteria, a fig and hibiscus. From the Reptonesque thatched summerhouse the view is of parkland and the Downs. By contrast the formal garden to the east falls into three intimate areas divided by alleys and hedges. The kitchen garden is meticulously kept and very productive. Water in octagonal pool forms the centre of a formal arrangement of magnolias and shrub roses which lies between the vegetables and the stables and is screened from the kitchen garden by a belt of shrubs, viburnums, *Garrya elliptica*, lilacs and crab apples. Beyond all this is a satisfying simple web of beech hedges and box clipped into balls, making palisades which enclose different-sized spaces of grass and lead to a specimen Japanese maple.

CORSHAM COURT   6
Corsham, Chippenham, Wiltshire.   Tel: (0249) 712214
The Lord Methuen

4m W of Chippenham on A4   ● Open Jan – Nov, daily except Mon and Fri, 2.00 – 4.30 p.m. and until 6.00 p.m. from Good Friday – Sept   ● Best season:

spring • *Entrance: £1.20* • *Parking* • *Toilet facilities* • *Suitable for wheelchairs* • *Dogs on lead* • *House open* • **Grade III**

Approaching from Chippenham, look out for a glimpse of this house on your left, once framed by an avenue of elms now replaced by some sickly-looking lime trees. Surrounded by a landscape of 'Capability' Brown's devising finished off by Humphrey Repton (the lake and boat-house particularly) it is an example of this kind of gardening at its best. Rare and exotic trees look entirely at home: black walnut, Californian redwood, cedars, Wellingtonias, and the most astonishing layered Oriental plane tree shading beeches, oaks, sycamores and Spanish chestnuts. The bath-house designed by Brown is a treat and one can get through it into a world of entirely different mood. The Bradford porch leads out into a small enclosed flower garden with catalpa trees. Repton's roses trained over metal arches encircling a round pond is a rare surviving example of the elegance of early nineteenth-century flower gardens. Here the flower borders contain the unusual *Clerodendrum trichotomum* and enormous iron supports for roses and *Clematis* x *jackmanii*. There is a box-edged garden, hornbeam allée, good urns and arbours and seats. In spring the park becomes sheets and sheets of bulbs under magnolia trees and in August there are handsome hydrangeas and willow gentians.

THE COURTS 7
Holt, Bradford-on-Avon, Wiltshire. Tel: (0225) 782340
The National Trust

3m SW of Melksham, 3m N of Trowbridge, 2m E of Bradford-on-Avon on B3107 • *Open April – Oct, daily except Sat, 2.00 – 5.00 p.m. and out of season by appointment* • *Best season: summer* • *Entrance: £1.00* • *Parking at the village hall* • *Suitable for wheelchairs* • *Dogs on lead* • **Grade III**

Created by Sir George Hastings in 1900-1911, this has been an impressive garden and is still well worth visiting for both the plants and ideas. Extensive bog and water plants. The formal layout is noteworthy such as the use of the eighteenth-century house as a backdrop and the transition from 'rooms' about the house which are formal and progress into wild, bog and orchard gardens beyond. Lots of good Edwardian features such as stone walls and paths, pergolas, hedges, ponds and terraces. A garden in the Hidcote mould.

FITZ HOUSE 8
Teffont Magna, Salisbury, Wiltshire. Tel: (072276) 257
Major and Mrs Mordaunt-Hare

10m W of Salisbury on B3089 • *Open Easter – Sept, Sun, 2.00 – 6.00 p.m. Also for NGS* • *Best season: spring/summer* • *Entrance: £1.50, children 75p* • *Parking* • *Teas* • *Partly suitable for wheelchairs* • **Grade IV**

Teffont Magna is an exquisite village threaded along a chalk stream which runs also through the garden of Fitz House. What more could a gardener wish for than the mottled stone of a sixteenth-century house as a backdrop for a garden and a stream to water it. Good hedges form the 'bones' of this garden infilled with massed spring bulbs and handsome shrub planting such as azaleas and roses. A good scented garden.

GREAT CHALFIELD MANOR 9
Melksham, Wiltshire. Tel: (0225) 64446
The National Trust

3m SW of Melksham on B3107 ● *Open 3rd April – Oct, Tues – Thurs by guided tours only at 12.15, 2.15, 3.00, 3.45, and 4.30 p.m. Closed on public holidays. Parties by written appointment on other days* ● *Entrance: £2.50* ● *Parking* ● *House open* ● ***Grade III***

This house and garden were rescued in the early 1900s by Mr Robert Fuller. The setting is extremely romantic, lost among tree-lined lanes and water meadows. One crosses a stream to enter the courtyard in front of the house with the parish church on the left and garden all tucked behind. Behind the house the land falls away to an orchard and to the lower moat which is spring-fed. The courtyard garden has a topiary house planted in 1911. The large lawn or pleasaunce has two topiary houses and a gazebo, all made by Mr Fuller, with a border below. The garden is not for plantsmen but its magic lies in the setting, the mill leat, nine hundred foot long, and in the fact that it is profoundly English and ancient.

HAZELBURY MANOR 10
Nr Box, Wiltshire. Tel: (0225) 810715
Mr and Mrs I.D. Pollard

5m SW of Chippenham. From Box take A365 to Melksham, turn left onto B3109 and left again at Chapel Plaister ● *Open for NGS 6th, 7th, 27th, 28th May, 14th, 15th, 21st, 22nd July, 2.00 – 6.00 p.m.* ● *Entrance: £2.00, children £1.00* ● *Parking* ● *Refreshments* ● *Toilet facilities* ● *Dogs* ● *Plants for sale* ● ***Grade III***

Very extensive formal gardens about a sprawling Elizabethan house, immaculately restored and rejuvenated by its present owner. The massive rock garden at the front of the house is impressive although it couldn't be called in keeping with the house and makes as big a twentieth-century statement as the earlier Edwardian garden. This formal garden has a vast lawn banked up on either side by high walks shaded by pleached hornbeams. Every inch is extremely well looked after. In spring the alleys are all carpeted with brilliant polyanthus, cowslips and wallflowers. Mammoth herbaceous borders blaze in summer. A more private and intimate garden nestles in the fortifications on the other side of the house. Almost Chaucerian in feeling this is a medieval bower with old apple trees and irises and climbing roses. Beyond the fortifications is a new plantation of specimen trees, mostly conifers. Very impressive.

HEALE HOUSE   11
Middle Woodford, Salisbury, Wiltshire. Tel: (0722) 73504
Major David and Lady Anne Rasch

4m N of Salisbury between A360 and A345 ● *Open Easter to Autumn, Mons –
Sats, 1st Sun of the month and Bank Holidays, 11.00 a.m. – 5.00 p.m.*
● *Entrance: £1.50* ● *Parking* ● *Teas on NGS days* ● *Toilet facilities*
● *Suitable for wheelchairs* ● *Dogs on leads* ● *Plants for sale* ● *Shop and plant
centre open all year (10.00 a.m. – 5.30 p.m.)* ● *House not open except to groups
of 20 or more booked in advance* ● ***Grade II***

What must have been a superlative Edwardian garden has been reduced and
revitalized at Heale to adapt to today's problems. A tributary of the Avon
meanders through it providing the perfect boundary and obvious site for the
sealing-wax red Japanese bridge and the thatched tea-house which straddles
the water. This was made with the help of four Japanese gardeners in 1910 and
extends under the shade of *Magnolia* x *soulangiana* along the boggy banks
planted with bog arums, *Rodgersia aesculifolia*, candelabra primulas and irises.
There are two terraces immediately beside the house, one rampant with
alchemilla, spurges and irises and the other has two stone lily ponds and two
small borders given height by nine-foot high wooden pyramids bearing
clematis and honeysuckle. A slightly lost border contains mostly hybrid musk
roses backed by a simple but effective rustic trellis. The walled kitchen garden
is possibly the most successful part of this garden – it achieves a very satisfying
marriage between practicality and pleasure. It is not a regimented vegetable
garden but the formal nature of rows of potatoes, etc are made a feature and
plots are divided by espaliered trees, pergolas and hedges. The wonderful flint
and brick wall protects *Abutilon vitifolium* and an ancient fig. This is a walled
garden where one is encouraged to linger on the seats and in the shaded
arbours and enjoy and admire the extraordinary tranquillity of the place. The
nursery is a treasure trove of good plants and also sells clever iron cages for
supporting old-fashioned roses. Look out for the ancient mulberry and the
Judas tree.

HILLBARN HOUSE   12
Great Bedwyn, Hungerford, Wiltshire.
Mr and Mrs A.J. Buchanan

S of A4 between Hungerford and Marlborough. N side of the main street
● *Open 24th June, 16th Sept, 2.00 – 6.00 p.m.* ● *Entrance: £1.50, children
50p* ● *Parking in village* ● *Teas* ● *Toilet facilities* ● ***Grade III***

An excellent example of how exciting gardens can be when they are not in the
least grand or when they occupy difficult spaces. It has the perfect sunny
terrace, dotted with tubs of agapanthus and clipped bay trees. Beyond this is
a lawn and a wall with pleached lime trees to one side, beneath which is a pink
and white border of foxgloves, roses and Japanese anemones. On the opposite
side a good border is bolstered by evergreen shrubs such as *Viburnum davidii*

and an old pear tree dripping with single white roses. More fruit trees girdle the croquet lawn above the lawn. Quite different in mood is the neatness of the parterre rolled out in front of the white weatherboard pavilion, its box edges filled with musk roses, peonies and cotton lavender. A tunnel of hornbeam, always a thrilling idea, has windows allowing one to see the potager on one side and the swimming pool on the other. The unmatched neatness of this now very fashionable mixture of vegetable and flower growing – the herb garden is a chessboard sentinelled by standard roses – is quite something. An ebullient informal border breaks the regimentation easily, its colour scheme reduced to silver pink and blue. There is that most delightful thing – a walk underplanted with hellebores. More hornbeams cut as a scalloped hedge on stilts are used to hide the tennis court.

IFORD MANOR   13
Iford, Bradford-on-Avon, Wiltshire. Tel: (02216) 2364
Mr and Mrs J.J.W. Hignett

2½m SW of Bradford-on-Avon on A36 ● Open Wed and Sun, May to August, 2.00 – 5.00 p.m. and Summer Bank Holidays. Other times by appointment ● Best season: spring/summer ● Entrance: £1.00 ● Parking in village ● Teas on Sun ● Toilet facilities ● Grade I

It is always illuminating to see a famous architect and landscape gardener's own garden. Harold Peto found himself a near-ideal house in the steep valley through which the Avon slides languorously towards Bath. The topography lent itself to the strong architectural framework favoured by Peto and the creation of areas of entirely differing moods. The overriding intention is Italianate with a preponderance of cypresses, juniper, box and yew, punctuated at every turn by sarcophagi, urns, terracotta, marble seats and statues, columns, fountains and loggias. In a different vein is a meadow of naturalised bulbs, most spectacularly martagon lilies. A path leads from here to 'the cloisters' – an Italian-Romanesque building of Harold Peto's confection made with fragments collected from Italy. From here one can admire the whole, and the breath-taking valley and the walled kitchen garden on the other side.

KELLAWAYS   14
Chippenham, Wiltshire. Tel: (02497) 4203
Mrs D. Hoskins

3m NE of Chippenham on the East Tytherton road ● Open March – Nov by appointment and 17th June ● Best season: June ● Entrance: £1.00, children 20p and by collection box ● Parking ● Teas ● Toilet facilities ● Suitable for wheelchairs ● Plants for sale ● Grade IV

June is the time to visit because of the old roses which, cleverly underplanted, predominate throughout. The Cotswold-stone seventeenth-century house has a stone terrace on the walled garden side bursting with thyme and wild strawberries. The clemency of the walls mean that the owner can grow joyous things like sun roses, *Carpenteria californica* and other frailties. A serious cottage garden.

LACOCK ABBEY 15
Lacock, Chippenham, Wiltshire.   Tel: (024973) 227
The National Trust

3m S of Chippenham off A350 ● *Open April – 4th Nov, daily except Good Friday, 12 noon – 5.30 p.m. Closed Good Friday* ● *Best season: spring* ● *Entrance: £1.00 (cloisters and grounds)* ● *Parking* ● *Toilet facilities* ● *Suitable for wheelchairs* ● *Dogs on lead* ● *National Trust shop in village* ● *House open except Tues* ● **Grade IV**

This thirteenth-century abbey was turned into a private house after the Restoration. Gothicized by Sanderson Millar, it possesses no garden as such but a delightful parkland with the River Avon running through it and meadowland beyond. Cedar trees and floods of crocuses in the early spring followed by daffodils are the best features. A cottage in the village has hollyhocks up to the bedroom windows in August, worth seeing.

LAKE HOUSE 16
Amesbury, Wiltshire.
Captain O.N. Bailey

7m N of Salisbury W off the A345 to Amesbury ● *Open 29th April, 1st July, 2.00 – 6.30 p.m.* ● *Best season: spring/summer* ● *Entrance: £1.00, children free* ● *Parking* ● *Teas* ● *Toilet facilities* ● **Grade IV**

Part of the rich belt of gardens on the network of views round Salisbury which includes Wilton and Heale House. It has the River Avon flowing through water meadows and a backdrop of a flinty-walled Jacobean manor house. Features include herbaceous planting and a woodland garden.

LONGLEAT HOUSE 17
Warminster, Wiltshire.   Tel: (09853) 551
The Marquess of Bath

4½m SE of Frome on A362 ● *Open daily except 25th Dec, Easter – Sept, 10.00 a.m. – 6.00 p.m., rest of the year, 10.00 a.m. – 4.00 p.m.* ● *Entrance: £1.00, coaches free (garden only)* ● *Parking* ● *Helicopter landing pad available by prior request* ● *Refreshments: café, licensed restaurant, kiosks* ● *Picnic area by lake* ● *Toilet facilities* ● *Suitable for wheelchairs* ● *Dogs* ● *Plants for sale* ● *Shop* ● *House open* ● **Grade II**

This garden has been rearranged and tinkered with by most of the great names in English landscape history. There is nothing left to show today of the two earliest gardens here, the Elizabethan and that made by London and Wise in the 1680s which must have been one of the most elaborate ever made in England. Sadly it was barely half a century before 'Capability' Brown ironed out the formality and created a chain of lakes set amongst clumps of trees and hanging woods – best admired today from 'Heaven's Gate.' This was slightly altered by Repton in 1804 and added to in the 1870s when it became fashionable to collect exotic trees such as Wellingtonias and monkey puzzles and groves of rhododendrons and azaleas. In this century the fortunes of the garden came under the guiding hand of Russell Page. The park remains both beautiful and rewarding for the dendrologist. The formal garden focused on the orangery to the south of the house was redeveloped in the nineteenth century. It was simplified and improved upon by Russell Page to great effect. The orangery itself is a dream of wisteria and lemon-scented verbenas. The garden is open to visitors to dusk on summer evenings and this is when it is at its best. Elsewhere there are the distractions of the safari park and other exhibitions devised to appeal to the general public.

MOMPESSON HOUSE   18
The Close, Salisbury, Wiltshire. Tel: (0722) 335659
The National Trust

In centre of Salisbury, N side of Chorister's Green in the Cathedral close   ● Open April – 4th Nov, daily except Thurs and Fri, 12 noon – 5.30 p.m. Last admission 5.00 p.m.   ● Entrance: £2.00   ● Parking charged for in close ● Toilet facilities   ● Suitable for wheelchairs in garden and ground floor of house   ● House open   ● Grade IV

If visiting Salisbury, the Cathedral and the close are a must, so if you have been fortunate enough to find a parking space, take time also to visit this small walled garden. Summer is best, with the old-fashioned roses in bloom, but it is attractive throughout the open season. The Trust notes that the house contains an important collection of drinking glasses, so if they are your thing you can take them in too.

OARE HOUSE   19
Oare, Nr Pewsey, Wiltshire. Tel: (0672) 62613
Mr H. Keswick

2m N of Pewsey on A345   ● Open 29th April, 29th July, 2.00 – 6.00 p.m. ● Best season: spring/summer   ● Entrance: 60p, children 20p   ● Parking ● Teas on NGS days   ● Toilet facilities   ● Partly suitable for wheelchairs ● Grade III

The 1740 house was extended by Clough Williams Ellis in the 1920s and the garden created from 1920 to 1960 first by Sir Geoffrey Fry and now by Mr Henry Keswick. It is tantalising to glimpse this house from the road, set back as it is behind towering lime avenues and beech hedges – and when in spring magnolias flower and the grass is awash with narcissi you know the real garden must be something. To the south of the house is an intimate, formal 'library garden' of yew hedges reached by a wisteria-covered pergola – a gap in the hedge leads the eye down a pleached lime walk to a loggia. Next to this is a narrow secret garden called 'the ship'. On the western side of the house an immense terrace either side and on the far end the pool garden and far away a wooded hillside with a ride cut in it on axis with the house. The borders are necessarily substantial and planted as they should be with big shrubs and quantities of roses. The swimming pool area forms a separate garden handled with a similar understanding of scale and mass planting. The kitchen garden contains all the best things arranged in a purposeful manner with Irish yews, espalier fruit trees, vegetables and an herbaceous border edged with lavender. All this is a model of maintenance on a large scale.

ROCHE COURT SCULPTURE GARDEN 20
East Winterslow, Nr Salisbury, Wiltshire.
Tel: (0980) 862204/863015
Mrs M. Ponsonby

5m E of Salisbury, S off A30 ● *Open April – Sept, Sat and Sun only, 11.00 a.m. – 5.00 p.m. Weekdays by appointment* ● *Parking* ● *Partly suitable for wheelchairs* ● **Grade IV**

This is an exhibition of modern garden or 'public-place' sculpture by such noted practitioners as Armitage, Flanagan, Frink and by dead sculptors in the modern idiom like Gill and Hepworth. All works are for sale and information about them can be obtained from the New Art Centre, 41 Sloane Street, London SW1, Tel: (01) 235 5844. The garden itself, with pleasant views of Wiltshire downland, is eminently suited to its rôle as open air gallery.

SHELDON MANOR 21
Chippenham, Wiltshire. Tel: (0249) 652440
Major M.A. Gibbs

1½m W of Chippenham, S off A420 ● *Open 27th March – 2nd Oct, Sun, Thurs and Bank Holidays* ● *Best season: June* ● *Entrance: £1.00, children over 11, 50p, under 11 free* ● *Parking* ● *Refreshments* ● *Toilet facilities* ● *Suitable for wheelchairs* ● *House open (£2.25 house and garden)* ● **Grade IV**

An ancient house whose gardens are enclosed by barns and walls. The wonderful courts in front of the house have mostly been put to lawn but a whiff of formality remains in the form of yew hedges and lavender. It is best to visit in late June when the good collection of old-fashioned shrub roses, grown in grass, are blazing. The swimming pool is worth seeing as an example of the use of pleached trees and stone work to save it from looking as glaring as most do. Among the rare and interesting shrubs and plants look out for

Rosa gigantea 'Cooperi', *Grevillea sulphurea*, callistemon and romneya, a white Judas tree and the Chilean fire bush.

STOURHEAD 22
Stourton, Wiltshire. Tel: (0747) 840348
The National Trust

3m NW of Mere at Stourton off the B3092 ● Open daily, 8.00 a.m. – 7.00 p.m. (or sunset if earlier) ● Best season: May for rhododendrons – wonderful in winter when empty ● Entrance: Mar – Oct, £3.00, Nov – Feb, £2.00 ● Parking ● Refreshments: Spread Eagle Inn lunches, bar snacks ● Toilet facilities ● Suitable for wheelchairs ● Shop ● House open different times (£3.00 extra) ● Grade I

Many people go to Stourhead to see the rhododendrons, which are astonishing. However they are not part of the original visionary design by Henry Hoare II in 1741–80, a paragon in its day and almost the greatest surviving garden of its kind. The sequence of arcadian images is revealed gradually if one follows a route anti-clockwise around the lake, having come from the house along the top and seen the lake from above. Each experience is doubly inspiring in that one enjoys the eye-catcher across the lake, almost unattainable and mirage-like, and when one reaches one's goal – always some other vision lures one on – the boat-house, the Temple of Flora, the bridge, Temple of Apollo, rock bridge, cascade (these two are tucked away) the pantheon, thatched cottage and the grotto. The view from the Temple of Apollo (1765) was described by Horace Walpole as 'one of the most picturesque scenes in the world' by which he meant that it was as fine as a painting. To gain a better idea of how these buildings would have looked had the surrounding planting remained as it was originally, take a walk by Turner's Paddock Lake below the cascade. Between 1791 and 1838 Richard Colt Hoare planted many new species particularly from America, tulip trees, swamp cypresses, Indian bean trees – the beginning of an arboretum. He also introduced *Rhododendron ponticum*. From 1894 the sixth Baronet replaced these with the latest kinds of hybrid rhododendron and azaleas, and a large number of copper beeches and conifers, such as the Japanese white pine, Sitka spruce and Californian nutmeg – all are record-sized specimens now.

THOMPSON'S HILL 23
Sherston, Nr Malmesbury, Wiltshire. Tel: (0666) 840766
Mr and Mrs J.C. Cooper

On B4040. At Sherston turn left opposite church down hill, then bear right up Thompson's Hill ● Open 17th June, 2.00 – 6.30 p.m. ● Best season: June ● Entrance: £1.00, children free ● Parking in road ● Grade II

Faultlessly-maintained half-acre garden created over the last six years on derelict ground. Terraced area behind house, planted in grey colours, enclosed by clipped yew hedges and three Gothic arches with climbing roses and clematis. Beyond, set in lawns, are island beds with mixed herbaceous planting. Old roses and grouped prunus add height and colour. An example of what can be achieved with taste and energy on an unpropitious site.

WILTON HOUSE   24
Wilton, Salisbury, Wiltshire.   Tel: (0722) 743115
The Earl of Pembroke

2½m W of Salisbury on A30 in the town centre   ● Open 24th March – 15th Oct, Tues, Sats and Bank Holiday Mons, 11.00 a.m. – 6.00 p.m., Suns 1.00 – 6.00 p.m. Last admission 5.15 p.m.   ● Entrance: grounds only £1.30, children 90p (inc. adventure playground) ● Parking (well-shaded for leaving dogs in cars) ● Refreshments: restaurant ● Toilet facilities ● Suitable for wheelchairs ● Plants for sale in garden centre separate from main house and garden area ● Shop ● Grade II

The first garden that one sees at Wilton is almost the most recent. The front (north) courtyard of the house has been laid out to a design by David Vicary using formal pleached limes, lavender and a really torrential fountain which baffles the traffic noise on the A30. It has created a cool green place of immense style which manages to answer the architecture of the house. Dotted about this garden are statues, which along with the grotto facade (sadly not viewable), are the last vestiges of one of the earliest gardens here – the complex garden to the south front laid out by Isaac de Cans in 1633. Today it is almost impossible to imagine the elaborations of this garden when one sees only the stretch down to the River Nadder and the Palladian bridge of 1737. Beyond is the vista to Sir William Chamber's pavilion. Visitors are not allowed into the nineteenth-century terraced garden on the west side but a walk down the broad gravel under the cedars to the east of the house brings one to the recently established rose garden, which although a bit lost, has a large collection of old-fashioned roses. Beyond this is a summerhouse and a statue from the Arundel collection; there are plans to build a water garden here soon. For children there is a good adventure playground.

YORKSHIRE (North)

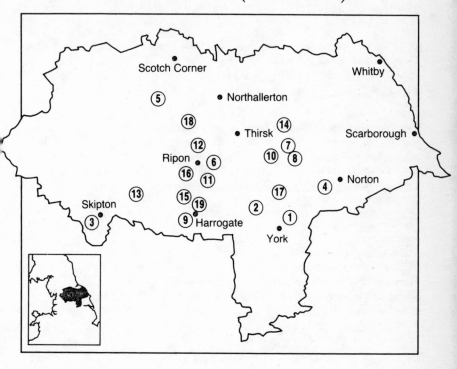

ASKHAM BRYAN COLLEGE OF AGRICULTURE AND HORTICULTURE 1
York, North Yorkshire. Tel: (0904) 702121
North Yorkshire County Council

4m SW of York on A64 ● *Open for special groups by appointment and on 2nd June, 1.30 – 5.30 p.m.* ● *Entrance: free on college open days* ● *Parking £1.00 per car* ● *Toilet facilities* ● *Suitable for wheelchairs* ● *Plants for sale* ● *Grade II*

As Askham Bryan is one of the prime centres for the teaching of practical amenity-horticulture, it is not surprising that it has high-quality decorative gardens. There are comprehensive collections of tropical plants in the greenhouses and outside, herbaceous borders, lawns, shrubs and a small arboretum. Although primarily established for teaching, it now has a very pleasant recreational role to fill. Almost all the plants are clearly labelled.

BENINGBROUGH HALL 2
Beningbrough, North Yorkshire. Tel: (0904) 470666
The National Trust

*8m NW of York off A19 York-Thirsk road at Shipton ● Open April, Sat, Sun
and Easter (13th – 19th April), daily, 12 noon – 6 p.m. May – Oct, Tues, Wed,
Thurs, Sat, Sun and Bank Holiday Mon. 12 noon – 6.00 p.m. Last admission
5.30 p.m. ● Best season: spring and summer ● Entrance: £1.90 ● Parking
● Teas ● Toilet facilities ● Suitable for wheelchairs ● House open at extra
charge. Guided tours and parties by prior appointment ● Grade III*

The main formal garden comprising geometrically-patterned parterres was
originally laid out at the time the house was constructed, but was replaced
during the late eighteenth century with sweeping lawns and specimen trees,
part of an estate of 365 acres. Although generally well-ordered, this is
essentially a pleasure garden with a historic framework amongst which
considerable recent planting has been integrated. The wilderness and two
privy gardens have been restored to eighteenth-century standards, and there is
a nineteenth-century American garden and a Victorian conservatory. In
conjunction with the imposing Georgian house it is well worthy of a visit.

BROUGHTON HALL 3
Broughton, Nr Skipton, North Yorkshire. Tel: (0756) 2267
Mr H.R. Tempest

*4m W of Skipton on the A59, take first left after the Bull Inn ● Open Bank
Holiday Suns only or by arrangement with the owner ● Entrance: £1.00
● Parking ● Toilet facilities ● Suitable for wheelchairs ● Grade III*

As well as being a pleasant country house in parklands, this is of interest to the
gardening historian as one of the best surviving examples of the Victorian
designer Nesfield who spent 30 years laying out the garden. He also sited
statues in the park and planted a semi-natural landscape, but it is the parterre
on the walled terrace which will most interest Nesfield fans. It has been
restored to his design, alas omitting the blue and white gravels he preferred.
Nesfield was successful in his time, working for Kew and submitting plans for
the forecourt of Buckingham Palace (which might have been rather fun in
coloured gravels).

CASTLE HOWARD 4
Malton, North Yorkshire. Tel: (065384) 333
Castle Howard Estates Ltd

*5m SW of Malton off A64 York – Scarborough road ● Open 20th March – Oct,
daily, 10.00 – 4.30 p.m. ● Entrance: £4.00, OAP £3.00, children £2.00
(house and garden) ● Parking ● Refreshments: cafeteria ● Toilet facilities
● Partly suitable for wheelchairs ● Plants for sale in large plant centre ● Shop
● House open ● Grade I*

Described as one of the finest examples of 'The Heroic Age of English Landscape Architecture' the grounds were first designed by Sir John Vanburgh assisted by Nicholas Hawksmoor to complement the castle designed by Vanburgh. This layout still generally exists, although in recent times features have been added. Although known principally as a very fine landscape, there is also much for the enthusiastic garden lover. The rose garden developed during the past few years has one of the largest collections of old-fashioned and species roses in Europe. Way Wood and the adjacent area accommodate a very fine collection of rhododendrons, an adjunct to the newly extended arboretum which will soon be one of the largest and most important in the United Kingdom. Most of the plants are well labelled.

CONSTABLE BURTON HALL 5
Leyburn, North Yorkshire. Tel: (0677) 50428
Mr Charles Wyvill

3m E of Leyburn on A684 ● *Open April – 4th Aug, daily, 9.00 a.m. – 6.00 p.m.* ● *Best season: spring* ● *Entrance: 50p* ● *Parking* ● *Partly suitable for wheelchairs* ● *House open (1768)* ● **Grade IV**

A pleasant garden to visit in beautiful countryside with large specimen trees in a parkland setting probably contemporary with the John Carr house. Essentially a strolling garden rather than one for the plantsperson. Despite obvious signs of labour shortage it is holding its own.

COPT HEWICK HALL 6
Copt Hewick, Nr Ripon, North Yorkshire. Tel: (0765) 3946
Earl and Countess of Ronaldshay

2m E of Ripon, 1½m W of A1 at Dishforth roundabout ● *Open 3rd, 24th June, 2.00 – 5.30 p.m.* ● *Entrance: £1.00, OAP 75p, children free* ● *Parking* ● *Teas* ● *Suitable for wheelchairs* ● *Plants for sale* ● **Grade III**

Laid out during the Victorian period and with some of those features still remaining, this is an interesting place for the keen plantsperson as it contains a range of choice, unusual and tender plants not often associated with northern gardens. The old walled rose garden is a delight, filled with a collection of old-fashioned, shrub and species roses. Amongst the specimen trees and shrubs growing in this garden are arbutus and halesia.

DUNCOMBE PARK 7
Helmsley, North Yorkshire. Tel: (0439) 70213
Trustees of Duncombe Park

1m SW of Helmsley on road S of Castle ● *Open May – Aug, Wed, 10.00 a.m. – 4.00 p.m.* ● *Entrance: £1.00* ● *Parking in town where tickets obtainable. No cars in park* ● *Suitable for wheelchairs* ● *Dogs on lead* ● **Grade III**

A fine terrace established in 1715 with a domed rotunda by Vanburgh at one end and at the other a round Doric temple. Below is one of the earliest ha-has. Beyond the woodland below the terrace, one can glimpse the river and its cascades. On the other side of the terrace are formal yew hedges. There is a secret garden, a ruined orangery, a Tuscan temple and a wood said to hold the tallest lime and the tallest ash.

FOUNTAINS ABBEY
(see Studley Royal page 421)

GILLING CASTLE   8
Gilling East, North Yorkshire.   Tel: (04393) 207
The Right Reverend the Abbot of Ampleforth

18m N of York on B1363 York – Helmsley road   ● Open July and August, daily, 1.00 p.m. – dusk   ● Entrance: 70p, children free   ● Parking
● Grade III

A lovely garden in outstanding scenery. The terraces have been constructed on the south-facing side of the garden, four of them tumbling down the slope from an expansive lawn at the top. Many old-fashioned flowers grow in the borders with a backdrop of majestic trees.

HARLOW CAR GARDENS   9
Crag Lane, Beckwithshaw, Harrogate, North Yorkshire.
Tel: (0423) 565418
Northern Horticultural Society

1½m W of centre of Harrogate off B6162 Otley road   ● Open all year, daily, 9.00 a.m. – 7.30 p.m. or dusk   ● Entrance: £2.00, OAP £1.50, accompanied children free. NHS and RHS members free. Reduced rates for parties by appointment   ● Parking   ● Refreshments: morning coffee, lunch, teas, picnics, 10.00 a.m. – 7.00 p.m.   ● Toilet facilities   ● Partly suitable for wheelchairs ● Guide dogs only   ● Gift shop   ● Grade III

A 60-acre site, formerly farmland, established in 1948 by the Northern Horticultural Society as a centre for garden plants trials in the north of England. Now also provides a wide range of horticultural courses for amateur gardeners. It is said that if a plant prospers at Harlow Car it will grow anywhere in the north. Hosts the National collections of heather and rhubarb cultivars as well as those of hypericum, dryopteris and polypodium. Extensive streamside planting with one of the best collections of moisture-loving plants in the north of England. Large collections of rhododendrons, roses and alpines. Boasts a very fine alpine house and two extensive rock gardens. The arboretum regrettably shows some signs of neglect and some of the shrub borders are rather jaded.

NEWBURGH PRIORY

10

Coxwold, North Yorkshire. Tel: (03476) 435
Sir George Wombwell, Bt

*3½m SE of Thirsk on A19, turn E to Coxwold ● Open mid-May to Aug, Wed
and Sun, 2.00 - 6.00 p.m. Also Easter Mon and Aug Bank Holiday Mon.
Parties of 25 or more on other days by appointment at reduced rates ● Entrance:
70p, children 30p ● Parking. Coaches by appointment ● Refreshments and
picnics ● Toilet facilities ● Suitable for wheelchairs ● Dogs ● House open 2.30
- 4.45 p.m. (extra charge) ● Grade III*

The house (formerly a twelfth-century priory) has been the home of one family
since 1538. Topiary is the first thing to strike the visitor, with a vast earl's
coronet in yew at the entrance, celebrating a former owner, Earl Fauconberg.
The house frontage is also decorated with topiary and, at the side, an avenue
of peacocks, birds and dogs recalls Francis Bacon's observation: 'they be for
children'. A tree-lined avenue leads to the wild water garden, created by the
late owner in 1938 on a sloping hillside. Below is an alpine trough-garden and
rock plants. The walled kitchen garden appears productive, and the overall
atmosphere is of time past rather than time present.

NEWBY HALL

11

Nr Ripon, North Yorkshire. Tel: (0423) 322583
Mr and Mrs Robin Compton

*4m SE of Ripon on B6265 3m W of A1 ● Open 24th March - 29th Oct, daily
except Mon (but open Bank Holiday Mons), 11.00 a.m. - 5.30 p.m. ● Best
season: spring for the laburnum walk ● Entrance: £2.00, OAP £1.80, children
£1.50 (house and gardens £3.60, OAP £3.00, children £2.00). Reduced rate
for parties by appointment ● Parking ● Refreshments: licensed restaurant open
11.00 a.m. ● Toilet facilities ● Suitable for wheelchairs (provided) ● Dogs on
lead ● Plants for sale ● Shop ● House open from 12 noon ● Grade II*

The family home of the owners who have set an exceptionally high standard of
maintenance while retaining the atmosphere of an established and still lived-
in country house. Newby Hall is seventeenth-century with additions and
interior by Robert Adam, set in 25 acres of open parkland and some features
remain from the eighteenth century such as east to west walk marked by
Venetian statuary, backed by yew and purple plum. The south face has long
wide green slopes down to the River Ure with herbaceous borders on either
side backed by clipped hedges and flowering shrubs. Cross walks lead to
smaller gardens full of interest. These include species roses, tropical walled,
rock and the stepped water gardens as well as a fine woodland area attributed
to Ellen Willmott. Facilities for children. Special events are held in June, July
and September such as craft fairs and historic car rallies with their own
admission prices.

NORTON CONYERS   12
Ripon, North Yorkshire.   Tel: (076584) 333
Sir James Graham, Bt

3½m N of Ripon. Follow Wath sign on A61 Ripon – Thirsk road ● *Open all year, Mon – Fri, 9.00 a.m. – 5.00 p.m., Sat and Sun, 2.00 – 5.00 p.m.* ● *Entrance: 50p, children free* ● *Parking* ● *Teas* ● *Partly suitable for wheelchairs* ● *Dogs on lead* ● *Plants for sale* ● *House open Suns in June and early Sept. Also Bank Holiday Sun and Mon and every day early Aug* ● *Grade III*

The lure of the garden is very much with the past and particularly the association of the house with Charlotte Brontë who made it one of the models for Thornfield Hall in *Jane Eyre*. Norton Conyers has a historic feel that transcends the planting which is pleasant but modest. Most plantings are of the cottage-garden type, although the gardens themselves are quite extensive.

PARCEVALL HALL GARDENS   13
Appletreewick, Pateley Bridge, North Yorkshire. Tel: (075672) 311
Walsingham College (Yorkshire Properties) Ltd

1m NE of Appletreewick off B6265 Pateley Bridge – Skipton road ● *Open Easter – Oct, daily, 10.00 a.m. – 6.00 p.m. and for NGS* ● *Best season: spring* ● *Entrance: £1.00, children 50p* ● *Parking* ● *Picnics in orchard* ● *Plants for sale* ● *Grade III*

A garden of great interest to the plantsperson, many of Sir William Milner's treasures having survived years of neglect. The garden is currently being restored and is well worth a visit, if merely to enjoy the spectacular views from the terrace. A fine range of rhododendrons, many originally collected in China, still grow happily here. Fishponds. Rock garden.

RIEVAULX TERRACE AND TEMPLES   14
Rievaulx, Helmsley, North Yorkshire.   Tel: (04396) 340
The National Trust

2½m NW of Helmsley on B1257 ● *Open April – Oct, daily, 10.30 a.m. – 6.00 p.m. or dusk if earlier. Last admission 5.30 p.m. Ionic Temple closed 1.00 – 2.00 p.m.* ● *Entrance: £1.50, children 70p* ● *Parking. Coach park 200 yards* ● *Picnics* ● *Toilet facilities* ● *Suitable for wheelchairs on terrace. Steps to temples* ● *Dogs on lead* ● *Shop and information centre* ● *Two eighteenth-century temples and exhibition of landscape design in basement of Ionic temple* ● *Grade II*

This is a unique example of the eighteenth-century passion for the romantic and the picturesque – that is, making landscape look like a picture. The work was done at the behest of Thomas Duncombe around 1754 and consists of a half-mile-long serpentine grass terrace high above Ryedale with fine views. At one end is a Palladian-style Ionic temple with furniture by William Kent and elaborate ceilings. At the other end is a Tuscan temple with a raised platform from which are spectacular views of the Rye Valley. The concept is wonderfully achieved, but those who expect gardens to have flowers must prepare their minds for higher things.

RIPLEY CASTLE 15
Ripley, Harrogate, North Yorkshire. Tel: (0423) 770152
Sir Thomas Ingilby, Bt

2½m N of Harrogate off A61 Harrogate – Ripon road • *Open Good Friday to end Oct, 11.00 a.m. – 5.00 p.m.* • *Best season: spring* • *Entrance: 85p, OAP 60p, children 50p. Reduced rates for large parties by appointment* • *Parking* • *Refreshments: morning coffee and tea, picnics* • *Toilet facilities* • *Suitable for wheelchairs* • *Dogs on lead* • *Gift shop* • *House open at extra charge* • *Grade III*

A mid-eighteenth-century 'Capability' Brown landscape with formal gardens developed by Peter Aram for a family that has been here since the thirteenth century. A beautiful landscape, especially during spring at daffodil time. Magnificent specimen trees. The formal areas have seen better days, but the current owner is making considerable strides in their restoration. Lake with attractive Victorian iron bridge. Eighteenth-century orangery and summer houses. Vegetable garden. Woodland walk to a temple with fine views.

STUDLEY ROYAL AND FOUNTAINS ABBEY 16
Ripon, North Yorkshire. Tel: (076586) 333
The National Trust

2m SW of Ripon, 9m N of Harrogate. Follow Studley Roger sign off B6265 Ripon – Pateley Bridge road • *Deer park open all year during daylight. Abbey and garden open all year, daily (except 24th, 25th Dec and Fri in Nov – Jan) as follows: Jan – March and Nov – Dec, 10.00 a.m. – 5.00 p.m. or dusk if earlier. April – June and Sept, 10.00 a.m. – 7.00 p.m. July and Aug, 10.00 a.m. – 8.00 p.m. Oct, 10.00 a.m. – 6.00 p.m. or dusk if earlier* • *Entrance: deer park free. Gardens £2.40, children £1.00* • *Teas* • *Toilet facilities* • *Suitable for wheelchairs* • *Gift shop* • *Grade I*

The gardens were created by John Aislabie, who had been Chancellor of the Exchequer but whose finances were 'ruined' by the South Sea Bubble in 1720 and who retired here to his estate in 1722 and worked until his death in 1742 to make one of the finest water-gardens in the country. The lakes, grotto springs, formal canal and water features plus buildings such as the Temple of Piety turn what is essentially a landscape with large trees and sweeping lawns into one of the most stunning of green gardens. Furthermore, there is the association with the largest and most complete Cistercian foundation in Europe described by the *Oxford Companion* as probably the noblest monastic ruin in Christendom. This can be seen in the distance from the 'surprise view', through a door in a small building.

SUTTON PARK   17
**Sutton-in-the-Forest, York, North Yorkshire.   Tel: (0347) 810249
Mrs N.M.D. Sheffield**

*8m N of York on B1363 ● Open April – 1st Oct, daily except Sat, 11.00 a.m. – 5.30 p.m. Parties at other times by appointment at reduced rates ● Parking. Coaches by appointment ● Refreshments: tea room and restaurant. Picnics ● Toilet facilities ● Suitable for wheelchairs ● Plants sometimes for sale ● Shop ● Georgian house open Easter weekend, April, Sun from 1.30 p.m., May – 12th Sept, Sun, Tues and Bank Holiday Mondays from 1.30 p.m. Also ice-house and nature trail ● **Grade III***

One of the most distinguished English garden designers of recent times, Percy Cane, came to this Georgian house and its terraced site in 1962 with its views over parkland said to have been moulded by 'Capability' Brown. Cane was inspired to take up his profession after a visit to Harold Peto's Easton Lodge. He started the elegant planting which has been most carefully expanded by the present owners. There are several fine features on the terraces – a tall beech hedge curved to take a marble seat, ironwork gazebos and everywhere soft stone. The woodland walk leads to a temple.

THORP PERROW ARBORETUM   18
**Firby, Bedale, North Yorkshire.   Tel: (0325) 462811
Sir John Ropner, Bt**

*2m S of Bedale, signposted off B6268 Masham road ● Open April – Oct during daylight hours ● Best season: spring and autumn ● Entrance: £1.00, OAP and children 50p ● Parking ● Picnic area ● **Grade II***

The arboretum was established some 50 years ago on open farmland by Sir Leonard Ropner and is one of the finest collections of trees in the north of England, containing over 2000 species. Unfortunately the arboretum suffered some years of neglect and the present owner is currently undertaking restoration. While many of the trees will never regain their natural habit owing to crowding and lack of pruning, the collection is still undisputedly one of the most comprehensive in the North.

VALLEY GARDENS   19
**1 Valley Drive, Harrogate, North Yorkshire.   Tel: (0423) 500600
Harrogate Borough Council**

In centre of Harrogate, main entrance is near Pump Museum ● Open daily during daylight hours ● Best season: spring and summer ● Entrance: free

● *Parking*   ● *Refreshments: morning coffee, light lunches, teas*   ● *Toilet facilities*   ● *Suitable for wheelchairs*   ● *Dogs*   ● *Grade III*

One of the best-known public gardens in the north of England laid out earlier this century at the time Harrogate was fashionable as a spa. This is the site of the annual Great Spring Flower Show which sadly causes damage each year, from which areas of the gardens are slow to recover. While the stream garden and rock features have gone into decline in recent years, the standard of formal bedding remains very high. A very fine dahlia display is an annual feature.

THE GRADING SYSTEM

This is the most subjective aspect of the *Guide* and one which may cause some disagreement on the part of owners as well as visitors. We stress that its purpose is to serve as an indication to visitors in order to give them some advance information about the status of the garden as viewed by our inspectors and editors. Readers will appreciate that direct comparisons cannot be made between a huge estate like Chatsworth with its staff of professional experts and a tiny plantsman's garden in a terraced house, tended with dedication by a single owner. This being said, both may be excellent of their kind and therefore be worthy of consideration for a visit, and considered by the *Guide* to be at the top of their class. Conversely a lesser grading does not imply any criticism of a garden but is an attempt to guide the potential reader as to its relative merits if a choice has to be made between several gardens. Broadly speaking the intention of the four grades is as follows:

Grade I Amongst the best gardens in the world in terms of design and content. Many are of historic importance, but some are of recent origin. Overseas visitors to Britain or Ireland are recommended to include them in their itinerary.

Grade II Gardens of high quality, though not perhaps as unique as Grade I, and worth travelling a considerable distance to visit. Sometimes the property as a whole, and the general ambience, make the visit particularly rewarding.

Grade III These are gardens which our inspectors suggest it would be worth driving fifty miles or more to visit. They may have some special feature of design or plant content while not being considered as justifying a higher grade overall.

Grade IV Gardens of considerable merit and well worth visiting when in the region.

YORKSHIRE
(South & West)

ARTHINGTON HALL

1

Arthington, Otley, West Yorkshire. Tel: (0532) 842115
Mr C.E.W. Sheepshanks

5m E of Otley off A659 ● *Open by appointment only* ● *Entrance: £1.00,*
children 20p ● *Parking* ● *Teas* ● *Suitable for wheelchairs* ● ***Grade III***

A large garden which is improving all the time. Set in beautiful countryside
with lovely views it is being enhanced by a developing tree collection,
especially maples, and carefully tended woodland walks. There is an area of
partly walled garden, greenhouses and both fruit and vegetable gardens.

BRAMHAM PARK 2
Bramham, Nr Wetherby, West Yorkshire. Tel: (0937) 844265
Mr and Mrs G. Lane Fox

5m S of Wetherby just off northbound A1 ● *Open Easter and Spring Bank Holiday weekends, 11th June - 31st August, Sun, Tues, Wed, Thurs, 1.15 - 5.30 p.m. Last admission 5.00 p.m.* ● *Entrance: £1.50, OAP 80p, children 50p (house and garden £2.00, OAP £1.30, children £1.00)* ● *Parking* ● *Toilet facilities* ● *Partly suitable for wheelchairs* ● *House open June - August at extra charge* ● ***Grade II***

Created by Robert Benson after the style of Le Nôtre some 250 years ago, this is one of the few landscape gardens in the French style to survive in this country. Although the great storm of 1962 removed many specimen beeches and disrupted the layout of the avenues, the original concept has been maintained and is being perpetuated. Apart from its uniqueness of design, the gardens also have a substantial rose garden which provides summer-long colour and an interesting herbaceous border. However it is the splendid architectural features and the trees which would have been familiar to the garden's creator, in his day Chancellor of the Exchequer, and as the visitor wonders at the beauty of this garden he may well muse how many Chancellors have left such a legacy to the nation.

EAST RIDDLESDEN HALL 3
Bradford Road, Keighley, West Yorkshire. Tel: (0535) 607075
The National Trust

1m NE of Keighley on S side of A650 and 3m NW of Bingley ● *Open May - June, Sept - Oct, Wed - Sun, 2.00 - 5.30 p.m., July - Aug, Wed - Sun and Bank Holiday Mon, 12 noon - 5.30 p.m., April weekends only* ● *Entrance: £1.50, accompanied children 70p, parties of 15 or more £1.30 per person, children 60p* ● *Parking* ● *Teas* ● *Toilet facilities* ● *Suitable for wheelchairs: not in refreshment room* ● *Dogs on lead* ● *Shop* ● *House open* ● ***Grade IV***

A traditional seventeenth-century Yorkshire manor house. Neglected through much of nineteenth and twentieth centuries and restored 1983 - 84 by the National Trust. The great barn is considered one of the finest in the north of England. A well- tended formal walled garden of modest size and a monastic fish pond in grounds running down to the river.

GOLDEN ACRE PARK 4
Otley Road, Leeds, West Yorkshire. Tel: (0523) 463504
Leeds City Council

Off A660 Leeds - Otley road at approach to Bramhope ● *Open daily during daylight* ● *Entrance: free* ● *Parking* ● *Refreshments: morning coffee, teas, lunches* ● *Toilet facilities* ● *Suitable for wheelchairs* ● *Dogs* ● ***Grade II***

Until 1945 when it was purchased by Leeds Corporation for £18,500 this was a privately-owned pleasure park. Since then it has been developed as an important public park and minor botanic garden. It is sited on a pleasant undulating site leading down to a lake. Extensively-planted tree collection with most specimens labelled. Rhododendrons are a feature in the spring, along with alpine plants both in the rock garden and in the alpine house. Golden Acre Park is noted for its very fine collection of houseleeks or sempervivums as well as its heather collection. Demonstration plots are maintained where instruction is provided for home gardeners.

HAREWOOD HOUSE 5
Harewood, Leeds, West Yorkshire. Tel: (0532) 886225
The Earl and Countess of Harewood

7m N of Leeds on A61 ● Open Easter weekend – Oct, daily, 10.00 a.m. – 5.00 p.m. and 2nd Sun in Feb, March and Nov ● Best season: early June and early Oct ● Entrance: £1.75, children 75p ● Parking ● Refreshments: light lunches, teas, etc., restaurant and bar, picnic area ● Toilet facilities ● Partly suitable for wheelchairs ● Dogs on lead ● Plants for sale ● Shop ● House open 11.00 a.m. – 5.00 p.m. Last admission 4.30 p.m. £3.30 ● Grade II

Originally laid out in the 1770s by 'Capability' Brown the gardens and park still retain many of his characteristic features, most notably in a majestic lake and well-wooded horizon to the park, although many of his trees have been lost. Nineteenth-century rhododendrons obscure the edge of his lake but afford a fine sight reflected on its surface when flowering in early June. Other features in this woodland setting are a vaguely Japanese bog garden below the lake's cascade. Sir Charles Barry's terrace of the 1840s adds a formal contrast with its justly renowned Victorian parterres and fountains, herbaceous border and roses. Large quantities of trees and shrubs in these excellently maintained grounds ensure a long season of interest.

THE HOLLIES 6
Weetwood Lane, Leeds, West Yorkshire. Tel: (0523) 463504
Leeds City Council

Entrance off Weetwood Lane, off A660 Leeds – Otley road ● Open daily during daylight ● Best season: spring ● Entrance: free ● Parking ● Toilet facilities ● Partly suitable for wheelchairs ● Grade III

The original layout is believed to be Victorian. The gardens were given to Leeds Corporation in 1921 by the Brown family in memory of a relative killed during World War I. The fine informal, largely woodland garden features woody plants, especially rhododendrons, many rarely seen growing in this part of the North. Ferns flourish and a varied collection of hydrangeas provide late summer colour. Many slightly tender subjects such as eucryphia, embothrium and drimys thrive in the pleasant micro-climate.

30 LATCHMERE ROAD   7
Leeds, West Yorkshire. Tel: (0532) 751261
Mr and Mrs Joe Brown

*NW of Leeds off A6120, along Fillingfir Drive ● Open by appointment to
horticultural societies and garden clubs, and every Sun from 24th June – 5th
Aug (excluding 8th July), 2.30 – 5.30 p.m. ● Entrance: 50p, children 25p
● Suitable for wheelchairs ● Plants for sale ● Grade III*

A council-house garden of exceptional merit created from scratch over the last
20 years by Mr and Mrs Brown, this is now one of the finest examples of
garden design in a small garden. Herbaceous plants, ferns, climbers and
shrubs all contribute to a series of mini-features which the visitor passes
through in a controlled circuit of the garden. These features include a clematis
collection, chamomile lawn, sink gardens, pools, patio and limestone garden.

LING BEECHES   8
Ling Lane, Scarcroft, Leeds, West Yorkshire. Tel: (0532) 892450
Mr and Mrs Arnold Rakusen

*7m NE of Leeds in Ling Lane, Scarcroft off A58 Leeds – Wetherby road ● Open
20th May, 16th Sept, 2.00 – 5.30 p.m. and by appointment ● Best season:
spring and summer ● Entrance: £1.00, children 50p ● Parking ● Teas
● Partly suitable for wheelchairs ● Plants for sale ● Grade III*

A two-acre woodland garden created during the past 30 years by Mrs Arnold
Rakusen amongst handsome stands of beech, oak, rowan and pine. Well-
arranged plantings of choice and unusual ground-cover plants, especially
foliage subjects. An excellent collection of ferns associate with bulbs and
spring-flowering hellebores. The tasteful plantings offer lessons for novice
gardeners, and there will also be ideas for those whose emphasis is on labour-
saving plants.

LISTER PARK   9
Keighley Road, Bradford, West Yorkshire. Tel: (0274) 493313
City of Bradford Metropolitan Council

*1½m N of Bradford centre (Forster Square) on A650 Bradford – Keighley road
● Open all year, daily during daylight hours ● Best season: spring and summer
● Entrance: free ● Parking in surrounding streets ● Light refreshments: daily
except Mon, 10.00 a.m. – 4.00 p.m. ● Toilet facilities ● Suitable for
wheelchairs ● Dogs on lead ● Cartwright Hall, City Art Gallery and Museum
open, April – Sept, Tues – Sun, 10.00 a.m. – 6.00 p.m., Oct – Mar, Tues – Sun,
10.00 a.m. – 5.00 p.m. ● Grade IV*

This used to be a well-tended park with an excellent garden and botanical
garden, including greenhouses with tropical plants. It is now a disaster, very
poorly maintained and a sad example of how councils, under pressure from

their political masters, make savings which result in neglect, and, it may appear, disinterest. The botanical garden still exists but appears untended. The only reason for including it in this guide is that there is a formal floral display in front of Cartwright Hall and an interesting floral clock, a rare example of Victorian ingenuity which is well worth seeing by those living in or passing through the city, perhaps to visit the National Museum of Photography, Film and TV.

LOTHERTON HALL 10
Aberford, West Yorkshire. Tel: (0532) 463510
Leeds City Council

3½m NE of Garforth on B1217 ● *Open all year, daily, 10.30 a.m. – dusk* ● *Entrance: free* ● *Parking. Coaches by appointment* ● *Refreshments and picnics* ● *Toilet facilities* ● *Dogs except in bird garden* ● *Shop* ● *House open. Bird garden closed Mon. Working shire horses* ● *Grade III*

A 10-acre garden which grows surprisingly tender shrubs and climbers rare in this raw Northern climate but here protected by walls and tree shelters. The design is thought to owe something to Ellen Willmott and is rather an Edwardian period piece. Formal rose garden, an avenue of yews leading to a white summerhouse, walled garden, sunken garden with lily pond, a rockery glen of 1912 and a ha-ha now filled in and planted with primulas, astilbes and meconopsis. Sports lovers will be interested to see the tennis court, one of the earliest of brick construction.

NOSTELL PRIORY 11
Nr Wakefield, West Yorkshire. Tel: (0924) 863892
The National Trust

6m SE of Wakefield on A638 ● *Open Easter – Oct, 12 noon – 5.00 p.m., Sun and Bank Holidays, 11.00 a.m. – 5.00 p.m.* ● *Best season: summer for rose garden* ● *Entrance: £1.30, children 60p, (house and garden £2.40, children £1.20)* ● *Parking* ● *Light refreshments and teas* ● *Toilet facilities inc. disabled* ● *Suitable for wheelchairs* ● *Dogs on lead* ● *Shop* ● *House open from 12 noon* ● *Grade III*

An eighteenth-century mansion set in open parkland with an attractive lake and a variety of well-established trees. A fine, well-tended and well-labelled rose garden is the main gardening feature. There is a children's playground and a picnic area. Special events and fairs are held during the season, some in marquees in front of the house, with a special admission charge (not applied if house and garden only visited).

ROUNDHAY PARK 12
Roundhay Road, Leeds, West Yorkshire. Tel: (0523) 463504
Leeds City Council

*Off A58 Roundhay Road from Leeds City centre • Open daily in daylight hours • Entrance: free • Parking • Refreshments: light snacks • Toilet facilities • Suitable for wheelchairs • Dogs • **Grade II***

The intensively-cultivated canal gardens area was formerly the kitchen and ornamental gardens of the Nicholson family who sold the site to the Leeds Corporation in 1871. The extensive parkland with its fine trees is an excellent setting for the canal gardens with their formal bedding and generous collections of tropical plants in greenhouses. The collections are constantly being added to and are a Mecca for enthusiastic gardeners.

SHEFFIELD BOTANICAL GARDENS 13
Sheffield, South Yorkshire. Tel: (0742) 671115
Sheffield Council

*½m from A625, 1½m SW of Sheffield centre • Open daily, daylight hours • Entrance: free • Parking in surrounding streets • Toilet facilities inc. disabled • Suitable for wheelchairs • Dogs on lead • Plants for sale occasionally, by Friends of Botanical Society • **Grade II***

A fine example of a botanical garden well-tended by a local authority, with support from and participation by local gardening societies and helpers. Flower displays are changed seasonally and are of high quality. All plants are well-labelled, including those in the special woodland area. A small aviary and an aquarium provide additional features. The gardens, though close to Sheffield centre, are secluded with good seating and grass areas suitable for children and recreation.

SILVER BIRCHES 14
Ling Lane, Scarcroft, Leeds, West Yorkshire. Tel: (0532) 892335
Mr S.C. Thompson

*7m NE of Leeds in Ling Lane, Scarcroft off A58 Leeds – Wetherby road • Open for NGS 22nd, 29th May, 2.00 – 6.00 p.m. and by appointment June – Oct for parties • Entrance: £1.00, children 50p • Parking • Teas • Partly suitable for wheelchairs • Plants for sale • **Grade III***

A two and a half-acre garden with tastefully-added shrubs and conifers. Foliage plants are a significant component in the design. There are also good collections of roses, heathers and climbers as well as open water with a range of aquatic plants.

TEMPLE NEWSAM 15
Leeds, West Yorkshire. Tel: (0532) 645535
Leeds City Council

Signposted off junction of A63 and A6120 ring road E of Leeds ● Open daily, 9.00 a.m. – dusk ● Best season: mid-June – mid-Oct ● Entrance free ● Parking ● Teas and snacks ● Toilet facilities ● Suitable for wheelchairs ● Shop ● House open daily except Mon, 10.30 a.m. – 6.15 p.m., 85p, OAP and children 35p ● Grade IV

A pleasant oasis surrounded by urban Leeds. Set in the remnants of a 'Capability' Brown landscape of the 1760s (much reduced by a golf course and open-cast mining) are a wide diversity of gardens. Around the house an Italian paved garden and a Jacobean-style parterre surrounded by pleached lime walks are poorly maintained. A rhododendron and azalea walk leads to small ponds with a bog garden and arboretum, beyond which is a large walled rose garden and greenhouses containing collections of ivies, cacti and some rather dashing climbing pelargoniums.

WENTWORTH CASTLE 16
Stainborough, Barnsley, South Yorkshire. Tel: (0226) 285426
Barnsley Metropolitan Borough Council

Off M1 at Junction 37, 2m down minor road signposted Stainborough ● Opening times being reviewed ● Best season: spring ● Entrance: free ● Parking ● Toilet facilities ● House occupied by Northern College ● Grade II

One of the most exciting gardens in Yorkshire, laid out mainly under the direction of William Wentworth in 1740, it is currently undergoing a complete review of its activities. Contains one of the finest collections of rhododendrons in the North. These have been established during the past 15 years and form an invaluable educational resource. The owners and tenants at Wentworth are putting together an important development package which will preserve the fabric of the garden and yet enable its already valuable collections to be expanded.

YORK GATE 17
Church Lane, Leeds, West Yorkshire. Tel: (0532) 678240
Mrs Sybil B. Spencer

Off A660 Leeds – Otley road, behind Adel Church ● Open 2nd, 3rd June, 2.00 – 6.00 p.m. ● Entrance: £1.00, accompanied children free ● Parking, but no coaches ● Refreshments ● Partly suitable for wheelchairs ● Plants for sale ● Grade II

Bought by the owner and her late husband in 1951 this was a bleak farmhouse and an unpromising area of land. When her husband died, her son took over the design and in a tragically short life he achieved a garden of impeccable taste and style, using local stone, cobble stones and gravel to create a structure of great interest. As to the design, Arthur Hellyer remarks on its debt to Hidcote, but notes that many of the ideas used there in 10 acres are here confined to barely one. He also comments on the clever use of eye-catching ornaments and topiary. 'This is a garden made for discovery' he says, as 'from no vantage point is it possible to see the whole ... Nor is any route of exploration specially indicated'. This is also a plantsperson's garden maintaining a quality collection arranged in clearly defined model features. These include an extraordinary miniature pinetum as well as fern, peony and iris borders and an exquisite silver and white border. A garden of rare delight.

YORKSHIRE SCULPTURE PARK   18
Bretton Hall College, Wakefield, West Yorkshire.
Tel: (0924) 830302
Yorkshire Sculpture Park Charitable Trust

3m NW of Barnsley, 7½m SW of Wakefield on outskirts of West Bretton village, near Monk Bretton. Leave M1 at junction 38 or 39 ● *Open daily except 25th, 26th Dec and 1st Jan, 10.00 a.m. – 4.00 p.m.* ● *Entrance: free* ● *Parking* ● *Refreshments in café* ● *Toilet facilities* ● *Partly suitable for wheelchairs* ● *Dogs on lead* ● **Grade IV**

A lecturer at the college initiated this great project for Britain's first permanent sculpture park in 1977, which was the 25th anniversary of the famous Battersea Park exhibitions of sculpture. The Yorkshire Arts Association was set up by a permanent facility the same year. The Palladian-style house and its 260 acres of formal gardens, woods, lakes and parkland provide a fine setting for both temporary exhibitions and the permanent collection that is being built up from them. Work is not bought or given, but available on extended loan from artists, arts councils and, in a few cases from the Tate Gallery. The layout here makes it possible to view sculpture in 'garden' settings as well as the 'public' settings that demand a more monumental approach by the sculptor.

IRELAND

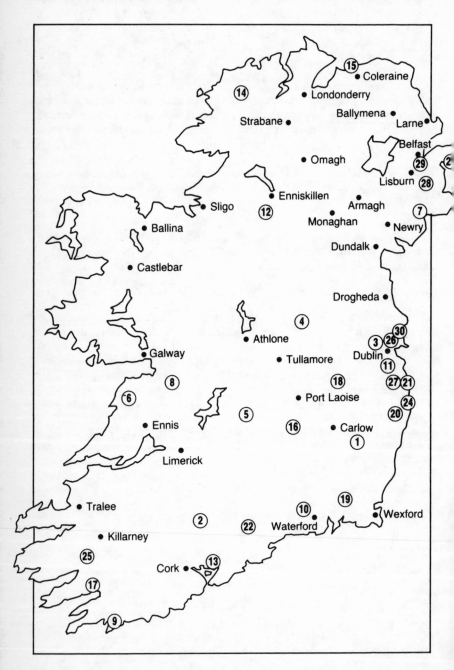

ALTAMONT   1
Tullow, Co Carlow, Republic of Ireland.   Tel: (0503) 57128
Mr and Mrs North

5m from Tullow, about 1m off main Tullow – Bunclody road ● Open Easter –
Oct, Suns, 2.00 – 6.00 p.m. Other times by appointment ● Entrance: IR£1.00,
children free ● Parking ● Home-made teas ● Partly suitable for wheelchairs
● Dogs on lead ● Plants for sale ● Grade III

The lily-filled lake surrounded by fine, mature trees forms a backdrop for a
gently sloping lawn. A central walkway formally planted with Irish yews and
roses leads from the house to the lake. There is a beautiful fern-leaved beech,
and some much more ancient beeches forming the 'Nun's walk'. A long walk
through the demesne leads to the River Slaney with diversions to a bog
garden, through a glen of ancient oaks undercarpeted with bluebells in spring.
Mrs North's passion for trees is evident in the recent planting, and she has
selected old-fashioned roses for her rose beds.

ANNE'S GROVE   2
Castletownroche, Co Cork, Republic of Ireland.   Tel: (022) 26145
Mr and Mrs F.P. Grove Annesley

2m N of village of Castletownroche, between Fermoy and Mallow ● Open Easter
– Sept, Mon – Fri, 10.00 a.m. – 5.00 p.m., Sun, 1.00 – 6.00 p.m. Closed Sat
● Entrance: IR£1.80, OAP IR£1.00 ● Parking ● Picnics ● Partly suitable
for wheelchairs ● Dogs on lead ● Grade I

This is an archetypal 'Robinsonian' alias wild garden, but such tags are not
helpful. Rhododendron species and cultivars arch over and spill towards the
pathways, carpeting them with fallen blossoms. Steep paths descend at various
places into the valley of the Awbeg river (which inspired Edmund Spenser).
The statuesque conifers planted in the valley make a colourful tapestry behind
the river garden, with *Primula florindae* and *P. japonica* cultivars in profusion.
Perhaps least successful is the formal garden, maintained with bedding and a
short herbaceous border. The glory of Anne's Grove is the collection of
rhododendron spp. wherein hidden, visitors may see surprises – a superb
Juniperus recurva 'Castlewellan', a mature handkerchief tree (*Davidia involucrata*) and other exotic, flowering trees. Here is bird-song and the crystal-clear
Awbeg, water-buttercups and primroses – peaceful groves.

BEECH PARK   3
Clonsilla, Co Dublin, Republic of Ireland.   Tel: (01) 212216
Mrs June Shackleton

1m from Clonsilla village on road to Lucan, 10m W of Dublin ● Open on first
Sun of months March – Nov, 2.00 – 6.00 p.m.   ● Entrance: IR£2.00
● Parking ● Home-made teas ● Toilet facilities ● Suitable for wheelchairs
● Plants for sale ● Grade II

In an old walled garden of a Regency house, once bedded with vegetables in season, are raised beds and herbaceous borders brim-full of the choicest perennials and dwarf shrubs. The gems of this highly personal, indeed eclectic, collection begun about 1960 are celmisias (New Zealand mountain daisies), yet the raised beds contain many unusual and uncommon plants, all deliberately selected and superbly cultivated. The herbaceous borders which encircle the walled garden and line its intersecting pathways are planted with as great attention to excellence, and the collection of perennials is outstanding – meconopsis (esp. *M.* x *sheldonii*) phlox, papaver and iris cultivars are striking in season, and a listing of the entire assemblage would occupy a small book. The plants range from old-fashioned, cottage-garden types, some forgotten elsewhere, to the newest and best. David Shackleton who created this garden, garnering cultivars from Ireland and Britain, died in 1988; his idiosyncratic garden is a wonderfully vivid memorial.

BELVEDERE 4
Mullingar, Co Westmeath, Republic of Ireland.
Tel: (044) 40861
Westmeath County Council

4m from Mullingar town, on Tullamore road ● *Open May – Sept, 12 noon – 6.30 p.m.* ● *Entrance: IR£1.00, children IR50p* ● *Parking* ● *Refreshments in restored stables* ● *Toilet facilities* ● *Suitable for wheelchairs* ● *Dogs on lead* ● *Shop* ● *House open* ● *Grade IV*

The Jealous Wall is one of those typically Gothic-Irish follies, built in 1760 to separate two squabbling brothers. It looks antique and is impressive. Otherwise this garden does not abound in interest but there are some fine trees and a large walled garden and it is pleasant to be on the terraces dropping in steps to the shores of Lough Ennel, with views of its waters and islands.

BIRR CASTLE 5
Birr, Co Offaly, Republic of Ireland. Tel: (0509) 20056
Earl and Countess of Rosse

In town of Birr, 60m W of Dublin ● *Open daily, 9.00 a.m. – 1.00 p.m., 2.00 – 6.00 p.m. Closed 25th Dec* ● *Entrance: IR£2.30, children IR£1.50. Annual membership scheme* ● *Parking outside castle gates* ● *Refreshments outside castle gate, picnics in walled garden* ● *Toilet facilities* ● *Suitable for wheelchairs* ● *Dogs on lead* ● *Plants for sale* ● *Shop* ● *Annual exhibition featuring some aspect of the history of Birr Castle or the Earls of Rosse* ● *Grade I*

The Victorian Gothic castle dominates vistas which strike through the park and at whose centre is the slumbering 'Leviathan' (a giant telescope which made Birr famous last century). Around, in profusion, are rare trees and shrubs especially many raised from seed received from central China in the mid-1900s. Over one of the rivers is a beautiful suspension bridge, and hidden amongst laurels is a Victorian fernery with recently restored water-works. Evergreen conifers, golden willows, carpets of daffodils, and world-record box hedges, magnolias in the river garden, a new cherry avenue and the original plant of *Paeonia* 'Anne Rosse' are mere selections of the many attractions at Birr. It is invigorating to walk around the lake, glimpsing the castle, examining the shrubs and trees (some of which are specially labelled), and revelling in the peace and quiet of central Ireland – three counties can be visited in one brief walk. It is fair to add that the beauties of this garden, which owe so much to Anne, Countess of Rosse, have given her international fame as a gardener.

THE BURREN 6
Co Clare, Republic of Ireland. Tel: (065) 88030
Coillte Teoranta (Irish Forestry Board)

North-western Clare, approached from main Galway – Ennis road ● Open daily all year. Never closed ● Entrance: free ● No parking problems (except in busy places during Sept) ● Refreshments: tea rooms, Ballyvaughan; Sheedy's Spa View Hotel, Lisdoonvarna ● Dogs ● Burren Display Centre, Kilfenon, 5m from Lisdoonvarna open, Easter – Oct, daily, and in winter by appointment by ringing (065) 88030 ● Grade I

Mankind did not assist in creating this enigmatic place which was shaped by nature over 500 million years. From afar it is a desolate, barren rock-scape, perhaps more akin to an outer planet. But the limestone rock weathers to rich soil, its natural fissures providing sheltered crannies for plants, and on it, aided by abundant rain, peat-hummocks form habitats for acid- loving species. Botanists abound (in season) and can be spotted easily as they photograph gentians, bottoms uppermost. The spectacle of spring gentians and mountain avens in May (optimal time around 15th May) is worth seeing once, but far, far too many people think May is the only time to visit The Burren. Mid-winter is as good as any; mid-summer a riot of orchids; early autumn mellow with rowan berries and hazel nuts. As a natural rock-garden The Burren has few equals, its flora a rich mixture of arctic and sub-tropical plants – maidenhair ferns and mountain catspaws, Irish orchids and autumn lady's tresses, rock-roses and bloody cranesbills. There are caves and dolmens, castles (with medieval banquets – whatever they may be) and sandy beaches. Comfortable, tough walking shoes are essential; aided by a ramblers' map (several excellent maps are readily available), endless days can be enjoyed walking the 'pavements grey' and the green roads. This was John Betjeman's 'Stony seaboard, far and foreign ...' – but remember to avoid Lisdoonvarna in September unless seeking a companion. By the way, the flowers are protected by law from the light-fingered.

CASTLEWELLAN NATIONAL ARBORETUM 7
Castlewellan, Co Down, Northern Ireland.
Forest Service, Dept of Agriculture (Northern Ireland)

In Castlewellan town, 25m from Belfast, 3m from Newcastle ● *Open all year*
● *Entrance: fee for forest park collected in high season* ● *Parking inc. disabled*
● *Refreshments: summer only* ● *Toilet facilities* ● *Partly suitable for
wheelchairs* ● *Dogs on lead* ● **Grade I**

The walled garden, now called the Annesley Garden, contains an outstanding
collection of mature trees and shrubs, many planted before the turn of the
century by Lord Annesley. Original specimens of some of Castlewellan's
cultivars thrive here, in fine condition. In the spring and summer there are
many rhododendrons in bloom, and scarlet Chilean fire-bushes (*Embothrium
coccineum*). In early autumn, the snow-carpet is the fallen petals of the
unequalled collection of eucryphia. The arboretum has a formal axis, with two
fountain pools and steps. An herbaceous border runs along part of this.
Beyond the walls is a new garden, planted with heathers, dwarf conifers and
limes, and with flowering trees (malus, prunus, etc.). Walks lead into the
forest and beside the lough. A caravan and camping ground within the forest-
park provides a wonderful base for exploring this part of Ireland and for
visiting the other County Down gardens. Castlewellan is well known to
everyone for the bilious golden Leyland cypress that came from here – don't
be dismayed – the arboretum contains many more wonderful plants, some
unique, all in their prime. The maintenance is exceptionally good.

COOLE PARK 8
Gort, Co Galway, Republic of Ireland.
Coillte Teoranta (Irish Forestry Board)

2m N of Gort on main Galway road ● *Open all year* ● *Parking* ● *Toilet
facilities* ● *Suitable for wheelchairs* ● *Dogs* ● *House demolished* ● **Grade III**

This was one of W.B. Yeats' haunts. The house, home of the famous literary
figure Lady Gregory, was demolished years ago as an act of thoughtless
vandalism and much of the demesne is now planted with conifers. However,
beside the remains of the house are two magnificent plane trees, an old
mulberry and other exotic trees. In the walled garden is the famous
'Autograph' tree (a copper beech) with the fading initials of the Irish literati
including George Bernard Shaw. The walled garden could be greatly
improved if the present authorities stopped the horrendous clipping of the
shrubs. Walk to the lake and see the swans and linger in the magnificent avenue
at the entrance.

CREAGH 9
Skibbereen, Co Cork, Republic of Ireland. Tel: (028) 21267
Mr Peter Harold Barry

4m from Skibbereen on road to Baltimore – concealed entrance ● *Open April –*
Sept, daily, 10.00 a.m. – 6.00 p.m. ● *Entrance: IR£1.50, children free*
● *Parking at house* ● *Suitable for wheelchairs* ● *Dogs on lead* ● **Grade III**

Definitely a garden for those who seek solitude and silence, far from traffic.
Paths lead through woodland underplanted with rhododendron species and
cultivars, and down to the sea. A serpentine mill-pond is now fringed with
gunnera, cordyline and hydrangea, the bold effect inspired by the paintings of
'Le Douanier' Rousseau. There are some fine tender species, including *Telopea*
truncata, Rhododendron 'Sesterianum', a magnificent *Vitex agnus-castus*, and
feathery *Azara microphylla* 'Variegata'. A valiant garden lovingly maintained
by the elderly owner, wherein one feels the wilderness is slowly winning,
creating a truly wild, Irish pleasaunce.

CURRAGHMORE 10
Portlaw, Co Waterford, Republic of Ireland. Tel: (051) 87102
The Marquis of Waterford

In Portlaw village, 9m from Waterford centre ● *Open May – Sept, Thurs, 2.00*
– 5.00 p.m. Also open public holidays ● *Entrance: IR£1.00, children IR75p*
● *Parking* ● *Suitable for wheelchairs* ● *House open by prior appointment only*
● **Grade III**

Some parts of the garden are of early design e.g. the Shell House of 1754
personally decorated by the Countess of Tyrone. However, the main interest
is the landscaping, the artificial lake and the views across to the mountains.
May and June are the best months to see the azaleas, bluebells and
rhododendrons.

FERNHILL 11
Sandyford, Co Dublin, Republic of Ireland. Tel: (01) 956000
Mrs Sally Walker

On main Dublin – Enniskerry road, 8m from central Dublin ● *Open March –*
Nov, Tues – Sat, 11 a.m. – 5.00 p.m., Suns, 2.00 – 6.00 p.m. ● *Entrance:*
IR£2.00, OAP and children IR£1.00 ● *Parking* ● *Toilet facilities* ● *Partly*
suitable for wheelchairs ● *Dogs on lead* ● *Plants for sale* ● **Grade II**

The plantings of rhododendron species and cultivars in Fernhill provide
spectacles of colour from early spring into mid-summer; many of the more
tender rhododendrons flourish here. The garden is situated on the eastern
slope of the Dublin Mountains and has a laurel lawn, some fine nineteenth-
century plantings and an excellent flowering specimen of *Michelia doltsopa*.
The walkways through the wooded areas wind steeply past many other shrubs,

principally those that thrive on acid soil – pieris and camellia are also outstanding as is the raised laurel lawn. There is a small rock garden and a water garden near the house, and drifts of daffodils in the spring. A sculpture exhibition has become an annual feature at Fernhill.

FLORENCE COURT 12
Florence Court, Co Fermanagh, Northern Ireland.
Tel: (036582) 249
The National Trust

7m SW of Enniskillen, 1m W of village ● *Open all year, 10.00 a.m. – 1 hour before dusk (grounds only). Parties by arrangement* ● *Entrance: £1.50* ● *Parking* ● *Refreshments: teas and lunches in North Pavilion* ● *Toilet facilities* ● *Suitable for wheelchairs in garden only* ● *Dogs on lead* ● *Shop* ● *Eighteenth-century house open* ● ***Grade III***

The original, the mother of all Irish yews (*Taxus baccata* 'Fastigiata') still grows in the laurel-infested woodland about a quarter of a mile from the splendid mansion at Florence Court. Well worth the walk; the path allows glimpses of the mountains and the fine 'Brownian' park in front of the house. Some fine weeping beeches and old rhododendrons grow near the house, and work is in progress on revitalizing the walled garden. Strong shoes essential (especially in rainy season!) if you wish to pay respects to the venerable, 250-year-old tree. Ice-house. The nearby caves (open to public) are worth visiting too making a rewarding day out, with some fine views.

FOTA 13
Fota Estate, Carrigtwohill, Co Cork, Republic of Ireland.
Tel: (021) 276871
University College, Cork, Republic of Ireland

9m E of Cork city, on road to Cobh ● *Open April – Sept, daily, 10.00 a.m. – 6.00 p.m., Sun, 11.00 a.m. – 6.00 p.m., Oct, 2.00 – 6.00 p.m.* ● *Entrance: free for arboretum* ● *Parking beside arboretum (also serving Fota Wildlife Park). IR£1.30* ● *Refreshments at Wildlife Park* ● *Toilet facilities at Wildlife Park and in Fota House* ● *Suitable for wheelchairs* ● *Dogs on lead* ● *Shop in Wildlife Park* ● *House open, separate charge* ● ***Grade II***

Many of the superb specimen trees in this garden are undoubtedly among the best examples in Ireland and Britain. By the house is a cedar of Lebanon, undercarpeted with cyclamen; a handkerchief tree (*Davidia involucrata*), exquisite pieris, contorted tree-ferns, *Magnolia campbellii* and much, much more. A banana palm lingers in the border with fuchsia and watsonia cultivars. The Italian garden is, however, a mere shadow, and the orangery derelict, its sentinel *Phoenix dactylifera* patiently waiting the outcome of present uncertainties. At the time of writing the whole island is under a sale-option which may lead to large-scale development altering its unique character. Meanwhile the arboretum slumbers, needful of a clear guiding spirit, but still a delight for those who enjoy trees and shrubs.

GLENVEAGH CASTLE 14
Glenveagh National Park, Chuchill, Letterkenny, Co Donegal, Republic of Ireland. Tel: (074) 37088/37090
National Parks and Monuments Service; Office of Public Works

10m W of Letterkenny ● *Open Easter week, May – Sept, Mon – Sat, 10.30 a.m. – 6.00 p.m., Sun, 12 noon – 6.00 p.m. Other times by arrangement* ● *Entrance: IR£1.00, reductions for groups, OAP, etc.* ● *Parking at Visitor Centre. Access to garden and castle by official minicoaches only* ● *Refreshments* ● *Toilet facilities* ● *Shop* ● *House open, IR£1.00* ● ***Grade I***

The centre-piece of the Glenveagh National Park is the garden around Glenveagh Castle. The castle is set beside a mountain lough encircled with high, peat-blanketed mountains, in the middle of windswept moorlands, a most unpromising site. But, as in so many Irish gardens, surprises are countless. The lower lawn garden has fringing shrubberies, and, beyond, steep pathways wind through oak woods in which are planted scented, white-flowered rhododendrons, and numerous other tender shrubs from southern lands. Terraced enclosures with terracotta pots of plants and sculpture are encountered unexpectedly. The jardin potager at the castle has rank on rank of ornamental vegetables and flowering herbs. This is a paradise for plantsmen and gardeners keen on seeing fine specimens of unusual aspect – *Pseudopanax ferox, Fascicularia pitcairniifolia*, and many more. Sadly, Glenveagh's great stairway on the mountain is closed to the public, and there have been other changes closing off parts of this wonderland. Linger, and walk the mountain sides. Take the last bus back to the remarkable heather-roofed Visitor Centre with its imaginative landscaping (except the appallingly trained rowans!)

GUY L. WILSON DAFFODIL GARDEN 15
University of Ulster, Coleraine, Co Londonderry, Northern Ireland.
Tel: (0265) 44141
University of Ulster

On Culmore road, about 1m N of Coleraine town on road to Portstewart ● *Open daily* ● *Best season: spring* ● *Entrance: free* ● *Parking* ● *Dogs on lead* ● ***Grade II***

The daffodils in this garden represent one of the National collections (established under the patronage of the National Council for the Conservation of Plants and Gardens although it was commenced long before the NCCPG scheme). It is principally based on Irish-bred cultivars particularly those of Guy Wilson; however, among the 1000 plus cultivars represented are daffodils from New Zealand and the USA, as well as Britain, and there are both old and modern cultivars. The daffodils are interplanted with shrubs in island beds. The setting is attractive, but the garden now shows signs of diminished care and attention due to cut-backs by the university. Vandalism clearly is a problem – flowers wantonly damaged and picked daffodils strewn on paths were seen on a recent visit. The labels have all been removed (to prevent theft) which makes a nonsense of the collection as an educational facility. The purpose of such a collection is to allow people to look and learn – we must sympathise with the problems faced by the university and hope that some imaginative scheme can be devised to allow visitors to discover the name of the host of daffodils.

HEYWOOD 16

Salesian College, Ballinakill, Co Laois, Republic of Ireland.
Tel: (0502) 3334
Salesian Order

Outside Ballinakill village. 3m from Abbeyleix (turn E in town following sign to Ballinakill) ● *Open daily* ● *Entrance: free (donations gratefully received)* ● *Parking* ● *Partly suitable for wheelchairs* ● *Dogs on lead* ● ***Grade III***

Edwin Lutyens' walled garden with pergola and lawns is acknowledged as his finest small-scale work in Ireland. It is a gem, now restored close to its original state as far as the walls and ornaments are concerned. The planting is being restored, in the style of Gertrude Jekyll with the advice of Graham Stuart Thomas. On the driveway leading towards the school buildings is an eighteenth-century folly. There is a long way to go before the garden is again sparkling, but it is still well worth visiting. Please, please do offer financial support when you have visited Heywood – it is a part of our heritage we cannot afford to neglect.

ILNACULLIN 17

(commonly known as Garinish Island)
Glengarriff, Co Cork, Republic of Ireland. Tel: (027) 63040
National Parks and Monuments Service, Office of Public Works

On an island in Bantry Bay ● *Open April – Sept, daily, 10.00 a.m. – 6.30 p.m., Sun, 1.00 – 6.00 p.m.* ● *Entrance: IR£1.30, children and students IR50p. Travel is by boat, charge for which is IR£5 return fare* ● *Toilet facilities* ● ***Grade I***

The boat trip across the sheltered inlets of Bantry Bay, past sun-bathing seals, with views of the Caha Mountains, is doubly rewarding; landing at the slipway you gain entrance to one of Ireland's gardening jewels begun in the early 1900s. Most visitors cluster around the Casita and reflecting pool, designed by Harold Peto, to enjoy (on clear days) spectacular scenery, and some quite indifferent annual bedding. But walk beyond, to the Temple of the Winds, through shrubberies filled with plants usually confined indoors – tree ferns, Southern Hemisphere conifers, rhododendron species and cultivars. A flight of stone steps leads to the Martello tower, and thence the path returns to the walled garden and Italianate garden. Plant enthusiasts can spend many happy hours with such delights as *Lyonothamnus aspleniifolius* and a myriad of manuka; take a picnic and linger; if wet, bring boots or strong shoes and an umbrella. Wonderful.

JAPANESE GARDEN   18
Irish National Stud, Tully, Kildare, Co Kildare, Republic of Ireland.
Tel: (045) 21617
Irish National Stud

1m outside Kildare town, 25m SW of Dublin   ● *Open Easter Sunday – Oct, daily 10.30 a.m. – 5.00 p.m., Sun, 2.00 – 5.30 p.m. Guided tours on request* ● *Entrance: IR£1.50, students IR£1.00, children IR80p* ● *Parking* ● *Refreshments* ● *Toilet facilities* ● *Plants for sale* ● *Shop* ● *The Irish National Stud and Horse Museum open* ● **Grade II**

Created between the years 1906-1910. Devised by Colonel William Hall-Walker (later Lord Wavertree), a wealthy Scotsman of a famous brewery family and laid out by the Japanese Eida and his son Minory, the gardens, symbolising the 'Life of Man' are acclaimed as the finest Japanese gardens in Europe. This is not a plantsman's garden, for few of the plants are Japanese; to be sure there are some excellent old maples, but many of the trees and shrubs are clipped and shaped beyond reason. The overshadowing Scots pines are exquisite. A pathway meanders through artificial caves, into a watery stream, past the tranquil ponds and on to the weeping trees of the grave. Beautiful stone lanterns grace the garden which is in the style of a Japanese 'tea garden'. On a misty day with smoke from a distant fire billowing across this visitor recalls it as mysterious, beautiful.

JOHN F. KENNEDY ARBORETUM   19
New Ross, Co Wexford, Republic of Ireland.   Tel: (051) 88171
Coillte Teoranta (Irish Forestry Board)

8m S of New Ross   ● *Open daily*   ● *Entrance: free*   ● *Parking: fee IR£2.00, season ticket IR£8.00, other charges for buses* ● *Refreshments: café May – Sept. April weekends only. Picnic area* ● *Toilet facilities* ● *Suitable for wheelchairs* ● *Dogs on lead* ● *Visitor Centre with Kennedy memorial and video* ● **Grade II**

A modern spacious arboretum laid out in botanical sequence with rides; from the summit of a nearby hill is a superb panorama of the park and Co Wexford. Best to begin at the viewpoint – turn left just beyond the main entrance and drive to summit car park to see the layout. At the arboretum be prepared for a long walk – fortunately those not keen on gardening tend to linger near the café so that the distant reaches are quiet and empty. Planting began in 1960s and now 4500 different trees and shrubs are growing, ranging from conifers to flowering shrubs. Most species are represented by several specimens, and keen plantsmen can linger long examining the groups. Good labelling. A colourful planting of dwarf conifers is on the western side, a small lake on the east. While primarily a scientific collection, the arboretum is now achieving an established elegance.

KILMACURRAGH 20
Rathdrum, Co Wicklow, Republic of Ireland.
Coillte Teoranta (Irish Forestry Board)

From village of Rathdrum. 25m S of Dublin ● *Open all year for those on foot, through turn stile* ● *Entrance: free* ● *Parking at gate only* ● *Dogs on lead* ● *House derelict* ● *Grade I*

This garden is rated highly because of its atmosphere and magnificent ancient plants. It has no visitor facilities, but is open without hindrance to those who can find it. Behind the derelict eye-sore of the house there is an incomparable avenue composed of alternating Irish yews and crimson rhododendrons – 'magical' is an overworked word, but the pattern of fallen blossoms on this pathway in May *is* magical. Beyond, paths wind through the arboretum, under rhododendrons taller and older than in most other gardens. The trees at Kilmacurragh include many unequalled specimens – rare conifers abound. If you can, visit it when the crocus blossom in the meadow, when the rhododendron flowers are tumbling down, at any time for elegant decrepitude. A secret pleasaunce; one hesitates to recommend it – for its secret then is lost.

KILRUDDERY 21
Bray, Co Wicklow, Republic of Ireland.   Tel: (01) 863405
Earl and Countess of Meath

1m S of Bray on road to Greystones ● *Open May, June, Sept, daily, 1.00 – 5.00 p.m.* ● *Entrance: IR£1.00, OAP and students IR50p. Children under 12 must be accompanied* ● *Parking* ● *Toilet facilities* ● *Partly suitable for wheelchairs* ● *Dogs on lead* ● *House open with conducted tours at extra charge* ● *Grade III*

The joy of Killruddery, a seventeenth-century garden with nineteenth-century embellishments is the formal hedges, known as 'The Angles' set beside the formal canals which lead to a ride into the distant hills. There is a collection of nineteenth-century French cast statuary, a sylvan theatre created in beech, and a fountain pool enclosed in a beech hedge too. The excellent conservatory (nineteenth-century), alas, has a perspex dome. The landscape features are unique, and Killruddery deserves to be better known, but it is not a garden for keen plantsmen without designer tastes.

LISMORE CASTLE 22
Lismore, Co Waterford, Republic of Ireland. Tel: (058) 54424
Duke and Duchess of Devonshire

Entrance in Lismore town ● *Open 8th May – 8th Sept, daily except Sat, 1.45 – 4.45 p.m.* ● *Entrance: IR£1.00, children IR50p* ● *Parking* ● **Grade III**

Do not come to Ireland just to see Lismore Castle gardens, but the situation of the castle overlooking the River Blackwater is stunning. Entering through the gatehouse, there are two gardens, the upper reached by a stairway in the gatehouse and terraced with patches of vegetables; and the reduced glass-house by Joseph Paxton (an interesting ridge-furrow house). The view from the main axis to the church spire is fine. In the lower garden are a few meritricious plants, but the principal feature, an ancient yew-walk carpeted softly with the dropped leaves, is wonderful. For that only can this be regarded as a garden of note – the rest is mundane. Yet Edmund Spenser is said to have written *The Fairie Queene* here, and it is the Irish home of the Duke of Devonshire who has Chatsworth (see page 82) to console him in England.

MOUNT STEWART HOUSE, GARDEN AND TEMPLE OF THE WINDS 23
Greyabbey, Newtownards, Co Down, Northern Ireland.
Tel: (024774) 387
The National Trust

On Ards Peninsula, 5m from Newtownards on road (A20) to Portaferry, 15m E of Belfast ● *Open 13th – 22nd April, daily, 12 noon – 6.00 p.m. April and May, Sept and Oct, Sat, Sun and Bank Holidays only, 12 noon – 6.00 p.m. June, July and Aug, daily, 12 noon – 6.00 p.m.* ● *Entrance: £2.50 to garden and Temple of Winds. Parties outside normal opening hours at extra charge* ● *Parking 300 yards* ● *Refreshments: light refreshments and teas same time as house. Lunches and high teas July and Aug* ● *Toilet facilities* ● *Partly suitable for wheelchairs* ● *Dogs on lead* ● *House open at extra charge* ● **Grade I**

Of all Ireland's gardens this is The One not to miss. Any adjective that evokes beauty can be applied to it, and it's fun too. In the gardens in front of the house is a collection of statuary, satirising British political and public figures – dodos, monkeys and boars. The planting here is formal, with rectangular beds of 'hot' and 'cool' colours. Beyond in the informal gardens are mature trees and shrubs, a botanical collection with few equals, planted with great panache and maintained with outstanding attention to detail. Spires of giant lilies (cardiocrinum), aspiring eucalyptus, banks of rhododendrons, ferns and blue poppies, rivers of candelabra primulas – and much more. Walk along the lakeside path to the hill that affords a view over the lake to the house. Rare tender shrubs such as *Metrosideros umbellata* flourish here outside the walled family cemetery. Leading from it is the Jubilee Avenue and its statue of a white stag. Mount Stewart is a whole day for those keen on plants and it should be seen several times during the year truly to savour its rich tapestry of plants and water, buildings and trees. The Temple of the Winds, James 'Athenian' Stuart's banqueting hall of 1785, is also memorable.

MOUNT USHER   24
Ashford, Co Wicklow, Republic of Ireland.
Tel: (0404) 40116/40205
Mrs Madelaine Jay

At Ashford, on main Dublin – Wexford road, 30m S of Dublin ● *Open 17th March – Oct, Mon – Sat, 10.30 a.m. – 6.00 p.m., Sun, 11.00 a.m. – 6.00 p.m.* ● *Entrance: IR£2.00, OAP, students and children IR£1.30* ● *Parking* ● *Refreshments: tea rooms* ● *Toilet facilities* ● *Partly suitable for wheelchairs* ● *Plants for sale* ● *Shop* ● *Grade II*

The Vartry river babbles through this exquisite garden over gentle weirs and under bridges which allow visitors to meander through the collections. Mount Usher is a plant-lovers' paradise. *Pinus montezumae* is always first port-of-call, a shimmering tree, magnificent when the bluebells are in flower. The philosophy of Mount Usher eschews chemicals of all kinds, and the lawns are cut in a cycle which allows the bulbs and wildflowers in them to seed naturally. Throughout there are drifts of rhododendrons, fine trees and shrubs including many that are difficult to cultivate outdoors in other parts of Britain and Ireland. The grove of eucalyptus at the lower end of the valley is memorable; a kiwi-fruit vine (*Actinidia chinensis*) cloaks the piers of a bridge, and beside the tennis court is the gigantic original *Eucryphia* x *nymansensis* 'Mount Usher'. In spring bulbs and magnolias, in summer a procession of rhododendrons, in autumn russet and crimson leaves falling from maples – a garden for all seasons.

MUCKROSS HOUSE   25
Killarney National Park, Killarney, Co Kerry, Republic of Ireland.
Tel: (064) 31947/31440
National Parks and Monument Service; Office of Public Works

4m from centre of Killarney, on road to Kenmare ● *Open for pedestrians all year, with car access, 8.00 a.m. – 5.00 p.m., Aug, 8.00 a.m. – 9.00 p.m.* ● *Entrance: free* ● *Parking* ● *Restaurant* ● *Toilet facilities* ● *Suitable for wheelchairs* ● *Dogs on lead* ● *Craft shop* ● *House open, 17th March – June, Sept – Oct, daily, 9.00 a.m. – 6.00 p.m. July – Aug, daily, 9.00 a.m. – 7.00 p.m. Rest of year, daily, 11.00 a.m. – 5.00 p.m. Charge made* ● *Grade II*

The garden around Muckross House is almost incidental to the spectacle of the lakes and mountains of Killarney. It is principally renowned as a viewing area for the wild grandeur of the mountains. The lawns sweep to clumps of old rhododendrons and Scots pines, and there is a huge natural rock garden which is plagued with noisy children in high season. There is no peace here except on wet winter days. But leave the garden and take the lough-side trails, and enjoy the wildwoods with their unique assemblages of plants – *Sorbus anglica* (English whitebeam), yew and, above all, the almost eternal strawberry tree (*Arbutus unedo*). There is a mystical yew woodland carpeted with mosses. Throughout the National Park the cursed *Rhododendron ponticum* is being slowly and successfully eliminated. Would that the jarveys could go too; don't be tempted to pay for their extravagant transport from the town – the car park is free and beside the house!

NATIONAL BOTANIC GARDENS, GLASNEVIN 26
Glasnevin, Dublin 9, Republic of Ireland.
Tel: (01) 377596/374388
Department of Agriculture and Food

1m N of central Dublin ● Open daily except 25th Dec, summer, 9.00 a.m. – 6.00 p.m., winter, 9.00 a.m. – 4.30 p.m. Opening times for glasshouses are posted at entrance ● Entrance: free ● Parking very limited in summer and at weekends ● Refreshments: arrangements for groups only may be made in advance by writing to the Director ● Toilet facilities ● Suitable for wheelchairs except for main Palm House ● Shop ● Grade I

A fine garden which still retains its Victorian exactitude with close-cut lawns and succulent carpet-bedding (in summer only!), but with an air of decrepitude, and the visitor facilities are parsimonious. The plant collection generally is fine, but in places the shrubs and trees are past their best. In the winter, the glasshouses are worth visiting; by spring there are daffodil-crowded lawns and flowering cherries; the summer highlight is the double, curving herbaceous border, and in autumn the fruit-laden trees and russet foliage can be magical. The Turner conservatory (1843–1869), the finest in Ireland, will be dismantled over 1990 for complete restoration. Glasnevin is undoubtedly worth visiting, especially by gardeners with a strong interest in shrubs and perennials; soil conditions preclude large-scale rhododendron planting, and anyone passionate about alpines will be very disappointed. Highlights are hard to enumerate, but a few outstanding plants may be mentioned: *Zelkova carpinifolia* (especially in winter a marvellous 'architectural' tree) the Chain tent (*c.* 1836) with ancient wisteria; *Picea omorika* (at pond); *Fascicularia pitcairniifolia* and *Ochagavia carnea* (at Cactus house); cycads in Palm House; *Parrotia persica* (near entrance, wonderful in February and October); and of course 'The Last Rose of Summer'!

POWERSCOURT 27
Enniskerry, Co Wicklow, Republic of Ireland. Tel: (01) 867676
Mr and Mrs Slazenger

15m S of Dublin, just outside village of Enniskerry ● Open March – Oct, 9.00 a.m. – 5.30 p.m. ● Entrance: IR£1.90, children IR85p. Separate charge for

waterfall • *Parking* • *Refreshments: licensed restaurant* • *Toilet facilities*
• *Partly suitable for wheelchairs* • *Dogs on lead* • *Plants for sale* • *Shop*
• *House a ruin after a fire in 1974. Craft show and children's play area*
• **Grade II**

In some ways Powerscourt is overrated – the so-called Japanese garden is merely a miscellany of red-painted bridges and stone lanterns set in a valley. In other ways it is beyond compare. Its central axis formed by the ceremonious stairway leading down to the Triton Pond and jet, stretches beyond to the Great Sugarloaf Mountain and is justly famous – it can be glimpsed in a few minutes (and that is what many tourists do). Avoid the Japanese garden, and the high-priced garden centre, and give the indifferent herbaceous border a miss too and walk along the terrace towards the Pepperpot, through the mature conifers which Lord Powerscourt collected – a big-cone pine (*Pinus coulteri*), the tallest in Ireland and Britain, is here. Wander on, to the edge of the pond, and look up, along the stairway, past the monumental terraces to the facade of the burnt-out house. That's the view of Powerscourt that is breathtaking – a man-made amphitheatre guarded by winged horses. Statuary and the famous perspective gate; an avenue of monkey puzzles and a beech wood along the avenue; these add to Powerscourt's glory.

ROWALLANE 28
Saintfield, Co Down, Northern Ireland. Tel: (0238) 510131
The National Trust

½m S of Saintfield on A7, Belfast – Downpatrick road • *Open 1st – 12th April, booked parties only. 13th April – Oct, daily, Mon – Fri, 10.30 a.m. – 6.00 p.m. Nov – March 1991, Mon – Fri, 9.00 a.m. – 5.00 p.m. Closed 25th, 26th Dec and Jan 1st. Special times for parties by arrangement* • *Entrance: April – Oct, £1.50, Nov – March, 50p. Parties outside normal hours extra charge by appointment* • *Parking* • *Refreshments: tea rooms with light refreshments, April – Sept, 2.00 – 6.00 p.m.* • *Toilet facilities* • *Partly suitable for wheelchairs* • *Dogs on lead* • *Trust shop* • **Grade I**

While famous as a 50-acre rhododendron garden, and certainly excellent in this regard, Rowallane has much more to interest keen gardeners. In summer, the walled garden blossoms in lemon and blue, while hoheria cast white petals in the wind. In secluded places, a handkerchief tree blows; there is a pale-yellow-leaved pieris, a restored Victorian bandstand (music-filled on summer weekends) and orchid meadows. Rock garden with primula, meconopsis, heathers etc. and several areas of natural wild flowers. Any season will be interesting, and for the real enthusiast there are rhododendron species and cultivars in bloom from October to August. The original plant of *Viburnum plicatum* 'Rowallane' is in the walled garden as is the original *Chaenomeles* x *superba* 'Rowallane'; a feature is made of *Hypericum* 'Rowallane' at the entrance to the walled garden.

ROYAL BOTANIC GARDEN PARK 29
Stranmillis, Belfast, Co Antrim, Northern Ireland.
Tel: (02332) 381996
Belfast Corporation Parks Department

Between Queen's University and the Ulster Museum, Stranmillis ● *Open daily* ● *Entrance: free* ● *Parking outside* ● *Refreshments: facilities in the Ulster Museum* ● *Toilet facilities* ● *Suitable for wheelchairs* ● *Dogs on lead* ● *Grade III*

Established in 1827, this became a public park in 1895. Today it has lots of vulgar bedding for general admiration; it is well done but not to everyone's taste. The curvilinear iron and glass conservatory (1839–1852) is one of the finest Victorian glasshouses (Richard Turner built only the wings; the dome is by Young of Edinburgh). It was restored in the 1970s and contains a small collection of tropical plants with massed displays of 'pot mums' and the like in season (again well-grown and finely displayed, but not everyone's favourite). The Tropical Ravine House is the greater delight, and also recently restored. This is 'High Victoriana', with ferns, bananas, lush tropical vines and tree ferns, goldfish in the Amazon lily pond, and a waterfall worked with a chain-pull! Marvellous, evocative of by-gone crinoline days.

TALBOT BOTANIC GARDEN 30
Malahide Castle, Malahide, Co Dublin, Republic of Ireland.
Tel: (01) 450940 Dublin County Council

Outside Malahide, 10m N of Dublin ● *Open May – Sept, daily, 2.00 – 4.30 p.m. Conducted tour of walled garden 2.00 p.m., Weds* ● *Entrance: IR50p, children free if accompanied* ● *Parking* ● *Refreshments: lunches and teas in castle* ● *Suitable for wheelchairs* ● *Dogs on lead* ● *Shop in castle* ● *House open, additional charge for tours* ● *Grade II*

Malahide Castle was the home of the Talbot family for many centuries; following the death of Lord Talbot de Malahide it was acquired by Dublin County Council. The garden consists of three parts – the outer demesne (now occupied by playing fields, well-kept lawns and shrubberies, pathways); the main shrubberies (open to the public as above) and the walled garden (open only by special arrangement and on Wednesdays for guided tours). The main shrubberies planted by Lord Talbot contain a varied mixture of trees and shrubs, some of which are outstanding and rare. However, the finest part of the collection is in the walled garden – here Lord Talbot planted such exotics as *Telopea truncata*, *Bomarea caldasii*, *Garrya* x *issaquahensis*, and numerous others. Olearia was a favourite genus and is well represented here. Australasian genera are also represented (e.g. pittosporum, grevillea, cya-thodes, acacia) *Berberis valdiviana* and *Pseudopanax ferox* lurk in an out-of-the-way corner. By the castle is a large cedar of Lebanon with cyclamen below, and a spacious lawn. The pity is that so many of the shrubs are still clipped into uncomfortable shapes, and that very few of the plants are fully labelled.

SCOTLAND

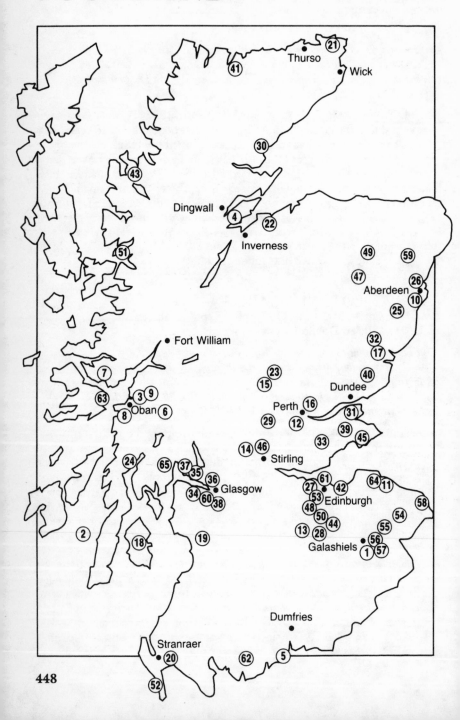

448

ABBOTSFORD 1
Melrose, Roxburghshire, Borders. Tel: (0896) 2043
Mrs P. Maxwell-Scott

3m W of Melrose on A6091, turn SW on to B6360. Just S of A72 ● *Open mid-March – Oct, Mon – Sat, 10.00 a.m. – 5.00 p.m., Sun, 2.00 – 5.00 p.m.*
● *Entrance: not decided at time of going to press, reduced rate for parties*
● *Parking* ● *Teas and picnics* ● *Toilet facilities* ● *Suitable for wheelchairs.*
Disabled enter by private entrance ● *Shop* ● *House open* ● **Grade IV**

Sir Walter Scott's magnificent house, built between 1817 and 1821 to satisfy his yearning to become a laird, has a garden that is rich in Scottish allusions. A yew hedge to the south of the house has medallions from an old cross inset, and a fountain in the same formal garden came from the same cross. The River Tweed flows past the house and there are fine views across a stretch of garden. Herbaceous beds lead to a gothic-type fern house filled with other plants beside ferns, such as orchids. The dedicated Scott scholar will find most interest in the house, amongst historical relics collected by the laird himself.

ACHAMORE GARDENS 2
Isle of Gigha, Argyll, Strathclyde. Tel: (05835) 267
Mr Malcolm Potier

Take A83 to Tayinloan then by ferry to Gigha ● *Open daily April – October*
● *Best season: spring* ● *Entrance: £2.00, OAP and children £1.00, collecting box* ● *Refreshments at hotel* ● *Toilet facilities* ● *Partly suitable for wheelchairs* ● *Dogs on lead* ● *Plants for sale* ● **Grade II**

An amazing idea to create such a superb garden on the Isle of Gigha. The journey there is via most beautiful countryside finishing up with the ferry trip, surrounded by squawking sea birds. In 1944 Sir James Horlick purchased the whole island with the sole purpose to create a garden in which to grow the rare and unusual. This was accomplished with the advice of James Russell. A delightful woodland landscape was planted with a vast collection of rarities from around the world. The garden is especially rich in fine specimens of tender rhododendrons such as *R. lindleyii*, *R. fragrantissimum*, and *R. macabeanum* to name but a few. The overall effect of the garden is tropical. There are many varieties of camellias, cordylines, primulas and Asiatic exotica. A great number of genera are represented by very good specimens, thriving in Gigha's mildness. There is a very fine *Pinus montezumae* in the walled garden; drifts of Asiatic primulas feature around the especially pretty woodland pond. The rhododendrons are unsurpassed in variety, quality and sheer visual magnitude. Gigha is a must, a Mecca for the keen plantsman and avid gardener. Few gardens outside the national botanic collections can claim such diversity and rarity within their confines. Although It is true that in recent years the number of gardeners has been reduced and there has been a slight air of neglect, the island now has a new owner who is said to wish to preserve the character of Gigha and keep it open to the public.

ACHNACLOICH 3
Connel, Argyll, Strathclyde. Tel: (063171) 221
Mrs T.E. Nelson

3m E of Connel off A85 ● *Open 1st April – 23rd June, 4th Aug – mid-Oct,*
daily, 10.00 a.m. – 6.00 p.m. ● *Best season: April – June* ● *Entrance: 50p*
● *Parking* ● *Suitable for wheelchairs* ● *Dogs on lead* ● *Grade III*

A castellated Scottish baronial house situated above the loch on a rocky cliff.
The woodland garden consists of a series of interlined glades with unusual
rhododendrons, azaleas, magnolias and shrubs. Also a good display of
primulas around a woodland burn with footbridge. Massed bulbs in front of
the house in spring. Fine views.

ALLANGRANGE 4
Munlochy, Black Isle, Ross & Cromarty, Highlands.
Tel: (046381) 249
Major and Mrs A. Cameron

Signposted from A9, 5m N of Inverness ● *Open three Suns in May, June and*
July, under Scottish Gardens Scheme, 2.00 – 5.30 p.m., dates N.A. ● *Best*
season: May – July ● *Entrance: 50p, children 20p* ● *Parking: 50p* ● *Teas*
● *Toilet facilities in house* ● *Suitable for wheelchairs* ● *Dogs on lead*
● *Grade III*

A very attractive garden which spills down the hillside in a series of descending
terraces in a formal layout which incorporates a 'white' garden and a 'mauve'
garden. There is also a small pool garden, and to the rear of the house a
developing woodland garden with unusual rhododendrons, primulas, meconopsis and cardiocrinums. Well worth the detour from the A9.

ARBIGLAND 5
Kirkbean, Dumfries & Galloway. Tel: (038788) 283
Captain and Mrs J.B. Blackett

From New Abbey, signposted on A710 Solway coast road ● *Open May - Sept,*
Sun, Tues and Thurs, 2.00 – 6.00 p.m. ● *Best season: early-May – mid-June,*
Sept ● *Entrance: £1.00, children 50p, under 5 free* ● *Parking free* ● *Teas,*
picnics on beach ● *Toilet facilities* ● *Dogs on lead* ● *Secluded private sandy*
beach which can be used by visitors ● *Grade III*

The ancient 'broadwalk' leads down towards the sea and the woodland garden.
One area, called 'Japan' takes its name from the Japanese maples and azaleas
which have been arranged around a small burn. Nearby is a large pool,
especially attractive in the autumn when it reflects the colours of the trees that
surround it. The formal sunken garden has been created on the foundations of
the original house. The old walled garden, at present disused, dates from the
original eighteenth-century house.

ARDANAISEIG GARDEN AND HOTEL 6
Kilchrenan, Argyll, Strathclyde. Tel: (08662) 264
Mr and Mrs J.M. Brown and family

4m E from Kilchrenan on route B845 ● *Open mid-April – mid-Oct, 8.00 a.m. – 9.00 p.m.* ● *Best season: April, May, July, Oct* ● *Entrance: £1.00, children free. Collecting box at car park* ● *Parking* ● *Refreshments at hotel, no children under 8* ● *Toilet facilities at hotel* ● *Dogs on lead* ● *Plants for sale* ● *Hotel open, formerly Scottish baronial house* ● ***Grade III***

A woodland garden of early nineteenth-century origin attractively situated on the shores of Loch Awe with a fascinating collection of rare and unusual shrubs and trees. Some particularly fine examples of species and hybrid rhododendrons, and walled gardens with roses and herbaceous borders. The autumn colourings of the trees are also well worth seeing.

ARDTORNISH 7
Lochaline, Morvern, Highlands. Tel: (096784) 288 (Estate office)
Mrs John Raven

30m from Corran. From Corran ferry, S of Fort William, cross to Morvern and take route left on A861 towards Lochaline, then left on A884. Gardens 2m before Lochaline on left ● *Open April – Oct, 10.00 a.m. – 5.00 p.m.* ● *Best season: April, May and Oct* ● *Entrance: £1.00, children free. Collecting box* ● *Parking* ● *Dogs on lead* ● *Plants for sale in kitchen garden* ● *12 flats in the house available for self-catering accommodation* ● ***Grade III***

A plantsman's garden with an extensive collection of unusual shrubs, deciduous trees and rhododendrons set against a background of conifers, a loch and outstanding highland scenery. The gardens have developed over the past 100 years or more following the first house on the site established by a distiller from London in the 1850s. They are on a steeply sloping site and rainfall is heavy. Mrs Raven's late husband wrote a book about their other garden. Docwra's Manor in Hertfordshire (see page 179) and it was his ambition to establish a plantsman's paradise here. Apart from the area around the house, there is a pleasing air of informality about the gardens which include a boggy primula garden, Bob's Glen with *Rhododendron thomsonii* and *prattii* and a larger glen with still more species and hybrid rhododendrons. There is an alpine meadow and a flourishing kitchen garden.

ARDUAINE GARDENS 8
by Oban, Argyll, Strathclyde.
Mr H. and Mr M.E. Wright

On the A816, 18m S of Oban, 6m N of Kilmartin ● *Open April – Sept, daily except Thurs and Fri, 10.00 a.m. – 6.00 p.m.* ● *Entrance: £1.00, children free* ● *Parking: Loch Melfort Hotel by arrangement* ● *Refreshments at hotel* ● *Toilet facilities* ● *Dogs on lead* ● ***Grade II***

Although not included in many guide books, Arduaine (pronounced Ardoony if you are asking the way) is a very special place. Visitors are gently welcomed and guided round a maze of intertwining pathways which run up and down hills and amongst lawns and a series of interlocking ponds. The romance of the setting overlooking the lovely Asknish Bay is equal to the romance of the gardens' history. Created in the 1900s by J.A. Campbell they were much neglected after 1945 but were tended by a faithful nanny until they were sold in 1971 to the Wright brothers. Here is one of the best collections of rhododendrons in Scotland, as well as many other interesting trees and shrubs from Australasia as well as herbaceous plants all planted in harmony with a great understanding of colour and texture.

BARGUILLEAN 9
Taynuilt, Argyll, Strathclyde. Tel: (08662) 375
Mr Sam S. MacDonald

3m from Taynuilt. Minor road to Kilmore off A85 • *Open daily, March – Oct, 8.00 a.m. – 9.00 p.m.* • *Best season: April – June* • *Entrance: 50p, children free* • *Parking* • *Dogs on lead* • *Plants for sale* • *Grade III*

Nine-acre woodland garden with rhododendrons, azaleas, primulas, conifers and a number of rare and unusual trees and shrubs on a highland hillside overlooking a loch and with views towards Ben Cruachan. The central feature is a pool backed by a rocky crag. A very peaceful garden, showing what can be achieved in a difficult location. Good nursery garden. Much wildlife on and around the loch.

BEECHGROVE GARDEN 10
Beechgrove Terrace, Aberdeen, Grampian. Tel: (0224) 625233
BBC Scotland

1½m from city centre • *Open all day until dusk* • *Entrance: free except on SGS day when 50p* • *Teas on SGS day* • *Toilet facilities* • *Suitable for wheelchairs* • *Dogs* • *Grade III*

Beechgrove garden has been developed for use by the BBC Scotland's gardening programme of the same name. It is a relatively new garden, relying heavily on public demonstration aspects for home-owner education. Having said that, it is a highly instructive garden to visit since so many features are presented in various different ways i.e. paving, fencing, garden pools, fruit trees, vegetables, soft fruits, not to mention the vast array of ornamental trees, shrubs, flowers, alpines etc. that are grown to perfection in ways applicable to the home gardener. There is something of interest for every gardening taste.

BELHAVEN HOUSE 11
Belhaven, Dunbar, Lothian. Tel: (0368) 62392
Sir George Taylor

On the outskirts of Dunbar, route A1087 – Belhaven • Open 22nd April, 2.00 – 6.00 p.m. and at other times by appointment • Entrance: 60p • Parking • Dogs • Grade II

Sir George Taylor's associations with Royal Botanic Garden, Edinburgh and as Director of Kew Gardens has brought about the development of a small, but fascinating garden, filled with a great many treasured trees, shrubs, and herbaceous plants. The peat garden is very good, but it is the trough garden that excels. Some 20 troughs are heavily planted with very choice alpines and rockery plants of great variety. It is a good garden for the keen plantsperson. The Old House, Belhaven, commercial nursery and garden is nearby and is open daily March – Sept, excl. Tues, 10.00 a.m. – 5.00 p.m. Tel: (0368) 63223. This area of Scotland has great physical beauty and is quite unlike any other areas of Great Britain.

BELL'S CHERRYBANK GARDENS 12
Cherrybank, Perth, Tayside. Tel: (0738) 21111
Arthur Bell & Co Ltd

On A9 into Perth city centre. Gardens located S of main road • Open May – Oct, 11.00 a.m. – 5.30 p.m. • Entrance: not decided at time of going to press • Parking • Refreshments: light teas and picnic areas • Toilet facilities • Suitable for wheelchairs • Guide dogs only • House open April – Oct, Tues, Thurs, Sat and Sun, 11.00 a.m. – 5.30 p.m. • Grade III

This is a modern garden surrounding the commercial offices of Arthur Bell and Sons Ltd, whisky distillers. It is in fact two gardens, the first laid out in the early 1970s, plus the Scottish National heather collection begun in 1983. Apart from the heathers, the plant collections are not outstanding, but they are well-maintained and beautifully laid out. Interest is sustained throughout the total of eighteen acres by water features, modern sculptures, pleasant vistas, a tiny putting green, tubular bells and an aviary. The children's play area includes a roundabout for wheelchair-bound children. A remarkable sundial designed by Ian Hamilton-Finlay the sculptor is here (see page 470 for his garden, Little Sparta).

BIGGAR PARK 13
Biggar, Lanarkshire, Strathclyde. Tel: (0899) 20185
Capt and Mrs David Barnes

S end of Biggar on A702, 30m SW of Edinburgh • Open 10th June, 10.00 a.m. – 5.30 p.m., 15th July, 2.00 – 6.00 p.m. Visitors welcome by appointment • Entrance: £1.00, children 25p • Parking • Refreshments • Toilet facilities • Suitable for wheelchairs • Dogs on lead • Grade II

A Japanese garden of tranquillity welcomes one to this well-planned 10-acre plantsman's garden. Woodland walk, a small arboretum, a well-planted ornamental pond and herbaceous borders have all been carefully designed to give year-round interest, greatly aided by Susan Barnes' efficient labelling. The centrepiece, however, must be the outstanding walled garden reached through a fine rockery bank beside the eighteenth-century mansion house. The view through the wrought-iron gate stretches the length of a 50 yard double herbaceous border attractively backed by swags of thick ornamental rope hanging from rose 'pillars', whilst either side is divided into intensively planted sections divided by pleasing grass paths.

BLAIQUHOYLE 14
Port of Menteith, by Stirling, Central.
Tel: (08775) 210
Lt Colonel and Mrs J.D. Patullo

2m E of Lake of Menteith, 3m W of Thornhill on A8733 • *Open last Sun in May, June, July, 2.00 – 5.30 p.m., or by appointment* • *Entrance: £1.00, OAP and children 50p* • *Parking* • *Toilet facilities* • *Partly suitable for wheelchairs* • *Dogs on lead* • *Plants for sale* • *Grade II*

One of the choicest of the 'private' gardens in Scotland, both the garden and the arboretum were originally laid out by George Crabbie (of ginger wine fame) at the beginning of this century. It is a plantsman's garden of 16 acres with magnificent views across to the Lake of Menteith. The renowned arboretum leads down to the ornamental lake and the walled garden bursts with herbaceous plants, roses, fruit and vegetables. Even more attractive are the sweeping lawns which surround and lead into a large, but easily assimilated variety of mature shrubs, trees, rhododendrons, azaleas, primulas, ground-cover plants and heathers.

BOLFRACKS 15
Aberfeldy, Perthshire, Tayside.   Tel: (0887) 20207
Mr J.D. Hutchison

2m W of Aberfeldy on A827 towards Loch Tay • *Open mid-April – mid-Oct, daily, 10.00 a.m. – 6.00 p.m.* • *Entrance: £1.00, concessions 50p Honesty box at gate* • *Limited parking* • *Plants for sale occasionally* • *Grade IV*

There has been a garden on this site for 200 years, but the present garden was started by the owners' parents in the 1920s and reshaped by the owner over the last 20 years. Three acres of walled plantsman's garden, well laid out and planned to demonstrate the potential of an exposed hillside with a northerly aspect. Astounding views over the Tay Valley are matched by the garden's own interesting features. Gentians do well on this soil. Fine masses of bulbs in spring and good autumn colour. Peat walls and stream garden. A small wild garden is presently being laid out.

BRANKLYN GARDEN   16
Dundee Road, Perth, Tayside.   Tel: (0738) 25535
National Trust for Scotland

½m from Queen's Bridge on A85 • Open March – Oct, daily, 9.30 a.m. to sunset • Best season: early summer • Entrance: £1.20, OAP and children 60p Parties £1.00 (50p) per person • Parking ¼m from entrance. Disabled parking at gate • Toilet facilities • Paths too narrow for wheelchairs • Plants for sale • NTS sales table • Grade III

John and Dorothy Renton created this garden nearly in sight of the centre of Perth and certainly within sound. Work commenced in 1922 and in 1955 Dorothy was awarded the Veitch Memorial Medal by the Royal Horticultural Society. Branklyn extends to about three acres with the main interest being in alpine and ericaceous plants in its magnificent scree rock garden on the side of the tennis court. There is a splendid collection of dwarf rhododendrons. The National Trust took over the garden in 1968, following the death of Dorothy Renton in 1966 and of her husband the following year and a substantial restructuring and improvement programme is taking place over this winter. It is to be hoped that this essential work will restore Branklyn to its rightful position as an outstanding plantsman's garden with its main feature what has been described as 'a true rock-gardener's paradise'. It is impossible to describe all the splendid things to be found here from the fine trees to the comprehensive collection of dwarf and smaller rhododendrons, the meconopsis to the cyprepediums, and the garden will repay many visits.

BRECHIN CASTLE   17
Brechin, Tayside.   Tel: (03562) 4566 (Estate office)
The Earl and Countess of Dalhousie

1m from Brechin, route A94 • Open May – end June, 2.00 – 6.00 p.m. • Best season: late May, early June • Entrance: 50p, children 10p • Parking • Teas in garden • Grade II

The main axis of the walled garden is punctuated by a series of individual features. At the first one of these, four Lawson cypresses, a view down steps to the pond garden below is obtained. Subsequent events include a laburnum grove, a birch grove and a cherry grove, all flanked by castellated clipped yew hedges. Arguably one of the best walled gardens in Scotland. The eighteenth-century castle itself is half a mile away, approached by more recent plantings of azaleas and situated on a rocky cliff overlooking the River South Esk.

BRODICK CASTLE   18
Isle of Arran, Strathclyde.   Tel: (0770) 2202
National Trust for Scotland and Cunninghame District Council

On Isle of Arran, 2m from Brodick. Ferry from Ardrossan or Kintyre • Open 24th – 27th March, daily, 1.00 – 5.00 p.m., 28th March – 29th April and 2nd

– 14th Oct, Mon, Wed, Sat, 1.00 – 5.00 p.m., 28th April – 1st Oct, daily, 1.00 – 5.00 p.m. ● *Best season: late April/early May (woodland garden), May – Aug (formal garden)* ● *Entrance: castle and garden £2.10, children £1.05* ● *Parking free* ● *Refreshments* ● *Toilet facilities* ● *Partly suitable for wheelchairs* ● *Dogs on lead* ● *Shop* ● *Castle open as garden* ● **Grade I**

High above the shores of the Firth of Clyde and guarding three approaches to Western Scotland is this red-brick castle, a sign that Arran has been the scene of many territorial disputes over the centuries. Its garden was an overgrown jungle of rhododendrons until the Duchess of Montrose arrived after World War I; she was much helped after 1930 when her daughter married John Boscawen of Tresco Abbey (see page 72). Many of the trees and plants here came by boat from Tresco in the Scillies. Others came from subscriptions to the second generation of great plant-hunters like Kingdon-Ward and, in particular, George Forrest, one of the greatest of all collectors. Plants from the Himalayas, Burma and China, normally considered tender, flourish in the Gulf Stream climate. A good display of primulas in bog garden. The walled formal garden to the east of the castle is over 250 years old and has recently been restored as a Victorian garden with herbaceous plants, annuals and roses. It is impossible to list all the treasures of the woodland garden but perhaps the most surprising is the huge size of the specimens in the lower rhododendron walk where *R. sinogrande* are found, larger than a normal tree with blooms up to two feet long. Memorable views over Brodick Bay.

CARNELL 19
Hurlford, Ayrshire, Strathclyde. Tel: (056384) 236
Mr and Mrs J.R. Findlay and Mrs J.B. Findlay (The Garden House)

4m from Kilmarnock, 6m from Mauchline on A719, 1½m on Ayrshire side of A76 ● *Open 29th July, 2.00 – 6.00 p.m.* ● *Entrance: £1.00, children under 12 free* ● *Parking free* ● *Refreshments on day of opening* ● *Dogs on lead* ● *Plants for sale.* ● *Sixteenth-century peel tower* ● **Grade III**

Exquisite example of 100 yards of linear herbaceous borders facing a rectangular pool with informal planting as a contrast on the opposite bank. Also interesting rock garden, lilies. Walled garden. Burmese and Japanese features. Garden adjacent to house currently being developed. All plants and vegetables grown with organic compost produced *in situ*.

CASTLE KENNEDY AND LOCHINCH GARDENS 20
Stranraer, Wigtownshire, Dumfries & Galloway.
Tel: (0776) 2024
The Earl and Countess of Stair

3m from Stranraer on A75 ● *Open April – Sept, daily, 10.00 a.m. – 5.00 p.m.* ● *Best season: April/May* ● *Entrance: £1.50, OAP £1.00, children 50p*

Party rates on application ● *Parking* ● *Teas* ● *Toilet facilities* ● *Partly suitable for wheelchairs* ● *Dogs on lead* ● *Plants for sale* ● *Shop* ● **Grade I**

In 1716, Castle Kennedy, the home of the Earls of Stair, was destroyed by fire. This gave an excuse for Lord Stair to develop this huge area in a novel way, in the light of his principles as an 'improving landowner'. The Earl supervised the work himself although he employed garden designers such as William Boutcher. Part of the manual work was done by unoccupied dragoons who built banks up from the loch shores, somewhat in the style of irregular fortifications, so that informality was combined with massive formal gardens in the seventeenth-century French style with criss-cross avenues and allées of large specimen trees. The gardens were restored in the nineteenth century by which time the exotica imported from many parts of the world had had time to mature. In 1849 the great avenue from the circular pool to the new castle was planted with what has become the best avenue of araucarias in the UK. Many of Sir Joseph Hooker's original rhododendron introductions from his Himalayan expeditions were planted here, now forming the backbone of one of Britain's finest rhododendron collections. The massive specimens of *Rhododendron arboreum* are one of the spectacles of Scottish spring. The grounds are heavily planted with specimen conifers: abies, cryptomeria, pinus, *Pseudotsuga sciadopitys*, sequoia etc. The gardens around the new castle, Lochinch, are separate, screened by walls and hedges. These are more conventional with lawns, flowerbeds and shrub borders. Unusual herbaceous plants, exotica and fine Japanese cherries are much in evidence. A wonderful place; full of spectacular spring colour.

CASTLE OF MEY
Caithness, Highlands
H.M. Queen Elizabeth the Queen Mother

21

1½m from Mey ● *Open for SGS* ● *Entrance: 70p, OAP and children under 12, 40p* ● *Parking* ● *Teas* ● *Toilet facilities* ● *Suitable for wheelchairs* ● *Dogs* ● **Grade I**

Now the home of H.M. the Queen Mother, Castle of Mey is situated on the shore of the Pentland Firth with magnificent views to the Orkneys. The castle – a completely-restored late sixteenth- century tower house (not open) – sports a lovely small garden of particular charm in the Jekyll style. Within its walls H.M. the Queen Mother has collected her favourite flowers; many were gifts and have special meaning. The personal private feeling pervades the whole garden which is especially well planted and maintained. The colour schemes are very good, blending the garden with the vast natural panorama within which it is situated. The mild sea-temperate climate allows many unusual half-hardy plants to be grown to perfection.

CAWDOR CASTLE 22
Cawdor, Nairn, Highlands.   Tel: (06677) 615
The Earl of Cawdor

*Between Inverness and Nairn on the B9090 off the A96 • Open May – Sept,
daily, 10.00 a.m. – 5.30 p.m. • Best season: summer • Entrance: £2.75, OAP
and disabled £2.00, children £1.50. Family ticket £9.00. Parties of 20 or more
on application • Parking • Refreshments: restaurant, teas and picnics
• Toilet facilities • Partly suitable for wheelchairs • Plants for sale • Shop
• House open • Grade II*

Cawdor Castle, frequently referred to as one of the Highlands' most romantic
castles, is a superb fourteenth-century Scottish keep and seventeenth-century
fortifications. The surrounding parkland is very beautiful and well-kept,
though not in the grand tradition of 'classic' landscapes. There are very fine
views of castle, park and this lovely Scottish countryside. To the side of the
castle is the formal garden, perennial borders, and numerous beds filled with
all manner of perennials and annuals. The rose garden is well stocked with old
shrubs and modern varieties. The rustic arches and arbours are pleasant. There
is an abundance of lavender and pinks completing the Edwardian feel.
Specimen trees, especially the ancient oaks, are of note. The overall effect is
one of strong romance, although sadly marred by a tendency toward heavy
commercialization. That aside, Cawdor is a pleasant visit for the whole family;
the garden a riot of colour most of the summer season.

CLUNY HOUSE 23
Aberfeldy, Perthshire, Tayside.   Tel: (0887) 20795
Mr and Mrs J. Mattingley

*20m NW of Perth. N of Aberfeldy, over the Wade Bridge, take the Weem to
Strathtay road. Cluny House is signposted about 3m along this road • Open
March – Oct, 10.00 a.m. – 6.00 p.m. • Best season: spring, early summer or
late autumn • Entrance: £1.00, children free • Limited parking • Plants
for sale and plant and seed list available on request • Grade III*

A five-acre woodland garden, renowned for its Himalayan plants, primulas,
rhododendrons, lilies and meconopsis. A network of paths leads through the
woodland, occasionally revealing spectacular views over the surrounding
Perthshire countryside, Strathtay to Ben Lawers. An outstanding collection of
rare Asiatic plants is contained in this garden; note especially the rare
primulas, the meconopsis and the giant lilies. Good autumn colour.

CRARAE GLEN GARDEN 24
Minard, by Inverary, Argyll, Strathclyde.   Tel: (0546) 86614
Crarae Gardens Charitable Trust

*1m from Minard on A83 • Open daily, summer, 9.00 a.m. – 6.00 p.m.,
winter, daylight hours • Best season: spring and autumn • Entrance: £1.70,*

children 70p, wheelchairs free ● *Parking* ● *Refreshments: teas and coffee*
● *Toilet facilities* ● *Suitable for wheelchairs* ● *Dogs on short lead* ● *Plants for
sale* ● *Shop* ● **Grade II**

The gardens as they are today were started by the present baronet's
grandmother Grace Campbell. Her nephew was the English plant hunter
Reginald Farrer (1880–1920) who also made and wrote about a famous rock
garden. After World War I he collected in Burma, near the border of China,
and died there. The garden winds up and down and along paths and over
bridges crossing gushing streams, splendid torrents and waterfalls, mostly
under canopies of great rhododendrons. A fine collection of rare and exotic
trees and shrubs. The whole is admirably maintained.

CRATHES CASTLE GARDEN   25
Crathes Castle, Banchory, Grampian. Tel: **(033044) 651**
National Trust for Scotland

3m E of Banchory and 15m W of Aberdeen on A93 ● *Open daily, 9.30 a.m. –
dusk* ● *Entrance: £2.00, children £1.00* ● *Parking 200 yards from gardens,
signposted* ● *Refreshments: licensed restaurant* ● *Toilet facilities* ● *Suitable
for wheelchairs* ● *No dogs in garden, but nature/dog trail in grounds* ● *Plants
for sale* ● *National Trust Shop* ● *House open, to include gardens £2.80,
children £1.70* ● **Grade I**

The first view of Crathes is a breath-taking one – the image of a fairy castle set
in flowing lawns. The building looks much as it did in mid-sixteenth century
but there is no record of how the garden then looked, although the yew
topiary of 1702 survives. Sir James Burnett, who came here in 1926, was a
keen collector and his wife was an inspired herbaceous planter, and the garden
today is their achievement. In all there are eight gardens each reflecting a
different theme. Rare shrubs reflect Burnett's interest in the Far East where he
served in the army. Splendid wide herbaceous borders with clever plant
associations are Lady Burnett's heritage, most famous of which is the white
border. There are many specialist areas such as the trough garden and a
collection of grasses; the large greenhouses contain a unique collection of
carnations. Extensive wild gardens and grounds with picnic areas, with 15
miles of marked trails. Often compared to Hidcote but with evident
inspiration from Jekyll, Crathes has wonders for the plantsperson, the
designer and the ordinary visitor.

CRUICKSHANK BOTANIC GARDEN   26
St Machar Drive, Old Aberdeen, Grampian. Tel: **(0224) 272701**
The Cruickshank Trust and University of Aberdeen

1½m N from city centre in Old Aberdeen off Tillydrone Avenue ● *Open all
year, Mon – Fri, 8.30 a.m. – 4.30 p.m., May – Sept, Sat and Sun, 2.00 – 5.00*

p.m. • *Entrance: free* • *Parking. Coaches by appointment only* • *Picnics*
• *Suitable for wheelchairs* • *Dogs on lead* • **Grade III**

This serves a dual purpose, a collection for research and teaching and a public place for recreation and for proselytising ideas for design and planting. The glasshouses contain succulents and there is a sunken garden, a rock and water garden, a woodland border, patio garden and long herbaceous border. The woodland area is attractive, dating from late Victorian times; there are lawns and fine specimen trees.

DALMENY PARK 27
Mons Hill, South Queensferry, Lothian. Tel: (031) 3311784
The Earl of Roseberry

Between South Queensferry and Edinburgh. 7m from the city centre along the Firth of Forth • *Open May – Oct, Sun – Thurs, 2.00 – 5.30 p.m. and for SGS* • *Entrance: 60p, children under 14 free* • *Parking* • *Teas* • **Grade III**

Dalmeny's greatest feature is the Gothic house and its exceptionally fine collections. The gardens are all but gone, though the extensive grounds are heavily planted with good mature trees. Dalmeny is mentioned for one reason – its superb snowdrop wood. Open for charity two Sundays in March, the snowdrop wood must be seen to be believed. Five acres of beech woods atop a hill overlooking the Firth of Forth are drifted with countless wild snowdrops. The views back to Edinburgh are particularly lovely. This is undoubtedly Britain's best snowdrop wood; a spectacle never to be forgotten once seen.

DAWYCK BOTANIC GARDEN 28
Stobo, Peebleshire, Borders. Tel: (07216) 254
Royal Botanic Garden, Edinburgh

8m SW of Peebles, 28m from Edinburgh on B712 • *Open April – Sept, 10.00 a.m. – 5.00 p.m.* • *Best season: spring and autumn* • *Entrance: 70p per car* • *Parking* • *Partly suitable for wheelchairs* • *Guide dogs only* • **Grade IV**

The home of the famous Dawyck beech, the garden has a large variety of interesting mature trees. These provide an impressive backcloth for many species of flowering shrubs, especially in the spring. There are pleasant woodland walks rich in wildlife interest.

DRUMMOND CASTLE 29
Muthill, Nr Crieff, Perthshire, Tayside. Tel: (076481) 321
Grimsthorpe and Drummond Castle Trust Ltd

2m S of Crieff on A822 • *Open April – Oct, Wed and Sun, 2.00 – 5.00 p.m.* • *Best season: June and July* • *Entrance: £1.20, concessions 60p* • *Parking*

300 yards past main entrance ● *Toilet facilities* ● *Partly suitable for wheelchairs* ● ***Grade I***

The gardens to this fine castle were first laid out in 1630 by John Drummond, 2nd Earl of Perth. Next to the castle, across a courtyard, is the house and below both is the great parterre garden with, at its centre, the famous sundial made by the master mason to Charles I. When the garden was revived by Lewis Kennedy, who worked at Drummond from 1818 to 1860, he achieved what the *Oxford Companion* calls 'effectively the re-creation of an idea of the seventeenth-century Scottish garden'. The long St Andrew's cross design has Italian, French and Dutch influences. Beautiful white marble Italian statuary is set in arbours along the southern borders, giving an overall sense of tranquillity and order. The *Oxford Companion* believes that the old arrangement of filling the 'compartments' of the cross with shrubs and herbaceous plants was more effective than today's style in which some may feel the structure is too prominent. The fruit and vegetable gardens and glasshouses should also be visited.

DUNROBIN GARDENS   30
Golspie, Sutherland, Highlands.   Tel: (04083) 3177/3268
The Sutherland Trust

1m N of Golspie on A9 ● *Open June – mid-Sept, Mon – Sat, 10.30 a.m. – 5.00 p.m., Sun, 1.00 – 5.00 p.m* ● *Entrance: £2.20, children £1.10* ● *Parking* ● *Toilet facilities* ● *Shop* ● *House open* ● ***Grade II***

These Victorian formal gardens were designed in the grand French style to echo the architecture of Dunrobin Castle which rises high above them and looks out over the Moray Firth. They were laid out by the architect, Charles Barry, in 1850, when there was a staff of 40 gardeners. Rescued from near dereliction five years ago, there is a staff of only four gardeners now. Descending the stone terraces, one can see the round garden (evocative of the Scottish shield, the head gardener suggests), rose beds, grove, parterre and herbaceous borders laid out beneath. The round ponds, some with fountains, are a particular feature, together with the summer-house and wrought-iron Westminster gates. The garden is under development – a rhododendron and fern bank has been planted, and other features are planned, within the limitations of a south-east facing site on sandy soil. In the policies (estate lands) there are many woodland walks.

EARLSHALL CASTLE   31
Leuchars, Fife.   Tel: (033483) 205
Major and Mrs D.R. Baxter, Baron and Baroness of Earlshall

Follow signs from centre of Leuchars, A919 ● *Open Good Friday, Easter Sat, Sun and Mon, June – 3rd Sun in Sept, daily except Tues, 2.00 – 6.00 p.m. Parties by appointment* ● *Best season: July and Aug* ● *Entrance: £2.50, OAP*

£2.00, children £1.00 • *Parking free* • *Refreshments* • *Suitable for wheelchairs in garden* • *Guide dogs only* • *Plants for sale occasionally* • *Shop* • *House open as gardens* • **Grade II**

A walled garden situated beside the restored sixteenth-century castle divided by yew hedges into a series of external 'rooms'. The most significant of these contains topiary 'chessmen', and there is also a secret garden, orchard garden, herbaceous border and 'bowling green' with rose terrace, and an attractively laid-out kitchen garden. Interesting garden architecture includes a gardener's cottage, dowry house, summer-house and arbour, all bearing the stamp of Sir Robert Lorimer's eye for detail. Lorimer, famous for Kellie Castle (see page 468) believed in gardens as a place of repose and solitude, formal near the house but becoming 'less trim as it gets further ... and then naturally marries with the demesne that lies beyond'. Altogether, a most delightful retreat from the world outside.

EDZELL CASTLE   32
Edzell, Nr Brechin, Angus, Tayside. Tel: (031) 556840
Department of the Environment

4m N of Brechin. Take A94 and after 2m fork left on B966 • *Open April – Sept, Mon – Sat, 9.30 a.m. – 7.00 p.m., Sun, 2.00 – 7.00 p.m.* • *Entrance: 75p, OAP and children 50p, reduced rates for parties* • *Parking* • *Toilet facilities* • *Suitable for wheelchairs* • *Dogs* • *Ruins* • **Grade I**

In 1604 Sir David Lindsay made a remarkable small walled garden at his fortress at Edzell; it remains today probably the oldest complete and unaltered garden in the country. By the time they came into the custody of H.M. Office of Works in 1932, the garden and castle had lain in ruins for over 150 years. Although the plantings are new, dating from the 1930s, they are elaborate examples in the manner of the period of the early seventeenth century. Meticulously-kept parterres of box, lawn, and bedding are contained within walls of unique and curious design. There are 43 panels of alternating chequered niches and sculptured symbolic figures. There are large recesses below for bee skeps. The whole is laid out to be viewed from a corner garden-house and the windows of the now-ruined castle. The village of Edzel is quite small and a charming example of an ordered Victorian Scottish highland village. There are shops, a tea room and a small hotel. A must for lovers of the historical and romantic.

FALKLAND PALACE GARDEN   33
Falkland, Fife. Tel: (0337) 57397
National Trust for Scotland

11m N of Kirkcaldy via A912 • *Open 24th March – Sept, Mon – Sat, 10.00 a.m. – 6.00 p.m., Sun, 2.00 – 6.00 p.m., Oct, Sat, 10.00 a.m. – 6.00 p.m., Sun, 2.00 – 6.00 p.m.* • *Entrance: garden only, £1.30, children 65p, Palace*

and garden, £2.10, children £1.05 ● *Parking 100 yards from palace*
● *Refreshments in village, picnic area in orchard* ● *Toilet facilities plus ramp*
● *Suitable for wheelchairs* ● *National Trust shop* ● *House open* ● ***Grade IV***

This was originally the kitchen garden for the sixteenth-century palace where Mary Queen of Scots played as a girl. In World War II it became a forest nursery but was remodelled soon afterwards. On a compact scale, this 11-acre area contains everything: rose garden, herb garden, herbaceous borders and orchard. In addition, visitors may gain admission from the garden to the royal tennis court (i.e. real tennis) where occasional competitions of this old game are still staged. Features include an outdoor chequers game in the herb garden. Interesting village houses nearby.

FINLAYSTONE 34
Langbank, Renfrewshire, Strathclyde. Tel: (047554) 285
Mr George Gordon Macmillan of Macmillan

On A8 20m from Glasgow, follow large signpost W of Langbank ● *Open all year, daily, 11.00 a.m. – 5.00 p.m.* ● *Best season: spring and autumn*
● *Entrance: £1.00, children 60p* ● *Parking* ● *Refreshments* ● *Toilet facilities* ● *Suitable for wheelchairs* ● *Dogs on lead (off lead in woodland)*
● *Shop open at weekends* ● *House open, April – Aug, Suns, 2.30 – 4.30 p.m.*
● ***Grade III***

Designed, enhanced and tended over the last 50 years by Lady Macmillan, much respected doyenne of Scottish gardens and her family, this spacious garden is imaginatively laid out over 10 acres with a further 70 acres of mature woodland walks. Large, elegant lawns framed by long herbaceous borders, interesting shrubberies and mature copper beech look down over the River Clyde. John Knox's tree, a Celtic paving 'maze' laid out by Lady Macmillan's daughter-in-law Jane, a paved fragrant garden with the handicapped in mind and a new bog garden are all added attractions.

GEILSTON HOUSE 35
Nr Cardross, Dunbartonshire, Strathclyde. Tel: (0389) 841467
Miss M.E. Bell

1m W of Cardross on A814 ● *Open 26th May, 2.00 – 5.30 p.m. Other times by appointment* ● *Best season: May, Oct* ● *Entrance: £1.00, accompanied children under 12 free* ● *Parking* ● *Teas on open day* ● *Suitable for wheelchairs* ● *Plants for sale* ● ***Grade III***

A well-maintained walled garden with herbaceous borders and a heather garden which contains about ninety different varieties. Adjoining this garden is a small woodland 'glen garden' where rare and unusual shrubs, trees, rhododendrons and azaleas flourish on the banks of a small burn in picturesque surroundings. The autumn colour is also worth experiencing.

GLASGOW BOTANICAL GARDEN 36
Great Western Road, Glasgow, Strathclyde.
Tel: (041) 3342422
Glasgow Corporation

In the centre of Glasgow, corner of Great Western Road and Queen Margaret Drive • *Open daily, 7.00 a.m. – dusk* • *Entrance: free* • *Parking outside* • *Toilet facilities* • *Suitable for wheelchairs* • *Dogs on lead* • *Grade IV*

A pleasant afternoon's walk, but disappointing from a horticultural point of view particularly as such famous botanists as William Hooker and David Douglas were associated with the garden in the past. A few shiny bedding displays do not disguise the fact that apart from a nice herbaceous border the 40 acres of trees, shrubs, herb and teaching gardens are sometimes uninspired, frequently sparse and occasionally downright unkempt. It is worth a visit if only for the rusting old Kibble Palace glasshouse of 1873 where statues peer through temperate zone plants set in yards of bare, carefully hoed earth. Neighbouring glasshouses offer a comprehensive, if pedestrianly displayed, selection of foliage plants and National collections of orchids and begonias which must be lovely in season.

GLENARN 37
Rhu, Dunbartonshire, Strathclyde. Tel: (0436820) 493
Michael and Sue Thornley

40m NW of Glasgow on Pier Road opposite Rhu Marina • *Open 21st March – 21st June, dawn to dusk* • *Entrance: £1.00* • *Parking* • *Refreshments on special open days only* • *Toilet facilities* • *Dogs on lead* • *A few plants for sale* • *Grade III*

Established in the 1930s in a Victorian garden by the Gibson family and fed by the famous plant expeditions of that decade, this is a very special woodland garden. Well-kept paths meander round a 10-acre sheltered bowl, sometimes tunnelling under superb giant species rhododendrons (including a *falconeri* grown from Hooker's original seed in 1849), sometimes allowing a glorious vista across the garden to the Clyde estuary, and sometimes stopping the visitor short to gaze with unstinted admiration at 40 foot magnolias, piris, olearias, eucryphias and hoherias. Michael and Sue Thornley, both professional architects, acquired Glenarn six years ago and with almost no help are successfully replanting and restoring where necessary, whilst still retaining the special atmosphere created by such magnificent growth. An especially pleasing finale is provided by winding down through a nook-and-cranny, quarry garden – sadly not suitable for those who find walking very difficult.

GREEN BANK GARDENS 38
Nr Clarkston Toll, Glasgow, Strathclyde. Tel: (041639) 3281
National Trust for Scotland

Take A726 to Clarkston, turn off opposite railway station, follow signs • Open all year, 9.30 a.m. – sunset • Best season: spring and summer • Entrance: £1.10, children 55p • Parking • Refreshments • Toilet facilities • Suitable for wheelchairs • Dogs on lead, but not in walled garden • Plants for sale • Shop • Grade II

Large old walled garden of eighteenth-century house divided into many sections, all of which are imaginatively planted. The colour combinations are especially good. All the plants are in very good condition and admirably labelled. An old hard tennis court in the corner has been converted into a spacious and pleasant area for the disabled. There are many raised beds, a raised pond with a permanently running pump which makes a good splashing noise. Also there is wheelchair access to the glasshouse and potting shed to allow disabled people to work here. Woodland walks are filled with spring bulbs and shrubs and there are usually Highland cattle in the paddock.

HILL OF TARVIT 39
Cupar, Fife. Tel: (0334) 53127
National Trust for Scotland

2½m S of Cupar off A916 • Open daily, 10.00 a.m. – sunset • Entrance: £1.00, children 50p • Parking • Refreshments and picnic area • Toilet facilities • Partly suitable for wheelchairs • Plants for sale • Shop • House open 24th – 27th March and 28th April – Sept, daily, 2.00 – 6.00 p.m., 1st – 23rd April and 1st – 29th Oct, Sat and Sun, 2.00 – 6.00 p.m. Last tour 5.30 p.m. • Grade II

The garden surrounds the charming Edwardian mansion designed in 1906 for a jute magnate by Sir Robert Lorimer who also laid out the grounds. There is a lovely rose garden and delightful woodland walk to a toposcope. There are many beds and small borders filled with unusual perennials, annuals, heaths and heathers. The grounds contain many unusual ornamental trees and shrubs now reaching full maturity. The views over Fife are particularly fine. The garden is maintained by the National Trust which regularly upgrades the plantings to include newer and unusual specimens. A good garden for amateur and keen plantsperson alike.

HOUSE OF PITMUIES 40
Guthrie, by Forfar, Tayside. Tel: (02412) 245
Mrs Farquhar Ogilvie

1½m from Friockheim, route A932 • Open daily, Easter or 1st April (whichever is earlier) – Oct, 2.00 – 5.00 p.m. and at other times by appointment • Best season: June and July • *Entrance: £1.00 by collection box* • *Parking* • *Toilet facilities* • *Partly suitable for wheelchairs* • *Dogs on lead* • *Plants for sale* • *House open for parties by appointment* • **Grade II**

In the grounds of an attractive eighteenth-century house and courtyard, these beautiful walled gardens lead down towards a small river with an informal riverside walk and two unusual buildings, a turreted dovecote and a Gothic wash-house. There are rhododendron glades with other unusual trees and shrubs, but pride of place must go to the spectacular semi-formal gardens behind the house. Exquisite old-fashioned roses with a series of long borders containing a dramatic palette of massed delphiniums and other herbaceous perennials in July, constitute one of the most memorable displays of its type to be found in Scotland.

HOUSE OF TONGUE   41
Tongue, by Lairg, Sutherland, Highlands.   Tel: (084755) 209
Countess of Sutherland

1m N of Tongue off A838 • *Open 4th Aug, 2.00 – 6.00 p.m.* • *Entrance: £1.00, children 50p* • *Parking* • **Grade II**

Sheltered from wind and salt by tall trees, this walled garden is a haven in an otherwise exposed environment. Adjoining the seventeenth-century house, it is laid-out after the traditional Scottish acre with gravel and grass walks between herbaceous beds and hedged vegetable plots and orchard. A stepped beech-hedged walk leads up to a high terrace which commands a fine view over the Kyle of Tongue. The centre-piece of the garden is Lord Reay's sundial (1714) – a sculpted obelisk of unusual design.

INVERESK LODGE AND VILLAGE   42
Nr Musselburgh, East Lothian, Lothian.   Tel: (031) 2265922
Various owners inc. National Trust for Scotland (Lodge)

6m E of Edinburgh, S of Musselburgh via A6124 • *Open all year, Mon – Fri, 10.00 a.m. – 4.30 p.m., Sun, 2.00 – 5.00 p.m.* • *Best season: summer* • *Entrance: 50p, children 25p, honesty box* • *Parking* • *Lodge open as gardens* • **Grade II**

Inveresk Lodge, a large seventeenth-century house in the village of Inveresk, now owned by the National Trust for Scotland, is situated on a steeply sloping site. The high stone retaining walls are well-planted with a wide range of climbers. There are numerous flower beds; a particularly good border is devoted to shrub roses. A peat bed permits a greater diversity of planting. The garden has been completely remade since it came under the ownership of the National Trust for Scotland. No attempt has been made to recreate a period style. The garden is 'modern' in most respects; semi-formal, well planted, very well-maintained and offers a wide selection of plants flowering from spring through autumn. The village itself is a unique, unspoilt example of eighteenth-century villa development with houses dating from the late seventeenth and early eighteenth centuries. All have well laid-out gardens enclosed by high walls and containing a wide range of shrubs and trees as well as some unusual plants. Open one day under SGS by admission ticket to cover all gardens. Plant stall and teas.

INVEREWE GARDEN 43
Poolewe, Ross & Cromarty, Highlands. Tel: (044586) 356
National Trust for Scotland

6m NE of Gairloch on A832 ● *Open all year, daily, 9.30 a.m. – sunset* ● *Entrance: £2.00, £1.60 party rate, OAP, students, YHA, SYHA and children £1.00* ● *Parking* ● *Refreshments* ● *Toilet facilities* ● *Partly suitable for wheelchairs* ● *Plants for sale* ● *Shop* ● **Grade I**

This garden is spectacular. Created in 1865 on the shores of the sea loch, Loch Ewe, it covers the entire Am Ploc Ard peninsular. Planned as a wild garden around one dwarf willow on peat and sandstone, it has been developed as a series of walks through herbaceous and rock gardens, a wet valley, a rhododendron walk and a curved vegetable garden and orchard. This is a plantsman's garden (labelling is discreet) containing many sub-tropical species from Australia, New Zealand, China and the Americas, sheltered by mature beech, oak and pine trees. New Zealand alpines include the National collection of the genus Ourisia (1986). The garden is well-tended and way-marked. The gales of 1989 resulted in the loss of 80 specimen trees. Note: midge repellent is essential and on sale at main desk!

KAILZIE GARDENS 44
Peebles, Peebleshire, Borders. Tel: (0721) 20007
Mrs M.A. Richard

2½m from Peebles on B7062 ● *Open April – Oct, 11.00 a.m. – 5.30 p.m.* ● *Entrance: £1.00, children 50p* ● *Parking* ● *Tea room and restaurant* ● *Toilet facilities* ● *Suitable for wheelchairs* ● *Dogs on lead* ● *Plants for sale when available* ● *Shop* ● **Grade III**

'A Pleasure Garden' is the description in one of the advertisements for Kailzie (pronounced Kailie) and very apt it is too. The gardens of 17 acres are situated in a particularly attractive area of the beautiful Tweed Valley and are surrounded by breath-taking views. The Old Mansion Home was pulled down in 1962 and the vast walled garden, which still houses the magnificent greenhouse, was transformed by Angela Rich. From vegetables to a garden of meandering lawns and island beds full of interesting shrubs and herbaceous plants, there are many surprises including a herb garden, choice flower area, secret gardens, loving seats invitingly placed under garlanded arbours and several pieces of statuary which have been thoughtfully placed. A magnificent fountain at the end of the herbaceous borders leads on to woods and huge stately trees and from here you may stroll down the Mayor's walk which is lined with laburnum and underplanted with rhododendrons, azaleas, blue poppies and primulas. From here you can go to the small waterfowl lake.

KELLIE CASTLE 45
Pittenweem, Fife.   Tel: (03338) 271
National Trust for Scotland

3m NNW of Pittenweem on B9171   • Open all year, daily, 10.00 a.m. – sunset • Best season: summer   • Entrance: £1.00, children 50p (castle and garden £2.00, children £1.00)   • Parking 100 yards, closer parking for disabled • Refreshments in castle   • Toilet facilities, not for disabled   • Partly suitable for wheelchairs   • Shop   • House open, 24th – 27th March and 28th April – Sept, daily, 2.00 p.m. – 6.00 p.m., 1st – 27th April and 1st – 29th Oct, Sat and Sun, 2.00 p.m. – 6.00 p.m.   • Grade IV

The garden has no particular relationship to the sixteenth-century house, having been restored by Professor James Lorimer in early Victorian times. Entered by a door in a high wall, the garden is small (one acre) and inspires dreams within every gardener's reach. Simple borders, such as one of catmint only, capture the imagination as hundreds of bees and butterflies work the flowers. Areas of lawn are edged with box hedges, borders, arches and trellises. In one corner, behind a trellis, is a small romantic garden within a garden. Large, white-painted commemorative seats (reminiscent of Rennie Mackintosh's design) provide focal interest at the end of one of the walks.

KILBRYDE CASTLE 46
Dunblane, Perthshire, Central.   Tel: (0786) 823104
Sir Colin Campbell

Off A820 Dunblane – Doune road   • Open 1st, 22nd April, 6th, 27th May, 10th June, 8th July, 12th Aug, 16th Sept, 2.00 – 5.30 p.m. and also by appointment   • Best season: April – July   • Entrance: £1.00   • Parking • Partly suitable for wheelchairs   • Grade IV

A good example of a partly-mature 20-acre garden created over the last 10 years by the enthusiastic owner and his highly knowledgeable helper, who are constantly introducing new features and plant content. Imaginatively-placed borders filled with constant colour on wide lawns sloping down to a woodland water garden.

KILDRUMMY CASTLE GARDENS 47
Nr Alford, Aberdeen, Grampian.   Tel: (09755) 71264 and 71277
Kildrummy Castle Garden Trust

2m from Mossat, 10m from Alford, 17m from Huntly. Take A944 from Alford, following signs to Kildrummy, left on A97   • Open April – Oct, daily,

SCOTLAND

10.00 a.m. – 5.00 p.m. • *Entrance: £1.00, children 20p* • *Parking: car park free inside hotel main entrance. Coach park up hotel delivery entrance* • *Toilet facilities* • *Suitable for wheelchairs* • *Dogs on lead* • *Plants for sale* • *Kildrummy Castle Hotel open (09755 71288), for reservations* • *Visitor centre and video room* • *Woodland walks, children's play area* • ***Grade II***

This was once a famous Japanese water garden. Now a series of waterfall-linked pools run beneath a replica of the Auld Brig O'Bolgownie, and nearby a quarry garden shelters a superb collection of alpines, heathers and ericas. The quarry stone was used to build Kildrummy Castle which now lies in ruins above. Near the old quarry a waste tip has been transformed into a garden of rhododendrons, and old roller stones, millstones and staddle stones are used as features. The steep-sided glen shelters some normally tender plants such as the Chilean flame-bush and plants from New Zealand and water-loving plants such as hostas, primulas and veratrum. In all, a tranquil and unusual garden in a dramatic setting.

LAWHEAD CROFT   48
Tarbrax, Lanarkshire, Lothian.   Tel: (050185) 274
Sue and Hector Riddell

12m from Balerno, 6m from Carnwath on A70 • *Open 24th June, 22nd July, 2.00 – 6.00 p.m., parties by appointment* • *Best season: summer* • *Entrance: £1.00, children 20p* • *Parking* • *Refreshments on open days* • *Toilet facilities* • *Mostly suitable for wheelchairs* • *Dogs on lead* • *Plants for sale* • ***Grade IV***

Nearly 100ft up in the midst of the bleak Lanarkshire moors, Sue and Hector Riddell have planted shelter belts and laboriously carved out a luxuriant garden. Grass walks lead from one interesting border to another all full of unusual plants. Colour associations and leaf contrasts are carefully thought out. There is an enchanting series of garden rooms all with a different theme. A garden of great ideas including an excellent bonsai collection. Recently most of the vegetable garden has been swept away and replanted in a great sweep of curved, tiered and circular beds of spectacular and original design.

LEITH HALL   49
Kennethmont, by Huntly, Aberdeen, Grampian.
Tel: (0224) 572215
National Trust for Scotland

1m W of Kennethmont on B9002 and 34m NW of Aberdeen • *Open all year, daily, 9.30 a.m. – sunset* • *Entrance: donation, except SGS day in Aug when 40p, children 20p* • *Parking* • *Refreshments: picnic area and teas on SGS days* • *Toilet facilities* • *Dogs* • *Stalls on SGS day* • *House open inc. exhibition: 28th April – 1st Oct, 2.00 – 6.00 p.m. (last tour 5.15 p.m.) £2.10, children £1.05, parties £1.60, schools 80p* • ***Grade II***

Since it came into the care of the National Trust for Scotland, the gardens of Leith Hall have been expanded and upgraded. But it is the old garden, remote from the house, that offers the greatest pleasure to the garden enthusiast. This old garden comprises large borders and a large, well-stocked rock garden. The design is simple, romantic and allows a tremendous display of flowers during the whole of summer and early autumn. There are no lawns or open courtyards and no dominating architecture, just massive plantings of perennials and the odd rarity amongst the rocks. Like most gardens of the National Trust for Scotland the gardens of Leith are kept to a very high standard.

LITTLE SPARTA 50
Dunsyre, Nr Lanark, Lanarkshire, Strathclyde.
Tel: (089) 981252
Mr Ian Hamilton-Finlay

Turn off A721 at Newbigging for Dunsyre. 1m W of Dunsyre is an unmarked very rough farm track up to Little Sparta ● *Open by appointment in writing (SAE please)* ● *Best season: June* ● *Entrance: free* ● *Parking* ● *Guide dogs for the blind only* ● ***Grade I***

A clue as to what is hidden in Ian Hamilton-Finlay's totally unexpected garden is given on arrival at the gate to the property, where a beautifully-carved quotation from Heraclitus greets you. Hamilton-Finlay believes that a garden should appeal to all the senses and particularly should provoke thought, both serious and trivial, and he has therefore revived the art of emblematic gardening (which died out in Britain in the seventeenth century) and achieved an international reputation in the process. It is impossible to describe Little Sparta briefly, except to say that he has transformed a sizeable hill farmstead (starting in 1966 with the idea of establishing a testing-ground for his sculptures) into a garden full of images, allusions and symbols. Not all are easily understood or interpreted, which doesn't matter as this is a garden not a crossword puzzle. However, before visiting Littla Sparta it may help to read one of the many articles written about it – for example in the King and Rose book *Gardening with Style*.

LOCHALSH WOODLAND GARDEN 51
Balmacara, Highlands. Tel: (059986) 236
National Trust for Scotland

Just outside Kyle of Lochalsh, Plockton ● *Open all year, daily, in daylight hours* ● *Entrance: 80p, children 40p* ● *Parking* ● *Teas in Lochalsh House, Kyle of Lochalsh* ● *Toilet facilities* ● ***Grade II***

Although Lochalsh Woodland Garden is relatively new, started in 1979, it is being developed in established woodland at Lochalsh House. Many woodland plants and shrubs (rhododendrons, etc.) have been planted, but will take time to establish fully. Nonetheless, there are magnificent mature tree specimens and marvellous views of Lochalsh and some of Scotland's finest scenery. The garden is best in spring when the bulbs and rhododendrons provide a riot of colour. For a young garden there is much to learn by visiting.

LOGAN BOTANIC GARDEN
AND LOGAN HOUSE   52
Port Logan, by Stranraer, Dumfries & Galloway.
Tel: (077686) 231
Royal Botanic Gardens, Edinburgh/Sir Ninian Buchan-Hepburn, Bt

On B7065 ½m S of junction with A716 ● Open daily except Sat, April – Sept, 10.00 a.m. – 5.00 p.m. ● Best season: spring ● Entrance: 80p, concessions 40p ● Parking ● Teas ● Toilet facilities ● Suitable for wheelchairs ● Grade I

Logan is a fascinating sub-tropical garden situated on the southernmost tip of Scotland – the Rhinns of Galloway. The exceptionally mild climate allowed the creation of a formal garden in the Mediterranean style from the turn of the century. Now, under the care of The Royal Botanic Gardens Edinburgh, Logan is a rewarding collection of rare and unusual sub-tropical plants. Chusan palms (*Trachycarpus fortunei*), tree ferns (*Cyathea dealbata*), cabbage palms (*Cordyline australis*), and a large number of Australian and New Zealand plants are mixed with hardier temperate plants to give a unique air to this superb garden. Ancient magnolias and meconopsis (blue poppies of Tibet) make a magnificent spring show. Throughout the summer season there are endless banks of flowers appearing along meandering walks that lead to a formal pool filled with various water lilies – surrounded by tree ferns and vast cabbage palms. This garden is a must for the keen plantsman as many of Britain's finest specimens can be found here. The *Gunnera manicata*, by the entrance attains a leaf size greater than anywhere else in Britain. Logan is certainly one of Great Britain's finest and most unusual gardens. Logan House garden is open for one day for the SGS. The fine Queen Anne house has a garden with rare exotic tropical plants and shrubs.

MALLENY HOUSE GARDENS   53
Balerno, Midlothian, Lothian. Tel: (031449) 2283
National Trust for Scotland

In Balerno village, on A70 Edinburgh – Lanark road ● Open all year, 10.00 a.m. – dusk ● Best season: summer and autumn ● Entrance: £1.00, OAP 50p ● Parking ● Suitable for wheelchairs ● Grade III

Aptly described as the National Trust for Scotland's secret garden, Malleny seems an old and valued friend soon after meeting and reflects the thoughtful planning by the head gardener and his talented wife. An impressive Atlantic cedar reigns over this relatively small garden assisted by a square of early seventeenth-century clipped yews and yew hedges. As well as containing the N.C.C.P.G. collection of nineteenth-century shrub roses and a permanent display from the Scottish Bonsai Association, Malleny's 12ft herbaceous borders are superb as is the large glasshouse containing a continual display of flowering plants. Don't forget to admire the attractively laid-out herb and ornamental vegetable garden.

MANDERSTON 54
Duns, Borders. Tel: (0361) 83450
Mr Adrian Palmer

2m E of Duns on A6105 • *Open early May – Sept, Sun and Thurs, end May and Aug Bank Holiday Mons or parties by appointment* • *Best season: early Aug, woodland garden May and June* • *Entrance: £3.30 house and garden* • *Parking* • *Refreshments: tea room in grounds* • *Toilet facilities* • *Partly suitable for wheelchairs* • *Dogs on lead* • *Plants for sale* • *Shop* • *House open as for gardens* • *Grade II*

One of the last big classical houses to be built in Britain, Manderston was modelled on the famous Robert Adam house at Kedleston (see entry) owned by Lord Curzon to whom the owner here was related. Today Manderston has something for everyone. A formal terrace garden by the house overlooks a serpentine lake in a landscape created at the time of the original eighteenth-century house. On the far side is a woodland garden created in the mid-1950s renowned for its rhododendrons and azaleas. On the other side of the house, but set apart from it, is another formal garden with a pergola, roses and annuals. The greenhouse and nearby model dairy – finished in marble – are also well worth visiting.

MELLERSTAIN 55
Gordon, Etterick, Borders. Tel: (057381) 292
The Earl of Haddington

Halfway betwen Galashiels and Coldstream. Turn S in Gordon on A6089 and turn W after 2m or turn off B6397 2m N of Smailholm • *Open May – Sept, daily, except Sat, 12.30 – 5.00 p.m. and 15th July, 12.30 – 6.30 p.m.* • *Parking* • *Teas* • *Toilet facilities* • *Suitable for wheelchairs* • *House open, 12.30 – 5.00 p.m. (last admission 4.30 p.m.)* • *Grade I*

A bastion of formal garden layout with dignified terraces overlooking an 'arranged' landscape. The house of Mellerstain is a unique example of the work of the Adam family; both William and son, Robert, worked on the building. The garden is formal, comprised of very dignified terraces, ballustraded and 'lightly' planted with climbers and simple topiary. The great glory of the garden is the landscape complete with lake and woodlands in the style of Brown and Repton, but designed last century by Sir Reginald Blomfield. The view of the Cheviot Hills from the terraces is one of the finest to be found in this lovely area of the Scottish Borders. Mellerstain is a must for lovers of the formal landscape.

MERTOUN 56
St Boswells, Roxburghshire, Borders.   Tel: (0835) 23236
The Duke of Sutherland

*2m NE of St Boswells on B6404   ● Open April – Sept, Sat and Sun, 2.00 – 6.00
p.m.   ● Best season: spring and summer   ● Entrance: £1.00, OAP and children
50p   ● Parking   ● Toilet facilities   ● Suitable for wheelchairs   ● Grade III*

Overlooking the Tweed and with Mertoun House in the background this is a
lovely garden to wander round and admire the mature specimen trees, azaleas,
daffodils and a most attractive ornamental pond flanked by a good herbaceous
border. The focal point is the immaculate three-acre walled garden which is
everything a proper kitchen garden should be. Walking up from a 1567
dovecote, thought to be the oldest in the country, through a healthy orchard
the visitor reaches the traditional box hedges, raised beds and glasshouses of
the main area. Neat rows of vegetables, herbs and bright flowers for the house
vie for attention with the pruning of the figs and peaches in the well-stocked
glasshouses.

MONTEVIOT 57
Nr Jedburgh, Borders.   Tel: (08353) 380
Earl and Countess of Ancram

*Turn off A68 on B6400 to Nisbet. Entrance second turning on right   ● Open 1st
July, 2.00 – 5.00 p.m.   ● Best season: July and August   ● Entrance: £1.00,
OAP 50p, children under 14 free   ● Parking free   ● Refreshments in Woodland
centre, ½m from house   ● Toilet facilities   ● Partly suitable for wheelchairs
● Dogs on lead   ● Plants for sale   ● Grade III*

The river garden designed by Percy Cane in 1960s which runs down to the
River Teviot is currently being restored with herbaceous perennials and
shrubs. Beside it, the semi-enclosed terraced rose gardens overlooking the
river below have a large collection of hybrid teas, floribundas and shrubs.
Beside the house is an attractive formal herb garden. The pinetum is full of
unusual trees reaching great heights, and nearby a water garden has recently
been created, planted with unusual rhododendrons and azaleas. A circular
route around the gardens is also currently planned. Fine views.

NETHERBYRES 58
Eyemouth, Berwickshire, Borders.   Tel: (08907) 50337
Lieutenant-Colonel S.J. Furness

*¼m from Eyemouth on A1107   ● Closed temporarily   ● Best season: July, early
Aug   ● Entrance: 70p, children 30p   ● Parking by house   ● Suitable for
wheelchairs   ● Plants for sale on SGS days   ● Grade III*

The house built by William Craw in 1750 and developed by Sir Samuel Brown
in the nineteenth century has a very unusual eighteenth-century walled garden

of elliptical shape, possibly to reduce wind turbulence. It is orientated towards the south-east to capture the maximum sunshine. The gardens are largely formal, based around a central urn, with herbaceous and annual borders and roses. A Victorian greenhouse is soon to make way for a two-storey summer-house. The kitchen garden, divided from the formal area by a yew hedge, is also attracive in its own right.

PITMEDDEN GARDEN 59
Pittmedden, Gordon, Grampian. Tel: (06513) 2352
National Trust for Scotland

1m W of Pitmedden village on A920 and 1m N of Udny. 14m N of Aberdeen
● Grounds open all year, daily, 9.30 a.m. – sunset. Gardens open 28th April –
1st Oct, daily, 10.00 a.m. – 6.00 p.m. ● Entrance: 28th April – 1st Oct £1.70,
children 80p. Remainder of year £1.00, children 50p ● Parking
● Refreshments: picnic area ● Toilet facilities inc. disabled ● Suitable for
wheelchairs and wheelchairs supplied ● Dogs ● Museum of Farming Life open
● Grade I

Like Edzell Castle, the great garden of Pitmedden exhibits the taste of seventeenth-century garden makers and their love of patterns made to be viewed from above. The rectangular garden is enclosed by high terraces on three sides and by a wall on the fourth. Very ornamental patterns are cut in box on a grand scale, infilled with rather garish annuals. The overall impact is striking when viewed from either of two period stone gazebos with ogee roofs or when walking along the terraces. Simple topiary and box hedging are abundant. There is a rather curious contemporary fountain made from fragments preserved at Pitmedden and others from the Cross Fountain at Linlithgow. There is a small herb garden near the tea room. Fine borders of herbaceous plants outline the parterre garden on the south and west. When the National Trust for Scotland received Pitmedden in 1952 all that survived was the masonry. Since nothing remained of the original plans, contemporary plans for Holyroodhouse Palace gardens were used in recreating what is seen today. A garden well worth visiting any time of the year.

POLLOK HOUSE 60
Glasgow, Strathclyde. Tel: (041) 6320274
City of Glasgow District Council

3½m from city centre, well signposted. A736 in Pollakshaws ● Open all year,
weekdays, 10.00 a.m. – 5.00 p.m., Sun, 2.00 – 5.00 p.m. Closed 25th Dec and
1st Jan ● Entrance: free ● Parking ● Teas (reservations (041) 6497547
● Toilet facilities ● Suitable for wheelchairs ● House open and gallery
● Grade II

Everyone should visit the Burrell Collection, Scotland's gem, and Pollok House and gardens are thrown in free. A visit to Pollok House offers a full day's entertainment. The house itself, an Adam design, features a lovely formal terrace of box parterres, beautifully planted and maintained by Glasgow Parks. There are lovely borders near the water and a nineteenth-century woodland garden on the ridge nearby. Stone gazebos with ogee roofs. The grounds are famous for their bluebells in spring. Pollok House holds the famous Stirling Maxwell collection of European decorative arts.

In the grounds is the 1985 Museum of the Year, the Burrell Collection, one of the world's finest private collections of the decorative arts. The building was designed to encompass the surrounding woodland. The parkland around is beautifully planted and maintained.

ROYAL BOTANIC GARDEN 61
Edinburgh, Lothian. Tel: (031) 5527171
Department of Agriculture and Fisheries for Scotland

1½m N of city centre in Leith Walk above Cannongate ● *Open all year, Mon – Sat, 9.00 a.m. – sunset, Sun, 11.00 a.m. – sunset (1 hour before sunset during BST)* ● *Entrance: free* ● *Parking* ● *Toilet facilities* ● *Suitable for wheelchairs* ● *Exhibition hall and Inverleigh Visitor Centre open* ● ***Grade I***

Set on a hillside with magnificent panoramic views of the city, the Royal Botanic Garden of Edinburgh is one of the finest botanic gardens of the world; arguably the finest garden, physically, of its type in Britain. The 75 acres of gardens are filled with hundreds of thousands of plants, trees and shrubs from all over the world with a particular emphasis on Himalayan and Chinese species. The rhododendron collection is vast, the rock garden is easily the finest in the world. The conservatories hold enormous collections of tropical, sub-tropical and xerophytic plants. The home demonstration gardens are very well done. The perennial border is one of the largest in the UK, approaching 600 feet. The many paths meander through numerous areas of specific interest, all beautifully planted and maintained to the very highest degree. The overall standard of horticulture is superb. The specimen trees are amongst the finest in Britain – the birch collection is unexcelled. This is a garden that is forever being improved and replanted.

THREAVE SCHOOL OF GARDENING 62
Stewartry, Castle Douglas, Dumfries & Galloway. Tel: (0556) 2575
National Trust for Scotland

1m W of Castle Douglas off A75 ● *Open all year, daily, 9.00 a.m. – sunset.*
● *Entrance: £2.00, children £1.00, parties £1.60, schools 80p* ● *Parking*
● *Refreshments: restaurant 24th March – Oct, daily, 10.00 a.m. – 5.00 p.m.*
● *Toilet facilities* ● *Suitable for wheelchairs* ● *Shop* ● *Visitor centre.*
Exhibition 24th March – Oct, daily, 9.00 a.m. – 6.00 p.m. ● ***Grade II***

Nearly 1500 acres of policies (estates), woodland and gardens used as a school since 1960 and catering for young aspiring gardeners. Numerous perennials, annuals, trees and shrubs are used in innovative ways and maintained to a high standard by the resident students of gardening. For the visitor the main interest is a modern design relying heavily on island beds, which can be compared and contrasted with other layouts. Threave is famous for its collection of daffodils and is lovely in the spring when these are complemented by the rhododendrons and flowering trees and shrubs. It is an instructive and useful garden to visit rather than a garden of great design or beauty.

TOROSAY CASTLE AND GARDENS 63
Craignure, Isle of Mull, Argyll, Strathclyde. Tel: (06802) 421
Mr Christopher James

1½m from Craignure. Steamer 6 times daily from Oban to Craignure. Motor boat during high season. Miniature steam railway from Craignure ferry. Lochaline to Finnish, then 7m S on A849. ● *Open all year, daily, sunrise – sunset* ● *Best season: May* ● *Entrance: £1.00, OAP, students, children 50p* ● *Teas* ● *Toilet facilities* ● *Partly suitable for wheelchairs* ● *Dogs on lead* ● *Shop* ● *Castle open, mid-April – mid-Oct, 10.30 a.m. – 5.30 p.m. Admission extra* ● ***Grade II***

House in baronial castle style by Bryce (1858). Main garden formal Italian based on a series of descending terraces with unusual statue walk. Vaguely reminiscent of Powis Castle (see entry) this is a dramatic contrast with the rugged island scenery. The peripheral gardens are also a contrast – an informal water garden and Japanese garden looking out over Duart Bay; also a small rock garden. Rhododendrons and azaleas are a feature but less important than in other west-coast gardens. Collection of Australian and New Zealand trees and shrubs.

TYNINGHAME HOUSE 64
Tyninghame, Nr East Linton, Lothian. Tel: (0620) 860559
Mr Kit Martin

25m E of Edinburgh between Haddington and Dunbar. N of A1, 2m E of A198 ● *Garden may not open in 1990* ● *Entrance: SGS* ● *Parking* ● *Suitable for wheelchairs* ● ***Grade II***

Tyninghame is renowned for the gardens created by the Dowager Lady Haddington from 1947 onwards, which have been described as of 'ravishing beauty'. They consist of a formal rose garden, terraces, a secret garden, an Italian garden and an area of woodland. When her husband died in 1986, her son reluctantly sold the house, but those who worried about the garden's future needed not to fear, as the conversion and addition of two houses was handled by Kit Martin with great sensitivity. Tyninghame is close to the sea, with fine views, and those who are able to visit it on the open days will have a rare opportunity of seeing how the unique character of the garden has been maintained, perhaps enhanced, by the architectural changes around it.

YOUNGER BOTANIC GARDEN 65
Benmore, Strathclyde. Tel: (0369) 6261
Royal Botanic Gardens Edinburgh

Dunoon, Strathclyde. 1m from junction of A885 and A815 ● *Open daily,*
April – Oct, 10.00 a.m. – 6.00 p.m. ● *Best season: May to June* ● *Entrance:*
30p, OAP and children 15p ● *Parking: 10p* ● *Teas at main entrance* ● *Toilet*
facilities ● *Suitable for wheelchairs* ● ***Grade I***

Benmore's 100 acres of woodland gardens have been under development since
1820. The gardens are approached along Britain's finest Wellingtonia
(*Sequoiadendron giganteum*) avenue. The tallest is more than 150 feet.
Numerous other fine specimen conifers are to be found throughout the
gardens. There are exceptionally fine monkey puzzles (*Araucaria araucana*)
that retain their lower branches. But Benmore is most famous for its extensive
rhododendron and magnolia collections on the hillside beside the River
Eachaig in one of Britain's most breath-taking natural settings; the Highlands
at their best. A myriad of paths take the visitor along the mountainside
through vast plantations of rare shrubs and trees. Marvellous vistas open from
time to time. The only obviously man-made feature is a great rectangular lawn
enclosed on three sides by walls but open to the mountains on the fourth. This
garden is bisected by borders filled with a collection of dwarf conifers. A
handsome pavilion overlooks it all. There are other informal beds filled with
Australian and New Zealand shrubs and herbaceous plants; a large collection
of heathers. Benmore is well worth a visit both for its natural beauty and its
vast specimen plant collections. Be prepared for a full day's outing, a great deal
of walking, and rain.

TELEPHONE NUMBERS
Except where specifically requested to be excluded, telephone numbers
to which enquiries may be directed are given for each property. To
maintain the support and cooperation of private owners it is suggested
that the telephone be used with discretion. Where visits are by
appointment, the telephone can of course be used except where written
application, particularly for parties, is specifically requested. Code
numbers are given in brackets. For the Republic of Ireland when
phoning from the United Kingdom dial 353 plus area code plus
number (except Dublin numbers which are 0001 plus number). In all
cases where visits by parties are proposed, owners should be advised in
advance and arrangements preferably confirmed in writing.
London Telephone Codes: From May 1990 all London telephone
numbers with the prefix 01 will be changed. The new prefix will be
either 071 or 081. Details of these new numbers are available from
British Telecom. During the changeover period in 1990 all London
telephone numbers dialled with their 01 prefix will be redirected.

WALES

Holyhead

Colwyn
Bay

Bangor ㉑ ㉒⑳

Rhyl ⑭

②

Caernarfon

Betws-y-Coed

Wrexham ⑬

⑯

Llangollen

⑳㉔ ④

⑦

㉓

⑪

⑥

Dolgellau

⑮ ⑰

③

Welshpool

㉖

㉒

Newtown

Aberystwyth

⑤

Aberaeron

㉗

⑱

Lampeter

Cardigan ⑲

①

Fishguard

㉕

Brecon

⑩

⑨

Monmouth

Llanelli

Swansea

Merthyr Tydfil

⑧

Newport

Cardiff

⑫

BLAENGWRFACH ISAF 1
Bancyffordd, Dyfed. Tel: (055932) 2604
Mrs Gail Farmer

2m W of Llandyssul on Newcastle Emlyn road. First left by Halfmoon pub, 1½m until farm track on right ● *Open April – Jun, Sept and Oct, 10.30 a.m. – 5.30 p.m. or by appointment* ● *Best season: spring* ● *Entrance: 75p, children free* ● *Parking very limited* ● *Teas 1m away in village* ● *Plants for sale* ● *Shop, adjacent craft workshops* ● **Grade III**

Open to the public for the first time in 1990 and created over the last 15 years from a green field site, this is essentially a cottage garden, but recent plantings of trees and shrubs to attract wildlife and plants suitable for pressed flowers give great diversity. Good autumn colour.

BODNANT GARDEN 2
Tal-y-Cafn, Colwyn Bay, Gwynedd. Tel: (0492) 650460
The National Trust

7m S of Llandudno, just off A470 ● *Open 17th March – Oct, daily, 10.00 a.m. – 5.00 p.m. Last admission 4.30 p.m.* ● *Best season: May and June* ● *Entrance: £2.20, pre-booked parties of 20 or more £1.80 per person* ● *Official car park 50 yards from garden nursery* ● *Teas and light refreshments, picnic area in car park* ● *Toilet facilities* ● *Partly suitable for wheelchairs* ● *Plants for sale* ● **Grade I**

Bodnant is one of the finest gardens in the country not only for the magnificent collections of rhododendrons, camellias and magnolias but also for its beautiful setting above the River Conway and the magnificent views of the Snowdonia range. The gardens which extend to 80 acres have several interesting features, the most well known being the laburnum arch which is an overwhelming mass of bloom in early June. Others include the dell garden and a lily pool. The whole effect has been created by successive generations of the Aberconway family (who bought Bodnant in 1874), aided by the garden staff, including three generations of Puddles.

BRYNHYFRYD 3
Corris, Machynlleth, Gwynedd. Tel: (065473) 278
Mrs David Paish

6m N of Machynlleth off A487 ● *Open all year round by appointment only* ● *Entrance: collecting box* ● *Parking* ● *Toilet facilities* ● **Grade II**

This four-acre mountainside garden has been the subject of TV's *Gardeners' World* and justifiably so. Containing an enormous diversity of plant material, it is extremely steep, which makes for an interesting visit, especially during the latter half of May when the species rhododendrons and primulas are flowering. Good specimens of arbutus, halesias, hoherias and magnolias.

BRYNMELYN   4
Cymerau Isaf, Blaenau Ffestiniog, Gwynedd.   Tel: (076676) 2684
Mr and Mrs A.S. Taylor

*2m SW of Blaenau Ffestiniog on A496 ● Open all year round by appointment
● Best season: spring to autumn ● Entrance: collecting box ● Parking in lay-by
opposite junction to Manod (¼m to garden) ● Toilet facilities ● Grade III*

An interesting garden, not only for its range of plant material, but also for its
wild mountainside-setting. Divided into smaller gardens each with its own
theme and character, it lends itself well to the overall informal style and its
nature reserve and woodland setting.

CARROG   5
Llanddeiniol, Llanon, Nr Aberystwyth, Dyfed.   Tel: (09748) 369
Mr and Mrs Geoffrey Williams

*6m S of Aberystwyth on private road off A487 ● Open by appointment ● Best
season: summer ● Entrance: 75p ● Parking ● Toilet facilities ● Suitable for
wheelchairs ● Dogs on lead ● Grade II*

From the flowers of varied spring bulbs to the autumn colours of rare maples
and birches, this garden is alive with interest for the plant lover. Grass paths
wend amongst collections of sorbus, eucalyptus and sweetly scented old-
fashioned roses, with rhododendrons flowering well into summer. The walled
garden is home for many treasures such as fremontodendron, rare lilac species
and *Abutilon megapotamicum*.

CEFN BERE   6
Cae Deintur, Dolgellau, Gwynedd.   Tel: (0341) 422768
Mr and Mrs Maldwyn Thomas

*N of Bala – Barmouth road (not by-pass) near Dolgellau, turn at top of the
main bridge, turn right within 200 yards, then 2nd right behind school and up
hill ● Open spring and summer months by appointment only ● Entrance:
collecting box ● Parking at roadside ● Refreshments in Dolgellau ● Toilet
facilities ● Grade III*

This relatively small garden has a very diverse plant collection amassed over
the last 35 years. Planted informally but within a formal framework, it is a
delight to both amateur and professional gardeners alike. The alpine house,
bulb and peat frames are well worth seeing; so too are the old-fashioned roses.

CHIRK CASTLE 7
Chirk, Clwyd. Tel: (0691) 777701
The National Trust

½m W of Chirk village off A5, up private drive of 1½m ● Open April – Sept, daily except Mon and Sat, 12 noon - 6.00 p.m., Oct, Sat and Sun only, 12 noon - 6.00 p.m. Open Bank Holiday Mons ● Best season: spring ● Entrance: £2.50 (Castle and garden) ● Parking 200 yards from garden ● Refreshments: light lunches and teas, picnic area in car park ● Toilet facilities ● Partly suitable for wheelchairs ● Shop ● House open: Good Friday, end March – Sept, daily except Mon and Sat, 12 noon – 5.00 p.m. Open Bank Holiday Mons ● Grade II

A six-acre garden of trees and flowering shrubs including rhododendrons and azaleas. There are interesting formal gardens with some excellent nineteenth-century topiary in yew. Also a rockery garden, herbaceous borders, a ha-ha and a folly. The castle dates from 1300 but is set in an eighteenth-century landscaped park.

CLYNE GARDENS 8
Black Pill, Swansea, West Glamorgan. Tel: (0792) 401737
Swansea City Council

From Swansea take Mumbles road, turn right at Woodman Roast Inn ● Open all year ● Best season: spring ● Entrance: free ● Parking ● Refreshments at Woodman Roast Inn ● Toilet facilities ● Suitable for wheelchairs ● Dogs on lead ● Grade II

A large (50 acres) well-kept garden to interest everyone from the beginner to the more knowledgeable. There is a stream running through the bog area, fed by a lake via a waterfall and spanned by a Japanese bridge. A tower, built by Admiral Algernon Vivian, the last private owner of the garden, from which to view his rhododendrons, is now dwarfed by them.

COLBY ESTATE 9
Colby Lodge, Amroth, Narberth, Dyfed. Tel: (0558) 822800
The National Trust

Adjoining Amroth beside Carmarthen Bay ● Open 31st March – 3rd Nov, daily, 10.00 a.m. – 5.00 p.m. and in winter during daylight hours ● Best season: April and May ● Entrance: £1.00, children 50p ● Parking 50 yards from garden. Disabled may park closer ● Toilet facilities ● Partly suitable for wheelchairs ● Grade III

This early nineteenth-century estate garden round a Nash-style house is now mainly woodland with some formal gardens. The walled garden is planted informally for ornamental effect. The woodland garden is planted extensively with rhododendrons and contains some interesting tree species.

THE DINGLE 10
Crundale, Haverfordwest, Dyfed.   Tel: (0437) 764370
Mrs A.J. Jones

3m NW of Haverfordwest • *Open daily except Tues, mid-March – Oct, 10.00 a.m. – 6.00 p.m.* • *Best season: spring – autumn* • *Entrance: 70p, children 35p* • *Parking* • *Teas* • *Toilet facilities* • *Suitable for wheelchairs* • *Plants for sale, small nursery* • *Shop* • **Grade III**

A plantsman's secluded garden where foliage and plant structure play an important part in the layout and design. There is a collection of many rare and unusual plants, including over 150 different old-fashioned and species roses. Formal beds, scree beds, herbaceous borders, water garden and woodland walks all blend within an informal framework.

DOLWEN 11
Cefn Coch, Llanrhaedr-ym-Mochnant, Powys.   Tel: (069189) 411
Mrs Frances Denby

On B4580 Oswestry – Llanrhaedr road. Turn right in village at Three Tuns Inn • *Open May – Sept, Fri and last Sun in May – Aug, 2.00 – 4.30 p.m.* • *Entrance: 50p* • *Parking* • *Refreshments* • *Toilet facilities* • *Plants for sale* • *Shop* • **Grade II**

A woodland and water garden situated high in the hills with very good views. The owner has used the land to good advantage. The whole area is very rocky and large boulders have been used imaginatively to create pools and support bridges across a stream. There is an interesting collection of waterside plants.

DYFFRYN BOTANIC GARDEN 12
St Nicholas, Cardiff, South Glamorgan.   Tel: (0222) 593328

4m W of Cardiff on A4232 turn S on A4050 and then W to Dyffryn • *Open March – Oct, daily, 9.00 a.m. – dusk* • *Entrance: free* • *Parking* • *Refreshments and picnics* • *Toilet facilities* • *Suitable for wheelchairs* • *Dogs on lead* • *Plants for sale* • *Shop* • *House now a conference centre run by Mid Glamorgan and South Glamorgan County Councils. Open air theatre in garden* • **Grade II**

Dyffryn has been described as The Garden of Wales and one of Wales' best-kept secrets. An Edwardian garden, created out of a Victorian original between 1906 and 1914, it was designed by Thomas Mawson, a leading landscape architect rather overshadowed by his contemporary Lutyens. When the owner died, the garden (and Mawson's services) were retained by his son, Reginald Cory, a distinguished horticulturalist whose special interest was Eastern plants such as those brought here by E.H. Wilson. To the south of the fine house is a large open lawn with ornamental lily pond and, to the west, a series of 'rooms' each enclosed by yew. These are the Roman garden, the paved court, the swimming pool garden and the round garden. Beyond these is the west garden with large beds and borders and fine trees and shrubs. There is also a Japanese garden and a begonia garden. There is a vine walk, particularly splendid in its autumn colours, which is also the time to visit the arboretum which contains some of the finest *Acer griseum* (paperback maple) in the country. Also a large greenhouse and a cacti collection in the special house in the rose garden.

ERDDIG 13
Wrexham, Clwyd.   Tel: (0978) 355314
The National Trust

2m S of Wrexham off A525   ● Open April – June, Sept – 14th Oct, daily except Thurs and Fri (but open Good Friday), 11.00 a.m. – 6.00 p.m., July and August, daily except Fri, 11.00 a.m. – 6.00 p.m.   ● Best season: spring ● Entrance: £1.50 (house and garden £3.50)   ● Parking 200 yards from garden   ● Refreshments: light teas and lunches, picnic area in car park   ● Toilet facilities inc. disabled   ● Suitable for wheelchairs (wheelchairs provided but house difficult)   ● Dogs on lead in grounds   ● Plants for sale   ● Joiners shop manufacturing quality garden furniture   ● House open. Also Visitor Centre, open days with farming demonstration. For details telephone (0978) 264470 ● Grade II

Erddig's gardens, a rare example of early eighteenth-century formal design, were almost lost along with the house. They have been carefully restored. The large walled garden contains varieties of fruit trees known to have been grown there during that period and there is a canal garden and fish pool. South of the canal walk is a Victorian flower garden. Later Victorian additions include the parterre and walk. The garden contains the national ivy collection and also a narcissus collection. Parties may have conducted tours with the head gardener each afternoon.

GLANABER 14
Llanasa, Prestatyn, Clwyd.   Tel: (07456) 4977
Mrs J.M.P. Spiller

3m SE of Prestatyn   ● Open daily, 10.30 a.m. – 5.30 p.m. and 29th, 30th June, 1st, 2nd July for NGS   ● Best season: spring, summer, autumn   ● Entrance: collecting box   ● Parking   ● Refreshments: morning coffee, farmhouse lunch, cream teas (restaurant open Easter – Sept)   ● Toilet facilities   ● Suitable for wheelchairs   ● Plants for sale   ● Craft shop   ● Grade III

A peaceful and tranquil garden set in a Welsh conservation village. Created by the present owner over the last 12 years with underlying cottage-garden theme. Interesting water gardens with duck pond and fish/lily pond. Display of old tools and machinery, a garden shop, a craft shop and a restaurant make this more than just another garden to visit.

GLEBE HOUSE   15
Guilsford, Welshpool, Powys.   Tel: (0938) 553602
Mrs Jenkins and Mrs Habberley

3m N of Welshpool off A490 (Llanfyllin)   ● Open by appointment and 15th April, 29th July, 2.00 - 6.00 p.m.   ● Entrance: 70p, children 10p   ● Parking ● Refreshments   ● Toilet facilities   ● Suitable for wheelchairs   ● Plants for sale ● Grade II

This is a real cottage garden. A series of small gardens lead off from each other, with a mixture of shrubs, herbaceous plants, roses, herbs and fruit. Backing everything and climbing up the walls and trees is a large collection of clematis, said to total 130 varieties.

HAFOD GARREGOG   16
Nantmor, Penrhyndeudraeth, Gwynedd.   Tel: (076686) 282
Mr and Mrs Hugh Mason

5m N of Penrhyndeudraeth   ● Open April - Sept by appointment and on 13th May, 23rd, 24th June, 10.30 a.m. - 5.30 p.m.   ● Entrance: collecting box ● Parking   ● Teas on NGS days only   ● Toilet facilities   ● Partly suitable for wheelchairs   ● Dogs on lead   ● Plants for sale on NGS days   ● Grade III

A small garden created by the owners since 1971 in a woodland setting with fine mountain views above the River Hafod. The garden is essentially rhododendrons and azaleas, with a lot of other colour especially foliage colour provided by shrubs. There is a vegetable garden and water garden.

THE HILL COTTAGE   17
Bausley, Crew Green, Powys.   Tel: (0743) 884320
Mr and Mrs A.T. Bareham

8m NE of Welshpool via A458 Shrewsbury   ● Open for NGS, dates N.A. and by appointment only   ● Entrance: donations in collecting box   ● Parking   ● Toilet facilities   ● Plants for sale   ● Grade II

This is a very steep garden. There are areas of lawn surrounding shrub and conifer beds. A sheltered terrace overlooks the garden. It has numerous containers planted with alpines. There is also an area of rock garden and scree beds with an interesting range of plants.

PANT-YR-HOLIAD   18
Rhydlewis, Llandysul, Dyfed.   Tel: (023975) 493
Mr and Mrs G. Taylor

From Cardigan take coast road to Brynhoffnant. Take B4334 towards Rhydlewis for 1m, turn left and garden 2nd left   ● Open Easter - Sept, Wed, Fri and Sun, 2.00 - 5.00 p.m.   ● Best season: spring   ● Entrance: £1.00, children 50p

● *Parking* ● *Teas by appointment* ● *Toilet facilities* ● *Partly suitable for wheelchairs* ● *Plants for sale* ● **Grade II**

This five-acre woodland garden was created by the owners in part of a farmstead. It has many unusual trees and shrubs, rhododendrons and azaleas. There is a bog garden and pool with rare breed ducks. In the more open areas of the garden are terraced beds containing alpines and a herb garden. A recently constructed summer walk where herbaceous plants predominate should be a very pleasant area when more mature.

PENRALLT FFYNNON 19
Cwm-Cou, Newcastle Emlyn, Dyfed. Tel: (0239) 710654
Mr R.D. Lord

3m NW of Newcastle Emlyn, 10m E of Cardigan ● *Open by appointment all year round* ● *Entrance: collecting box* ● *Limited parking* ● *Suitable for wheelchairs* ● **Grade III**

Created over the last 18 years for all-year-round interest, this is still a young garden in many respects with certain trees and shrubs needing time to mature. It is an informal garden with a great diversity of plants and many different species of prunus, sorbus, acer, malus, salix and rhododendron.

PENRHYN CASTLE 20
Bangor, Gwynedd. Tel: (0248) 353084
The National Trust

3m E of Bangor on A5122 ● *Open April – 4th Nov, daily, except Tues, 11.00 a.m. – 6.00 p.m.* ● *Best season: spring and summer* ● *Entrance: £1.10, children 60p. Castle and garden: £2.80* ● *Parking* ● *Refreshments: light lunches and teas, picnic in grounds* ● *Toilet facilities inc. disabled* ● *Suitable for wheelchairs, golf buggy available for garden and park* ● *Dogs on lead in grounds only* ● *Shop* ● *Castle and museum open as for gardens, 12 noon – 5.00 p.m.* ● **Grade II**

Large garden covering 40 acres with some fine specimen trees, shrubs and a Victorian walled garden in terraces with pools, lawns and a wild garden. Although the site of the house dates from the eighteenth century, the gardens are very much early Victorian, dating from the building of the present castle by Thomas Hopper.

PLAS NEWYDD 21
Llanfairpwll, Anglesey, Gwynedd. Tel: (0248) 714795
The National Trust/The Marquess of Anglesey

1m SW of Llanfairpwll ● *Open April – Sept, daily except Sat, 12 noon – 5.00 p.m., 5th Oct – 4th Nov, Fri and Sun only, 12 noon – 5.00 p.m. In July and*

Aug gardens open at 11.00 a.m. Last admission 4.30 p.m. • *Best season: spring* • *Entrance: £1.10 (house and garden £2.40)* • *Parking ¼m from house and garden* • *Refreshments: light lunches and teas* • *Toilet facilities inc. disabled* • *Suitable for wheelchairs* • *Shop* • *House open inc. military museum* • **Grade III**

An eighteenth-century house by James Wyatt, also an attraction because it contains Rex Whistler's largest wall painting. An informal open-plan garden with shrub plantings in the lawns and parkland. There is a formal Italian-style rose garden to the front of the house. A special rhododendron garden is open in the spring when the gardens are at their best.

PLAS PENHELIG 22
Aberdovey, Gwynedd. Tel: (065472) 676
Mr and Mrs A.C. Richardson

At Aberdovey, between the two railway bridges • *Open mid-June – mid-Oct, Wed – Sun, 2.30 – 5.30 p.m.* • *Best season: spring* • *Entrance: collecting box* • *Parking* • *Teas* • *Toilet facilities* • *Suitable for wheelchairs* • *Plants for sale* • **Grade II**

A traditional Edwardian estate garden of seven acres reclaimed over the past 10 years. An informal garden with lawns, terraces, pools, fountains, orchard, rock garden and herbaceous borders. Spring bulbs, azaleas, rhododendrons, magnolias, euphorbias, roses and some mature tree heathers of immense size. The jewel is the half-acre walled kitchen garden, including 900 square feet of glass with vines and peaches.

PLAS-YN-RHIW 23
Pwllheli, Gwynedd. Tel: (0758) 88219
The National Trust

12m from Pwllheli on S coast road to Aberdaron • *Open April – Sept, daily except Sat, 12 noon – 5.00 p.m., 7th Oct – 4th Nov, Sun only, 12 noon – 4.00 p.m. Last admission ¼ hour before closing* • *Best season: spring* • *Entrance: £1.10. House and garden: £2.20, family ticket £5.50, parties of 20 or more £1.80 per person* • *Parking 80 yards from house and garden. No coaches* • *Toilet facilities inc. disabled* • *Shop* • *House open* • **Grade III**

Essentially a cottage garden around a partly medieval manor house, on west shore of Hell's Mouth Bay. Flowering trees and shrubs, rhododendrons, camellias and magnolias, divided by formal box hedges and grass paths extending to three quarters of an acre. The Trust has recently extended Plas-yn-Rhiw to include 150 acres of woodland, purchased from the Forestry Commission. Snowdrop wood on high ground above garden.

PORTMEIRION 24
Penrhyndeudraeth, Gwynedd.

2m SE of Porthmadog near A487 ● *Open throughout the year* ● *Parking and refreshments at hotel (which may be closed during winter) (0766) 770228* ● *Many areas suitable for wheelchairs* ● *Dogs on lead* ● **Grade II**

Architect Clough Williams-Ellis' wild essay into the picturesque is a triumph of eclecticism with Gothic, Renaissance and Victorian styled buildings arranged as a village around a harbour set in 85 acres of spendidly gardened woodland. It provides one of Britain's most stimulating objects for an excursion and during the period of the June festival in nearby Criccieth there are nine other good gardens open in the district. Write to Criccieth Festival Office, PO Box 3, Criccieth, Gwynedd LL52 0BW for details.

POST HOUSE GARDENS 25
Cwmbach, Whitland, Dyfed.   Tel: (09948) 213
Mrs Jo Kenaghan

From Carmarthen W on A40, take B4298 through Meidrim. Leave by centre lane signposted Llanboidy, turn right at crossroads signposted Blaenwaun then right at next crossroads to Cwmbach ● *Open all year during daylight hours* ● *Best season: spring and early summer* ● *Entrance: 50p, children free* ● *Parking in official car park* ● *Refreshments by appointment* ● *Toilet facilities* ● *Partly suitable for wheelchairs* ● *Plants for sale* ● **Grade II**

Four to five acres of woodland valley garden, begun in 1978, wind along the bank of the River Sien. Many rare and unusual trees and shrubs, including 150 species and hybrid rhododendrons, carpeted with snowdrops, anemones, bluebells and wild orchids in the spring. There is a bog garden and a large pool stocked with carp and orfe. Old roses climb into many of the trees in early summer. A glasshouse, built on what was once a water mill, houses the more tender plants and a conservatory contains plants from many parts of the world.

POWIS CASTLE 26
Welshpool, Powys.   Tel: (0938) 4336
The National Trust

¾m from Welshpool on A483, well signposted ● *Open April – June, and Sept – 4th Nov, daily except Mon and Tues. In July and Aug, daily except Mon but open Bank Holiday Mon, 11.00 a.m. – 6.00 p.m. 11th Nov – 24th March 1991, Suns only, 2.00 – 4.30 p.m. Last admission ½ hour before closing* ● *Entrance: £2.50 (Castle and garden £3.00)* ● *Parking* ● *Refreshments: Teas and light lunches* ● *Toilet facilities* ● *Partly suitable for wheelchairs* ● *Plants for sale* ● *Shop* ● *Castle open at extra charge* ● **Grade I**

This is a garden originally laid out in 1720 based on even earlier designs. Its most notable features are broad hanging terraces interestingly planted with huge clipped yews. On the second terrace, brick alcoves opposite fine lead urns and figures above the orangery below. Some fruit trees remain on the terraces where in the nineteenth century advantage was taken of the micro-climate to grow fruit and vegetables until a kitchen garden was established. The latter is now a flower garden. Unusual and tender plants and climbers prosper in the shelter of walls and hedges. This garden is not for the faint-hearted because it is very steep, but it's well worth the effort to relish the views which are as fine as any, anywhere. A good collection of old roses. Excellent guide book available with lists of plants.

WINLLAN 27
Talsarn, Lampeter, Dyfed.   Tel: (0570) 470612
Mr and Mrs Ian Callan

8m NNW of Lampeter on B4342 ● *Open by appointment May – Sept and 17th June, 2.00 – 5.30 p.m.* ● *Best season: spring and summer* ● *Entrance: £1.00, children 50p, under 12 free* ● *Parking* ● *Teas* ● *Toilet facilities* ● *Partly suitable for wheelchairs* ● *Dogs on lead (but not on NGS day)* ● *Plants for sale on open day* ● *Shop* ● **Grade IV**

Essentially a wildlife garden but includes a good conventional garden, with fruit and vegetables, terrace beds and shrub borders, containing many fine species roses. The wildlife garden has many different features, perhaps the most important being the old hay meadow, the wood and the pond. It is worth mentioning that all of these areas have a very good display of wild flowers – eye-bright burnet, spotted orchid and corncockle to name but a few.

TELEPHONE NUMBERS
Except where specifically requested to be excluded, telephone numbers to which enquiries may be directed are given for each property. To maintain the support and cooperation of private owners it is suggested that the telephone be used with discretion. Where visits are by appointment, the telephone can of course be used except where written application, particularly for parties, is specifically requested. Code numbers are given in brackets. For the Republic of Ireland when phoning from the United Kingdom dial 353 plus area code plus number (except Dublin numbers which are 0001 plus number). In all cases where visits by parties are proposed, owners should be advised in advance and arrangements preferably confirmed in writing.

London Telephone Codes: From May 1990 all London telephone numbers with the prefix 01 will be changed. The new prefix will be either 071 or 081. Details of these new numbers are available from British Telecom. During the changeover period in 1990 all London telephone numbers dialled with their 01 prefix will be redirected.

Acknowledgements

Our thanks to everyone who has helped with the preparation of the *Guide* – to owners, custodians, professional gardening staff, and many others. In particular, we thank our inspectors and those who advised them. Some of those who have given advice do not wish to be listed, and, although anonymous they have been every bit as valuable. We are also obliged to National Garden Scheme participants, to staff of the National Trust and Scottish Garden Scheme organisers for their cooperation. The names which follow include inspectors (but not all of them) and advisors: Rachel Anderson, Rosie Atkins, Lady Bacon, Mrs David Barnes, Anne Bates, Kenneth and Gillian Beckett, Susan Berry, Jill Billington, Kathryn Bradley-Hole, Lady Cave, Anne Chamberlain, Anne Collins, Beatrice Cowan, Simon Cramp, Jo and Rosie Currie, Rose Davey, Daphne Dormer, Bill Drower, Julie Edmonstone, Matthew Fattorini, Diana Fernsby, Michael and Freda Fisher, Adrian and Audrey Gale, Camilla Harford, Ronald Higgins, Steve Hipkin, Pam Hoare, Tessa Hobbs, David Howard, Sandy Hunt, Jill Husselby, Freda James, Rosemarie Johnson, Vanessa Johnstone, Mary Keen, Jo Kenaghan, John Last, Jean Laughton, Malcolm Lyell, Charles Lyte, Janet Macnutt, Pat McCrostie, Deirdre McSharry, Lucinda Parry, John and Carol Pease, Stephen Player, Lorna Ramsay, Edwina Robarts, Lady Smith-Ryland, Mr and Mrs Gerald Sterck, Vera Taggart, Sally Tamplin, Mr and Mrs G. Taylor, Bill Tobias, Caroline Todhunter, James Truscott, Sally Walker, Christopher Whitmey, Cynthia Wickham. The editors also express their appreciation of the dedicated assistance of Lizzie Boyd, Angie Hipkin, Hilary Hodgson and Wendy Turner.

The authors and publisher are grateful for permission to reproduce extracts from *Four Quartets* by T.S. Eliot, published by Faber & Faber Ltd.

Your Comments

The next edition of the *Guide* will be improved if readers will write to tell us
(i) if gardens are not included which you think should be
(ii) if you visit a garden in the guide and want to confirm its merits or propose an up-grading
(iii) if you visit a garden and believe its merits are overestimated by our inspector.

Report forms on the following pages can be used for this purpose, or you may just send your comments on a sheet of paper. Handwriting is not always distinct, so if possible please print difficult words and Latin names for plants. Also please print your name clearly. All those who write will help to improve the standards of garden visiting by making good gardens open to the public known to a wider circle. The great thing is to enjoy your garden visiting, just as our inspectors have done. Happy visting in 1990.

Send your comments to The Good Gardens Guide, Barrie & Jenkins Ltd, 20 Vauxhall Bridge Road, London SW1V 2SA.

Report Form

To the Editors of The Good Gardens Guide, Barrie & Jenkins Ltd,
20 Vauxhall Bridge Road, London SW1V 2SA.

GARDEN

Name:

Address:

Tel:

Name of owner(s):

DETAILS

Location:

Opening times:

Best season:

Entrance charge:

Plants for sale:

House open/times:

DESCRIPTION

Type of garden:

Features/condition:

Please continue overleaf

Brief details of its main characteristics:

Name:

Address:

Date of visit:

Signed:

Report Form

To the Editors of The Good Gardens Guide, Barrie & Jenkins Ltd, 20 Vauxhall Bridge Road, London SW1V 2SA.

GARDEN

Name:

Address:

Tel:

Name of owner(s):

DETAILS

Location:

Opening times:

Best season:

Entrance charge:

Plants for sale:

House open/times:

DESCRIPTION

Type of garden:

Features/condition:

Please continue overleaf

Brief details of its main characteristics:

Name:

Address:

Date of visit:

Signed:

Report Form

To the Editors of The Good Gardens Guide, Barrie & Jenkins Ltd,
20 Vauxhall Bridge Road, London SW1V 2SA.

GARDEN

Name:

Address:

Tel:

Name of owner(s):

DETAILS

Location:

Opening times:

Best season:

Entrance charge:

Plants for sale:

House open/times:

DESCRIPTION

Type of garden:

Features/condition:

Please continue overleaf

Brief details of its main characteristics:

Name:

Address:

Date of visit:

Signed: